Evolutionary Psychopathology

Evolutionary Psychopathology

A Unified Approach

MARCO DEL GIUDICE

OXFORD
UNIVERSITY PRESS

OXFORD
UNIVERSITY PRESS

Oxford University Press is a department of the University of Oxford. It furthers the University's objective of excellence in research, scholarship, and education by publishing worldwide. Oxford is a registered trade mark of Oxford University Press in the UK and certain other countries.

Published in the United States of America by Oxford University Press
198 Madison Avenue, New York, NY 10016, United States of America.

Library of Congress Cataloging-in-Publication Data
Names: Del Giudice, Marco, author.
Title: Evolutionary psychopathology : a unified approach / Marco Del Giudice.
Description: New York, NY : Oxford University Press, [2018]
Identifiers: LCCN 2018008306 | ISBN 9780190246846 (hardback) |
ISBN 9780190670146 (epub)
Subjects: LCSH: Psychology, Pathological. | BISAC: PSYCHOLOGY /
Clinical Psychology. | PSYCHOLOGY / Developmental / General.
Classification: LCC RC454.4 .D45 2018 | DDC 616.89—dc23
LC record available at https://lccn.loc.gov/2018008306

Per Alice,
il nostro viaggio più dolce

CONTENTS

ACKNOWLEDGMENTS

As I was working on this book I was lucky to be able to discuss evolution, psychopathology, and everything in between with many exceptional people around the world. Some of them kindly provided feedback on earlier chapter drafts. My warmest thanks to Riadh Abed, Paul Andrews, Jay Belsky, Brian Boutwell, Martin Brüne, Lee Copping, Bernie Crespi, Colin DeYoung, Bruce Ellis, Dan Fessler, Willem Frankenhuis, Steve Gangestad, Marco Garzitto, Paul Gilbert, Phil Kavanagh, Leif Kennair, Dario Maestripieri, Michelle Martel, Geoffrey Miller, Lars Penke, George Richardson, William Skiba, Alfonso Troisi, Paul Watson, and Ron Yeo.

This is the present: looking back, my gratitude goes to the years at the Center for Cognitive Science in Turin, where Bruno Bara and Livia Colle gave me the time, space, and intellectual freedom to find my own path (it took a while). I also want to acknowledge a special debt to Giovanni Liotti, whose work had a tremendous impact on me as an undergraduate and made me realize the power of evolutionary ideas in clinical psychology. In retrospect, it was his pioneering book with Vittorio Guidano (Guidano & Liotti, 1983) that set me on the quest for an integrated theory of psychopathology.

I have seen many book authors thank their spouses for love, help, patience, and support; now is my turn, and I can't find words good enough to say how incredibly grateful I am. Writing a book is like running a marathon, and my wife Romina ran with me all the way. Finally, Sarah Harrington at Oxford University Press provided invaluable advice and turned the editorial process into a smooth, enjoyable experience.

ACKNOWLEDGMENTS

INTRODUCTION

After decades of pioneering efforts and hard-fought intellectual battles, evolutionary ideas are finally starting to permeate the behavioral sciences. Psychologists and psychiatrists have always recognized that humans are biological organisms and that our thinking, feeling brain is a product of evolution just like the rest of our body. It took much longer to start using the tools of evolutionary biology to explain human behavior and the neural and mental processes that control it. While the integration with biology is still at an early stage, there is little doubt that the influence of evolutionary ideas in psychology is growing rapidly (Buss, 2015). As in other disciplines, the Darwinian insight of natural selection transforms the intellectual landscape, eating through the concepts it touches and changing them in fundamental ways like a "universal acid" (Dennett, 1995).

The theory of evolution is not only a necessary foundation for the study of normal behavior, but also a powerful tool to understand mental disorders and the (often blurry) interface between normality and psychopathology. Using evolutionary concepts to explain vulnerability to disease is the goal of evolutionary medicine, another long-awaited scientific movement that is now reaching critical mass (Gluckman et al., 2016; Nesse, 2011; Stearns & Medzhitov, 2016; Stearns et al., 2010). The convergence of evolutionary approaches in psychology and medicine should make psychopathology an ideal arena for integration and discovery. And, indeed, interest in the discipline is high—the past 10 years have seen the publication of new and influential models (e.g., Crespi & Badcock, 2008), a major textbook (Brüne, 2015), and many empirical studies guided by evolutionary hypotheses. At the same time, it is clear that evolutionary psychopathology has yet to realize its true potential. Its main limitation probably lies in its fragmentation—not just healthy theoretical pluralism, but lack of an overarching framework that would help researchers draw connections between individual models of particular conditions and systematically explore their relations.

The loose conceptual structure of the discipline might explain why, despite the limitations of existing taxonomies such as the one embodied in the *Diagnostic and Statistical Manual of Mental Disorders* (DSM; American Psychiatric Association, 2013), evolutionary psychopathology has not yet produced an alternative set of classification principles rooted in biological concepts. Seminal attempts in this direction (McGuire & Troisi, 1998; Stevens & Price, 2000) have failed to gather a broad consensus and have not been followed up in the research literature. In the meantime, other approaches have been gaining ground: most notably, structural models of psychopathology based on empirical comorbidity patterns have yielded some important results and are rapidly becoming mainstream (e.g., Caspi et al., 2014; Kotov et al., 2017). Evolutionary scholars have been watching this game from the sidelines, even though their approach is uniquely suited to identify the functional mechanisms that underlie correlations between symptoms and disorders. A related limitation of our discipline is its lack of integration with models of normal individual differences in personality and cognition (Kennair, 2011). Moreover, the developmental dimension of mental disorders has often been neglected—a limitation shared with large sectors of mainstream psychiatry and evolutionary psychology (Del Giudice & Ellis, 2016). In sum, the evolutionary study of mental disorders is advancing locally—with new models and empirical studies of specific conditions—but lagging behind at the more global level of theoretical integration and classification.

With this book, I aim to make a bold move toward a truly unified approach to evolutionary psychopathology. The conceptual basis for the integrative framework I am advancing is *life history theory*, a branch of evolutionary biology that deals with fitness tradeoffs and allocations across the life span, with far-reaching implications for the structure and organization of individual differences (Del Giudice, 2014*a*, 2014*b*; Del Giudice et al., 2015). The goal is not to replace existing models of particular mental disorders, although the framework does suggest a number of revisions and extensions to current ideas. Instead, a life history framework offers the means to understand patterns of comorbidity between disorders from a functional perspective, link them to meaningful clusters of risk and protective factors, and make sense of the data on sex differences, age of onset, and other important epidemiological features. Building on this foundation, I describe and detail the *fast-slow-defense (FSD) model*, a new classification system based on the distinction between *fast spectrum* (F-type), *slow spectrum* (S-type), and *defense activation* (D-type) disorders. The FSD model represents the first biologically informed alternative to empirical structural models. The updated version presented in this book substantially extends the original life history model I introduced in a series of earlier papers (Del Giudice, 2014*a*, 2014*b*, 2016*c*, 2016*d*).

It goes without saying that the goal is ambitious, even intimidating: an attempt to "climb Mount Impossible" (Kennair, 2010)—or, with a different metaphor, find a common language for what is still a chaotic Babel of disciplines, models, and approaches (Del Giudice, 2014*b*). Still, I believe this may be the right time for a major step toward integration. In some ways, this book picks up where McGuire and Troisi (1998) left off with their classic *Darwinian Psychiatry*. Twenty years later, life history theory—only hinted at in that book—has become a major influence in evolutionary psychology and medicine. Meanwhile, genetics and neurobiology have made striking advances, developmental psychopathology has blossomed, and computational modeling has begun to transform the way we think about mental disorders (Del Giudice, 2016*c*). I strived to do justice to these changes and illustrate how evolutionary models can be integrated more fully with genetics, neurobiology, and computational psychiatry. A key feature of McGuire and Troisi's approach was their emphasis on psychological mechanisms, including the motivational systems that guide behavior toward evolved goals such as mating, status, and attachment. I retained that emphasis and extended it to self-regulation processes (e.g., executive functions) and neurobiological mechanisms. Even more importantly, I made an effort to situate mental disorders within the broader landscape of individual and sex differences in personality, intelligence, and cognitive skills.

SCOPE OF THE BOOK

Psychopathology can be approached from two sides, that of basic research—with questions about the etiology, epidemiology, and classification of disorders—and that of intervention. This book lies squarely on the side of basic research. Its goal is to advance a unified theoretical framework and a novel taxonomy of disorders, not to provide directions for therapy or prevention. This does not mean that an evolutionary understanding of psychopathology is useless for clinicians; on the contrary, it offers a wealth of insights that can make a real difference, from basic principles about the nature of motivation and defenses to sophisticated ideas about the potential costs and benefits of symptoms. In the hands of a skilled therapist, evolutionary models are unrivaled in their power to improve self- and other-understanding and help patients make sense of the complexities and contradictions of life. Moreover, the general theory of motivation and behavior embedded in this approach can inform clinical strategies and suggest ways to manage and improve the therapeutic relationship (see Cortina & Liotti, 2014; Gilbert, 1992, 1995, 2002; Gilbert & Bailey, 2000; Liotti & Gilbert, 2011; McGuire & Troisi, 1998). I am confident that clinicians will find much useful material in this book. At the same time, it is fair to say that—at least until now—evolutionary approaches have yielded little in the way of novel techniques and intervention strategies (Kennair, 2010, 2011). I suspect that the clinical implications of evolutionary models may not be fully revealed until future technological breakthroughs widen the range of therapeutic possibilities beyond what is feasible today. As things stand today, I believe that our discipline is poised to make major contributions to the functional description and classification of mental disorders, with a cascade of implications for research in areas as diverse as epidemiology, neurobiology, and psychiatric genetics. This is where I focused my effort in this book. Clinical applications will follow in due time, even if it may take a few decades to get there.

I wrote this book with two types of readers in mind. Readers of the first kind have a primary background in psychiatry or psychopathology and an interest in evolution. For them, Part I of the book begins with a primer on key biological concepts and an introduction to the mind as a network of evolved information-processing mechanisms. Both of these topics are vast, and it is impossible to offer more than a cursory overview in the space of a few chapters. For those who enjoy reading suggestions, I recommend Nettle (2009*c*) and Futuyma (2017) as friendly introductions to evolutionary biology, and the handbook edited by Buss (2015) as an in-depth account of contemporary evolutionary psychology (see also Workman & Reader, 2014). Readers of the second type are those with a background in evolutionary psychology, anthropology, or biology who wish to deepen their understanding of mental disorders or contribute to this fascinating area of research. Each of the chapters in Part III begins with an overview of a particular disorder or group of disorders. While I strived to make these overviews as informative and up to date as possible, they are necessarily brief and include only a summary description of the condition's symptoms and the underlying cognitive and emotional processes. Also, pathological conditions are presented from a researcher's perspective, without the clinical detail and emotional richness of good case descriptions. It may be worth stressing that the book focuses specifically on evolutionary models of mental disorders and is not intended as a standalone psychopathology textbook.

An integrative book of this kind draws on many different areas of research, each with its own literature and thousands of potentially relevant publications. In selecting empirical references, I privileged meta-analyses, large-scale studies, and systematic reviews. I noted some cases in which reliable evidence of this kind was not available, for example regarding the neurobiological correlates of some disorders. To increase the robustness of the evidence presented in the book, I ultimately decided to sidestep the literature on genetic association studies targeting specific candidate genes (e.g., genes coding for the serotonin transporter or various types of dopamine receptors). While these studies have yielded many intriguing findings, there are serious and growing concerns about their replicability (see Chapter 3). The decision to eschew candidate gene studies does not imply a blanket indictment of the field; however, it is probably wise to suspend judgment until the solid findings are sorted from the statistical artifacts.

ORGANIZATION OF THE BOOK

The structure of this book is straightforward. Part I provides the necessary background for the remaining chapters. Specifically, Chapter 1 introduces key biological concepts and provides a brief evolutionary overview of human behavior and development. Chapter 2 zooms in to the mind/brain and discusses the adaptive nature of psychological mechanisms. In this chapter, I examine some mechanisms that play an especially prominent role in the etiology of mental disorders, and review key neurobiological systems (from brain monoamines to sex hormones) with a focus on their behavioral functions. Chapter 3 is about individual and sex differences, their evolution, and their emergence in development through the interplay of genetic and environmental factors. I consider cognitive ability as well as personality since both contribute in important ways to the risk of psychopathology. In Chapter 4, I introduce the basics of life history theory, including the crucial concept of *life history strategies*. I then discuss how life history strategies organize human variation in personality, cognition, and neurobiology. In doing this, I advance some new ideas about the organization of life history strategies in our species. The model I sketch in this chapter goes beyond classic accounts of life history variation and suggests a host of novel hypotheses.

Having laid out a working theory of normal behavior, I turn to the nature of disorders in Part II of the book. Chapter 5 introduces the main tenets of evolutionary psychopathology, discusses the biological reasons for our vulnerability to disease, and reviews various kinds of "undesirable conditions" that may be regarded as mental disorders (whether or not they represent true dysfunctions). The chapter also addresses some important points regarding the structure and classification of disorders and considers the strengths and weaknesses of other emerging approaches to psychopathology. Chapter 6 is the heart of the book: this is where I present the life history framework, explore its implications, and detail the classification criteria of the FSD model. Ideally, Chapter 6 should be read twice—after Chapter 5 as an introduction to the FSD model, then again after the analytical chapters of Part III as a synthesis and recapitulation of the framework.

In Part III of the book, I apply the concepts and criteria developed in Part II to a range of common mental disorders. Chapters 7 to 20 all follow the same template. The first section of each chapter is an overview of the disorder(s), including a survey of findings on genetic and environmental factors, sex differences, and developmental patterns. When relevant, I also summarize key neurobiological correlates of the disorder and/or recent computational work that helps illuminate the logic of its symptoms. This initial overview is followed by a critical review of the main evolutionary models of the disorder. The final section of the chapter applies the criteria introduced in Chapter 6 to classify the disorder within the FSD model and, in some cases, identify functionally distinct subtypes within the standard diagnostic categories. Part IV of the book consists of a concluding chapter (Chapter 21) where I share some thoughts on the future of the discipline and discuss promising directions for research.

ABBREVIATIONS

ACRONYMS FOR BRAIN REGIONS AND STRUCTURES

ACC	anterior cingulate cortex
BNST	bed nucleus of the stria terminalis
DLPFC	dorsolateral prefrontal cortex
DMPFC	dorsomedial prefrontal cortex
DPFC	dorsal prefrontal cortex
DPC	dorsal parietal cortex
IFG	inferior frontal gyrus
IPL	inferior parietal lobule
LC	locus coeruleus
MPFC	medial prefrontal cortex
NAcc	nucleus accumbens
OFC	orbitofrontal cortex
PAG	periaqueductal gray
PCC	posterior cingulate cortex
PVN	paraventricular nucleus
SN	substantia nigra
SON	supraoptic nucleus
STN	subthalamic nucleus
STS	superior temporal sulcus
TPJ	temporoparietal junction
VLPFC	ventrolateral prefrontal cortex
VMPFC	ventromedial prefrontal cortex
VTA	ventral tegmental area

ACRONYMS FOR NEUROENDOCRINE SYSTEMS, HORMONES, AND NEUROTRANSMITTERS

5-HT	serotonin
ACh	acetylcholine

ACTH	adrenocorticotropic hormone
AVP	vasopressin
CRH	corticotropin-releasing hormone
DA	dopamine
DHEA	dehydroepiandrosterone
DHEAS	dehydroepiandrosterone sulfate
FSH	follicle-stimulating hormone
GABA	γ-aminobutyric acid
GnRH	gonadotropin-releasing hormone
HPA	hypothalamic-pituitary-adrenal (axis)
HPG	hypothalamic-pituitary-gonadal (axis)
HPT	hypothalamic-pituitary-thyroid (axis)
IGF-1	insulin-like growth factor 1
LH	luteinizing hormone
NE	norepinephrine
OT	oxytocin

ACRONYMS FOR COMMON MENTAL DISORDERS

ADHD	attention-deficit/hyperactivity disorder
AN	anorexia nervosa
APD	avoidant personality disorder
ASD	autism spectrum disorder
ASPD	antisocial personality disorder
BD	bipolar disorder
BED	binge-eating disorder
BN	bulimia nervosa
BPD	borderline personality disorder
CD	conduct disorder
ED	eating disorder
GAD	generalized anxiety disorder
MDD	major depressive disorder
NPD	narcissistic personality disorder
OCD	obsessive-compulsive disorder
OCPD	obsessive-compulsive personality disorder
ODD	oppositional-defiant disorder
PDD	persistent depressive disorder
PTSD	posttraumatic stress disorder
SAD	social anxiety disorder
SPD	schizotypal personality disorder
SSD	schizophrenia spectrum disorder
SUD	substance use disorder

PART I

Foundations

1

Human Nature in a Nutshell

A unified approach to psychopathology would be impossible without an integrated working model of the mind and its functions. In Part I of the book (Chapters 1–4), I draw on evolutionary psychology, anthropology, and neuroscience to sketch such a model. This initial chapter has two goals—first, to present a brief overview of human behavior and development from an evolutionary perspective and, second, to introduce a toolkit of biological concepts and theories that provide the necessary background for the remainder of the book.

WHO WE ARE

Homo sapiens is an ape whose lineage separated from that of chimpanzees and bonobos 5–7 millions of years ago and acquired its modern anatomical features in Africa about 300,000 years ago (Hublin et al., 2017; Jobling et al., 2004). Until the invention of agriculture at the end of the latest glacial period—a mere 12,000 years ago—human subsistence worldwide was based on hunting, fishing, and gathering. The use of sophisticated foraging techniques that make extensive use of manufactured tools is part of the *human adaptive complex*—a suite of coevolved traits that contribute to define the ecology of our species (Kaplan et al., 2000). The human adaptive complex includes the exploitation of high-quality food sources (e.g., large game, protected items such as shells and roots) through learning- and technology-intensive acquisition techniques; a large brain to enable massive amounts of learning and information storage; a long period of dependence before sexual maturity to support brain development and learning; a multigeneration system of resource transfers (flowing from grandparents to parents to children) to subsidize our slow, energetically costly developmental trajectory; provision of food, protection, and other resources from both mothers and fathers (biparental investment), supported by marriage and long-term bonding between sexual partners; low mortality rates; and networks of cooperative arrangements among kin and unrelated individuals, which permit extensive food sharing and group coordination, further reducing mortality (Kaplan et al., 2007). Another major function of group cooperation throughout human evolution has been that of enabling collective aggression against other groups, from small-scale fights and raids to all-out wars between enemy coalitions (Bowles, 2009; Bowles & Gintis, 2011; Keeley, 1996; Tooby & Cosmides, 2010).

Social and Cultural Brains

The ever-increasing complexity of human social dynamics—including those generated by pair bonding, multigeneration transfers, extended cooperation, and conflict between and within groups—worked in synergy with foraging and tool-making to favor the evolution of larger brains and increased cognitive abilities (Alexander, 1989; Bailey & Geary, 2009; Dunbar, 1993; Dunbar & Shultz, 2007, 2010; Flinn et al., 2005). The social organization of foragers over the past 300,000 years was likely characterized by a nested hierarchy of groups, from small bands of 30–50 people to large tribes of perhaps 1,000 or 2,000 individuals, with an intermediate level ("clans" or "villages") numbering 100–200 units. In short, the social world of our distant ancestors comprised hundreds of individuals, connected by various degrees of kinship and organized in groups and subgroups of variable size. This level of social complexity would not have been possible without language, which is possibly the most distinctive of all human traits (Birdsell, 1973; Dessalles, 2007; Dunbar, 1993; Pinker, 1994). Language and the cooperative sharing of information that it permits have entrenched humans in the *cognitive niche*—a unique foraging niche in which problem-solving based on cause–effect reasoning, transmitted knowledge, and social coordination are employed to overcome other organisms' defenses in order to feed on them (examples are hunting large game, constructing weapons and traps, and detoxifying plants by cooking; Pinker, 2010; Tooby & DeVore, 1987).

The information-sharing skills that define the cognitive niche also enable cultural transmission on a massive scale (Dean et al., 2014; Richerson & Boyd, 2005; Tomasello, 2009). Humans possess a vast range of transmission devices that include direct observation and imitation, teaching, storytelling, drawing, and (much more recently) reading and writing. Cultural transmission engenders a complex interplay between individual and social learning—and, more generally, between innovation and conformity, with their complementary costs and benefits for individuals and groups (Dean et al., 2014; Nettle, 2009*a*; Richerson & Boyd, 2005). The ability to build a cumulative culture has been a key factor in the propagation of human populations across the continents and their adaptation to a strikingly broad range of climatic and ecological conditions (Flinn et al., 2005; Nettle, 2009*b*).

Agriculture and Recent Human Evolution

In evolutionary terms, the invention of agriculture belongs to the very recent past. The earliest traces of farming in the Middle East go back to about

12,000 years, that is, roughly 500 generations ago. And yet, agriculture has been a major watershed in our evolutionary history. With the advent of farming, vital resources such as land and cattle could be accumulated, stolen, and defended; the outcome was a dramatic increase in social stratification, power/wealth inequality, and warfare, as well in the scale of cooperative networks. All these trends further intensified with the appearance of cities and states around 6,000 years ago (Kaplan et al., 2009; Powers & Lehmann, 2014). At the same time, food production increased by orders of magnitude, enabling unprecedented levels of demographic expansion and population density. The effects of these demographic changes reverberated through virtually every aspect of life—from diet and social interactions to the spread of infectious diseases (Cochran & Harpending, 2009).

Largely as a consequence of population growth, the rate of genetic change in humans seems to have accelerated dramatically over the past 10,000 years (Enard et al., 2014; Fu et al., 2013; Hawks et al., 2007). Genes showing evidence of recent evolutionary change include several that are expressed in the nervous system and some that have been associated with the risk for specific mental disorders (e.g., Grossman et al., 2013; López Herráez et al., 2009; Polimanti & Gelernter, 2017; Schrider & Kern, 2017). The once contentious notion that the evolution of human brain and behavior has accelerated in the recent past is becoming increasingly accepted. What is still controversial (despite being biologically plausible) is the idea that populations inhabiting different ecologies and living in different social and cultural systems may have evolved systematic differences in genes that affect personality and cognition (Frost, 2011; Frost & Harpending, 2015; Wade, 2014; Winegard et al., 2017).

Using the Past to Understand the Present: Proximate and Ultimate Explanations

The central premise of evolutionary psychology is that our present minds embody the deep historical past, having been shaped across millions of years by the changing demands of the human ecology. Tinbergen (1963) famously pointed out that any biological system can be explained in four ways; that is, from the standpoint of *mechanism* (What is the system like? How does it work?); that of *ontogeny* or *development* (How does the system change over the organism's life course?); that of *phylogeny* (What is the system's history? How has it changed through evolution, and how does it differ between related species?); and, finally, that of *adaptation* (Why did the system evolve into its present form? What evolutionary advantages did it provide?).

Ontogenetic and mechanistic explanations concern the way an organism works in the present—in biological parlance, they are *proximate* explanations. *Ultimate* explanations (phylogeny and adaptation) consider the organism in relation to the past and the evolutionary forces that shaped its body and behavior. The two levels are pragmatically distinct but not mutually exclusive;

on the contrary, proximate and ultimate questions are complementary and synergistic. Just as knowing the adaptive purpose of a mechanism can illuminate its functioning, understanding the mechanics and development of a trait constrains the range of plausible adaptive explanations for its evolution (Mayr, 1963; Scott-Phillips et al., 2011). The standard approach in psychology, medicine, and neuroscience is to focus almost exclusively on the proximate level of analysis. Evolutionary disciplines take the next logical step by asking questions about adaptation—which, as Darwin was the first to realize, ultimately reduce to questions about *reproduction*. The goal of the next section is to unpack the logic of natural selection and clarify the meaning of crucial terms such as fitness, adaptation, and maladaptation.

NATURAL SELECTION AND ADAPTATION

The concept of natural selection (Darwin, 1859) is the cornerstone of evolutionary biology. Natural selection occurs in a population of reproducing individuals whenever these conditions are met: (a) resources are limited, so that unconstrained reproduction is impossible; (b) individuals differ from one another in their morphological, physiological, and behavioral traits, or *phenotypes*; (c) at least some phenotypic traits correlate with an individual's ability to successfully reproduce, leaving more descendants in the next generation; and (d) phenotypes are inherited, meaning that they are transmitted to descendants with some reliability. When these conditions apply, individuals that are better able to reproduce leave more descendants; in turn, those descendants tend to carry the traits that favored reproduction in the preceding generations. Over time, successful traits tend to become more common—that is, they are selected for because of their positive effects on reproductive success or *fitness*. Traits that enhance fitness are called *adaptive*, while those that reduce it are called *maladaptive*; if a trait has no impact on fitness, it is considered *neutral* with respect to natural selection. Note that natural selection is an abstract process and does not require specific mechanisms of inheritance (such as DNA replication) in order to work. All it requires is the combination of heritable variation and differential reproduction based on that variation.

The basic measure of Darwinian fitness is an individual's lifetime reproductive success, or the total number of that individual's offspring that survive to maturity. (Fitness calculations become more complex when population growth and fluctuations in the environment are taken into account; see Hunt & Hodgson, 2010.) While surviving is usually a condition for reproduction, the catchphrase "survival of the fittest" is somewhat misleading, as survival without reproduction is an evolutionary dead end. It does not matter how well an organism is able to survive; if it fails to leave descendants, its enhanced survival abilities will not be passed down to the next generation and will eventually disappear. Organisms thus need to trade longer survival against increased reproduction, which is the real currency of evolution.

Inclusive Fitness

While individual reproduction is an important component of fitness, it still fails to fully capture the logic of natural selection. Indeed, many important and widespread phenomena—including altruism and self-sacrifice—involve a *loss* of individual fitness and may seem paradoxical or maladaptive on the face of it. Hamilton (1964) was the first to show that, in order to account for these apparent contradictions, the straightforward idea of fitness as individual reproduction must be replaced by the related but more sophisticated concept of *inclusive fitness*. Inclusive fitness theory—also known, somewhat improperly, as *kin selection*—provides a unified account of natural selection that includes social behavior in all its forms (Bourke, 2011; Grafen, 2009; West et al., 2007). In a nutshell, the theory shows that natural selection does not maximize individual reproductive success, but a different quantity called inclusive fitness. Inclusive fitness is the sum of the contribution of an individual (actor) to its own reproduction and its contribution to the reproduction of other individuals (recipients), the latter weighted by a coefficient of *relatedness* that summarizes the average genetic similarity between actor and recipient. In other words, an individual can increase its inclusive fitness in two ways: by increasing its own reproductive success (direct fitness) and by increasing that of genetically similar individuals (indirect fitness).

Relatedness is $r = 0$ between two individuals of a population picked at random and $r = 1$ between two genetic clones (such as identical twins). The relatedness coefficient may even become negative if the recipient is *less* genetically similar to the actor than a random member of the population (for example because the recipient belongs to a different population; see Grafen, 1985). Diploid organisms such as humans have two sets of chromosomes, one from each parent; as a result, relatedness between family members is high but considerably less than perfect. In simplified terms, the relatedness between parent and child is $r = 0.5$, the same as that between two full siblings; that between grandparent and grandchild is $r = 0.25$, the same as that between two half-siblings; and so on.

Inclusive fitness theory is encapsulated by the expression known as *Hamilton's rule*:

$$M + rN > 0$$

The rule states that a behavior—or any other phenotype with social effects—will be selected for if its effect on the actor's fitness (M) and its relatedness-weighted effect on the recipient's fitness (rN) sum to a positive quantity. Note that M and N can be either positive (benefits) or negative (costs); likewise, r can range from positive to negative, as noted earlier. In the specific case of altruism, the effect of behavior is by definition a cost C for the actor and a benefit B for the recipient. By treating both B and C as positive quantities, one gets the standard version of Hamilton's rule for altruism:

$$rB > C$$

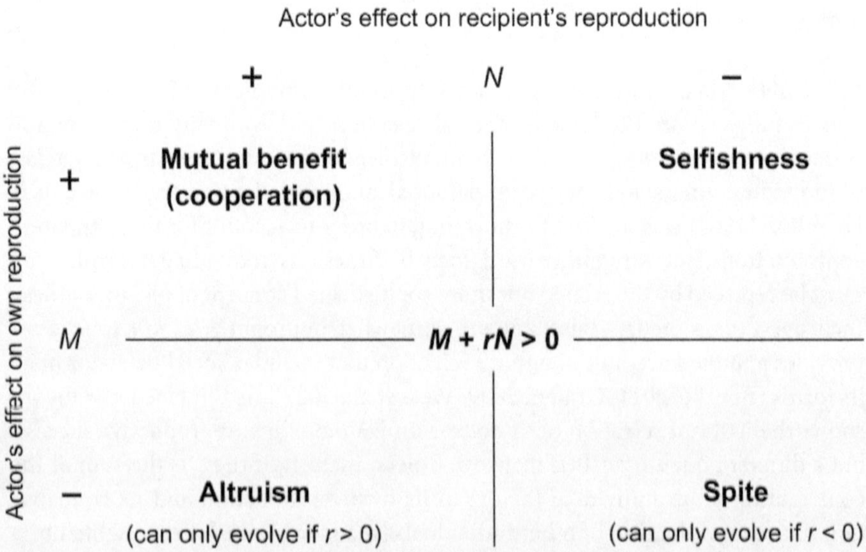

Figure 1.1. Hamilton's rule applied to the four main types of social interaction. A trait or behavior can be *mutually beneficial/cooperative* if both actor and recipient benefit from the interaction; *altruistic* if the actor incurs a cost in order to provide a benefit to the recipient; *selfish* if the actor benefits by inflicting a loss on the recipient; or *spiteful* if the actor incurs a cost in order to inflict a loss on the recipient. Whereas cooperation and selfishness can potentially evolve at any level of relatedness (depending on the exact balance of costs and benefits), altruism can only evolve if actor and recipient are positively related, and spite can only evolve if they are negatively related.

Altruism will be selected for if the benefit enjoyed by the recipient, weighted by the relatedness between actor and recipient (rB), is larger than the cost incurred by the actor (C). This means that costly altruistic behavior can evolve, provided that the benefit for the recipient and/or the relatedness between actor and recipient are sufficiently high. Also, biological altruism can only evolve when relatedness is positive ($r > 0$). However, the implications of inclusive fitness are not limited to altruism; Hamilton's rule can be applied to all kinds of social interactions, as shown in Figure 1.1 (see Bourke, 2011; West et al., 2007, 2011).

Adaptive/Maladaptive Versus Desirable/Undesirable

In the evolutionary disciplines, the terms "adaptive" and "maladaptive" refer to the overall fitness effect of a trait. All traits have costs as well as benefits; to be adaptive, a trait does not have to be cost-free, but only to yield a positive net contribution to the organism's inclusive fitness. These notions of adaptation and maladaptation contrast sharply with how the same terms are usually employed in psychology and psychiatry. In these disciplines, "adaptive" traits and behaviors are those that promote health, safety, subjective well-being, and mutually rewarding social relations; whereas socially undesirable, aversive, or health-damaging traits are viewed as "maladaptive" (see Nesse & Jackson, 2006). It is paramount to realize that these definitions of adaptation and maladaptation are conceptually orthogonal. Unsettling as it may be, the logic of natural selection promotes reproductive success rather than happiness, or even health per se (Cosmides & Tooby, 1999; Gluckman et al., 2011; Nesse, 2004*a*). Biologically adaptive traits may or may not be socially desirable or conducive to health and well-being; conversely, traits that consistently reduce well-being and adversely impact an individual's health can be selected for—as long as they lead to enhanced reproduction. In this book, I always refer to adaptive and maladaptive traits in the biological sense, and employ the terms "desirable" and "undesirable" to denote the implications of a trait for health, well-being, or social values.

Adaptations

By constantly weeding out unsuccessful variation, natural selection produces modifications of existing phenotypes, leading to the accumulation of characteristics that are organized to enhance survival and reproductive success. *Adaptations* are inherited and reliably developing phenotypes that have been selected for because of their causal role in enhancing the fitness of individuals that possess them (Williams, 1966). Through this process, adaptations acquire biological functions and the appearance of purposeful design: the immune system functions to protect organisms from pathogens, the heart functions as a pump for blood, and so on.

While adaptations are (by definition) a product of evolution, evolution does not always produce adaptations; likewise, not every characteristic of an organism is automatically an adaptation. For example, traits may become fixated in a population by *drift*, a random process by which neutral or even deleterious characteristics become more prevalent due to chance fluctuations in the frequency of traits. A neutral or weakly maladaptive trait may also spread by "hitchhiking" on another, positively selected trait to which it happens to be developmentally or genetically linked. In addition, many traits are not adaptations in themselves but rather *byproducts* of other adaptations. The sound the heart makes when it beats, the white color of bones, and the human chin are all nonfunctional byproducts of natural selection. A variety of approaches can be employed to identify adaptations and distinguish them from other types of traits. The most common methods include making phylogenetic comparisons between different species, including extinct ones (e.g., early hominids); estimating the fitness costs and benefits of a trait by measuring its associations with survival and reproduction; and building mathematical models of trait evolution that can be compared with empirical data or used to evaluate the plausibility of alternative hypothetical scenarios (Schmitt & Pilcher, 2004). Adaptations often show evidence of *special design*: the main features that indicate special design are economy, efficiency, complexity, precision, specialization, and reliability in service of a trait's function. These features can be used to identify and "reverse-engineer" adaptations by framing them as solutions to specific biological problems (Tooby & Cosmides, 2015; Williams, 1966).

The IMA Principle

The logic of adaptation through natural selection has an important implication: as evolution proceeds, individual organisms are selected to develop and behave in ways that maximize their (expected) inclusive fitness. One does not have to assume that individuals are intentionally or consciously maximizing their fitness; they only need to function *as if* they were attempting to do so. This has been aptly described as the *individual-as-maximizing agent* or IMA principle (Grafen, 1999, 2006, 2009). Crucially, it can be shown that maximizing one's inclusive fitness is equivalent to maximizing the replication of one's genetic variants (*alleles*) in future generations, since—by definition—recipients who are more closely related are also more likely to carry copies of the actor's own alleles.

This deep equivalence is the source of Dawkin's much misunderstood metaphor of the "selfish gene": individual organisms can be selected to behave altruistically (thus sacrificing their individual fitness), but only because doing so ultimately enhances the replication of their genes (Dawkins, 1976). Note that, in inclusive fitness theory, a gene is an abstract unit of inheritance, not a protein- or RNA-coding sequence of DNA as in molecular biology. For example, epigenetic mechanisms such as DNA methylation influence gene expression without modifying the underlying DNA sequence (Feil & Fraga, 2012; Jones, 2012; Ledón-Rettig et al., 2013). In some cases, epigenetic modifications can be transmitted from parent to offspring, even across multiple generations (Day & Bonduriansky, 2011; Ledón-Rettig et al., 2013; Meaney, 2010). Provided they follow the same pattern of transmission as the individual's DNA, stable epigenetic marks can be assimilated to genes from the standpoint of inclusive fitness and natural selection (Lu & Bourrat, 2017).

Of course, the IMA principle does not imply that a given individual will necessarily achieve high fitness; what is maximized by natural selection is only an individual's statistical *expectation*, not the realized outcome in any particular case. Even more crucially, optimization does not imply unconstrained "perfection" in the design of organisms and adaptations. Fitness maximization always takes place within the constraints and tradeoffs imposed by the laws of physics, the characteristics of the environment, the phenotypic results of previous evolution, and the existence of evolutionary conflicts of interest (see later discussion). Furthermore, the IMA principle can only be expected to hold when the environment is sufficiently similar to that in which the organism evolved—which, in the case of contemporary humans, is often debatable (more on this in Chapter 5).

Group Selection

Some influential evolutionary scholars have invoked *group selection* as an alternative explanation of the evolution of cooperation and altruism in humans (e.g.,

Bowles & Gintis, 2011; Sober & Wilson, 1998; Wilson, 2012). The basic idea of modern group selection (or *multilevel selection*) is that competition for reproduction occurs simultaneously at two levels, between different groups within the broader population and between individuals within each group. While competition within groups tends to favor selfishness, competition between groups favors altruism; this means that altruism toward group members can be selected for as long as it is counterbalanced by a sufficient benefit for the group as a whole.

As it turns out, multilevel selection and inclusive fitness theory are mathematically equivalent and differ only in how they partition the costs and benefits of social traits (Marshall, 2011; West et al., 2007, 2011; West & Gardner, 2013). Whereas inclusive fitness partitions fitness effects between actors and recipients, multilevel selection partitions them between individuals and their broader social groups. The evolution of altruism by group selection can be explained just as well from the standpoint of inclusive fitness, since mechanisms of group formation increase relatedness within groups relative to that between groups. As a result, helping group members leads to an indirect fitness benefit that can be so strong as to override large costs in direct fitness. Depending on the question being asked, describing the evolution of a trait in terms of group selection rather than inclusive fitness may be mathematically more convenient or provide additional insight (Goodnight, 2013). The bottom line is that—despite frequent claims to the contrary—group/multilevel selection is not an alternative evolutionary process, but only a redescription of natural selection from a different point of view.

Evolutionary Conflicts

The very idea of evolution by natural selection is predicated on competition among alternative forms—including alternative alleles of the same gene that compete for replication and representation in future generations. Inclusive fitness theory shows how this fundamental conflict of interest can give rise to cooperation and even altruism given the right combination of factors (costs, benefits, and relatedness). At the same time, the logic of inclusive fitness shines a spotlight on the fact that cooperation is usually fragile and coexists with conflict in most kinds of social relationships (Bourke, 2011).

The clearest examples of evolutionary conflict are those involving predators and parasites, including the pathogens that constantly assault larger organisms. Here, relatedness is not an issue, and interactions between organisms are entirely driven by direct costs and benefits. Predator–prey and pathogen–host interactions usually evolve into endless "arms races" in which the evolution of better offensive mechanisms is followed by that of more effective defenses, which selects for even better offenses, and so on. However, other outcomes are possible as well. Pathogens may benefit by becoming *less* virulent if doing so helps them spread more effectively: this is especially likely when contagion occurs through personal contact (e.g., coughing, sexual intercourse) rather than through indirect channels such as insects or bodily waste. Sometimes, as in the case of gut microbes, pathogens turn into symbionts and engage in mutually beneficial exchanges with their hosts instead of harming them.

Parent–Offspring Conflict

At the opposite end of the spectrum, the highest levels of cooperation and altruism are found between close relatives. Humans are no exception to this pattern, as documented by the extensive cross-cultural evidence of favoritism toward kin (e.g., Burton-Cheller & Dunbar, 2014; Hooper et al., 2015; Madsen et al., 2007). Still, as long as relatedness is less than perfect ($r < 1$), Hamilton's rule leaves room for conflicts of interest between family members. An especially pervasive kind of evolutionary conflict is *parent–offspring conflict* (Trivers, 1974; see Schlomer et al., 2011 for a nontechnical introduction). Leaving aside paternity uncertainty, the relatedness between a parent and its offspring has a constant value ($r = 0.5$ in diploid species). This implies that—all else being equal—parents are selected to value the welfare of all their offspring to the same degree. However, each offspring should value *itself* ($r = 1$) more highly than its siblings and half-siblings ($r = 0.5$ or less). As a result, parents and offspring can be expected to disagree about the optimal distribution of resources among siblings: the parent would maximize its inclusive fitness by dividing resources (e.g., food) equally, but each sibling would maximize its inclusive fitness by getting a larger share of the pie at the expense of present and future siblings (Figure 1.2). The same logic applies to other types of parental investment, such as time and protection. In fact, *any* trait or behavior that benefits the offspring at a cost to the parent (or vice versa) can be subject to parent–offspring conflict.

In humans, parent–offspring conflict theory has been employed to explain mother–infant conflicts about the timing of weaning, conflicts between siblings in step-families, and even conflicts between young adults and their parents over the choice of romantic partners (e.g., Apostolou, 2014; Buunk et al., 2008; Fouts et al., 2005; Schlomer et al., 2010; van den Berg et al., 2013). Parent–offspring conflict on fetal nutrition and growth during pregnancy has a profound impact on prenatal physiology and is the ultimate explanation for the occurrence of gestational hypertension and diabetes (Haig, 1993; Schlomer et al., 2011). Of particular importance for psychopathology, the regulation of maternal cortisol and other stress-related hormones during pregnancy may also be subject to similar conflicts (Del Giudice, 2012*a*; Gangestad et al., 2012; Mokkonen et al., 2016).

Intragenomic Conflict

Even within a single individual, different parts of the genome may not always share the same evolutionary interests, leading to *intragenomic conflict*. For instance, maternally derived genes (i.e., genes on the chromosomes inherited from the mother) have relatedness $r = 0.5$ with the maternally derived genes in each of the individual's siblings. The situation is symmetric for paternal genes only if all siblings in a family can be expected to have the same father. With any degree of multiple paternity, some of the siblings are going to be half-siblings; from the perspective of paternally derived genes, this implies that relatedness between siblings is not 0.5 but a smaller quantity—much smaller if multiple paternity is common

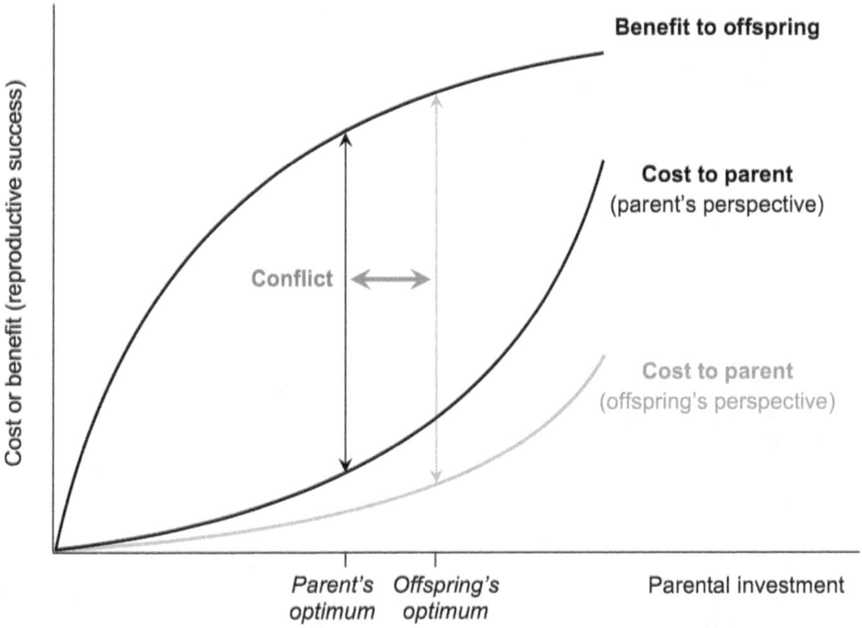

Figure 1.2. The logic of parent–offspring conflict. The offspring benefits from parental investment; at the same time, the parent incurs a reproductive cost because resources invested in the current offspring cannot be invested in future offspring. From the offspring's perspective, this cost is discounted by the relatedness with future siblings. As a result, the optimal level of investment in the current offspring (i.e., the level that maximizes the difference between benefits and costs) is higher from the offspring's perspective than from the parent's perspective, engendering a conflict of interest between the two parties.

in a certain species or population. Because of this asymmetry in relatedness, maternally derived genes can benefit by taking the mother's side in parent–offspring conflict (for example by reducing the growth rate of the fetus) while paternally derived genes benefit by siding with the offspring (Haig, 1997; Úbeda & Haig, 2003).

For most genes, the intrinsic conflict between patrilineal and matrilineal fitness is ultimately irrelevant because they carry no molecular memory of whether they were inherited from the mother or the father. However, at least a hundred genes in the human genome bear epigenetic marks that partially or completely inactivate them depending on their parent of origin (Barlow & Bartolomei, 2014; Davies et al., 2008; Gregg et al., 2010; Schalkwyk et al., 2010; Wilkins et al., 2016). These *imprinted genes* may evolve so as to shift the balance of parent–offspring conflict in favor of the mother (if maternally expressed) or the offspring (if paternally expressed; Figure 1.3). Many imprinted genes are expressed in the placenta, where they can participate in conflicts on parental investment—for instance by enhancing or suppressing fetal growth. Others are expressed in the brain, where they can potentially influence a wide range of behavioral traits subject to parent–offspring conflict (Haig, 2000; Úbeda & Gardner, 2010, 2011, 2012;

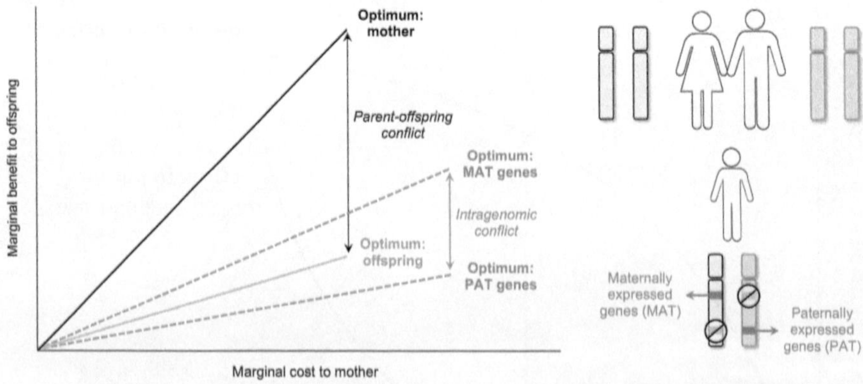

Figure 1.3. The logic of intragenomic conflict between imprinted genes. Because of parent–offspring conflict, the mother favors a higher benefit/cost ratio for parental investment than the offspring. However, paternally expressed genes within the offspring are less related to future siblings than maternally expressed genes; for this reason, they also favor a lower benefit/cost ratio than their maternally expressed counterparts. Paternally expressed genes may evolve as "resource enhancers" (genes that tend to maximize the investment provided by the mother, e.g., by increasing growth rate in fetuses or hunger in infants) whereas maternally expressed genes may evolve as "resources inhibitors" that counteract the action of resource enhancers. When both parents contribute to parental investment, more complex patterns may evolve; for example, if paternal investment increases over time, paternally expressed genes may behave as resource enhancers early in life but resource inhibitors later on (Úbeda, 2008).

Wilkins & Haig, 2003; for a review of alternative theories, see Patten et al., 2014). Intragenomic conflicts are not limited to imprinted genes but may also involve sexual chromosomes, mitochondrial genes, or "selfish" strands of DNA that—for various reasons—follow inheritance rules that differ from those of the rest of the genome (Burt & Trivers, 2006).

Because it breaks down the unity of the individual, intragenomic conflict works against the IMA principle: if different parts of the genome have divergent interests, selection cannot maximize any single measure of fitness. In most cases, however, the IMA principle remains valid as an approximation—because most genes within the genome have convergent interests being replicated and transmitted together, and because different sets of conflicting genes are likely to pull the phenotype in different directions, partly canceling out each other's effects (West & Gardner, 2013). Still, at a deeper level, the individual does not function as a fully self-consistent unit, but more like a compromise among competing interests within a collective of genetic "factions" (Haig, 2014).

SEX AND MATING

As in other sexual organisms, the biology of mating shapes human behavior in myriad ways. Social dynamics acquire much of their meaning from their direct and indirect connections with mating and reproduction; moreover, the selection forces that originate from sexual competition are ultimately responsible for many important differences between the psychologies of males and females.

Sexual Selection

In species that reproduce sexually, phenotypic traits can be selected for because they increase the quality or number of an individual's mates (Darwin, 1871). This can happen in two ways: by making individuals compete more effectively with rivals of the same sex, or by making them more attractive to potential mates of the opposite sex. Selection that arises from competition for mates is called *sexual selection* (Andersson & Simmons, 2006; Kuijper et al., 2012). While some authors draw a clear-cut distinction between natural selection (driven by survival) and sexual selection (driven by mating), it is more useful and logically consistent to define natural selection broadly in terms of inclusive fitness and treat sexual selection as a special case (Clutton-Brock & Huchard, 2013). Sexual selection is just one of many possible forms of *social selection*, in which traits are selected by other individuals through competition and choice (Lyon & Montgomerie, 2012; West-Eberhard, 1983). Examples of nonsexual social selection are the evolution of altruistic tendencies that increase one's attractiveness as a partner for cooperation and sharing, or the evolution of "cute" features that elicit interest in parents and make them more willing to protect their infants and children (Bogin, 1997; Locke & Bogin, 2006; Nesse, 2007).

Sexual selection drives the evolution of two main types of traits: *weapons* (traits used to physically compete with same-sex rivals) and *displays* (traits used to attract members of the opposite sex or repel same-sex rivals). In most species, males engage in physical competition and develop extravagant displays, while females play the role of the choosing sex. This is connected to the fact that females in those species provide most or all of the parental investment, including feeding, protection, and the physiological costs of eggs or pregnancy (Janicke et al., 2016; Kokko & Jennions, 2008; Trivers, 1972). However, several species exist in which males contribute to parental investment and mate choice is more reciprocal, and there are a minority of species in which sex roles are "reversed" (that is, females compete while males choose and provide for the offspring; Clutton-Brock, 2007; Janicke et al., 2016). In general, the sex that provides less parental care can reproduce at a higher rate and thus benefits more from investing time and energy in seeking multiple sexual partners. However, the evolutionary dynamics of sex roles are complex and depend on several interacting factors, such as uncertainty of paternity and the relative proportion of males to females in a population, or *sex ratio* (Kokko & Jennions, 2008). A common outcome of those dynamics is the evolution of alternative mating strategies, usually in males. For example, some males may fight for dominance or territory while others avoid competition and attempt to "sneak" copulations with unguarded females. Or, some may specialize in parenting while others become highly competitive in the attempt to mate with as many partners as possible (Stiver & Alonzo, 2009; Taborsky & Brockmann, 2010).

The most fascinating products of sexual selection arise from mate choice. Selection based on sexual displays has a peculiar self-reinforcing nature: the displaying sex is constantly under selection to express more extreme versions of the trait, which in turn raises the bar for mate selection in the choosing sex. This process has the quality of an arms race between the displaying and choosing sex and explains the evolution of extravagant displays, such as the peacock's tail and the bowerbird's nest. The two basic mechanisms of selection via mate choice are *runaway* sexual selection (also known as Fisherian or "sexy sons" selection) and selection for *fitness indicators* (also known as "viability indicators", "genetic indicators", or "good genes" selection). In runaway selection, genes that determine the development of a trait in one sex become statistically linked with genes that control preference for the trait in the other sex, giving rise to a rapid and self-reinforcing selection dynamics. In fitness indicator selection, the trait becomes a display because it reveals the condition or "quality" of the bearer, including absence of deleterious genetic mutations (low *mutation load*), freedom from pathogens and other parasites (low *parasite load*), good nutritional status, and low exposure to stress during development. Note that the term "fitness" in this context indicates an individual's health and condition, not reproductive success or inclusive fitness. The various aspects of an individual's quality are often interdependent—for example, individuals who are healthier because of their low mutation load are often better able to secure high-quality food. Also, when both sexes contribute to parental investment, a mate in good condition is not only able to provide good genes for one's offspring but also high-quality investment—such as better food or better protection and defense of the young. Runaway and fitness indicator selection are best seen as extremes on a continuum, and even traits that originate from runaway processes tend to become fitness indicators as evolution proceeds (Chandler et al., 2013; Kokko et al., 2002; Kuijper et al., 2012).

A trait may function as a fitness indicator because it requires high levels of energy, strength, skill, health, or precise coordination in the expression of many different genes during development. Whatever the mechanism, a fitness indicator must be highly condition-dependent, which also means highly *vulnerable* to various sorts of disruptions—including deleterious mutations, infections, malnutrition, stress, and toxins (Geary, 2015). An indicator of condition is only useful if it discriminates well between individuals of different quality (Figure 1.4); as a result, sexually selected traits tend to show an especially wide range of individual variation. When a fitness indicator is established, other traits may evolve as *amplifiers*. An amplifier is a trait that, while not a fitness indicator itself, functions to increase the condition-sensitivity of an indicator. For example, a decorative pattern on a bird's tail (the amplifier) may make it easier for partners and rivals to evaluate the length of the tail (the indicator; Castellano & Cermelli, 2010; Hasson, 1990).

Outcomes of Sexual Selection

Sexual selection often drives the evolution of sex differences in morphology and behavior, but it can also produce similarities between the sexes, especially when

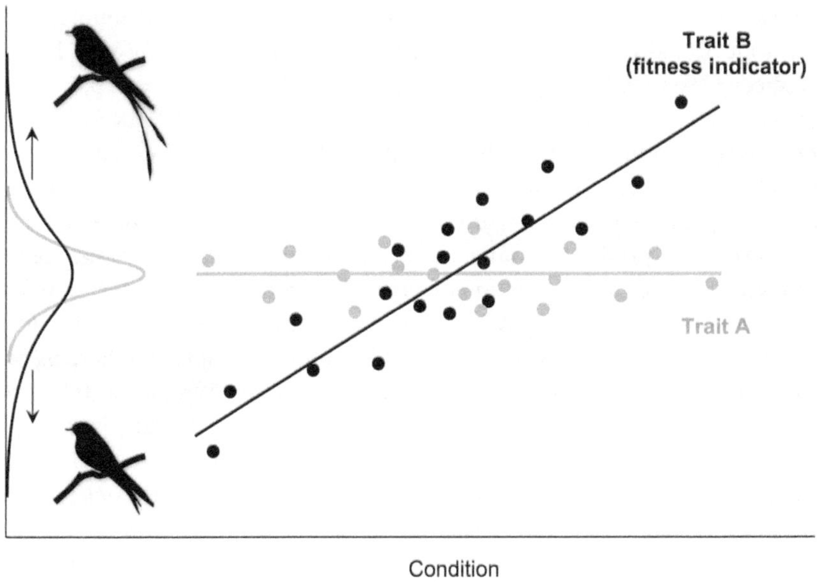

Figure 1.4. Fitness indicator traits are highly dependent on individual condition (e.g., low mutation and parasite load, good nutrition). As a result, they tend to show larger individual variation than other traits (see the distributions on the left).

partner choice is mutual rather than unilateral. Of course, the sexes may diverge even under mutual choice if males and females base their selection on different traits and qualities (Clutton-Brock, 2007). In the biological literature, discussions of sexual selection usually center on morphological traits (e.g., body size, weapons such as claws and horns, ornaments) and on the behaviors involved in the utilization of those traits during contests and courtship (e.g., fighting rituals, courtship dances). However, *cognitive* traits are equally plausible targets of sexual selection. Selection for elaborate songs in bird translates into selection for learning abilities and memory capacity; in species with complex social behaviors, cognitive ability and social intelligence play important roles in both courtship and competition. Selection for cognitive abilities is especially likely to produce similarity between the sexes even when mate choice is unilateral, since the cognitive processes required to evaluate the quality of a display (e.g., a complex bird song) may have to be just as sophisticated as those needed to produce the display itself (Boogert et al., 2011; DeVoogd, 2004; Keagy et al., 2012; Miller, 2000).

Human Mating Systems

Human mating systems are remarkably flexible but, under the surface of cultural and ecological variation, there are some powerful common themes. To begin, *marriage* is a universal feature of human mating. Marriage in the traditional form is a social contract based on an enduring reproductive bond between a man and a woman. Cross-culturally, this contract implies a sexual division of labor: while both parents may contribute to provisioning, women disproportionally engage in childcare in every single society that has been studied (Geary, 2005, 2010; Walker et al., 2011). In all likelihood, pair bonding in our prehuman ancestors originally involved polygynous unions between a male and multiple females (Chapais, 2008, 2011). Today, about 80% of human societies allow polygyny; however, even in polygynous systems most marriages are monogamous, and only a minority of men actually have more than one wife. In contrast, polyandry (a woman marrying multiple men) is extremely rare and limited to marginal, resource-poor ecological contexts (Marlowe, 2003). The rate and intensity of polygyny increased dramatically after agriculture caused a rapid increase in social stratification and wealth inequality; the harems of ancient kings and emperors provide the most dramatic examples of this process (Kaplan et al., 2009; Walker et al., 2011). More recently, socially imposed monogamy has been replacing polygyny in a growing number of cultures, beginning in ancient Greece and Rome and spreading throughout Europe during the Middle Ages (Henrich et al., 2012; MacDonald, 1995*a*; Scheidel, 2009). Across history and cultures, the reproductive success of men has been more variable than that of women, indicating a stronger intensity of sexual selection. Men are more likely than women to leave few or no descendants, but also to father really large numbers of offspring; this general pattern is attenuated in monogamous societies and in foragers, and amplified in polygynous and agrarian societies (Betzig, 2012; Brown et al., 2009).

Humans are clearly adapted for long-term pair bonding—whether monogamous or polygynous—with romantic love serving as a universal psychological mechanism of commitment. Consistent with a central role of pair bonding in offspring provisioning, marriages are most stable when men and women contribute about equally to family subsistence. At the same time, long-term bonding coexists with short-term, uncommitted sexual relationships and with the pervasive occurrence of extramarital affairs (Fletcher et al., 2015; Quinlan, 2008; Schmitt, 2015*a*). Paternity rates in humans are difficult to estimate, but the available evidence indicates high variability: extra-pair paternity may range from 1–2% (the most common scenario) to 10–20% depending on the specific cultural and social context (Anderson, 2006; Larmuseau et al., 2016; Scelza, 2011).

The interplay between long- and short-term mating is one of the defining features of human reproduction (Buss, 2003; Gangestad & Simpson, 2000; Schmitt, 2015*a*). Short-term mating with little or no parental investment can be highly adaptive for men, although there are also potential costs (including sexually transmitted diseases, retaliation from partners and relatives, and loss of reputation). Women benefit comparatively less from mating with many partners because their maximum rate of reproduction is severely limited by pregnancy and lactation. The main determinant of a woman's reproductive success is not her number of sexual partners, but the amount of resources—both material and social—that she can invest or leverage to the benefit of her children. However, short-term sexual relationships have advantages for women as well, from the direct exchange of sex for resources or protection to the chance of mating with a man of higher genetic quality than her long-term partner (sometimes called "gene shopping"). Also, short-term sexual encounters may facilitate mate switching for women who find themselves in unsatisfactory relationships (Gangestad & Simpson, 2000; Greiling & Buss, 2000).

Parental Choice

Another peculiar aspect of human mating is the fact that parents and other close relatives often play an important role in the choice of marriage partners. Parental influence on mate choice can range from subtle to extreme, as in the case of arranged marriages. In both forager and agricultural societies, parental arrangement of marriage is the norm for daughters and a common occurrence for sons. While direct courtship is also widespread and may coexist with parental arrangement to some degree, it is often the case that parents have the last word on whether marriage proposals are accepted (Apostolou, 2010; Walker et al., 2011). Intriguingly, the preferences of parents and those of offspring can be expected to diverge somewhat as a result of parent–offspring conflict, promoting disagreement within families about the choice of the "right" partner (Apostolou, 2007, 2014; Buunk et al., 2008; van den Berg et al., 2013).

Mating Preferences and Strategies

Owing to the fact that both men and women contribute to parental investment, human mating has a strong component of mutual choice (Miller, 2000; Stewart-Williams & Thomas, 2013). When they look for long-term partners, both men and women value traits such as physical attractiveness (a reliable predictor of health; Kalick et al., 1998; Nedelec & Beaver, 2014; Tybur & Gangestad, 2011), intelligence, creativity, humor (a correlate of intelligence; Greengross & Miller, 2011; Hone et al., 2015), social status, industriousness, dependability, and kindness. At the same time, the sexes show some robust differences in their areas of competition and in their preferences for various desirable traits (Buss, 2003; Conroy-Beam et al., 2015; Davies & Shackelford, 2008).

On average, men show a stronger preference for attractiveness and beauty—especially for features that signal youth or high fecundity. (Following biological usage, in this book I use *fecundity* to denote an individual's potential for reproduction and *fertility* to indicate that individual's total number of offspring). In contrast, women are more attracted to indicators of status, resources (e.g., good financial prospects), and physical strength, and tend to prefer partners older than themselves (Gangestad & Scheyd, 2005; Grillot et al., 2014; Kenrick & Keefe, 1992; Shackelford et al., 2005). Preferences for creativity and humor production are also stronger in women than in men (Beaussart et al., 2012; Clegg et al., 2011; Hone et al., 2015; Nettle & Clegg, 2006; Shackelford et al., 2005). Finally, women are more attracted to indicators of a man's willingness to invest in them and their children, such as kindness, generosity, parenting skills, and an interest in infants (Brase, 2006; La Cerra, 1994; Lukaszewski & Roney, 2010). The genetic evidence supports the hypothesis that sexual selection has been involved in the evolution of traits such as height, intelligence, and creativity (Verweij et al., 2014).

This general pattern of mating preferences is modulated by many personal, contextual, and social factors. For example, when men are looking for short-term sexual partners, they become much less selective about personality and tend to prioritize physical cues of current fecundity (e.g., breasts, buttocks) over cues of youth and health (e.g., facial features, symmetry; Confer et al., 2010; Currie & Little, 2009; Lu & Chang, 2012; Zelazniewicz & Pawlowski, 2011). Conversely, women prefer higher dominance and stronger masculine features in their short-term partners (Aitken et al., 2013; Little et al., 2011; Thornhill & Gangestad, 2008). In environments with high levels of pathogens, women's preference for indicators of health increases relative to that for dependability and paternal quality (Gangestad & Simpson, 2000; Lee & Zietsch, 2011; Tybur & Gangestad, 2011). Also, sex differences on several dimensions of mate preferences (e.g., social status, financial prospects, age) are attenuated in countries with higher gender equality in income and access to jobs (Zentner & Mitura, 2012; see also Schmitt, 2012). Depending on the social context, individual preferences may interact more or less strongly with those of parents. When parents evaluate their offspring's potential partners, they systematically place less importance on physical attractiveness and more importance on traits such as good family background, financial prospects, religiosity, and kindness—all indicators that prospective in-laws are going to invest in their offspring and bring benefits to the whole family (Apostolou, 2008*a*, 2008*b*, 2011, 2014; Buunk et al., 2008; Dubbs & Buunk, 2010; Perilloux et al., 2011).

Alternative Mating Strategies

Human mate preferences are complex and partially contradictory. As such, they leave room for a variety of viable mating strategies. This is especially true of male strategies, for two main reasons: first, female preferences are more complex and multidimensional; second, men have a wider range of pathways toward reproductive success, from long-term investment in a woman and her children ("dad" strategies) to uncommitted relationships with multiple sexual partners ("cad" strategies). Throughout our evolutionary history, men's strategies have changed and diversified with each major social transition. Considerable evidence indicates that dominance contests involving physical force and aggression have been the predominant mechanism of male sexual selection in ancestral humans and continue to play a significant role today (Puts, 2010; Hill, Hunt et al., 2013). This includes collective aggression between groups; in fact, capturing women was one of the main objectives of raids and wars in traditional societies (Kaplan et al., 2009). As paternal investment became an increasingly larger component of the human adaptive complex, some of the traits selected as weapons in male–male contests (e.g., upper body strength, throwing ability) may have been partially repurposed as provisioning tools in hunting, fishing, farming, and other forms of manual labor (see Geary, 2010).

The growing interdependence between group members caused by technological advancements and the consequent increase in role specialization—with multiple niches for hunters, tool-makers, healers, warriors, and many others—is likely to have had two important effects on mating competition. First, in a highly interdependent group, the benefits of dominance must be balanced against the need to maintain group cohesion and cooperation. By limiting the adaptive value of naked physical aggression, social interdependence must have intensified selection for social intelligence and political skills and probably favored nonphysical forms of competition (such as public speaking and "verbal duels"; Locke & Bogin, 2006; Puts, 2010). Second, technological and social interdependence make it possible to gain social status and resources by acquiring valuable skills, expertise, and knowledge, thus opening up alternative routes to mating success that do not depend on physical dominance.

In the evolutionary literature, this duality is often captured by the distinction between *dominance*, or social status acquired with the threat of force, and *prestige*, or social status freely conferred by others (Henrich & Gil-White, 2001). The importance of prestige in human societies likely increased with agriculture. As society became increasingly stratified, the number of specialized domains of skills and knowledge grew to unprecedented levels; also, for the first time, it was possible to accumulate wealth and pass it down to one's descendants (e.g., Borgerhoff Mulder, 1987; Cronk, 1991). All the while, dominance competition escalated with the rise of chiefs and warlords and the intensification of polygyny (Kaplan et al., 2009; Puts, 2010). More recently, socially imposed monogamy and state-managed law enforcement have contributed to reduce—but by no means eliminate—the benefits of dominance contests (Winegard et al., 2014). With the expansion of prestige-based competition during human evolution, the scope for direct mate choice by women (and their relatives) has increased considerably, likely resulting in stronger selection on display traits such as humor, verbal skills, and artistic creativity (Klasios, 2013; Miller, 2000; Puts, 2010). The partial divergence between parents' and offspring's preferences may also have contributed to select for *variation* in mating strategies: under parental choice, traits that are especially valuable to parents (such as religiosity and provisioning skills) can lead to reproductive success just as reliably as traits that appeal directly to the preferences of potential mates (Apostolou, 2014).

SOCIAL RELATIONSHIPS

Being an intensely social species, we spend most of our time interacting with other people in a variety of roles and situations. Human social dynamics are driven by the intricate interplay between cooperation and competition with other group members. From a biological standpoint, prosocial behaviors (such as cooperation, helping, and reciprocity) and aggressive, coercive behaviors can be seen as different types of strategies for gaining status and resources (Hawley, 2014*a*, 2014*b*). As described in the previous section, mating accounts for a large amount of competition revolving around dominance, prestige, and attractiveness. While direct mating competition in women is based more on physical attractiveness than on status and wealth, women do compete intensely with one another as they try to secure both material resources and social resources such as friends and allies (Benenson, 2013, 2014; Campbell, 2004; Geary et al., 2014).

Generally speaking, both males and females must balance "getting along" and "getting ahead" within their group; however, the two sexes solve this problem in somewhat different ways. Male groups are larger, show stable status hierarchies determined by one-on-one competition, and tend to be organized around shared goals and activities. Female groups are characterized by fluid, shifting hierarchies and high levels of emotional intimacy, sharing, and reciprocity. In female groups, overt competition and displays of superiority are usually discouraged; in addition, female competition largely avoids physical confrontation and instead employs relational forms of aggression such as gossiping, dismissive nonverbal behaviors, and social exclusion or ostracism (Archer, 2009; Benenson, 2013, 2014; Campbell, 1999, 2004; Geary, 2010; Geary et al., 2003, 2014). While female aggression is usually tempered by caring and egalitarian concerns, there are many exceptions to this pattern; for example, wives in polygynous marriages often compete fiercely with one another for sexual attention, status within the family, and resources for their children (Geary et al., 2014).

Cooperation, Altruism, and Morality

Across societies, cooperation and altruism are greatly facilitated when they occur between close relatives (Burton-Cheller & Dunbar, 2014; Hooper et al., 2015; Madsen et al., 2007; Stewart-Williams, 2007). Even between nonrelatives, there is evidence that facial resemblance and other cues of potential relatedness lead to increased trust and altruistic dispositions (DeBruine et al., 2008; Lieberman et al., 2007); indeed, friends tend to be significantly more genetically similar to one another than to strangers (Christakis & Fowler, 2014). Of course, cooperation is not limited to relatives and often takes place between unrelated or weakly related individuals. People are highly sensitive to reciprocity in cooperative exchanges, and they are more likely to benefit someone if they expect that he or she will return the favor in time. This is known as *reciprocal altruism* (Trivers, 1971), although, from the standpoint of inclusive fitness, it is more correctly described as a kind of mutually beneficial cooperation (see Figure 1.1; West et al., 2007, 2011). Of course, reciprocity can be exploited by cheaters who enjoy its immediate benefits but then fail to reciprocate; this creates the opportunity for social and cognitive arms races in which increased ability to exploit and manipulate others coevolves with better skills for predicting behavior, detecting manipulation, and identifying and remembering cheaters (Cosmides & Tooby, 2015; Cosmides et al., 2010; Flinn et al., 2005).

Large-Scale Cooperation and the Evolution of Moral Norms

Human cooperation can take place on an extraordinarily large scale, easily involving hundreds, thousands, or even millions of individuals depending on the available technologies and means of communication. To achieve this feat, we rely on a rich toolkit of psychological and cultural mechanisms. Two of these mechanisms are *reputation*—people constantly exchange information about the cooperative or selfish behavior of others—and *punishment* (West et al., 2011). Punishment occurs more frequently in larger communities, suggesting that it is an effective mechanism for promoting cooperation beyond the narrow circle of relatives and reciprocal exchange partners. The correlation with group size is especially strong for "altruistic" punishment, in which people willingly incur a personal cost to punish a violator (Henrich et al., 2010; Marlowe et al., 2008). On an even larger scale, *moral norms* seem to play a crucial role in suppressing—or at least regulating—selfish behavior and enabling large-scale cooperation with strangers. Moral reasoning is rooted in a multitude of evolved emotional mechanisms that regulate responses to harm (e.g., empathy), reactions to fairness and unfairness (e.g., gratitude, anger), hierarchical relations (e.g., respect, shame), and even contamination by pathogens and toxins (disgust; Haidt, 2007; Haidt & Kesebir, 2010; see Chapter 2). At the same time, human morality has been extended and organized with the cultural evolution of powerful institutions such as religions and systems of law (Norenzayan & Shariff, 2008; Norenzayan et al., 2016). Moral norms do more than just enable large-scale cooperation. First, they help maintain cohesion by marking the boundaries of the in-group. Second, they permit flexible social coordination by helping people choose sides in conflicts and disputes through moral judgment—that is, based on the moral rightness or wrongness of actions rather than simply on the identity of the conflicting parties. Potentially, this mechanism can prevent any particular individual from gaining too much power, while also avoiding the inevitable escalation of conflict that would result from the formation of rigid alliances (DeScioli & Kurzban, 2013; Haidt & Kesebir, 2010).

The biological and cultural evolution of moral norms creates more opportunities for social arms races. In this case, self-serving moral reasoning (e.g., hypocrisy, self-justification, advocating moral rules that promote one's personal interest) can be expected to coevolve with a mentality of suspicion and with the ability to detect insincere or self-interested moral convictions (Haidt & Kesebir, 2010; Tooby & Cosmides, 2010). Also, reciprocity and moral norms provide the conditions for social selection on credible displays of altruism, fairness, empathy, and generosity. If individuals who display these traits are chosen more often as social partners, the resulting selection pressures can favor a rapid increase of altruistic and cooperative dispositions within a population (Nesse, 2007). At the same time, selection for effective coordination between coalition members may explain pervasive group phenomena such as emotional contagion and conformity (Tooby & Cosmides, 2010). Social selection for altruism and other moral virtues is likely to overlap with sexual selection for the same traits. For example, men are more likely to engage in competitive displays of generosity, altruism, and self-sacrifice when they are being observed by women, consistent with an especially strong role for moral traits in female mate choice (Iredale et al., 2008; McAndrew & Perilloux, 2012; Miller, 2007; Tognetti et al., 2012).

Group Cohesion and Splitting

Group-splitting dynamics are a universal feature of human relationships, from forager bands to modern organizations such as business companies and political parties (Fox, 2004; Hart & Van Vugt, 2006; Walker & Hill, 2014). In group splitting or *fission*, some members leave the original group either to form a new group or to join an existing one. The trajectory of group splitting is accompanied by the escalation of conflict and by the progressive reinforcement of the subgroup's identity in opposition to that of the larger group. In traditional societies, common causes of splitting include stealing, free-riding, and other violations of reciprocity, as well as sexual affairs and—more generally—competition over scarce resources or mates. Competition between political or spiritual leaders often catalyzes group splitting: charismatic leaders play a dual role in this process as they foster cohesion within their faction while instigating conflict with adversaries (Bandy, 2004; Price & Stevens, 1999; Sani, 2008). Predictably, human groups often split at least partially along kinship lines, so that the members of a subgroup are more closely related with one another than with the rest of the group (Walker & Hill, 2014). Splitting becomes increasingly likely as groups become larger and the face-to-face mechanisms that promote cohesion and conflict resolution become progressively less effective. However, organized religions and other structured systems of moral norms can succeed in maintaining group cohesion on a much larger scale. Also, the prospect of conflict with a large competing coalition can powerfully motivate smaller groups to form alliances and merge with one another (Bandy, 2004; Haidt & Kesebir, 2010; Tooby & Cosmides, 2010).

DEVELOPMENT

Individuals change as they move through their life cycle—they grow, mature, decay, develop new traits and lose old ones. Some traits develop smoothly and gradually, while others change dramatically over a short period of time. The relation between evolution and development is deep and bidirectional: while all developmental processes are shaped by natural selection, selection can only modify the traits of an organism by acting on the developmental processes that build them (West-Eberhard, 2003). Any plausible model of human nature must take into account the developmental dimension of behavior and consider the interplay between physical and behavioral change over the life course.

Key Developmental Concepts

Plasticity and Canalization

As a rule, developmental processes are highly *canalized*—that is, they are designed to achieve their target phenotypic outcome despite fluctuations in the environment, perturbations of metabolic processes, mutations in an individual's genome or epigenome, and other sources of random noise. Canalization ensures that individuals of the same species will reliably develop the same basic anatomy and physiology despite being exposed to a wide range of external and internal conditions. At the same time, many phenotypes show some degree of plasticity and can vary in response to the specific environment encountered in development (Debat & David, 2001). While undirected plasticity is usually constrained by natural selection, organisms can evolve mechanisms of adaptive plasticity that respond to specific aspects of the environment in a way that maximizes fitness (DeWitt & Scheiner, 2004; Pigliucci, 2005; Schlichting & Pigliucci, 1998; see Chapter 3).

Ontogenetic and Deferred Adaptations

A developmental perspective suggests a useful distinction between *ontogenetic* and *deferred* adaptations. Ontogenetic adaptations are selected to serve their adaptive function at a specific time in development and often disappear when they are no longer needed. Examples include the placenta, a fetal organ that provides nourishment and other vital functions during prenatal development and is discarded immediately after birth; heat-producing brown fat in infants, which provides enhanced thermoregulation during a critical survival phase and is typically lost in adults; and infantile reflexes such as the suckling reflex (Bjorklund, 1997; Oppenheim, 1981). A subtler example is "neonatal imitation" of facial expressions in newborns. Neonatal imitation disappears around two months of age and—contrary to widespread belief—is not a precursor of later imitation skills. Instead, the primary function of this captivating phenomenon seems that of eliciting parents' attention and facilitating early social interactions (Byrne, 2005). Many other aspects of cognition in infancy and childhood can be interpreted as ontogenetic adaptations with age-limited functions (Bjorklund & Ellis, 2014).

Deferred adaptations are phenotypes that appear in childhood but function—at least in part—to prepare children for adult behavior, and do not express their fitness-enhancing potential until sexual maturity (Hernández Blasi & Bjorklund, 2003). Play is an important example of deferred adaptation. A major function of play in humans and other mammals seems to be that of training the organism to deal with unexpected events, as well as regulating the long-term development of the neuromuscular system. Similarly, play parenting and play fighting are universal, sex-typical behaviors that foster the development of specialized adult skills in males and females (Byers & Walker, 1995; Geary, 2010; Pellegrini, 2013; Spinka et al., 2001).

Stages and Transitions

The human life cycle can be described as a sequence of functionally distinct stages, with transitions between stages usually controlled by hormonal mechanisms (Bogin & Smith, 1996). This pattern is especially clear before sexual maturity; by segmenting development into modular blocks, stages prevent interference

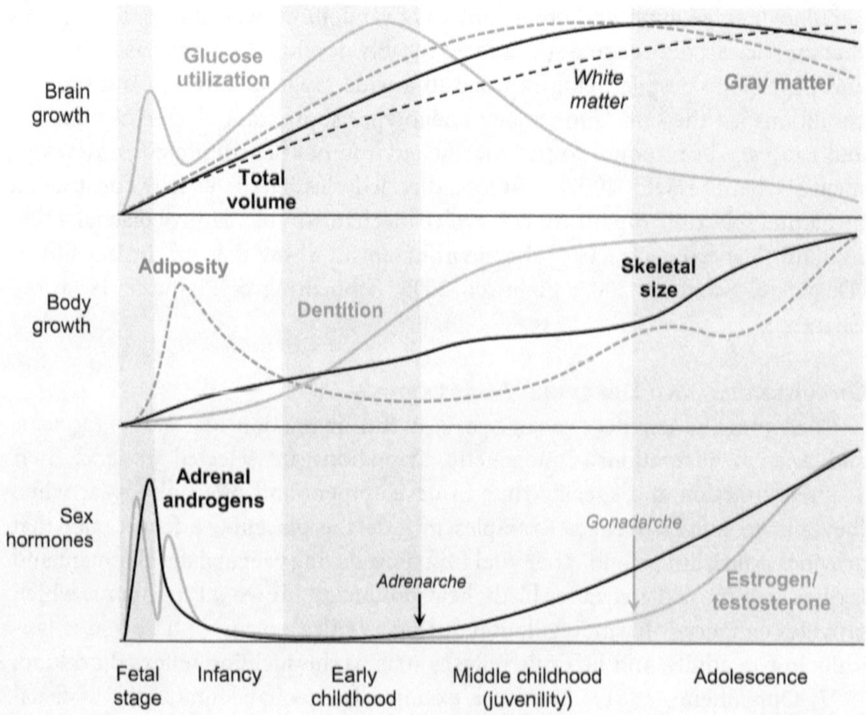

Figure 1.5. Developmental trajectories of human growth and sex hormones production, from conception to sexual maturity. Adapted with permission from Del Giudice (2014c).

between competing functions—for example by ensuring that body growth is complete before switching on the reproductive system—and permit tight coordination in the emergence of physical and behavioral adaptations. Figure 1.5 summarizes the main stages of human development from conception to adulthood.

Fetal Development

The fetal stage is a critical phase of development; it takes place within the environment provided by the mother and further buffered by the placenta (which, as noted earlier, is made up of fetal tissue and can be regarded as an organ of the fetus). Fertilized eggs face extremely high mortality—between 30% and 70% of conceptions do not survive to birth—partly as a result of maternal "screening" mechanisms that trigger spontaneous abortion in the presence of genetically abnormal or malformed zygotes (Brosens et al., 2014; Bruckner et al., 2012; Forbes, 1997). Pregnancy involves a mixture of cooperation and conflict between the mother and the fetus, with a bidirectional network of physiological signals involved in the regulation of fetal nutrition, growth, and even maternal behavior (Del Giudice, 2012*a*; Haig, 1993, 2010; Schlomer et al., 2011; Sherman & Flaxman, 2002). The initial development of the brain is a key function of the fetal stage. During pregnancy, sex hormones are produced both by the mother (mainly estrogen and small amounts of androgens) and by male fetuses during the second trimester (large amounts of androgens, particularly testosterone). Prenatal sex hormones have profound organizational effects on the developing brain and play an important role in the establishment of sex differences in behavior (Berenbaum & Beltz, 2011; Constantinescu & Hines, 2012; Hines, 2011).

Infancy

In mammals, infancy is defined as the period in which the mother provides nourishment to her offspring through lactation. In traditional human societies, weaning occurs around 2–3 years of age. Lactation provides the resources for sustained brain growth and allows infants to accumulate fat stores that will support brain metabolism after weaning. Infancy is marked by rapid cognitive maturation, including the development of basic linguistic competence (Bogin & Smith, 1996; Locke & Bogin, 2006). Intriguingly, the first months of life are marked by a peak of testosterone production in male infants (Figure 1.5), which further contributes to sex-specific brain organization (Hines, 2011). After this early phase of activity, the testes become inactive until puberty and androgen levels drop accordingly.

Infants are fully dependent on their caregivers for survival; within the first year of life they form attachment relationships characterized by intense desire for closeness and separation anxiety, with the mother usually serving as the primary attachment figure (Cassidy, 2008; Marvin & Britner, 2008). And, indeed, infancy is a dangerous time: across cultures and history, 20–30% of newborns have died before the first year of life, with disease as the leading cause and another major contribution being infanticide and abandonment. Mortality remained high through childhood, so that 20–30% of the children who survived the first year still failed to reach puberty (Hrdy, 1999; Volk & Atkinson, 2013). Such high levels of mortality inevitably created strong selection pressures for ontogenetic adaptations designed to help fetuses, infants, and children survive the dangers of early development, even at a cost to later health or reproduction (Jones, 2009).

Childhood

Early childhood (about 3 to 7 years of age) is a uniquely human stage of development (Bogin & Smith, 1996). While other mammals begin to feed themselves right after weaning, humans spend several more years in which they fully depend on adults for feeding. Childhood permits extended brain growth while freeing the mother from lactation, thus shortening the interval between pregnancies and increasing women's potential fertility. Glucose utilization by the brain peaks in early childhood, at around 4 years of age (Kuzawa et al., 2014). The transition from infancy to childhood is marked by a gradual increase in growth hormone, which then takes over as the main regulator of physical growth (Hochberg & Albertsson-Wikland, 2008). The cognitive breakthroughs of early childhood include the emergence of imitation and a dramatic increase in the ability to attribute mental states to other people, or *mentalizing* (also known as *folk psychology* and *theory of mind*; Bjorklund & Causey, 2018; Bjorklund & Ellis, 2014; see Chapter 2).

The next stage of human development is middle childhood (about 7 to 11 years in Western industrialized countries). Middle childhood is analogous to *juvenility* in primates and other mammals—a stage in which the young is still sexually immature but no longer dependent on adults for feeding and protection (Bogin & Smith, 1996). Middle childhood starts with the eruption of the first permanent teeth and the awakening of the adrenal gland (*adrenarche*), which begins to secrete increasing amounts of adrenal androgens, such as dehydroepiandrosterone (DHEA) and its sulfate (DHEAS; Figure 1.5). Adrenal androgens have a broad range of effects; notably, they promote neural plasticity and shift the allocation of energy away from the brain and toward the accumulation of muscle and fat in preparation for puberty. They can also be converted to other androgens (e.g., testosterone) and estrogens in the brain, thus activating sexually differentiated pathways while further organizing brain development in a sex-specific manner (Campbell, 2006, 2011; Del Giudice et al., 2009; Del Giudice, 2014*c*; Kuzawa et al., 2014).

Middle childhood witnesses the emergence or intensification of sex differences in many domains—for example aggression and social play—as well as the first appearance of sexual and romantic attractions (Del Giudice, 2014*c*). The changes of middle childhood include dramatic increases in self-control and motor skills, which enables juveniles to help with domestic tasks such as foraging, preparing food, and taking care of younger siblings (Kramer, 2011). In total, middle childhood is a phase that combines intensive social learning and *integration* into one's group and culture with the emergence of social *competition* for status among peers (Del Giudice, 2014*c*). It also marks the first major peak in the onset of psychopathology (Costello et al., 2003; Kessler et al., 2005).

Adolescence

Adolescence begins with a characteristic growth spurt and the onset of sex hormone production by the gonads (*gonadarche*). This is a phase of rapid physical and behavioral transformation that ends with the completion of growth and the achievement of full sexual maturity. In industrialized countries, the mean age of the first period in girls (*menarche*) has decreased from 15–17 to 12–13 years owing to improved nutrition and health (Parent et al., 2003). Girls remain infecund for some years after menarche, whereas boys become fecund shortly after the peak of their growth spurt. As in middle childhood, rising levels of sex hormones during puberty seem to have both activational and organizational roles on brain function (Bogin & Smith, 1996; Hines, 2011; Locke & Bogin, 2006; Romeo, 2003). Sexual motivation and status competition become central in adolescence; this motivational shift is paralleled by enhanced sensitivity to social cues and evaluation by peers, a dramatic rise in risk-taking behavior (especially in boys), and a surge in parent–child conflicts (Blakemore & Robbins, 2012; Ellis et al., 2012; Steinberg et al., 2008). In adolescence, the brain as a whole becomes smaller due to the loss of gray matter that accompanies cortical maturation; however, the development of axonal connections (reflected in increasing white matter volume) continues well into adulthood (Figure 1.5; Blakemore et al., 2010; Casey et al., 2011).

Adulthood and Senescence

While the segmentation of the life cycle becomes less clear-cut after sexual maturity, several important transitions take place in adulthood. For example, the birth of a child is associated with extensive hormonal and behavioral changes in both parents (Edelstein et al., 2015; Gettler, 2014). From this vantage point, parenthood can be viewed as a functionally meaningful life stage even if it is not tied to a particular age. Another key transition for women is that of menopause, which marks the end of their reproductive window. Some aspects of behavior in old age may have been selected for in the context of specific human traits such as multigenerational provision and helping by grandparents (Gurven & Kaplan, 2009).

After maturity, bodily and brain functions gradually deteriorate as part of *senescence*, resulting in a pattern of increasing mortality over time (Jones et al., 2014). Even if senescence impairs health and accelerates death, evolutionary models show that it can be optimal for organisms to allow their body to decay if later mortality is compensated for by increased reproduction earlier in life. In other words, senescence is not something that organisms endure passively, but (at least in part) an evolved design feature that depends on a specific balance of fitness costs and benefits (Kaplan & Robson, 2009; Kirkwood, 1990). The evolution of senescence powerfully illustrates the distinction between adaptive and desirable traits and underscores the role of natural selection in shaping the whole life cycle, from conception to death.

2

The Evolved Mind

In modern psychological terms, the mind can be described as a network of information-processing mechanisms whose function is to control and regulate behavior. These mechanisms are mainly instantiated in the brain, although some processing may take place in the rest of the nervous system and even outside of it (e.g., the immune system collects and integrates information about pathogen threats and can modulate brain functioning via hormonal signals). The mechanisms that enable and govern our behavior today have been shaped by the ecology and behavior of our ancestors across countless generations; the mind/brain can then be studied as an evolved "computational organ"—or, more precisely, a collection of specialized organs that perform various kinds of computations (Barrett, 2015; Carruthers, 2006). In this chapter, I introduce the idea that psychological mechanisms are adaptations and consider some of its most important implications. I then examine three aspects of mental functioning that are especially relevant to the disorders discussed later in the book: motivation and emotion, decision-making and self-regulation, and the distinction between mentalistic and mechanistic cognition. Throughout the chapter, I focus on the biological and computational functions of psychological mechanisms and touch only briefly on their localization in the brain. I conclude with an overview of key neurobiological systems, from brain monoamines such as dopamine and serotonin to sex- and stress-related hormones.

PSYCHOLOGICAL MECHANISMS AS ADAPTATIONS

As discussed in Chapter 1, the individual-as-maximizing agent (IMA) principle predicts that an organism's behavior will tend to maximize its expected fitness, at least in environments sufficiently similar to that in which the behavior originally evolved. However, fitness cannot be maximized directly but only indirectly by being successful at foraging, avoiding pathogens and predators, finding and attracting mates, and so on. Moreover, inclusive fitness does not map neatly on individual reproductive success, and some of its components (e.g., indirect or subtle effects on the reproduction of related recipients) may be difficult or impossible to observe within a lifetime. As a result, any individual trying to directly maximize its own fitness would face a hopeless task. The black-box observation that behavior tends to maximize fitness does not imply that organisms possess a general "fitness maximization mechanism"; rather, behavior is likely to be controlled by multiple systems that specialize in reaching narrower fitness-related goals such as finding and choosing food or improving one's social status. A key tenet of evolutionary psychology is that people should be viewed as "adaptation executors" rather than direct "fitness maximizers" (Tooby & Cosmides, 1992, 2015).

Another important reason to focus on psychological adaptations is that they are the best candidates for the truly universal features of human nature. While human behavior shows many regularities, specific behavioral patterns are usually variable and contingent on learning, ecological and social conditions, and individual differences. Psychological mechanisms embody the computational rules that enable learning and behavioral flexibility; thus, the basic design features of a mechanism—or, more precisely, the evolved processes that control and regulate its development—can be universal even if the resulting behaviors are highly variable and context-dependent (Barrett, 2015; Bjorklund et al., 2007; Tooby & Cosmides, 1992).

The Environment of Evolutionary Adaptedness

Biological adaptation is a historical concept; in essence, all claims about adaptation are claims about the past. Traits that promote fitness in a certain environment may become neutral or maladaptive if the environment changes. While natural selection is expected—all else being equal—to weed out traits that have become detrimental to fitness, the process may often take a long time. This generates the potential for *mismatch* between an organism's adaptations and its present environment.

The environment in which a given trait evolved is often referred to as its *environment of evolutionary adaptedness* (EEA). Despite some misrepresentations in the literature, the EEA is not a specific time or place (e.g., the African savannah or the Pleistocene), but a statistical composite of those aspects of the environment that have shaped the evolution of a given trait across space, time, and generations. For this reason, different adaptations within the same organism can have widely different EEAs (Durrant & Ellis, 2003; Tooby & Cosmides, 1990). Consider two human adaptations: language and shivering in response to cold. While language originated in the human lineage no more than 2 million years ago, the shivering response has a much more ancient history and is shared with other warm-blooded vertebrates. Likewise, the dimensions of the environment that shaped shivering and language show virtually no overlap—factors such as external temperature and metabolic rates are crucial for the evolution of shivering but irrelevant to that of language. Because the EEA is not a specific environment, it does not have to be static; on the contrary, the amount and type of environmental variation experienced during the evolution of a trait is an important component of that trait's EEA.

For example, metabolic processes can evolve to maximize survival in unpredictable environments in which food abundance is suddenly followed by starvation.

Functional Specialization

In the most general sense, the overarching function of the mind/brain as a whole is to generate predictions in the service of action (Bar, 2007; Barrett, 2015; Clark, 2013). At the same time, there are strong reasons to believe that the mind—including "higher" mental functions such as reasoning and decision-making—is composed of a large number of evolved computational mechanisms, each specialized to process a specific kind of input (Barrett, 2015; Carruthers, 2006). Note that, in the broad sense employed here, computation refers to the manipulation of information regardless of its format (e.g., symbolic representations, distributed activations within a neural network; see Piccinini & Scarantino, 2011). Functional specialization (often discussed as *modularity* or *domain specificity*) is a common outcome of natural selection because it promotes computational efficiency, increases robustness (the mind as a whole can function even if a particular mechanism is damaged or perturbed), and facilitates rapid evolution as it allows selection to modify and fine tune the design of a mechanism without affecting the rest of the system (Tooby & Cosmides, 1990, 1992, 2015). As a rule, psychological mechanisms do not work as indivisible units but can be further decomposed into a number of simpler elements, some of which may be shared with other mechanisms. Because of the nested and partially overlapping nature of mental adaptations, psychological taxonomies are necessarily "fuzzy," and there are multiple valid ways of drawing boundaries between different systems and subsystems.

The question of how psychological mechanisms interact to produce flexible, adaptive behavior is still largely unanswered. In principle, the components of mind might be arranged in a hierarchical structure whereby higher level mechanisms monitor and control the activity of lower level ones, or in a horizontal structure whereby multiple interacting mechanisms work in parallel and compete for the control of behavior (e.g., Minsky, 1988; see Barrett, 2015, Carruthers, 2006). Still another alternative is a "soft" hierarchy in which interactions are mainly horizontal, but some mechanisms exert asymmetric influences or even "veto power" over others (e.g., through unidirectional inhibitory inputs).

The Nature of Specialized Mechanisms

Over the years, the issue of specialization has generated much debate but also a lot of conceptual confusion. Contrary to widespread misconceptions, functional specialization does *not* entail that a mechanism will process its input in an automatic or reflex-like fashion; that it will be unresponsive to contextual factors and conscious control; that it will be "encapsulated" or impermeable to information exchange with other mechanisms; that it will be present and functional from birth; or that it will follow innate rules that cannot be modified by learning. Instead, the operating characteristics of any given mechanisms should depend on its particular evolved function; for instance, specialized decision-making mechanisms may be *designed* to integrate a broad range of inputs, interact with other systems, and respond in a flexible way to contextual factors. Other mechanisms may respond automatically and inflexibly but depend heavily on learning—a dramatic example of the latter is Pavlovian (classical) aversive conditioning. More generally, learning is by no means antithetical to evolved specialization; on the contrary, psychological mechanisms may require a considerable amount of experience and environmental input to fully acquire their functionality. Conversely, adaptive learning processes must embody at least some assumptions about the expected structure of the world and/or be biased to attend to certain kinds of stimuli—in other words, they must be functionally specialized to some degree (see Barrett, 2015; Barrett & Kurzban, 2006).

The popularity of the idea that specialized mechanism are rapid, automatic, nonconscious, and associative whereas domain-general mechanisms are slow, controlled, conscious, and rule-based can be linked to the rise of dual-systems theories of cognition. In their early versions, these theories contrasted a rapid and intuitive "System 1" with a slow and deliberative "System 2" (Evans, 2008). More recently, however, dual-systems theorists have considerably softened the distinction and acknowledged that psychological mechanisms may show combinations of both types of attributes (e.g., both automatic *and* rule-based). Accordingly, the classic System 1–System2 distinction has been recast as a much narrower contrast between multiple "Type 1" systems that require little or no access to working memory and multiple "Type 2" systems that rely on working memory to support hypothetical thinking and the simulation of mental scenarios (Evans & Stanovich, 2013).

In current evolutionary thinking, the domain of a mechanism is defined by the formal properties of its input and does not have to correspond to a narrow type of *content* such as food items, predators, or sexual partners. Psychological mechanisms can specialize to process abstract properties such as the temporal or logical sequence of a chain of events; also, their domain of operation can be extremely wide (e.g., "all physical objects" or "all rewarding stimuli"). Thus, a given mechanism can serve multiple functions and be recruited to perform different kinds of tasks (Anderson, 2010). On this view, the distinction between domain-specific and domain-general mechanisms loses meaning: *all* evolved mechanisms have a domain, however wide and abstractly defined (Barrett & Kurzban, 2006). This meaning of functional specialization is broader than the one usually found in neuroscience, where the term is employed to describe brain areas that specifically respond to certain content categories (e.g., faces, places, tools) or certain types of task (e.g., language comprehension, spatial orientation; Kanwisher, 2010). It is also useful to distinguish between a mechanism's *proper* domain—the input it was selected to process in the EEA—and its *actual* domain: that is, the input it processes in the present (Sperber, 1994). Sensory mechanisms that evolved to detect high-calorie sugars in food can now be activated by artificial sweeteners without any nutritive value; mentalizing processes that evolved in the context of face-to-face relationships can be applied to fictional characters in novels and movies. Over time, the proper domain of a mechanism and the range of functions it performs can change as individuals are exposed to novel selection pressures.

It is important to stress that functional modularity is not the same as *anatomical* modularity at the macroscopic level of visible brain structures. In neuroscience, modules are usually defined as clusters of brain regions that show strong anatomical connections, correlated variation in size, or correlated activity patterns (e.g., Gómez-Robles et al., 2014; Meunier et al., 2010). Since neural communication is more efficient at shorter distances, it is reasonable to expect some overlap between functional and anatomical modularity. To be sure, the human brain has a markedly modular organization, which seems to have facilitated the semi-independent evolution of different regions and structures (Barger et al., 2014; Gómez-Robles et al., 2014; Kanwisher, 2010; Wig, 2017). However, there is no reason that psychological mechanisms should always be localized within narrow areas of the brain; on the contrary, some mechanisms may be widely distributed across brain regions and include both cortical and subcortical structures. The analogy with bodily organs is a useful one. Whereas the liver is highly localized, the immune system is spread across the whole body; the circulatory system is similarly distributed, but it also includes some localized structures (e.g., the heart). In all these examples, a mechanism's degree of localization is ultimately dictated by its biological function.

The flip side of specialization is that different psychological mechanisms may partly rely on the same processes. Powerful computational principles such as Bayesian inference (see later discussion) and reinforcement learning can be successfully applied to a wide range of information-processing tasks including perception, reasoning, decision-making, and action control (Clark, 2013; Dayan, 2012; Dayan & Daw, 2008; Geisler & Diehl, 2003; Gopnik & Bonawitz, 2015; Kacelink, 2012; Vilares & Körding, 2011). In this sense, those computational principles can be regarded as domain-general, even if the mechanisms that employ them have their own specialized domains (Carruthers, 2006). Also, most models of the mind postulate the existence of shared cognitive workspaces (e.g., working memory) that can be accessed by multiple mechanisms to carry out their specific tasks.

MOTIVATION AND EMOTION

Motivational systems (also called *behavioral systems* in the ethological literature) are psychological mechanisms that organize behavior by orienting an individual toward biologically significant goals, tracking its progress toward those goals, responding to opportunities or obstacles, and promoting learning of goal-related strategies and skills (see Aunger & Curtis, 2013; Carruthers, 2006). In some cases, the goal of a motivational system is to keep a certain parameter close to its set point (homeostasis), as in the regulation of drinking and fluid intake. An example of social homeostasis comes from infant attachment, where a key goal of the system is to maintain physical proximity to the caregiver. In other instances, motivational systems are designed to flexibly adjust their goals in response to circumstances, as in the regulation of mating and dominance behaviors (e.g., the adaptive goals of high-ranking individuals are often different from those of low-ranking ones).

Importantly, the goals of a system need not be consciously represented by the individual. In extreme case, they may not be represented at all; bacteria manage to effectively swim toward nutrients without any internal representations of the reason for their behavior—or even of the direction in which they are swimming (see Dennett, 2009). In more complex organisms, motivational systems may rely on multiple sources of information about the state of the individual and its environment. For example, the pituitary gland constantly collects and integrates information about the volume and dilution of the blood, which in turn informs the system that controls thirst and fluid intake. The same logic applies to social motivations. In Chapter 1, I discussed how coefficients of relatedness play a crucial role in the cost-benefit analysis of cooperation and altruism. In the real world, relatedness is not a known quantity, but has to be estimated by combining various sources of information about other individuals. Some relatedness cues are weak and probabilistic (e.g., physical resemblance), while others are clear-cut and very accurate (e.g., having been nursed by the same mother). In humans, there is evidence that relatedness estimates are computed based on multiple cues and used to modulate altruistic behavior, sexual attraction, and other social motivations (Lieberman et al., 2007; Tooby et al., 2008). The information summaries employed by motivational systems can be described as *internal regulatory variables* (Tooby & Cosmides, 2008, 2015; Tooby et al., 2008). In all likelihood, most of the regulatory variables in the human brain are computed outside of consciousness and are largely or fully inaccessible to introspection.

While organisms have multiple biological goals, they cannot pursue all of them at the same time. Determining and managing priorities is thus a central task of motivational mechanisms. A key component of any motivational system is the set of rules that determine when and how strongly it will become activated, based on internal and/or external cues and the associated regulatory variables. A system's "rules of engagement" may be more or less complex and may depend on the activation state of other systems. The motivation to eat is partly determined by an individual's internal state (e.g., stomach fullness, blood glucose), but the sight and smell of delicious food may induce hunger even when internal cues alone would not. Conversely, hunger may be suppressed when other high-priority systems are activated, for example in presence of an immediate danger such as a venomous snake. Finally, motivational systems receive input from cognitive appraisals—a snake in a glass box may evoke a very different response than the same snake crawling on the floor. When two or more systems with incompatible goals become activated at the same time, the resulting motivational conflict may require the intervention of specialized regulatory mechanisms, as I discuss later in this chapter.

Emotions

When motivational systems are activated, they trigger the onset of emotions (such as fear and joy) and other feelings such as hunger, sexual arousal, and safety. The line between emotions and feelings is a blurred one and may have to do more with the conventions of language than with biological and psychological reality. Both emotions and feelings have affective *valence*—they are either subjectively positive (rewarding) or negative (aversive)—and both contribute to regulate behavior in similar ways. In an evolutionary perspective, emotions and feelings are best understood as *modes of functioning* of the brain that coordinate physiological, cognitive, and behavioral responses to fitness-relevant events and situations. In other words, they are superordinate psychological mechanisms designed to coordinate the activity of other mechanisms, including those involved in attention, perception, memory, learning, and physiological regulation (Al-Shawaf et al., 2016; Nesse, 1990, 2004*a*; Nesse & Ellsworth, 2009; Tooby & Cosmides, 1990, 2008). To illustrate, fear activates immediate physiological changes in circulation, respiration, and digestion; increases perceptual acuity and improves the quick detection of threats; increases the salience of conceptual categories such as "dangerous" and "safe" (e.g., a closet may suddenly be perceived as a hiding place); directs memory to threat- and escape-relevant information; activates powerful learning systems (fear conditioning); makes some behavioral responses (e.g., running) more likely; and, depending on context, may result in facial and vocal expressions that communicate the presence of a threat to others (Tooby & Cosmides, 2008). Accordingly, affective experiences are associated with the activation of multiple brain regions, with considerable overlap between different emotions (Lindquist et al., 2012; more on this later). Depending on their function, emotions may or may not have specific nonverbal markers (e.g., a characteristic facial expression). While clearly expressing anger may be adaptive, other emotions such as jealousy may be strategically designed to have no obvious external cues (Al-Shawaf et al., 2016; Sznycer et al., 2017).

An important function of some emotions is to recalibrate the value of motivational regulatory variables, both in the affected individual and in others. Intense fear in response to a life-endangering threat may switch the internal representation of the environment from safe to unsafe. Expressing anger in response to a slight may increase the implicit "weight" that others assign to the welfare of the angry individual, making it more likely that the latter will be treated fairly in the future. More generally, emotional expressions elicit emotional states in others, which then feed back on the individual's own emotions in a loop of reciprocal regulation (Gilbert, 2015; Tooby & Cosmides, 2008, 2015; Tooby et al., 2008). Given their central role in changing and updating internal representations, it is not surprising that emotions can be exploited to manipulate others, either by producing simulated or exaggerated emotional displays (e.g., pretending to be angry or hurt) or by strategically eliciting affective states (e.g., inducing guilt; Al-Shawaf et al., 2016).

Emotions and Motivational Systems

Motivational systems control goal-directed behavior by deploying adaptive emotional programs in response to cues and events that activate the system, indicate success or progress toward the system's proximate goal, or indicate failure or obstacles to achieving the goal. For example, a sudden scream in the dark is likely to activate the fear system, whose goal is to avoid or escape an immediate threat. The system's activation is marked by the emotion of fear; in turn, fear orchestrates a complex suite of responses, possibly including escape behaviors such as hiding or running away. If one manages to avoid the threat (motivational success), fear will subside and be replaced by relief and a feeling of security; after a while, the fear system will deactivate and give way to other motivational priorities (e.g., hunger). If the threat cannot be avoided (motivational failure), the system may switch from fear to despair, trigger extreme defensive programs such as fainting, or activate the aggression motivational system in an attempt to fight back the threat.

In sum, motivational systems set the goals of behavior and monitor cues of success and failure in the pursuit of those goals. Motivational systems affect behavior indirectly by triggering emotions, which in turn coordinate adaptive suites of physiological, cognitive, and behavioral responses. Different motivational systems may deploy similar or identical emotions in the service of different goals. Anger may be triggered by the aggression system in response to a physical threat, by the attachment system in response to separation from a caregiver, or by the pair bonding system in response to a partner's infidelity (see later discussion for details). Conversely, it is quite possible that emotion terms such as "anger" and "love" actually refer to families of related but motivationally distinct mechanisms. Romantic love has many aspects in common with parental love, has likely evolved out of it, and depends on some of the same psychological and physiological mechanisms (Crespi, 2016*a*; Esch & Stefano, 2005; Feldman, 2017; Panksepp, 1998). Still, the two differ in important respects and have been shaped by selection to serve different adaptive goals. While aggressive anger overlaps with attachment-related anger well enough that the same word may be used to describe both, the two may differ in subtle ways and be mediated by partially distinct mechanisms.

The intricate relationship between motivation and emotion has two important implications. First, most affective labels have low motivational specificity—knowing that a person feels angry or ashamed says relatively little about his or her goals and motivational state. Second, emotions come in functionally related families that reflect the underlying structure of motivational systems. To the extent that motivational systems are functionally related to one another and/or rely on similar affective mechanisms, the phenotypic map of emotions can be expected to contain many fuzzy, overlapping clusters rather than a small number of sharply defined "basic" categories (Nesse, 2004*a*; Nesse & Ellsworth, 2009; Sznycer et al., 2017). In this perspective, there is also no clear-cut distinction between short-lived emotions and long-lasting moods. However, while emotions are tied to the action of specific motivational systems, moods are more likely the product of regulatory processes that affect multiple systems at once.

Human Motivational Systems

Table 2.1 shows a nonexhaustive list of motivational systems in humans (see Aunger & Curtis, 2013; Gilbert, 1995, 2015; Keltner et al., 2006; Kenrick et al.,

Table 2.1 A Partial List of Human Motivational Systems

Motivational system	Proximate goals	Examples of associated emotions/feelings
Aggression system	Counter immediate threats by threatening or inflicting harm Harm and/or control other individuals/organisms (e.g., prey)	*Activation:* anger, rage, excitement *Success:* relief, satisfaction *Failure:* frustration, fear
Fear system	Avoid or escape immediate threats	*Activation:* fear, freezing (attentive immobility), panic *Success:* relief, safety *Failure:* shock, despair, tonic immobility
Security system	Detect and prevent potential threats	*Activation:* anxiety, wariness, apprehension *Success:* relief, safety *Failure:* fear, guilt
Disgust system	Avoid contact with pathogens and/or toxins (pathogen disgust) Avoid undesirable sexual contacts (sexual disgust) Condemn moral violations (moral disgust)	*Activation:* disgust, repulsion, nausea *Success:* relief *Failure:* discomfort, shame, guilt
Status system	Improve, maintain, and display status (dominance and/or prestige) Defer/submit to higher status individuals	*Activation:* ambition, anxiety, envy, embarrassment *Success:* confidence, pride, admiration, awe *Failure:* frustration, shame, anger, sadness
Mating system	Find, attract, and select sexual partners Engage in sexual intercourse Conceive offspring	*Activation:* excitement, arousal, desire, embarrassment *Success:* pleasure, joy, confidence, pride *Failure:* frustration, sadness, anxiety, shame
Attachment system	Maintain proximity and availability of caregivers	*Activation:* loneliness, anxiety, fear, anger *Success:* joy, safety, relief, comfort *Failure:* sadness, despair, loneliness

Caregiving system	Protect and provision offspring and other dependent individuals	*Activation:* solicitude, compassion, anxiety *Success:* joy, satisfaction, pride *Failure:* sadness, guilt
Pair bonding system	Form and maintain long-term relationships with sexual partners Prevent and/or detect infidelity	*Activation:* romantic love, jealousy *Success:* joy, security *Failure:* sadness, loneliness, anger
Affiliation system	Form and maintain relationships with group members (e.g., friends)	*Activation:* sympathy, loneliness, anxiety, fear *Success:* joy, security, belonging *Failure:* sadness, loneliness
Reciprocity system	Find and select cooperation partners Cooperate, trade favors and resources Monitor and enforce fairness	*Activation:* trust, suspiciousness, envy, indignation *Success:* joy, satisfaction, pride, gratitude *Failure:* sadness, anger, guilt
Acquisition system	Acquire, accumulate, and defend resources	*Activation:* desire, greed, envy, anxiety *Success:* joy, satisfaction, pride, security *Failure:* frustration, sadness, anger
Play system	Acquire and improve skills (physical, social, cognitive) Display skills and other attractive traits Promote social bonding	*Activation:* excitement, engagement *Success:* joy, confidence *Failure:* frustration, boredom
Curiosity system	Acquire knowledge Explore the environment	*Activation:* curiosity, excitement, surprise *Success:* satisfaction, pride, confidence, insight *Failure:* frustration, boredom, anxiety, confusion

2010; McGuire & Troisi, 1998; Panksepp, 1998, 2011; Toronchuk & Ellis, 2013). Each system has one or more proximate goals and a characteristic set of emotions that correspond to its activation, success, and failure. For brevity, the list does not include the many feeling-regulated systems that mediate basic physiological needs such as eating, drinking, sleeping, and temperature regulation. Some scholars have argued for a small core of motivational/emotional systems that are phylogenetically ancient and exist in homologous forms across mammalian species (e.g., Panksepp, 1998, 2011). While these criteria apply to some important systems such as fear and attachment, there is no a priori reason to restrict one's attention to mechanisms that are shared by all mammals. Each species faces its own set of ecological and social challenges, which in turn drive the evolution of specialized motivational systems and goals. Among other things, the human adaptive complex includes extended cooperation with non-kin, extensive reliance on technology and information transmission, pair bonding, and multigeneration transfer of resources. These traits have been critical to human fitness for thousands of generations and have shaped their own sets of motivations and associated emotions such as jealousy, greed, and curiosity (Al-Shawaf et al., 2016; Aunger & Curtis, 2013).

Aggression System

Aggression is a basic motivation to harm or threaten other organisms, including—but not limited to—individuals of the same species. Aggression is often deployed as a defensive strategy by immediate threats to oneself, one's kin, or one's allies (*reactive* aggression). Reactive aggression is marked by intense arousal, anger, or rage, and can be triggered by high levels of fear (Panksepp, 1998, 2011). For this reason, aggression and fear are sometimes discussed together as part of a unitary "fight-or-flight" or "fight-flight-freeze" system (e.g., Corr, 2013). However, aggressive motivations are not necessarily defensive; a prime example of *proactive* aggression is hunting, which involves extreme aggression toward prey but no anger. Proactive aggression is instrumental and cold-blooded, and may even be accompanied by feelings of pleasure and excitement (Elbert et al., 2010; Panksepp, 1998). In humans, proactive aggression is also a key component of group conflicts and wars, in the course of which the enemy is dehumanized and effectively treated like prey (Wrangham, 1999). Proactive aggression can be employed to reinforce dominance hierarchies, take or steal resources, and more generally control the behavior of other individuals. Importantly, humans can use language to make threats, hurt another individual's reputation, exclude him or her from the group, incite others to violence, and so on; thus, *verbal* and *relational* aggression play an important role in our species alongside physical aggression (Archer, 2009).

Fear System

The fear system is an ancient defensive mechanism that motivates organisms to avoid or escape immediate threats. This system can be activated by a multitude of cues and situations, and many specific fears are acquired through learning. However, some types of stimuli elicit fear with no need for learning (e.g., sudden loud noises) or after minimal exposure (e.g., snakes, spiders, angry male faces; LoBue & Rakison, 2013; Mallan et al., 2013; Öhman, 2009). The existence of so-called "innate fears" is highly adaptive; when even a single exposure to a certain recurring threat can lead to death, trial-and-error learning is simply too dangerous to be an option. *Tonic* and *attentive immobility* are important components of the fear system. Attentive immobility or "freezing" occurs in preparation for escape or fighting; tonic immobility is a kind of paralysis or fainting without loss of consciousness, a last resort defense when harm is inevitable. Freezing and tonic immobility can be associated with analgesia, emotional numbing, and dissociative experiences (Hagenaars et al., 2014; Nijenhuis et al., 1998).

Security System

Like the fear system, the security system is an ancient mechanism designed to protect organisms from threats. The crucial difference is that fear is triggered by immediate threats, whereas security motivation is activated by *potential* threats—that is, threats that are relatively rare and difficult to detect but may have catastrophic consequences, such as predators or contaminating pathogens (Boyer & Liénard, 2006; Woody & Szechtman, 2011). Immediate threats evoke fear and escape/fight behaviors; in contrast, activation of the security system is marked by anxiety, wariness, and precautionary repetitive behaviors such as checking and exploration, which are designed to gather further information about the presence of potential risks. Indeed, the security system tends to inhibit fear, preventing flight/panic responses to permit cautious exploration (Graeff, 2004). By its nature, the security system is activated by subtle and indirect cues of danger; once activated, is not easily switched off because the *absence* of a potential threat is hard or even impossible to determine with certainty, and there are no clear signals indicating whether precautionary behaviors have been successful. In humans, security motivation often involves heightened perceptions of responsibility, and failing to avert a preventable threat may lead to painful feelings of guilt.

Disgust System

The disgust system is a defensive mechanism whose original function is preventing contact with pathogens and/or toxins through ingestion of contaminated foods, drinks, or waste products; manipulation of contaminated objects; and contact with infected people (*pathogen* disgust; Curtis, 2011; Toronchuk & Ellis, 2013). Pathogen disgust promotes physical avoidance, expulsion (e.g., vomiting), and cleaning behaviors. Disgust can also trigger activation of the security system; indeed, the two systems often work in synergy. Over evolutionary history, the disgust system has been coopted and differentiated to deal with other kinds of threats (Rozin et al., 2008; Tybur et al., 2013). In particular, *sexual* disgust is designed to prevent sexual contact with partners that would be detrimental to fitness, for example because they are too old, too genetically similar (e.g., siblings and other close kin), or prone to sexually transmitted diseases (e.g., highly promiscuous individuals). Finally, disgust in our species is deeply connected to morality: violations of moral norms and taboos can elicit disgust and feelings of uncleanliness and contamination (e.g., Chapman et al., 2009). A likely function of *moral* disgust is to motivate and coordinate social distancing from individuals who violate moral rules (Tybur et al.,

2013). While failure to avoid contact with disgusting objects leads to intense physical discomfort, motivational failures in the sexual and moral domains may evoke self-evaluative emotions such as shame and guilt.

Status System

Dominance hierarchies are extremely common in animals, and so is the existence of specialized motivational systems designed to deal with the challenges of social rank. Dominance systems have a dual function: that of enhancing or defending one's rank and that of submitting to higher ranking individuals to avoid punishment and retaliation (McGuire & Troisi, 1998; Toronchuk & Ellis, 2013). In our species, social hierarchies reflect both physical dominance and skill-based prestige; the more general concept of a "status system" covers both aspects, emphasizing the complex nature of human competition (Anderson et al., 2015; Aunger & Curtis, 2013; see also Keltner et al., 2006). The status system is activated by challenges to one's dominance rank or prestige (from provocations and disrespectful acts to situations that involve social judgments), but also by opportunities to rise in the social hierarchy. The emotions associated with the system's success include pride and confidence, whereas failure may trigger shame, frustration, anger, and sadness. Importantly, voluntary deference to high-status individuals such as leaders and teachers can evoke a range of positive emotions such as admiration and awe (Keltner et al., 2006). Dominance competition often elicits aggression, and the two systems are deeply connected on a functional level (Anderson et al., 2015; Toronchuk & Ellis, 2013).

Mating System

The mating system plays a critical role in reproduction by motivating sexual behavior, from courtship and mate choice to copulation. The system is activated by the presence or prospect of attractive partners and draws on a broad range of feelings and emotions, from excitement to embarrassment to sexual arousal (Al-Shawaf et al., 2016; McGuire & Troisi, 1998; Panksepp, 1998). Ultimately, the function of the mating system is to conceive offspring; however, its core proximate goals are sexual pleasure and intercourse rather than conception per se. Sexual desire can thus become largely decoupled from reproduction, for example as a result of effective birth control. At the same time, there are some indications that a conscious desire to have children may be an evolved feature of mating motivation in humans, particularly in women (Brase & Brase, 2012; Rotkirch, 2007; Rotkirch et al., 2011).

Attachment System

Like most young mammals, infants and children are vulnerable and depend on adults for feeding and protection. The attachment system is designed to monitor and maintain the proximity and availability of caregivers; physical separations quickly activate the system, as do perceptions of danger, pain, and discomfort. Emotional responses to separation include anxiety and angry protests, whereas a sensitive response from the caregiver reliably deactivates the system and evokes feelings of safety and relief. In infancy and childhood, attachment has high motivational priority, consistent with its critical role in ensuring survival. When activated, the attachment system inhibits play and curiosity; conversely, the presence of an available attachment figure works as a "secure base" for exploration (Kobak & Madsen, 2008; Marvin & Britner, 2008; Posada et al., 2013). In all likelihood, the mammalian attachment system originally evolved from mating-related mechanisms promoting physical proximity and contact. In our species, attachment has been coopted as a building block of close relationships in adulthood, including those with romantic partners and friends (Crespi, 2016*a*; Del Giudice, 2009*a*; Fletcher et al., 2015; Panksepp, 1998). Specifically, most intimate relationships involve an attachment component as they provide comfort, reassurance, and safety in times of distress.

Caregiving System

Mirroring the biological function of the attachment system, the caregiving system motivates parents and other caregivers to protect and nurture their dependent young (Brown et al., 2012; Cassidy, 2008; Panksepp, 1998, 2011). As a species, humans show many features of *cooperative breeding*: across societies, care and protection are provided not just by parents but by multiple individuals including older siblings, grandparents, and friends (Hrdy, 2005; Kramer, 2010). Thus, caregiving motivations are not restricted to one's biological offspring; conversely, children are predisposed to form multiple attachment relationships in addition to the one with their primary caregiver (usually the mother; Howes & Spieker, 2008). Caregiving is primarily activated by displays of vulnerability and/or distress (e.g., crying, cute baby-like features) and involves a range of emotions from anxious solicitude to parental love. Failures of the caregiving motivation can trigger powerful negative emotions, including sadness and guilt. Like attachment, caregiving is a vital component of close relationships between adults, particularly intimate friends and romantic partners.

Pair Bonding System

Pair bonding is a central feature of the human adaptive complex. It has likely evolved from the integration of sexual attraction with attachment and caregiving—two motivations rooted in parent–child relations—and reused to enable long-term bonding between sexual partners. In part, romantic love can be seen as a blend of emotions associated with these three systems; at the same time, the psychology of love also shows unique features and evidence of functional specialization. For example, being in love temporarily inhibits the desire for alternative sexual partners, thus working as a "commitment device" in view of shared parental investment (Eastwick, 2009; Fletcher et al., 2015; Quinlan, 2008). Also, romantic love is powerfully associated with jealousy, an emotional mechanism designed to prevent infidelity by partners (Buss, 2000, 2013). For these reasons, it makes sense to postulate a specialized pair bonding system with the specific goal of forming and maintaining couple relationships (Aunger & Curtis, 2013), partly by coordinating other motivational systems such as mating, attachment, caregiving, and reciprocity.

Affiliation System

Affiliation is a key motivational substrate of group living; its function is to enable and sustain long-term relationships with extended kin and other group members, including friends and allies. Long-term friendships have been documented in many animal species, including a number of primates (Seyfarth & Cheney, 2012). As with pair bonding, the psychology of affiliation significantly overlaps with that of attachment; at the same time, friendship and group membership appear sufficiently distinct from parent–child relations to warrant the hypothesis of a specialized motivational system (Aunger & Curtis, 2013; Bugental, 2000; Kenrick et al., 2010). The affiliation system can be activated by the perception of shared interests and goals, but also by threatening situations or a lack of social resources (isolation, rejection). Successful affiliation evokes feelings of security and belonging, promotes the formation of a shared group identity, and favors cooperation and reciprocity.

Reciprocity System

While the affiliation system promotes affective bonding with other group members, the reciprocity system deals with cooperation and with the exchange of favors and resources. Cooperation and reciprocal exchange are greatly facilitated when they occur within families and groups, but they also take place between strangers, or—under certain conditions—even between enemies (Bugental, 2000; Keltner et al., 2006; McGuire & Troisi, 1998). While extensive cooperation networks of non-kin are unique to humans, other primates do engage in more limited forms of reciprocity, for example in the context of grooming and food sharing (Jaeggi et al., 2013; Jaeggi & Gurven, 2013; Engelmann et al., 2015). The reciprocity system can be activated by opportunities such as the presence of a capable and trustworthy partner or by obstacles such as cheating and unfairness. In humans, reciprocity is supported by specialized cognitive mechanisms that monitor violations of rules and keep track of partners' contributions and reputations over time (Cosmides & Tooby, 2013, 2015). Failures of reciprocity may arouse intense anger or guilt, depending on whether one is the victim or the perpetrator. Both friendships and long-term couple relationships involve elements of reciprocity, although friends and partners are considerably more tolerant than strangers in tracking each other's contributions over time (e.g., Xue & Silk, 2012).

Acquisition System

An obvious but sometimes overlooked characteristic of our species is the extent to which we store and accumulate resources for future use. Material wealth—whether in the form of land, cattle, houses, or money—provides immediate adaptive benefits as it improves both mating success (especially in men) and the survival of children (Borgerhoff Mulder & Beheim, 2011; Cronk, 1991; Koster, 2011; Nettle & Pollet, 2008). Moreover, stored resources reduce risk by working as a buffer against periods of scarcity and can be passed down from one generation to the next, with cumulative effects on long-term fitness (Borgerhoff Mulder et al., 2009; Winterhalder et al., 1999). Unsurprisingly, humans have strong motivations to acquire resources, accumulate them, and defend them against theft, as well as a distinct psychology of ownership based on emotions such as desire, envy, and greed. The acquisition system likely has its evolutionary roots in the mechanisms that mediate foraging and food hoarding (Aunger & Curtis, 2013; Preston, 2014; Preston & Vickers, 2014). The specific goals of the acquisition system depend on its interaction with other motivations such as mating and pair bonding. For example, saving resources for future family needs in the context of a long-term relationship is not the same as acquiring costly luxury goods to boost success in courtship and short-term mating (Griskevicius et al., 2007; Sundie et al., 2011).

Play System

Play is virtually universal in mammals and absorbs a large fraction of juveniles' time and energy. The overarching function of play is to enable self-training in a range of adaptive skills; fighting, parenting, and foraging are prominent recurring themes across species. More specific functions are regulating neuromuscular development and learning how to cope with unexpected events (Burghardt, 2005; Byers & Walker, 1995; Spinka et al., 2001). While play motivation clearly constitutes an independent psychological mechanism (Panksepp, 1998), it always works in synergy with other motivational systems that provide the momentary goals of play and the relevant behavioral/emotional repertoires. For example, rough-and tumble play involves the playful coordination of the aggression, fear, and status systems. Cognitive skills are also exercised through play, as when children play games of memory, numbers, and language (e.g., Locke & Bogin, 2006). Finally, play promotes social bonding in synergy with the affiliation system (Toronchuk & Ellis, 2013) and can be an effective way to *display* skills and other attractive traits (e.g., physical strength, intelligence) to potential allies and future partners. A notable aspect of play in humans is that adults also play, not only with children but also with other adults. Bonding and displaying are likely to be the main functions of adult play, compared with the primary training role of play in childhood.

Curiosity System

Curiosity is the motivation to acquire knowledge and has been long recognized as a fundamental motive in animals (Aunger & Curtis, 2013; Loewenstein, 1994). Information-seeking is essential to build models of the world and improve one's ability to make inferences and predictions (Gottlieb et al., 2013). In humans, knowledge can be used to build social prestige or increase one's value as a social partner (Dessalles, 2007). Far from being a "cold" cognitive task, the acquisition of information is regulated by a wide range of emotions and feelings, from excitement and surprise to boredom, frustration, and anxiety. Curiosity and exploration are often discussed in association with play, and play is certainly a powerful way to gather information about oneself, other people, and the environment. Even pretend play based on unrealistic scenarios can play a critical role in building sophisticated causal models of the world (Weisberg & Gopnik, 2013). However, there are many ways to acquire knowledge that do not rely on play; moreover, language permits massive transfer of information without the need for first-hand experience. In humans, adaptations for learning seem to be matched by adaptations for *teaching*, the deliberate transmission of knowledge and skills (Csibra & Gergely, 2006).

Defensive Mechanisms and the Smoke Detector Principle

Several of the mechanisms described in the previous section—most notably the fear, security, and disgust systems—can be understood as defenses whose function is to protect an individual from physical or social damage. The compromises involved in the design of defensive mechanisms have important implications for behavior, which are encapsulated by the *smoke detector principle* (Nesse, 2001*a*, 2005*a*). By necessity, the calibration of defenses involves a tradeoff between the rate of false negatives (failing to activate a defense mechanism when a threat is present) and that of false positives or "false alarms" (mistakenly activating the mechanism when no threat is present). A more sensitive system—for example one with a lower threshold for experiencing disgust—offers enhanced protection from false negatives (e.g., accidentally eating contaminated food) but does so at the cost of an increased risk of false positives (e.g., rejecting safe food items). It is often the case that false negatives have potentially catastrophic consequences, while false positives have only minor costs. Under such conditions, natural selection favors a high rate of false positives, leading to the evolution of hair-trigger defenses that often activate when no actual threat is present (Figure 2.1).

The smoke detector principle applies to all sorts of defensive mechanisms, including physiological defenses such as fever and vomiting (Nesse, 2001*a*). The principle has two key implications. First, high rates of errors and inappropriate responding may be adaptive features of a system rather than signs of dysfunction.

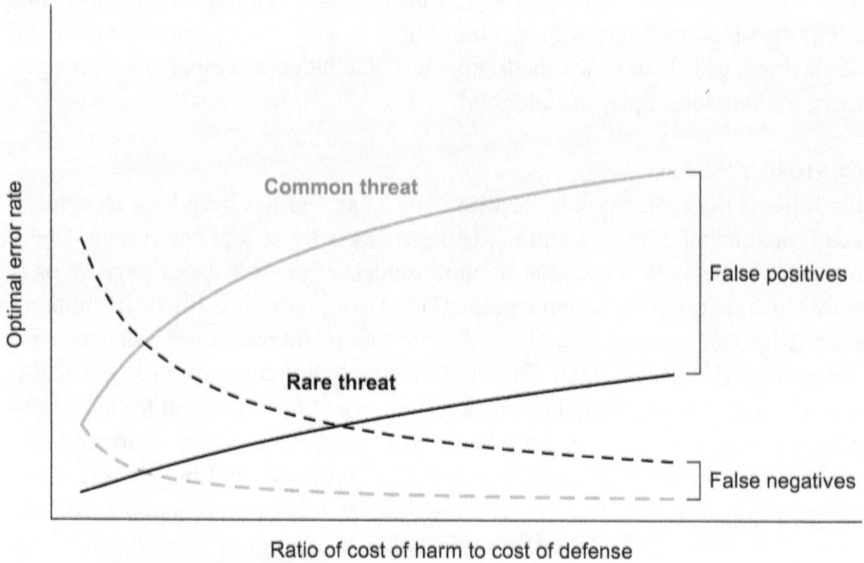

Figure 2.1. The smoke detector principle in the calibration of defensive mechanisms. When threats are common (gray line) and/or the fitness cost of potential harm is large relative to the cost of the defense, it is adaptive to accept a high rate of false positives (activating the defense even if no threat is present) in order to reduce the rate of false negatives (failing to activate the defense when a threat is present).

Second, blocking or attenuating an adaptive defense (e.g., taking fever-reducing or anxiety-reducing drugs) may have little of no adverse effects most of the times, precisely because many instances of activation are likely to be false positives rather than necessary responses (Nesse & Jackson, 2006).

Motivation and Emotion in the Brain

Motivation is the engine of the mind, and motivational systems coordinate brain activity at all levels, from the brainstem to the cortex. Studies of motivation and emotion show an important role for the thalamus, hypothalamus, and other subcortical structures such as the amygdala, the bed nucleus of the stria terminalis (BNST), the periaqueductal gray (PAG), and the ventral striatum (including the nucleus accumbens, NAcc). The amygdala is a central node in this network (often referred to as the *limbic system*) and plays a key role in encoding salience and orienting attention to motivationally relevant stimuli. The main cortical areas involved in affective processes are the medial temporal lobe (including the hippocampus and parahippocampal gyrus), the insula, the anterior and posterior cingulate cortex (ACC and PCC), the dorsomedial prefrontal cortex (DMPFC), and the ventromedial prefrontal cortex (VMPFC, including the orbitofrontal cortex, OFC; see Lindquist et al., 2012; Panksepp, 2011; Toronchuk & Ellis, 2013). A map of these brain regions is shown in Figure 2.2. Acronyms for the brain regions discussed in the book are listed in Box 2.1.

DECISION-MAKING AND SELF-REGULATION

Decision-making and self-regulation are intrinsic features of goal-directed behavior. Virtually all of an organism's actions can be described as choices between potential alternatives; the organism's biological goals determine which actions should be favored or avoided and how their outcomes should be evaluated. In other words, the distinction between motivation, decision-making, and self-regulation is largely artificial—they are all facets of the general problem of adaptive behavior control. Still, the distinction makes it easier to look at the problem from complementary perspectives and facilitates discussion of some important concepts.

Decision-Making

Bayesian Optimality and the Role of Heuristics

Adaptive behavior requires organisms to make approximately optimal (or at least "good enough") decisions given their own state and that of the environment. However, organisms cannot know the environment directly but only imperfectly through their senses; moreover, conditions are always changing in more or less predictable ways, and the outcomes of actions cannot be anticipated

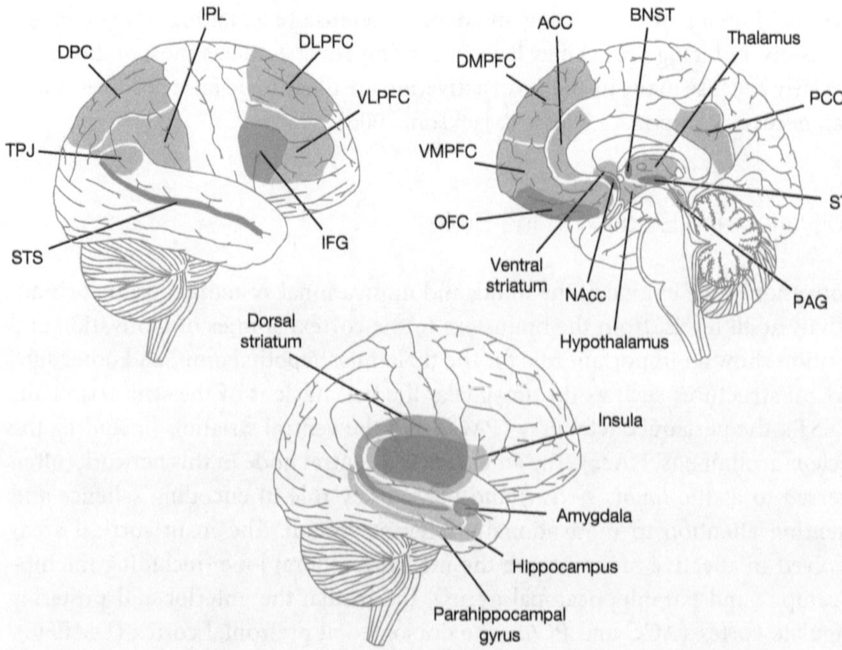

Figure 2.2. Map of the brain structures discussed in this chapter. ACC = anterior cingulate cortex. BNST = bed nucleus of the stria terminalis. DLPFC = dorsolateral prefrontal cortex. DMPFC = dorsomedial prefrontal cortex. DPC = dorsal parietal cortex. IFG = inferior frontal gyrus. IPL = inferior parietal lobule. NAcc = nucleus accumbens. OFC = orbitofrontal cortex. PCC = posterior cingulate cortex. STN = subthalamic nucleus. STS = superior temporal sulcus. TPJ = temporoparietal junction. VLPFC = ventrolateral prefrontal cortex. VMPFC = ventromedial prefrontal cortex.

with certainty. In a stochastic world filled with uncertainty and noise, decision-making crucially depends on the ability to estimate and combine probabilities. When making inferences and predictions, current sources of information must be integrated with previous expectations, which in turn may result from learning, evolved predispositions, or both. The optimal way to combine probabilistic information is described by the equation known as *Bayes' rule*:

$$P(A|B) = \frac{P(A)P(B|A)}{P(B)}$$

In a nutshell, the rule describes how the probability of event A (e.g., the probability that it will rain today) changes after observing event B (e.g., clouds in the sky). *P(A)* is the previous expectation or *prior* (in the example, the probability of rain on any given day), while *P(A|B)* is the conditional probability of A given that B has occurred—that is, an updated or *posterior* probability based on all the available evidence. To obtain the posterior probability, the prior is multiplied by the conditional probability of B given A (the probability of observing clouds on a

Box 2.1

Acronyms for Brain Regions and Structures

ACC: anterior cingulate cortex
BNST: bed nucleus of the stria terminalis
DLPFC: dorsolateral prefrontal cortex
DMPFC: dorsomedial prefrontal cortex
DPFC: dorsal prefrontal cortex
DPC: dorsal parietal cortex
IFG: inferior frontal gyrus
IPL: inferior parietal lobule
LC: locus coeruleus
MPFC: medial prefrontal cortex
NAcc: nucleus accumbens
OFC: orbitofrontal cortex
PAG: periaqueductal gray
PCC: posterior cingulate cortex
PVN: paraventricular nucleus
SN: substantia nigra
SON: supraoptic nucleus
STN: subthalamic nucleus
STS: superior temporal sulcus
TPJ: temporoparietal junction
VLPFC: ventrolateral prefrontal cortex
VMPFC: ventromedial prefrontal cortex
VTA: ventral tegmental area

rainy day) and divided by the overall probability of B (the probability of observing clouds averaged across rainy and nonrainy days). From another perspective, the logic of Bayes' rule consists of using prior expectations to make a prediction about the state of the world, then updating one's expectations based on the discrepancy between the predicted and observed state (*prediction error*). Bayes' rule is the foundation of an expanding family of models that cover all kinds of psychological processes, from perception and memory to motor and cognitive control (Clark, 2013; Dayan & Daw, 2008; Jacobs & Kruschke, 2011; Jiang et al., 2014; Mathys et al., 2011; Vilares & Körding, 2011).

Given that optimal decision-making must conform to Bayes' rule, the IMA principle implies that organisms will generally tend to behave *as if* they were performing Bayesian computations to maximize their expected fitness. In this sense, adaptation and Bayesian decision-making are two sides of the same coin (Geisler & Diehl, 2003; Trimmer & Houston, 2014). Notably, the smoke detector principle described in the previous section is a straightforward application of Bayes' rule to the optimal calibration of defenses. However, actual psychological mechanisms do not work by literally applying Bayes' rule to probabilities, not least because full-fledged Bayesian computations for realistic problems are too complex and time-consuming to be solved in real time. Instead, selection favors the evolution of mechanisms that employ Bayesian approximations or even "rules of thumb" (*heuristics*) that mimic the results of Bayesian logic by performing much simpler operations, often relying on limited amounts of information (Castellano, 2015; Lange & Dukas, 2009; Mathys et al., 2011; Sanborn & Chater, 2016; Trimmer & Houston, 2014). On the positive side, heuristics can be fast and cognitively efficient; precisely because of their simplicity, they also tend to be very robust to perturbations in the environment, sensory and processing noise, and unreliable information (Gigerenzer, 2008; Gigerenzer & Brighton, 2009). At the same time, heuristics usually work by making implicit assumptions about the environment; a heuristic that produces near-optimal behavior in a certain context may fail spectacularly if conditions change. From this vantage point, emotions and motivational systems can be framed as sophisticated heuristic devices. They embody assumptions (for example about pathogens, children, or status hierarchies) that have been shaped and refined in the EEA and coordinate fast behavioral responses that are likely—but not guaranteed—to be adaptive in most situations (Johnson-Laird & Oatley, 1992).

Tradeoffs in Decision-Making

Even well-adapted decision-makers face a number of unavoidable tradeoffs. A ubiquitous tradeoff is that between *speed* and *accuracy* (Chittka et al., 2009; Keramati et al., 2011; Trimmer et al., 2008). Waiting to collect more information from the environment reduces the margin of error for a decision; at the same time it delays action, which can be costly for the organism. Speed–accuracy tradeoffs also occur when engaging in more detailed computations (e.g., a systematic exploration of all the options instead of a quick decisional heuristic) would permit better decisions but also take longer to complete. Similar tradeoffs involve the flexibility of a system, or its ability to effectively handle a variety of inputs and situations. While flexibility can be useful, it usually comes at a cost in terms of other desirable qualities such as speed and robustness. For example, learning mechanisms that build a detailed internal model of the environment (instead of simply storing stimulus–response associations or other summary representations) provide enhanced flexibility and accuracy; however, they also require complex and lengthy computations to make decisions, and are more sensitive to the effects of noise in the processing machinery (Daw & Dayan, 2014; Daw et al., 2005; Dayan & Daw, 2008).

In many cases, future decision-making can be improved by spending time and energy to explore the environment and try out new behaviors. Of course, the time spent exploring and learning cannot be used to pursue rewards and thus comes at an immediate cost for the organism. This is the essence of the *exploration–exploitation* tradeoff (Bland & Schaefer, 2012; Dayan & Daw, 2008). Exploration–exploitation tradeoffs may occur at different time scales. An animal searching for food in a new environment faces a short-term tradeoff between eating the first items it finds and exploring in the hope of finding better or more abundant food. On a developmental scale, the time that young animals spend playing and learning represents a long-term investment in exploration at the expense of immediate exploitation (Berger-Tal et al., 2014; Eliassen et al., 2007).

Risk Sensitivity and Time Discounting

Decision-makers deal with risk whenever the result of an action cannot be predicted with certainty. In biology and economics, risk is defined as *unpredictable variation in outcomes* or "expected uncertainty" (Bland & Schaefer, 2012; Kacelnik & Bateson, 1997; Smallwood, 1996). Whereas some actions offer a narrow range of possible outcomes (low risk), others entail widely variable outcomes (high risk), with the potential for large gains as well as large losses. For example, hunting large but hard-to-catch prey is riskier than feeding on smaller but easily caught animals. Risk-sensitive organisms do not only weigh expected outcomes, but also choose among options based on outcome variability.

Whether natural selection favors positive or negative attitudes toward risk crucially depends on the shape of the relationship between outcomes and fitness (Figure 2.3). When better outcomes yield diminishing fitness returns (e.g., a satiated animal benefits less from eating larger amounts of food), a smaller variance in outcomes is associated with higher expected fitness, and *risk aversion* becomes optimal. Since riskier actions often yield larger expected rewards, risk-averse organisms routinely face *risk–reward* tradeoffs (Sih & Del Giudice, 2012). When better outcomes are associated with increasing returns (e.g., a starving animal would benefit disproportionately more by eating a larger amount of food),

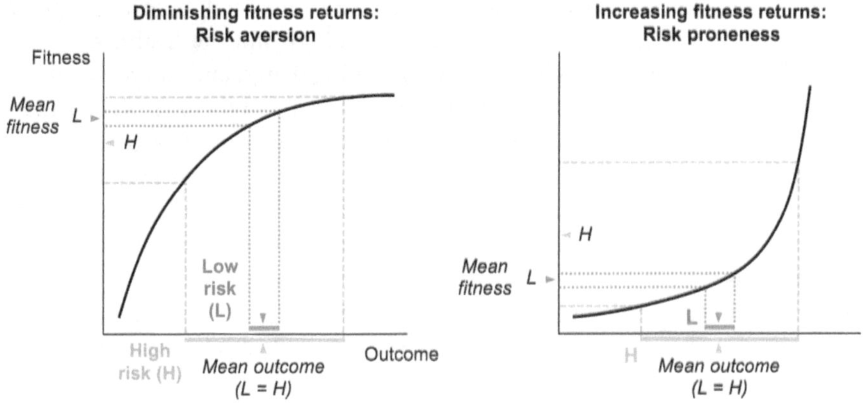

Figure 2.3. The logic of risk sensitivity. When better outcomes yield diminishing fitness returns (concave function on the left), low-risk options with smaller variance have higher mean fitness and risk aversion is favored. With increasing fitness returns (convex function on the right), high-risk options with larger variance have higher mean fitness and risk proneness is favored. Adapted with permission from Frankenhuis & Del Giudice (2012).

the expected fitness is maximized by choosing options with higher variance, and *risk proneness* is favored by selection. Risk proneness puts a premium on variance, so that risky options can be preferred even if they have a worse expected outcome. In many real-world scenarios, the fitness consequences of an action are more complex than the simple functions shown in Figure 2.3 and involve multiple thresholds where fitness returns switch from increasing to diminishing and vice versa (Hurly, 2003; Kuznar, 2002; Mishra, 2014). To illustrate, a foraging animal may be risk prone when near starvation (increasing returns), become risk averse once satiated (diminishing returns), but switch to risk proneness again if gaining more energy allows it to reproduce or compete more effectively for status (increasing returns).

In addition to variance, the timing of outcomes plays a critical role in decision-making. It is often the case that larger rewards can be gained by choosing to wait for a longer time. However, waiting for larger rewards also has two downsides: first, conditions may change so that the reward may no longer be available (in the extreme, the organism might die before getting the reward); second, waiting may have opportunity costs as it prevents the organism from engaging in other rewarding activities (Fawcett et al., 2012; Stephens et al., 2004). For these and other reasons, organisms tend to *discount* the future; that is, they subjectively regard delayed gains as less valuable (and delayed losses as less aversive). Moreover, selection often favors a steeper discounting rate for short delays, so that rewards lose most of their subjective value in the initial phase of the waiting period (Fawcett et al., 2012; Green & Myerson, 1996). The key implication of the evolutionary literature on time discounting is that impulsive decision-making (choosing smaller immediate rewards instead of waiting for larger ones) is not necessarily irrational, and may actually be adaptive under a broad range of conditions.

The concept of risk as unpredictable variation does not fully correspond to how risk is usually conceptualized in psychology and the health sciences. "Risky behaviors" such as fighting, stealing, taking drugs, and unprotected sex are primarily defined by a high likelihood of negative outcomes rather than outcome variance per se. However, the same behaviors can often be reframed as involving increased variance—for example, winning a fight may lead to a gain in dominance, whereas losing may bring social defeat in addition to physical harm (Mishra, 2014). More generally, the psychological concept of risk-taking involves a mixture of increased outcome variance and steep discounting of future rewards and/or future harm (e.g., drinking may bring about social advantages in the short term despite its long-term health consequences; see Fox & Tannenbaum, 2011).

Self-Regulation

There are three main ways to think about self-regulation. In the broadest sense, the term describes the control strategies that organisms use to enact their decisions and reach their goals in spite of disturbances such as noise, errors, and unpredictable changes in the environment. More narrowly, self-regulation refers to a set of processes that do not have well-defined goals such as avoiding threats or finding sexual partners, but rather modulate the activity of multiple motivational systems at once. These mechanisms are useful to coordinate an individual's motivational state across domains or resolve conflicts between incompatible motivations. Finally, some psychological mechanisms support conscious, deliberate forms of self-regulation or self-control. The mechanisms involved in deliberate self-control are usually labeled *executive functions* to distinguish them from more automatic and/or less accessible regulatory processes (Barkley, 2001, 2012; Carver & Scheier, 2011; Del Giudice, 2015*a*; Goldstein & Naglieri, 2014; Hofmann et al., 2012).

Feedback and Feedforward Control

Feedback and *feedforward control* are the basic building blocks of self-regulation, from simple motor coordination all the way up to the complexities of social interactions (Albertos & Mareels, 2010; Bechhoefer, 2005; Del Giudice, 2015*a*; Wolpert et al., 2003). In feedback or *closed-loop* control, the outcomes of behavior are constantly monitored and used to generate corrective actions, often by reducing the discrepancy between the current state of the system and the desired one (i.e., the goal). Feedback control is a powerful strategy for reaching a desired state even when the outcomes of one's actions cannot be accurately predicted and/or when one lacks a good model of the environment. Feedback loops can be easily nested within one another, creating a hierarchy of goals and subgoals. Nested feedback loops allow a complex control task to be split into simpler, smaller tasks, and permit high levels of flexibility and accuracy (see Carver & Scheier, 2011).

In feedforward or *open-loop* control, an action or sequence of actions is initiated and carried out with no further feedback about the state of the system. Reflexes represent the simplest kind of open-loop control, as in the automatic withdrawal response that occurs on touching a burning object. Indeed, the optimal regulation of defensive mechanisms often involves a rapid initial open-loop response that is then adjusted by slower feedback processes (Shudo et al., 2003). More complex versions of feedforward regulation are based on predictive models and may involve strategic planning, simulation of future events, and integration of existing knowledge about the rules that govern the system and the influence of contextual variables. While feedforward control can be faster and more robust than its feedback counterpart, it requires a considerable amount of contextual information and a detailed model of the environment and the organism's actions.

Feedback and feedforward strategies have complementary strengths and weaknesses, and selection promotes the integration of both kinds of processes in the mind/brain (e.g., Braver et al., 2009; Wolpert et al., 2003). In the self-regulation literature, this duality is reflected in the distinction between *reactive* and *proactive* control processes. Reactive processes are "late correction" feedback mechanisms that detect and respond to interferences and unexpected events after they occur. Proactive processes anticipate future events and prepare the organism for action based on goal-relevant information; they represent a prime example of model-based feedforward regulation (Braver, 2012; Tops et al., 2010).

Approach, Avoidance, and Inhibition

Classic theories of motivation posit a fundamental distinction between approach motivations elicited by rewarding stimuli and avoidance motivations elicited by threats and punishments (see Carver & Scheier, 2011; Corr, 2013). In a broader perspective, approach and avoidance can be seen as general regulatory processes that are involved in the operation of most motivational systems. The fear system may trigger either avoidance (flight) or approach behaviors (fight) in different situations; the mating system promotes approach to desirable sexual partner but also avoidance of unattractive ones; and the same food may be rewarding when one is hungry but aversive when one has had too much to eat. There is evidence of specialized psychological mechanisms that regulate the overall balance between approach and avoidance across motivational domains, based on expectations about the future likelihood of rewarding and aversive events; these mechanisms are likely responsible for long-lasting mood states including anxious, euphoric, and depressed moods (Harmon-Jones & Harmon-Jones, 2015; Nettle & Bateson, 2012; Tops et al., 2010; Trimmer et al., 2013).

Reinforcement sensitivity theory (RST; Gray & McNaughton, 2000; Corr, 2013) is a popular approach–avoidance model that postulates the existence of three major systems: a *behavioral approach system* (BAS) that mediates approach to rewards, a *fight-flight-freeze system* (FFFS) that mediates active avoidance of threats and largely overlaps with the fear system described earlier, and a *behavioral inhibition system* (BIS) that suppresses immediate behavioral responses when there is a motivational conflict between the BAS and the FFFS. In reinforcement sensitivity theory, the BIS is associated with anxiety and promotes exploration or cautious approach to ambiguous stimuli. In all likelihood, the security system described in the previous section derives from basic conflict resolution mechanisms such as the BIS.

The inhibition of behavioral responses is an essential psychological function and is not limited to the specific case of the BIS. Indeed, the brain contains multiple inhibitory pathways that mediate both reactive forms of inhibition (stopping in response to an unexpected event) and proactive ones (preparing to stop or suppress a certain behavior in view of a superordinate goal; Aron, 2011; Diamond, 2013). Inhibition can occur automatically or as the result of a deliberate decision; in fact, the ability to consciously override cognitive and behavioral responses is a central component of self-control.

Executive Functions

Executive functions are deliberate, self-directed processes that regulate the operation of other psychological mechanisms. The core executive functions are usually described as *inhibition* (the ability to override dominant or prepotent responses), *updating* (the ability to monitor and modify the contents of working memory), and *flexibility* or *shifting* (the ability to switch fluidly and rapidly among tasks, strategies, and contexts). In general, different executive processes tend to reinforce one another—for example, maintaining a goal in working memory makes it easier to inhibit incompatible goals and responses. At the same time, inhibition and flexibility often have opposite effects on task performance, creating the opportunity for executive tradeoffs (Blackwell et al., 2014; Miyake & Friedman, 2012). Planning and problem-solving can be regarded as higher order abilities that depend critically on core executive functions (Diamond, 2013). In a broader perspective, the family of executive functions can be expanded to include self-directed actions such as emotional regulation, internal speech, and mental "play" used to simulate and generate novel action sequences and problem-solving strategies (Barkley, 2001, 2012).

The common theme of executive functions is their orientation toward the future. In different ways, executive processes contribute to detach behavior from immediate, short-term goals in order to maximize the long-term outcomes for the individual. In humans, they facilitate social interactions and provide critical support to social behaviors that extend in time, such as delayed reciprocity, long-term cooperation, and romantic pair bonding. Executive functions are also involved in social competition, because they enable effective deception as well as self-defense against emotional and cognitive manipulation by others (Barkley, 2001, 2012; Denckla, 1996).

Decision-Making and Self-Regulation in the Brain

Given the functional overlap among motivation, decision-making, and self-regulation, it is not surprising that several brain regions have been found to participate in all these aspects of mental functioning (Figure 2.2). Medial prefrontal areas (VMPFC/OFC), the PCC, and the striatum work together to process rewards and punishments and integrate the motivational value of stimuli with contextual information. These regions are crucially involved in the evaluation of risk and delayed rewards; the hippocampus and amygdala contribute as well, probably because they integrate current stimuli with representations of past and future events and their emotional significance (Aston-Jones & Cohen, 2005; Harmon-Jones & Harmon-Jones, 2015; Moore & Depue, 2016; Pessiglione & Lebreton, 2015; Peters & Büchel, 2011; Rilling, 2011).

The cingulate cortex—particularly the ACC—responds to prediction errors, novelty, risk, and uncertainty, and is one of the main neural correlates of executive functions (Cavanagh & Frank, 2014; Chung et al., 2014). Executive functions also depend on the lateral and medial prefrontal cortex, in combination with the insula and other parietal regions. Specifically, DLPFC activation (particularly in the right hemisphere) is a robust correlate of self-control, risk aversion, and future-oriented decision-making and is implicated in both proactive and reactive control (Braver, 2012; Chung et al., 2014; Knoch & Nash, 2015). The brain contains multiple inhibitory pathways involving lateral and medial prefrontal regions as well as the dorsal striatum. Many of these pathways have a common final node in the subthalamic nucleus (STN). STN activity controls motor inhibition and contributes to regulate the tradeoff between speed and accuracy in decision-making (Aron, 2011; Cavanagh et al., 2011).

MENTALISTIC AND MECHANISTIC COGNITION

From the perspective of agents with minds, the world contains two radically different kinds of things: mindless physical objects and other agents with minds of their own. The distinction between *mentalistic* and *mechanistic* cognition (Badcock, 2004; Crespi & Badcock, 2008) crisply differentiates between two types of psychological mechanisms: those designed to interact with physical objects and those specialized to interact with other minds. The separation between mentalistic and mechanistic cognition is far from complete, since many cognitive processes (e.g., attentional orienting, reinforcement learning, cause–effect reasoning) can be applied to both social and nonsocial information (Heyes, 2014; Parkinson & Wheatley, 2015; Schaafsma et al., 2015). At the same time, there is considerable evidence of functional specialization in the mechanisms that mediate our interactions with the "world of things" on the one hand and the "world of minds" on the other.

Mentalistic Cognition

Mentalistic cognition—also known as *mentalizing, theory of mind*, and *folk psychology*—is an umbrella term for the psychological mechanisms that allow us to infer, represent, and respond to the mental states of other individuals. The attribution of mental states to another agent has been called the *intentional stance* (Dennett, 1971). In essence, the intentional stance is an evolved heuristic for predicting behavior using a simplified model of the agent's mind based on intuitive concepts like beliefs, desires, and emotions; this is incomparably more powerful and efficient than attempting to use a detailed physical model of the agent to predict its behavior. Mentalistic processes do not necessarily depend on explicit or conscious representations of others' mental states. For example, while the ability to follow gaze does not require a representation of the gazing individual's perceptual and attentional states, it is designed to operate on the assumption that there are certain systematic links between gaze direction, attention, and perception.

Mentalizing is best described as a complex mosaic of mechanisms rather than a single ability (Barrett, 2015; Frith & Frith, 2010; Schaafsma et al., 2015). Some of those mechanisms are automatic, others deliberate; some are strongly connected to emotional processes, while others depend on cause–effect reasoning; some are evolutionarily ancient, while others have evolved only recently. Whereas some components of mentalistic cognition are highly specialized for mentalistic inference (e.g., recognition of emotional expressions), others have a broader range of functions (e.g., face recognition); finally, some mechanisms may support or replace mentalizing in daily life without being specifically designed to process social information (e.g., attentional orienting; Heyes, 2014). A strong case can be made that mentalizing mechanisms originally evolved to predict the behavior of other people and were later adapted to represent and interpret one's own mental states; self-directed mind-reading or *metacognition* dramatically increases the ability to regulate one's cognitive processes—thus overlapping with executive functions—and communicate them to other people (Carruthers, 2009).

Mentalizing and Motivation

The ability to read and infer other people's mental states can be used for competition and exploitation as well as cooperation. Mentalistic skills are the basis for Machiavellian intelligence and enable people to outwit, deceive, and manipulate others to their own advantage (Byrne & Whiten, 1989; Flinn et al., 2005). In fact, mathematical models indicate that competition promotes the evolution of sophisticated mentalistic cognition more strongly than cooperation. When cooperative interactions are more frequent than competitive ones, selection is likely to favor moderate levels of mentalizing, which are sufficient to form and maintain shared goals between cooperation partners. In a competitive social environment, however, it is crucial to have better mentalistic skills than one's opponents in order to predict and outsmart their moves (Devaine et al., 2014). This idea is consistent with evidence that competitive interactions activate mentalizing-related brain areas more strongly than cooperation (Decety et al., 2004).

To a remarkable degree, the mentalistic processes deployed in social interactions are modulated by the individual's motivational state. For example, empathic emotional responses to another person's joy or distress are favored in the context of cooperation, affiliation, and caregiving but inhibited by aggression and dominance competition. Likewise, activation of some motivational systems such as the fear and disgust systems may temporarily inhibit sophisticated mentalizing to promote rapid, stereotyped defensive responses (Liotti & Gilbert, 2011). Intriguingly, there is evidence that prosocial and hostile mentalistic abilities are negatively correlated in children, suggesting that they rely on partially distinct mechanisms (Ronald et al., 2005).

Mechanistic Cognition

Mechanistic cognition deals with objects whose behavior can be effectively predicted by applying cause–effect reasoning or input–output rules. Two mechanistic domains with a long evolutionary history are *folk physics* (the intuitive understanding of objects and physical laws) and *folk biology* (the intuitive understanding of biological organisms and their physiology; Geary, 2010). However, the same "systemizing" abilities can be employed to make sense of many other rule-based domains, from abstract ones such as mathematics and music to social ones such as law and economics (Baron-Cohen, 2003). As with mentalizing, mechanistic cognition depends on multiple mechanisms, some of which show evidence of specialized design. For instance, children process information about animals and plants differently, and do so in ways that are tailored to the characteristics of each biological category (Atran, 1998; Broesch et al., 2014; Greif et al., 2006). The domain of folk physics includes important specialized abilities such as spatial navigation, three-dimensional visualization, and tool use.

There is evidence that mentalistic and mechanistic cognition depend on different brain networks, and—even more importantly—that they tend to inhibit one another when people face social versus physical tasks (Jack et al., 2013). Indeed, there may be intrinsic tradeoffs between mentalistic and mechanistic reasoning, possibly because they employ incompatible heuristics that generate contradictory predictions; however, the exact nature of these tradeoffs is still poorly understood.

Mentalistic and Mechanistic Cognition in the Brain

Many different brain structures contribute to mentalizing; for example, the recognition of emotional expressions recruits several regions discussed previously in relation to motivation and emotion, including the ACC, DMPFC, and VLPFC (Lindquist et al., 2012). In addition, studies of mentalizing converge on a network that includes the temporoparietal junction (TPJ), superior temporal sulcus (STS), inferior parietal lobule (IPL), and inferior frontal gyrus (IFG, a subregion of the VLPFC), as well as medial prefrontal areas (Figure 2.2). These cortical structures serve a diverse set of functions—biological motion detection in the STS, imitation and action understanding in the IPL and IFG, and so on (Frith & Frith, 2010; Schaafsma et al., 2015). The brain correlates of mentalistic cognition overlap with the *default mode network*, which includes the superior temporal lobe and TPJ, IPL, IFG, PCC and adjacent parietal regions, and medial prefrontal areas. Coordinated activation of the default network is associated with both introspective, self-referential thought and other-directed mentalizing. Mechanistic cognition is also very heterogeneous, but there is only scant evidence on the neural basis of key mechanistic skills such as folk physics and folk biology. There are indications that physical reasoning activates the *dorsal attention network*, which comprises the dorsal parietal cortex together with some prefrontal and temporal regions; its activity is weakly negatively coupled with that of the default mode network (Broyd et al., 2009; Dixon et al., 2017; Fischer et al., 2016; Jack et al., 2013).

KEY NEUROBIOLOGICAL SYSTEMS

In this section, I review a number of important neurobiological systems: brain monoamines and "social" neuropeptides, excitatory and inhibitory neurotransmitters (glutamate and GABA), sex hormones, and the stress response system. Instead of detailing these systems at the molecular level—receptor types, synthesis and degradation enzymes, specific genetic variants—I focus on their main biological functions and their role in the psychological processes discussed so far. One should keep in mind that, despite decades of animal and human research on these systems, our understanding of their role in behavior and personality is still tentative and provisional. Reasons for this state of things include the prevalence of small-sample studies (that inevitably produce many spurious and contradictory findings); the technical challenges of measuring neurobiological function in vivo; the methodological and statistical problems involved in detecting the effects of individual genes; and the remarkable complexity of the systems themselves (see Chapter 3). Acronyms for the neurotransmitters, hormones, and neuroendocrine systems discussed in the book are listed in Box 2.2.

Brain Monoamines

Dopamine

The main sources of dopamine (DA) in the brain are the ventral tegmental area (VTA) and the substantia nigra (SN). Neurons in the SN project to the dorsal

---

Box 2.2

Acronyms for Neuroendocrine Systems, Hormones, and Neurotransmitters

5-HT: serotonin
ACh: acetylcholine
ACTH: adrenocorticotropic hormone
AVP: vasopressin
CRH: corticotropin-releasing hormone
DA: dopamine
DHEA: dehydroepiandrosterone
DHEAS: dehydroepiandrosterone sulfate
FSH: follicle-stimulating hormone
GABA: γ-aminobutyric acid
GnRH: gonadotropin-releasing hormone
HPA: hypothalamic-pituitary-adrenal (axis)
HPG: hypothalamic-pituitary-gonadal (axis)
HPT: hypothalamic-pituitary-thyroid (axis)
IGF-1: insulin-like growth factor 1
LH: luteinizing hormone
NE: norepinephrine
OT: oxytocin

---

striatum, whereas VTA neurons project to the prefrontal cortex (*mesocortical* pathway), the ventral striatum (including the NAcc), and other motivation- and emotion-related regions such as the hippocampus, cingulate cortex, and amygdala (*mesolimbic* pathway; see Figure 2.4). In turn, many of these structures project back to dopaminergic nuclei. Dopamine has been classically involved in reward learning; more broadly, it mediates psychological reactivity to both positive and negative events, likely by encoding the salience of stimuli and/or the individual's ability to control the outcome of actions. Dopaminergic activity modulates multiple motivational systems—chiefly the aggression system (by facilitating active approach), the mating system (by increasing sexual desire and facilitating orgasm), and the acquisition system (by increasing the reward value of desirable items). Dopamine also plays a complex role in regulating hunger and food intake (Frank et al., 2009; Friston et al., 2014; Giuliano & Clément, 2005; Kayser et al., 2014; Miczek & Fish, 2006; Moore & Depue, 2016; Panksepp, 2011; Preston & Vickers, 2014; Ramos et al., 2005; Toronchuk & Ellis, 2013).

From the standpoint of self-regulation, dopamine is a key determinant of approach motivation and represents the main neurobiological substrate of the BAS. In particular, dopamine is more strongly linked to appetitive ("wanting") than to consummatory aspects of approach motivation ("liking"). The reciprocal connections between the VTA, ventral striatum, and prefrontal cortex contribute to regulate risk sensitivity, executive flexibility, and both speed–accuracy and

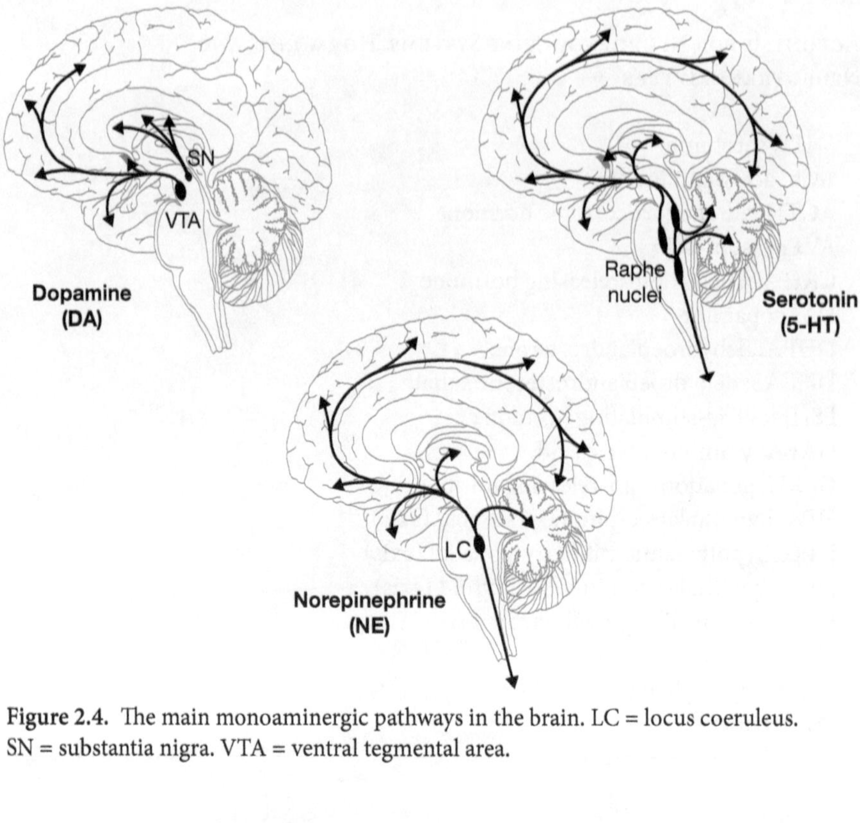

Figure 2.4. The main monoaminergic pathways in the brain. LC = locus coeruleus. SN = substantia nigra. VTA = ventral tegmental area.

exploration–exploitation tradeoffs in decision-making. The effects of dopamine on these parameters may be nonlinear and depends critically on the specific site of release. In particular, prefrontal and striatal dopamine have opposing influences on some aspects of cognition and behavior; notably, prefrontal (mesocortical) dopaminergic activity is associated with behavioral persistence, whereas striatal (mesolimbic) dopamine facilitates flexibility—consistent with an executive tradeoff between flexibility and inhibition (see earlier discussion). High DA levels in the striatum—but not in prefrontal areas—have been associated with risk proneness, speed over accuracy, and exploitation over exploration; however, there is still debate concerning potential associations between *reduced* striatal dopaminergic function, impulsivity, and risk-taking (Cools, 2011; Corr et al., 2013; DeYoung, 2013; Gatzke-Kopp, 2011; Kayser et al., 2014; Sullivan & Brake, 2003; van Schouwenberg et al., 2010; Wiecki & Frank, 2013; Zisner & Beauchaine, 2015). Finally, dopaminergic function may affect mentalizing, as increased DA levels seem to reduce empathic concerns about inflicting harm to others (Crockett et al., 2015).

Serotonin

In the brain, serotonin (5-HT) is synthesized in the brainstem raphe nuclei and distributed widely across cortical and subcortical structures (Figure 2.4). This monoamine is derived from tryptophan, an amino acid that cannot be synthesized by humans and must be acquired from food. The original biological function of serotonin is that of regulating metabolism and energy allocation (Andrews et al., 2015); as a neuromodulator, it shows a broad range of effects, including a complex pattern of antagonistic and synergistic interactions with dopamine. For example, serotonin suppresses dopaminergic activity in the VTA and SN and inhibits dopamine release in the ventral striatum, but facilitates reward processing in the dopaminergic system (Cools et al., 2011; Rogers, 2011). Serotonin is involved in aversive learning and threat avoidance and modulates several motivational systems—including key defensive systems such as fear, security, and disgust. Specifically, serotonergic activity potentiates disgust and upregulates security motivation by promoting anticipatory anxiety; at the same time, it downregulates the expression of some fear and panic responses and suppresses reactive aggression, but not proactive aggression. In the mating domain, serotonergic activity inhibits sexual desire, arousal, and orgasm; serotonin also reduces hunger and suppresses food intake (Canteras & Graeff, 2014; Corr et al., 2013; Giuliano & Clément, 2005; Graeff, 2004; Lam et al., 2010; Manuck et al., 2006; Mickzek & Fish, 2006; Pfaus, 2009; Ramos et al., 2005; Toronchuk & Ellis, 2013; van Goozen et al., 2007; Vicario et al., 2017).

The serotonergic system plays important roles in self-regulation, mainly as a source of behavioral constraint and withdrawal motivation. High serotonin levels are robustly associated with inhibition in response to threats and aversive stimuli (i.e., BIS activation), risk aversion, and reduced time discounting with increased preference for delayed rewards (Carver et al., 2015; Cools et al., 2011; Corr et al., 2013; Moore & Depue, 2016; Rogers, 2011; Tops et al., 2010). In contrast, the role of serotonin in executive flexibility is unclear, and the empirical findings are inconsistent (Cools et al., 2011; Faulkner & Deakin, 2014). Serotonin has also been found to promote prosocial and cooperative behavior, responsivity to social norms, and empathic aversion to inflicting harm to others (Bilderbeck et al., 2014; Crockett et al., 2015; Rogers, 2011).

Norepinephrine

Norepinephrine (NE) is released in the general circulation by the medulla of the adrenal gland and plays a central role in the stress response system. In the central nervous system, norepinephrine is produced in the locus coeruleus (LC) and transported to many brain areas, with reciprocal connections between the LC and prefrontal and cingulate regions, amygdala, hypothalamus, and other structures (Figure 2.4). Norepinephrine increases arousal and vigilance and facilitates reactive aggression (Miczek & Fish, 2006; Moore & Depue, 2016). Phasic NE spikes are associated with novel or surprising stimuli and contribute to reorient attention and behavior toward the unexpected event. They also promote engagement and performance by amplifying task-related information while filtering out irrelevant stimuli. In contrast, high tonic levels of the neurotransmitter depress phasic activity and facilitate exploration, flexibility, and distractibility. The balance of exploration versus exploitation in noradrenergic activity is regulated by inputs from other regions of the brain, primarily the ACC and OFC (Adams et al., 2012; Aston-Jones & Cohen, 2005; Bouret & Sara, 2005; Yu & Dayan, 2005).

Neuropeptides

Oxytocin

Oxytocin (OT) is produced in the supraoptic and paraventricular nuclei of the hypothalamus (SON and PVN). From there, oxytocin is released as a hormone in the bloodstream through the pituitary gland and as a neuromodulator in various brain regions including the striatum, amygdala, hippocampus, and VTA. The overarching psychological function of oxytocin is to motivate and maintain social bonds, from mother–child relationships to cooperation in extended groups. Oxytocinergic activity modulates the attachment and caregiving systems, the mating system (e.g., OT is released during orgasm), the pair bonding systems, the affiliation system, and the reciprocity system. Importantly, oxytocin is released in response to both relational opportunities (e.g., a beginning romantic relationship) and relational threats (e.g., abandonment, rejection), and seems to specifically promote investment in developing or vulnerable social bonds (Bos et al., 2012; Brown et al., 2012; Crespi, 2016*a*; Gangestad, 2016; van Anders et al., 2011). High OT levels also tend to suppress hunger and food intake (Lam et al., 2010; Lawson et al., 2015). Oxytocin works as an enhancer of mentalizing—it facilitates empathy, emotion reading, and social learning. Depending on context, oxytocin can enhance trust and cooperation with social partners; at the same time, it has been found to inhibit cooperation with strangers and out-group members (Bos et al., 2012; Crespi, 2016*a*; Hurlemann et al., 2010).

Vasopressin

The peptide vasopressin (AVP) is closely related to oxytocin; like oxytocin, it is synthesized in the SON and PVN, released in the pituitary, and transported throughout the brain as a neuromodulator. However, the two peptides have largely contrasting effects, for example on patterns of neural activity in the amygdala. Vasopressin is involved in social aggression and promotes mating, courtship behaviors, and status competition (especially in males). There is some evidence that AVP also contributes to caregiving and may specifically regulate aggression in the context of offspring defense. Recent evidence in humans suggests a potential involvement of AVP in high-risk cooperation among men (Bos et al., 2012; Brunnlieb et al., 2016; Panksepp, 2011; Sanchez et al., 2009; Toronchuk & Ellis, 2013).

Opioids

Several opioid molecules are produced in the brain, mostly in the hypothalamus and brainstem. Opioid receptors are highly expressed in the brainstem, amygdala, striatum, and prefrontal cortex (especially the OFC). β-endorphin is the most potent and well-studied of the endogenous opioids and contributes to modulate pain (with an analgesic function) as well as reward processing (particularly the consummatory or "liking" component). Opioids are crucially involved in the formation and maintenance of social bonds. Grooming, affectionate touch, and laughter all stimulate opioid release; more broadly, opioid levels increase in response to closeness and affiliative behaviors and drop following separations. Low opioid levels increase the need for social stimulation and promote activation of the attachment, caregiving, and affiliation systems. Opioids also participate in play and mating (sexual pleasure) and have stimulatory effects on hunger and food intake (Machin & Dunbar, 2011; Moore & Depue, 2016; Panksepp, 1998, 2011; Yeomans & Gray, 2002).

Glutamate and GABA

Glutamate

The amino acid glutamate is the main excitatory neurotransmitter and one of the most abundant molecules in the brain. Glutamate is involved in virtually all brain processes and plays a key role in regulating neural plasticity. As a neuromodulator, glutamate tends to increase the excitability of neural networks; glutamatergic projections to the NAcc from prefrontal and limbic areas contribute to regulate approach and avoidance motivation, with important effects on the BIS, BAS, fear, and aggression systems (Floresco, 2015; Miczek & Fish, 2006; Panksepp, 2011). Both dopaminergic and serotonergic neurons have been found to co-release glutamate, which may contribute to modulate the psychological effects of these monoamines (Fischer et al., 2015).

GABA

GABA is produced by a widely distributed system of interneurons in the brain cortex and is the main inhibitory neurotransmitter/neuromodulator. GABA has broad anxiolytic effects and plays a crucial role in dampening the activity of defensive systems such as the BIS and the security system (Moore & Depue, 2016). GABAergic activity is also involved in the modulation of the aggression system; the relation between GABA and aggression seems to be nonlinear, with enhanced aggression at moderate GABA levels but suppressed aggression at high levels (Miczek & Fish, 2006).

The Stress Response System

The stress response system is an integrated neuroendocrine network that coordinates the organism's response to a wide range of metabolic and behavioral challenges. Its main components are the autonomic nervous system and the hypothalamic-pituitary-adrenal (HPA) axis. The whole-body adjustments mediated by the stress response system are captured by the term *allostasis*—the maintenance of stability through change (Sterling & Eyer, 1988). The system receives input from the amygdala, hippocampus, and prefrontal and cingulate regions, but also from other organs and systems in the body (including the immune system). It responds to both threats and opportunities by reorienting attentional focus, increasing the organism's readiness for action (e.g., by regulating heart/respiratory rate and blood flow to various organs), mobilizing energy by triggering glucose release into the bloodstream, shifting the balance between different memory and learning processes, suppressing or enhancing reproductive physiology, regulating immune function, and many other effects (see Del Giudice et al., 2011; Ellis & Del Giudice, 2014; Flinn, 2006, Flinn et al., 2011; Gunnar & Quevedo, 2007; Miller G. E. et al., 2011). In short, the stress response system functions as a central node in the integration of physiology and behavior and shows extensive bidirectional interactions with all the neurobiological systems described in this section.

Autonomic Nervous System

The autonomic nervous system is composed of two branches, *sympathetic* and *parasympathetic*. Autonomic branches innervate most bodily organs; their complementary physiological effects result in a dynamic equilibrium in which parasympathetic activation suppresses sympathetic-induced arousal. The parasympathetic system employs acetylcholine (ACh) as its main neurotransmitter. Parasympathetic activity promotes digestive and reproductive functions, reduces the heart and respiratory rate, and sustains attention and social engagement (Lovallo & Sollers, 2007; Porges, 2001, 2007). Disengagement of the parasympathetic "brake" provides a way to quickly increase arousal and reorient attention toward unexpected events. Parasympathetic activation is involved in the regulation of many social behaviors including mating, caregiving, affiliation, and play; it is also a robust physiological correlate of disgust (Ottaviani et al., 2013). Signaling in the sympathetic system is based on two catecholamines, epinephrine (E) and NE. Sympathetic activity is coordinated by the LC (see earlier discussion); from there, its activation follows two routes—a fast pathway mediated by direct innervation of the brain and other organs, and a slower pathway in which sympathetic fibers project to the medulla of the adrenal gland, which in turn releases E and NE in the circulatory system. Sympathetic effects on physiology include increased heart and respiration rate, increased blood supply to skeletal muscles, glucose release in the bloodstream, and suppression of vegetative functions.

Motivational systems often recruit both branches of the autonomic system with complementary functions. For example, parasympathetic activation promotes sexual arousal, whereas sympathetic activity peaks during orgasm (Giuliano & Clément, 2005; Krüger et al., 2003; Salonia et al., 2010). In responding to danger and threats, the sympathetic branch promotes fight-or-flight behaviors, whereas the parasympathetic one mediates freezing and fainting (Porges, 2007). While the sympathetic and parasympathetic systems usually operate in a reciprocal fashion, they can also become strongly activated at the same time. This occurs during attentive immobility (freezing) and in situations that demand high arousal and readiness to action but also tight self-control (e.g., skydiving; Allison et al., 2012).

HPA Axis

The HPA axis mounts long-term responses to metabolic and social challenges through the release of cortisol, a hormone with a wide range of physiological and behavioral effects. Hypothalamic neurons secrete corticotropin-releasing hormone (CRH) and AVP in response to inputs from multiple brain regions such as the LC, amygdala, and hippocampus. CRH and AVP are transported to various brain areas—including the LC, where they modulate sympathetic activity—and to the pituitary gland, where they stimulate release of adrenocorticotropic hormone (ACTH) in the bloodstream, together with other molecules such as β-endorphin. ACTH then reaches the cortex of the adrenal gland, where it triggers cortisol release (Figure 2.5). Cortisol begins to rise within minutes from the onset of a stressor, and some of its effects may last for several hours. Rising cortisol levels activate the glucocorticoid receptor (GR) at various levels of the axis (Figure 2.5), providing negative feedback that ultimately deactivates the system. Initially, cortisol potentiates sympathetic activity, but later contributes to dampen it and suppress some of its effects (Del Giudice et al., 2011; Flinn, 2006; Gunnar & Quevedo, 2007).

As a neuromodulator, CRH has a range of psychological effects that include facilitating anxiety, enhancing the formation of emotional memories, and suppressing hunger. Cortisol mobilizes energetic (glucose) and attentional resources, and modulates motivation and self-regulation on a broad scale (Ellis & Del Giudice, 2014; Moore & Depue, 2016). The HPA axis is activated by both

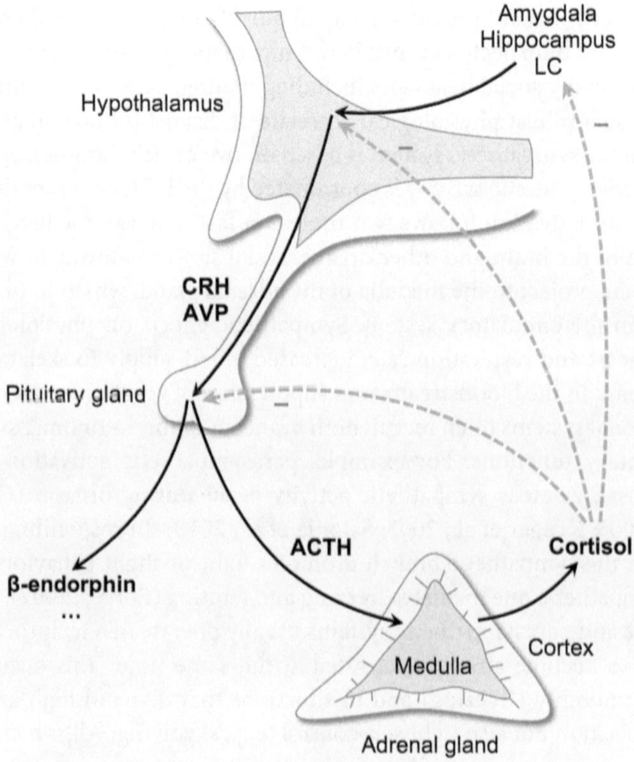

Figure 2.5. The hypothalamic-pituitary-adrenal (HPA) axis. Cortisol exerts negative feedback on the axis at multiple levels through the glucocorticoid receptor. ACTH = adrenocorticotropic hormone. AVP = vasopressin. CRH = corticotropin releasing hormone. LC = locus coeruleus.

threats and opportunities, such as the presence of a potential sexual partner (e.g., Roney et al., 2007). Events that involve social judgment and/or uncontrollability arouse strong, sustained HPA responses (Dickerson & Kemeny, 2004). While cortisol has important benefits, maintaining high levels of this hormone also has substantial costs for the organism; thus, periods of chronic HPA activation are usually followed by a "rebound" below the initial level that can last weeks or even months after the end of the stressor (Miller G. E. et al., 2007).

Sex Hormones

Sex hormones are the end products of another neuroendocrine system, the hypothalamic-pituitary-gonadal (HPG) axis. Hypothalamic neurons release gonadotropin-releasing hormone (GnRH) in the pituitary gland, where luteinizing hormone (LH) and follicle-stimulating hormone (FSH) are secreted into the blood. In response to LH/FSH signals, the ovaries and testes release androgens (mainly testosterone), estrogens (mainly estradiol), and progesterone. Androgens and progesterone are also produced in the cortex of the adrenal gland. The metabolism and action of sex hormones is complex; for example, adrenal androgens dehydroepiandrosterone (DHEA) and dehydroepiandrosterone sulfate (DHEAS) can be converted to testosterone, which in turn can be converted to estradiol. Sex hormones regulate sexual development, reproduction, and fecundity and have a striking range of behavioral and cognitive effects. There are strong bidirectional influences between the HPG and HPA axis, as well as among sex hormones, monoamines, and neuropeptides (Bos et al., 2012; Toronchuk & Ellis, 2013; van Anders et al., 2011).

The main motivational effects of testosterone are on the mating, status, aggression, and fear systems. In both sexes, testosterone promotes competition for dominance and status, mates, and resources. Specifically, testosterone stimulates aggression, suppresses fear, and is crucially involved in courtship and sexual behavior (Bos et al., 2012; Cashdan, 1995; Eisenegger et al., 2011; Harris et al., 1996; Mazur & Booth, 1998; Zilioli & Bird, 2017). Testosterone also increases approach motivation and risk-taking, particularly in competitive contexts; at the same time, it decreases trust and affiliation (Apicella et al., 2015; Bos et al., 2012; Crespi, 2016*a*). Testosterone levels in men decline when they enter committed romantic relationships (e.g., marriage) and become fathers; this is consistent with the idea that testosterone plays a role in courtship and relationship initiation but interferes with long-term pair bonding and parental investment. There is some evidence that similar effects may occur in women as well (Barrett et al., 2013; Carré & Archer, 2018; Gettler, 2014; Roney & Gettler, 2015). In women, estrogen and progesterone levels change across the menstrual cycle and jointly contribute to regulate motivational states. Estrogens and progesterone often have opposite effects on psychological processes; for example, estrogens tend to increase sexual motivation and decrease hunger and food intake, whereas progesterone inhibits desire and promotes hunger (Hirschberg, 2012; Roney & Simmons, 2013).

Sex hormones and social neuropeptides are functionally linked: estrogens increase oxytocin synthesis and release, while testosterone has a stimulating effect on vasopressin. Indeed, neuropeptides probably mediate some of the psychological effects of sex hormones. In general terms, activity of the estrogen–OT pathway tends to promote nurturance, prosocial affiliation, and mentalizing, whereas the testosterone–AVP pathway promotes self-oriented behaviors, reduced mentalizing, and a focus on threats and rewards (Bos et al., 2012; Crespi, 2016*a*; van Anders et al., 2011). However, things are likely more complicated than suggested by this schematic account; for example, testosterone and vasopressin can actually promote caregiving motivation, especially in situations that involve protection of a vulnerable partner or child (Gettler, 2014; van Anders et al., 2011). There is also initial evidence that testosterone can stimulate oxytocin release and vice versa, at least in caregiving contexts (Gangestad, 2016; Weisman et al., 2014).

3

Individual and Sex Differences

In the previous chapter, I focused on universal psychological mechanisms such as motivational systems, executive functions, and mentalizing processes. These systems are part of the blueprint of the human mind, and their basic design is the same across individuals and populations. Here, I take the complementary perspective and consider the origin and structure of psychological *differences* between people. Since psychopathology is inextricably linked to normal variation in personality and cognition (Krueger & Tackett, 2006; Rodriguez-Seijas et al., 2015), a unified approach to mental disorders must incorporate a sophisticated understanding of both individual and sex differences. I begin this chapter with an overview of the many biological processes that can produce and maintain variation in phenotypic traits. I then go on to examine the structure of personality and cognitive ability, their evolutionary and neurobiological underpinnings, and some important patterns of sex differences. Finally, I address the role of genetic and environmental factors in the development of individual differences over the life course.

THE EVOLUTION OF VARIATION

Individual differences in morphology, physiology, and behavior are ubiquitous in nature. Patterns of variation can range from quantitative differences along continuous traits (e.g., smaller vs. larger body size) to sharply demarcated alternative forms or "morphs" (e.g., winged vs. wingless locusts). Individual differences in phenotype can arise through a striking variety of evolutionary and developmental processes (Figure 3.1). To disentangle this complexity, it is useful to start from the broad distinction between genetic and nongenetic sources of variation, keeping in mind that variation in any specific trait may reflect the joint contribution of multiple mechanisms and processes.

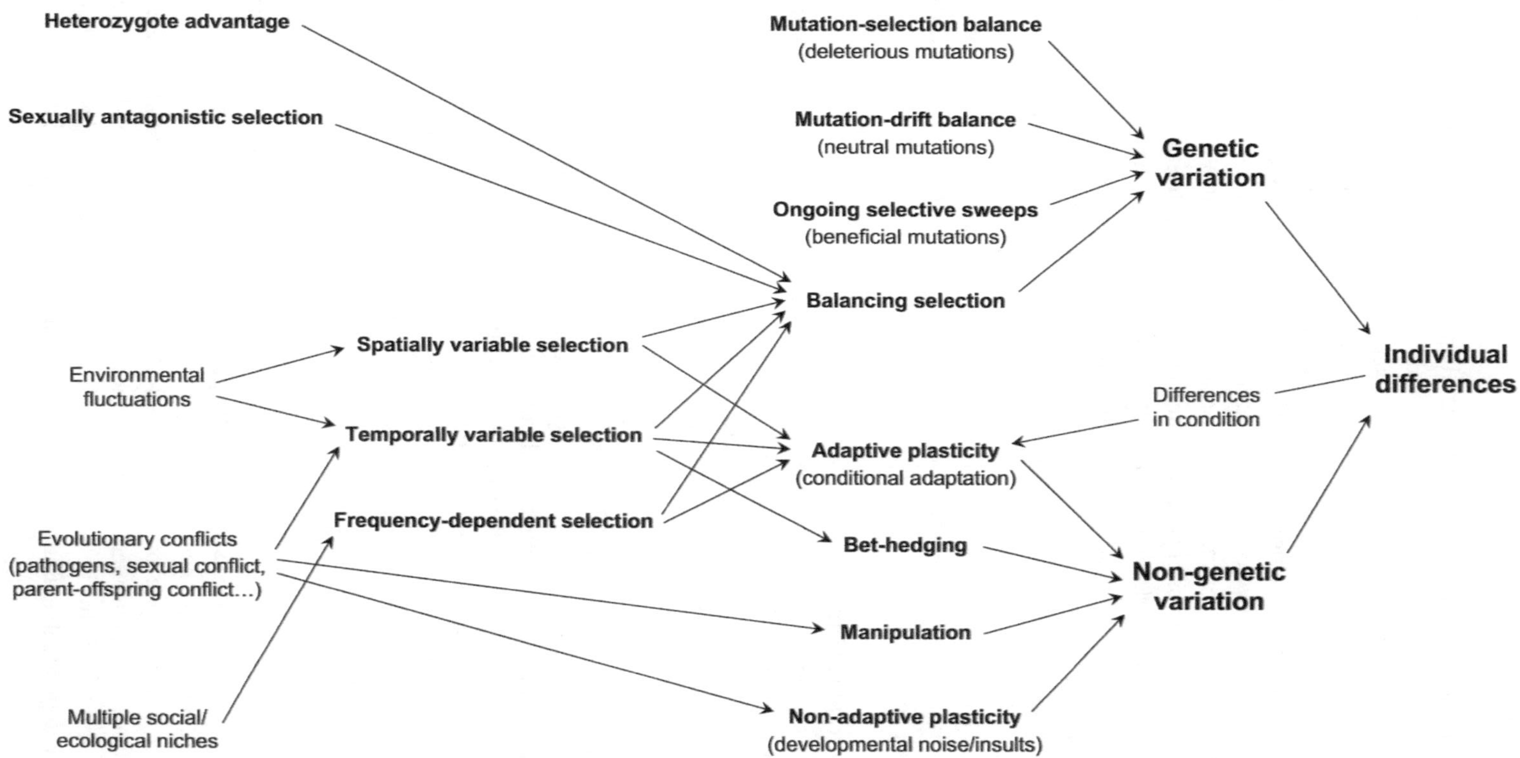

Figure 3.1. Multiple pathways in the evolution and development of individual differences.

Genetic Variation

Genetic variation (*polymorphism*) is constantly produced as new mutations arise in each generation—not just single-nucleotide substitutions but also deletions, insertions, and duplications of entire DNA segments. Most de novo mutations have deleterious effects, and selection tends to eliminate them over time. However, the elimination of harmful alleles can take many generations and is especially slow when the effects of a mutation are recessive (i.e., they are only expressed when an individual inherits two copies of the same allele). As a result, any given individual ends up carrying a smaller or larger amount of harmful alleles (mutation load). The endless process of generation and elimination of deleterious mutations is known as *mutation-selection balance*. Other mutations are neutral with respect to fitness and may either go extinct or spread in a population by random drift (*mutation-drift balance*). When mutations are beneficial, they tend to spread in relation to their positive effects on fitness. A *selective sweep* is the process through which a new beneficial allele replaces the existing, less beneficial ones. Selective sweeps can take hundreds or thousands of generations to complete; all the while, the population remains genetically polymorphic (see Miller, 2011; Mitchell-Olds et al., 2007; Penke, 2011).

Balancing Selection

Mutation-selection balance, mutation-drift balance, and selective sweeps are all cases in which genetic variation persists as a side effect of evolutionary inertia (i.e., natural selection occurs slowly and coexists with random drift). However, multiple alleles can be actively maintained in a population if the fitness effect of a given allele is not constant but changes across time, space, or individuals. This process is known as *balancing selection* (Dingemanse & Réale, 2013; Gangestad, 2011; Mitchell-Olds et al., 2007; Penke, 2011). A simple form of balancing selection occurs when there is a *heterozygote advantage*, as in the case of malaria resistance: if individuals with two discordant alleles (heterozygotes) have the highest fitness, no allele can displace the other, and variation may persist indefinitely. Another kind of balancing selection is *sexually antagonistic selection*, which takes place when a certain allele has positive fitness effects in one sex but negative effects in the other. Balancing selection may also occur when the direction of selection keeps changing across time and/or space. Variable selection pressures are often tied to fluctuations in the environment, both physical (e.g., availability of food, risk of predation) and social (e.g., population density, sex ratio). However, temporally variable selection can also arise from evolutionary conflicts and the resulting arm races—such as between pathogens and hosts, predators and prey, or parents and offspring (Gangestad, 2011).

Another major source of balancing selection is *frequency-dependent selection*. In frequency-dependent selection, the fitness of a trait depends on how common the trait is in the population. Alternative mating strategies are often frequency-dependent; to illustrate, males who avoid competition and try to sneak copulations (Chapter 1) can only be successful if most of the other males follow a territorial strategy. As sneaky strategists become more common they also become less successful, and the direction of selection switches from positive to negative. As the cycle repeats, the alleles that contribute to different strategies persist in the population. Frequency-dependent selection can be a powerful source of genetic variation when individuals can fill multiple ecological and social niches, broadly defined to include alternative roles and strategies in domains such as foraging, mating, and cooperation (Figueredo et al., 2011; Montiglio et al., 2013; Wolf & McNamara, 2012).

Nongenetic Variation

While genes contribute significantly to individual differences in most traits, there are other mechanisms of variation that do not involve heritable differences in DNA sequence. Nongenetic variation can be mediated by a variety of specific processes, from epigenetic modifications to social learning. In general terms, *developmental plasticity* can be defined as an organism's ability to produce distinct phenotypes when exposed to different environments during development (Nettle & Bateson, 2015; Schlichting & Pigliucci, 1998; West-Eberhard, 2003). Plasticity can be shaped by selection to maximize fitness through phenotype–environment matching, or *conditional adaptation* (Boyce & Ellis, 2005). Mechanisms of adaptive plasticity track the state of the environment and use that information to adjust the developing phenotype, for example by triggering the development of costly defenses when early cues indicate a high risk of predation. Because adaptive plasticity involves durable change, it is inherently forward-looking; that is, it involves predicting and preparing for a future state of the environment, often based on the earliest available cues (e.g., maternal hormones during fetal development may indicate high levels of stress in the mother, which in turn may correlate with predation risk). Indeed, sometimes there is a long delay between a plastic response to the environment and its fitness-enhancing effects, as when exposure to a certain cue during infancy directs the expression of a trait that affects survival and/or reproduction in adulthood. Anticipatory processes of this kind are often referred to as *predictive-adaptive responses* (Bateson et al., 2014; Gluckman et al., 2005).

The input for adaptive plasticity is not restricted to information from the external environment. Individuals may also adjust their phenotypic development based on information about their own condition; labels for this type of process include *facultative calibration* and *somatic state-based plasticity* (Luttbeg & Sih, 2010; Nettle & Bateson, 2015; Rickard et al., 2014). For example, it is often the case that individuals who are small or weak (e.g., because of poor nutrition or high mutation load) have less to gain from being physically aggressive. It may then be adaptive to calibrate the development of aggression to one's physical size and strength. In this way, individual differences in one trait become the source of individual differences in other traits. As discussed in Chapter 1, the condition-dependent traits that drive facultative calibration are more likely to arise through social or sexual selection.

Like genetic mutations, plasticity is not necessarily adaptive and in fact can be quite disruptive. Developmental processes can be perturbed in myriad ways, resulting in neutral or maladaptive variation when disturbances exceed the canalization ability of the organism. Most developmental perturbations and insults arise from random events such as accidents, exposure to toxins, and nutritional fluctuations. A special kind of nonadaptive plasticity is that resulting from active manipulation by other organisms in the context of evolutionary conflict. In the context of parent–offspring conflict, mothers may use prenatal hormones to shape the development of their offspring in partly self-interested ways (Del Giudice, 2012*a*). Also, pathogens often manipulate the physiology and behavior of their hosts (Kramer & Bressan, 2015; Poulin, 2010). The protozoan *Toxoplasma gondii* can affect the behavior of host animals (e.g., cats) by altering the synthesis of dopamine and other neurotransmitters. There have been speculations that being infected by *Toxoplasma* may permanently alter personality in humans, although the evidence is weak and effects have not replicated in the largest studies (Cook et al., 2015; Flegr, 2013; Lindová et al., 2012; Sugden et al., 2016). Finally, the same processes that mediate adaptive plasticity early in life may cause maladaptive byproducts later on. This is especially likely if selection is strongest in early development, for example because of high mortality risk in infants: traits that boost survival during this critical initial phase can persist even if they become mildly harmful in adulthood (Nettle & Bateson, 2015).

Another limit of adaptive plasticity is that it can only evolve if the environment is sufficiently predictable and the available cues are at least moderately reliable. An alternative to plasticity in the face of unpredictable fluctuations is *bet-hedging*, a strategy that provides "insurance" against large fitness fluctuations by randomly diversifying the phenotype of offspring (Philippi & Seger, 1989; Starrfelt & Kokko, 2012). Bet-hedging mechanisms purposefully generate undirected variation, making it more likely that at least some offspring in a generation will end up with a well-matched phenotype regardless of the future state of the environment.

Genetic variation, plasticity, and bet-hedging are not mutually exclusive and can easily coexist within the same species or population. As shown in Figure 3.1, similar ecological conditions—such as environments characterized by large fluctuations across time—can select for different types of variation, depending on additional factors such as the rate and distribution of fluctuations or the precise costs and benefits of plasticity (e.g., Sadeh et al., 2009; Svanbäck et al., 2009; Svardal et al., 2011). In principle, the same developmental mechanisms can mediate both adaptive plasticity and random bet-hedging at the same time, making it more difficult to differentiate between the two (Donaldson-Matasci et al., 2013). Individual variation often reflects a mixture of genetic and nongenetic sources of variation, and disentangling the evolutionary processes implicated in its origin and maintenance can be extremely challenging (Arslan & Penke, 2015*a*).

INDIVIDUAL DIFFERENCES

Historically, psychological research on individual differences has branched into two largely separate fields dealing with personality on one side and intelligence or cognitive ability on the other. This disciplinary split reflects a deeper distinction between two aspects of individual variation that can be loosely described as *function* and *functionality*. Although motivational and self-regulatory systems share a universal structure, the details of their functional organization are highly variable. Different individuals may prioritize different goals, follow different strategies to reach those goals, or strike a different balance in the many tradeoffs involved in the regulation of behavior. This kind of variation is essentially *strategic* as it reflects alternative "settings" of the same underlying processes. In turn, individual differences in functional settings can often be explained by invoking differences in the values of key regulatory variables. Such strategic variation in the functional settings of psychological mechanisms can be contrasted with variation in how well those mechanisms perform their tasks with speed, efficiency, and reliability—in a word, their functionality (Del Giudice, 2014*b*).

Personality

Differences in Motivation and Self-Regulation

Personality traits describe stable patterns of thought, emotion, and behavior that occur across a broad range of contexts and situations. In a functional perspective, personality emerges from individual differences in motivation and self-regulation, which in turn determine consistent differences in the appraisal of situations, the type and intensity of the emotions evoked by those situations, and the resulting behavioral tendencies (Denissen & Penke, 2008; DeYoung, 2015; Wood et al., 2015). The basic level of analysis for personality, then, is that of motivational mechanisms such as attachment and aggression and self-regulatory processes such as time discounting. Motivational traits identified at this level are usually "narrow" in that they are only relevant to a particular type of situation (e.g., contexts and events that activate the fear system). By contrast, individual differences in self-regulation can have broad-ranging effects that spill over multiple motivational domains.

Functionally meaningful personality traits can be identified in relation to all the motivational systems described in Chapter 2. For example, individual differences in aggression are easily mapped onto aggression subtypes—proactive and reactive as well as physical, verbal, and relational (e.g., Archer, 2009; Card et al., 2008; Raine et al., 2006). Researchers have assessed individual differences in sensitivity to disgust in the pathogen, sexual, and moral domains (Sparks et al., 2018; Tybur et al., 2009, 2011), developed measures of acquisitiveness (Preston & Vickers, 2014), and described stable individual differences in patterns of cooperative behavior (e.g., Kurzban & Houser, 2005). In the mating domain, *sex drive* quantifies the overall intensity of sexual desire and the motivational salience of sexual rewards (Lippa, 2009), while *sociosexuality* offers a more nuanced description of individual mating strategies. Specifically, *unrestricted* sociosexual attitudes reflect a desire for uncommitted sex with many short-term partners or "short-term orientation"; conversely, "long-term orientation" captures the desire for committed romantic relationships or long-term pair bonding. Mixed sociosexual strategies involve a combination of short- and long-term mating orientation (Jackson & Kirkpatrick, 2007; Simpson & Gangestad, 1991; Simpson et al., 2004).

As an extended example of personality traits defined at the level of motivational systems, consider individual styles of romantic attachment. As children interact with their caregivers, they develop characteristic patterns of emotions and behavior when stressful events activate their attachment system (Marvin & Britner, 2008). In adults, attachment patterns generalize and become trait-like styles of interaction with romantic partners, close friends, and other potential attachment figures. Individual differences in romantic attachment map on two main dimensions, *avoidance* and *anxiety*. Avoidant people tend to avoid intimacy, minimize their emotional needs, and develop a self-reliant attitude, whereas anxious people tend to be emotionally dependent, worry about abandonment and loneliness, and become angry and distressed when their partners are not readily available (Mikulincer & Shaver, 2016). Securely attached people are low in both avoidance and anxiety and enjoy emotional closeness without fearing dependence or asking their partners for constant reassurance. From the standpoint of internal regulatory variables, individual differences in attachment partly reflect "internal working models" that include one's sense of being worthy of love, generalized expectations about partners' availability as caregivers, and perceptions of the world as a safe or dangerous place (Bretherton & Munholland, 2008; Mikulincer et al., 2003). From an evolutionary perspective, the primary function of romantic attachment is to regulate commitment and investment in long-term relationships; consistent with this view, attachment styles correlate with sociosexuality and predict patterns of couple stability, infidelity, jealousy, and many other aspects of relationship functioning (Del Giudice, 2009*a*; Gillath & Schachner, 2006; Mikulincer & Shaver, 2016; Stefanou & McCabe, 2012). Because of the deep functional connections among the attachment, security, and fear systems, attachment styles also correlate with individual differences in attention and response to threats (Ein-Dor, 2015; Ein-Dor et al., 2011).

The same general approach can be extended to individual differences in decision-making and self-regulation. A key personality trait in this area is *risk-taking*; another is *sensation seeking*, the tendency to seek out novel, stimulating, and emotionally intense experiences (Zuckerman, 2007). A number of studies have shown that the same individual may show different levels of risk-taking in different domains such as mating, social competition, and exploration (e.g., Kruger et al., 2007; Weber et al., 2002; Wilke et al., 2014). This makes biological sense because risk sensitivity should be calibrated to contextual and personal factors—for example, the individual's need or the value of expected rewards—that can easily vary across domains (Mishra, 2014). While domain-specific approaches to risk can be informative, it is also true that some of the putative domains of risk-taking described in this body of literature probably do not reflect risk proneness in a technical sense but rather other motivational traits, such as sociosexuality and disgust sensitivity. Moreover, risk-taking scores in the more plausible domains tend to be positively correlated with one another, suggesting that a general factor of risk sensitivity exists above and beyond domain-specific attitudes (Frey et al., 2017). For simplicity, I will treat risk-taking as a generalized trait in the remainder of this book.

Arguably, the most important dimension of individual differences in self-regulation is *impulsivity*, defined as a stable tendency to act without deliberation and without consideration of future consequences. Impulsivity reflects a combination of behavioral disinhibition and future discounting, and it correlates with both risk-taking and sensation seeking (DeYoung, 2011). In addition, the distinction between reactive and proactive control discussed in Chapter 2 has been used to identify reactive and proactive *coping styles* in a number of species, including humans (Del Giudice, 2015*a*; Koolhaas et al. 1999; Réale et al., 2010; see also Braver, 2012). Just like their motivational counterparts, self-regulatory traits are likely to depend on regulatory variables such as the individual's condition (which determines whether the outcomes of risk-taking have increasing or decreasing returns) and the predictability of future rewards (e.g., Ermer et al., 2008; Mishra, 2014).

Broad Personality Factors

If one considers the fact that the mind contains a multiplicity of motivational and self-regulatory systems and that each system may accommodate several dimensions of variation, it becomes apparent that there are dozens if not hundreds of personality traits potentially worthy of description. However, studies of personality descriptors across languages and cultures show that the structure of individual differences can be reasonably approximated with about five broad factors, the so-called "Big Five." The five factors identified in this way are *agreeableness* (kindness, trust, altruism, cooperation, social compliance, and politeness), *conscientiousness* (self-control, restraint, orderliness, dependability, and industriousness), *neuroticism* (negative emotionality and emotional instability), *extraversion* (positive emotionality, sociability, assertiveness, and dominance), and *openness to experience* (imagination, intellectual curiosity, and aesthetic appreciation; see Costa & McCrae, 1995; McCrae & Costa, 2003). Each of these factors can be decomposed into multiple narrower traits (*aspects* or *facets*), which can often be linked more directly to specific motivational and self-regulatory mechanisms (DeYoung et al., 2007; Saucier, 2009).

Factors such as the Big Five are best regarded as descriptive summaries that capture broadband patterns of covariation between many functionally specific dimensions of personality (Ashton & Lee, 2005; Krueger & Marton, 2006; Wood et al., 2015). For example, extraversion reflects individual differences in the functioning of the status and affiliation systems, and—more generally—in responsivity to rewards and activity of the behavioral approach system (BAS). Likewise, conscientiousness describes coordinated variation in multiple self-regulatory processes such as inhibition and time discounting; agreeableness captures broad dispositions toward cooperation and altruism; and so on (Corr et al., 2013; DeYoung, 2010, 2015). These patterns of covariation may arise for a number of reasons. At the ultimate level, different traits may vary together because they act in a synergistic way to promote adaptation; within extraversion, assertiveness and dominance may be especially effective at gaining social status when they are coupled with high levels of sociability (Nettle, 2011*a*). Similarly, different traits may evolve to depend on the same underlying regulatory variables or be calibrated to the same aspects of individual condition (Buss, 2011; DeYoung, 2015). At the proximate level, different psychological mechanisms may share the same functional processes, be modulated by the same neurobiological pathways, or respond to the same cues from the environment—all potential sources of covariation between traits.

Although the Big Five offer a parsimonious approximation of the structure of personality, they inevitably leave out many specific dimensions of variation. Still, even specific traits that are not part of the model can be mapped on the descriptive space of the Big Five based on their correlations with those factors. In this sense, the five-factor model of personality can be employed as a common frame of reference or "coordinate system" for individual differences. For instance, attachment styles are not explicitly represented in the five-factor model; at the same time, attachment anxiety and avoidance show sizable positive correlations with neuroticism and negative correlations with conscientiousness and agreeableness (Noftle & Shaver, 2006). Traits that describe mating strategies and sexuality are also conspicuously absent from the five-factor model despite their evolutionary and personal significance (Schmitt & Buss, 2000). Research has shown that high sex drive, unrestricted sociosexuality, and short-term orientation are reliably associated with low levels of conscientiousness and agreeableness (and less consistently so with high levels of extraversion, neuroticism, and openness); long-term orientation and relationship exclusivity show the opposite pattern (Banai & Pavela, 2015; Bourdage et al., 2007; Del Giudice, Klimczuk et al., 2014; Holtzman & Strube, 2013; Schmitt & Buss, 2000).

Another broad dimension of personality that is not well represented in the five-factor model is *honesty-humility* (sincerity, honesty, modesty, and fair-mindedness). The honesty-humility factor is a key component of the six-factor HEXACO model of personality (Ashton & Lee, 2008; Lee & Ashton, 2012) and shows only moderate overlap with the Big Five version of agreeableness (the HEXACO also includes an agreeableness factor, but with a somewhat different content). On the opposite side of the moral spectrum one finds the "dark triad," a set of correlated traits—*psychopathy*, *narcissism*, and *Machiavellianism*—that share a common core of manipulativeness, callousness, and lack of affective empathy (Furnham et al., 2013; Jones & Figueredo, 2013; Muris et al., 2017; Paulhus, 2014). In particular, Machiavellianism is defined by a calculating, deliberately manipulative approach to interpersonal relationships; psychopathic traits include impulsive and antisocial tendencies, whereas narcissism is characterized by grandiosity, need for attention, and a sense of entitlement. All these traits are associated with low levels of agreeableness and honesty-humility (with correlations in the −.40 to −.60 range); on top of this, each trait in the triad shows specific correlations with other factors, such as conscientiousness and extraversion (Book et al., 2015; Furnham et al., 2013; Jonason et al., 2013; Muris et al., 2017; O'Boyle et al., 2015; Veselka et al., 2012).

Higher Order Personality Factors

The dimensions of variation described by the Big Five are not completely independent from one another. Two main patterns of covariation emerge from the empirical data: first, agreeableness is positively correlated with conscientiousness and negatively correlated with neuroticism; second, extraversion is positively correlated with openness to experience (correlations range from about .20 to .40). This suggests the existence of two higher order factors or *metatraits* that account for correlations at the level of broad factors (Figure 3.2). The first metatrait—*alpha* or *stability*—describes a combination of self-control, emotional stability, and prosociality (high agreeableness, high conscientiousness, low neuroticism). The second—*beta* or *plasticity*—brings together exploration and active social engagement (high extraversion, high openness), both of which reflect a highly responsive BAS. (Note that the "plasticity" label for this metatrait has nothing to do with the concept of developmental plasticity discussed earlier.) The existence of alpha and beta is probably related to pervasive tradeoffs in the regulation of goals, including that between exploration and exploitation (Corr et al., 2013; DeYoung, 2006, 2015; Digman, 1997; Saucier, 2009; Saucier et al., 2014; Segarra et al., 2014). Alpha shows robust negative associations with the dark triad and impulsivity, whereas beta is positively related to both impulsivity and sensation seeking (Corr et al., 2013; DeYoung, 2011; Jonason et al., 2013).

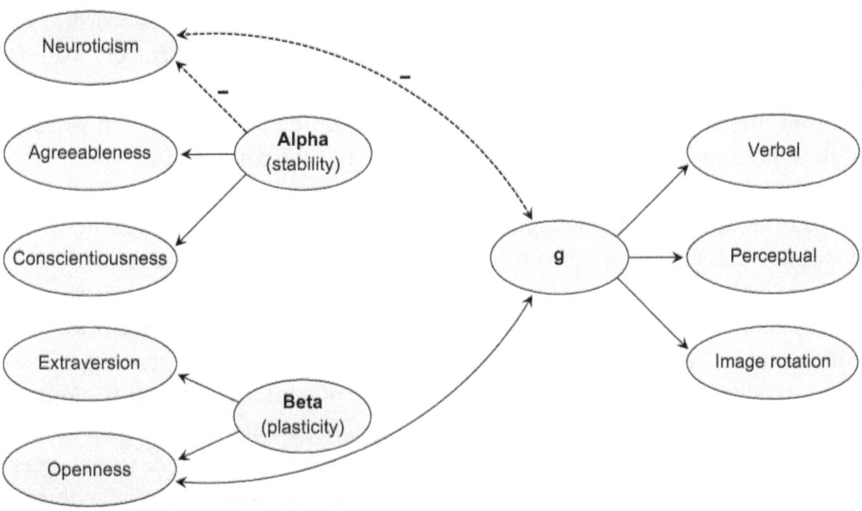

Figure 3.2. The broadband structure of personality and cognitive ability. Curved arrows represent correlations between personality traits and general intelligence (g).

Some researchers have identified an even broader trait sitting at the top of the personality hierarchy, the *general factor of personality* (GFP). The GFP is defined by high levels of both alpha and beta—in short, a distillate of socially desirable personality, curious and extraverted but also kind, altruistic, self-controlled, and emotionally stable (Figueredo et al., 2011, 2015; Musek, 2007; Rushton & Irwing, 2009; van der Linden et al., 2010). Unfortunately, the socially desirable nature of the GFP and other methodological issues make it hard to decide to what extent this factor reflects substantive differences in behavior, a general dimension of positive self-evaluation, and/or measurement artifacts (e.g., Chang et al., 2012; Erdle & Rushton, 2011; Muncer, 2011; Revelle & Wilt, 2013; Rushton, 2012). The debate on the nature and significance of the GFP continues to this date, and there is still no clear consensus in the literature. On the one hand, GFP scores predict job performance and show positive correlations with measures of "emotional intelligence" (e.g., recognition of facial expressions), consistent with the idea that this factor captures aspects of social competence. On the other hand, there is evidence suggesting that the GFP is strongly contaminated by positive self-evaluation biases and socially desirable responding; as a result, people's self-rated position on the GFP correlates weakly (if at all) with how they are rated by others (Davies et al., 2015; Dunkel et al., 2016; Gnambs, 2013; Pelt et al., 2017; van der Linden et al., 2017).

Neurobiological Correlates

The neurobiological basis of personality ultimately resides in the neural systems that control motivation and self-regulation. Since broad personality factors represent summaries of correlated variation across multiple systems, it is unsurprising that individual differences in the Big Five are associated with differential activity in many regions of the brain, from subcortical structures such as the amygdala and striatum to the prefrontal cortex (Kennis et al., 2013). Personality is also correlated to variation in brain structure; for instance, people high in neuroticism tend to have a larger left amygdala and smaller medial prefrontal cortex (MPFC) and anterior cingulate cortex (ACC) (Mincic, 2015).

From the molecular standpoint, a key duality in the neurobiology of personality is the association between metatrait alpha and serotonergic function on the one hand, and beta and dopaminergic function on the other hand (DeYoung, 2010, 2013, 2015). Both openness and extraversion are associated with increased dopaminergic signaling; more specifically, dopamine is implicated in the assertiveness and dominance facets of extraversion, whereas sociability is primarily modulated by opioids. Increased dopaminergic activity is also likely to contribute to the *industriousness* facets of conscientiousness (persistence, achievement striving), which empirically correlate with both alpha and beta (DeYoung, 2013). Individual differences in serotonin signaling are associated with conscientiousness, agreeableness, and neuroticism. Moreover, neuroticism has been linked to the stress response system and its signaling molecules—norepinephrine, corticotropin-releasing hormone (CRH), and cortisol—in addition to glutamate and GABA (Allen & DeYoung, 2017; DeYoung, 2010; more on this in Chapter 6).

Impulsivity is negatively correlated with alpha and positively correlated with beta; accordingly, individual differences in impulsivity show associations with both serotonergic and dopaminergic signaling as well as relations with other molecules such as NE, GABA, and endogenous opioids (Dalley & Roiser, 2012).

Evolutionary Models

In general, evolutionary scholars have singled out variable selection—whether spatial, temporal, or frequency-dependent—as the most plausible explanation for the maintenance of individual differences in personality. Being high versus low in any of the Big Five carries different combinations of costs and benefits, and what is the most adaptive combination may change across space, time, or social niches. For example, high extraversion facilitates access to status and resources, promotes exploration, and increases mating success; however, it also increases the risk of social conflict, accidents, and diseases (including sexually transmitted ones). Given these costs and benefits, low levels of extraversion may be favored in stable social and ecological environments, whereas high extraversion may be adaptive in novel or socially fluid contexts. Similarly, the costs of neuroticism for relationships and health can be offset by an increased ability to anticipate, detect, and deal with social threats and other dangers—an instance of the smoke detector principle. Highly conscientious people are more persistent and capable of delaying gratification in view of future goals but also more rigid and less able to take advantage of unexpected opportunities (Denissen & Penke, 2008; de Vries et al., 2016; Dickman, 1990; Nettle, 2011*a*).

In principle, variable selection can maintain both genetic and nongenetic variation in personality, including developmental plasticity in response to critical aspects of the environment. So far, the evidence on the genetic and fitness correlates of personality is most consistent with variable selection (and balancing selection at the genetic level), although specific cost-benefit hypotheses are difficult to test conclusively (de Vries et al., 2016; Penke & Jokela, 2016). There is also cross-cultural evidence that extraversion in men—but not women—is typically associated with high fertility, possibly implying a net fitness advantage and a history of mutation-selection balance in addition to balancing selection. Finally, recent genetic data point to a contribution of rare mutations to variation in neuroticism (e.g., Alvergne et al., 2010; Bailey et al., 2013; Berg et al., 2014; Gurven et al., 2014; Hill, Arslan et al., 2018; Jokela, 2012; Skirbekk & Blekesaune, 2014).

To the extent that personality traits are plastic, they can be facultatively calibrated to an individual's condition. Specifically, extraversion may be partly calibrated to other traits that increase one's potential for social success and dominance, such as physical attractiveness and formidability (Buss, 2011; Lukaszewski & Roney, 2011). However, the evidence for this kind of facultative adjustment is still very mixed (Haysom et al., 2015; Lukaszewski & von Rueden, 2015; Zietsch, 2016). It is also worth noting that a certain amount of variation in personality may be the nonadaptive result of manipulation. Pathogens such as *Toxoplasma* can manipulate host behavior by altering the synthesis of a number of neurotransmitters. Benign microbes in the gut produce key neurotransmitters such as dopamine, serotonin, and GABA, and evidence is accumulating that they are able to affect various aspects of cognition and behavior including eating, sleeping, stress reactivity, and memory (Alcock et al., 2014; Dinan & Cryan, 2012). Another speculative idea is that mothers may indirectly manipulate the future personality of their children by changing their exposure to cortisol and other hormones during pregnancy and lactation (Del Giudice, 2012*a*; Grey et al., 2013).

An important but rarely addressed question is whether human personality may have changed in recent evolutionary times; a related question is what proportion of the genetic variation we observe today is explained by the fact that we are in the middle of ongoing selective sweeps (Miller, 2011). With the invention of agriculture and money, traits like conscientiousness, self-control, and orientation toward the future (low time discounting) may have become especially adaptive (Cochran & Harpending, 2009). Likewise, increased population density and the rise of organized religion and law enforcement may have selected for higher levels of sociability and agreeableness—a sort of self-domestication (Frost, 2011; Frost & Harpending, 2015). Even more intriguingly, it is possible that the recent explosion in social stratification and in the number of available social/occupational niches may have selected for more variability and specialization in individual profiles of behavior and cognition. Consistent with this hypothesis, a study of personality in the Tsimane (a forager-horticulturalist population of Bolivia) was unable to recover the standard Big Five and instead found evidence for only two broad factors of "prosociality" and "industriousness" (largely a combination of conscientiousness, agreeableness, and extraversion; Gurven et al., 2013). Cross-cultural data also show that correlations between the Big Five become weaker as societies become more complex, which suggests increasing diversification of individual personalities (Lukaszewski et al., 2017).

Cognitive Ability

General Intelligence: The g Factor

The domain of cognitive abilities is vast and comprises many specialized types of information processing, which have been classically dived into broad categories of perception, attention, memory, reasoning, and language. In spite of the variety and multiplicity of cognitive processes, individual differences in cognition have a surprisingly simple structure due to an empirical phenomenon called the *positive manifold*. The positive manifold is a pervasive pattern of positive correlations between people's performance on cognitive tasks across widely different areas and domains. For example, people who perform better on memory tasks also tend to be better at mathematical reasoning, have a larger vocabulary and better comprehension skills, and even respond more quickly in tasks that measure simple reaction times. The positive manifold points to the existence of a strong general factor of ability called *general intelligence, general cognitive ability*, or simply *g*. When people are presented with a diverse set of cognitive tasks, the g factor alone typically accounts for about half of the variance in their performance. An individual's *intelligence quotient* or IQ score can be interpreted as a standardized estimate of g based on a specific selection of tests (Deary et al., 2010; Hunt, 2011; Jensen, 1998).

Individual differences in g are revealed most clearly in the ability to learn new information quickly and efficiently and to deal with complex, abstract reasoning tasks (Gottfredson, 2002). However, g itself is not a specific capacity or mechanism, but is instead a statistical representation of individual variation across tasks and domains. In turn, variation in the positive manifold is likely due to broad differences in the speed, efficiency, and accuracy of information processing in the brain, even if some particular brain networks may contribute more strongly to performance across tasks (see later discussion). Much theoretical confusion in the literature flows from the misconception that g corresponds to some domain-general cognitive process, and its corollary that the existence of g somehow contradicts the functionally specialized nature of psychological mechanisms (e.g., Chiappe & MacDonald, 2005; van Schaik et al., 2012; see Lee, 2009).

General intelligence is mostly uncorrelated with personality, with two main exceptions. First, there is a reliable positive correlation (about .30) between g and openness to experience, particularly the facets that measure intellectual curiosity rather than imagination and aesthetic interests. Second, intelligence shows a weaker negative correlation with neuroticism (about −.15), possibly because of a shared effect of mutation load on both traits. Although correlations with extraversion are sometimes reported, they tend to be very small and inconsistent across studies (Ackerman & Heggestad, 1997; Bartels et al., 2012; DeYoung & Gray, 2009; Wolf & Ackerman, 2005). In the area of self-regulation, g is most strongly associated with individual differences in executive functions. Correlations between executive functions and intelligence are highest for working memory updating (about .70) and lowest for flexibility/shifting (about .20; Friedman et al., 2008).

Broad Ability Factors

While the importance of g is hard to understate, individual differences in cognition cannot be fully described by a single general dimension. The g factor is best regarded as the apex of a hierarchy, followed by a number of more specialized factors. As it turns out, most of the variation at the level below g can be summarized by just three factors, as described in the *verbal-perceptual-image rotation model* of intelligence (VPR; Johnson & Bouchard, 2005; Major et al., 2012). The *verbal* factor includes verbal comprehension and reasoning skills, vocabulary, and fluency. The domain of visuospatial abilities comprises two correlated factors: the *perceptual* factor includes speed of perceptual processing, visual memory, visualization, and abstract/mechanical reasoning; the *image rotation* factor is more specific and captures the ability to rotate mental images of two- and three-dimensional objects (Figure 3.2).

Once variation in g is accounted for, a second major dimension of individual differences emerges that pits verbal ability against perceptual/rotation abilities. In general, people who are better at verbal tasks also perform well in visuospatial tasks (positive manifold) because of their higher general ability. Controlling for differences in g reveals the existence of a tradeoff between verbal and perceptual/

rotation skills, so that people who are *relatively* better at verbal tasks compared with their general ability level tend to be *relatively* worse at spatial and rotation tasks (and vice versa). A possible reason for this tradeoff lies in the serial nature of verbal processing contrasted with the parallel nature of the operations involved in perceptual and rotation tasks. Another tradeoff identified in this way is that between abilities that require focused attention on details and those that involve diffuse attention to multiple cues simultaneously (Hunt, 2011; Johnson & Bouchard, 2007; Johnson, Jung et al., 2008). Moving further down the hierarchy, one can identify many narrow abilities that map more directly on specific cognitive processes, such as verbal working memory or three-dimensional mental rotation. However, narrow abilities of this kind tend to explain comparatively little variation in performance beyond that contributed by the broader factors.

Neurobiological Correlates

Cognitive ability is associated with individual differences in both brain structure and function. To begin with, g correlates with the total volume of the brain, with estimates ranging from .25 to .40. Beyond brain volume, g is also associated with the thickness of the cortex and the structural integrity of connection fibers in the white matter. Structurally intact fibers seem to enhance cognitive ability by supporting fast information transfer between connected brain areas. Other indices of connection efficiency within brain networks have been also linked to higher levels of g (Deary et al., 2010; Gignac & Bates, 2017; Penke et al., 2012; Pietschnig et al., 2015; Ritchie et al., 2015). At a finer scale, studies have identified a specific network that makes an especially large contribution to general cognitive ability. This network comprises the lateral prefrontal cortex, the parietal lobe, the cingulate cortex (mainly the ACC), and the white matter fibers that connect frontal and parietal regions. According to the *parieto-frontal integration theory* of intelligence (P-FIT), these regions form an integrated circuit that supports working memory, abstract reasoning, and response selection (Jung & Haier, 2007). Notably, this network overlaps with the dorsal attention network that has been associated with mechanistic cognition (Chapter 2). Within the parieto-frontal network, gray matter volume, white matter integrity, and stronger activation during tasks all predict higher levels of g (Barbey et al., 2014; Basten et al., 2015; Deary et al., 2010). Moreover, cognitive ability is associated with increased volume and activity of the striatum, suggesting an involvement of dopamine signaling and a possible neurobiological basis for the correlation between intelligence and openness to experience (Basten et al., 2015; Schlagenhauf et al., 2013).

As for the neural correlates of broad ability factors, verbal skills are mainly supported by a network of prefrontal and temporal regions in the left hemisphere. Perceptual and rotation skills are associated with information processing pathways in the parietal and temporal lobes, with an especially strong contribution from the right parietal cortex (Colom et al., 2009; Gläscher et al., 2009; Hunt, 2011). The contrast between a left-hemisphere bias in verbal ability and a right-hemisphere bias in perceptual and rotation tasks may help explain the verbal–rotation tradeoff at the neurobiological level (Johnson & Bouchard, 2007).

Evolutionary Models

The sheer complexity of the brain and the large number of genes expressed in neural tissue have led some researchers to hypothesize that mutation-selection balance would be the main driver of individual differences in intelligence, in combination with nonadaptive plasticity caused by developmental insults and disturbances. From this perspective, sexual selection through mate choice for low levels of mutation and parasite load is a highly plausible explanation for the evolution of condition dependence in brain development (Miller, 2000; Penke et al., 2007); social selection for high-intelligence cooperation partners may have played a similar role. It has been known for some time that mutation load plays a major role at the very low end of intelligence (i.e., intellectual disability), and there is evidence that lack of damaging mutations contributes to cognitive performance at the very high end (see Arslan & Penke, 2015*b*; Penke & Jokela, 2016; Spain et al., 2016). The contribution of mutations to variation in g within the normal range has been more elusive, but recent findings indicate that about half of the genetic variation in general intelligence is in fact due to rare variants, consistent with a mutation-selection model (Hill, Arslan et al., 2018). It is still unclear what evolutionary processes might explain the remaining effect of common genetic variation. Over the next few years, our understanding of the evolution of intelligence should improve dramatically with the availability of new, high-resolution genetic data and more sophisticated analytic techniques (Plomin & von Stumm, 2018).

SEX DIFFERENCES

Just like individual differences, systematic differences between the behavior of males and that of females are extremely common in nature. While sexual selection is a powerful source of sex differences, it is not the only one. In highly social species, other forms of social selection—including selection for cooperation partners—may easily operate in sexually differentiated ways, leading to the evolution of distinct behavioral profiles. At the same time, males and females often face different ecological pressures that are not directly related to mating and social selection, for example because they specialize in different subsistence tasks (e.g., hunting vs. gathering) or are subject to different health risks. All these processes can produce differences in the *average* level of a trait but may also result in sex differences in *variability*. Across species, it is common for males to be more phenotypically variable than females (Wyman & Rowe, 2014). There are two main reasons for this general pattern. First, males typically undergo stronger sexual selection for condition-dependent traits, which tend to be especially variable. Second, males often have a wider spectrum of alternative mating strategies, which in turn are associated with different behavioral profiles. Humans are no exception: men are somewhat more variable than women in many areas of personality and cognition, and, as a result, they are often overrepresented at both the high and the low end of the same traits (Archer & Mehdikhani, 2003; Del Giudice, 2015*b*).

The development of psychological sex differences critically involves sex hormones, from early organizational effects on brain development to multiple waves of activational effects in middle childhood, puberty, and beyond (Constantinescu & Hines, 2012; Geary, 2010; Hines, 2011). Hormonal mechanisms modulate social learning and in turn are regulated by feedback from the environment. While many sex differences in behavior have the same direction across populations and cultures (e.g., on average, men are always more physically aggressive than women), their size often varies depending on a combination of social and ecological factors, from mortality rates and sex ratios to cultural norms regarding gender equality (e.g., Conroy-Beam et al., 2015; Schmitt, 2015*b*; Zentner & Mitura, 2012).

Sex Differences in Personality

The largest sex differences in the Big Five are found in neuroticism and agreeableness, with women scoring higher in both traits. The size of these differences ranges from about 0.3 to 0.4 standard deviations (SD). Women are also somewhat more conscientious and extraverted (about 0.1 SD), while there are no consistent differences in openness to experience. The size of these effects shows some cross-cultural variation; as a rule, sex differences in personality tend to be *larger* in more gender-egalitarian countries (Lippa, 2010; Schmitt, 2015*b*). Combining sex differences on individual Big Five traits into multivariate profiles for the two sexes yields a global difference equivalent to approximately 1 SD (Del Giudice, 2009*b*). Even if broad factors such as the Big Five show reliable sex differences, their heterogeneity masks some important patterns that only become apparent when one examines narrow personality traits. For example, the relatively small sex difference in extraversion hides two larger effects of opposite sign, with males higher in dominance and assertiveness but lower in gregariousness and sociability (Costa et al., 2001; Del Giudice, 2015*b*). Combining narrow personality traits into multivariate profiles yields a global male–female difference of more than 2 SD, which is an extremely large effect by psychological standards (Del Giudice et al., 2012; Del Giudice, 2013).

Sex differences emerge even more clearly at the level of specific motivational and self-regulatory traits. Males are more physically and verbally aggressive than females, while females use more relational aggression (e.g., spreading rumors, threatening social exclusion); the combined difference across aggression types amounts to about 1 SD in adults (Archer, 2009; Card et al., 2008; Del Giudice, 2009*b*). Risk-taking and sensation seeking are also consistently higher in men (0.2 to 0.4 SD), while sex differences in impulsivity are considerably smaller (less than 0.1 SD; Byrnes et al., 1999; Cross et al., 2011).

Across cultures, men report a stronger desire for sexual variety, higher sex drive, and more unrestricted sociosexuality than women (differences range from about 0.5 to 0.7 SD). Sex differences in sociosexuality—but not sex drive—tend to become smaller in more gender-egalitarian countries (Lippa, 2009; Schmitt &

International Sexuality Description Project, 2003). Romantic attachment styles are also sexually differentiated, with higher avoidance in men and higher anxiety in women. These differences are relatively small (about 0.1 to 0.2 SD across cultures); however, there is evidence that broad dimensions such as avoidance and anxiety mask the existence of larger sex differences at the level of narrower attachment facets such as self-reliance and neediness, similarly to what happens with the Big Five (Del Giudice, 2011, 2016*a*). Disgust sensitivity is another motivational trait with clear relevance for psychopathology. Disgust sensitivity is consistently higher in women, but the effect is much larger in sexual disgust (more than 1 SD) than in pathogen and moral disgust (about 0.4 and 0.2 SD, respectively; Sparks et al., 2018; Tybur et al., 2009, 2011; Tybur & de Vries, 2013).

Sex Differences in Cognitive Ability

Despite the fact that the brain is 10–15% larger in men (corresponding to a standardized difference of 1.4 to 2 SD), sex differences in the average level of general intelligence are either nonexistent or very small (see Pietschnig et al., 2015; Ritchie et al., 2017). However, males show more *variability* in cognitive ability and are at higher risk for intellectual disability; as a result, they are overrepresented at both the high and (especially) low end of the distribution of IQ (Johnson, Carothers et al., 2008; Wai et al., 2012). The absence of average sex differences in general intelligence stands in contrast with the marked sexual differentiation found in the other ability factors. On the rotation–verbal dimension of the VPR model, women show higher verbal ability while men show better perceptual and rotation skills (about 0.6 SD). Intriguingly, sex differences in brain volume have been specifically associated with differences in visuospatial abilities rather than general intelligence (Burgaleta et al., 2012). Sex-related effects are even stronger on the focus–diffusion dimension: while men are better at tasks requiring a narrow attentional focus, women perform better in tasks involving diffusion of attention (about 0.9 SD). On top of these average differences, men show more variability than women in both these cognitive dimensions (Halpern et al., 2007; Johnson & Bouchard, 2007).

Sex differences are also apparent at the level of narrower ability facets. For instance, women outperform men in memory for object location—likely as a result of selection for gathering skills—and tend to use different strategies for spatial navigation and wayfinding. Another major axis of sexual differentiation is that of mechanistic versus mentalistic cognition. In general, females perform better in mentalistic tasks such as decoding nonverbal behavior, interpreting emotional expressions, and attributing beliefs and other states of mind. They also show increased resting activity in the default mode network. This advantage in mentalizing—especially in one-to-one and small-group interactions—is likely due to the higher demands posed by the complexity of female social networks, the fluid and indirect nature of female competition, and women's primary role in caregiving (see Baron-Cohen, 2003; Benenson, 2014; Del Giudice, 2015*b*; Geary,

2010; Ritchie et al., 2017). Mechanistic reasoning overlaps considerably with perceptual and rotation abilities, suggesting that sex differences in mechanistic versus mentalistic cognition may be closely linked to those in the verbal–rotation dimension. Sex differences in this domain are not limited to cognitive abilities but have a large motivational component as well. This is well illustrated by the difference between males and females in their interest for things-related versus people-related occupations, which is both large (about 1.2 SD) and extremely robust across time and cultures (Lippa, 2010; Morris, 2016; see also Baron-Cohen, 2003).

Sexual Orientation

To conclude this section, it is worth considering how sex differences in personality and cognition intersect with sexual orientation. While homosexual behaviors are fairly common across animal species (Bailey & Zuk, 2009), the existence of *exclusive* homosexuality is an evolutionary puzzle because of its potentially dramatic effects on reproduction and fertility. Many evolutionary hypotheses have been advanced over the years, including speculations that homosexuality may confer an inclusive fitness advantage—either by increasing investment in the children of other family members or by reducing mating competition among siblings (e.g., Apostolou, 2013; VanderLaan et al., 2013). There are preliminary indications that the same genetic factors that predispose some people to homosexuality may increase mating and reproductive success in their heterosexual relatives; moreover, at least some of these effects seem to work in a sexually antagonistic way (e.g., alleles that predispose to homosexuality in males increase mating success in heterosexual females; Camperio Ciani & Pellizzari, 2012; Camperio Ciani et al., 2008; Zietsch et al., 2008). In addition to genetic factors, there is evidence of prenatal effects in both sexes. In females (but not males), higher exposure to androgens during fetal development increases the odds of homosexuality. In males, the odds are increased by having older brothers (Blanchard, 2018*a*, 2018*b*; Breedlove, 2017). The latter effect seems to be linked to immunological interactions between male fetuses and the mother across successive pregnancies; however, its evolutionary logic is still unclear (Blanchard, 2008; Bogaert et al., 2017).

At the level of the Big Five, the personality profile of gay men is shifted toward the female average (higher agreeableness, neuroticism, and conscientiousness than heterosexual men). Symmetrically, personality traits in lesbian women show a shift in the direction of the male average (lower neuroticism and agreeableness than heterosexual women). On average, bisexual and gay men tend to have very similar personality profiles; in contrast, the average profile of bisexual women is intermediate between that of lesbians and heterosexual women (Lippa, 2005, 2008). The same general pattern is found in the domain of cognitive abilities. Gay men have better verbal skills than heterosexual men but worse perceptual-rotation skills; lesbians score lower than heterosexual women in verbal tasks but higher in perceptual and rotation tasks, although the pattern is much weaker than in men (LeVay, 2017; Peters et al., 2007; Rahman, 2005; Xu et al., 2017).

This shift toward the opposite sex does not apply to all traits, however; in particular, gay men are just as sociosexually unrestricted as heterosexual men (and have more sex partners on average), while lesbians match heterosexual women in sociosexual attitudes and behavior (Schmitt, 2007). In sum, homosexuality in both men and women is associated with a psychological mosaic of sex-typical and sex-atypical traits (LeVay, 2017).

GENES AND ENVIRONMENTS

Individual differences reflect the joint contribution of genetic and nongenetic influences, including the environmental factors that serve as inputs for plasticity and learning mechanisms. In the end, all these sources of variation can only affect the phenotype by acting on the organism's developmental processes; conversely, the evolved nature of developmental processes determines how genetic and nongenetic factors combine and how much they contribute to individual variation.

Heritability

A simple way to quantify the contribution of genetic factors to individual variation is a trait's *heritability* (Johnson et al., 2011; Visscher et al., 2008). In the narrow sense—the one employed here and in most of the literature—heritability is the proportion of variance in a trait accounted for by *additive* genetic effects. To the extent that genetic effects are additive, the phenotypic similarity between two individuals is proportional to their genetic similarity. Narrow-sense heritability excludes the effects of statistical interactions between dominant and recessive alleles, between multiple genes within the genome (*epistasis*), or between genetic and environmental factors. The classic methods for measuring heritability include twin and adoption studies; more recently, it has become feasible to directly estimate the genetic similarity between nonrelatives via genome sequencing. In principle, heritability is a statistic of a specific population and may not generalize beyond the original context in which it is measured. In practice, though, heritability estimates for psychological traits are remarkably stable and do not change much across times and places (Knopik et al., 2017; Polderman et al., 2015; Sesardic, 2005; Yang et al., 2010).

At a first approximation, both personality and cognitive traits are about 50% heritable—that is, additive genetic effects explain about half of their variance. Studies of personality in animals find the same general result (Briley & Tucker-Drob, 2017; Deary et al., 2010; Dochtermann et al., 2015; Turkheimer et al., 2014). A closer look reveals some important distinctions between the two domains. Individual differences in cognitive ability crystallize before puberty and become increasingly more heritable with age, from about 20% in early childhood to more than 60% in adulthood. Moreover, different cognitive skills are largely influenced by the same set of genetic factors. These so-called "generalist genes" probably control some nonspecific properties of the brain—such as white matter integrity—which in turn determine overall processing speed and efficiency. In contrast, the stability of personality increases steadily over the first 20–30 years of life; heritability peaks in infancy at 75% and declines to about 55% in young adulthood. Personality does not show any evidence of generalist genes; instead, variation in personality is influenced by a large number of distinct genetic sources, consistent with the idea that the Big Five and other broad traits summarize the combined action of multiple mechanisms (Bleidorn et al., 2014; Briley & Tucker-Drob, 2017; Penke & Jokela, 2016).

While estimating the heritability of a trait is relatively straightforward, identifying the particular genes that determine individual differences has proved extremely challenging. The data from large-scale association studies support the idea that variation in psychological traits is highly polygenic—that is, individual differences are caused by hundreds or thousands of genes, each with a tiny effect on the final phenotype. Save for rare mutations associated with intellectual disability, each of the few variants that have been reliably identified so far accounts for less than 1% (and usually less than 0.1%) of the total variance in personality and intelligence (Chabris et al., 2015; Munafò & Flint, 2011; Plomin & von Stumm, 2018). If the effects of individual genes are so vanishingly small, candidate gene studies that target specific variants, such as the 7-repeat allele of the dopamine receptor 4 gene (*DRD4*), have extremely low chances of identifying real genetic effects. Although small-sample studies of candidate genes are still common in psychology, they are likely to suffer from exceedingly high levels of false positives; accordingly, their findings often fail to replicate in larger association studies (Dick et al., 2015; Duncan et al., 2014; Penke & Jokela, 2016).

Environmental Effects

A useful way to think about environmental effects is to frame the relations between genotypes and phenotypes as *reaction norms*. The reaction norm of a genotype is a function that describes how different states of the environment result in different values of the phenotype (Figure 3.3). Reaction norms capture the plastic potential of genotypes (DeWitt & Scheiner, 2004; Schlichting & Pigliucci, 1998). A flat reaction norm indicates absence of plasticity, while differences in the range of phenotypic expression correspond to individual differences in plasticity. (For linear reaction norms, as those shown in Figure 3.3, a steeper slope equals higher plasticity.) Variation in the shape of reaction norms results in *genotype-environment interactions* (G×E; see Grigorenko et al., 2016; Manuck & McCaffery, 2014; Rutter et al., 2006). In the presence of G×E interactions, genetic and environmental factors are no longer additive: the same genotype has different effects depending on the environmental conditions in which it is expressed—or, equivalently, the same environmental conditions have different effects on individuals with different genotypes (see Figure 3.3). To illustrate, consider two genotypes,

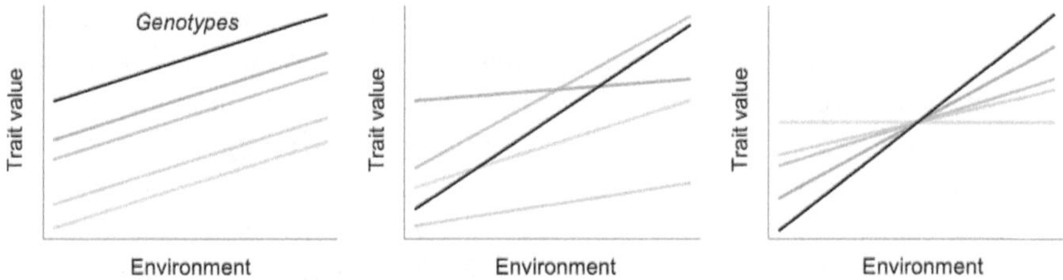

Figure 3.3. A reaction norm describes the relation between environmental states and phenotypic outcomes (trait values) for a given genotype. In the left panel, genetic and environmental effects are fully additive, and reaction norms are parallel (equal slope). The center panel shows a G×E interaction in which different genotypes have different slopes and intercepts. The right panel shows a G×E interaction in which reaction norms with different slopes cross at an intermediate point, but diverge for both high and low values of the environmental variable.

A and B. Individuals with genotype A show low aggression regardless of their environment, whereas individuals with genotype B become highly aggressive if they experience violent interactions with peers. In this scenario, the difference between genotypes A and B is only expressed in violent environments; conversely, growing up in a violent environment does not increases aggression across the board, but only in individuals with genotype B.

When environmental factors contribute to the development of individual differences, they can do so in two distinct ways. *Shared* environmental influences increase the similarity between siblings raised in the same family, whereas *nonshared* influences act independently on each sibling (and thus tend to make siblings different from one another). Nonshared environmental effects may result from siblings' unique experiences (e.g., different schools, friends, illnesses), but also from ostensibly shared events that end up affecting siblings in different ways. For example, economic hardship may play out as a nonshared influence on the development of two siblings if one of them starts working while the other stays home to help.

The results of twin studies indicate that environmental effects on adult personality and cognition are largely nonshared, with a small or even negligible role for shared effects. As a rule, individual differences in adults are about 50% heritable, while nonshared environmental influences explain another 40–50% of variance. The effect of the shared environment accounts for less than 10% of variance and is often close to zero, although shared influences tend to play a larger role in infancy and childhood compared with adulthood (Briley & Tucker-Drob, 2017). These figures must be interpreted with some care for a number of reasons. First, they do not account for G×E interactions or the effects of dominance and epistasis. When genes interact with the nonshared environment, twin studies yield inflated estimates of "pure" nonshared effects, whereas G×E interactions with the shared environment inflate the size of heritability. Similarly, the effects of genetic dominance may be confounded with either shared environmental or additive genetic influences (see Chen et al., 2015; Johnson et al., 2011). Second, twin studies tend to underestimate the weight of shared environmental effects for statistical reasons (Burt, 2014). Third, in many studies, the weight of the nonshared environment is inflated by the presence of measurement error in the trait. Another confound is that many aspects of the environment—including life events that affect families, such as divorce and accidents—are themselves influenced by heritable differences between individuals, giving rise to *genotype–environment correlations* (see Jaffee, 2016; Knopik et al., 2017; Polderman et al. 2015). That said, the evidence consistently shows that the environment affects psychological development in ways that are largely unique to each individual; simply growing up in the same family does little to make people more similar, especially once they become adults.

Differential Susceptibility

Individual differences in plasticity have important implications for models of development, as they imply that the same aspects of the environment may have strong effects on some individuals but only weak or negligible effects on others. According to theories of *differential susceptibility*, many of the same factors that determine increased sensitivity to the effects of "negative" aspects of the environments, such as stress, danger, and adversity, also confer enhanced responsivity to "positive" qualities, such as safety and emotional support. In other words, susceptible individuals respond to the quality of their environment "for better *and* for worse" (Belsky et al., 2007; Boyce & Ellis, 2005; Ellis, Boyce et al., 2011). Differential susceptibility gives rise to crossover person–environment interactions of the kind shown in the right panel of Figure 3.3. When susceptibility is restricted to the effects of negative environments, most researchers speak of *vulnerability* to stressors, although the same pattern can be produced by conditional adaptation to adversity. Finally, individual factors may specifically increase susceptibility to positive environments (*vantage sensitivity*; Pluess, 2015; Pluess & Belsky, 2013). However, evolutionary considerations suggest that vulnerability and differential susceptibility are more likely to evolve than vantage sensitivity under most conditions (Del Giudice, 2017).

A plausible scenario for the evolution of differential susceptibility involves frequency-dependent selection, whereby the fitness of susceptible individuals increases with the proportion of non-susceptible individuals in the population. Another possibility is that variation in susceptibility evolved as a bet-hedging strategy aimed at diversifying the offspring's phenotypes by making some of them refractory to their parent's behavior and other contextual influences (see Ellis, Boyce et al., 2011; Frankenhuis et al., 2016). Susceptibility is partly a function of an individual's genotype, although there is evidence that early experiences and prenatal factors such as maternal stress may also modulate susceptibility to later environmental influences. To the extent that they reflect the combined effects of genotype and early environment, differential susceptibility and other forms of person–environment interplay are best described as phenotype–environment interactions (P×E) that unfold over time rather than simple G×E interactions (see Del Giudice, 2015*c*).

So far, the evidence points to negative emotionality, "difficult" temperamental traits, and high physiological reactivity of the stress response system as phenotypic mediators of susceptibility in childhood, although results are not always consistent (e.g., Laceulle et al., 2014; Slagt et al., 2016). In fact, individual differences in reactivity to the environment may depend on the joint contribution of most of the neurobiological systems discussed in Chapter 2—including brain monoamines, neuropeptides, and GABA (Ellis, Boyce et al., 2011; Moore & Depue, 2016). Genetic studies of differential susceptibility have mainly focused on candidate genes in serotonergic and dopaminergic pathways. This line of research has yielded some promising results; of particular interest, a number of randomized experimental studies have shown G×E effects consistent with differential susceptibility (e.g., Bakermans-Kranenburg & van IJzendoorn, 2015; Belsky & Pluess, 2013; van IJzendoorn & Bakermans-Kranenburg, 2015; van IJzendoorn et al., 2012). It remains to be seen whether these findings will hold up in larger genomic studies.

Sensitive Periods and Switch Points

Sensitive Periods

In the development of individual differences, some phases of the life cycle are more critical and influential than others. *Sensitive periods* are windows of time during which the organism is especially open to environmental inputs. From the standpoint of adaptive plasticity, individuals in a sensitive period are responding to contextual cues about the present and/or future state of their environment. Fetal development, the first 5–7 years of life, the transition to middle childhood, and adolescence have been singled out by many researchers as sensitive periods in the origin of psychological traits. Different periods involve heightened sensitivity to different aspects of the environment, from maternal hormones and nutrition during fetal development to social experiences with peers starting from middle childhood (Blakemore & Mills, 2014; Byrne et al., 2017; Del Giudice & Belsky, 2011; Ellis et al., 2012; Fawcett & Frankenhuis, 2015).

A biological approach yields some important insights into the logic of sensitive periods. Evolutionary models predict that, all else being equal, plasticity should decrease across the life course, and early experience should have a disproportionate effect on later development. However, there are many exceptions and qualifications to this general pattern. In long-lived organisms with lengthy reproductive spans, such as ourselves, selection is expected to favor an initial plasticity peak followed by an extended phase of moderate plasticity (Fischer et al., 2014). Moreover, different sources of information may become available at different stages (e.g., family relations in infancy vs. peer relations in middle childhood and adolescence), leading to the evolution of multiple sensitive periods (Fawcett & Frankenhuis, 2015).

Evolutionary models also predict that there should often be a delay between the time at which information is collected and the time at which it starts affecting the phenotype. This is especially likely to occur if environmental cues are only moderately reliable, so that it takes time to accumulate valid information about the world (Fischer et al., 2014). Thus, periods of maximal openness to the environment may paradoxically be characterized by little or no visible change—individuals may be storing information that they will use only later. Conversely, early experiences may have strong immediate influences on behavior, but their effects may be designed to dissipate at later stages if the behavior in question is a transient ontogenetic adaptation (see Chapter 1). To illustrate, patterns of parent–child attachment develop in infancy following a sensitive period in the first 1–2 years of life. Avoidance and anxiety in infants are strongly predicted by their parents' caregiving behavior and attachment representations and show very little evidence of genetic influences. By contrast, avoidance and anxiety in young adults are about 40% heritable and only weakly related to attachment styles in infancy (see Barbaro et al., 2017*a*; Del Giudice, 2015*d*; Fraley et al., 2013). This is consistent with the idea that early attachment styles partly function as ontogenetic adaptations: by closely matching their behavior to their parents' caregiving style, children maximize the amount of protection and investment they can receive during the most vulnerable, dangerous phase of their life (Del Giudice, 2009*a*). At an even deeper level, the existence of parent–offspring conflict means that children should not passively accept the influence of their parents—instead, they should show a certain amount of developmental "resistance" to parental shaping. While it is difficult to directly test this hypothesis, parent–offspring conflict may contribute to explain why family experiences have only small and inconsistent effects on the development of adult personality.

Developmental Switch Points

The concept of a developmental switch point is a modern extension of the classic idea of a sensitive period (West-Eberhard, 2003). A *developmental switch* is a regulatory mechanism that activates at a specific point in development, collects input from the external environment and/or the internal state of the organism, and shifts the individual along alternative pathways that lead to different phenotypic outcomes (Figure 3.4). Developmental switches are often implemented through hormonal signals; their activation controls the coordinated expression of multiple sets of genes—both those involved in the regulatory mechanism itself and those involved in the expression of the new phenotype. Alternative phenotypes are produced by the expression of modular "packages" of genes specific to each phenotype in addition to stage-specific genes activated by the switch. A key aspect of developmental switches is that they integrate environmental information with variation in the genes that regulate the switch; for example, genetic factors may influence the location of the threshold for switching between phenotypes (see Figure 3.4). The embodied effects of past experiences and conditions may also modulate the switch (through epigenetic modifications and other mechanisms), allowing the organism to integrate information over time and across life stages. Like a sensitive period, a developmental switch point implies heightened sensitivity to the environment, but with a crucial difference: since genetic and environmental inputs

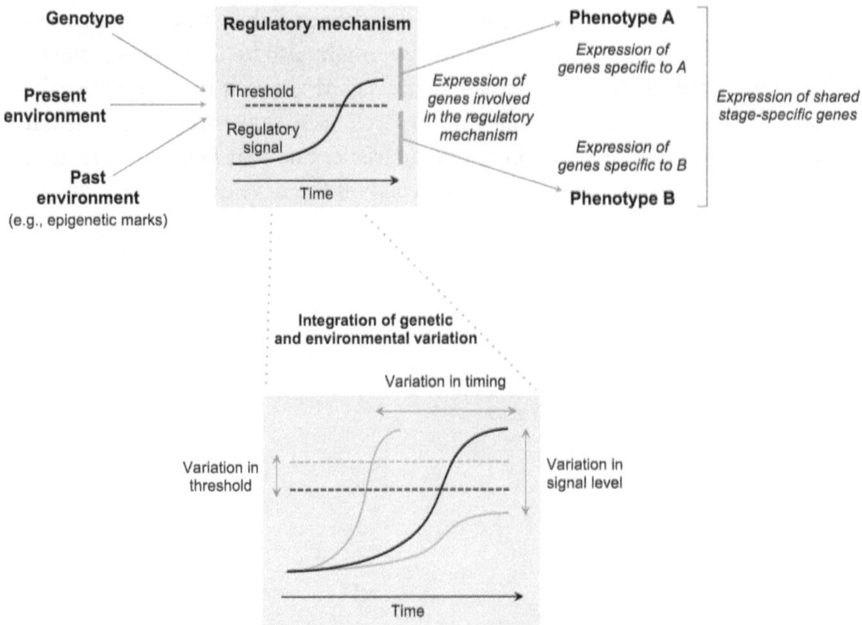

Figure 3.4. The logic of developmental switches. A regulatory mechanism integrates information from the environment with the individual's genotype. As a result, that individual's developmental trajectory is channeled along alternative pathways—here, A and B—depending on whether a threshold is crossed within the mechanism. The location of the threshold, the intensity of the signal, and the timing of the switch point depend on the joint action of the present environment, the embodied effect of past environmental conditions, and variation in the genes involved in the regulatory mechanism. The simplified logic of this binary switch can be extended to the development of continuous traits. Adapted with permission from Del Giudice (2014d).

converge in the regulatory mechanism, a developmental switch has the potential to amplify both environmental *and* genetic influences on the phenotype. In other words, activation of a switch may increase the individual's susceptibility to some aspects of the environment, but may also reveal the effects of previously unexpressed genetic factors.

Puberty is clearly a major switch point in physical and psychological development. The physiological mechanism of puberty is regulated by the hormones secreted by the hypothalamic-pituitary-gonadal (HPG) axis (Ellis, 2013). Another important switch point is the transition from early to middle childhood, at around 6–8 years of age; here, the regulatory signal is provided by adrenal androgens following the onset of adrenarche (Chapter 1). In middle childhood, behavioral plasticity and heightened social learning go hand in hand with the expression of new genetic influences on psychological traits such as aggression, prosocial behavior, and cognitive skills (Del Giudice, 2014*d*; Del Giudice et al., 2009). The social feedback that children receive in this phase—for example about their attractiveness and competitive ability—may feed into the regulation of puberty timing and shape behavioral strategies in adolescence. Other life transitions, such as the birth of one's first child or menopause, might also be usefully described as switch points, although the evidence in this regard is much more tentative (Del Giudice & Belsky, 2011). Viewing the life cycle as a sequence of concatenated stages and switch points is a productive heuristic, one that helps illuminate the intricacies of genotype–environment interplay in the development of individual and sex differences.

4

Life History Strategies

As apparent from the summary presented in Chapter 3, the landscape of individual differences is complex and multidimensional. Making sense of this complexity requires deeper organizing principles that can explain why different traits cluster together into broader patterns, and how those patterns develop over time in response to genetic and environmental influences. In this chapter, I introduce *life history theory*, an evolutionary approach to species and individual differences that offers much-needed support for this task. The concepts of life history theory can be used to connect variation in personality, growth, and physiology within an integrated functional model of development. In light of this, it is not surprising that life history–inspired approaches are becoming increasingly central in evolutionary psychology and anthropology (Del Giudice et al., 2015; Jones, 2015; Kuzawa & Bragg, 2012). After an overview of key ideas and results, I discuss the concept of the fast–slow continuum of life history variation and its applications to individual differences in nonhuman animals. I then review the literature on human life history variation and present a synthesis of the correlates of fast and slow strategies in our species. I end by discussing the role of environmental and genetic factors in the development of individual strategies.

LIFE HISTORY THEORY

All living organisms deal with the inescapable fact that energy and time are limited resources. Individuals must live within finite budgets—themselves earned through expenditures of time and energy—and can never spend more than they have available. While a larger body may increase survival and promote reproductive success, the calories that have been invested in growth are no longer available for reproduction. Developing skills through exploration and play may be highly beneficial in the future, but the time devoted to these activities cannot be used to find mates and raise offspring in the present. In sum, the allocation of a finite budget entails tradeoffs; natural selection favors individuals who allocate resources between competing activities in a way that maximizes fitness within their ecological niche. Life history theory describes the key tradeoffs faced by organisms over their life cycle and provides a framework to model the evolution of different patterns of allocation, or *life history strategies* (Roff, 2002; Stearns, 1992; see Del Giudice et al., 2015). As I detail later, life history strategies have profound ramifications that affect virtually every aspect of an organism's development and behavior.

Fundamental Life History Tradeoffs

Activities that promote fitness ultimately do so by contributing to survival or reproduction (of self and/or related individuals). Organisms can channel resources into two main forms of investment: *somatic effort* and *reproductive effort*. Somatic effort consists of all those activities that increase an individual's survival or its future reproductive potential. At a minimum, somatic effort comprises growth, body maintenance (e.g., tissue repair, immune function), and survival activities such as predator avoidance and predator defense. However, there is much more to somatic effort than staying alive and building a larger body. Developmental activities such as learning, exercise, and play contribute to increase reproductive potential through the accumulation of competence, knowledge, and skills. Social status and possession of external resources such as nests, territories, and wealth can also contribute massively to reproductive success. In total, somatic effort builds up and maintains stocks of *embodied capital*—investment in self that can be translated into future reproduction (Geary, 2002; Hill & Kaplan, 1999; Kaplan et al., 2000).

Reproductive effort directly channels resources into the replication of genes. This can be done in three distinct ways: through *mating effort* (finding and attracting mates, conceiving offspring), *parenting effort* (investing resources in already conceived offspring), and *nepotistic effort* (investing in other related individuals). Reproductive effort is thus a broad category and includes many activities that do not involve sex and mating—such as parents saving resources for their children and children helping their parents take care of younger siblings.

Because of limited time and energy, there are tradeoffs between somatic and reproductive effort, as well as between different components within each category. In addition, many if not most traits have contrasting effects on different components (e.g., heightened sexual motivation may increase mating effort at the expense of parenting effort) or on the same component at two different points in time (e.g., heightened HPA reactivity to stressors may promote survival in childhood but increase the risk of chronic diseases in adulthood). The many tradeoffs that result can be described and modeled at various levels of detail, from broad and general to narrow and specific (see Roff, 2002). Most research in life history theory has focused on three fundamental tradeoffs: current versus future reproduction, quality versus quantity of offspring, and mating versus parenting effort.

Current Versus Future Reproduction

The tradeoff between current and future reproduction is arguably the main allocation problem in life history evolution. At any point in time, energy can be devoted to reproduction in the present or spent in somatic effort, thus facilitating future opportunities to reproduce. On the one hand, trying to reproduce too early can be ineffective if one does not have the necessary resources and competitive skills. Moreover, reproduction is costly and prevents resources from being invested in embodied capital, thus lowering the chances of surviving and reproducing in the future (this is known as the "cost of reproduction"; Williams, 1966). On the other hand, waiting is also dangerous as it increases one's chances of dying before leaving descendants (for an example of this tradeoff in humans, see Hayward et al., 2015). To solve this general problem, organisms typically have a juvenile phase during which reproductive effort is zero, and they stop growing when allocation to reproduction is likely to increases fitness more than growth. Even after maturity, adjusting reproductive timing remains a critical task for individuals and can have major effects on fitness.

Quality Versus Quantity of Offspring

The second major tradeoff concerns a division within the resources allocated to current reproduction, namely allocation to increase offspring *quality* (e.g., size, health, survival, or competitive ability) versus allocation to increase offspring *quantity*. This tradeoff arises because parents have limited resources to invest in reproduction, and any additional offspring reduces the average investment per offspring in terms of parental care, provision of resources, and so on. Parental investment often plays an important role in offspring survival, but can also contribute to offspring's somatic capital more broadly by increasing their health, skills, and status (see Kaplan, 1996). Quality–quantity tradeoffs are often difficult to demonstrate empirically, but there is evidence that they operate in human populations (e.g., Jones & Bliege Bird, 2014; Lawson et al., 2012; Meij et al., 2009).

Mating Versus Parenting Effort

In sexually reproducing species, finding and attracting mates takes time and may involve considerable energy expenditures (e.g., costly displays, competition with rivals) as well as exposure to danger (e.g., increased predation risk, sexually transmitted diseases). Individuals who already have offspring have the option of investing time and energy to increase their survival and quality. When mating effort and parental investment compete for time and resources, a tradeoff arises so that the opportunity of gaining additional mating must be weighed against a reduction in the fitness of existing offspring (Kokko & Jennions, 2008; Trivers, 1972). The mating–parenting tradeoff partly overlaps with the quality–quantity tradeoff, although offspring number can be regulated by many means other than mating—such as egg production, spontaneous abortion, or even infanticide. Also, the distinction between mating and parenting is not always a sharp one; when the ability to care and invest in offspring is a desirable trait in a mate, the same behaviors (e.g., protecting offspring, showing good provisioning skills) may contribute to both mating and parenting effort at the same time (Stiver & Alonzo, 2009).

Life History Strategies

Taken together, the allocation decisions made in response to life history tradeoffs constitute an organism's life history strategy. Variation in life history strategies can be found between species, populations, and individuals. The basic components of an organism's life history strategy are its age at maturity and its schedule of survival and reproduction across the life course (Roff, 2002). In a broader perspective, life history strategies are expressed as synergistic combinations of coadapted morphological, physiological, and behavioral traits (Braendle et al., 2011). To illustrate, in many organisms the transition to sexual maturity involves a range of dramatic behavioral shifts, including the activation of motivational systems that support mating and parental care. Life history strategies that delay reproduction should be characterized not only by slower physical growth, but also by protracted behavioral immaturity and inhibition of reproduction-oriented motivational systems (and the neurobiological pathways that support them). Self-regulation should also be affected; for example, risk aversion is especially beneficial for individuals who delay reproduction because it reduces the probability of dying before reaching maturity (van Doorn et al., 2009). Conversely, a strategy of early reproduction and high mating effort can only be successful if supported by a suite of appropriate morphological (e.g., muscle mass, sexual displays) and behavioral traits (e.g., aggression, risk-taking).

The bottom line is that life history strategies organize behavior and cognition across domains; in doing so, they generate systematic patterns of correlation between traits (Del Giudice, 2014*a*, 2015*a*; Réale et al., 2010; Stamps, 2007; Wolf et al., 2007). In species with complex social lives, the correlates of life history strategies extend to future-oriented behaviors such as cooperation, pair bonding, and the multigenerational transmission of knowledge and resources. Correlations between life history–related traits can vary depending on context, sex, and life stage; moreover, a tradeoff between two traits does not necessarily result in a negative correlation. Individual differences in resources and condition tend to engender positive associations between traits—for example, individuals with larger energy budgets and better somatic capital can afford to invest more than others in both offspring quality *and* quantity. Such positive associations may reduce or even reverse the negative correlations that would be produced by life history tradeoffs alone (Reznick et al., 2000).

Variation in Life History Strategies

A central insight of life history theory is that different ecological conditions favor different allocation strategies, and mathematical models show that the effects of ecological factors on life history evolution can be quite complex. The standard approach is to model life history outcomes as a function of *extrinsic mortality*—the risk of death due to difficult-to-avoid causes such as predation, accidents, and epidemics (Charlesworth, 1994; Roff, 2002). The broader concept of *extrinsic morbidity-mortality* also includes unavoidable causes of damage and disability that contribute to decrease an organism's reproductive potential (e.g., the long-term consequences of nonlethal injuries and diseases; Ellis et al., 2009). Another important factor is the degree of unpredictable variation in environmental conditions. Finally, resource availability sets the baseline for all sorts of allocation problems (Ellis et al., 2009).

In general, high extrinsic mortality in adults selects for early maturation and reproduction, early senescence, and concentration of reproductive effort in a shorter period of time; high mortality in juveniles also favors early maturation, but promotes life history strategies that spread reproductive effort over an extended window. Like high mortality, unpredictable variation in adult mortality usually selects for concentrated reproductive effort and early reproduction; however, these effects depend strongly on the details of an organism's ecology. By contrast, unpredictable variation in juvenile (but not adult) mortality favors delayed maturation and an extended reproductive schedule (Charlesworth, 1994; Roff, 2002). In humans, mortality rates tend to be strongly correlated across the life course, making this distinction less relevant than in other species (Ellis et al., 2009). Population growth is another important determinant of life history evolution. All else being equal, earlier reproduction is favored in expanding populations; conversely, later maturation and reproduction are more beneficial in stable or even shrinking populations (Charlesworth, 1994; Jones & Bliege Bird, 2014). In models of the quality–quantity tradeoff, higher extrinsic mortality favors quantity over quality—a larger number of offspring and lower levels of investment in somatic capital in each—while resource availability tends to increase the optimal number of offspring, all else being equal (Harpending et al., 1990; Kaplan, 1996).

These general predictions come from models that consider life history evolution at the level of entire populations or species. However, real-world populations usually display a great deal of individual variation in life history traits. Individual differences in life history strategies may originate from any of the evolutionary and developmental processes reviewed in Chapter 3. As mortality and resource availability fluctuate across time and space, they create variable selection for alternative life histories; frequency-dependent selection may also occur, for example, when the success of a parenting-oriented strategy depends on the frequency of mating-oriented strategists in the population (Sinervo et al., 2008). Another theoretical possibility is that alternative combinations of life history traits may yield essentially equivalent fitness (neutrality). Together, these evolutionary processes can maintain both genetic and nongenetic variation in life histories.

Adaptive developmental plasticity is an especially important source of individual differences in life histories. As with any other trait, life history strategies and allocations can be modeled as reaction norms that respond to cues about key aspects of the environment such as mortality, unpredictability, and resource availability (e.g., Berrigan & Koella, 1994; Fischer et al., 2011). A common assumption in evolutionary psychology and anthropology is that plastic responses to recurrent changes in environmental characteristics mirror the evolutionary responses to the same characteristics at the population level; notably, cues of extrinsic morbidity-mortality and unpredictability are expected to induce earlier reproduction and lower investment in offspring quality (Belsky et al., 1991; Ellis et al., 2009). While this assumption works reasonably well under some conditions, the details of a population's demography may affect individual responses in ways that do not necessarily match population-level responses (Baldini, 2015). Despite their encouraging empirical success, many current ideas about the development of life history strategies are based on heuristic analogies with population models, and will likely need to be revised or extended as the underlying theory becomes more sophisticated.

Sex Differences

Males and females usually face different tradeoffs as a result of sexual selection, which leads to the evolution of sexually differentiated life history strategies. Species-typical patterns of sexual selection determine systematic sex differences in reproductive timing, allocation to mating and parenting, age-specific mortality, and investment in different components of embodied capital. For example, when male–male competition is intense, males tend to mature later than females to accumulate competitive ability (e.g., McDonald, 1993; Roff, 2002). In addition, males and females often have different reaction norms and respond differently to the same environmental cues. This point is well illustrated by *reproductive suppression*: since females invest heavily in offspring, they are more likely than males to respond to cues of temporary energetic scarcity (or other unfavorable conditions) by delaying reproduction through a variety of mechanisms ranging from suppression of ovarian function and sexual motivation to spontaneous abortion (Beehner & Lu, 2013; Ellison, 2001).

Allocation Mechanisms

The adaptive regulation of life history strategies depends on the coordinated action of multiple physiological and psychological mechanisms, which in turn requires distributed systems of communication and control. Endocrine systems are precisely this kind of communication devices and play pivotal roles in coordinating life history–related traits (Finch & Rose, 1995; Lancaster & Sinervo, 2011). Hormones released at one site (e.g., the gonads, the adrenal cortex) are "picked up" by receptors at multiple other sites (e.g., internal organs, brain structures) and can affect them in a modular fashion. Hormonal signals can simultaneously regulate many different features and modulate allocation decisions at various timescales, from short-term adjustments to major transitions between life stages.

The endocrine systems involved in life history allocations are remarkably conserved across species. Major life history regulators in vertebrates include the HPA and HPG axes, the hypothalamic-pituitary-thyroid (HPT) axis, the insulin/insulin-like growth factor 1 (IGF-1) signaling system, and pathways involving neuropeptides and cytokines (the signaling molecules of the immune system). In male vertebrates, testosterone increases mating effort at the expense of parenting and survival. In both vertebrates and invertebrates, IGF-1 promotes faster growth and reproduction at the expense of longevity (Gerish & Antebi, 2011; Hau & Wingfield, 2011; Lancaster & Sinervo, 2011; Swanson & Dantzer, 2014;

Zilioli & Bird, 2017). All these systems are characterized by extensive interplay and cross-regulation; however, some nodes in the endocrine network may play key decision-making roles by integrating information from multiple sources and redistributing it to other systems. The HPA axis plays such a coordination role in life history development as it encodes and integrates information about many features of the environment that modulate life history strategies—from danger and unpredictability to energetic resources and social support (Crespi et al., 2013; Del Giudice et al., 2011, 2015; Ellis & Del Giudice, 2014).

Because life history allocations are contingent on environmental circumstances, psychological processes ultimately guide many allocation decisions, whether mediated by endocrine processes or not. For example, cortisol release in response to a threat is the last step in a decisional cascade that begins with perception, continues with the appraisal of the event as threatening, and culminates with the secretion of CRH in the hypothalamus. In turn, CRH and cortisol may feed back on the brain regions involved in appraising and evaluating threats so that different levels of the control cascade influence one another. Over a longer time span, life history decisions should partly depend on integrative regulatory variables that summarize the quality and predictability of an individual's ecology. In humans, the unconscious regulatory variables that drive life history allocations may be reflected in conscious appraisals of mortality and unpredictability, which in turn can be assessed by asking people to rate their perceived control on the environment or subjectively estimate their life expectancy (e.g., Chisholm, 1999*b*; Mittal & Griskevicius, 2014).

THE FAST–SLOW CONTINUUM

Life history strategies are often analyzed at the level of specific traits such as maturation timing and number of offspring. At the same time, variation in one trait is usually correlated to variation in other traits, giving rise to broader patterns of differences between species and individuals. An especially important pattern is that described by the *fast–slow continuum* of life history variation. The concept originates from the finding that the life histories of different species can be roughly arranged on a continuum, from "fast" (early maturation and reproduction, fast growth, small body size, short life span, large numbers of offspring, and low investment in offspring quality) to "slow" (late maturation and reproduction, slow growth, large body size, and long life span, with relatively few offspring and high parental investment in each) (Jeschke et al., 2008; Sæther, 1987; Promislow & Harvey, 1990; Figure 4.1). Among mammals, mice and voles are close to the fast end of the continuum, whereas elephants and whales are close to the slow end.

Some years ago, two well-known comparative studies cast doubts on the robustness of the fast–slow continuum and suggested that its apparent coherence may be an artifact of variation in body size. After size was controlled for, the continuum seemed to dissolve into multiple independent dimensions or end up being

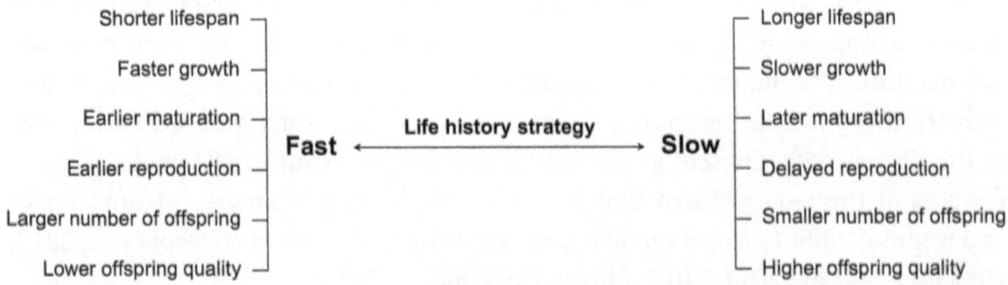

Figure 4.1. The fast-slow continuum of life history variation in mammals. Adapted with permission from Del Giudice (2015a).

defined by a very different set of traits (Bielby et al., 2007; Jeschke & Kokko, 2009). However, both studies suffered from serious methodological problems; a later reanalysis of the data showed that, despite some meaningful differences between species—for example, offspring quantity is a "fast" trait in mammals and birds but not in fish—the fast–slow continuum remains a stable dimension of variation even controlling for differences in body size (Del Giudice, 2014*b*).

Origins of the Fast–Slow Continuum

The fast–slow continuum captures a pattern that was initially described by mathematical models of *r/K selection* (MacArthur & Wilson, 1967; Pianka, 1970). In this context, the letter *r* is used to denote the growth rate of a population, whereas *K* indicates the maximum population size (also known as the environment's "carrying capacity"). According to *r/K* models, life history evolution is primarily driven by the organism's population density. In stable and densely populated environments that promote intense competition, *K-selection* maximizes population size by favoring slow growth, late reproduction, and a small number of offspring. In fluctuating or sparsely populated ecologies, the population size remains far below the carrying capacity, and *r-selection* maximizes the population growth rate by promoting fast maturation, early reproduction, and a large number of offspring.

Later modeling work has confirmed some important aspects of the early *r/K* models—most notably, the general prediction that stable ecologies promote the ability to maintain a large population size whereas fluctuating ecologies promote rapid population growth (Engen et al., 2013; Lande et al., 2009). In contrast, the proposed links between general patterns of *r/K* selection and specific life history traits such as age at maturity and offspring number are not robust, as they depend on the details of the tradeoffs experienced by a particular organism (Jeschke et al., 2008; Roff, 2002). Thus, models of *r/K* selection do not offer a satisfactory explanation of the fast–slow continuum, even if they provide insight into how selection works in different types of ecology. The limitations of *r/K* models have led evolutionary biologists to focus on extrinsic mortality as a driver of life history evolution.

In part, the fast–slow continuum emerges from basic constraints on the relationships among mortality, age at maturity, metabolism, and body size (Brown et al., 2004; Roff, 2002; Savage et al., 2004). But different life history traits may also coevolve because they adaptively respond to the same characteristics of the environment. For example, high levels of extrinsic morbidity-mortality tend to favor early maturation and reproduction but also lower investment in offspring quality and increased mating effort. These functional commonalities between different tradeoffs may be stable enough to account for the robustness of the fast–slow continuum. Still, mathematical models of life history evolution tend to focus on one trait or tradeoff at a time, and a general formal theory of the fast–slow continuum is still lacking (Jeschke et al., 2008; Mathot & Frankenhuis, 2018). This is why it is critical to distinguish between the fast–slow continuum as an empirical pattern of life history variation and the specific theories—such as *r*/*K* selection—that attempt to explain the evolution of that pattern. In the psychological literature, the distinction is often blurred, and the terms "*r*-selected" and "*K*-selected" are sometimes used as synonyms of "fast" and "slow" in spite of their different implications (e.g., Boutwell, Barnes, Beaver et al., 2015*a*; Brüne, 2015).

The Fast–Slow Continuum and Individual Differences

Variation in life history strategies occurs both between and within populations, and the fast–slow continuum can be used to describe individual differences in addition to differences between species. An important challenge to applying this concept to individual variation is that life history tradeoffs may combine in different ways within different species, giving rise to multiple "versions" of the continuum. At the same time, all organisms face some basic allocation problems, such as the tradeoff between current and future reproduction; this can be expected to impart a similar overall structure to individual variation across species. The main advantage of the fast–slow distinction at the individual level is that it offers an integrative principle for the study of individual differences—not just in basic reproductive traits but also in physiology, behavior, and developmental trajectories. Most crucially, the fast–slow distinction is a powerful heuristic for the study of personality and the connections between personality and physiology.

In biology, the configurations of traits associated with fast and slow strategies are usually described as *pace-of-life syndromes* (Réale et al., 2010). Evolutionary models and empirical data lend support to the idea that fast strategies are typically associated with impulsivity, risk-taking, and risk-related traits such as boldness, aggression (particularly in males), and fast but superficial exploration (e.g., Cole & Quinn, 2014; Coppens et al., 2010; Hall et al., 2015; Stamps, 2007; van Doorn et al., 2009). Other models suggest that ecological conditions should affect exploration–exploitation tradeoffs in a way consistent with pace-of-life syndromes. On a developmental time scale, high levels of mortality and unpredictability should reduce investment in learning and knowledge acquisition early in life (a form of somatic capital); in the short term, reduced life expectancy favors faster exploration and higher investment in resource exploitation (Berger-Tal et al., 2014; Eliassen et al., 2007).

Other behavioral correlates of life history strategies show more variability across species and contexts. This is the case of the association between fast life histories, increased mating effort, and lower parental investment (e.g., Patrick & Browning 2011; Patrick et al., 2012). How these traits fit within broader pace-of-life syndromes is likely to depend on a species' mating system and on the details of mating–parenting tradeoffs. More recently, researchers have attempted to extend pace-of-life syndromes to cognition and self-regulation. For instance, there are reasons to expect that fast strategists should typically favor speed over accuracy in decision-making tasks (Sih & Del Giudice, 2012). More speculatively, the ecological dimensions associated with the fast–slow continuum may favor individual differences in the balance between feedback and feedforward control of behavior, as reflected for example in reactive versus proactive control processes. In the animal literature, the standard view is that slow strategies are associated with reactive (feedback) regulation whereas fast strategies favor proactive (feedforward) control (Coppens et al., 2010). This prediction is plausible for simple forms of impulsive open-loop control; however, some animals also engage in more sophisticated forms of feedforward regulation based on predictive models and long-term planning, which should be especially beneficial in the context of slow life history strategies (Del Giudice, 2015*a*).

On the physiological side, most research on nonhuman animals has focused on stress reactivity and metabolic rates. A commonly observed pattern is that fast (bold, proactive) individuals tend to show low reactivity of the HPA axis and high reactivity of the sympathetic nervous system, whereas slow (fearful, reactive) individuals show high HPA and low sympathetic reactivity (Carere et al., 2010; Coppens et al., 2010; Réale et al., 2010). This account is probably too simple to capture the full range of individual variation in stress physiology, at least in humans. In our species, fast life history traits can be associated with both hyper- and hyporeactivity of the HPA axis, depending on age, sex, and the amount of exposure to chronic stressors (Del Giudice et al., 2011; Ellis & Del Giudice, 2014; see later discussion). In contrast with stress physiology, research on pace-of-life syndromes and metabolic rates has failed to yield any consistent pattern across species. The initial hypothesis was that fast individuals would show higher metabolic rates—that is, higher energy expenditure at rest and during activity (Biro & Stamps, 2010). This correlation has been confirmed in some species, but in many others it has been found to be absent or even reversed (e.g., Careau et al., 2015; Le Galliard et al., 2013). Such extreme variability is consistent with mathematical models showing that the optimal relation between risk-taking and metabolic expenditure can easily switch direction depending on the details of an organism's ecology (Houston, 2010).

In conclusion, a key insight from the literature on pace-of-life syndromes is that some traits are reliably associated with life history strategies, while others show more complex patterns that vary across species and contexts. Impulsivity and risk-taking are the most consistent personality correlates of fast strategies across species; the contributions of other traits, such as mating styles and parental provisioning, must be understood on a case-by-case basis as the associations found in one species may not generalize to others. Just as importantly, not all traits should be expected to correlate with life histories in a simple linear fashion. To illustrate, exploratory behavior may cluster with either fast or slow personalities depending on whether it reflects risk-taking (e.g., exposing oneself to predators to find better mating opportunities) or risk avoidance (e.g., searching the surroundings to make sure there are no hidden dangers). A similar logic applies to life history–related traits such as proactive versus reactive control strategies and hyper- versus hyporeactive patterns of stress physiology. The simplicity and heuristic power of the fast–slow distinction must always be balanced by careful consideration of the specific tradeoffs and challenges faced by a particular organism.

HUMAN LIFE HISTORY STRATEGIES

In the 1980s and 1990s, psychologists and anthropologists started to explore the idea that variation in life history strategies may contribute to the organization of individual differences in our species. The first organic contribution in this sense was made by Rushton (1985, 1987), who advanced a theory of individual and population differences based on the concept of *r*/*K* selection. Rushton's theory became extremely controversial because it focused on differences between major racial groups—by postulating a pattern of increasing *K*-selection from blacks to whites to East Asians—and emphasized the role of genetic factors over that of environmental influences (see Black et al., 2017). From a developmental perspective, Draper and Harpending (1982, 1988) suggested that mating strategies are influenced by early social cues, such as father presence versus absence during childhood. Belsky and colleagues (1991) built on those insights and developed an influential model of how the quality of parent–child and family relationships shapes key life history decisions contributing to individual variation in social and sexual behavior and in the timing of sexual maturation. Over the years, these seminal contributions have grown into a large and diverse research literature that employs life history concepts to explain patterns of individual differences in humans (see Black et al., 2017; Chisholm, 1999*a*; Del Giudice et al., 2015).

Here I present a synthesis of this literature, focusing on the fast–slow continuum and its implications for behavior and neurobiology. In my discussion, I distinguish between a *basic* and an *extended* model of human life history strategies. The basic model describes a set of core traits that define the main axis of variation in pace-of-life syndromes in our species. The extended model is more speculative and goes beyond the basic model by taking into account the contribution of some unique features of the human ecology, such as dual status hierarchies (dominance/prestige) and multigeneration resource transfers. These evolutionary innovations have likely selected for differentiation within fast and slow strategies, resulting in multiple behavioral, cognitive, and neurobiological profiles at both ends of the continuum.

The Basic Model

The Fast–Slow Continuum in Humans

Among the defining features of the human life history are a long life span and a remarkably broad window for reproduction, with additional opportunities for nepotistic effort in old age (e.g., grandparenting) but also in childhood (helping). While reproduction can be distributed over an extended period of time, each offspring requires many years of investment by the mother and other family members. This constellation of factors suggests that, compared with most other species, variation on the human fast–slow continuum should be driven less by differences in current versus future reproduction and more by other tradeoffs, such as quality versus quantity and mating versus parenting. In particular, while the timing of sexual maturity (e.g., menarche in girls) and that of first birth obviously play a role in defining an individual's life history trajectory, their net impact on total fertility is relatively small because reproductive effort can be allocated with considerable flexibility over a span of decades (Borgerhoff Mulder, 1989). The complexity of human mate choice, marriage practices, and social constraints on sexual behavior further complicates the relations between maturation and reproduction. While some societies maintain a strong temporal link between puberty and marriage in females, the association is often weakened by other factors—especially in industrialized countries, where nutritional factors have pushed down the age of puberty to unprecedented levels (Deardorff et al., 2005; Dunbar et al., 2008; Sandler et al., 1984; Udry & Cliquet, 1982). This applies even more strongly to men, who are not limited by pregnancy and lactation and can potentially have many children in a short time with different sexual partners. The reproductive rate of men is constrained by that of their female partners, so that their allocation in quality versus quantity depends to a larger extent on their investment in mating versus parenting (the dad/cad dichotomy discussed in Chapter 1).

On the face of it, the remarkable intensity of parental investment in our species should amplify the quality–quantity tradeoff; however, there are some complicating factors that make predictions less than straightforward. On the one hand, the balance between quality and quantity becomes even more critical when resources and wealth can be transferred across multiple generations. On the other hand, older children and adolescents are not just recipients of investment but can contribute to the family economy by taking care of younger siblings, foraging, and so on. If the cost of having additional children is partly repaid by the children's help, the quality–quantity tradeoff is likely to become less stringent (Lawson & Borgerhoff Mulder, 2016). Intriguingly, the fact that human offspring can contribute to their parents' reproduction while they remain in the family of origin implies that allocations between current and future reproduction may be partly driven by tradeoffs between mating effort (one's own reproduction) and nepotistic effort (the parents' reproduction).

In total, the correlates of human life history strategies should prominently include traits that modulate mating and parenting in addition to those that modulate reproductive timing and longevity. Against this background, there are reasons to predict systematic sex differences in the traits that define the fast–slow continuum. Fast strategies in males should be primarily associated with increased mating effort and risky competition. Fast strategies in females should be more tightly linked to early sexual maturation and childbearing, since decisions about reproductive timing are especially critical for women; however, these relations are not expected to be particularly strong for the reasons discussed earlier. Finally, women engaging in fast strategies should be less ready than men to forgo parental investment because maternal care is critical for infant survival. Instead, fast strategies in females should often correlate with behaviors directed at obtaining help and resources from others, including relatives and sexual partners (Chisholm, 1999*a*; Del Giudice, 2009*a*; Del Giudice et al., 2011; Harpending & Draper, 1988).

Motivation, Decision-Making, and Self-Regulation

In line with animal research on pace-of-life syndromes, human research has shown that impulsivity, risk-taking, and sensation seeking are systematically associated with fast life history traits such as early intercourse, early childbearing in females, unrestricted sociosexuality, larger numbers of sexual partners, reduced long-term mating orientation, and increased mortality. Future discounting and heightened mating competition reduce the benefits of reciprocal long-term relationships; in motivational terms, affiliation and reciprocity are downregulated, whereas status seeking and aggression are upregulated. The resulting behavioral pattern is marked by exploitative and socially antagonistic tendencies; these tendencies may be expressed in different forms in males and females, for example through physical versus relational aggression (see Belsky et al., 1991; Borowsky et al., 2009; Brezina et al., 2009; Chen & Vazsonyi, 2011; Copping et al., 2013*a*, 2013*b*, 2014*a*; Curry et al., 2008; Dunkel & Decker, 2010; Figueredo & Jacobs, 2010; Figueredo et al., 2004, 2005, 2007; Kahn et al., 2002; Kruger et al., 2008; Nettle, 2011*b*; Romer et al., 2011; Wang et al., 2009; White et al., 1994). Early maturation and precocious sexuality promote investment in current reproduction at the expense of future reproductive success (especially in females); at the same time, they accelerate the motivational shift toward mating and status competition, effectively curtailing the exploration and learning phase of childhood. From the standpoint of exploration–exploitation tradeoffs, this can be viewed as a reduction of exploration on a developmental scale, resulting in lower somatic capital in the form of knowledge and skills.

Disgust sensitivity is another dimension of individual differences with links to the fast–slow continuum. To begin, high disgust sensitivity is broadly associated with measures of risk aversion. Moral and sexual disgust correlate with higher agreeableness, conscientiousness, and honesty-humility; and sexual disgust specifically predicts restricted sociosexuality (Al-Shawaf et al., 2015; Sparks et al., 2018; Tybur et al., 2009, 2015; Tybur & de Vries, 2013). These findings suggest that the disgust system is implicated in the regulation of life history–related behaviors. In particular, sexual and moral disgust show the most consistent pattern of correlations with other indicators of slow strategies.

Romantic attachment styles have wide-ranging influences on sexuality, mating, and couple stability, but their relations with life history strategies are somewhat complex. Secure attachment styles are consistently associated with slow life history traits (e.g., Chisholm, 1999*b*; Chisholm et al., 2005; Del Giudice, 2009*a*). Avoidance predicts unrestricted sociosexuality, reduced long-term orientation, and low commitment to partners (Brennan & Shaver, 1995; Jackson & Kirkpatrick, 2007; Tempelhof & Allen, 2008). Given the central role of pair bonding in long-term parental investment, avoidant attachment—which, on average, is higher in men—can be generally interpreted as a mediator of reduced parenting effort. However, some inconsistent findings indicate that avoidance may capture multiple functional mechanisms. High levels of romantic avoidance are found both in people with very early sexual debut and in those who delay intercourse (Gentzler & Kerns, 2004); this suggests that, at least for some people, avoidant attachment may actually reflect a partial downregulation of the mating system, consistent with slower life history strategies. A related speculative hypothesis is that, in women, avoidance may sometimes increase as part of a broader response of reproductive suppression following intense relational stressors (Del Giudice, 2009*a*, 2011).

The core function of attachment anxiety is to maximize investment from partners and relatives, and high anxiety seems to be a common correlate of fast strategies in women (Del Giudice, 2009*a*). However, anxiety shows small and inconsistent relations with sociosexuality, again suggesting a degree of functional heterogeneity (Brennan & Shaver, 1995; Del Giudice, 2016*a*; Jackson & Kirkpatrick, 2007). Anxiously attached people find it very difficult to break up with their partners, and, when they do, they often leave open the option of getting back together. Accordingly, elevated anxiety does not predict relationship dissolution in longitudinal studies (Collins & Gillath, 2012; Henderson et al., 1997; Jang et al., 2002; Quirk et al., 2016; Stewart & Harkness, 2015). While attachment anxiety causes tension between partners and lowers their romantic satisfaction, it also contributes to keep them together, thus acting as a stabilizing factor as far as long-term investment is concerned. For this reason, a small to moderate amount of anxiety is probably not inconsistent with slow strategies, especially in women. To summarize, secure romantic attachment is consistently associated with slow strategies, but insecure strategies may play different functional roles at the two ends of the continuum. This invites caution in treating insecurity as an unambiguous marker of fast life history. A better approach is to focus on the temporal *stability* of romantic attachments, which is only in part a function of security (see Del Giudice, 2014*a*).

Some authors have proposed that individual differences in executive functions may be an important correlate of life history strategies in humans (e.g., Figueredo & Jacobs, 2010; Figueredo et al., 2006). This idea deserves closer examination. Disinhibition is a central component of impulsivity, but the cognitive laboratory tasks used to assess inhibition in studies of executive functions show only small to moderate correlations with impulsive behavior in real-life situations. Compared with self-reports of impulsivity, laboratory measures of inhibition are more strongly associated with IQ and less strongly associated with antisocial behavior, suggesting a confounding effect of general intelligence (Duckworth & Kern, 2011; White et al., 1994). While some findings indicate that cognitive inhibition tasks may predict life history–relevant outcomes such as faithfulness to romantic partners (e.g., Pronk et al., 2011), performance on these tasks is best regarded as a weak correlate of life history strategy. Another core executive function is flexibility/shifting. Flexibility is only weakly correlated with intelligence and shows inconsistent associations with impulsivity; in fact, high flexibility seems to be a *negative* predictor of the ability to suppress impulses and delay gratification (Hofmann et al., 2012; Miyake & Friedman, 2012; but see Fleming et al., 2016). These findings suggest that alternative life history strategies may involve a partial tradeoff between inhibition and flexibility; specifically, relatively low levels of executive flexibility may enable forms of proactive control based on persistence and long-term planning (Del Giudice, 2015*a*; Mittal et al., 2015).

Personality Factors

At a higher level of abstraction, the behavioral correlates of life history strategies can be framed within the five-factor model of personality. Among the Big Five, agreeableness and conscientiousness show the most consistent pattern of associations with slow traits such as restricted sociosexuality, long-term mating orientation, couple stability, secure attachment to parents in infancy and romantic partners in adulthood, reduced sex drive, low impulsivity, and risk aversion across domains (e.g., Baams et al., 2014; Banai & Pavela, 2015; Bourdage et al., 2007; DeYoung, 2011; Holtzman & Strube, 2013; Jonason et al., 2013; Noftle & Shaver, 2006; Orzeck & Lung, 2005; Markey & Markey, 2007; Schmitt & Buss, 2000; Wiebe, 2004; Young et al., 2017; see Del Giudice, 2012*b*). Conscientiousness and (to a smaller extent) agreeableness are also the most reliable personality predictors of physical health and longevity; the contribution of neuroticism is mixed and may depend on the specific facets considered (Bogg & Roberts, 2004; Chapman & Goldberg, 2011; Clarke & Robertson, 2005; Hill, Weiss et al., 2017; Jackson et al., 2015; Jokela et al., 2013; Martin et al., 2007; Weiss & Costa, 2005; Weller & Tikir, 2011). The life history correlates of neuroticism are much less straightforward; for example, high neuroticism tends to predict increased short-term mating in women but reduced short-term mating in men, with much cross-cultural variation. There is also evidence that slow life history–related traits can be associated with social anxiety and insecurity, which is consistent with a general profile of risk aversion and behavioral inhibition (Schmitt & Shackelford, 2008; Sherman et al., 2013). As a first approximation, then, metatrait alpha can be treated as a broadband correlate of slow strategies, with the caveat that neuroticism may be elevated at both ends of the continuum (see also Del Giudice, 2014*a*).

A very different picture emerges for extraversion and openness, the two components of metatrait beta. From the standpoint of life history strategies, both are "hybrid" traits that include both fast and slow facets. In particular, the assertiveness and dominance facets of extraversion—but not the warmth and sociability facets—are associated with risk-taking and unrestricted sociosexuality (Lucas et al., 2000; MacDonald, 1995*b*). Accordingly, extraversion has been found to correlate with both short- and long-term mating orientation (Holtzman & Strube, 2013). Similarly, short-term mating orientation is associated with the imagination, aesthetics, and nonconformity facets of openness, but not with those that relate to intellectual curiosity (see Del Giudice, 2012*b*; Manson, 2017). As a result, metatrait beta is a poor indicator of fast strategy despite its overall positive correlations with impulsivity and risk-taking.

Outside the five-factor model, honesty-humility is another important correlate of slow life history strategies. Like agreeableness and conscientiousness, honesty-humility is associated with restricted sociosexuality, risk aversion, and future orientation (low time discounting; Ashton & Lee, 2008; Ashton et al., 2010; Bourdage et al., 2007; Manson, 2015). Conversely, dark triad traits correlate with unrestricted sociosexuality, aggression, reduced cooperation, and high time discounting (Jonason et al., 2010, 2015; Lee, Ashton et al., 2013; Schmitt et al., 2017). While many personality correlates of fast life histories are regarded as harmful and socially undesirable, it would be a mistake to idealize slow strategies by underplaying their biological and psychological costs. For example, conscientiousness and future orientation are mixed blessings: individuals high on these traits are inevitably less able to take advantage of unexpected opportunities in the present and may find it more difficult to adapt to changing or novel circumstances. High levels of self-control can lead to rigidity and conformity, and both agreeableness and honesty-humility expose people to the risk of being exploited (Ashton & Lee, 2008; Block & Block, 1980; de Vries et al., 2016; DeYoung et al., 2002; Dickman, 1990).

Some researchers working in a life history perspective have argued that the general factor of personality (GFP) should be regarded as the core personality correlate of slow strategies (Figueredo et al., 2004, 2007, 2011, 2015; Figueredo & Rushton, 2009). In Chapter 3, I discussed the uncertain status of the GFP as an objective personality factor. Even if the GFP captures some aspects of social competence, it is not ideal as a general indicator of life history strategy. The first reason is that the GFP is affected by evaluative biases and distortions, more so than other personality traits (Davies et al., 2015; Dunkel et al., 2016). The second and most important reason is that the GFP reflects a mixture of slow traits (agreeableness and conscientiousness) and hybrid traits that, if anything, tend to align more strongly with the fast end of the continuum (extraversion and openness). I suggest that a "splitting" approach to personality and life histories based on traits such as agreeableness, conscientiousness, impulsivity, and honesty-humility is more accurate—and potentially more fruitful—than the prevailing "lumping" approach based on the GFP. The same caveats apply to global behavioral scales of life history strategy such as the Arizona Life History Battery and the Mini-K (Figueredo, 2007). These scales mainly reflect a combination of agreeableness, conscientiousness, and extraversion (Manson, 2015, 2017; Olderbak et al., 2014). Like the GFP, they combine traits with somewhat different functional implications, even within the scope of the basic model; in addition, they fail to capture the subtler patterns of individual variation described in the extended model (e.g., slow profiles that combine high conscientiousness and low agreeableness; see later discussion).

Because of these limitations, global scales are less than ideal as tools for mapping the correlations between life history strategies and psychopathology (for a more detailed argument, see Copping et al., 2014*b*, 2017).

It can be useful to conclude this section on personality with a note on the relations between personality traits and reproductive outcomes such as total fertility and age at first birth. While these outcomes are theoretically important from a life history perspective, in modern populations they are confounded by powerful, evolutionarily novel factors such as effective technologies for birth control and abortion. In many societies, it is possible to have sexual relations with multiple partners without any effect on one's reproductive status; in fact, people with a strong desire for sexual variety—a trait that would have promoted faster strategies in past conditions—may end up postponing the decision to become parents and decide to have few children, if any. The net effect is to increase the relative fertility of people with personality traits that favor long-term commitment and a desire for children (e.g., Richardson et al., 2017; Woodley of Menie et al., 2017). Openness to experience provides a striking illustration of this phenomenon: while higher openness predicts unrestricted sociosexuality and more sexual partners, it is also consistently associated with later reproduction and lower fertility in both the United States and Norway (Berg et al., 2014; Jokela et al., 2011; Skirbekk & Blekesaune, 2014). Confirming that this is a recent development, historical data show that the negative influence of openness on fertility has been increasing steadily over the 20th century, from a nonsignificant trend for people born in the 1920s to a strong negative effect for those born in the 1960s (Jokela, 2012). Extraversion is the only personality trait that seems to be consistently associated with increased fertility across time and societies (Alvergne et al., 2010; Bailey et al., 2013; Jokela, 2012; Berg et al., 2014).

Cognitive Ability

From a theoretical standpoint, there are no reasons to expect strong associations between life history strategies and general cognitive ability. The animal literature points to differences in cognitive style (e.g., speed vs. accuracy) rather than in overall efficiency, consistent with the idea that life history strategies primarily organize individual differences in function rather than functionality (Sih & Del Giudice, 2012). Still, there may be some minor sources of shared variation between general intelligence (g) and the fast–slow continuum. Brain development is a form of somatic investment; individuals who pursue faster strategies may invest less in maintenance mechanisms such as buffering of deleterious mutations and tissue repair. Also, high levels of stress and adversity in childhood tend to entrain faster strategies; to the extent that cognitive development is also affected by early stress, one can predict a correlation between faster strategies and lower intelligence. This effect is unlikely to be substantial considering that individual differences in g are largely under genetic control and respond only weakly to environmental factors, especially in adults. The results of human research support this prediction: correlations between general intelligence and composites of slow life history–related traits tend to be small, typically below .10 (Figueredo et al.,

2014; Loehlin et al., 2015; Woodley, 2011; Woodley of Menie & Madison, 2015). However, the correlation may be stronger in populations exposed to extremely high levels of adversity and deprivation (e.g., prison inmates; Dunkel et al., 2014).

Neurobiological Correlates

While the developmental and behavioral correlates of human life history strategies have been mapped with reasonable confidence, there has been very little work on their neurobiological underpinnings. Here, I propose some initial generalizations about the neurobiology of fast and slow strategies. As I noted in Chapter 2, the present state of knowledge on the behavioral implications of molecules such as dopamine, serotonin, and oxytocin is still provisional in many respects; thus, the content of this section should be regarded as especially tentative and open to revision.

Taken together, the traits associated with fast and slow strategies point to a central role of serotonin in regulating variation on the fast–slow continuum. Specifically, the neurobiological evidence indicates that fast strategies should be systematically associated with reduced serotonergic activity, whereas slow strategies should be associated with upregulated serotonin. The place of dopamine in this scheme is more complex. In many ways, serotonin and mesolimbic dopamine have contrasting effects on key life history–related traits including risk-taking, inhibition, time discounting, sexuality, and cooperation. At the same time, metatrait beta and behavioral approach system (BAS) activation are not exclusively associated with fast strategies; in particular, dopamine seems to play an important "energizing" role in promoting key components of conscientiousness, such as industriousness, persistence, and achievement striving (Chapter 3). Moreover, there is still no consensus in the literature as to whether impulsivity and risk-taking are always associated with hyperdopaminergic functioning or may also be prompted by reduced dopamine levels in mesolimbic pathways. In total, upregulated mesolimbic dopamine is likely to be a common neurobiological correlate of fast strategies, but there may be exceptions to this pattern: for example, dopaminergic enhancement may promote conscientiousness in some variants of slow strategies, and hypo-dopaminergic function may be involved in some forms of impulsivity.

Other important contributions to life history regulation come from sex hormones. Androgens (including, but not limited to, testosterone) tend to suppress affiliation and promote mating effort, competition, and aggression in both sexes. In women, estrogens may also play a similar role (Cashdan, 1995). At the neuropsychological level, differences in self-regulation should be reflected in patterns of dorsolateral prefrontal cortex (DLPFC) activity, with dampened activation in fast strategies and increased activation in slow strategies. However, the evidence linking cortical activation to self-regulation comes mostly from laboratory tasks; it is possible that DPLFC activity may be only weakly correlated with real-world manifestations of impulsivity and risk-taking. The role of IGF-1 in the regulation of life history tradeoffs across species makes this hormone an intriguing candidate for future research, especially considering its involvement in brain development and functioning throughout the life course (Aleman & Torres-Aleman, 2009; Swanson & Dantzer, 2014).

Other plausible neurobiological correlates of life history variation are likely to operate in more complex and/or sexually differentiated ways. Fast strategies in men should correlate with high vasopressin and low oxytocin levels, although there may be important exceptions to this pattern (see the extended model presented later). In contrast, women who engage in fast strategies often show anxious attachment styles, which in turn correlate with elevated oxytocin and/or oxytocinergic reactivity to relational threats (Marazziti et al., 2006; Weisman et al., 2013). Oxytocin also enhances mentalizing, which is a critical asset in many aspects of female competition (e.g., relational aggression).

The stress response system plays a critical role in coordinating life history allocations across organs and systems, but the relation between patterns of stress reactivity and life history strategies is not a simple one. According to the *adaptive calibration model* of individual differences in stress physiology (ACM; Del Giudice et al., 2011; Ellis & Del Giudice, 2014; Ellis et al., 2017), fast strategies can be associated with two distinct patterns of reactivity: a hyperreactive *vigilant* pattern characterized by anxiety and/or reactive aggression, and a hyporeactive *unemotional* pattern (possibly more common in men) with high levels of risk-taking and proactive aggression. Similarly, slow strategies can be associated with highly responsive *sensitive* patterns but also with moderately responsive, *buffered* patterns (Figure 4.2). While a life history perspective can shed light on the relations between stress reactivity and behavior, the very complexity of those relations implies that individual differences in stress physiology cannot be used as straightforward markers of life history strategy.

Limitations of the Fast–Slow Distinction

The distinction between fast and slow strategies is a powerful integrative concept, but it is important to remember that it only accounts for a limited amount of variation in personality and behavior. It can be useful to think of the fast–slow continuum as the broadest level of analysis in the organization of individual differences. The other levels are just as important—for example, many important differences between males and females are better understood as reflecting sex-specific constraints on specific tradeoffs (e.g., mating vs. parenting) rather than global differences on the fast–slow continuum. While the fast–slow distinction can be invaluable as an initial classification principle, it cannot (and should not) substitute for a detailed, multilevel account of individual and sex differences.

Consistent with this view, the life history–related traits described in this section are only moderately correlated with one another, leaving room for much individual variation and many exceptions to the general pattern. Part of the reason may lie in the existence of multiple behavioral profiles within fast and slow strategies, as I discuss later in the extended model. Another reason is that life history–relevant behaviors reflect a multitude of influences that do not always act consistently on individuals. For example, physically attractive people have more sexual partners, and attractive men also tend to be more sociosexually unrestricted (Lukaszewski

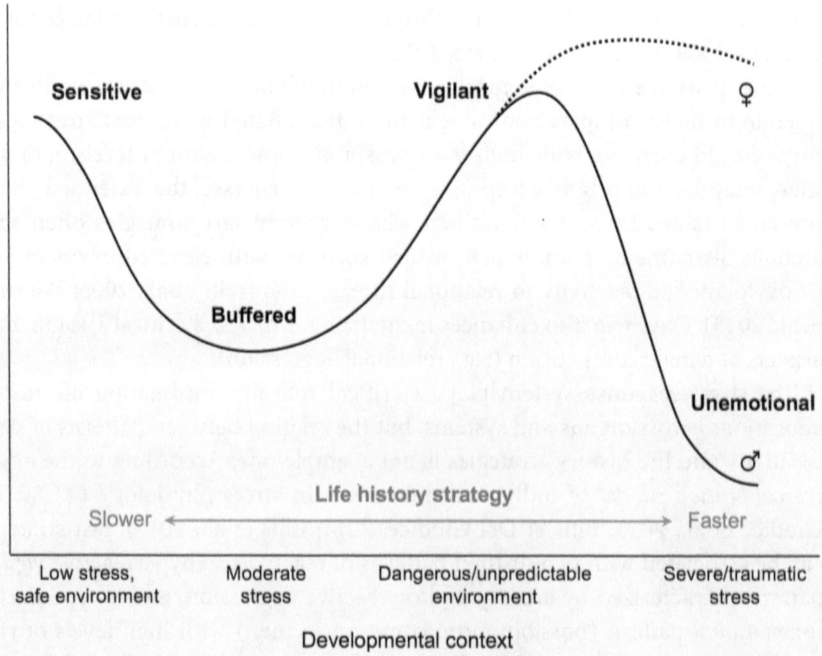

Figure 4.2. Patterns of reactivity in the adaptive calibration model of stress physiology (ACM). SRS = stress response system. Adapted with permission from Del Giudice et al. (2011).

et al., 2014; Perilloux et al., 2013; Weeden & Sabini, 2007). However, attractiveness is likely unrelated to most of the other genetic and ecological factors that affect life history development. Also, the availability and cultural legitimacy of contraception in different communities may dramatically alter the associations between life history–related traits such as sociosexuality and life history outcomes such as age at first reproduction. Finally, some individuals are simply less constrained than others because of superior wealth and status, an especially favorable environment, or similar advantages. Those individuals can afford to allocate their resources more flexibly, as reflected in mixed sociosexual strategies that combine short- and long-term mating.

The Extended Model: Differentiation Within the Fast–Slow Continuum

The Ecological Context of Differentiation

Some features of human ecology discussed in Chapter 1 have significant implications for the evolution and differentiation of life history strategies. To begin, the rise of dual status hierarchies has led to the emergence of prestige competition as an alternative pathway to mating and reproduction. In contrast with physical dominance, prestige can be acquired in myriad different ways: this includes displays of moral wisdom and political intelligence, artistic talent, and valuable technical skills—from hunting and tool-making to all sorts of specialized knowledge. Compared with dominance competition, prestige competition also requires less aggression and more cooperation (Cheng et al., 2010). While verbal and artistic creativity can directly contribute to courtship by functioning as fitness displays, technical activities contribute to mating success only indirectly, by raising the social standing of skilled individuals and—particularly since the invention of agriculture and money—enabling the long-term accumulation of wealth. Even if effective wealth transmission is a recent phenomenon on an evolutionary scale, it has likely amplified existing selection pressures by allowing successful individuals to boost the fitness of many relatives at once, potentially for several generations instead of the typical two (children and grandchildren). In the context of male provisioning and multigeneration resource transfers (both pre-existing features of the human adaptive complex), wealth accumulation becomes especially significant for men as an extended form of parental and/or nepotistic effort (see Jones, 2015). For this reason, selection on behaviors favoring the acquisition of prestige and wealth through technical skills must have been significantly stronger in men than in women.

The agricultural revolution almost certainly played a key role in the diversification of human life history strategies, above and beyond selection for specialized technical skills. For example, the transition from relatively egalitarian hierarchies to highly stratified, unequal, and even despotic societies (Boehm, 1999; Kaplan et al., 2009; Powers & Lehmann, 2014) increased the scope for extreme forms of aggressive competition for power and resources that would have been severely punished in small-scale forager groups, further amplifying the dominance/prestige dichotomy. Importantly, aggressive competition in large-scale, stratified societies can take many different routes, both legitimate (e.g., "cultures of honor" in pastoral societies, despotism) and illegitimate (criminality; Durrant & Ward, 2015).

Prestige competition, social interdependence, and the rising value of both social and technical skills are likely explanations for the evolution of our remarkable capacities for both mentalistic and mechanistic reasoning. High levels of mentalistic ability are especially valuable in courtship and competition via social manipulation. In fact, cooperation and reciprocity do not seem to require the same degree of mentalistic sophistication (Chapter 2). The need for highly developed mentalistic cognition is even lower for individuals who achieve status and resources by specializing in technical skills that depend on mechanistic reasoning, especially in view of the likely existence of cognitive tradeoffs between mentalistic and mechanistic abilities.

Multiple Profiles Within Fast and Slow Strategies

In the basic model, fast strategies are associated with antagonistic, exploitative behaviors and overt dominance competition (particularly in males). However, an alternative way to channel mating effort is to invest in prestige competition and courtship with a combination of verbal skills, enhanced mentalizing, and creativity (specifically of the verbal and/or artistic kind; Del Giudice et al., 2010; Miller, 1999, 2000). In particular, successful courtship and interpersonal influence are promoted by mind-reading or *cognitive* empathy and not necessarily by *affective* empathy, which is the tendency to resonate with other people's feelings on an emotional level (Slaughter et al., 2015; Wlodarski, 2015). The cognitive and behavioral strategies that arise from these alternative pathways can be labeled *antagonistic/exploitative* and *seductive/creative*. The antagonistic/exploitative and seductive/creative profiles define two separable regions in the behavioral space of fast strategies—variations on a common theme of high mating effort, impulsivity, and risk-taking (Figure 4.3). The key features of the seductive/creative profile are increased mentalizing, verbal ability, and creativity coupled with relatively low levels of aggression and physical dominance competition (Johnson et al., 2007). The personality factor most closely linked to this constellation of traits is openness to experience, particularly the imagination and aesthetics facets. At the level of brain functioning, upregulated mentalizing can be expected to correlate with elevated oxytocin, and possibly with heightened activation of the default mode network (Chapter 2).

The extended model of fast strategies overcomes some limitations of the basic model by positing a range of partially differentiated strategies instead of a single constellation of life history–related traits. As an illustration, it is useful to consider how the two models deal with individual variation in the personality traits of the dark triad. The basic model regards the dark triad as a correlate of fast life histories, with no further differentiation between psychopathy, narcissism, and Machiavellianism. By contrast, the extended model makes it possible to draw finer distinctions between these traits, which are moderately but not perfectly correlated with each other. Whereas psychopathic traits fall squarely in the domain of the antagonistic/exploitative profile, narcissistic traits are functionally closer to the seductive/creative profile. Within the triad, narcissism shows the smallest correlations with aggression and is associated with high levels of cognitive empathy. Narcissistic traits help people achieve leadership status in groups, and have been found to increase leadership effectiveness when they are present in moderate amounts (Grijalva, Harms et al., 2015; Jonason et al., 2013, 2015; Nagler et al., 2014; Ritter et al., 2011; Wai & Tiliopoulos, 2012). Machiavellianism seems to occupy an intermediate place between the two fast profiles described here. Somewhat counterintuitively, people with Machiavellian personalities tend to have relatively poor mind-reading abilities. At the same time, they are highly motivated to reason about other people's states of mind and exploit them to their own advantage; they are also capable of rapidly and flexibly adjusting their behavior to changes in the social context (Bereczkei, 2015; Esperger & Bereczkei, 2012; Lyons et al., 2010). Another important dimension of personality that fits the seductive/creative profile is *schizotypy*, the tendency to experience low-level psychotic phenomena, such as hallucinations and paranoid thoughts. Schizotypal personality traits are associated with artistic creativity and upregulated mentalizing; people high in schizotypy show increased success in short-term mating and

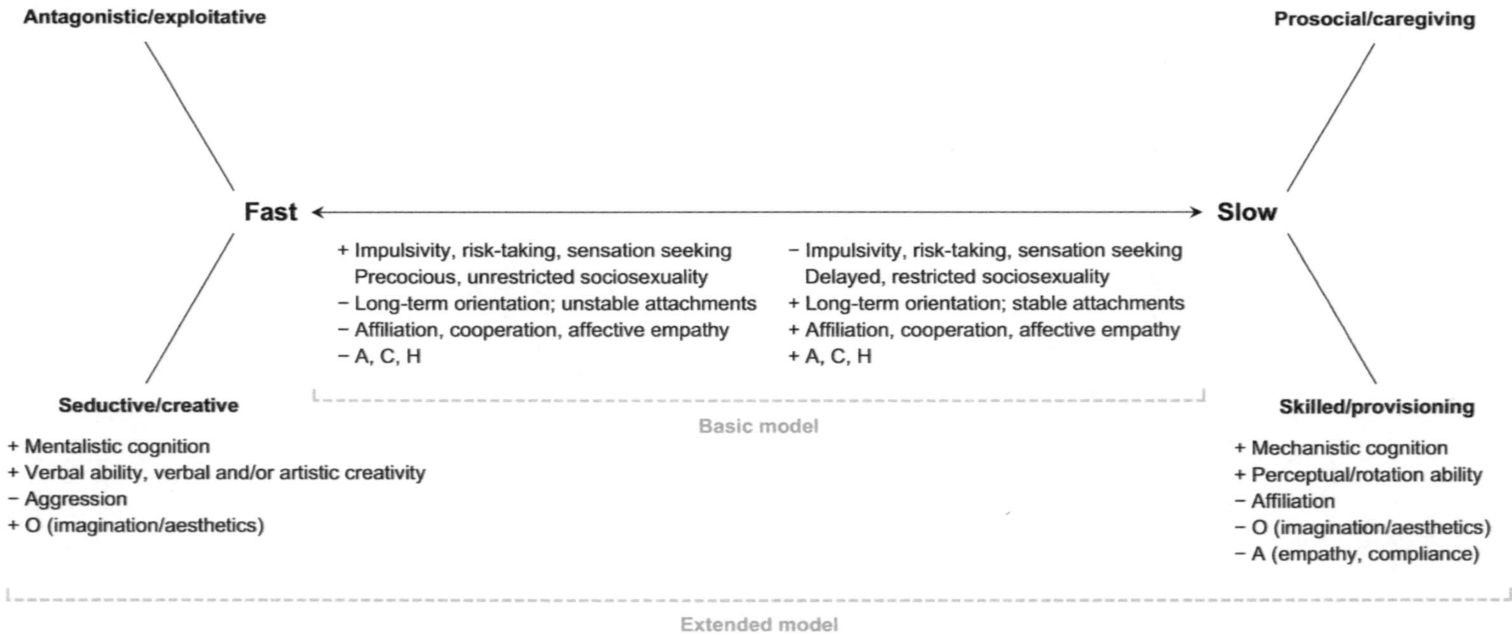

Figure 4.3. Key correlates of human life history strategies in the basic and extended model (see Table 4.1. for a more detailed list of traits). A = agreeableness. C = conscientiousness. H = honesty-humility. O = openness to experience.

other traits indicative of a fast strategy (Chapter 8; see also Del Giudice et al., 2010, 2014; Nettle, 2001, 2006*a*; Shaner et al., 2004).

Turning to slow strategies, the basic model focuses on traits that favor direct parental investment, such as affiliation, pair bonding, and secure attachment styles. All these traits imply a prosocial, nurturing attitude and are functionally associated with affective empathy. The resulting profile can be labeled as *prosocial/caregiving*; people with this constellation of traits can be expected to be sensitive partners and parents and score at the high end of agreeableness. However, direct caregiving is not the only route to successful parental investment. Especially for men, another option is to contribute mainly with status and resources—both of which can be acquired through mastery of technical skills, broadly defined (Del Giudice et al., 2010).

This male-typical reproductive strategy creates a niche for a *skilled/provisioning* profile in addition to the prosocial/caregiving one (Figure 4.3). The specific ecology of this profile changes the relative value of the traits associated with slow life histories in the basic model. Skilled/provisioning strategies clearly benefit from enhanced mechanistic cognition but do not require high levels of empathy, social skills, and artistic imagination; in fact, the latter may positively interfere with the development of technical proficiency. The expected cognitive profile is one of enhanced mechanistic reasoning and visuospatial abilities combined with reduced mentalizing. These are all important facets of *autistic-like traits* (Baron-Cohen et al., 2001). Autistic-like traits comprise poor social and communication skills, heightened attention to details, restricted imagination, and a tendency to engage in highly focused, repetitive activities. While autistic-like traits are associated with increased risk for autism (Chapter 10), they are continuously distributed in the general population and do not imply the presence of a disorder. The extended life history model provides a broader context for the hypothesis that autistic-like traits have been selected as part of a high-investment, long-term mating strategy at the slow end of the continuum (Del Giudice et al., 2010, 2014*a*). The increasing diversification of social roles and technical skills sparked by the invention of agriculture is likely to have boosted the evolutionary benefits of skilled/provisioning strategies over the past 10,000 years (Del Giudice et al., 2010; Spikins, 2009). A related and intriguing possibility is that, while people with this profile are relatively ineffective in direct courtship, they may compensate by appealing to the mating preferences of parents (see Chapter 1).

Compared with the prosocial/caregiving profile, the expected personality correlates of skilled/provisioning strategies include low imagination (a facet of openness to experience) and moderate or low agreeableness, particularly in facets related to empathy and social compliance (for evidence of differential associations between facets of agreeableness and mentalizing skills, see Allen et al., 2017). At the neurobiological level, these traits should be associated with a downregulated oxytocinergic system (see Crespi, 2016*a*); dampened activation of the default mode network is another plausible correlate of this profile (Allen et al., 2017). From a developmental perspective, skilled/provisioning strategies should involve a long phase of sexual immaturity, which can be mediated by hormonal and/

or motivational mechanisms (later puberty, delayed sexual interests and debut; see Forbes & Dahl, 2010). Protracted immaturity affords skilled/provisioning strategists ample time to engage in developmental exploration and accumulate specialized somatic capital that will become valuable later on. Accordingly, this profile might be associated with a combination of attachment avoidance and restricted sociosexuality, consistent with a partial suppression of the mating system.

The nature of the traits that define the seductive/creative and skilled/provisioning profiles suggests that sex hormones may play a complex role in the development of these strategies. The seductive/creative profile is characterized by female-typical traits such as high investment in mentalizing, elevated oxytocin, and low physical aggression, which point to downregulation of androgen pathways and/or estrogen upregulation. However, the same traits coexist with a male-typical pattern of unrestricted sociosexuality and risk-taking, which are generally associated with elevated androgen levels. This paradoxical combination of motivational and cognitive features suggests a mixed neurobiological makeup, with elements of both up- and downregulation in different aspects of sex hormone signaling. A hypothetical example of how this could happen in practice would be the combination of (a) elevated androgen production and (b) suppressed responsivity to androgens in the brain mechanisms that mediate cognitive abilities such as mentalizing and verbal processing (e.g., through downregulation of androgen receptors). Alternatively, conversion of testosterone to estrogen within specific brain areas may produce a similar effect. Still another possibility is that mixed male-typical and female-typical features arise from alternating patterns of hormone secretion over time. For instance, low levels of prenatal androgens (which may have a stronger influence on cognitive processes that develop in childhood, including language and mentalizing) may be followed by elevated androgen levels during middle childhood and puberty (with stronger organizational and activational effects on mating- and competition-related systems). The specular scenarios apply to the skilled/provisioning profile, in which exaggerated male-typical cognitive traits (high mechanistic ability and visuospatial skills, poor mentalizing) coexist with a feminized motivational pattern of low mating effort and restricted sociosexuality.

Table 4.1 summarizes the most important traits associated with fast and slow strategies in the basic and extended model. The table is not meant to be exhaustive and is open to future additions and refinements. In particular, it may be possible to describe other major clusters of life history–related traits in addition to the four profiles described here. Importantly, the strategic profiles I just sketched are not meant as rigidly separated categories, and some people may combine aspects of more than one profile. More generally, the fact that cognitive and behavioral tradeoffs are only probabilistic allows for the existence of unusual combinations of fast and slow traits in some atypical individuals (e.g., high levels of both mentalistic and mechanistic skills; see Crespi & Badcock, 2008).

It can be useful to conclude this section by stressing the limitations of the labels I used to identify life history profiles. These labels are convenient pointers to clusters of functionally related traits and should not be interpreted too literally

Table 4.1 Correlates of Fast and Slow Life History Strategies in Humans (Basic and Extended Model)

Domain/level of analysis	Fast strategies	Slow strategies
Personality factors	*Antagonistic/exploitative profile (basic model)*	*Prosocial/caregiving profile (basic model)*
	Low agreeableness	High agreeableness
	Low conscientiousness	High conscientiousness
	Low honesty-humility	High honesty-humility
	Seductive/creative profile	*Skilled/provisioning profile*
	High openness (imagination/aesthetics)	Low openness (imagination/aesthetics)
		Moderate/low agreeableness (empathy, compliance)
Motivation	*Antagonistic/exploitative profile (basic model)*	*Prosocial/caregiving profile (basic model)*
	Precocious sexuality	Delayed sexuality
	Unrestricted sociosexuality	Restricted sociosexuality
	Unstable, insecure romantic attachments	Stable romantic attachments (usually secure)
	Reduced long-term mating orientation	Increased long-term mating orientation
	Low affiliation	High affiliation
	Exploitative attitudes	Cooperative attitudes
	Low disgust sensitivity (especially sexual/moral)	High disgust sensitivity (especially sexual/moral)
	Seductive/creative profile	*Skilled/provisioning profile*
	Low aggression	Low affiliation

Decision-making, self-regulation	*Antagonistic/exploitative profile (basic model)*	*Prosocial/caregiving profile (basic model)*
	High impulsivity	Low impulsivity
	High time discounting (present orientation)	Low time discounting (future orientation)
	High sensation seeking	Low sensation seeking
	Risk proneness	Risk aversion
Cognitive ability	*Seductive/creative profile*	*Skilled/provisioning profile*
	High mentalistic cognition	Low mentalistic cognition
	Low mechanistic cognition	High mechanistic cognition
	High verbal ability	High visuospatial ability (perceptual/rotation)
	High verbal and/or artistic creativity	
Sexual maturation	Early, fast maturation (especially females)	Late, slow maturation (especially females)
Early environment	Harsh and/or unpredictable	Safe, predictable
	High exposure to stressors	Low exposure to stressors
	Negative family relations	Positive family relations

or narrowly. For example, naming a fast profile "seductive/creative" does not imply that creativity is found exclusively at the fast end of the continuum, but only that a particular kind of fast strategies is characterized by high levels of verbal/artistic creativity. Accordingly, verbal/artistic creativity predicts success in short-term mating (especially in men) and tends to correlate with lower honesty-humility (Clegg et al., 2011; Nettle & Clegg, 2006; Silvia et al., 2011). However, these correlations are only moderate, and artistic skills can be found along the whole life history spectrum. One should also remember that creativity is not only verbal and artistic: technically inclined people with autistic-like features may be quite creative in discovering new facts, developing theories and generalizations, or inventing novel tools and techniques (Kell et al., 2013; Simonton, 1999). Similar caveats apply to other labels such as "prosocial" or "provisioning"; despite their exploitative tendencies, fast strategists are clearly capable of behaving prosocially—for example, people high in Machiavellian traits often acquire status and influence by flexibly combining prosocial and coercive behaviors (Hawley, 2014*a*, 2014*b*).

Sex Differences

The issue of sex differences in life history strategies is complicated by the fact that the male distribution is shifted toward the fast end of the spectrum for many of the relevant traits. On average, men are more unrestricted and show higher risk-taking and sensation seeking; they are also lower in agreeableness, honesty-humility, and disgust sensitivity, particularly in the sexual domain (in contrast, there are only minor sex differences in impulsivity and conscientiousness). The reason is that these traits are crucially involved in the mating–parenting tradeoff, and males tend to invest in mating effort more than females even net of individual differences in life history strategies. As noted earlier, concluding that males are faster strategists than females can be misleading; a more accurate statement is that the correlates of the fast–slow continuum are partially differentiated by sex because the two sexes face somewhat different constraints and tradeoffs.

Regarding the behavioral profiles described in the extended model, females who engage in slow strategies are expected to show more prosocial/caregiving traits than males. In contrast, skilled/provisioning profiles should be strongly male-biased, given the sexual asymmetries in the costs and benefits of direct versus indirect parental investment. At the fast end of the continuum, antagonistic/exploitative traits should be more common in males, although similar motivational dispositions can manifest themselves in different ways in males and females (e.g., physical vs. relational aggression, avoidant vs. anxious romantic attachment styles). Seductive/creative strategies can be adaptive in both men and women; accordingly, large sex differences are not expected in this profile (see Del Giudice et al., 2010). However, the principle of higher variability in male mating strategies suggests that men should still be more likely to develop *extreme* versions of seductive/creative traits.

The Development of Life History Strategies

The expression of life history–related traits is a complex developmental process that unfolds according to the biological functions of each life stage. Risk-taking and sensation seeking peak during puberty while agreeableness and conscientiousness drop to their lowest point—a pattern consistent with the contrasting roles played by these traits in the regulation of mating and sexual competition (Ellis et al., 2012; Soto et al., 2011; Steinberg et al., 2008). Even before puberty, the transition to middle childhood is a turning point in the development of motivational systems, including those that regulate status, aggression, mating, and attachment; it also marks a phase of rapid maturation in self-regulation, moral reasoning, verbal ability, and both mentalistic and mechanistic skills (Del Giudice, 2014*c*; Del Giudice et al., 2009). For many of the life history–related traits discussed in the preceding sections, individual and sex differences emerge or intensify in middle childhood; other important changes occur during puberty, when the mating system becomes fully functional. In total, the transition to middle childhood and the onset of puberty function as two major switch points in life history development (Del Giudice & Belsky, 2011). The timing of these events is itself a component of a person's life history strategy: especially in females, early maturation and puberty contribute to prioritize current reproduction and should be associated with faster strategies, net of individual differences in nutrition and energetic resources (Belsky, 2012; Belsky et al., 1991; Ellis, 2013). The development of cognition, motivation, and self-regulation does not end with adolescence; indeed, personality traits do not reach their maximum stability until the third or fourth decade of life. This suggests that life history strategies are partially open to revision for a large portion of the life course—possibly depending on factors such as success in mating and reproduction, major environmental fluctuations, or unexpected changes in health, wealth, or status.

Environmental Factors

Starting with the seminal work by Draper and Harpending (1982) and Belsky and colleagues (1991), research on life history development has focused on conditional adaptation and stressed the role of environmental factors. At the heart of this approach is the idea that harsh (high morbidity-mortality) and/or unpredictable environments increase stress on parents and families, leading to negative and conflictual family relationships, insensitive parenting, and low levels of warmth and affection. Developmental processes track the quality of the child's environment and translate early adversity into faster life history strategies, including accelerated sexual maturation—especially in girls—and sexual debut (Belsky, 2012; James & Ellis, 2013; Nettle, 2011*b*). On this view, life history plasticity works in part as a predictive-adaptive response since children use the quality of family relations as a cue of the environment they will face as adults (safe/predictable vs. dangerous/unpredictable). An alternative but not incompatible interpretation of the empirical data is that early stressors inflict permanent damage on the organism—thus increasing later morbidity-mortality—and that life history strategies are facultatively calibrated to internal cues of somatic damage (Rickard et al., 2014; Wells, 2012).

A considerable body of research is consistent with the hypothesis that early harshness and unpredictability modulate the development of life history–related traits such as sociosexuality, impulsivity, and risk-taking; accelerate the transition to middle childhood (adrenarche) in both sexes; and anticipate puberty and childbearing in girls (e.g., Belsky J. et al., 2012, 2015; Brumbach et al., 2009; Carver et al., 2014; Ellis & Essex, 2007; Ellis, Shirtcliff et al., 2011; Lukaszewski, 2015; McCullough et al., 2013; Mendle et al., 2011; Nettle et al., 2011, 2013; Quinlan, 2010; Placek & Quinlan, 2012; Sheppard et al., 2016; Simpson, Griskevicius et al., 2012; Szepsenwol et al., 2017; Tither & Ellis, 2008). However, correlations between early environmental effects and puberty timing are typically small; in addition to measurement error, this may be partly explained by the overwhelming effects of modern nutrition on puberty, or reflect the comparatively minor role of maturation timing in the regulation of human reproductive patterns (Sheppard et al., 2016).

On the whole, the developmental evidence supports the idea that family relations mediate the effect of broader ecological factors such as socioeconomic status and mortality rates. However, ecological factors probably affect development in a number of other ways—including through influences on fetal development or direct exposure to danger and violence (Copping & Campbell, 2015; Nettle, 2011*b*). While early work emphasized the centrality of family experience in the first 5–7 years of life, more recent findings suggest that prenatal stress may also contribute to accelerate maturation and shift development toward faster strategies (Belsky et al., 2015; Nettle et al., 2011, 2013; see Del Giudice, 2014*d*). With few exceptions, psychological research has also neglected the influence of pathogen stress on life history development. The frequency and severity of early exposure to pathogens and parasites (e.g., prenatal infections, childhood diseases) are likely to work as reliable cues of mortality and influence life history allocations, either independently or in interaction with psychosocial factors (e.g., Abrams & Miller, 2011; Beckes & Simpson, 2009; Caudell & Quinlan, 2012; Waynforth, 2012).

At the physiological level, the stress response system is a central mechanism in life history development. This neurobiological system is ideally suited to integrate information about the environment across the life course, from prenatal nutrition and maternal stress hormones to psychosocial stressors in childhood and beyond (Del Giudice, 2014*d*; Del Giudice et al., 2011; Flinn et al., 2011). From a psychological standpoint, attachment security in infancy and childhood has been proposed as an important mediator of the effects of family stress (Belsky et al., 1991; Chisholm, 1993, 1999*a*, 1999*b*; Chisholm et al., 2005; Del Giudice, 2009*a*). Fast strategies are associated with insecure attachment patterns and may show an especially strong link with attachment *disorganization* in the first years of life. Disorganized children show inconsistent patterns of attachment (e.g., contradictory mixtures of avoidance and anxiety) or bizarre, dissociated behaviors such as freezing, suggesting that their interactions with the caregiver simultaneously activate attachment and fear. The causes of disorganization range from unresolved traumatic experiences in parents to downright maltreatment and abuse (Lyons-Ruth & Jacobvitz, 2008; van IJzendoorn et al., 1999). Attachment styles and stress physiology are intimately connected as secure attachment relationships shield the child from contextual sources of stress and dampen the reactivity of the HPA axis (e.g., Bernard & Dozier, 2010; Sung et al., 2016; see Pietromonaco & Powers, 2015). Other indications that psychological mechanisms may contribute to mediate life history development come from experimental studies in which life history–relevant behaviors such as risk-taking can be modulated by contextual cues of mortality, unpredictability, or resource scarcity (e.g., Griskevicius et al., 2011; Pepper & Nettle, 2014).

Genetic Factors and G×E Interactions

While most developmental research has focused on environmental effects, genetic factors clearly play a substantial role in life history development. The behavioral traits associated with life history strategies are about 50% heritable, and the same is true of life history events such as puberty timing and age at reproduction (e.g., Bezdjian et al., 2011; Figueredo et al., 2004; MacDonald, 1997; Rowe, 2002; Towne et al., 2005). As a rule, studies of life history plasticity do not include genetic information or attempt to control for genetic effects by indirect means (e.g., comparing siblings within the same family). Since many aspects of children's environment—including divorce, harsh parenting, and socioeconomic status—are affected by their parents' heritable phenotypes, correlations between environmental factors and life history–related traits reflect an unknown mixture of true causal effects of the environment and gene–environment correlations (Barbaro et al., 2017*b*; Gaydosh et al., 2017). For example, the same genetic factors that promote harsh parenting and couple conflict in parents may also promote impulsivity and aggression in children (Schlomer & Cleveland, 2014).

A related problem for models of life history plasticity is that ecological factors such as mortality and unpredictability should mainly operate on families as a whole, giving rise to shared environmental effects. But, as discussed in Chapter 3, shared environmental influences on personality and cognition decline rapidly after childhood and become small or even negligible in adulthood. At present, theories of differential susceptibility offer the only account of adaptive plasticity that is potentially compatible with the results of twin studies (Del Giudice, 2016*b*). Some individuals—possibly those who display negative emotionality and high physiological reactivity early in life—may be predisposed to adjust their strategy based on contextual influences, while others may follow highly canalized trajectories that place them at different locations on the fast–slow continuum regardless of the quality of the environment (Schlomer & Cleveland, 2014).

Population Differences

While the main focus of this chapter is on individual and sex differences, it is important to touch on the controversial topic of population differences in life history strategies. As I noted in Chapter 1, different human populations have likely followed somewhat different trajectories of genetic evolution, and this includes life history traits and their psychological correlates. All the major ecological determinants of life history variation—morbidity-mortality, unpredictability, resource availability—show considerable variation across societies and geographic regions (e.g., Caudell & Quinlan, 2012; Marlowe, 2005; Quinlan & Quinlan, 2007). At the same time, key life history traits such as growth rates and puberty timing show systematic differences, both between countries and between racial/ethnic groups within the same country. In the United States, for example, blacks reach puberty and start having sex significantly earlier than non-Hispanic whites, with Hispanics in between (Biro et al., 2010; Cavazos-Rehg et al., 2009; Haydon et al., 2012; Sun, 2002). Most likely, this pattern reflects a mixture of genetic effects, differences in nutrition, and differential exposure to stressors and other environmental factors. A scenario of partial genetic divergence between populations is supported by the genomic data, which show evidence of recent selection (over the past 2,000 years) for life history traits such as age at menarche (Field et al., 2016). Other traits, such as risk-taking, sociosexuality, and attachment security, show systematic relations with mortality and fertility rates across countries (Mata et al., 2016; Schmitt, 2005; Schmitt, Alcalay et al., 2003).

Basic life history traits such as mortality, fertility, and puberty timing in different populations are relatively easy to quantify; however, the measurement of group differences in personality is fraught with methodological problems that make it difficult to assess the behavioral correlates of life history strategies at this level of analysis. Personality scales show different measurement characteristics in different cultures, and the correlates of personality traits at the group level often contradict those observed at the individual level; for example, the average self-reported conscientiousness across countries and US states is a *positive* predictor of mortality, crime, corruption, and administrative inefficiency (Church et al., 2011; Mõttus et al., 2010; Rentfrow et al., 2008). One possible explanation of this pattern is that people in different groups and cultures use different reference points to evaluate personality, but research in this area is still preliminary. Similar confounds may operate between racial/ethnic groups, where personality comparisons show small effects and many inconsistencies between facets of the same trait (Foldes et al., 2008). Whatever future research will conclude about population differences in life history–related traits, it seems reasonably clear that general intelligence is not a major correlate of the fast–slow continuum in humans and that group differences in IQ—by far the most contentious aspect of Rushton's theory (Rushton, 1985, 2000)—are unlikely to be explained by differences in life history strategy (Meisenberg & Woodley, 2013; Woodley of Menie & Madison, 2015).

PART II

A Unified Approach

5

Evolution and Mental Disorders

In Part II of the book, I build on the concepts and models presented in Part I to develop a unified evolutionary approach to psychopathology. In this chapter, I introduce the core principles of evolutionary psychopathology and discuss the biological reasons for our vulnerability to mental disorders. I draw a pragmatic distinction between narrow-sense disorders that involve dysfunctions and broad-sense disorders that are merely undesirable, and present a detailed evolutionary taxonomy of undesirable conditions. In the last section, I address some important and hotly debated questions about the nature and structure of mental disorders. In doing so, I briefly review other emerging approaches to psychopathology and discuss their strengths and limitations from an evolutionary perspective.

WHAT IS A DISORDER?

The concept of a disorder is frustratingly difficult to define with precision (Nesse, 2001*b*). Intuitively, calling something a disorder implies a deviation from a desirable state that is perceived as normal. In the latest edition of the American Psychiatric Association's *Diagnostic and Statistical Manual* (DSM-5; American Psychiatric Association, 2013), mental disorders are said to involve "a dysfunction in the psychological, biological, or developmental processes underlying mental functioning" (p. 20), usually accompanied by significant distress or social impairment. However, the crucial term "dysfunction" is left undefined. The *Research Domain Criteria* (RDoC) promoted by the National Institute of Mental Health define mental disorders as dysfunctions in neural circuits, but similarly fail to specify what counts as a dysfunction (Cuthbert & Insel, 2013; Sanislow et al., 2010).

From an evolutionary perspective, an especially fruitful approach is to define disorders as conditions that involve *harmful dysfunctions* (Wakefield, 1992, 1999*a*, 1999*b*, 2011, 2015). To fulfill the dysfunction criterion, a condition must be caused by the failure of a biological mechanism to perform its evolved function. To fulfill the harm criterion, it must inflict some harm or damage on the affected person, as judged by sociocultural standards. This definition is a hybrid of objective (dysfunction) and subjective (harm) elements. On the one hand, it recognizes that social and cultural values contribute to shape perceptions of illness; on the other hand, it ties the concept of dysfunction to that of evolved function. In order to understand pathology, one needs to understand the biological functions of the relevant mechanisms as well as the structure of the environment in which they evolved (their environment of evolutionary adaptedness or EEA; Nesse, 2001*b*; Troisi & McGuire, 2002; Wakefield, 2015).

The definition of disorders as harmful dysfunctions has attracted a fair amount of criticism (e.g., Lilienfeld & Marino, 1999; Roe & Murphy, 2011; Troisi, 2015), but its implications are often misunderstood. When properly framed, it provides a remarkably useful heuristic for thinking about disorders. Four points should be kept in mind to avoid common errors of interpretation. First, evolved mechanisms must be defined broadly: major organs like the heart are mechanisms, but so are specialized brain areas, microscopic cellular structures, and biochemical pathways. Second, dysfunctions can occur in many different ways and for a wide variety of reasons, both internal and external—from mutations and infections to injuries and wounds. Third, the concept of dysfunction is fuzzy rather than all-or-none as evolved mechanisms can show varying degrees of functionality. Obvious instances of dysfunction are surrounded by borderline cases for which there are no clear-cut demarcating criteria. For example, there is no univocal threshold between "normal" blood pressure and hypertension, but the functionality of the circulatory system clearly decreases as blood pressure increases. The simplest cases are those in which the transition is strongly nonlinear (e.g., a sudden drop in functionality beyond a certain point), but gradual loss of function is also possible. Finally and crucially, "dysfunctional" is *not* synonymous with "maladaptive." It is quite possible for a dysfunction to be selectively neutral, for example because it occurs too late in life to impact an individual's fitness or because changes in the environment reduce its damaging effects. Myopia—a failure of the crystalline lens to project a focused image on the retina—remains a dysfunction even if glasses and contact lenses can easily neutralize its negative impact on survival. Conversely, even a properly functioning mechanism can have maladaptive consequences, for example if there is a mismatch between the present environment and the EEA for that mechanism (e.g., an evolved taste for sweet foods may become maladaptive with the advent of refined sugars and sedentary lifestyles).

The harmful dysfunction criterion poses a serious challenge to current classifications of mental disorders. Although the DSM purports to be a catalog of dysfunctions, only some of its diagnostic categories involve a clear-cut failure of evolved mechanisms; many psychopathological conditions likely arise from functional processes, and some may be biologically adaptive despite their costs and undesirable effects (see later discussion). A rigorous application of the harmful dysfunction criterion would require taking those conditions out of the DSM and reclassifying them as normal manifestations of our evolved psychology (e.g., Kennair, 2014; Wakefield, 2015). Of course, people with those conditions would not stop seeking treatment to alleviate their distress. Fever and pain are widely medicated even if they are not diseases but functional, adaptive defenses (note that there are also genuinely dysfunctional instances of fever and pain). Cosmides and Tooby (1999) used the label "treatable conditions" to include a wide range of conditions that compromise well-being and may prompt people to seek treatment regardless of whether they represent true dysfunctions or not.

A Pragmatic Approach

I anticipate that, in the long run, biologically informed taxonomies of disorders will increasingly conform to the harmful dysfunction criterion by excluding some conditions, reclassifying some conditions as manifestations of adaptive defenses, or introducing new conceptual distinctions like the one between true pathologies and "pseudopathologies" (Crawford & Anderson, 1989). I also believe that this change should happen gradually, for two reasons. First, overturning the current classification system in one fell swoop is not a realistic goal; attempts in this sense may actually backfire and delay the adoption of evolutionary ideas in the field. Second, our knowledge of many if not most condition is still insufficient to make clear-cut decisions about the functionality or lack thereof of the relevant mechanisms; at the present state of research, it would be a mistake to make premature decisions for the sake of conceptual rigor.

In this book I adopt a pragmatic approach by distinguishing between *narrow-sense* disorders (harmful dysfunctions) and *broad-sense* disorders—that is, undesirable conditions that are currently diagnosed as disorders but may or may not represent genuine dysfunctions. In the remainder, I will employ the term "disorder" in the broad sense, not least to avoid confusion in using standard labels such as "obsessive-compulsive disorder" or "personality disorder." At the same time, I will strive to be as precise as possible in distinguishing between different kinds of biological explanations and explicitly note when a particular evolutionary model claims that a condition is a dysfunction in the narrow sense. I regard this as an initial, realistic step toward a biologically informed approach to psychopathology (Del Giudice, 2014*b*).

A TAXONOMY OF UNDESIRABLE CONDITIONS

Because biological mechanisms are designed by natural selection to serve adaptive goals, understanding the function of a mechanism typically brings order and simplicity to what would otherwise be a mass of disconnected facts and observations about its workings. This is why the study of biological *function* has an intrinsic tendency toward increasingly elegant, economic explanations. The study of *dysfunctions* has a very different character. Things can go wrong for any number of reasons, from external insults to internal failures; complex mechanisms can break down in many different ways, and, even when they function properly, they may produce all sorts of negative side effects. This is why taxonomies of disorders—both in psychopathology and in medicine at large—resemble lengthy, redundant troubleshooting manuals more than elegant explanations of how mechanisms work (Wakefield, 1999*c*). This does not mean, however, that such taxonomies cannot be informed by deeper functional principles. To the extent that multiple mechanisms work in a coordinated fashion and patterns of functioning vary systematically between people, models of individual differences can be used to illuminate broad tendencies in the risk for various disorders and their co-occurrence (Chapter 6). This is even truer if broad-sense disorders include a certain proportion of adaptive conditions in addition to genuine dysfunctions.

At a more fundamental level, evolutionary principles can be successfully used to explain why organisms are vulnerable to disorders at all. As it turns out, there are only a handful of general explanations for vulnerability to disorders, in striking contrast with the variety and diversity of the disorders themselves (Nesse, 2005*b*, 2015). First of all, natural selection is limited in the problems it can solve—it cannot just eliminate all deleterious mutations or make organisms invulnerable to accidents. Other limits to the power of selection stem from intrinsic design tradeoffs (e.g., speed vs. accuracy, body mass vs. ability to dissipate heat) and the fact that every innovation must build on the already existing phenotype of the organism, which in turn constrains the possible outcomes of evolution. Second, even when selection can solve a problem in principle, it is often too slow to prevent disorders from occurring. Fast-replicating parasites coevolve with their hosts, finding new ways to attack them and sidestep their defenses; positive selection for a trait can have negative side effects on other traits that take many generations to be eliminated; rapid changes in the environment create the potential for mismatches between the evolved function of a mechanism and its present effects. Third, selection maximizes genetic replication rather than health, well-being, or even survival; many traits that enhance reproduction have substantial costs, and adaptive defenses can be painful and distressing. Tradeoffs between health and fitness are further amplified by the existence of evolutionary conflicts, both between individuals and between different sets of genes within the same individual (Crespi, 2010).

A complementary approach is to draw some basic distinctions between the various biological processes that may give rise to undesirable conditions (Figure 5.1; Del Giudice & Ellis, 2016; see also Cosmides & Tooby, 1999; Kennair, 2003). The first distinction is that between harmful dysfunctions (narrow-sense disorders) and conditions that involve functionally intact mechanisms. Within the latter category, it is useful to distinguish between mechanisms that are currently maladaptive because of evolutionary mismatches and mechanisms that are not just functional, but also adaptive in their present environment. Finally, even mechanisms that are adaptive at a population level (i.e., increase inclusive fitness *on average*) may still lead to maladaptive outcomes for specific individuals. Such "instance failures" of adaptive mechanisms (Cosmides & Tooby, 1999) can be contrasted with phenotypes that are socially or psychologically undesirable but ultimately beneficial to the individual's fitness. Distinguishing between individual and average fitness permits a finer grained analysis of the interplay between adaptation and maladaptation in psychopathology (Frankenhuis & Del Giudice, 2012).

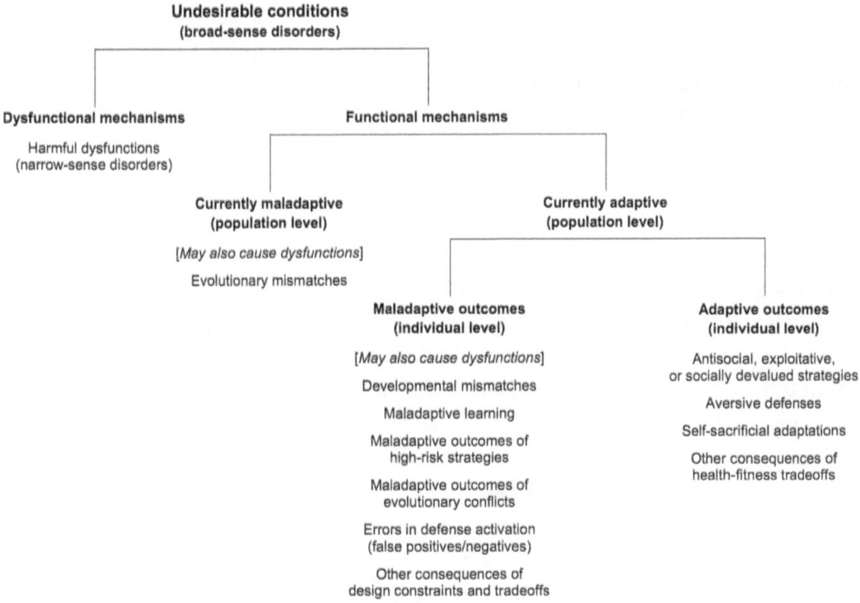

Figure 5.1. An evolutionary taxonomy of undesirable conditions (broad-sense disorders). Adapted with permission from Del Giudice & Ellis (2016).

The taxonomy in Figure 5.1 is a useful tool for comparing alternative evolutionary hypotheses about the origin of disorders. Still, the distinctions on which it is based are necessarily approximate: a given condition may involve a combination of biological and etiological processes, each reflecting a different category in the taxonomy. Clear-cut distinctions would only be possible if each condition depended on a single mechanism and a single etiological process. In reality, disorders often result from the interplay between multiple mechanisms, and different steps in the etiological pathway may well require different evolutionary explanations. For example, the maladaptive outcomes of a functional mechanism may induce secondary dysfunctions in other mechanisms. The evolved preference for sugary and fatty foods (a functional mechanism) may lead to obesity because of a mismatch with modern nutrition (a maladaptive outcome), which in turn increases the risk of heart failure (a harmful dysfunction). Conversely, a dysfunction that occurs in one mechanism may cause functional but undesirable reactions in other mechanisms. Accumulation of fluid in the lungs or *edema* (a dysfunction) may trigger severe cough (a functional defensive mechanism); damaged face processing mechanisms in the brain (a dysfunction) may start feeding contradictory information to other intact regions, leading to delusional feelings that a familiar person has been replaced by an identical impostor (a harmful dysfunction known as Capgras syndrome; see Hirstein & Ramachandran, 1997). At a deeper level, it is useful to remember that even individual fitness is only valid as an approximation because different genetic factions may have partially conflicting interests. For example, a condition that is adaptive for maternally derived genes may be maladaptive from the perspective of paternally derived genes. With all these caveats in mind, I now examine the four categories of Figure 5.1 in more detail. The illustrative examples I bring up in this section are discussed more extensively in Part III of the book.

Harmful Dysfunctions

All biological and artificial mechanisms—no matter how well designed—are vulnerable to malfunctions, failures, and breakdowns. Even if developmental processes are canalized against perturbations, they can deviate from their target phenotype as random events and disturbances accumulate over time. More dramatically, evolved mechanisms may cease to perform their functions because of accidents or environmental insults, from brain injuries to toxins. Exposure to extreme or prolonged stressors can exceed the regulatory capacity of response mechanisms such as the fear system, the security system, or the stress response system. Chronic exposure to adversity may interfere with the ability of the stress response system to promote allostasis, resulting in long-term dysregulation (*allostatic load*; see Beauchaine et al., 2011; Ellis & Del Giudice, 2014; Juster et al., 2011). The environment is not the only source of threats to functionality, as mechanisms can break down owing to the effects of deleterious genetic or epigenetic mutations (Crespi, 2000, 2010). Sometimes a single mutation in a critical pathway is sufficient to cause a disorder; more often, disorders may arise from the cumulative impact of small-effect mutations, possibly in conjunction with environmental stressors. Mutation load has been proposed as a likely explanation for the persistence of common, heritable, and harmful mental disorders like autism and schizophrenia (Keller & Miller, 2006).

Attacks and manipulations by pathogens (viruses, bacteria, and other parasites) are another common cause of biological dysfunction. Infectious diseases—especially when they occur in early development—have been associated with increased risk for mental disorders such as autism, schizophrenia, and depression (Benros et al., 2012; Patterson, 2011). The roles of pathogens and mutations in the etiology of mental disorders are not mutually exclusive. Just like mutations, infections can perturb developmental processes at critical stages; even if they have different origins, mutation and pathogen load can ultimately converge on the same neurobiological pathways and act synergistically to cause pathological outcomes. In addition to their direct effects on individual organisms, pathogens contribute indirectly to the risk of harmful dysfunctions by shaping the evolution of defenses across generations. Pathogens and hosts are constantly involved in coevolutionary arms races so that, for every improvement in defensive mechanisms, new means of offense are selected for on the other side. Coevolutionary arms races tend to produce increasingly complex offense–defense mechanisms (consider the intricacy of the immune system); however, the very complexity of those mechanisms may render them more vulnerable to failures and dysfunctions (Nesse, 2001*b*). The same general argument extends to the evolution of mechanisms involved in social and sexual competition between conspecifics (e.g., mentalistic skills).

As a rule, sexually selected traits tend to be more condition-dependent—and thus more vulnerable to dysfunctions—than other phenotypes. This contributes to explain why males are generally more vulnerable to both harmful mutations and environmental insults. Female-specific vulnerabilities may exist for traits that have been under stronger sexual selection in females (Geary, 2015), but they should be considerably less common than their male-specific counterparts. Females also enjoy additional protection from deleterious X-linked mutations: they carry two copies of the X chromosome, and different copies are randomly expressed in different cells of the body (Migeon, 2007). Finally, dysfunctions in older people may simply result from senescence as brain mechanisms decay over time due to the accumulation of damage and lack of repair.

Evolutionary Mismatches

Thanks to natural selection, evolving organisms tend to become progressively more successful at surviving and reproducing in their environment. The environment, however, is not a static background: conditions change all the time because of external events (e.g., geological or climatic change), social and technological evolution (e.g., increased population density, antibiotics), and coevolutionary processes between species (e.g., agriculture, new pathogen strains). If environmental changes are rapid and extensive, previously adaptive mechanisms may suddenly become maladaptive and bring about all sorts of unintended and/or undesirable consequences. Thanks to cultural evolution and technological progress, humans have gained unprecedented power to alter their social and physical environment but, in doing so, have also created enormous opportunity for evolutionary mismatch.

Evolutionary mismatch may occur when an evolved mechanism encounters a novel environmental context that falls outside of the range that was recurrently encountered over its evolutionary history (the EEA). In the new context, a functional mechanism can give rise to maladaptive outcomes or even induce dysfunctions in other mechanisms. Evolutionary mismatches are likely to be implicated in the etiology of several mental disorders. In modern societies, for example, the media expose people to a relentless stream of images of unrealistically attractive "competitors"—an artificial, evolutionarily novel kind of social stimulus. It has been hypothesized that such exposure hyperactivates the evolved mechanisms that regulate female competition for attractiveness and status, thus contributing to the rising incidence of eating disorders (Abed, 1998).

Other instances of potential mismatch are less obvious. Sanitation in developed countries determines a lack of exposure to common microorganisms ("old friends") during development. These novel hygienic conditions appear to interfere with the early ontogenetic processes that train the immune system and calibrate its functioning parameters. The resulting states of chronic inflammation may increase the risk for a range of physical and mental disorders, including depression (Miller & Raison, 2016; Raison & Miller, 2013*a*). Another intriguing example is the effect of age segregation within peer groups. As a result of formal schooling and other age-segregated activities in modern societies, adolescents spend most of their time with peers of approximately the same age. This is an evolutionary novel and unusual arrangement: in traditional cultures, adolescents play in mixed-age groups that include both other adolescents and younger children, and not infrequently they are expected to take care of infants and toddlers. Continual interactions with infants and younger children activate the caregiving system and stimulate prosocial, nurturant behaviors. The available evidence indicates that exclusive, same-age adolescent groups may contribute to exacerbate the intensity of so-called *externalizing* behaviors such as physical and verbal aggression, defiance, attention seeking, and risk-taking (Ellis et al., 2012; Gray, 2011).

The very process of adaptation constantly generates subtle forms of mismatch that may contribute to the etiology of undesirable conditions. When a trait has been subjected to strong recent selection, the resulting adaptive changes may co-occur with maladaptive side effects caused by other traits that happen to be genetically and/or developmentally linked to the trait under selection. Similarly, recently evolved adaptations are likely to show increased scope for dysregulation because they have yet to be "fine-tuned" by natural selection (Crespi, 2010). If one combines our species' rapid pace of social and technological change in with the evidence of accelerating genetic evolution over the past few millennia (Chapter 1), the probability that mismatches significantly contribute to human psychopathology becomes quite high. This point is reinforced by the findings of comparative studies that have tried to estimate the frequency of mental pathologies in other primates. Using behavioral criteria adapted from the DSM, researchers found very high rates of conditions matching the symptoms of depression, generalized anxiety, posttraumatic stress, and obsessive-compulsive disorder in captive chimpanzees that had been used in laboratory research. However, the prevalence of the same conditions in wild chimpanzee populations was extremely low, from less than 1% to about 3% (Ferdowsian et al., 2011, 2012).

Maladaptive Outcomes of Adaptive Mechanisms

Up to now, I have examined cases in which undesirable conditions are caused by failures of evolved design. Harmful dysfunctions occur when a biological mechanism fails to perform its evolved functions; evolutionary mismatches occur when an intact mechanism becomes maladaptive under novel environmental conditions. However, maladaptation at the individual level may systematically occur even when adaptive mechanisms perform their evolved functions in an environment that matches the EEA on the relevant dimensions. Adaptive mechanisms can produce maladaptive outcomes for a variety of reasons, typically due to unavoidable constraints, tradeoffs, and side effects (Frankenhuis & Del

Giudice, 2012). The ubiquity of maladaptive outcomes underscores the fact that biological optimality is very different from unconstrained perfection.

Developmental Mismatches

Developmental plasticity promotes fitness in variable environments by enabling conditional adaptation based on contextual cues. However, the validity and predictive accuracy of cues are usually far from perfect; although accuracy can often be improved by sampling the environment longer or more thoroughly, the potential benefit must be balanced against the required investment of time and effort. If there are tradeoffs between time spent sampling cues and time available to develop a specialized phenotype, selection favors organisms that accept some level of uncertainty and the consequent risk of mismatch (Frankenhuis & Del Giudice, 2012; Frankenhuis & Panchanathan, 2011). This type of tradeoff is not due to limitations in information processing; mismatches are expected to occur even if individuals employ contextual cues in the best possible way (that is, conforming to Bayesian principles). In unstable or changing environments, the risk of mismatch is magnified because individuals growing up in one kind of environment may suddenly end up in a different context where a different phenotype would be adaptive. For all these reasons, conditional adaptation is a fallible process, and a proportion of individuals end up developing mismatched phenotypes and suffering fitness costs as a result. Still, natural selection can favor conditional adaptation even if the costs of mismatch are high, as long as the average benefits of plasticity are larger than the average costs across individuals.

Like evolutionary mismatches, developmental mismatches are a potential cause of pathology. Metabolic mismatches between fetal undernutrition and availability of high-calorie food in childhood are a risk factor for type 2 diabetes and heart conditions (Rinaudo & Wang, 2012). Children raised in deprived, high-stress contexts such as Romanian orphanages may show blunted stress reactivity even many years after being adopted into supportive families, particularly if adoption occurs after the sensitive window of infancy (e.g., McLaughlin et al., 2015). The outcomes of developmental mismatches may or may not qualify as genuine dysfunctions; while type 2 diabetes is a clear example of metabolic dysregulation, blunted stress reactivity may represent an adaptive response to dangerous environments, a response produced by intact developmental processes when children are exposed to prolonged adversity (Del Giudice et al., 2011).

Maladaptive Learning

Developmental mismatches arise from constraints and tradeoffs in the use of information by mechanisms of adaptive plasticity. The larger point is that similar constraints and tradeoffs apply to all types of learning, from simple associative processes (e.g., Pavlovian conditioning) to social and cultural transmission. Natural selection only requires learning strategies to be adaptive on average, which typically allows for a substantial rate of errors and mistakes. In fact, strategies that result in a *majority* of errors can still be selected for if the errors have a relatively low cost and the benefits of correct learning are sufficiently large. For example, a tendency to readily infer causal relations between events that may easily be unrelated (e.g., conclude that eating a certain plant cures fever based on just a few observations) can be adaptive on the whole, even if it leads people to form many false beliefs and engage in useless superstitious behaviors (Foster & Kokko, 2009). Social learning is extremely efficient because it reduces the need to learn everything by direct trial and error; at the same time, learning from others or copying them also carries the risk of acquiring false beliefs and fitness-damaging behaviors. Even simple forms of social transmission can generate a mixture of adaptive and maladaptive cultural "traditions" (e.g., Franz & Matthews, 2010).

Some potential downsides of adaptive learning strategies become apparent when viewed from a developmental perspective. If the environment is characterized by significant uncertainty, a certain proportion of individuals may end up developing maladaptive behaviors because they receive incorrect information early on and then fail to update their internal models owing to (normally adaptive) self-reinforcing processes. For instance, people who form early representations of the world as dangerous or uncontrollable may become anxious and start avoiding situations that they perceive as threatening. Avoidance is usually an adaptive response to danger; in this case, however, it prevents anxious individuals from learning that the environment is actually safer than they believe, thus locking them in a state of exaggerated anxiety (Meacham & Bergstrom, 2016). Even if such catastrophic failures of learning mechanisms are statistically rare, they can be highly maladaptive for the individuals who experience them.

The relevance of these ideas for psychopathology is difficult to overstate if one considers that beliefs, schemata, expectations, and other learned cognitive constructs play an important role in the origin and maintenance of many psychological symptoms (Hofmann, 2014). The motivational systems discussed in Chapter 2 do not operate in a vacuum—they depend on multiple sources of information about oneself, other people, and the environment, from largely implicit regulatory variables to explicit representations and beliefs. To be effective, metacognitive forms of self-regulation crucially depend on correct self-knowledge—that is, information about one's own psychological functioning (Dimaggio et al., 2007; Wells, 2000). To the extent that psychological mechanisms rely on information acquired through learning, they are vulnerable to maladaptive outcomes owing to the intrinsic limitations of learning processes. Indeed, the massive capacity for individual and social learning required to exploit the cognitive niche may contribute to explain our species' seemingly unique vulnerability to mental disorders.

Maladaptive Outcomes of High-Risk Strategies

Risky adaptive strategies represent an important source of individual-level maladaptation. By definition, high-risk strategies involve the possibility of both large gains and large losses. The most dramatic examples come from "winner takes all" mating systems in which reproductive benefits are highly skewed toward top-ranking individuals. In such conditions, there is intense selection to compete for top rank, even if this implies a greater risk of injury. Male elephant seals engage in fierce fights that cause harm and sometimes death; still, they benefit—on average—from participating in fights because not participating would mean being shut out from reproduction.

In humans, externalizing behaviors such as defiance and physical aggression can be interpreted as high-risk tactics of social competition (Del Giudice et al., 2011; Ellis et al., 2012; Martel, 2013). Aggressive children and adolescents sometimes manage to become dominant, popular leaders in their group of peers. When they do not succeed the consequences can be dramatic, as they may become unpopular or rejected and even incur ostracism or physical harm. These outcomes can be individually maladaptive even if they result from an adaptive strategy designed to achieve dominance and social status. Similarly, some personality traits may facilitate mating or social competition at the cost of increased risk of harmful mental disorders. For example, schizotypal traits can boost mating success as part of a seductive/creative strategy, but they also increase the risk of schizophrenia (Nettle, 2001, 2006*a*; Shaner et al., 2004). Again, individually maladaptive outcomes do not necessarily lead to true dysfunctions; while schizophrenia is almost certainly dysfunctional, the anxiety, shame, and depression experienced by rejected aggressive children are more likely to stem from intact emotional responses to status loss.

Maladaptive Outcomes of Evolutionary Conflicts

Because of their intrinsically antagonistic logic, evolutionary conflicts are guaranteed to yield maladaptive outcomes for at least one of the parties involved. Consider the prenatal conflicts on nutrition that take place between the mother and the fetus. Each actor in this conflict is equipped with adaptations that are *designed* to reduce the other's fitness: for example, the fetus secretes hormones that increase blood pressure and glycemia to increase the flow of nutrients to the placenta beyond the mother's optimum. Moreover, the most adaptive outcomes for the mother are the least adaptive for the fetus and vice versa. In addition to the inevitable costs, conflict may occasionally escalate to dangerous levels, with severely maladaptive consequences for the parent, the offspring, or both. In the case of prenatal nutrition, the interplay between placental hormones and maternal countermeasures may result in severe hypertension and death of both mother and fetus (Haig, 1993; Schlomer et al., 2011). Similar dynamics may be involved in the regulation of sex- and stress-related hormones during pregnancy (Del Giudice, 2012*a*; Mokkonen et al., 2016). Elevated prenatal stress and cortisol levels have been associated with increased risk for a broad range of psychopathological conditions (Betts et al., 2015; Class et al., 2014; Glover, 2011; Khalife et al., 2013). To some extent, these developmental outcomes may arise as maladaptive side effects of parent–offspring conflict during pregnancy.

Intragenomic conflicts (such as those between maternally and paternally expressed genes) also tend to produce maladaptive outcomes for the person as a whole. In the presence of intragenomic conflict, the developing phenotype is subject to opposing forces, much like in a game of tug-of-war. The tension between different sets of genes with opposite effects increases phenotypic variability and, consequently, the likelihood of reaching maladaptive levels of trait expression. If for any reason the dynamic equilibrium is broken—for example because of disruptive mutations on one side of the conflict—the resulting unbalance may easily determine dysregulated or frankly pathological outcomes. Conflicts between brain-expressed imprinted genes seem to play a role in the development of some mental disorders, most notably autism, schizophrenia, and other psychotic conditions (Byars et al., 2014; Crespi & Badcock, 2008; Crespi et al., 2010; Wilkins, 2011).

Errors in Defense Activation

Defensive mechanisms can make two symmetric kinds of mistakes: they can fail to activate in the presence of a threat (false negatives) or become activated when no threat is present (false positives). Even when defenses are functional and optimally calibrated, errors cannot be completely avoided; given the tradeoffs between the costs of different types of errors, the smoke detector principle suggests that defensive systems should typically evolve to commit more false positives than false negatives (Chapter 2). The logic of the smoke detector principle can be employed to shed light on the etiology of conditions such as panic attacks, phobias, and generalized anxiety (Bateson et al., 2011; Nesse, 2005*a*; Nesse & Jackson, 2006). Adaptive defenses like fever, cough, and anxiety are typically aversive and frequently disabling; occasionally, inappropriate activation of a defensive mechanism may cause serious harm and lead to maladaptive outcomes for the individual. Because defenses are often calibrated to accept a certain proportion of false positives, the line between inappropriate activation of a functional mechanism and frank dysregulation can be blurred, and evidence of maladaptation is not enough to infer the presence of a dysfunction or mismatch.

Since many if not most defensive mechanisms are modulated by learning and acquired information (e.g., fear conditioning, learned taste aversion, regulatory variables that encode the safety of the environment), the problem of false alarms is compounded by that of maladaptive learning. For example, posttraumatic stress symptoms arise at least in part from defense-related learning processes such as associative fear conditioning and stress sensitization. For various reasons, these processes may lead to high rates of inappropriate activation, so that extreme fear and avoidance are repeatedly triggered by mild or innocuous cues. Mathematical models show that even optimal learning processes can occasionally fall into self-reinforcing vicious cycles, leading to maladaptive hyperactivation of defenses in a certain proportion of the population (Lissek & van Meurs, 2015; Meacham & Bergstrom, 2016).

Although they are less obvious and more difficult to recognize, the effects of false *negatives* can be just as problematic as those of false positives (Horwitz & Wakefield, 2012). Insensitivity to pain is an extremely dangerous condition; people who are congenitally unable to feel pain often die in childhood because they fail to notice injuries and illnesses (Nagasako et al., 2003). As pointed out by Nesse (1990), the fact that people rarely complain about "too little anxiety" or the "inability to feel fear" does not mean that such conditions do not exist or cannot be harmful to individuals, their relatives, and their social partners.

Other Constraints and Tradeoffs

The design of organisms is shaped by countless physical constraints that limit the range of phenotypic evolution and burden adaptations with undesirable side effects. Larger and stronger bodies are more expensive to build and maintain; walking upright necessarily makes humans more vulnerable to stumbling and falling. Unavoidable physical constraints are compounded by the legacy of previous history: natural selection builds incrementally on previous designs, and its inability to "start from scratch" introduces further constraints on adaptive design. The fact that human babies are delivered through the pelvic canal poses severe constraints on head size at birth; at the same time, selection for larger head size contributes to the occurrence of maladaptive obstetrical complications. Design tradeoffs are just as ubiquitous. Increasing the functionality of one system may interfere with the functionality of another; increasing the efficiency of a system early in life may lead to reduced efficiency when the organism gets older, and enhanced protection against a certain disease may increase vulnerability to a different condition. Constraints and tradeoffs in the design of adaptations are all potential causes of maladaptation at the individual level.

An important kind of tradeoff originates in what have been called *cliff-edged* fitness functions. Cliff-edged functions arise when phenotypic traits that are biologically adaptive within a certain range (e.g., head size at birth) rapidly become maladaptive if they exceed the limits of that range. Sometimes, the fitness associated with a trait increases up to an optimal level but decreases sharply once a threshold is crossed (Figure 5.2). When the fitness contribution of a trait follows a cliff-edged function, selection for higher trait levels may occasionally result in maladaptive phenotypes that overshoot the fitness optimum (Vercken et al., 2012). This mechanism has been suggested as a possible explanation for the persistence of genes that increase the risk of severe mental disorders such as schizophrenia (Nesse, 2004*b*). More generally, traits can reach maladaptive levels of expression owing to genetic, epigenetic, and/or environmental factors that contribute to push the phenotype in a certain direction, alone or in combination. In the simplest case, extreme levels of a trait may appear in the children of two people who are both high on that trait yet still within the adaptive range. Thus, *assortative mating*—the tendency for sexual partners to resemble one another on certain phenotypes, including behavioral and cognitive traits—can greatly increase the risk of maladaptive trait expression in the offspring (Peyrot et al., 2016).

Undesirable Adaptations

In the all scenarios reviewed so far, undesirable conditions arise either from dysfunctions or from the maladaptive outcomes of functional mechanisms. However, it may also be the case that *adaptive* outcomes are perceived as

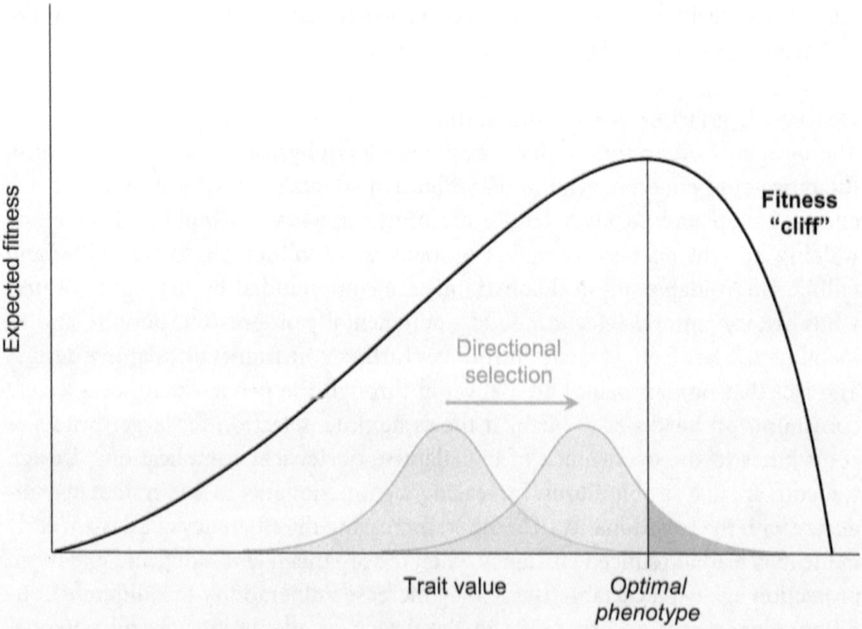

Figure 5.2. Cliff-edged fitness functions increase the risk of maladaptive outcomes. In this example, directional selection for higher values of the trait tends to shift the trait distribution toward the fitness optimum. As a result, some individuals may overshoot the optimal trait value and experience a substantial fitness loss.

undesirable or even mistakenly classified as narrow-sense disorders. This can happen when adaptations cause harm or distress to the "affected" person, inflict damage on other people, or conflict with shared social values. Distinguishing undesirable adaptations from maladaptive outcomes can be theoretically and empirically challenging, but is an essential step to understand the meaning and etiology of the relevant conditions (Nesse, 2004*a*; Nesse & Jackson, 2006).

Unsurprisingly, defensive mechanisms are a prime source of undesirable adaptations. When defenses are triggered inappropriately or respond with excessive intensity, it can be relatively easy to recognize the outcomes as maladaptive. However, many protective mechanisms have strongly aversive effects, which may be regarded as undesirable even when mechanisms are responding appropriately in the presence of actual threats. Sometimes, adaptive defensive processes can be altogether mistaken for dysfunctions, especially if their logic is incompletely understood and the correspondence between threat and response is imperfect (for reasons explained by the smoke detector principle). An example would be the misconception that coughing is a disease instead of a protective reflex. This has been called the "fallacy of mistaking defenses for diseases" and is a pervasive feature of mainstream approaches to psychopathology (Nesse & Jackson, 2006). Many diagnosable instances of emotional disorders—involving depression, anxiety, fear, and other negative emotions—may be best understood as unpleasant but adaptive responses to contextual factors. At the same time, severe instances of the same disorders are more likely to reflect at least some degree of dysregulation in the underlying mechanisms. Distinguishing adaptive defensive reactions from maladaptive outcomes and dysfunctional responses can be a daunting task because it requires a truly sophisticated understanding of the logic, costs, and benefits of the relevant defenses (for extended discussion, see Horwitz & Wakefield, 2012).

While aversive defenses primarily harm the person who expresses them, other conditions are classified as disorders mainly because they have undesirable effects on other people. For example, antisocial personality disorder (the DSM counterpart of psychopathy) can be understood as an extreme instance of antagonistic/exploitative strategies at the fast end of the life history continuum. From this vantage point, many putative dysfunctions associated with these conditions—low empathy, impulsivity, lack of guilt and remorse—can be interpreted as design features rather than failures (e.g., Barr & Quinsey, 2004; Glenn et al., 2011; Mealey, 1995). Still, antisocial personality profiles are routinely regarded as mental disorders regardless of whether they are biologically successful. This example forcefully illustrates the complications introduced by conflicts of interest between different social actors, which play a significant role in the subjective evaluation of which conditions qualify as disorders (Wakefield's harm criterion). Obsessive jealousy may feel useful and even desirable to the jealous person but painful and distressing to his or her partners; in cases like this, the problem of whose perspective one should take in deciding whether a condition is harmful is not a trivial one (Cosmides & Tooby, 1999). In other instances, individual strategies may be viewed as disorders because they conflict with the values of a certain group or society—to illustrate, conditions involving extreme shyness and social anxiety may be considered harmful in large cities and cultures that value extraversion but not necessarily so in small-scale, traditional societies based on kinship ties.

A final case to consider is that of "self-sacrificial" adaptations designed to inflict significant costs on the person who expresses them to the advantage of other people. Altruistic adaptations of this kind can be selected for if they benefit related individuals, who (depending on the context and level of analysis) may be close relatives, extended family members, or even members of the same extended social group. In principle, even suicide—the ultimate form of self-harming behavior—can be favored by natural selection if the potential benefits of surviving are smaller than the reproductive cost imposed on the individual's relatives (de Catanzaro, 1991). Accordingly, there is some evidence that perceptions of being a burden to one's family strongly predict suicidal ideation—especially when coupled with poor health, mating failures (e.g., divorce, rejection by a partner), social isolation, and other indicators of limited reproductive prospects (e.g., Brown et al., 2009; de Catanzaro, 1995). Self-sacrificial adaptations may also evolve in the context of sexual and/or social selection for altruism, cooperation, and other moral dispositions. Preferences for altruistic social partners may sustain runaway selection cycles for extreme levels of psychological traits such as need for acceptance, fear of rejection, and sensitivity to guilt and shame (Nesse, 2007). The idea that adaptive mechanisms may trigger pathological forms of altruism is starting to receive more attention in the evolutionary literature (see Oakley et al., 2012).

Fertility as a Measure of Adaptiveness

When one considers the possibility that a certain condition may be a biologically adaptive strategy, it is intuitive to look for evidence of enhanced fertility in individuals with that condition (e.g., Jacobson, 2016). This is obviously a useful piece of information, but simply equating individual fertility with adaptiveness can be misleading. While dramatic losses of fertility are virtually always maladaptive, subtler variations can often be interpreted in multiple ways; in most cases, there is no substitute for a full-fledged analysis that integrates multiple strands of evidence and reasoning, from mathematical models to demonstrations of special design (Schmitt & Pilcher, 2004).

A first reason why present fertility may not be a valid measure of past adaptiveness is the confounding effect of modern technologies for birth control and abortion, which can largely uncouple mating success from actual reproduction (Chapter 4). A second and more general reason is that natural selection does not maximize individual fertility but inclusive fitness—a weighted combination of an individual's reproduction and that of related individuals. As a result, even a significant loss of personal fitness can be compensated for by a sufficient gain in relatives or group members. This is why many studies of fertility in psychiatric patients also measure reproductive outcomes in parents, siblings, and offspring (e.g., Power et al., 2013). This point applies even more forcefully to self-sacrificial adaptations, which may dramatically reduce the individual's personal fitness for the benefit of others.

Finally and least intuitively, quality–quantity tradeoffs in life history allocation imply that sometimes the optimal strategy is to have *fewer* rather than more offspring. The adaptive nature of quality-oriented life history strategies only becomes apparent across multiple generations; this creates a formidable methodological challenge for studies of personality and psychopathology in humans, since the available data are normally restricted to just one cohort and rarely span two generations (e.g., Berg et al., 2014; MacCabe et al., 2009). Even if data on several generations became available, it would still be important to carefully consider how modern conditions—social welfare, medical advances, improved nutrition—may have altered the strength and nature of quality–quantity tradeoffs in our species, for example by increasing the health and survival of children who grow up under conditions of low parental investment.

THE SHAPE OF DISORDERS

I now consider two important questions about the phenotypic and causal structure of mental disorders: Are disorders best understood as discrete categories or as extremes of a continuum of variation? And what explains the covariation between the symptoms of a disorder? Many recent innovations and trends in psychopathology stem precisely from these questions, and the answers will shape the evolution of the discipline over the next decades. I also review the main features of some emerging approaches and discuss their strengths and limitations from the vantage point of evolutionary psychopathology.

Categories Versus Dimensions

In the classic psychiatric approach, mental disorders are regarded as qualitatively distinct categories, clearly separated from each other and from normal functioning. This categorical view of disorders derives from the European tradition of descriptive psychopathology and is a central feature of the neo-Kraepelinian perspective that has informed the DSM taxonomy since the 1980s. In this approach—named after the German psychiatrist Emil Kraepelin, who revolutionized the psychiatric classification of disorders in the 19th century—the symptoms that define a disorder are expected to occur together in a coherent "syndrome." This expectation rests on the assumption that each disorder is a homogeneous entity with a specific etiology; that is, a single underlying dysfunction that causes the observed symptoms (see Paris & Phillips, 2013).

The limits of the classic categorical model have become increasingly apparent over the decades. Attempts to isolate specific etiologies for mental disorders have been largely unsuccessful, consistent with the idea that most disorders reflect the activity of multiple mechanisms and may arise from multiple causal pathways—mutations, infections, environmental stressors—that happen to converge on the same downstream processes. Advances in clinical genetics and neuroscience have shown that, in many cases, diagnostic categories that were assumed to be unitary are in fact heterogeneous and comprise functionally distinct conditions with different etiologies and risk factors (Lilienfeld et al., 2013; Widiger & Gore, 2014). Another important development in this respect has been the increasing diffusion of a family of statistical procedures known as *taxometrics* (Waller & Meehl, 1998). Taxometric methods are designed to assess whether disorders represent nonarbitrary classes or *taxa*—that is, if they differ from normal behavior in kind and not just in degree (Figure 5.3). In contrast with the classic view, taxometric studies consistently indicate that most mental disorders are better described as extremes of normal variation rather than discrete categories. This means that, as a rule, the boundary between normality and pathology is arbitrary and does not reflect a discontinuity in the real world. (Of course, conventional distinctions are inevitable or even desirable when making practical decisions; e.g., who should receive treatment or qualify for insurance.) There are some likely exceptions to this general pattern: autism, schizotypy/schizophrenia, substance abuse, and some eating disorders may involve true discontinuities in addition to differences in degree. The somatic symptoms associated with certain subtypes of depressive and bipolar disorders also seem to have a taxonic nature (Coghill & Sonuga-Barke, 2012; Haslam et al., 2012).

The crisis of the classic view has gone hand in hand with two growing trends in psychopathology: the movement to replace categorical diagnoses with dimensional ones and the shift in focus from broad unitary syndromes to specific neural/

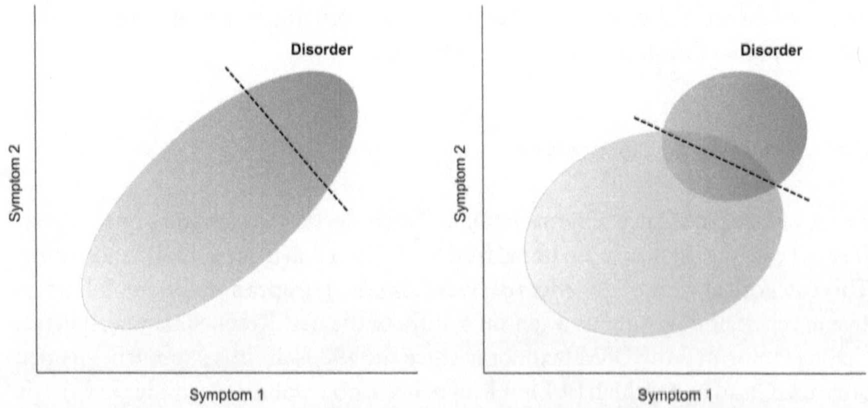

Figure 5.3. Mental disorders as dimensions vs. taxa. On the left, the disorder is the extreme of a distribution of symptoms, and the boundary between normality and pathology is arbitrary. On the right, the disorder is a discrete category (taxon), and the boundary between normality and pathology reflects a true discontinuity in the symptoms.

psychological mechanisms and their dysfunctions. One of the original goals of DSM-5 was precisely that of implementing a dimensional diagnostic system. The goal has been reached only in minimal part, and most diagnoses in the DSM are still categorical; however, the criteria for some disorders—notably autism and, to some extent, personality disorders—have been revised to be more consistent with a dimensional model (Widiger & Gore, 2014).

A dimensional view is also a key feature of the transdiagnostic approach to psychopathology (Carragher et al., 2015; Eaton et al., 2015; Forbes et al., 2016; Kotov et al., 2017; Krueger & Markon, 2006; Rodriguez-Seijas et al., 2015). This approach aims to identify broad factors of individual variation (*transdiagnostic factors*) that underlie both personality and mental disorders at a structural level. The classic structure of transdiagnostic models includes an *internalizing* factor characterized by negative emotionality (fear, depression, anxiety), an *externalizing* factor characterized by disinhibition, impulsivity, and aggression, and a *thought disorder* factor for psychotic symptoms. More recently, empirical studies have identified a general factor of psychopathology or *p factor*, which explains individual differences in susceptibility to mental disorders above and beyond the other transdiagnostic dimensions. An additional autism spectrum factor has also been proposed to account for autistic symptoms within the same structural model (Carragher et al., 2016; Caspi et al., 2014; Laceulle et al., 2015; Lahey et al., 2011, 2015; Noordhof et al., 2015; Patalay et al., 2015). At least in principle, the DSM-5 embraces the distinction between internalizing and externalizing disorders as a useful organizing framework for psychopathology (American Psychiatric Association, 2013, p. 13). The most sophisticated transdiagnostic model to date is the *hierarchical taxonomy of psychopathology* (HiTOP) advanced by Kotov and colleagues (2017). The HiTOP model is an attempt to synthesize much of the existing literature in the area. In its current form, it comprises five main dimensions or spectra: internalizing, externalizing-disinhibited, externalizing-antagonistic, thought disorder, and detachment. While the HiTOP does not include an autistic spectrum, it contains a tentative *somatoform* spectrum for pain disorder and other conditions marked by somatic symptoms. The hierarchical structure of the model allows for higher order factors above the main spectra, including a general p factor (Kotov et al., 2017).

The ongoing shift toward a focus on specific etiological processes is best represented by the RDoC approach. An explicit goal of RDoC is to break away from categorical diagnosis to embrace a fully dimensional view of psychiatric symptoms. Even more importantly, the RDoC approach focuses on individual, well-defined mechanisms (e.g., the attachment system, sleep–wakefulness circuits) to understand how specific dysfunctions in those systems translate into clinically relevant symptom dimensions. The dimensions identified in this way may sometimes cut across traditional diagnostic categories; for example, similar dysfunctions in sleep–wakefulness mechanisms may be involved in a broad range of disorders including depression, anxiety, and posttraumatic stress. One of the long-term goals of the RDoC approach is to reconstruct the classification of mental disorders from the bottom up, with the focal point firmly set at the neurobiological level of analysis (Cuthbert & Insel, 2013; Insel et al., 2010).

Evolutionary Perspective

From an evolutionary standpoint, broad-sense disorders are a highly heterogeneous assortment of conditions ranging from local dysfunctions to adaptive behavioral strategies (Figure 5.1). This state of things is incompatible with the classic categorical view of disorders as self-contained syndromes; however, it does not automatically support the equally rigid idea that *all* disorders must be intrinsically dimensional. The most reasonable prediction is that at least some disorders (or disorder subtypes) will turn out to reflect true qualitative differences in mental functioning. Categorical syndromes of this kind should often involve harmful dysfunctions, which are the most likely cause of discontinuity between normal and pathological behavior. At the same time, even the risk of experiencing a discrete, specific dysfunction is likely to depend—at least in part—on individual differences in the function and functionality of the relevant mechanisms. For this reason, most conditions should have at least *some* dimensional component, even when they involve taxonic differences; moreover, the main dimensions of clinical variation can be expected to overlap to a large degree with normal variation in personality and cognition, as postulated by the transdiagnostic approach.

Symptoms and Their Causes

Current descriptions of mental disorders are based on lists of symptoms, which raises the crucial question of what causes the symptoms to occur in specific combinations. The literature on psychopathology offers three main answers to this question (Figure 5.4). On the classic view, the symptoms that define a given disorder are caused by a single underlying dysfunction; conversely, statistical correlations between observable symptoms are explained by postulating the existence of a (typically unobserved) dysfunction. This "unitary disorder model" descends from the medical tradition and has contributed to shape the DSM classification, even if the DSM does not explicitly subscribe to a single-cause account of disorders. Some dysfunctions may be more likely to occur together because they share certain genetic or environmental risk factors; moreover, having one disorder may create vulnerabilities for other disorders, with the possibility of reciprocal causation (see Neale & Kendler, 1995). The key point is that, according to this model, whenever two disorders co-occur in the same person (*comorbidity*) it is because the person is experiencing both dysfunctions at the same time.

The RDoC approach is based on a different set of assumptions, rooted in experimental neuroscience rather than medicine. According to what could be labeled the "specific dysfunction model," symptoms and constellations of symptoms can be traced back to dysfunctions that affect specific neurobiological mechanisms. As a rule, disorders as conventionally defined are *not* unitary entities; instead, they reflect the combined effects of multiple dysfunctions occurring together (which may share some genetic or environmental risk factors). Crucially, a given dysfunction may be involved in the etiology of more than one disorder; the main explanation of comorbidity in this model is that ostensibly distinct diagnostic categories actually reflect the same underlying dysfunctions. Versions of the specific dysfunction model inform both the RDoC approach and the emerging field of computational psychiatry (Huys, Daw et al., 2015; Huys, Guitart-Masip et al., 2015*b*; Wang & Krystal, 2014; Wiecki et al., 2015). Computational psychiatry employs mathematical models of psychological and neural processes—such as decision-making, reinforcement learning, or synaptic excitation–inhibition—to identify the mechanisms involved in mental disorders and their dysfunctions. The neural and cognitive markers identified through computational modeling can then be measured experimentally and used to classify individuals into clusters, which may or may not correspond to conventional diagnostic categories.

A recent, radical alternative to both the unitary disorder model and the specific dysfunction model is the network approach to psychopathology (Borsboom & Cramer, 2013; Cramer et al., 2010*a*, 2010*b*; McNally, 2016). The network approach originates in psychometrics; in a nutshell, it rejects the classic idea that different symptoms are caused by a common unobserved dysfunction and embraces the alternative assumption that symptoms directly cause one another. For example, if depressed mood and concentration problems co-occur in depression, it is not because they reflect a common dysfunction but because depressed mood directly impairs concentration. Causal relationships between symptoms can be reciprocal, giving rise to feedback loops—sleep disturbances may worsen depressed mood, which in turn makes it more difficult to fall asleep, and so on. In total, psychiatric symptoms can be visualized as nodes of a large, interconnected causal network; disorders emerge as clusters of strongly

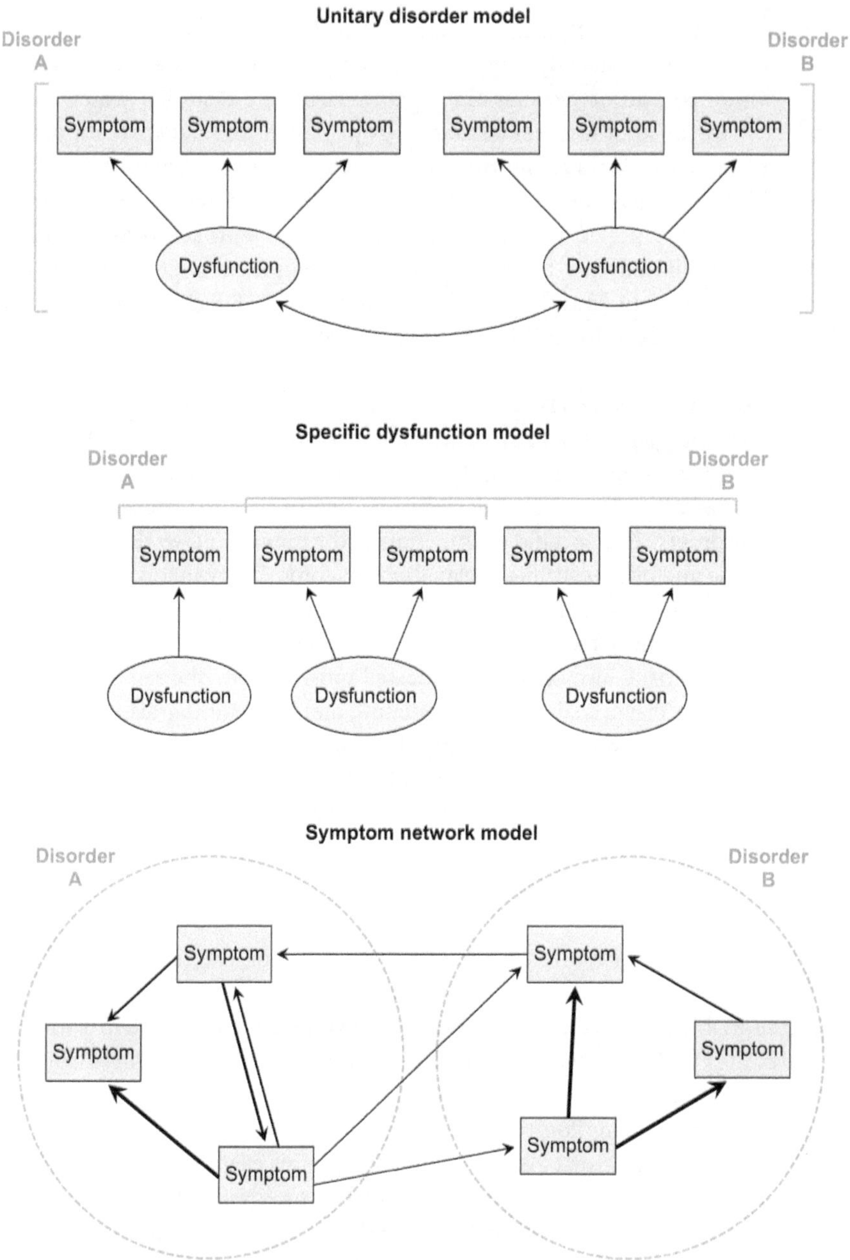

Figure 5.4. Three general models of the causal structure of mental disorders. Observed symptoms are shown as rectangles; dysfunctions are typically not observed or measured directly, and are shown as ellipses. In the unitary disorder model, the various symptoms of each disorder reflect a single underlying dysfunction. In the specific dysfunction model, a given disorder (conventionally defined) may involve multiple dysfunctions, and different disorders may share the same dysfunction. As a result, there is no simple correspondence between disorders and the underlying dysfunctions. In the symptom network model, symptoms directly cause one another, and disorders emerge as clusters of strongly connected symptoms (thicker arrows = stronger connections) without the need to postulate unobserved causal factors.

connected symptoms within the broader network. From this perspective, comorbidity occurs because disorders overlap (two or more clusters share some core symptoms) and/or because the symptoms of one disorder are causally connected to those of another disorder. In principle, the network approach can be extended to include intermediate variables, cognitive/neurobiological vulnerabilities, and other entities that are not observed symptoms (Cramer et al., 2010*b*). In practice, though, proponents of this approach favor the view that disorders literally *are* their symptoms, and empirical applications so far have been limited to "pure" symptom networks (e.g., Boschloo et al., 2015; Goekoop & Goekoop, 2014; Wigman et al., 2015).

Evolutionary Perspective

From an evolutionary perspective, there is no reason to expect that all mental disorders will share the same causal structure. In fact, it is quite plausible that different types of structural models are more appropriate to describe different types of disorders. The specific dysfunction and symptom network models are both valuable and offer plausible explanations of comorbidity that go beyond the assumptions of the classic view. In particular, the network approach shines a spotlight on the possibility that some symptoms may arise as a direct consequence of other symptoms; it also offers sophisticated tools to study the self-reinforcing cycles that often play a major role in initiating and maintaining disorders (e.g., Hofmann, 2014). However, a rigid application of the model (e.g., pure symptom networks that exclude other causal factors) is unlikely to be successful in the long run, given the sheer diversity of the biological processes that give rise to psychopathological conditions (Figure 5.1).

Strengths and Limitations of Current Approaches

Both the RDoC approach and computational psychiatry are consistent with the model of the mind as a network of specialized mechanisms presented in Chapter 2. At the same time, these approaches share a number of limitations, first and foremost the default assumption that clinical symptoms arise from dysfunctions in the underlying mechanisms. As I have discussed in this chapter, many conditions diagnosed as broad-sense disorders may not be true dysfunctions or, alternatively, may reflect a mixture of functional and dysfunctional processes. Another limitation—arguably inherited from the tradition of experimental neuroscience—is a strong emphasis on individual brain mechanisms coupled with a neglect of how multiple mechanisms coordinate their activity into broadband patterns of personality and physiology. Without the benefit of top-down insight into the nature of individual differences and their adaptive significance, a purely bottom-up approach is unlikely to succeed—especially when dealing with conditions that do not reflect harmful dysfunctions but rather mismatches, maladaptive outcomes, or undesirable adaptations.

Current instantiations of RDoC and computational psychiatry are also constrained by their focus on a relatively narrow subset of mechanisms and processes. For example, the "social processes" domain of RDoC includes affiliation and attachment but makes no mention of mating, sexuality, or dominance/status. These are striking omissions given the centrality of sex, mating, and dominance competition in the evolution and organization of behavior. While the "negative valence" domain of RDoC draws a useful functional distinction between fear and anxiety, key social emotions such as guilt and shame are framed as manifestations of the generic construct of "loss" (National Institute of Mental Health, 2018). In total, current RDoC domains and constructs fail to add up to a coherent account of motivation and self-regulation; hopefully, the situation will improve in future revisions of the framework. Similar considerations apply to models in computational psychiatry, which tend to focus on abstract, "domain-general" processes (e.g., reinforcement learning, synaptic potentiation) and fail to consider the fitness costs and benefits of behavior in specific adaptive domains (see Del Giudice, 2016*c*; more on this in Chapter 21).

As noted earlier, the network approach challenges simplistic assumptions about the nature of disorders and places a much-needed emphasis on the complex causal pathways that give rise to symptoms and their combinations. Also, this approach is less wedded to the assumption that symptoms reflect dysfunctions and can easily accommodate a variety of conditions, both adaptive and maladaptive. In practice, however, network models have been limited by a restrictive focus on symptoms and a neglect of shared causal mechanisms. As an example, consider somatic symptoms of depression such as sleep disturbances, restlessness, fatigue, and weight gain or loss. A network approach correctly stresses that these symptoms can directly influence each other—restlessness interferes with sleep, while disturbed sleep exacerbates fatigue (Cramer et al., 2010*a*). However, it is also true that all the relevant physiological mechanisms are modulated by the stress response system, and changes in cortisol levels may simultaneously induce clusters of somatic symptoms above and beyond their reciprocal influences (e.g., Miller, Chen et al., 2007; Taylor & Fink, 2008). More generally, regulatory mechanisms can be specifically designed to coordinate the activity of multiple specialized systems (Chapter 2). Ironically, a rigid application of the network approach can easily miss key aspects of the functional organization of behavior and encourage a skewed understanding of the etiology of disorders. Other limitations of this approach concern the statistical techniques used to model symptom networks, which tend to suffer from low replicability even in large samples (Forbes et al., 2017).

In contrast with the approaches reviewed so far, transdiagnostic models directly aim to identify broad top-down patterns in the structure of psychopathology. This line of research has yielded many important and heuristically valid findings, including the p factor and the internalizing–externalizing distinction. In addition, a transdiagnostic perspective has helped reveal deep patterns of continuity in the development of mental disorders across life stages (e.g., Lahey et al., 2014). The main limitation of this approach is the lack of a functional model of individual differences. In absence of deeper theoretical principles, researchers have no choice but to take patterns of correlations between symptoms at face value: the resulting dimensions can be statistically and empirically robust while still failing to "carve nature at its joints." In particular, I have argued that the same empirical findings that support the internalizing–externalizing distinction and the existence of a general p factor can be explained more satisfyingly within in a life history framework (Del Giudice, 2014*a*, 2016*d*; discussed in Chapter 6).

6

The Life History Framework and the FSD Model

The concepts discussed in Chapter 5 can be used to analyze specific symptoms and disorders in evolutionary terms (Brüne, 2015; McGuire & Troisi, 1998; Nesse, 2015). However, they still fall short of providing a coherent theoretical framework for the discipline. A compelling framework should meet four main challenges: (a) explain observed patterns of comorbidity between disorders; (b) address the problem of heterogeneity within diagnostic categories; (c) bridge psychopathology with normative individual differences in personality and cognition; and (d) make sense of the developmental features of mental disorders, including their life course trajectories and early risk factors. The life history framework I present in this chapter meets all these challenges and offers an alternative taxonomy of disorders based on functional criteria. In earlier versions of the framework I introduced the distinction between *fast spectrum* and *slow spectrum disorders* (Del Giudice, 2014*a*, 2014*b*, 2016*c*, 2016*d*). Here, I update and revise that initial formulation in a number of ways. In particular, I supplement the fast–slow spectrum distinction with the novel category of *defense activation disorders*. The tripartite distinction between fast spectrum, slow spectrum, and defense activation disorders is the foundation of the fast-slow-defense (FSD) model of psychopathology. I describe the FSD model and discuss its predictions about sex differences, developmental patterns, and risk factors for the three categories of disorders. At the end of the chapter, I explore some additional implications of the model, consider the role of general intelligence in the origin of psychopathology, and compare the FSD taxonomy with the structural models based on the transdiagnostic approach.

HOW TO READ THIS CHAPTER

This chapter presents a large amount of information, including a bird's eye view of the FSD model in its complete form. It is important to keep in mind that the reasons for sorting disorders into the three FSD categories and splitting them into functional subtypes are explained in detail in the analytical chapters of Part III (Chapters 7–20). The chapters of Part III also discuss limitations, anomalies, and unknowns with respect to the classification of each disorder. There are two reasons for introducing the full model before examining individual disorders in depth. First, many readers will likely find it useful to get a sense of the big picture before delving into the intricacies of diagnostic categories and their subtypes. Second, there is a practical advantage in placing all the information about the life history framework in a single reference chapter instead of dispersing it throughout the book. At the same time, some of the information presented here may become easier to appreciate when one is more familiar with the details of individual disorders. This is why I recommend coming back to this chapter after finishing Part III for a synthesis and recapitulation of the framework.

A FUNCTIONAL TAXONOMY OF MENTAL DISORDERS

Fast and Slow Spectrum Disorders

In Chapter 4, I discussed how life history strategies organize broad functional patterns of individual and sex differences. By coordinating variation across multiple traits, life history strategies also set the stage for the development of psychopathology. Different strategies and profiles are associated with differences in motivation, self-regulation, personality, cognition, and neurobiological functioning (Figure 4.3; Table 4.1), which in turn increase (or decrease) the risk of developing different types of mental disorders. As one moves along the fast–slow continuum, some symptoms and disorders should become more frequent, while others should become less likely to occur. This is the functional basis for the distinction between fast spectrum (or *F-type*) disorders and slow spectrum (or *S-type*) disorders—that is, disorders that cluster at the fast or slow end of the life history continuum (Del Giudice, 2014*a*). For example, fast strategists are more at risk for disorders that involve impulsivity and antisocial behavior; in contrast, slow strategists tend to develop disorders involving behavioral constraint, exaggerated self-control, or reduced sexual motivation. Moreover, alternative profiles within fast and slow strategies are associated with specific constellations of disorders; for example, schizophrenia and other psychotic disorders are characterized by exaggerated mentalistic cognition and arise mainly in the context of seductive/creative strategies; conversely, autism risk is associated with reduced mentalistic skills and other traits that define the skilled/provisioning profile (see Del Giudice et al., 2010, 2014*a*).

In sum, the core proposition of the life history framework is that risk for different types of mental disorders partly depends on broader patterns of individual differences, which in turn can be functionally understood as manifestations of alternative life history strategies. This correspondence makes it possible to classify disorders based on their connections with different strategies and profiles within those strategies. Interestingly, the distinction between fast and slow spectrum disorders recovers some classic ideas about *undercontrolled* versus *overcontrolled* profiles of self-regulation and their links to different clusters of mental disorders (e.g., Block, 2002; Block & Block, 1980; Huey & Weisz, 1997). However, the life history perspective has a wider scope and situates individual differences in self-regulation within a much larger network of interconnected traits that spans personality, cognitive abilities, and sexual maturation (Chapter 4).

A common misconception about the life history framework is that, since fast and slow spectrum disorders are functionally linked to adaptive patterns of individual differences, they should also be understood as adaptive strategies in their own respect. While this may apply to some particular conditions, the distinction between F-type and S-type disorders is much more general and does not depend on the assumption that mental disorders are adaptive. By modulating the expression of multiple traits and the functioning parameters of key psychological mechanisms, life history allocations can increase or decrease the risk for *all* kinds of broad-sense disorders, from harmful dysfunctions to adaptive strategies. To restate: the life history framework does not assume that all or even most mental disorders are adaptations; both the fast and slow spectrum of psychopathology include plenty of maladaptive and/or dysfunctional conditions alongside adaptive or potentially adaptive strategies.

Multiple Causal Pathways

A more detailed analysis based on the taxonomy presented in Chapter 5 suggests the existence of several potential pathways from life history strategy to psychopathology. To begin, adaptive life history–related traits may be regarded as symptoms because of their undesirable features. This is most likely to occur in relation to antisocial, exploitative, or socially devalued strategies (e.g., psychopathic traits, mild autistic symptoms). Other times, life history–related traits that are adaptive on average may yield individually maladaptive outcomes. An especially interesting case occurs when potentially adaptive traits (e.g., mentalistic cognition) are expressed at maladaptive levels—for example as a result of assortative mating between two individuals high (or low) on the same trait, or as a maladaptive side effect of intragenomic conflict. Consistent with this view, a number of mental disorders—most notably autism, schizophrenia, and attention-deficit/hyperactivity disorder (ADHD)—show fairly high rates of assortative mating, with correlations between partners in the .40–.50 range (Nordsletten et al., 2016). Finally, life history–related traits may directly or indirectly increase a person's vulnerability to specific types of dysfunctions. Upregulation of serotonergic signaling may render the system especially sensitive to mutations in serotonin-related genes; increased motivation for affiliation and reciprocity may make people vulnerable to developing harmful levels of guilt and shame (Oakley et al., 2012). In the etiology of dysfunctions, individual traits and vulnerabilities interact with a range of environmental insults such as infections, nutritional deficits, and psychosocial stressors. Intriguingly, fast traits such as risk proneness and sexual promiscuity may increase an individual's exposure to environmental risk factors (e.g., pathogens, injuries, traumatic events), further increasing the risk of harmful dysfunctions.

Because individual differences in life history affect the risk of psychopathology through multiple causal pathways, the life history framework does not apply only to "trait-like" disorders characterized by developmentally stable configurations of symptoms (e.g., autism, personality disorders), but also to "state-like" disorders whose onset reflects a distinct change in psychological functioning (e.g., eating disorders, depression; see Kennair, 2014). Importantly, the fact that stable life history–related traits (e.g., impulsivity, overcontrol) predispose people to develop some pathological conditions does not mean that treatments for those conditions should necessarily target the predisposing traits. Treatments that address specific symptoms and the psychological processes that maintain them can be highly effective in resolving a disorder (Kennair, 2007). However, it is also possible to design broadband interventions that seek to modify aspects of the patient's personality instead of focusing on a particular symptom or condition (Barlow, Sauer-Zavala et al., 2014; Norton & Paulus, 2016; Roberts et al., 2017). The evidence indicates that cognitive-behavioral treatments based on the two approaches are about equally effective (Pearl & Norton, 2017). This is not surprising: if mental disorders arise from complex causal pathways, it should often be possible to intervene at different levels with similar clinical results.

Defense Activation Disorders

As discussed in Chapter 5, defensive mechanisms are a major source of psychiatric symptoms. Many negative emotions—such as fear, anxiety, shame, and disgust—can be construed as self-protective reactions to social and nonsocial threats (Gilbert, 1992, 1995; Nesse, 2005*a*, 2015; Nesse & Jackson, 2006). To some degree, these emotions contribute to the phenomenology of many if not most mental disorders; for example, autism is often associated with social anxiety, and shame is a pervasive correlate of eating disorders (e.g., Allan & Goss, 2012). However, some disorders *primarily* consist of symptoms that reflect the activation of a defensive mechanism. I propose to group those conditions into a distinct functional category, that of defense activation or *D-type* disorders. Conditions such as phobias, panic, posttraumatic stress, generalized anxiety, and depression can be understood as manifestations of strongly activated defenses; of course, this does not mean that these conditions are necessarily beneficial to fitness. While there is no doubt that aversive reactions such as panic and anxiety *can* be adaptive, defense activation errors in absence of a threat may also yield maladaptive outcomes. Defensive mechanisms may also become damaged or dysregulated, giving rise to harmful dysfunctions. In short, D-type disorders may belong to any of the biological categories listed in Figure 5.1.

Defenses and the Fast–Slow Continuum

Danger, threats, and mortality risk are among the aspects of the environment that most strongly contribute to determine life history allocations. There is no doubt that life history strategies have broad implications for the regulation of defenses; however, the relations between life history variation and specific patterns of defense activation are far from straightforward. This is why the list of life history–related features in Table 4.1 is notably lacking in defense-related traits, with the exception of disgust sensitivity. The adaptive calibration model (ACM) model of stress physiology (introduced in Chapter 4) helps illustrate this concept. According to the model, hyperreactive profiles tend to develop at both the slow end (sensitive pattern) and the fast end of variation (vigilant pattern), while a subset of fast strategists develop hyporeactive profiles (unemotional pattern; Figure 4.2). Even if stress physiology has deep functional connections with life history strategies, those connections do not translate into a simple fast–slow gradient of stress reactivity.

More generally, there are reasons to predict that patterns of upregulated defenses should become more common at both ends of the fast–slow continuum (Del Giudice, 2014*a*; Lienard, 2011). In the context of fast life histories, hair-trigger defenses contribute to protect the person from immediate danger in a threatening, unpredictable environment. In the context of slow strategies, upregulated defenses may help prevent dangerous events and avoid potentially risky situations in the future, even if the present environment is reasonably safe and predictable. Protecting oneself against even minor sources of harm contributes to the long-term maintenance of somatic investment—a key priority for slow strategists, who make major investments in embodied capital. Also, when the environment is safe and threats are rare, the benefits of sensitive defenses can be afforded without paying the costs of hyperactivation. Chronic defense activation is much more likely to occur in stressful and chaotic environments that expose people to repeated, high-intensity threats.

These considerations suggest that, all else being equal, D-type conditions should arise relatively more often in dangerous, stressful environments—which is to say, contexts that also favor the development of fast life history strategies. Moreover, the behavioral traits associated with fast strategies (e.g., risk-taking, impulsivity) increase the chance of experiencing stressful events such as accidents, romantic breakups, and job losses; the cumulative effect of such events further contributes to increase defense activation and with it the risk of D-type disorders. At the level of personality traits, neuroticism is the principal marker of upregulated defense activation. Neuroticism covaries with low agreeableness and conscientiousness as part of metatrait alpha, and some of its facets measure antagonistic negative emotions such as anger and hostility. This pattern of correlations contributes to predict a stronger association between defense activation and F-type disorders compared with S-type disorders. In general, females have more to lose than men from both physical damage and social rejection (Archer, 2009; Benenson, 2013, 2014; Campbell, 2004; Martel, 2013); accordingly, D-type disorders can be expected to be markedly more

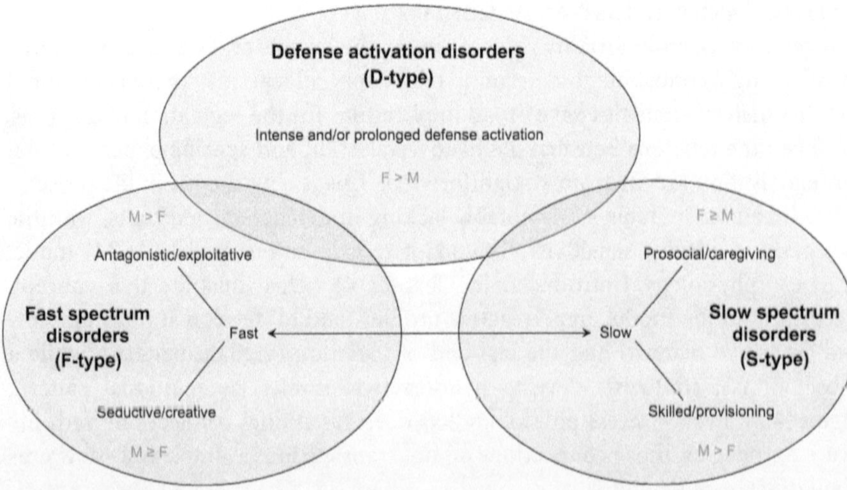

Figure 6.1. Conceptual structure of the FSD classification model. Overlap between disorder categories represents comorbidity. While defense activation disorders may arise at both ends of the fast-slow continuum, they are expected to occur more frequently in associations with fast spectrum disorders. F = females. M = males.

common in females, especially as one moves toward the fast end of the continuum. Figure 6.1 illustrates the relation between defense activation disorders and fast–slow spectrum disorders in the FSD model. As shown in the figure, D-type disorders occur at both ends of the fast–slow continuum; however, their specific symptoms may vary to some extent depending on the person's life history profile and comorbid conditions. For example, symptoms of worry involve a preoccupation with potential events in the future (e.g., losing one's job, becoming ill) rather than a focus on immediate threats (Chapter 15). Interestingly, the facets of neuroticism associated with worry tend to predict better physical health and increased longevity, in contrast with those associated with anxiety (Hill, Weiss et al., 2017). It is reasonable to hypothesize that D-type conditions involving intense worry may co-occur relatively more often with disorders in the slow spectrum given their future-oriented focus on harm prevention (see Fernandes et al., 2018).

The concept of defense activation disorders calls attention to the specular possibility that some conditions may primarily reflect a *lack* of activation of adaptive defenses in contexts that would require a vigorous response (pain insensitivity and immunosuppression are medical examples). Instances of systematic defense downregulation are more likely to occur in association with fast strategies, especially with behavioral profiles characterized by high levels of risk-taking. The underlying logic is that, in order to be successful, high-risk strategies require outright insensitivity to threats and dangers, including powerful social threats such as disapproval and rejection. Moreover, unresponsive strategies can mitigate the costs of inappropriate or excessive defense activation when the environment becomes too unpredictable or threatening (Del Giudice et al., 2011; Korte et al., 2005). In general, males benefit from risk-taking more than females; for this reason, they should also be more vulnerable to pathological forms of defense downregulation.

Evolutionary scholars have long pointed out that standard diagnostic systems may be neglecting the existence of conditions marked by a dangerous lack of defense activation (Horwitz & Wakefield, 2012; Nesse, 1990). Conditions of this kind could be labeled *defense inactivation disorders* (abbreviated as lowercase *d-type* disorders, to distinguish them from D-type disorders marked by exaggerated activation). The *Diagnostic and Statistical Manual* (DSM) includes many disorders characterized by defense hyperactivation, but virtually no conditions whose core symptoms reflect defense hypoactivation. The only potential exception is "disinhibited social engagement disorder," a childhood condition whose key symptom is lack of fear and reticence in approaching unfamiliar adults (American Psychiatric Association, 2013). Of course, several common disorders are characterized by a degree of defense inactivation—for example, insensitivity to fear is an important component of psychopathy (Fowles & Dindo, 2006; Hughes et al., 2012). However, failures of defense activation are not as dramatic and subjectively aversive as strong defensive reactions; as a result, even legitimate dysfunctions of this kind may not be regarded as pathological when they occur on their own (that is, they may fail to meet Wakefield's harm criterion). Given the dearth of information at this time, it would be premature to explicitly include this type of condition in the FSD model; still, this remains a fascinating area for future research.

Applying the Framework

The classification scheme summarized in Figure 6.1 can be employed with two distinct but complementary goals. The first goal is to map the large-scale structure of psychopathology by describing broad patterns of comorbidity between disorders (Del Giudice, 2016*d*). The second is to identify functionally heterogeneous conditions within existing diagnostic categories. Importantly, the FSD classification is not meant to replace specific evolutionary models of individual disorders; rather, the goal is to integrate and connect them under the theoretical umbrella of the life history framework.

Patterns of Comorbidity

The life history framework maps the structure of psychopathology on two main axes of variation: a primary axis aligned with the fast–slow continuum (risk for F-type versus S-type disorders) and a secondary axis that captures the tendency to display strong and/or sustained defense activation (risk for D-type disorders). In addition to these two axes of comorbidity, low cognitive ability contributes to increase the risk for most mental disorders, as I discuss in more detail later. Females are generally at higher risk for defense activation conditions than are males, while fast and slow spectrum disorders may show different associations with sex depending on their relations with specific life history profiles (e.g., disorders linked to the skilled/provisioning profile should be more common in males).

It is important to appreciate that, at this level of analysis, comorbidity is explained by the existence of underlying patterns of individual differences in the function and/or functionality of psychological processes. These differences are reflected in personality traits and profiles of motivation and cognitive ability (Table 4.1). From this perspective, two disorders may co-occur within individuals and families even in the absence of a shared underlying dysfunction (as postulated by the Research Domain Criteria [RDoC] approach) or a direct causal "bridge" between their symptoms (as assumed by the network approach). The idea that large-scale patterns of comorbidity stem from broad dimensions of individual variation rather than disorder-specific risk factors is in line with the spirit of the transdiagnostic approach. At the same time, the FSD model carves up the landscape of psychopathology in a way that only partially matches the internalizing–externalizing distinction and other features of the transdiagnostic model. In a later section, I compare the two models in detail and highlight the advantages of the FSD taxonomy.

While the broad dimensions described by the FSD model offer a useful first approximation of the structure of psychopathology, they are hardly exhaustive. Within each of the three main FSD categories (F-type, S-type, D-type) one finds smaller clusters of disorders that share particular traits or risk factors. Comorbidity clusters may arise from specific combinations of life history–related traits; for example the combination of increased mentalizing, high openness to experience, and disinhibition in the seductive/creative profile may increase the risk for a number of related conditions in the schizophrenia and bipolar spectrum. On an even finer scale, two disorders may co-occur because they share a specific causal factor—a particular dysfunction in the same psychological mechanisms or a certain set of genetic/epigenetic variants. This level of analysis is the one emphasized by the RDoC approach, which seeks to identify dysfunctions at the level of specific neurobiological mechanisms.

Functional Heterogeneity

Because diagnostic categories in the DSM are mainly based on symptom similarity, they may fail to capture important distinctions between conditions that have different functional underpinnings but show similar constellations of symptoms. The problem of heterogeneity is widely recognized in the discipline; however, there are many possible ways to draw distinctions within a diagnostic category, and without sound theoretical criteria the task of subtyping can become overwhelming. The FSD model can be used as a lens to identify meaningful variants within existing diagnostic categories. The life history correlates reviewed in Chapter 4 can be used as convergent "markers" to locate a condition (and its subtypes) within the functional space of Figure 6.1. For example, it is possible to describe fast and slow spectrum subtypes of eating disorders that are primarily characterized by differences in risk factors and associated personality features rather than specific symptoms (Chapter 13; Del Giudice, 2014*a*).

The task of identifying variants or subtypes within existing categories is not disconnected from that of describing large-scale comorbidity—in fact, the former is a precondition for the latter. As it turns out, not all disorders in the DSM can be assigned unambiguously to the fast or slow spectrum; in a number of cases, a life history analysis suggests the existence of functionally distinct conditions whose symptoms are similar enough that they are diagnosed as the same disorder in the DSM taxonomy. This is fully expected—the whole point of a functional approach is to redraw the boundaries between disorders based on their underlying organization *rather than* just symptom similarity. However, splitting existing categories into subtypes based on alternative criteria remains a radical move, considering that symptom similarity has played a central role in psychiatric classification for most of recent history. For example, arguing that attention and hyperactivity symptoms are best regarded as manifestations of at least three functionally distinct conditions instead of a unitary ADHD category (Chapter 11) may strike some as wildly unparsimonious (e.g., Martel, 2014). However, it is important to realize that—to the extent that DSM categories are internally heterogeneous—this is the inevitable consequence of any approach to classification based on functional rather than purely symptomatic criteria. In the life history framework, the parsimony lost at the level of individual categories is recovered at the level of broad functional distinctions (Figure 6.1) and the resulting large-scale model of comorbidity.

Contemporary approaches to psychopathology differ in how they deal with existing DSM categories. For example, most applications of the transdiagnostic approach are based on symptom scores derived from DSM checklists (e.g., Caspi et al., 2014; Lahey et al., 2015; for a recent exception, see Carragher et al., 2016). At least implicitly, then, they assume the validity and internal consistency of the corresponding criteria. What differentiates transdiagnostic models from the DSM taxonomy is that symptom scores are used to define broader, continuous dimensions of variation (e.g., internalizing, externalizing, thought disorders). As a consequence, this approach has much to say about comorbidity but is virtually silent on the issue of heterogeneity *within* existing diagnostic categories.

The RDoC and computational approaches do not share this limitation; in fact, an explicit goal of RDoC is to reconstruct the taxonomy of mental disorders by identifying specific etiological processes that may cut across existing diagnostic categories and groups. To the extent that this approach is successful, it will inevitably generate distinctions that are not well captured by standard criteria of symptom similarity. Still, there is an important difference between the RDoC approach and the life history framework. From the standpoint of RDoC, new diagnostic boundaries are expected to emerge from the bottom up as knowledge of neurobiological mechanisms and their potential dysfunctions accumulates; in contrast, the life history approach starts with broad, functionally meaningful distinctions (e.g., between fast and slow spectrum disorders) and uses them as heuristics to identify heterogeneity within existing categories. While the two approaches rest on different methodological premises, they are not incompatible—the focus on specific mechanisms promoted by RDoC can be a useful complement to the kind of top-down analysis encouraged by the FSD model.

Nomenclature

Applying the life history framework to specific disorders raises the issue of how to deal with existing diagnostic labels. In general, evolutionary models of mental disorders have focused on DSM categories such as schizophrenia and ADHD, usually taking them at face value (see Brüne, 2015; McGuire & Troisi, 1998). However, a life history perspective suggests that at least some of these categories contain distinct subtypes that belong to different functional spectra. A possible option would be to discard DSM labels altogether or reject the standard diagnostic criteria as invalid. I believe this would be a mistake: while the DSM has several well-known limitations, many of its categories have substantial validity and descriptive power. Even radical bottom-up attempts inspired by the network approach end up recovering clusters of symptoms that closely resemble the major conditions described in the DSM. Similarly, computational methods applied to brain imaging data often converge with classic diagnostic distinctions (e.g., Bansal et al., 2012; Boschloo et al., 2015; Haubold et al., 2012). Moreover, from a pragmatic standpoint there are simply no realistic alternatives, since most of the empirical evidence available today has been collected using criteria from the various editions of the DSM.

For these reasons, in the remainder of the book I will use the standard nomenclature to refer to individual conditions (see Box 6.1 for a list of acronyms). To identify putative subtypes of a given disorder, I will simply add the relevant FSD descriptor to the label, as in "fast spectrum ADHD," "F-type ADHD," or "F-ADHD." For variants that seem to fall outside the FSD classification, I will use the descriptor "O-type" (for "other"), as in "O-type ADHD" or "O-ADHD." Whenever necessary, I will point to limitations and weaknesses in the current DSM criteria for certain disorders. This solution should be regarded as provisional; one should always remember that boundaries between conditions might not be so clear-cut as implied by existing classification systems, and that future research will likely suggest new categories and labels that may eventually replace the ones in use today. Figure 6.2. shows the classification of common mental disorders in the current version of the FSD model.

Scope of the FSD Model

As discussed in Chapter 5, mental disorders form a highly heterogeneous collection, with many possible evolutionary explanations and myriad proximate causes. No single set of taxonomic criteria can possibly capture all the important distinctions within psychopathology. Moreover, it is reasonable to expect that different criteria will prove more or less useful depending on the specific goal at hand. The primary goal of the FSD model is to map the large-scale structure of psychopathology on functionally significant dimensions of individual variation and to do so at the broadest level of analysis, that of life history strategies (Figure 6.2).

Box 6.1

Acronyms for Common Mental Disorders

ADHD: attention-deficit/hyperactivity disorder
AN: anorexia nervosa
APD: avoidant personality disorder
ASD: autism spectrum disorder
ASPD: antisocial personality disorder
BD: bipolar disorder
BED: binge-eating disorder
BN: bulimia nervosa
BPD: borderline personality disorder
CD: conduct disorder
ED: eating disorder
GAD: generalized anxiety disorder
MDD: major depressive disorder
NPD: narcissistic personality disorder
OCD: obsessive-compulsive disorder
OCPD: obsessive-compulsive personality disorder
ODD: oppositional-defiant disorder
PDD: persistent depressive disorder
PTSD: posttraumatic stress disorder
SAD: social anxiety disorder
SPD: schizotypal personality disorder
SSD: schizophrenia spectrum disorder
SUD: substance use disorder

It is easy to see how this classification approach can be supplemented by narrower distinctions, for example based on the involvement of specific motivational or self-regulatory mechanisms. Some of the resulting categories would be similar to those of the DSM (e.g., eating disorders), though others would not (e.g., disorders of mating and status). Indeed, other evolutionary scholars have suggested that motivational domains can be used heuristically to classify mental disorders (e.g., McGuire & Troisi, 1998; Stevens & Price, 2000). Another interesting approach would be to classify disorders based on their genetic structure, for example by distinguishing conditions that depend mainly on the effects of rare and de novo mutations from those that are largely influenced by common genetic variants. Given that different criteria may offer different and complementary insights into the nature of psychopathology, a pluralistic attitude toward classification is most likely to succeed the long run. In this book I explore the potential of the FSD model, while mapping out its boundaries and taking note of its inevitable limitations.

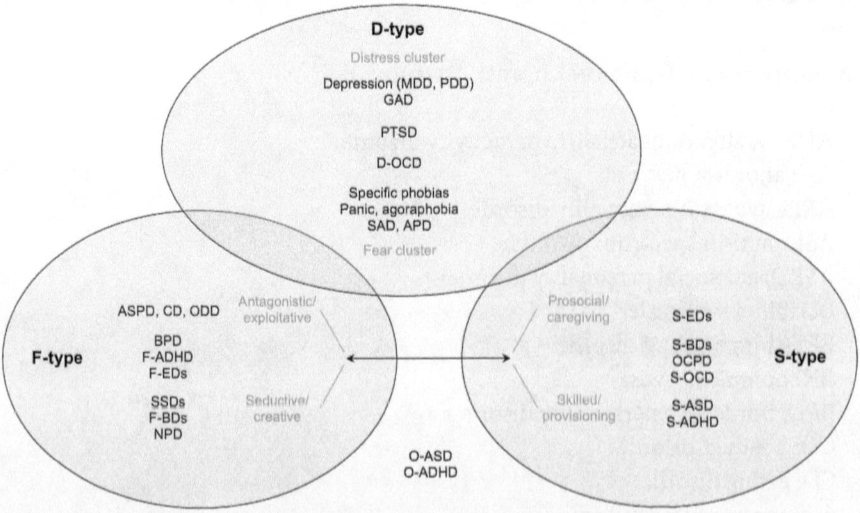

Figure 6.2. Fast spectrum (F-type), slow spectrum (S-type), and defense activation (D-type) disorders in the current version of the FSD model. Overlap between disorder categories represents comorbidity. Conditions that fall outside the FSD classification (O-type disorders) are shown at the bottom of the figure. ADHD = attention-deficit/hyperactivity disorder. APD = avoidant personality disorder. ASD = autism spectrum disorder. ASPD = antisocial personality disorder. BDs = bipolar disorders. BPD = borderline personality disorder. CD = conduct disorder. EDs = eating disorders. GAD = generalized anxiety disorder. MDD = major depressive disorder. NPD = narcissistic personality disorder. OCD = obsessive-compulsive disorder. OCPD = obsessive-compulsive personality disorder. ODD = oppositional-defiant disorder. PDD = persistent depressive disorder. PTSD = posttraumatic stress disorder. SAD = social anxiety disorder. SSDs = schizophrenia spectrum disorders.

FAST SPECTRUM DISORDERS

Fast spectrum disorders arise in connection with fast life history strategies and the corresponding behavioral, cognitive, and neurobiological traits. The idea that fast strategies predispose to psychopathology was proposed decades ago (Belsky et al., 1991; Draper & Harpending, 1982, 1988; MacMillan & Kofoed, 1984). Over the years, a number of conditions have been framed as either adaptive manifestations or maladaptive outcomes of fast-related traits: externalizing disorders (most notably psychopathy and its DSM counterpart, antisocial personality disorder), ADHD, borderline personality disorder, schizophrenia, and eating disorders (e.g., Barr & Quinsey, 2004; Brüne et al., 2010; Del Giudice et al., 2010; Figueredo & Jacobs, 2010; Frederick, 2012; MacMillan & Kofoed, 1984; Mealey, 1995; Salmon et al., 2009). In Part III of the book, I discuss individual disorders and their evolutionary origins in detail; here, I briefly summarize their classification according to the FSD model. In the current version of the model, the fast spectrum of psychopathology comprises the following conditions:

- A cluster of disorders marked by disruptive and antisocial behaviors, namely antisocial personality disorder (ASPD), conduct disorder (CD), and oppositional-defiant disorder (ODD).
- Most instances of schizophrenia spectrum disorders (SSDs).
- A high-frequency, fast spectrum subtype of bipolar disorders (F-BDs).
- A high-frequency, fast spectrum subtype of ADHD (F-ADHD) associated with antisocial/conduct disorders and psychosis risk.
- Personality disorders marked by high levels of antagonism, disinhibition, and/or psychoticism—most notably antisocial personality disorder (ASPD, also part of the conduct/antisocial cluster); schizotypal personality disorder (SPD, also part of the schizophrenia spectrum); borderline personality disorder (BPD); and narcissistic personality disorder (NPD).
- A fast spectrum subtype of eating disorders (F-EDs) marked by high impulsivity and neuroticism.

Among these conditions, antisocial and conduct disorders (ASPD, CD, and ODD) fit the prototype of the antagonistic/exploitative profile, whereas SSDs, F-BDs, and NPD are linked to the seductive/creative profile (Figure 6.2). The constellation of traits that characterizes BPD is intermediate between the antagonistic/exploitative and seductive/creative profiles. It is worth stressing that strategic profiles are not meant as rigidly separated categories, and some people may combine aspects of both. F-type disorders associated with different profiles (e.g., ASPD and BDs) may co-occur within individuals and families, though not as frequently as disorders that share the same functional correlates (e.g., SSDs and BDs).

Fast Spectrum Markers

A working list of fast spectrum markers is presented in Table 6.1. The table shows two largely overlapping sets of markers corresponding to the two strategic profiles discussed in Chapter 4. The main correlates of F-type disorders are low conscientiousness, agreeableness, and honesty-humility; high impulsivity and risk-taking; precocious and unrestricted sexuality; reduced long-term mating and stability of romantic attachments; low levels of disgust sensitivity (especially in the sexual and moral domains); and earlier/faster sexual maturation (especially in females). Markers such as high imagination and a verbally biased pattern of cognitive ability are typical of the seductive/creative profile. This list is not intended to be definitive and will have to be expanded and refined as further research details the neurobiological, hormonal, and genetic bases of human life history strategies and their variants. Tentative neurobiological correlates of the fast spectrum include reduced serotonergic activity, (typically) upregulated mesolimbic dopamine, reduced activity of the dorsolateral prefrontal cortex (DLPFC), and high androgen levels. The seductive/creative profile should be associated with elevated oxytocinergic

Table 6.1 Markers of Fast Spectrum Disorders (F-Type)

F-type markers	Antagonistic/exploitative profile	Seductive/creative profile
Personality factors	Low agreeableness Low conscientiousness Low honesty-humility	Low agreeableness Low conscientiousness Low honesty-humility High openness (imagination/aesthetics)
Motivation	Precocious sexuality Unrestricted sociosexuality Unstable romantic attachments Reduced long-term mating orientation Low disgust sensitivity (especially sexual/moral)	Precocious sexuality Unrestricted sociosexuality Unstable romantic attachments Reduced long-term mating orientation Low disgust sensitivity (especially sexual/moral)
Decision-making, self-regulation	High impulsivity High risk-taking and sensation seeking	High impulsivity High risk-taking and sensation seeking
Cognitive ability		High mentalistic cognition Low mechanistic cognition Verbal > visuospatial ability
Sexual maturation	Early, fast maturation (especially females)	Early, fast maturation (especially females)

function, increased activity of the default mode network, and a more complex pattern with respect to androgens and other sex hormones (Chapter 4).

A crucial point to keep in mind is that the life history markers listed in Table 6.1 may or may not play a *causal* role in the etiology of any given disorder. For example, impulsivity and risk-taking have a direct causal effect on the development of some externalizing symptoms (e.g., Lahey & Waldman, 2003). However, the robust association between externalizing symptoms and early sexual maturation (Chapter 7) does not mean that sexual maturation per se is a cause of externalizing behavior. The goal of Table 6.1 is not to detail the etiology of F-type disorders, but to present a list of convergent markers that can be used to classify a condition as belonging to the fast spectrum of psychopathology. Also note that certain life history markers—such as high mentalistic cognition or precocious sexuality—may show stronger associations with the less severe forms of a disorder, emerge only during remission phases, or appear more clearly in the unaffected relatives of diagnosed individuals. This is most likely to happen in disorders that reflect harmful dysfunctions or maladaptive outcomes, to the extent that they are associated with impairments (either temporary or permanent) in the functionality of neural and cognitive processes. To illustrate, openness/imagination and creativity are elevated in people with schizotypal personalities and in relatives of schizophrenic patients, but *not* in the patients themselves (Chapter 8). This does not make these traits less useful as markers of a functional connection between schizophrenia and the seductive/creative profile of the fast spectrum.

Sex Differences

The life history approach helps make predictions about systematic patterns of sex differences in psychopathology. On the whole, disorders linked to the antagonistic/exploitative profile should be more common in males; in females, the same underlying dispositions (such as impulsivity and risk-taking) may give rise to different behavioral manifestations because of the different costs and benefits of traits such as physical aggression and avoidant attachment. Consistent with this prediction, the prevalence of externalizing disorders is considerably higher in males (Martel, 2013). As noted in Chapter 4, theoretical considerations suggest a more or less balanced sex ratio in the seductive/creative profile. However, males may still be somewhat more at risk for the corresponding disorders, both because they show higher variability in personality and behavior (and are thus more likely to develop extreme levels of fast-related traits) and because they are generally more susceptible to dysfunctions, owing to stronger sexual selection and sensitivity to X-linked mutations. Disorders in the psychosis spectrum (SSDs and BDs) have similar prevalence in males and females (with slightly higher male risk for schizophrenia), while men are more likely to be diagnosed with NPD than are women (Aleman et al., 2003; Diflorio & Jones, 2010; Oltmanns & Powers, 2012; Räsänen et al., 2000; Stinson et al., 2008).

Borderline personality disorder combines features of both the antagonistic/exploitative and seductive/creative profiles and shows considerable genetic and phenotypic overlap with externalizing behaviors and some aspects of psychopathy (Crowell et al., 2013; Hunt et al., 2015; Oltmanns & Powers, 2012; Chapter 12). BPD is diagnosed more often in females, although some studies of community samples have found a balanced sex ratio, suggesting that self-selection may partly explain the female bias in clinical settings (Grant et al., 2004, 2008; Martel, 2013; Oltmanns & Powers, 2012; Silberschmidt et al., 2015). Finally, eating disorders (EDs) tap into sex-specific aspects of female physiology and psychology (Chapter 13) and are overwhelmingly more common in females. Not coincidentally, ED risk in males is strongly associated with non-heterosexual orientations (e.g., Feldman & Meyer, 2007; Russell & Keel, 2002; Yean et al., 2013).

Developmental Patterns

While mental disorders occur throughout the whole life course, different conditions show different developmental patterns—including typical age of onset, age-related peaks in prevalence, and trajectories of remission. In a life history perspective, the developmental characteristics of a given disorder should depend—at least in part—on its motivational underpinnings and the maturation trajectory of the relevant motivational systems. Within the fast spectrum, a useful distinction can be drawn between disorders that primarily involve social competition for dominance and status and those that relate more directly to courtship and mating. This distinction overlaps with that between the antagonistic/exploitative and seductive/creative profiles, but the correspondence is not exact (e.g., NPD is linked to the seductive/creative profile, but its core motivational signature is exaggerated competition for status; Russ et al., 2008). Competition-related disorders are likely to develop earlier, with a peak in middle childhood (Del Giudice, 2014*c*; Del Giudice et al., 2009). Middle childhood is a critical phase for status competition; both the status and aggression systems undergo important developmental shifts, likely under the influence of adrenal androgens. Other important changes occur in the attachment system as close relations with peers start to become salient alongside those with parents. While sexual and mating motivations begin to awaken in middle childhood, they only become fully active at puberty (following maturation of the HPG axis) and peak with the attainment of reproductive maturity, between adolescence and young adulthood (Ellis et al., 2012; Forbes & Dahl, 2010; Mundy et al., 2016). This developmental window is when courtship- and mating-related disorders are expected to arise most often. In general, F-type disorders can be expected to improve or remit starting from the third decade of life, after the peak of social and reproductive competition has ended and sex hormone levels begin to decline.

There are multiple reasons why the onset of competition-related disorders should first peak in middle childhood. To begin, the switch point of adrenarche amplifies individual and sex differences by activating a number of mechanisms and pathways involved in social competition. The resulting individual profiles may include adaptive strategies—some of which may be regarded as broad-sense disorders—as well as biologically maladaptive variants (e.g., detrimentally high or low levels of competition-related traits). Second, rapid changes in the activity of the relevant psychological mechanisms can make them temporarily vulnerable to dysfunctions. Third, competition with peers is likely to expose some children to stage-specific stressors and failures (e.g., peer rejection), which may trigger defensive responses or even result in behavioral and neurobiological dysregulation. Fourth, the intense social learning that takes place in middle childhood opens the way to potentially maladaptive learning at all levels—ineffective social skills, pathological levels of self-esteem, or "deviancy training" by antisocial peers (Dishion & Patterson, 2016). Finally, modern cultural practices may contribute to both developmental and evolutionary mismatches; for example, age segregation between children and adolescents both in schools and in out-of-school activities seems to exacerbate aggression and other problematic behaviors (Ellis et al., 2012). Similar arguments apply to the onset of mating-related disorders during puberty and adolescence.

These developmental predictions are supported by the empirical data. The onset of conduct/antisocial disorders such as CD and ODD shows a first peak in middle childhood and another around puberty, although there is a subgroup of children who follow a trajectory of elevated, persistent aggression starting from infancy (see Chapter 7). Eating disorders (which have deep connections with mating competition) typically emerge in adolescence, and the risk for psychosis spectrum disorders such as schizophrenia and BDs peaks in young adulthood (Costello et al., 2003; Hulvershorn & Nurnberger, 2014; Khandaker et al., 2014; Mitchell & Bulik, 2014). Developmental data on personality disorders are extremely scarce due to the long-standing assumption that these conditions should only be diagnosed in adults. However, narcissistic traits can be measured reliably starting from middle childhood; also, the constellation of traits that define BPD is already in place at age 12, indicating that this condition likely develops before puberty (Belsky et al., 2012; Sharp et al., 2012; Thomaes & Brummelman, 2016). As a rule, F-type conditions tend to remit or become milder in the third and fourth decades of life, although severe disorders such as schizophrenia may result in chronic or even lifelong impairment.

The distinction between competition- and mating-related disorders is heuristically useful, but does not fully explain the developmental course of F-type disorders. Another important factor to consider is the maturation schedule of specific psychological mechanisms. For example, the development of executive functions accelerates dramatically with the transition to middle childhood; in many cultures, the sophisticated self-control skills that emerge during this phase enable children to contribute significantly to family subsistence (Best et al., 2009; Del Giudice, 2014*c*). The rapid maturation of executive functions in middle childhood amplifies both adaptive and maladaptive individual differences; because of the increasing importance of self-control in children's daily life, latent dysfunctions that previously had little impact on behavior may grow into full-fledged disorders. The confluence of these developmental factors likely contributes to explain why the onset of ADHD peaks at the boundary between early and middle childhood (Kessler et al., 2005).

Differences in the developmental course of fast spectrum disorders intersect with sex differences in prevalence, with the result that childhood-onset conditions also tend to be more common in males. One reason noted earlier is that disorders that peak in childhood tend to be functionally linked to status competition. A complementary reason is that human males have been under stronger sexual selection than females and tend to mature later, a common pattern in species where males need to build up resources and competitive skills to succeed in mating competition. Traits that function as fitness indicators are more vulnerable to developmental disruptions, and slower maturation implies a broader window of susceptibility to stressors and insults experienced in early life (Geary, 2002, 2015; Martel, 2013). This kind of explanation is unlikely to apply to disorders that reflect adaptive or potentially adaptive behavioral strategies (e.g., conduct disorders) but may help explain the early onset of some male-biased conditions that seem to involve genuine dysfunctions, such as childhood-onset schizophrenia.

The Definition of "Childhood-Onset" Disorders

The preceding discussion highlights the need to draw clear distinctions between life stages in order to make sense of the developmental features of disorders. Early childhood, middle childhood, and adolescence are characterized by different functional and endocrine profiles and have widely different implications for the biological meaning of psychological symptoms. From this vantage point, the loose definitions of childhood found in the psychiatric literature are potentially problematic. In this area, most authors use the label "childhood-onset" for any disorder arising by 12 years of age; in doing so, they pool together individuals at very different stages of development, from children who have yet to undergo adrenarche to adolescents who are experiencing the beginning of puberty. Some adopt an even more inclusive definition that stretches to 18 years of age (e.g., Khandaker et al., 2014). To avoid conceptual confusion, it is important to keep in mind that standard conventions in the literature do not necessarily map on the biological boundaries between developmental stages.

A subtler but important point is that individual differences in life history strategy do not only affect the risk of developing S-type or F-type disorders at certain developmental stages, but also the timing of those stages and the transitions between them. For this reason, life history–related differences in maturation timing may further confound the conventional distinction between childhood- and adolescent-onset disorders when age is used as a proxy for the person's stage of development. Consider the hypothetical case of two disorders, an S-type condition A that emerges in middle childhood and an F-type condition B with onset in adolescence (Figure 6.3). Because fast strategies are associated with accelerated puberty (especially in females), condition B will peak early, and many cases will fall within the conventional age range for middle childhood; moreover, the cases with the earliest onset may also be the most severe as they tend to be linked to more extreme versions of fast strategies. The prediction is reversed for condition A: children will develop the disorder comparatively late, overlapping with the conventional age range for adolescence. Following standard conventions, a minority of cases of condition A would be classified as "adolescent-onset," while a majority of those of condition B (including the more severe ones) would be classified as "childhood-onset." If the two conditions had similar symptoms, they might be regarded as a single disorder despite their different functional underpinnings and hormonal correlates (e.g., adrenal androgens for disorder A, gonadal hormones for disorder B). Both the "childhood-onset" and "adolescent-onset" forms of this putative disorder would be functionally inconsistent, and would comprise mixtures of individuals with different underlying conditions and life history profiles.

Risk Factors

To make predictions about the probable risk factors for a disorder, it is crucial to consider its place in the evolutionary taxonomy of Figure 5.1. When dysfunctions play a major role in the etiology of a certain condition, one can

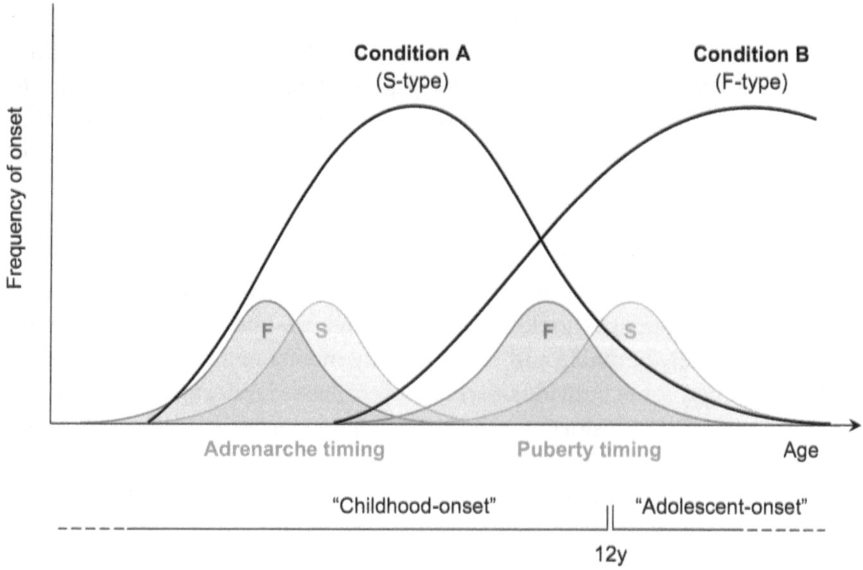

Figure 6.3. Conventional criteria for age of onset may be confounded by life history-related differences in maturation timing. Condition A is a slow spectrum disorder with onset in middle childhood, whereas condition B is a fast spectrum disorder with onset in adolescence. Following conventional age-based criteria, a minority of cases of condition A would be classified as "adolescent-onset," while a substantial proportion of cases of condition B would be classified as "childhood-onset." F = fast life history strategies. S = slow life history strategies.

reasonably expect that risk for that condition will be associated with deleterious mutations and environmental insults such as early infections, malnutrition, or exposure to toxins and other harmful chemicals. Even in the absence of narrow-sense dysfunctions, mutations and developmental stressors may also increase the likelihood that adaptive processes will yield individually maladaptive outcomes. There is considerable evidence that all the factors I just listed are implicated in the etiology of ADHD, schizophrenia, and BDs (e.g., Ahn et al., 2014; Benros et al., 2012; D'Onofrio et al., 2014; Ehli et al., 2012; Khandaker et al., 2014; Mitchell & Goldstein, 2014). For disorders that plausibly represent adaptive strategies on the fast spectrum, the life history framework predicts correlations with variables associated with harshness and unpredictability—including stressful life events, low socioeconomic status (SES), prenatal stress, negative family relationships, maltreatment, trauma, and peer victimization. These are the main environmental risk factors emphasized in the literature on developmental psychopathology, and they correlate with increased prevalence of fast spectrum conditions, from antisocial/conduct disorders and BPD to schizophrenia (Caspi et al., 2014; Fonagy & Luyten, 2016; Green J. G. et al., 2010; Hulvershorn & Nurnberger, 2014; Larsson et al., 2014; McMahon et al., 2003; Russell et al., 2014; Wadsworth et al., 2016; Waldman & Lahey, 2013). Since socioeconomic disadvantage (e.g., low SES) also increases exposure to developmental insults such as infections and malnutrition, risk factors of different kinds will typically occur together rather than in isolation. Moreover, some environmental factors (e.g., prenatal infections, exposure to maternal stress hormones) may increase the risk for F-type disorders by acting both as cues of harshness/unpredictability and as risk factors for harmful dysfunctions; internal cues of somatic damage may also contribute to the development of faster life history strategies by feeding into mechanisms of facultative calibration.

While environmental stressors can increase the risk for fast spectrum disorders, their influence should not be overestimated. Life history strategies are at least moderately heritable and may be partly maintained by balancing selection; accordingly, some individuals will follow canalized trajectories and develop a full suite of fast life history–related traits—and associated risk for psychopathology—even without being exposed to cues of harshness or unpredictability. Chronic stress is likely to have a stronger and longer lasting impact on infants and children who are highly susceptible to the quality of their environment. Another important caveat is that empirical correlations between contextual variables and mental disorders are not necessarily causal, but may be partially or fully explained by confounding factors such as family-level effects and genotype–environment correlations. For example, epidemiological studies that control for relatedness patterns indicate that the associations between antisocial behavior, schizophrenia, and neighborhood deprivation are driven to a considerable extent by self-selection, as families with a higher shared risk for criminality and/or psychosis also tend to live in more disadvantaged neighborhoods (Sariaslan et al., 2013, 2015).

Extending this line of reasoning, a life history perspective suggests that some associations between putative risk factors and psychopathological outcomes may arise from shared genetic effects on the strategies of parents and offspring. For example, low birth weight reliably predicts earlier sexual maturation (Hochberg, 2008, 2010; Nettle et al., 2013) as well as increased risk for F-type disorders including antisocial/conduct disorders and schizophrenia. In the standard view, low birth weight is an indicator of prenatal stress and poor nutrition, which in turn increase the risk of pathological dysregulation in the child. However, low birth weight can also be interpreted as an outcome of reduced energetic and metabolic investment by the mother; if mothers with faster strategies curtail parental investment in the growing fetus, they will tend to have smaller babies *and* transmit them heritable factors that predispose to earlier maturation and F-type disorders. Associations between birth weight, early maturation, and fast spectrum psychopathology may thus be explained—at least in part—by the effect of shared genetic and/or epigenetic variants. Conflicts about fetal nutrition between maternally and paternally expressed genes may further exacerbate this pattern (see Chapters 8–10).

Paternal age is another potential risk factor liable to be confounded with adaptive life history variation. Because sperm production involves frequent and repeated cell divisions, the number of de novo mutations in sperm increases gradually as men get older. For this reason, paternal age is often used as an indicator of mutation load in the offspring and is a robust risk factor for several psychiatric conditions, from autism to schizophrenia and BDs (D'Onofrio et al., 2014; Francioli et al., 2015; Malaspina et al., 2015). However, men with faster strategies are also likely to become fathers earlier in life (e.g., Moffitt & Caspi, 2005), suggesting that *low* paternal age should be a predictor of F-type disorders. From this vantage point, the overall association between paternal age and fast spectrum psychopathology is the sum of two contrasting effects: a risk-increasing effect of older age mediated by mutation load and a risk-increasing effect of younger age mediated by life history strategy. Consistent with this prediction, epidemiological data show a curvilinear relation between age and risk: in addition to older fathers, younger fathers (and mothers) show increased rates of mental disorders in their offspring—sometimes even more so, as in the case of ADHD and SSDs. Restricting the analysis to paternal siblings (which automatically controls for variation in the father's life history strategy) shows a linear increase of risk with advancing paternal age, which can be interpreted as the "purified" effect of mutation load (Chudal et al., 2015; D'Onofrio et al., 2014; Merikangas et al., 2017).

SLOW SPECTRUM DISORDERS

Slow spectrum disorders arise in connection with slow life history strategies and the corresponding phenotypic traits. The idea that not only fast strategies, but also slow strategies may set the stage for mental disorders is a recent development in evolutionary psychopathology (Del Giudice, 2014*a*; Del Giudice et al., 2010). In the current version of the FSD model, the slow spectrum of psychopathology comprises the following conditions:

- A high-functioning subtype of autism spectrum disorder, typically associated with normal or high intelligence (S-ASD).
- A low-frequency, slow spectrum subtype of bipolar disorders (S-BDs).
- A low-frequency, slow spectrum subtype of ADHD (S-ADHD) that overlaps with S-ASD.
- Personality disorders marked by high conscientiousness and/or agreeableness, including obsessive-compulsive personality disorder (OCPD).
- A slow spectrum subtype of obsessive-compulsive disorder (S-OCD) in which symptoms are primarily motivated by feelings of incompleteness/imperfection.
- A slow spectrum subtype of eating disorders (S-EDs), with two distinct personality variants characterized by high versus low levels of neuroticism.

Within the slow spectrum, S-ASD and S-ADHD match the features of the skilled/provisioning profile, whereas the low-neuroticism variant of S-EDs is linked to the prosocial/caregiving profile (Figure 6.2). Consistent with the idea that life history profiles are not rigid categories but extremes of a distribution of traits, all S-type disorders show a substantial degree of comorbidity with one another.

Slow Spectrum Markers

Table 6.2 shows a working list of slow spectrum markers. The main correlates of S-type disorders are high conscientiousness and honesty-humility, low impulsivity and risk-taking, increased long-term mating and romantic attachment stability, high levels of disgust sensitivity (especially in the sexual and moral domains), delayed and restricted sexuality, and slower sexual maturation (especially in females). Agreeableness is high in the prosocial/caregiving profile, but moderate to low in the skilled/provisioning profile because of reduced empathy and social compliance. Other correlates of the skilled/provisioning profile are low openness/imagination, enhanced visuospatial abilities, and a bias toward mechanistic reasoning. Tentative neurobiological correlates of the slow spectrum include increased serotonergic activity, (typically) downregulated mesolimbic

Table 6.2 MARKERS OF SLOW SPECTRUM DISORDERS (S-TYPE)

S-type markers	**Prosocial/caregiving profile**	**Skilled/provisioning profile**
Personality factors	High agreeableness	Moderate/low agreeableness (empathy, compliance)
	High conscientiousness	High conscientiousness
	High honesty-humility	High honesty-humility
		Low openness (imagination/ aesthetics)
Motivation	Delayed sexuality	Delayed sexuality
	Restricted sociosexuality	Restricted sociosexuality
	Stable romantic attachments	Stable romantic attachments
	High long-term mating orientation	High long-term mating orientation
	High disgust sensitivity (especially sexual/moral)	High disgust sensitivity (especially sexual/moral)
Decision-making, self-regulation	Low impulsivity	Low impulsivity
	Low risk-taking and sensation seeking	Low risk-taking and sensation seeking
Cognitive ability		Low mentalistic cognition
		High mechanistic cognition
		Visuospatial > verbal ability
Sexual maturation	Late, slow maturation (especially females)	Late, slow maturation (especially females)

dopamine, low androgen levels, and heightened DLPFC activity. Moreover, the skilled-provisioning profile should be associated with reduced oxytocinergic function, dampened activity of the default mode network, and a pattern of sex hormones capable of accounting for the combination of male-typical traits such as high visuospatial skills and female-typical traits such as restricted sociosexuality (Chapter 4).

Sex Differences

The skilled/provisioning profile is a male-typical variant of slow strategy; accordingly, the risk for disorders that fit this profile (S-ASD and S-ADHD) is substantially higher in males, with sex rations of at least 3:1 and up to 10:1 (Agnew-Blais & Seidman, 2014; Baxter et al., 2015). All else being equal, more females than males should display a prosocial/caregiving profile; at the same time, males are generally more vulnerable to disorders and dysfunctions. The combination of these effects should result in a balanced or female-biased prevalence for conditions associated with this profile. In the current version of the FSD taxonomy, the only disorder with a clear link to the prosocial/caregiving profile is a variant of S-type eating disorders (S-EDs); as noted earlier, the distribution of EDs is strongly female-biased at both ends of the continuum. OCPD is not strongly associated with a particular strategic profile; some studies report similar OCPD rates in males and females, while others find a slightly higher prevalence in men (de Reus & Emmelkamp, 2012; Grant et al., 2004; Samuels & Costa, 2012). Finally, the slow spectrum subtype of OCD is associated with both OCPD and ASD and is more common in males, though not as male-biased as autism (Chapter 20).

Developmental Patterns

The developmental trajectory of S-type disorders is harder to predict than that of their F-type counterparts. Slow strategies are less intensely focused on competition and mating and allocate the organism's resources over a longer time frame with substantial investment in parenting and/or nepotistic effort. All else being equal, then, the risk for this type of disorders should be more broadly distributed across the life span. This is certainly the case of OCPD, which peaks in the third decade of life and becomes more prevalent during the fourth and fifth decades (Albert et al., 2004; Diedrich & Volderholzer, 2015; Grant et al., 2004; Samuels & Costa, 2012). The slow spectrum subtype of OCD also has a wide risk window that extends from childhood throughout adulthood (Chapter 20).

This general prediction can be refined for disorders linked to the skilled/provisioning profile. An important aspect of this profile is a protracted phase of reproductive immaturity devoted to the accumulation of somatic capital through learning, exploration, and skills practice. Accordingly, disorders associated with this profile should involve delays or interruptions in the acquisition of age-typical skills, especially those relating to mating and social competition. The exact timing of onset is then going to depend on the specific mechanisms involved in the disorder. For example, mentalizing abilities undergo a major developmental transition in early childhood; this is when autism is typically diagnosed, although developmental delays in language and communication may appear already in the first 1–2 years (Bernier & Dawson, 2016). A counterintuitive prediction is that, all else being equal, disorders associated with the skilled/provisioning profile should tend to become *less* severe as mating competition gets more intense, in marked contrast with mating-related conditions within the fast spectrum. For slow strategists, the peak of mating effort should also begin somewhat later, often closer to adulthood than adolescence. The available evidence indicates that autism symptoms are stable across childhood but tend to improve in adulthood, with recovery rates estimated between 3% and 25% (Helt et al., 2008; Seltzer et al., 2004; Wu et al., 2016).

Risk Factors

Because slow life history strategies are more likely to develop in safe, predictable contexts, there should be a general tendency for S-type disorders to be associated with favorable family conditions, low levels of early stress, and high SES—all aspects of the environment that are usually regarded as *protective* factors against psychopathology. These counterintuitive associations should be more apparent for conditions that reflect alternative strategies rather than dysfunctional processes. Within the slow spectrum, OCPD is the best candidate for a potentially adaptive strategy (Chapter 12). Consistent with predictions, the risk of OCPD increases at higher levels of income and education and is associated with the lowest rates of exposure to traumatic events, neglect, and abuse among the personality disorders (Battle et al., 2004; Coid, 1999; Grant et al., 2004; Torgersen et al., 2001; Walsh et al., 2013; Yen et al., 2002). As in F-type disorders, the correlation between environmental stress and risk for psychopathology should be attenuated by genetic variation in life history strategies and individual differences in susceptibility.

The picture becomes more complicated for S-type disorders that involve harmful dysfunctions. On the one hand, socioeconomic disadvantage and chronic stress influence life history development by acting as cues of harshness/unpredictability; on the other hand, they can be expected to increase the risk of dysfunction regardless of the individual's position on the fast–slow continuum. In total, high SES should work as a risk factor for some aspects of slow spectrum psychopathology and as a protective factor for others; the net effect is going to depend on the relative weight of dysfunctions in the etiology of any given disorder. Some diagnostic categories comprise a spectrum of conditions, from functional and possibly adaptive variants to clearly dysfunctional ones, as well as different life history profiles. In those cases, epidemiological patterns with respect to SES may become quite complex. This is the case of ASD, which spans a broad range of severity—from mild symptoms at the boundary of normal personality to extremely dysfunctional cases with major intellectual disability. Autism is associated with many genetic and environmental risk factors, from deleterious mutations and advanced paternal age to prenatal infections and perinatal complications (Bernier & Dawson, 2016; Mandy & Lai, 2016). The prevalence of severe autism with intellectual disability—which, as I argue in Chapter 10, is a cluster of dysfunctional conditions outside the FSD classification—is either unrelated to SES or more common at lower socioeconomic levels. In contrast, several studies (particularly in the United States) have found associations between higher SES and risk for autism *without* intellectual disability, which comprises the bulk of the slow spectrum subtype of ASD. In part, this effect is explained by high-income, educated parents having better access to healthcare; however, there are indications that differential access does not fully account for the epidemiological findings (e.g., DiGuiseppi et al., 2016; Durkin et al., 2010; Hill et al., 2014; Leonard et al., 2011; Rai et al., 2012; Wu et al., 2016). The key point is that the pattern of socioeconomic risk for ASD is complex and nuanced, in contrast with the consistent negative association with SES found in F-type disorders.

As noted in a previous section, the effect of paternal age on mutation load is confounded with its functional role as a life history–related trait. In the fast spectrum, these two effects go in opposite directions; in the slow spectrum, they tend to reinforce one another. Unsurprisingly, higher paternal age is consistently associated with increased risk of ASD; a more interesting finding is that advancing *maternal* age is an equally strong predictor of autism spectrum conditions in the offspring (Idring et al., 2014; Lee & McGrath, 2015; Leonard et al., 2011; Sandin et al., 2013). From a purely genetic standpoint, this is a puzzling finding. The eggs of older mothers are more likely to carry chromosomal abnormalities, and there is recent evidence that de novo mutations increase slightly with maternal age (Wong et al., 2016). However, the overall effect on mutation load is much smaller than in the case of sperm; moreover, this explanation does not fit with the small or even negative correlations observed between maternal age and F-type disorders such as schizophrenia. Of course, the link between maternal age and ASD is easily explained from a life history perspective if women who engage in slower strategies tend to mature later, delay childbirth, *and* transmit risk factors for S-type disorders to their offspring.

DEFENSE ACTIVATION DISORDERS

Defense activation disorders are conditions that arise primarily from the intense and/or prolonged activation of evolved defensive mechanisms. There are many possible reasons for exaggerated defense activation, including undesirable but adaptive responses, neurobiological dysfunctions, evolutionary and developmental mismatches, and maladaptive learning. In previous versions of the life history framework, depression and generalized anxiety disorder (GAD) were described as nonspecific conditions that could arise at both ends of the fast–slow continuum (Del Giudice 2014*a*, 2014*b*; 2016*c*, 2016*d*). The FSD model builds on this idea by adding a distinct category for disorders of defense activation (Figure 6.2). These disorders share common predisposing traits and form a broad comorbidity cluster that connects with both F-type and S-type disorders. In the current version of the FSD model, D-type disorders comprise:

- Depressive disorders, including major depressive disorder (MDD) and persistent depressive disorder (PDD) or *dysthymia*.
- Generalized anxiety disorder (GAD).
- Posttraumatic stress disorder (PTSD).
- Specific phobias.
- Panic attacks, panic disorder, and agoraphobia.
- Social anxiety disorder (SAD, also known as "social phobia") and the largely overlapping diagnosis of avoidant personality disorder (APD).
- A defense activation subtype of obsessive-compulsive disorder (D-OCD) in which symptoms are primarily motivated by harm prevention.

In total, D-type disorders include most of the conditions classified as internalizing in the transdiagnostic approach; the main exceptions are eating disorders and "interstitial" conditions such as bipolar disorders and BPD, which correlate with multiple transdiagnostic factors (more on this later). In the DSM-5, D-type disorders are split into three main categories, namely "anxiety disorders," "depressive disorders," and "obsessive-compulsive and related disorders." Within the broader defense activation family it is possible to identify two smaller clusters of disorders: a *distress* cluster marked by anxious or depressed affect (depression and GAD) and a *fear* cluster in which the primary emotional experience is one of fear (panic disorder, most specific phobias, SAD, and APD). These labels were introduced by Watson (2005) and are often employed in the transdiagnostic approach to describe the lower level structure of the internalizing spectrum (e.g., Carragher et al., 2015; Kotov et al., 2017). The distinction between distress and fear disorders is useful but should not be employed too rigidly: anxiety-related symptoms such as avoidance and worry in response to a potential threat (e.g., public speaking in SAD) can easily coexist with intense fear or even panic when the threat materializes (Boyer & Bergstrom, 2011). While some authors include PTSD in the distress cluster, its symptoms reflect a mixture of distress and fear, suggesting that an intermediate classification may be more appropriate (Watson, 2005). Also, the central emotion in some phobias seems to be disgust rather than fear (Chapter 17).

The classification of a subtype of OCD as a D-type disorder is a major change from earlier versions of the taxonomy and deserves special comment. In the original description of the framework (which did not include defense activation disorders), I suggested that OCD could be subdivided into fast and slow spectrum subtypes based on the particular kind of symptoms shown by patients (specifically *reactive* vs. *autogenous* obsessions; see Chapter 20). However, the distinction turned out to be less clear and functionally meaningful than anticipated (Del Giudice, 2014*b*; Del Giudice et al., 2014*b*). In most patients, the symptoms of

OCD are motivated by the desire to prevent harm and reflect the activation of the security and/or disgust systems. In the updated FSD model, this variant of OCD is an obvious candidate for inclusion in the defense activation category (Berle & Phillips, 2006; Boyer & Liénard, 2006; Szechtman & Woody, 2004; Woody & Szechtman, 2011). Like other defense-related conditions, D-OCD occurs in conjunction with both F-type and S-type disorders, possibly with somewhat different constellations of obsessive symptoms (Chapter 20; Del Giudice et al., 2014*b*).

Markers of Defense Activation Disorders

Elevated neuroticism is the core personality correlate of D-type disorders (Hong & Cheung, 2015; Watson & Naragon-Gainey, 2014; Watson & Stasik, 2014). Neuroticism describes the tendency to experience frequent, intense negative emotions in response to challenging events, coupled with a pervasive appraisal of the world as threatening or beyond one's coping abilities. People high in neuroticism tend to be intolerant of uncertainty, pessimistic, sensitive to negative evaluations, and prone to rumination and worry. Evolutionary and neurobiological models of personality converge on the idea that neuroticism reflects heightened sensitivity of defensive psychological mechanisms designed to deal with multiple types of social and nonsocial threats (Allen & DeYoung, 2017; Barlow, Ellard et al., 2014; Denissen & Penke, 2008; DeYoung, 2015; Nettle, 2011*a*; Patrick & Bernat, 2006). These mechanisms include the behavioral inhibition system (BIS) and the security, fear, and disgust systems, but also components of other motivational systems (e.g., status, affiliation) that mediate the individual's response to potentially catastrophic social threats such as humiliation, rejection, and exclusion. From the standpoint of the smoke detector principle, neuroticism indicates a readiness to activate defenses so as to avoid false negatives—even at the cost of many false alarms and an increased risk of maladaptive outcomes (Bateson et al., 2011). Consistent with this interpretation, all D-type disorders share a background of elevated neuroticism; this pattern is so robust that the internalizing factor of the transdiagnostic model is almost perfectly correlated with the neuroticism factor of the Big Five (Barlow, Ellard et al., 2014; Griffith et al., 2010; Hengartner et al., 2016; Rodriguez-Seijas et al., 2015).

Neurobiological Correlates

In the brain, defensive responses are mediated by a complex network of anatomical structures and neurochemical pathways. The amygdala is often singled out as a neural "gateway" in the regulation of vigilance and responsivity to threats. Individual differences in neuroticism have been shown to correlate with the volume of the amygdala; there is also some evidence for systematic differences in amygdala reactivity, although the findings are not as consistent (Allen & DeYoung, 2017; Mincic, 2015). Other regions showing systematic anatomical and functional associations with neuroticism are the hippocampus and parahippocampal gyrus, the striatum, the dorsal prefrontal cortex (DPFC), the medial prefrontal cortex (MPFC), and the anterior cingulate cortex (ACC) (Bjørnebekk et al., 2013; Holmes et al., 2012; Servaas et al., 2013).

At the molecular level, glutamate and GABA exert important regulatory influences on anxiety, fear, and approach/avoidance motivation. Many defense activation symptoms—such as anxiety, depression, and panic—are associated with a physiological profile of reduced GABAergic activity as well as alterations in glutamatergic transmission. Moreover, one of the few genomic regions that have shown reliable associations with neuroticism includes the gene for a glutamate receptor (Kalueff & Nutt, 2007; Lener et al., 2016; Möhler, 2012; Sanacora et al., 2012; Smith, Anderson et al., 2015). Serotonin plays multiple and contrasting roles in the modulation of defenses as it inhibits fear but tends to *potentiate* the BIS, the security system, and the disgust system. Serotonergic activity is thus unlikely to show global correlations with neuroticism—and indeed, the evidence in this regard is mixed and inconsistent (Ormel et al., 2013). This is not to say that serotonin is not involved in the etiology of D-type disorders; however, its role is probably complex and nuanced, in contrast with the popular idea that depression and anxiety are caused by low serotonin levels. As I discuss in Chapter 14, a life history approach may help make sense of some contradictory findings concerning the role of serotonin in depression.

The stress response system is a key neurobiological node in the regulation of defensive processes. It mediates fight-flight-freeze responses (mainly through the sympathetic and parasympathetic nervous system), mobilizes energetic and cognitive resources in the face of sustained threats (mainly through the HPA axis), and contributes to the physiology of disgust (through parasympathetic activation). Despite its manifold contributions to defensive processes, it is important to remember that the stress response system is not a specialized defensive mechanism; rather, its main function is to coordinate physiological and behavioral allocations across a wide range of domains and in response to both positive and negative events. Defensive mechanisms recruit this system precisely because of its ability to rapidly and effectively regulate the state of the whole organism. There is evidence that both norepinephrine levels and HPA reactivity are implicated in negative emotionality, anxiety, and depression; also, variation in the gene for the CRH receptor 1 is reliably associated with neuroticism (Allen & DeYoung, 2017; Barlow, Sauer-Zavala et al., 2014; Charney & Nestler, 2009; Smith, Escott-Price et al., 2015). However, findings in this area are often contradictory and indicate that neuroticism and defense activation can be associated with both hyper- and hypoactivity of the HPA axis (Charney & Nestler, 2009; Ormel et al., 2013). A plausible solution to this paradox lies in the temporal dynamics of the HPA response: periods of sustained activation are usually followed by phases of hyporeactivity and low cortisol production, to promote recovery and/or to protect the organism from the severe side effects of prolonged exposure to glucocorticoids (Barlow, Sauer-Zavala et al., 2014; Miller, Chen et al., 2007). For this reason, the combination of intense stress and high HPA reactivity does not necessarily translate into a stable pattern of elevated cortisol. Instead, the expected trajectory is cyclical, with fluctuations between high and low HPA activity and cortisol levels—especially in chronically stressful contexts. In the language of the ACM model, it is important to distinguish between the temporary hypoactivity that follows response peaks in vigilant or sensitive patterns and the persistent lack of reactivity that characterizes stable unemotional patterns (Figure 4.2).

Sex Differences

With respect to sex differences, the general prediction is that D-type disorders should arise more often in females than in males. This is consistent with the higher level of neuroticism observed in women, which indicates a lower threshold for the activation of defenses and a generalized tendency toward risk avoidance. In line with this prediction, females are more at risk for all the disorders in this category. The largest sex differences are found in depression, GAD, PTSD, panic disorder, agoraphobia, and specific phobias (with sex ratios raging from 1.5:1 to 3:1), the smallest ones in OCD and SAD. While epidemiological studies in the general population consistently find higher female risk for OCD, clinical samples tend to be male-biased, suggesting that severe cases of this disorder may occur more often in males (Arch et al., 2013; Calamari et al., 2011; Fontenelle & Hasler, 2008; McLean & Anderson, 2009; McLean et al., 2011; Tolin & Foa, 2006; Valentiner et al., 2014).

The prediction of higher female risk for D-type disorders can be refined in at least two ways. First, males and females differ in their vulnerability to different kinds of threats; as a consequence, they tend to show somewhat different patterns of symptoms and risk factors even when they develop the same disorder. For example, loss of status has a stronger impact on depression in males, whereas females are more sensitive to social rejection and loss of social support; obsessions with contamination themes (linked to pathogen disgust) are more common in females than in males; and so on (de Mathis et al., 2011; Kendler et al., 2005; Martel, 2013; Nolen-Hoeksema & Hilt, 2009). Second, sex differences in defense activation should be small in infancy and early childhood, when boys and girls face the same threats and share essentially the same vulnerabilities. Starting from middle childhood, however, boys and girls begin to take part in different social worlds with specific sets of challenges; moreover, sex differences in muscle mass and strength, bone density, and adiposity become more pronounced, giving boys a definite advantage in dealing with physical danger (Del Giudice et al., 2009; Wells, 2007). These trends culminate in adolescence and young adulthood, which is when D-type disorders are expected to show the largest and most robust sex differences. As mating competition becomes more intense, males engage in more physical risk-taking and aggression; in contrast, sexually mature females become especially vulnerable to injuries and diseases that may compromise their fecundity or interfere with pregnancy and nursing. They are also physically weaker and thus less able to defend themselves from assaults and other threats. Consistent with this prediction, young boys and girls show similar levels of neuroticism and negative emotionality; sex differences in these traits appear in middle childhood, peak in adolescence and young adulthood, and decline starting from the third decade of life (Else-Quest et al., 2006; Soto et al., 2011).

The epidemiology of defense activation clearly reflects these developmental trends—for example, sex differences for strongly female-biased disorders such as PTSD and depression are either absent or attenuated during childhood (Costello et al., 2003; Nolen-Hoeksema & Hilt, 2009; Tolin & Foa, 2006). Note that many studies follow standard conventions and define "childhood" as the first 12 years of life, a window that includes middle childhood and the initial phase of puberty; thus, sex differences in early childhood are probably even smaller than the existing data indicate.

Developmental Patterns

The timing of onset of D-type disorders should mirror the development of the defensive mechanisms involved in each particular condition. In turn, the developmental trajectory of psychological defenses tracks the rise and fall of different kinds of threats over the life cycle, as well as the shifting balance between the costs and benefits of defense activation. Many social challenges related to status, mating, and affiliation become salient in middle childhood and even more so after puberty. Accordingly, conditions such as depression and SAD are rare in early childhood, become more common after puberty, and peak either in adolescence or young adulthood (Costello et al., 2011; Ledley et al., 2013; Nolen-Hoeksema & Hilt, 2009). The prevalence of panic disorder and agoraphobia also increases through adolescence and adulthood, with a secondary rise after age 40. These female-biased disorders are rooted in perceptions of physical and social vulnerability, and their developmental pattern seems to track the trajectory of the *actual* risk for physical diseases and other potential dangers (e.g., assault by strangers). Indeed, both panic and agoraphobia show sizable correlations with poor physical health, from cardiovascular and gastrointestinal conditions to diabetes and respiratory illnesses. In contrast, specific phobias—especially for animals, blood, and injections—have a distinct onset peak in childhood, which is the phase of maximal vulnerability to physical dangers of this kind. Childhood phobias tend to improve or remit as children grow up, although people who suffered from early phobias remain at higher risk for other D-type disorders later on (American Psychiatric Association, 2013; Arch et al., 2013; Beesdo-Baum & Knappe, 2014; Costello et al., 2011; Goodwin et al., 2014; Valentiner et al., 2014).

The developmental features of OCD are especially interesting when considered from a functional perspective. Overall, the risk of OCD peaks in young adulthood; however, more than one-third of cases develop much earlier, before 10–12 years of age (Calamari et al., 2011; Nakatani et al., 2011; Ruscio et al., 2010). As I argue in Chapter 20, early onset is particularly common in the slow subtype of OCD (S-OCD), which is marked by a high frequency of symptoms with themes of symmetry, ordering, repeating, hoarding, and cleaning. All these behaviors are fairly common in children; in nonclinical samples, they increase through early childhood and peak at the beginning of middle childhood (Boyer & Liénard, 2006; Laing et al., 2009). Disgust also plays a prominent role in OCD, and the disgust system only becomes fully mature in middle childhood, when children begin to eat the same food as adults (thanks to the eruption of permanent teeth) and become able to forage on their own. These new capabilities expose children to a whole new range of pathogen-related threats and emerge in synchrony with a dramatic increase in disgust sensitivity—which in turn may contribute to trigger the onset of OCD symptoms (Berle & Phillips, 2006; Del Giudice, 2014*c*; Rozin, 1990). In addition to disgust, middle childhood witnesses the rapid maturation of other psychological mechanisms, including executive functions and the acquisition system (collecting and hoarding behaviors are very common at this age). These developmental changes contribute to explain the emergence of benign compulsive-like behaviors in most children and the initial peak in the onset of OCD (Chapter 20).

A generalization that is often made in the developmental literature is that internalizing disorders show a first peak in adolescence, in contrast with the typical childhood onset of externalizing disorders (e.g., Martel, 2013). While this is clearly the case for depression and GAD, other internalizing disorders fail to conform to this simple pattern. Most specific phobias and a substantial proportion of OCD and SAD cases develop in childhood, while the prevalence of agoraphobia and panic disorder keeps increasing through adulthood with no adolescent peak. Reframing (most) internalizing conditions as disorders of defense activation encourages a richer and more sophisticated understanding of their developmental features, and helps avoid rigid generalizations by calling attention to the changing nature of threats and vulnerabilities throughout the life course.

Risk Factors

If D-type conditions are rooted in the upregulation of adaptive defensive mechanisms, the risk for this family of disorders should increase in environments that are dangerous, threatening, or particularly challenging. This is consistent with a large literature showing that D-type and F-type disorders share many important risk factors, from low SES and early stress to negative family relations, maltreatment, and trauma (Beesdo-Baum & Knappe, 2014; Furmark, 2002; Goodwin et al., 2014; Groh et al., 2012; Hammen, 2005; Hudson, 2005; Kendler et al., 2004; Madigan et al., 2013; McMahon et al., 2003; Rudenstine, 2014). In addition, experiencing a severe stressor at one point in life seems to amplify the risk that later challenging events will trigger the onset of disorders such as depression and GAD (Hammen, 2005; Kendler et al., 2011). Such "sensitization" or "kindling" effects are entirely consistent with the logic of the smoke detector principle. In Bayesian terms, experiencing adversity should lead people to increase their estimated probability that other threats will occur in the future. (As noted in Chapter 2, such estimates are most likely computed as a unconscious regulatory variables.) When the probability of encountering threats is high, it is optimal to lower the threshold for the activation of defenses (Figure 2.1); in turn, a lower threshold makes it more likely that a defensive mechanism will respond strongly when faced with new stressors or even in the absence of actual threats (false positives). Importantly, many common types of stressors—from accidents to divorce—do not occur at random but are influenced by the person's own behavior. Thus, fast personality traits such as impulsivity and risk-taking can indirectly increase vulnerability to D-type conditions (e.g., Hamilton et al., 2015; Kendler & Gardner, 2016; Snyder & Hankin, 2016).

While the data show a clear pattern of increased risk for D-type disorders in adverse and stressful environments, there are also some exceptions and caveats to consider. First of all, not all the disorders in this category fit the general pattern; in particular, the prevalence of OCD is largely independent from socioeconomic factors, and some studies have found increased risk at higher levels of SES (Brander et al., 2016; Fontenelle & Hasler, 2008; Goodwin et al., 2014). As I argue in Chapter 20, this may be partly explained by the existence of two distinct subtypes of OCD, a defense activation subtype and a slow spectrum subtype. Second, epidemiological studies have shown a nonlinear relation between stressful life events and depression: prevalence increases steeply at very high levels of stress but flattens out at low levels, so that even people growing up in extremely safe and protected environments suffer a nontrivial risk of depression (Kendler et al., 2004; see also Hudson, 2005). Third, the correlation between insecure attachment in childhood and internalizing disorders (which overlap significantly with D-type disorders) is reliably lower than that with externalizing disorders (about .15 versus .30; Groh et al., 2012). Fourth, symptoms of anxiety, depression, and stress are elevated in the offspring of older mothers, suggesting a functional link with slow life histories (Tearne et al., 2016). Taken together, these data converge on the idea that D-type disorders occur at both ends of the fast–slow continuum. At the same time, harshness and unpredictability are expected to increase the risk of both D-type and F-type disorders and amplify their observed comorbidity.

In contrast with the robust effects of adversity and early stress, mutations and developmental disturbances do not seem to have a major influence on the risk for D-type disorders (Doherty & Owen, 2014). The few available data suggest a somewhat elevated risk of being diagnosed with depression in the offspring of both younger and older fathers; however, the severity of depressive and anxious symptoms seems to be largely unrelated to paternal age. The data on OCD are inconclusive, as OCD risk has been associated with advancing paternal age in one study and advancing maternal age in another (Buizer-Voskamp et al., 2011; Steinhausen et al., 2013; Tearne et al., 2016; Wu, Liu et al., 2012). The relatively minor role played by this type of risk factors suggests that, as a rule, D-type disorders arise from the expression of functional defensive mechanisms rather than harmful dysfunctions. It does not follow that these conditions necessarily represent adaptive responses. Even properly functioning defenses are subject to activation errors, evolutionary/developmental mismatches, and maladaptive learning; moreover, mechanisms that are initially functional may become damaged or dysregulated following periods of chronic hyperactivation. In other words, conditions that start as adaptive response may sometimes morph into dysfunctions along the way. These complications make it especially difficult to adjudicate between alternative evolutionary explanations of depression and other defense-related conditions (Chapters 14–20).

FURTHER CONSIDERATIONS ON THE FSD MODEL

Curvilinear Effects of Adversity

An interesting feature of the FSD model is its ability to explain some puzzling empirical findings on the relation between exposure to adversity and psychological outcomes such as distress, well-being, and reactivity to stress and pain. While subjective distress and psychological disturbances predictably increase at high levels of adversity, they are also moderately elevated in people exposed to very *low* levels of adversity, giving rise to a J-shaped curve (Figure 6.4). Other data show that the probability of attempting suicide increases in people who report many stressful life events, but also in those who report very few (McFeeters et al., 2015; Seery, 2011; Seery et al., 2010). These findings are typically taken to mean that experiencing moderate levels of stress and adversity builds up resilience, promotes effective coping, and generally "inoculates" people against the impact of future stressors.

The FSD model suggests a deeper interpretation of the same findings based on life history concepts. As illustrated in Figure 6.4, higher levels of adversity favor the development of faster strategies and progressively increase the risk of F-type as well as D-type disorders (genotype–environment correlations may also contribute to this pattern). While low levels of adversity reduce the risk of

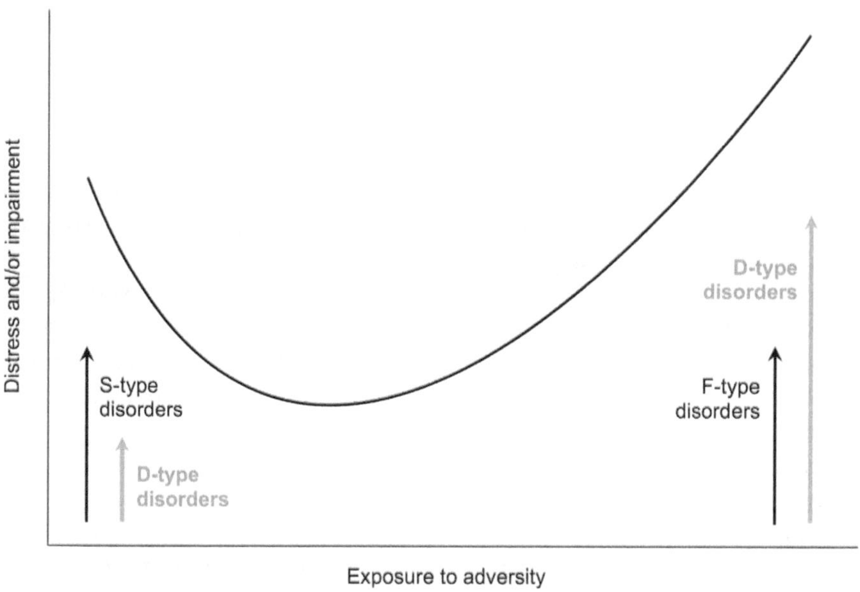

Figure 6.4. The FSD model explains the curvilinear effects of adversity on psychological distress. High levels of adversity tend to increase the risk of fast spectrum and defense activation disorders; low levels of adversity tend to increase the risk of slow spectrum disorders and, to a lesser degree, defense activation disorders. Note that both life history strategies and individual differences in defense activation are substantially heritable, and only partly influenced by contextual factors such as stress and adversity.

F-type disorders, they tend to entrain slower strategies and thus increase the risk of both S-type and D-type disorders; still, the overall risk for defense activation disorders in safe, protected environments remains lower than in severely stressful contexts. The combined result of these effects (represented as upward pointing arrows in Figure 6.4) is a J-shaped curve linking adversity to measures of distress, well-being, and psychiatric symptoms. This interpretation is supported by studies showing that both high and low exposure to adversity predict stronger physiological reactions to laboratory stressors, heightened pain perception, and more posttraumatic symptoms following distressing events such as the 9/11 attack (Seery, 2011; Seery et al., 2013). All these variables indicate upregulation of defensive mechanisms, which can be adaptive at both ends of the fast–slow continuum. Also consistent with this interpretation, studies have shown an inverted J-shaped relation between conscientiousness and well-being. Specifically, well-being increases with higher conscientiousness, but only up to a point; as one approaches the upper end of the scale, extreme conscientiousness morphs into "pathological" obsessive-compulsive personality and well-being drops again, though not as steeply (Carter et al., 2016).

The Role of General Intelligence

The emphasis placed by the FSD model on strategic variation in motivation and self-regulation should not obscure the role of cognitive ability in the origin of mental disorders. Some aspects of cognitive functioning do appear in the FSD model as life history markers; in particular, the seductive/creative and skilled/provisioning profiles are partially defined by different patterns of mentalistic/mechanistic skills and cognitive ability factors (verbal vs. perceptual/rotation). However, the chief dimension of variation in cognitive ability—general intelligence or g—is largely unrelated to individual differences in life history strategy and does not have a specific place in the classification model.

This does not mean that variation in g is unimportant for psychopathology—quite the opposite. To begin, lower levels of intelligence are associated with higher mutation load, which is a risk factor for many mental disorders (Arslan & Penke, 2015*b*; Penke & Jokela, 2016). Even variation in the middle range of g can be expected to affect the risk for psychopathology in a number of ways. In general, people with lower intelligence are less able to take care of their health and less likely to engage in prevention behaviors; as a result they are more exposed to multiple risk factors for mental and physical disorders (Gottfredson, 2004; Wraw et al., 2015). Low intelligence also increases the likelihood of maladaptive learning and may further reduce the viability of antisocial or socially devalued strategies, making it more likely that they will be diagnosed as disorders. For example, cognitive ability may be one of the factors that differentiate incarcerated psychopaths from "successful" ones in business, law, and other professions (Lilienfeld, Watts, & Francis-Smith, 2015; Spironelli et al., 2014). Intelligence may act as a protective factor during the onset of disorders by helping at-risk individuals compensate for psychological dysfunctions, avoid maladaptive outcomes, or stop self-reinforcing feedback loops between symptoms before they develop into full-blown conditions. Likewise, cognitive skills may promote recovery once a disorder has developed (e.g., high IQ is the main predictor of eventual remission from autism; Helt et al., 2008; Seltzer et al., 2004). Finally, there is a small but reliable negative correlation between g and neuroticism (Chapter 3), and neuroticism has been associated with smaller brain volume and reduced white matter integrity (Bjørnebekk et al., 2013). Thus, low intelligence may indirectly increase the risk for defense activation disorders. To reinforce this effect, poor performance in laboratory tests of executive functions (which are robustly associated with g) predicts a higher frequency of stressors that depend at least in part on one's behavior, as for example divorce and job loss; in turn, those stressors lead to increased levels of anxiety and depression (Snyder & Hankin, 2016).

All of the preceding suggest that low cognitive ability should work as a generalized risk factor for many kinds of psychiatric conditions. This is precisely what the evidence shows (Caspi et al., 2014; Castellanos-Ryan et al., 2016; Koenen et al., 2009; Neumann et al., 2016; Urfer-Parnas et al., 2010). The association should be especially strong for disorders that involve dysfunctions and/or clearly maladaptive outcomes. A case in point is schizophrenia, which shows remarkably strong associations with low premorbid intelligence. On average, the early IQ of people who will develop schizophrenia is about 0.5 SD lower than that of healthy controls, and declining IQ through adolescence is a powerful risk factor for this disorder (Khandaker et al., 2011; Koenen et al., 2009; MacCabe et al., 2010; Meier, Caspi et al., 2014; Woodberry et al., 2008). Symmetrically, negative associations with intelligence should be attenuated—or even reversed—for conditions that reflect adaptive or potentially adaptive strategies. For example, OCPD and NPD are not associated with low IQ, and there is some evidence that people with NPD tend to have above-average intelligence (Coid, 1999; Hengartner et al., 2014). Manic symptoms correlate with higher IQ, and the risk for bipolar disorders has been found to increase with higher academic performance (Hagenaars et al., 2016; Koenen et al., 2009; MacCabe et al., 2010; Smith, Anderson et al., 2015). The picture for autism is more complicated; while mild forms of ASD grade into the territory of adaptive strategies, the more severe cases—especially those with intellectual disability—are unquestionably dysfunctional. The overall correlation between autistic symptoms and IQ in children is somewhat negative (around −.20); however, genetic risk scores for autism based on common alleles also predict *higher* intelligence and academic success (Clarke et al., 2016; Hagenaars et al., 2016; Hoekstra et al., 2010). Taken together, these findings suggest that rare and de novo mutations (which tend to lower cognitive ability and are not included in genetic risk scores in the studies I just cited) are largely responsible for the dysfunctional aspects of ASD (more on this in Chapter 10).

Intelligence shows a significant degree of assortative mating, with correlations between partners of about .40 (Plomin & Deary, 2015; Vinkhuyzen et al., 2012). Assortative mating for intelligence may contribute to explain findings of partner similarity for some mental disorders. Indeed, the highest levels of similarity between partners have been documented in autism, schizophrenia, and ADHD (Nordsletten et al., 2016). As I discuss in Part III of the book, all these diagnostic categories include at least one subtype that is robustly associated with low IQ.

Intelligence and Socioeconomic Status

A final point to consider is the robust correlation that exists between g and measures of socioeconomic status. This association does not simply reflect the fact that better education and a stimulating family environment may increase performance on intelligence tests. On the contrary, there is strong evidence that intelligence plays an important *causal* role in determining an individual's eventual occupation and income and that the same genetic factors that raise g also tend to increase SES (see Gottfredson, 2011; Ericsson et al., 2017; Trzaskowski et al., 2014). The main implication for psychopathology is that some well-established associations between low SES and risk for psychiatric disorders are likely to be partly confounded by individual differences in intelligence. For example, the finding that autistic disorders with and without intellectual disability are differentially associated with socioeconomic factors (discussed in an earlier section) is consistent with the idea that genetic risk for intellectual disability is higher in low-SES families. The strong link between socioeconomic disadvantage and risk for ADHD should also be considered in this light, given that ADHD symptoms correlate with lower IQ owing to shared genetic factors (Clarke et al., 2016; Kuntsi et al., 2004).

Comparison with Transdiagnostic Models

The FSD taxonomy offers an evolutionary alternative to transdiagnostic models of the structure of mental disorders. Over the years, the original model based on the internalizing–externalizing distinction has evolved and become more complex. Most authors now include a thought disorder factor for SSDs and other psychotic conditions, and there have been initial attempts made to add a separate factor for the autism spectrum (e.g., Carragher et al., 2016; Kotov et al., 2011; Noordhof et al., 2015). The HiTOP model includes a detachment factor and splits the domain of externalizing symptoms into two overlapping spectra (disinhibition and antagonism; Kotov et al., 2017). Above and beyond these factors or spectra, it is possible to identify a "p factor" that reflects generalized risk for all kinds of mental disorders. The p factor is about 40% heritable, with a major influence of common genetic variants (Carragher et al., 2016; Caspi et al., 2014; Laceulle et al., 2015; Lahey et al., 2015; Neumann et al., 2016; Waldman et al., 2016).

While most conditions can be located within the model's structure with reasonable confidence, some disorders correlate strongly with more than one factor and are said to occupy "interstitial" positions: in particular, BPD and PTSD correlate with both the internalizing and externalizing factors, while BDs correlate with the internalizing and thought disorder factors. Also, OCD has been alternatively classified as an internalizing or thought disorder (Carragher et al., 2015; Caspi et al., 2014; Forbes et al., 2016; Kotov et al., 2017). Despite minor inconsistencies between different versions of the model, its basic structure has been empirically supported in many large studies. In this section, I compare the FSD and transdiagnostic models in some detail and discuss how the existing data on the structure of psychopathology can be interpreted and explained from a life history perspective.

Internalizing and Externalizing Disorders

In earlier discussions of the life history framework, I argued that the internalizing spectrum is not a fully coherent dimension of psychopathology as it comprises a mixture of functionally divergent conditions (Del Giudice, 2014*a*, 2016*d*). This criticism was based on the original version of the framework, which lacked a separate category for defense activation disorders. With the inclusion of D-type conditions, the FSD model has recovered key aspects of the internalizing spectrum, and its structure has become more similar to that of the standard transdiagnostic model. At the same time, some important differences remain. In the transdiagnostic approach, disorders are assigned to the internalizing category if they show strong empirical correlations with the internalizing factor. In contrast, the classification of D-type conditions relies on the functional criterion of whether the symptoms of a disorder primarily reflect the activation of defensive mechanisms. Thus, eating disorders are classified as internalizing because of their comorbidity with anxiety and depression but do not fit the FSD criteria for D-type conditions. In fact, the inclusion of EDs in the internalizing spectrum is problematic: when symptoms are clustered based on the associated personality profiles, a subtype of EDs turns out to be strongly associated with externalizing behaviors, while another subtype shows very little comorbidity with either depression or anxiety (Chapter 13). Even though interstitial conditions such as BPD and BDs have marked depressive components, from a life history perspective they are better understood as F-type and S-type conditions rather than pure disorders of defense activation. In sum, the internalizing spectrum of transdiagnostic models does include a functionally coherent "core" of defense-related conditions, but instead is rendered heterogeneous by the inclusion of other disorders such as EDs, BDs, and BPD.

Similar considerations apply to the externalizing spectrum. Antisocial and conduct disorders such as ASPD, CD, and ODD clearly form a coherent cluster linked to the antagonistic/exploitative profile. However, the status of ADHD is much less straightforward, even if this condition is routinely classified as externalizing because of its robust associations with CD and ODD (e.g., Castellanos-Ryan et al., 2016; Kotov et al., 2017). As I discuss in Chapter 11, the fast spectrum subtype of ADHD overlaps not just with antisocial conditions but also with schizophrenia and psychosis, whereas the slow spectrum subtype is closer to autism. I also argue ADHD contains a subtype that is mainly linked to low intelligence and has no functional connections with life history strategy (O-ADHD). This complex pattern challenges the classification of ADHD as a simple externalizing disorder. Substance use disorders (SUDs) are also routinely included in the externalizing spectrum (externalizing-disinhibited in the HiTOP) but are not covered in the current version of the FSD model. While there is a strong link between fast-related traits and risk for SUDs (e.g., Quintelier et al., 2013; Richardson et al., 2014, 2016;

Vincke, 2016), the picture is likely more complex: for instance, some personality profiles associated with substance use may be closer to the slow spectrum or more characteristic of D-type disorders such as depression and social anxiety (e.g., Bulley et al., 2016; Del Giudice, 2014*b*; Yeo et al., 2014). More generally, the FSD and transdiagnostic model differ in the structural role assigned to externalizing disorders. According to the transdiagnostic approach, the externalizing spectrum is one of the fundamental dimensions of psychopathology. In the FSD model, externalizing conditions such as ASPD, CD, ODD, and F-ADHD are only one subset within the broader category of fast spectrum disorders, which also includes a number of internalizing and interstitial disorders (BPD, the fast spectrum subtypes of BDs and EDs), thought disorders (SSDs), and other conditions (NPD). Figure 6.5 summarizes the relations between the FSD taxonomy and the main categories of the transdiagnostic model.

With respect to the internalizing–externalizing distinction, an important advantage of the FSD model is that it makes "interstitial" classifications unnecessary. For example, defense activation conditions can occur in association with both S-type and F-type disorders; thus, the fact that BPD is strongly comorbid with depression and anxiety does not create a classification problem. Another advantage of the FSD model is its parsimony: with just two main dimensions of variation (a bipolar fast–slow continuum and a defense activation axis), the model provides an integrated structural account of internalizing and externalizing conditions but also autism, psychosis, and disorders such as NPD and OCPD that still have no clear placement in the transdiagnostic model. However, the real added value of the FSD model lies in the underlying theoretical framework, which brings coherence to the taxonomy and increases its heuristic power. For example, on a purely descriptive level, the D-type cluster of conditions is similar to the internalizing spectrum of the transdiagnostic model. Still, framing the same conditions as disorders of evolved defensive mechanisms affords unique insights into their developmental and comorbidity patterns, risk factors, and other important features.

The p Factor

In the most recent versions of the transdiagnostic model, the p factor captures a dimension of generalized risk that is shared by all kinds of psychopathology. The FSD model does not include such a general factor, although it recognizes that low cognitive ability tends to increase the risk for many (but not all) mental disorders. From the standpoint of the FSD model, the p factor is an artifact that reflects a mixture of three functionally distinct dimensions of variation: risk for fast spectrum psychopathology, risk for defense activation disorders, and low intelligence. These dimensions are not just conceptually distinct but also statistically separable, although they are expected to correlate to some degree—first because stressful conditions increase the risk for both D-type and F-type disorders, and second because low intelligence is weakly associated with both defense activation (neuroticism) and fast life history–related traits (Chapter 4). The p factor remains approximately valid at a descriptive level, as some people *are* at higher risk for a wide range of psychiatric conditions. However, such a general factor fails to capture the

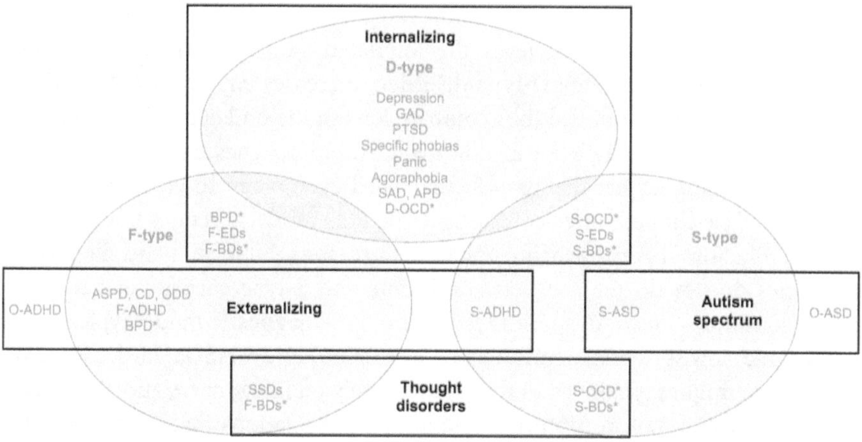

Figure 6.5. Relations between disorder categories in the FSD taxonomy and the main dimensions of transdiagnostic models. The internalizing spectrum includes defense activation (D-type) disorders as well as a number of F-type and S-type conditions, some of which are classified as "interstitial" (e.g., borderline personality disorder, bipolar disorders). The externalizing spectrum includes a number of F-type conditions (antisocial and conduct disorders; borderline personality disorder), in addition to attention-deficit/hyperactivity disorder (which has both F-type and S-type variants, and an O-type variant characterized by low intelligence and unrelated to life history variation). Thought disorders comprise schizophrenia spectrum disorders and bipolar disorders (which have both F-type and S-type variants); OCD is sometimes grouped with thought disorders, other times with internalizing disorders. In the FSD model, autism spectrum disorders include a slow spectrum subtype with normal/high intelligence, and an O-type variant with intellectual disability that is unrelated to life history variation. Asterisks denote conditions that are usually regarded as interstitial or have been classified in different spectra of the transdiagnostic model. ADHD = attention-deficit/hyperactivity disorder. APD = avoidant personality disorder. ASD = autism spectrum disorder. ASPD = antisocial personality disorder. BDs = bipolar disorders. BPD = borderline personality disorder. CD = conduct disorder. EDs = eating disorders. GAD = generalized anxiety disorder. NPD = narcissistic personality disorder. OCD = obsessive-compulsive disorder. OCPD = obsessive-compulsive personality disorder. ODD = oppositional-defiant disorder. PTSD = posttraumatic stress disorder. SAD = social anxiety disorder. SSDs = schizophrenia spectrum disorders.

specific risk for slow spectrum disorders beyond the component associated with low intelligence and/or elevated mutation load. More importantly, the p factor is not a coherent functional construct, emerging as it does from the combination of three separate sources of variation with different biological underpinnings.

This alternative interpretation of the p factor is supported by simulation results and consistent with the available empirical data. In a simulation study, I showed that the p factor, the internalizing factor, and the externalizing factor emerge reliably when standard data analysis methods are applied to virtual symptom scores generated from a continuum of risk for F-type versus S-type disorders (Del Giudice, 2016*d*). Adding a largely or completely unrelated dimension of variation in cognitive ability did not change the results. (Note that the simulation did not include a separate defense activation category as it was based on a previous version of the framework; however, the simulated model is formally equivalent to one in which the risk for D-type disorders increases equally at both ends of the fast–slow continuum, and thus compatible with the updated FSD taxonomy.) These findings demonstrate that standard analytic approaches are going to recover the "internalizing–externalizing–p factor" triad even when the true underlying structure of psychopathology conforms to the FSD model and does not include a unitary p factor. This happens for three main reasons. First, standard diagnostic categories do not distinguish between F-type and S-type variants of heterogeneous conditions. Second, studies testing the transdiagnostic model typically do not include slow spectrum conditions such as OCPD and S-ASD. Third, the factor analysis techniques employed in those studies rely on linear correlations between symptoms, which fail to capture the nonlinear associations that arise when the risk for a disorder (e.g., depression) increases at both ends of the fast–slow continuum (for details, see Del Giudice, 2016*d*).

Simulation results are further corroborated by the empirical correlations between the p factor and a range of cognitive, personality, and environmental variables. The available data show that high scores on the p factor are associated with indices of low intelligence and reduced neural integrity, including low IQ scores, neurological abnormalities, and damage to the retinal vasculature; fast spectrum markers such as low conscientiousness, low agreeableness, impulsivity, high time discounting, and reduced self-control; defense activation markers such as high neuroticism and negative emotionality; and high levels of early stress and adversity, which should increase the risk of both F-type and D-type disorders (Carver et al., 2017; Caspi et al., 2014; Castellanos-Ryan et al., 2016; Neumann et al., 2016; Waldman et al., 2016). This pattern of correlations is consistent with the idea that the p factor is a functionally heterogeneous construct, in line with the alternative interpretation advanced here.

ANALYSIS OF COMMON MENTAL DISORDERS

In this chapter, I presented an overview of the FSD model and listed the psychiatric conditions included in the current version of the taxonomy. In Part III of the book (Chapters 7–20) I examine those conditions in more depth. For each disorder (or group of disorders), I begin with an overview of key symptoms and correlates and summarize the evidence on the condition's genetic structure, comorbidity, developmental features, and risk factors. I then review the main evolutionary models of the disorder, examine them in relation to the taxonomy presented in Chapter 5, and present a selection of relevant empirical findings. Finally, I analyze each diagnostic category from the standpoint of the FSD model and consider the possibility that it may comprise functionally distinct subtypes.

PART III

Common Mental Disorders

7

Antisocial and Conduct Disorders

OVERVIEW

Psychopathy

Antisocial and conduct disorders form a cluster of related conditions at the core of the externalizing spectrum. The prototype of this cluster is psychopathy, a condition defined by a combination of affective/interpersonal traits—superficial charm, manipulativeness, callousness, and lack of remorse—and behavioral traits such as impulsivity, irresponsibility, and an antisocial or "parasitic" lifestyle. The affective/interpersonal component is usually labeled *primary psychopathy* and is associated with fearlessness and low anxiety (i.e., reduced activation of the behavioral inhibition system [BIS] and fear system); in the developmental literature, the childhood manifestations of primary psychopathy are referred to as *callous-unemotional traits*. The behavioral component is labeled *secondary psychopathy* and is strongly linked to sensation seeking and hyperactivation of the behavioral approach system ([BAS]; Broerman et al., 2014; Hughes et al., 2012; Roose et al., 2011; Vitale & Newman, 2013; Waldman & Lahey, 2013; Yildirim & Derksen, 2015*a*).

Psychopathic traits are continuously distributed in the population and are about 50% heritable, with virtually no contribution from the shared environment (Haslam et al., 2012; Vitale & Newman, 2013; Waldman & Rhee, 2006). Starting from middle childhood, fearlessness and callous-unemotional traits become associated with dampened reactivity to stressors, particularly in the sympathetic and HPA components of the stress response system (Alink et al., 2008; Del Giudice et al., 2011; Dindo & Fowles, 2011; Hawes et al., 2009; Lorber, 2004). While stress hyperreactivity correlates with reactive aggression (as in the vigilant pattern of the adaptive calibration model [ACM]; Chapter 4), hyporeactivity specifically predicts engagement in proactive, predatory aggression (as in the unemotional pattern). The physiological and emotional unresponsivity associated with callous-unemotional traits in childhood seems to develop gradually over the first years of life; recent evidence suggests that children who develop high levels of callous-unemotional traits in childhood tend to show *heightened* stress reactivity and fearfulness during infancy (Mills-Koonce et al., 2015).

There is ongoing debate as to whether overt antisocial behavior (e.g., stealing, physical assault) should be regarded as a core aspect of psychopathy or merely as a typical outcome of psychopathic traits. Despite the strong link between psychopathy and delinquency, many people with a psychopathic personality avoid incarceration, and "successful psychopaths" can actually thrive in competitive, high-risk professions—from politics and business to law enforcement, firefighting, and dangerous sports. Successful psychopaths show high levels of primary psychopathy and fearlessness but comparatively low levels of secondary psychopathy and disinhibition. Potential factors that differentiate between successful and unsuccessful psychopaths include executive functioning and self-control, conscientiousness, and general intelligence (Boccio & Beaver, 2015; Gao & Raine, 2010; Lilienfeld et al., 2012, 2014; Lilienfeld, Watts, & Francis Smith, 2015; Lilienfeld, Watts, Francis-Smith, et al., 2015; Mullins-Sweatt et al., 2010; Spironelli et al., 2014; Yildirim & Derksen, 2015*a*).

Antisocial and Conduct Disorders

Despite its centrality in the clinical and research literature, psychopathy is not included in the DSM as a diagnostic category. The DSM counterpart of psychopathy is antisocial personality disorder (ASPD), which is mainly defined by antisocial and criminal behavior, physical aggression, impulsivity, and irresponsibility. While psychopathy and ASPD are obviously related, the criteria for ASPD give little consideration to the affective/interpersonal facets of primary psychopathy and instead emphasize overt antisocial behaviors. As a result, a substantial proportion of those who qualify for the diagnosis of ASPD do not match the personality profile of a psychopath (Vitale & Newman, 2013). The heritability of ASPD is lower than that of psychopathy (about 40%), and shared environmental effects seem to play a somewhat larger role in its etiology (up to 10%, although not all studies support this conclusion; Kendler et al., 2008, 2012; Waldman & Rhee, 2006).

In the DSM system, ASPD can only be diagnosed in adults, as with the other personality disorders (see Chapter 12). However, antisocial and rule-breaking behaviors typically emerge much earlier in development. In addition to ASPD, the DSM-5 category of "disruptive, impulse control, and conduct disorders" includes two conditions that can be diagnosed in childhood and adolescence: oppositional defiant disorder (ODD) and conduct disorder (CD). The criteria for ODD include angry and irritable mood, vindictiveness, and argumentative or defiant behaviors (e.g., arguing with authority figures, deliberately annoying others, refusing to comply with rules); aggression in ODD is mostly reactive and linked to negative mood. The symptoms of CD are markedly more severe than those of ODD and comprise proactive aggressive behaviors (e.g., bullying, attacking someone with weapons, cruelty to animals, forcing someone into sexual activity), destruction of property, theft, deceitfulness, and serious rule violations (e.g., frequently running away from home, truancy).

All the disorders in the antisocial cluster share a common set of genetic influences, and there is a definite developmental tendency to progress from ODD to CD to ASPD. At each step in the sequence, about 25–30% of individuals move up to the more severe diagnosis; this means that most children and adolescents diagnosed with ODD never meet the criteria for CD, and most of those diagnosed with CD never meet the criteria for ASPD. However, the risk for ASPD in adulthood is much higher when conduct symptoms in childhood are coupled with callous-unemotional traits and/or a diagnosis of attention-deficit/hyperactivity disorder (ADHD; Chapter 11). The heritability of CD in childhood is about 50%; shared environmental effects range from about 10% to 30%, are largely or exclusively restricted to nonaggressive symptoms, and become stronger at increasing levels of socioeconomic disadvantage (Burt, 2014; Burt et al., 2016; Links et al., 2012; Taylor et al., 2013; Waldman & Lahey, 2013; Waldman & Rhee, 2006).

Antisocial and conduct disorders are strongly male-biased (with ratios ranging from 2:1 to 5:1) and show high rates of comorbidity with ADHD and defense activation disorders such as depression, generalized anxiety disorder (GAD), social anxiety disorder (SAD), and posttraumatic stress disorder (PTSD). The largest association at the genetic and phenotypic level is with substance use disorders (SUDs), to the extent that many authors regard substance use as a core component of the externalizing spectrum (Coid, 1999; Coid et al., 2006; Koenen et al., 2014; Links et al., 2012; McAdams et al., 2011; Slade, 2007; Verona et al., 2011).

Development and Course

There are multiple pathways to the onset of antisocial disorders. Developmental research on deviancy and delinquency has described four prototypical trajectories (Figure 7.1; Jennings & Reingle, 2012; Moffitt, 1993, 2003). While the majority of people are "abstainers" who show consistently low levels of antisocial behavior, studies consistently identify a small subgroup of individuals (around 5%) who display very high aggression and rule-breaking starting from infancy and continuing through the life course. This trajectory is variously referred to as *early-onset*, *life-course persistent*, or *childhood-onset*, even if defiant and aggressive behaviors are often in place by 2–3 years of age and may begin to emerge already during the first year of life (Lorber et al., 2015). The early-onset trajectory is strongly male-biased (about 10:1) and is frequently characterized by boldness, fearlessness, and lack of anxiety; this trajectory is associated with particularly high levels of callous-unemotional traits in childhood, as well as primary psychopathy and elevated risk of ASPD in adulthood (Byrd et al., 2016; Shaw et al., 2003; Waldman & Lahey, 2013; Yildirim & Derksen, 2012*a*).

In addition to the early-onset trajectory, developmental studies have identified a larger group characterized by so-called *adolescent-onset* of antisocial behavior. In fact, conduct problems in this group reach their peak in adolescence but emerge already in middle childhood (Del Giudice et al., 2009; Haltigan et al., 2011; Sentse

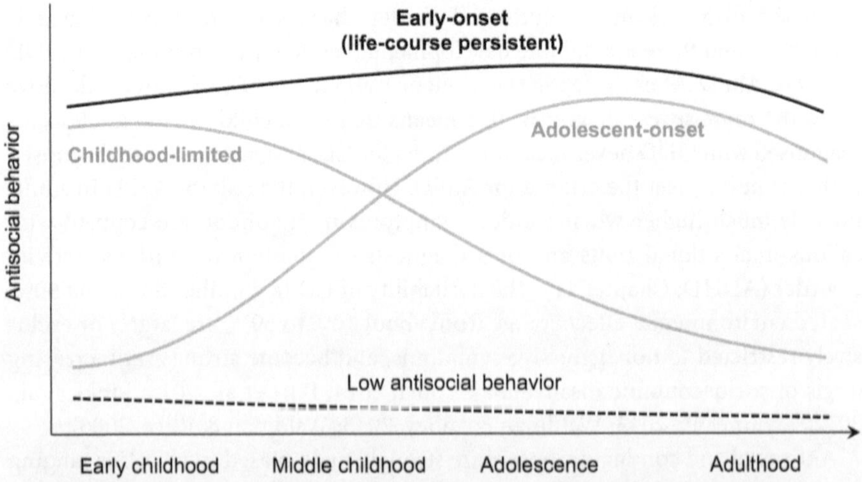

Figure 7.1. Common developmental trajectories of antisocial behavior. Note that "adolescent-onset" trajectories are characterized by a rapid increase of antisocial behavior during middle childhood.

et al., 2017). Another common label for this trajectory is *adolescent-limited*, based on the initial hypothesis that the gap between biological and social maturity experienced by adolescents would cause a temporary increase in deviancy in this age group (Moffitt, 1993). In fact, later research has shown that this pattern is not nearly as normative as previously believed and comprises between 10% and 20% of adolescents in most studies. People who follow adolescent-onset trajectories show relatively high levels of psychopathy and impulsivity and often continue to engage in antisocial behaviors into adulthood, even if the frequency of violent and delinquent acts decreases steadily with age (Jennings et al., 2016; Moffitt & Caspi, 2005; Moffitt et al., 2002; Sentse et al., 2017). Finally, some studies have identified a *childhood-limited* group characterized by high aggression and defiance in infancy and childhood, followed by a rapid decrease during middle childhood and adolescence. Childhood-limited trajectories are associated with comparatively low levels of psychopathy, and tend to predict later anxiety and depression more strongly than they predict violence and offending. For both childhood-limited and adolescent-onset trajectories, the developmental transition toward higher or lower levels of antisocial behavior usually takes place in middle childhood (Figure 7.1; Byrd et al., 2016; Jennings & Reingle, 2012; Moffitt et al., 2002; Sentse et al., 2017).

Moving from developmental trajectories to diagnostic categories, the risk for ODD and CD shows a first peak in middle childhood followed by another increase in adolescence. By definition, ASPD can only be diagnosed in adults; its prevalence peaks in early adulthood and diminishes steadily with age, particularly after the third decade. Notably, psychopathic traits decline more slowly than ASPD criteria across the life course, mostly due to the stability of the affective/interpersonal facets of primary psychopathy (Grant et al., 2004;

Slade, 2007; Torgersen et al., 2001; Vachon et al., 2013). The developmental course of antisocial and conduct disorders is intertwined with that of D-type conditions. Depression and anxiety in childhood tend to predict CD and ODD in adolescence, which in turn predict the onset of depression, GAD, and other defense-related conditions such as PTSD and SAD in adulthood. While early-onset antisocial behavior is associated with disorders such as depression, GAD, and PTSD, the childhood-limited subtype shows the highest risk for the onset of defense activation disorders later in life. This is consistent with the finding that anger and irritability in ODD specifically predict depression, whereas defiance and rule-breaking predict escalating conduct problems in adolescence and adulthood (Copeland et al., 2013; Costello et al., 2003, 2011; Moffitt et al., 2002; Sentse et al., 2017; Whelan et al., 2013).

Risk Factors

Antisocial and conduct disorders are associated with adversity, low socioeconomic status (SES), and a wide range of family stressors such as harsh discipline, maltreatment, abuse, neglect, and parental loss. Additionally, the risk for CD correlates with low birth weight, prenatal malnutrition, and birth complications; there is also some evidence that younger maternal age is a predictor of mixed externalizing and internalizing symptoms in children. In general, early-onset trajectories are associated with the highest levels of socioeconomic, familial, and prenatal risk factors, as well as low childhood IQ (Coid, 1999; Edwards & Hans, 2015; Grant et al., 2004; Koenen et al., 2014; Moffitt et al., 2002; Waldman & Lahey, 2013). At the same time, psychopathy in adulthood correlates only weakly with intelligence (less than −.10), and psychopathic traits are not systematically associated with indices of developmental perturbations such as low-grade *fluctuating asymmetry* between the left and right side of the body or minor physical anomalies (Blair, 2005; Coid, 1999; de Ribera et al., 2017; Harris et al., 2001; Lalumière et al., 2001). These findings suggest that persistent antisocial behavior may comprise different subtypes with different etiologies, perhaps reflecting variable combinations of genetic and environmental influences (e.g., Hawes et al., 2009).

At least for some people, social learning may play a role in the development of antisocial behavior: studies of children and adolescents support the idea that contact with delinquent peers and groups increases deviancy through "contagion effects" (Dishion & Patterson, 2016). Shared environmental factors seem to play a small but non-negligible role in the origin of both CD and ASPD, and there is initial evidence of G×E interactions between children's genetic risk of externalizing behavior and the characteristics of their peer groups (Salvatore et al., 2015). It is important to remember that many of the empirical associations between antisocial disorders and putative risk factors discussed here are likely to be confounded by genotype-environment correlations and shared genetic effects between parents and offspring.

EVOLUTIONARY MODELS

Evolutionary scholars have long stressed the adaptive role of aggressive and antisocial behavior as a high-risk strategy for social and mating competition (see Ellis et al., 2012; Glenn et al., 2011; Kruesi & Schowalter, 2006; Martel, 2013). In evolutionary psychopathology, antisocial disorders are usually regarded as costly but potentially adaptive strategies rather than behavioral dysfunctions. Some authors have focused specifically on the evolution of psychopathy, and argued that this condition embodies a "cheater" social strategy designed to exploit other people's trust and cooperative behavior while avoiding reciprocation (Harpending & Sobus, 1987; Mealey, 1995). Others have adopted a broader life history perspective and framed antisocial and conduct disorders (including psychopathy) as manifestations of fast strategies, emphasizing their sexual and reproductive correlates in addition to their effects on cooperation (Barr & Quinsey, 2004; Belsky et al., 1991; Boutwell et al., 2013; Del Giudice, 2014*a*; Draper & Harpending, 1988; Kruesi & Schowalter, 2006; MacMillan & Kofoed, 1984). Adaptive models of antisocial disorders are widely accepted in the literature and supported by a substantial amount of evidence; however, subtler questions remain about the potential role of evolutionary mismatches and the possibility that at least some instances of these disorders may reflect genuinely dysfunctional and/or maladaptive outcomes.

Psychopathy as a Cheater Strategy

Mathematical models of social evolution show that when selection favors generalized cooperation in a species or population, the spread of cooperative phenotypes creates a niche for cheaters who fail to reciprocate the benefits they receive. Cheater phenotypes have been described in many different species and range from simple biochemical mechanisms (for example in cooperating bacteria) to sophisticated behavioral tactics involving deception, false displays of cooperation and altruism, and high mobility to avoid detection and punishment (Bergmüller et al., 2010; Kurzban & Houser, 2005; McNally & Jackson, 2013). Since cheaters can only thrive in populations whose members are mostly cooperators, the evolution of cheating is subject to negative frequency-dependent selection—that is, cheater strategies are selected for when they are rare but selected against as soon as they become more common (Chapter 3).

An influential hypothesis in evolutionary psychopathology is that, in our species, psychopaths express a low-frequency cheater strategy based on deception and manipulation (Harpending & Sobus, 1987; Mealey, 1995). From this vantage point, traits such as superficial charm or lack of guilt and remorse can be framed as design features rather than social deficits. Of course, cheating strategies are not without downsides, and the potential fitness benefits of exploitation need to be balanced against the costs of punishment, retaliation, and ostracism that may befall cheaters when they are exposed. While these costs would have been especially high in small-scale forager societies characterized by intense social control, evolutionary constraints on the expression of psychopathic traits should have loosened considerably with the transition to agriculture and even further with the advent of cities and their anonymous crowds (see Chapter 4). The general idea that psychopathy represents a potentially adaptive strategy is consistent with the finding that even violent psychopaths who harm nonrelatives tend to spare closely related individuals, such as their own parents and children (Krupp et al., 2012, 2013).

Mealey (1995) presented the most detailed version of this model, in which she argued that there are two main pathways to the development of psychopathy. In Mealey's model, the first pathway is strongly based on genetic predisposition, with little or no role for environmental factors. Frequency-dependent selection on cheater phenotypes translates into balancing selection on alleles that increase or decrease the corresponding traits, which in turn contributes to maintain genotypic differences in the predisposition for psychopathy. Individuals at the extreme of this genotypic continuum express the full-blown cheater strategy (i.e., clinical psychopathy) regardless of their environment and conditions, at approximately similar rates across populations and cultures. The second pathway involves adaptive plasticity, either in response to harsh environmental conditions (conditional adaptation) or cues of strong competitive disadvantage such as low intelligence and/or attractiveness, poor health, and socioeconomic deprivation (facultative calibration). Even if both pathways ultimately lead to the development of psychopathy, only the second pathway should be associated with standard risk factors such as maltreatment, negative family relationships, and low SES.

The developmental predictions of Mealey's two-pathway model have turned out to be at odds with the empirical data on early-onset trajectories. In the early-onset group, unemotional traits and antisocial behavior emerge too early to enable the kind of adaptive plasticity envisioned by the model, and yet, this trajectory shows the strongest associations with maltreatment, socioeconomic disadvantage, and low intelligence. One possibility is that early-onset trajectories reflect dysfunctional outcomes rather than adaptive individual differences (more on this later). Another is that Mealey's genetic hypothesis only applies to a subset of children with this developmental pattern. Consistent with this view, persistent violent offending is associated with low IQ, perinatal complications, and minor physical anomalies (which indicate developmental stress and/or mutation load), but psychopathy per se is largely unrelated to these variables (Allen et al., 2013; Barr & Quinsey, 2004; Glenn et al., 2011). Another factor that was not explicitly considered by Mealey is the confounding effect of genotype–environment correlations. For example, psychopathic traits in children may elicit more aggression and harsher discipline from parents, and parents with a high genetic predisposition to psychopathy may be more likely to end up in low-SES occupations. In these plausible scenarios, one would expect to find sizable correlations between psychopathic traits and familial/socioeconomic variables even if the latter played no causal role in the development of psychopathy.

A related but somewhat distinct perspective on psychopathy comes from studies that employ economic games to detect individual differences in cooperation. In these studies, people with higher psychopathic traits tend to be significantly more "strategic" in their interactions with potential cooperation partners. In particular, they reciprocate high-value partners (i.e., those with the potential to provide large benefits in the future) but systematically defect on low-value ones (Gervais et al., 2013). In other words, psychopathy in the nonclinical range does not predict indiscriminate cheating but rather a highly selective, impersonal, and calculated approach to cooperation. While classic evolutionary models emphasize the high-risk benefits of systematic cheating (i.e., clinical psychopathy), these findings suggest that moderate levels of psychopathic traits may be adaptive in a broader range of conditions if they promote selective cooperation with strangers.

Life History Models of Antisocial Disorders

In a life history perspective, antisocial traits can be adaptive as a behavioral component of fast, mating-oriented strategies. MacMillan and Kofoed (1984) were the first to argue that ASPD represents an alternative reproductive strategy based on sexual opportunism, promiscuous short-term mating, and investment in offspring quantity at the expense of parental investment and care. Over the years, evidence has accumulated that disorders in the antisocial/conduct cluster are associated with faster sexual maturation and earlier age of intercourse, pregnancy, and fatherhood, as well as unrestricted sociosexuality, larger numbers of sexual partners, and harsh or uninvolved parenting (see Barr & Quinsey, 2004; Belsky et al., 1991; Del Giudice, 2014*a*; Dorn et al., 2008; Glenn et al., 2011; Gutiérrez et al., 2013; Kruesi & Schowalter, 2006; Negriff & Susman, 2011; Mendle, 2014). In addition, there are indications that the behavioral profile of psychopathy includes a pattern of precocious and coercive sexuality (Harris et al., 2007; Jonason et al., 2009, 2010).

A life history approach to antisocial disorders does not contradict the hypothesis of psychopathy as cheating; rather, it frames deception and reduced cooperation as facets of a broader behavioral and reproductive strategy. A life history perspective also expands the scope for balancing selection on genes involved in antisocial behavior and psychopathy, complementing the standard frequency-dependent account of cheater models with scenarios based on spatially and temporally variable selection. For example, recurrent fluctuations in a population's sex ratio may contribute to maintain genetic variation in life history strategies and the associated behavioral traits, including psychopathy (Del Giudice, 2012*b*).

In a series of papers, Boutwell and colleagues (Boutwell et al., 2013; Boutwell, Barnes et al., 2015) employed life history concepts to reinterpret the developmental evidence on antisocial trajectories. These authors argued that the early-onset trajectory is the developmental expression of a fast strategy, whereas the trajectory of abstainers represents the extreme of a slow strategy. People in the middle range of the fast–slow continuum are assumed to follow a normative adolescent-onset (or "adolescent-limited") trajectory. Boutwell and colleagues showed that life-course patterns of delinquency are associated with especially high levels of promiscuity and large numbers of sexual partners; they also documented that the correlation between delinquency and sexual behavior is partly explained by shared genetic factors (Boutwell, Nedelec et al., 2015). These findings are consistent with evidence that men with early-onset conduct problems tend to become fathers early in life and have more children than their less antisocial peers (Moffitt & Caspi, 2005; Moffitt et al., 2002).

The model by Boutwell and colleagues regards adolescent-onset patterns as normative and transitory, as originally proposed by Moffitt (1993); however, I noted earlier that this proposition has not been supported by developmental research. It is probably relevant that these authors based their analysis on longitudinal data starting from age 11. In all likelihood, the "life-course persistent" groups they identified include a mixture of early-onset trajectories beginning in infancy and "adolescent-onset" trajectories beginning in middle childhood. Likewise, the "adolescent-limited" groups in their studies probably include a substantial proportion of children who follow a childhood-limited pattern, which in turn is only weakly predictive of antisocial behavior in adulthood. The totality of the evidence indicates that both early-onset and adolescent-onset trajectories are associated with fast life history strategies; individuals in the early-onset group display a particularly extreme version of the corresponding traits, including fearlessness, callous-unemotional traits, and primary psychopathy. Despite these caveats, the model is an important step toward integrating the life history approach with the findings of developmental psychopathology.

While early- and adolescent-onset trajectories can be interpreted as manifestations of fast strategies, the functional underpinnings of the childhood-limited trajectory remain unclear. We also know little about the mechanisms that determine a drop in antisocial behavior during middle childhood. Some studies show a trajectory of increasing prosocial behavior and peer acceptance in the childhood-limited group (Barker et al., 2010; Veenstra et al., 2009); these findings suggest that, in these children, the developmental switch point of middle childhood may bring about a shift toward slower life history strategies, possibly in response to improved social and family conditions. A related possibility is that children in this group may be especially susceptible to the environment, and thus more responsive to improvements in the social context. This would be consistent with the fact that they display high levels of negative emotionality, irritability, and physiological reactivity in early childhood.

Other Evolutionary Scenarios

To conclude this section, it is useful to consider some counterpoints to the common view of antisocial disorders as adaptive or potentially adaptive strategies. To begin, the data indicate that persistent violent offending (but not psychopathy) is associated with a higher frequency of minor physical anomalies, which is an indicator of developmental perturbations and/or deleterious mutations (Barr & Quinsey, 2004). This suggests that early-onset trajectories (which predict persistent offending) may comprise a mixture of adaptive and dysfunctional phenotypes (see Glenn et al., 2011). Another possibility—which has not been explored in the evolutionary literature—is that psychopathic and antisocial traits are adaptive over most of their range but become maladaptive when expressed at extremely high levels. The fitness function of antisocial traits might be cliff-edged if, after a certain threshold, their potential costs (e.g., social ostracism, premature death or disability) systematically started to outweigh the reproductive benefits. As noted in Chapter 5, assortative mating is a common source of maladaptive trait expression; antisocial behavior is not only heritable, but also shows a high degree of assortative mating, with correlations between partners around .50. Assortative mating also occurs for personality traits in the Dark Triad, including psychopathy (Boutwell et al., 2012; Frisell et al., 2012; Kardum et al., 2017; Kruesi & Schowalter, 2006). In principle, the combination of high heritability and partner similarity can lead to maladaptive levels of trait expression in some of the children of moderately antisocial parents.

Another weakness of current models is their incomplete understanding of early-onset trajectories (e.g., Boutwell, Barnes et al., 2015). At the population level, antisocial behaviors peak between middle childhood and young adulthood, consistent with a functional interpretation in terms of dominance and mating competition. While adolescent-onset trajectories conform to this general pattern, the early-onset group represents a puzzling exception to the rule. From a purely proximate standpoint, this atypical developmental trajectory could be explained by the maturation schedule of the mechanisms that underlie fearlessness and callous-unemotional traits. Whereas the BAS and the status and mating systems undergo a rapid maturation phase between middle childhood and adolescence, the fear and security systems are already functional in infancy and early childhood because of their critical role in survival. Thus, boldness and fearlessness—the most distinctive features of the early-onset group—can be expected to emerge much earlier than sensation seeking or dominance orientation. That said, the adaptive benefits (if any) of displaying strong antisocial tendencies already in infancy and early childhood are unclear; in fact, aggression and defiance may have significant fitness costs if they contribute to elicit harsher punishment from parents (e.g., Jaffee et al., 2004; Pardini et al., 2008).

An intriguing possibility is that, in spite of their costs, aggressive traits in early development may serve a protective function against the challenges posed by antisocial parents, including the risk of abuse and infanticide (see Chapter 1). In other words, the traits displayed by children in the early-onset group might be best understood as ontogenetic adaptations to the likely behavior of their parents (who share the genetic predisposition to antisocial and violent behavior). Another possibility is that early aggression may play an adaptive function in competition with siblings, suggesting a role for parent–offspring conflict in the evolutionary origin of early-onset trajectories. Indeed, many of the contextual factors associated with faster life histories are also expected to exacerbate the intensity of parent–offspring conflict and, consequently, sibling competition for resources (see Schlomer et al., 2011). Alternatively, antisocial behavior in early development may arise as a byproduct of selection for the same kind of behavior in adulthood or as a maladaptive offshoot of excessive, inflexible trait expression. All these ideas are highly speculative; the point is that formulating a satisfactory model of early-onset trajectories will require a better understanding of the associated costs and benefits, with an eye to potential conflicts of interest between parents, children, and other family members. Finally, there is evidence that evolutionary mismatches in modern societies contribute to the development of antisocial psychopathology. In particular, age-segregated schooling separates adolescents from young children and infants and indirectly contributes to increase the frequency of externalizing and aggressive behaviors (Chapter 5; Ellis et al., 2012). The effects of this mismatch should be largely limited to adolescent-onset trajectories, and should become apparent in cross-cultural comparisons between societies with different patterns of age segregation.

FSD CLASSIFICATION

Antisocial and conduct disorders are prototypical F-type conditions and embody all the defining features of the antagonistic/exploitative profile. In addition to the evidence on mating and sexual maturation just reviewed, studies of romantic attachment consistently find associations between psychopathy, ASPD, and high levels of insecurity (both anxiety and avoidance). Externalizing symptoms in childhood are most strongly predicted by disorganized attachment to parents, which may be a precursor of the markedly insecure patterns observed in adulthood (Fearon & Belsky, 2011; Mack et al., 2011; Mikulincer & Shaver, 2016; Savard et al., 2015). Disorders in this cluster are also characterized by impulsivity, risk-taking, and sensation seeking; all these dimensions correlate more strongly with secondary than with primary psychopathy (Bagshaw et al., 2014; Birkás & Csathó, 2015; Dean et al., 2013; Fairchild et al., 2009; Figueredo & Jacobs, 2010; Zisner & Beauchaine, 2015). Of note, some studies of executive functions suggest that psychopaths are generally low in inhibition but not in flexibility/shifting, although the evidence in this respect is limited and there are contrasting findings. Overall, antisocial behavior correlates with reduced executive performance in both children and adults, an effect that seems to be only partly mediated by the lower IQ associated with some conditions in this cluster (Bagshaw et al., 2014; Dinn & Harris, 2000; Dolan, 2012; Morgan & Lilienfeld, 2000; Ogilvie et al., 2011).

At the level of broad personality traits, psychopathy and antisocial behavior are robustly associated with low levels of agreeableness, conscientiousness, and honesty-humility. In addition, primary psychopathy shows a mixed pattern of correlations with extraversion facets—positive for dominance and excitement seeking and negative for warmth and sociability—whereas secondary psychopathy is associated with facets of neuroticism that measure anger and hostility

(Gaughan et al., 2012; Jones et al., 2011; Lilienfeld, Watts, Francis Smith, Berg et al, 2015; O'Boyle et al., 2015; Samuel & Widiger, 2008).

In Chapter 4, I discussed how the balance between mechanistic and mentalistic cognition can be expected to vary across life history strategies and profiles, with the seductive/creative and prosocial/caregiving profiles showing the highest investment in mentalizing. Mentalistic skills are somewhat reduced across the externalizing spectrum, including psychopathy (e.g., Ali & Chamorro-Premuzic, 2010; Dolan & Fullam, 2004; Newbury-Helps et al., 2017; Sharp, 2008). Little is known about the specific types of errors made by people with these conditions in mentalizing tasks; at least in part, their poor performance may reflect a tendency to automatically attribute aggressive emotions and hostile motivations to others, which can function as an adaptive bias in violent, high-risk social contexts (e.g., Dodge, 1993, 2006; Mellentin et al., 2015; Schönenberg & Jusyte, 2014; Snyder et al., 2005).

Neurobiology

On the whole, neurobiological findings indicate that psychopathy and antisocial disorders are associated with downregulated serotonergic function (e.g., Fanning et al., 2014; Moul et al., 2013; Soderstrom et al., 2001, 2003; Susman, 2006). While some authors have speculated that low serotonin may be specific to secondary psychopathy (Yildirim & Derksen, 2015*a*), the supporting evidence is still very limited. As for the role of dopamine, the literature is contradictory and open to sharply divergent interpretations. In the nonclinical population, impulsivity is associated with higher levels of mesolimbic dopamine and increased reactivity to rewards. Dopaminergic upregulation in the mesolimbic pathway also seems to characterize psychopathy (Plichta & Scheres, 2014; Seara-Cardoso & Viding, 2015; Yildirim & Derksen, 2015*b*). At the same time, some evidence points to lower dopamine reactivity in externalizing conditions broadly defined, which has led some to argue that impulsivity and sensation seeking stem from dampened, rather than enhanced, mesolimbic function (Beauchaine & Thayer, 2015; Gatzke-Kopp, 2011; Zisner & Beauchaine, 2015). This interpretation is complicated by the fact that many of the relevant studies are confounded by alcohol/drug use and comorbid ADHD, both of which are associated with atypical patterns of dopaminergic regulation (see Plichta & Scheres, 2014; Chapter 11). At present, the evidence is still too fragmented to draw reliable conclusions.

A comparatively well-established neurobiological link is that between androgens and externalizing behavior. People with antisocial and conduct disorders tend to have higher levels of circulating testosterone, and studies of children with CD and ODD have found evidence of elevated adrenal androgens (DHEA, DHEAS) as well. Prenatal exposure to high concentrations of testosterone seems to contribute to increased aggression through organizational influences on brain development, although the magnitude of this effect is difficult to evaluate (Hönekopp & Watson, 2011; Marceau et al., 2015; Yildirim & Derksen, 2012*a*, 2012*b*). The functional connection between androgens and antisocial behavior is highlighted by the finding that boys with antisocial tendencies in childhood undergo a steeper increase in strength and muscularity during the transition to adolescence (Isen et al., 2015).

The literature on oxytocin (OT) and antisocial disorders is sparse; the available data support a negative correlation with OT levels, at least in males (e.g., Dadds et al., 2014; Levy et al., 2015). Of note, genetic polymorphisms in the OT receptor have been associated with antisocial behavior in a recent large-scale study (Hovey et al., 2016). Consistent with the data on reduced mentalizing and oxytocinergic activity, neuroimaging studies find decreased activity and functional connectivity of the default network in CD and psychopathy (Dalwani et al., 2014; Freeman et al., 2015; Lu et al., 2015; Zhou et al., 2016).

In summary, the neurobiology of antisocial and conduct disorders is characterized by reduced serotonergic and oxytocinergic function, elevated androgens at multiple developmental junctures, and—more tentatively—upregulated dopaminergic signaling in mesolimbic pathways. Findings of low default network activity corroborate those of reduced mentalizing abilities in this cluster of disorders. Associations with stress reactivity vary across conditions and age groups; both hyperreactive (vigilant) and hyporeactive (unemotional) patterns have been linked to aggression and defiance. This neurobiological pattern fits reasonably well with the predictions for the antagonistic/exploitative profile advanced in Chapter 4.

8

The Schizophrenia Spectrum

OVERVIEW

The Spectrum of Psychosis

The hallmark of psychotic disorders is loss of contact with external reality. The prototypical symptoms of psychosis are delusions (fixed, unrealistic beliefs that resist disconfirming evidence) and hallucinations (perceptual experiences that occur without an external stimulus). Delusions and hallucinations are referred to as *positive symptoms*—they "add" some unusual content to normal mental functioning—in contrast with *negative symptoms* such as flattened or constricted affect, social isolation, and anhedonia (a marked loss of interest and pleasure in rewarding activities). The third dimension of psychosis is *disorganization*, a heterogeneous symptom category that includes disorganized thinking and speech (e.g., flight of ideas, tangential or incoherent language) as well as disorganized motor behaviors such as agitation, immobility, and stereotyped or inappropriate movements (e.g., staring, mechanical imitation of gestures).

As shown in Figure 8.1, the spectrum of psychosis comprises a remarkably wide range of genetically and phenotypically related conditions. Classically, psychosis spectrum disorders are subdivided into two main clusters, schizophrenia spectrum disorders (SSDs) and bipolar disorders (BDs). Schizophrenia and the other SSDs are characterized by the presence of positive and/or negative symptoms, whereas the defining feature of the bipolar spectrum is extreme elevated mood (*mania*) alternating with depression. However, delusions and hallucinations can also occur in bipolar and depressive episodes, and both manic and depressive symptoms are quite common in schizophrenia (Combs et al., 2014; Trotman et al., 2013). In the DSM, the absence of clear-cut boundaries between SSDs, bipolar, and (to a lesser extent) depressive conditions is reflected in the hybrid category of "schizoaffective disorder," which is characterized by alternating phases of mainly psychotic and mainly affective symptoms.

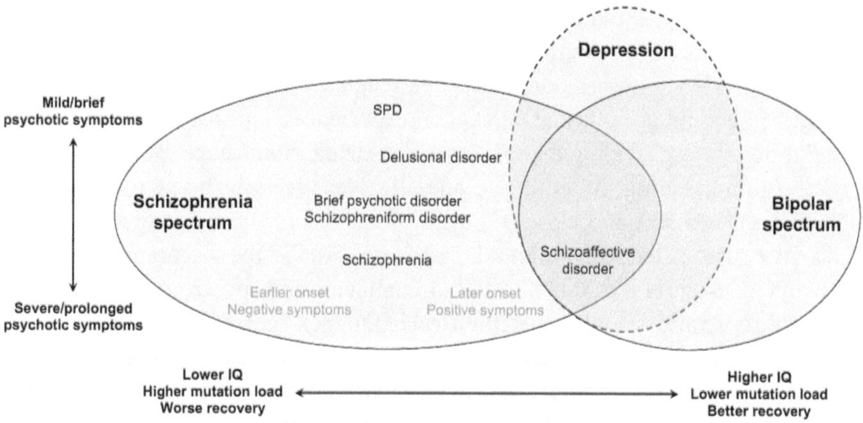

Figure 8.1. The spectrum of psychosis. Schizophrenia spectrum disorders (SSDs) and bipolar disorders blend into each other and can be arranged on a continuum of functionality, with the hybrid category of schizoaffective disorder in the middle. Within SSDs, later age of onset and a prevalence of positive symptoms (delusions, hallucinations) are associated with higher functionality and better prognosis. SPD = schizotypal personality disorder.

Within the psychosis spectrum there is a clear gradient of functionality (Figure 8.1); this gradient has important implications for evolutionary models of these disorders. As I discuss in more detail later, schizophrenia is associated with reduced IQ, extensive loss of gray matter during development, indicators of elevated mutation load, and low rates of remission and recovery. This is especially true of early-onset forms with predominantly negative symptoms. The pattern is attenuated in later-onset forms with high levels of positive and/or manic symptoms, and even more so in schizoaffective disorder. At the other end of the spectrum, bipolar disorders show comparatively small levels of deleterious mutations and neural atrophy; they also improve and remit more often than schizophrenia (e.g., Bansal et al., 2017; Černis et al., 2015; Ellison-Wright & Bullmore, 2010; Grozeva et al., 2010; Hagenaars et al., 2016; Hill, Reilly et al., 2013; Lewandowski et al., 2014; MacCabe et al., 2010; Potter & Nestor, 2010; Smith, Anderson et al., 2015). In keeping with standard diagnostic distinctions, here I focus specifically on SSDs and present the bipolar spectrum in Chapter 9; however, many of the concepts discussed in this chapter apply to the psychosis spectrum as a whole.

The Schizophrenia Spectrum

Schizotypy

As it often happens with mental disorders, the spectrum of schizophrenia extends all the way from normal variation in personality to severe, debilitating conditions. Schizotypy is the dimension of personality that underlies the schizophrenia spectrum (Claridge, 1997; Lenzenweger, 2010). Parallel to the distinction between the positive, negative, and disorganization symptoms of psychosis, the domain of schizotypal traits comprises three facets with the same names. Positive schizotypy includes a tendency toward odd beliefs and magical thinking (e.g., telepathy, paranormal phenomena), unusual perceptual experiences, and paranoid and "reference" thoughts (e.g., feeling that ordinary, unrelated events have special meaning or are communicating something to oneself). Negative schizotypy includes lack of social engagement and close friendships, flat or unresponsive affect, and social anxiety associated with paranoid tendencies. Finally, the disorganized facet of schizotypy describes a profile of oddity in behavior and speech (e.g., a tendency to use idiosyncratic or highly metaphorical language). Schizotypal traits are about 50% heritable, with no significant contribution from the shared environment. On average, females show higher levels of positive schizotypy, whereas males score higher on the negative and disorganized facets (Bora & Baysan Arabaci, 2009; Ericson et al., 2011; Raine, 1992; Ross et al., 2002; Williams & Barry, 2003).

The positive facet of schizotypy correlates with the imagination/aesthetics facets of openness to experience and is a reliable predictor of creativity and divergent thinking. People with high levels of this trait habituate more slowly to predictable stimuli and generate more unusual associations of ideas, partly owing to weaker inhibition of "irrelevant" contents and connections (Baas et al., 2016; Batey & Furnham, 2008; Kaufman & Paul, 2014; Miller & Tal, 2007; Nelson & Rawlings, 2010; Stoneham & Coughtrey, 2009; Zabelina et al., 2014). At a more abstract level, the production of unusual associations seems to reflect a shift from exploitation toward exploration with respect to internally generated stimuli (Baror & Bar, 2016), likely connected to the activation of the curiosity system (Chapter 2). In agreement with the age-old concept of the "mad genius," artists tend to be high in positive schizotypy (but comparatively low in negative schizotypy); among the creative professions, the risk of psychosis seems to be especially elevated in literary artists such as novelists and poets (Kyaga, 2015; Mason et al., 2015; Nettle, 2006*b*; Simonton, 1999, 2014). Intriguingly, there is evidence that a moderate reduction of white matter integrity in the brain is associated with both positive schizotypy and enhanced creative thinking, even controlling for IQ (Grazioplene et al., 2016; Jung et al., 2010).

Schizophrenia Spectrum Disorders

High levels of schizotypal traits may lead to impairment and severe discomfort in social relationships, even if cognitive and perceptual distortions never reach the status of actual psychotic symptoms—that is, they do not involve major breaks with external reality—or only do so for very brief periods of time. This quasi-psychotic pattern is captured by the diagnosis of schizotypal personality disorder (SPD). While some taxometric studies indicate that schizotypal personality is best described as a continuum from normality to pathology, there is also evidence that high schizotypy may reflect a qualitatively distinct category comprising about 10% of the population, as originally proposed by Meehl (1962). To date, the debate on the dimensional versus taxonic nature of schizotypy remains unresolved (Ahmed et al., 2012; Nelson et al., 2013).

Most people with schizotypal traits or SPD never develop clinical levels of psychotic symptoms. When a psychotic episode occurs, the DSM-5 provides a set of diagnostic categories that are mainly differentiated by the episode's duration: "brief psychotic disorder" when symptoms last less than 1 month, "schizophreniform disorder" for symptoms between 1 and 6 months, and schizophrenia for symptoms that last 6 months or more. These distinctions are based on arbitrary thresholds and do not reflect true qualitative differences between conditions. Sometimes, delusions occur in the absence of hallucinations and negative symptoms; the diagnosis of "delusional disorder" applies to isolated delusions that persist for less than 6 months (Figure 8.1).

Schizophrenia and other SSDs are quite heterogeneous, both in their presentation—which may involve virtually any combination of positive, negative, and disorganized symptoms—and in their genetic underpinnings (Arnedo et al., 2015; Chisholm et al., 2015). In general, a prevalence of negative symptoms is associated with earlier and more gradual onset of the disorder, and all these features predict worse recovery. SSDs with mainly positive symptoms have a better prognosis and tend to be associated with later age of onset. Auditory hallucinations (voices) are especially common, but visual hallucinations may also occur, especially in the more severe cases. Delusions usually involve paranoia and persecution, external mind/body control, grandiosity (having a special identity, exceptional powers, knowledge, or skills), love or sexual attraction, and jealousy; religious themes are also fairly prevalent in all types of delusions (American Psychiatric Association, 2013; Combs et al., 2014; Knowles et al., 2011). While schizophrenia as a whole is associated with reduced premorbid IQ (about 0.5 SD below controls), a number of studies have identified a high-IQ subtype characterized by fewer negative symptoms and more positive and manic symptoms (Černis et al., 2015; Hallmayer et al., 2005; Lewandowski et al., 2014; Potter & Nestor, 2010).

The predisposition to SSDs has a strong genetic component, with about 80% heritability. This value reflects the combined effect of multiple sources of genetic variation, including common alleles of small effects—many of which are shared with BDs—and rare variants of large effect that are more likely to be deleterious (more on this later). Some of the common variants that increase the risk for schizophrenia and BDs are also associated with higher openness and lower conscientiousness. The concordance for schizophrenia in identical twins is only moderate (close to 50%), consistent with an important role for epigenetic mechanisms and environmental risk factors in the etiology of the disorder (Haut et al., 2016; Knopik et al., 2017; Lee, Ripke et al., 2013; Lo et al., 2017; Ruderfer et al., 2014).

Overall, the prevalence of schizophrenia is about the same in males and females, even if males tend to develop more severe forms of the disorder (with higher levels of negative symptoms) and are strongly overrepresented in childhood-onset SSDs. Both schizoaffective disorder and delusional disorder are more common in females (up to 3:1) and tend to arise later in life. Until recently, it was widely assumed that schizophrenia occurred at an approximately constant rate across populations and countries. A new generation of epidemiological studies has disproved this belief and shown that rates vary systematically across countries by about an order of magnitude (from about 0.1% to 3%). Specifically, schizophrenia rates increase linearly as one moves farther away from the equator and toward colder climates; at the same time, darker-skinned populations show higher rates of the disorder after controlling for latitude (Kinney et al., 2009; McGrath et al., 2008). In adults, SSDs show especially high comorbidities with depression, generalized anxiety disorder (GAD), posttraumatic stress disorder (PTSD), and obsessive-compulsive disorder (OCD). Substance use disorders are also very common in the schizophrenia spectrum, and about 50% of people with a diagnosis of schizophrenia also have a history of substance abuse (American Psychiatric Association, 2013; Asarnow, 2013; Combs et al., 2014; Falkenburg & Tracy, 2014).

Neurobiological Correlates

Schizophrenia spectrum disorders are unusually well understood from a neurobiological standpoint. To begin, schizophrenia is associated with reduced brain volume and thinner cortical areas, especially in frontal and temporal regions (including the insula and hippocampus). These anatomical outcomes result from a progressive loss of gray matter throughout development. In fact, the pattern observed in SSDs is an exaggerated version of the pruning and thinning observed in normal brain maturation (see Figure 1.5) and seems to involve many of the same cellular mechanisms, which are partly regulated by glutamate and GABA. Reductions in gray matter are coupled with a pattern of reduced connectivity and white matter integrity between dorsolateral prefrontal areas and other brain regions, as well as hypoactivation of the dorsolateral prefrontal cortex (DLPFC). Importantly, fronto-parietal connections involving the DLPFC are among the key substrates of general intelligence (Chapter 3). At the same time, functional and anatomical connections are enhanced between the ventral striatum and the orbitofrontal cortex (OFC) and more generally within mesolimbic dopaminergic pathways (Alba-Ferrara & de Erausquin, 2013; Asarnow, 2013; Ellison-Wrigth & Bullmore, 2010; Fornito et al., 2013; Haut et al., 2016; Katz et al., 2016; Trotman et al., 2013).

Upregulated activity of the dopaminergic system is crucially involved in the etiology of SSDs and other psychotic disorders. The specific cellular processes involve exaggerated dopamine (DA) synthesis and synaptic release, particularly in the mesolimbic pathway. Some evidence suggests that hyperdopaminergic mesolimbic function is specifically associated with positive symptoms and positive schizotypal traits, whereas negative symptoms may reflect hypodopaminergic function in mesocortical pathways (Haut et al., 2016; Howes & Kapur, 2009; Howes et al., 2012; Maia & Frank, 2017; Woodward et al., 2011). In addition to hyperdopaminergic function, psychotic symptoms are associated with reduced glutamate signaling, mainly through downregulated expression of the N-methyl-D-aspartate (NMDA) glutamate receptor. The exact role of reduced glutamatergic function in psychosis is still unclear and may be fairly indirect. One of the functions of excitatory glutamatergic neurons is to stimulate inhibitory

GABAergic neurons; thus, low glutamate levels within specific pathways can indirectly increase excitatory brain activity. Even more importantly, NMDA signaling regulates DA synthesis and release, and glutamate is often co-released in the synapsis by dopaminergic neurons (Cannon, 2015; Corlett et al., 2009). Large genetic association studies of schizophrenia have identified several genes involved in dopaminergic, glutamatergic, and GABAergic pathways. However, variation in specific dopamine-related genes seems to play a minor role, suggesting that DA signaling may be altered as a downstream effect of other neurobiological processes, as, for example, glutamatergic activity (Edwards et al., 2016; Kavanagh et al., 2015; Pardiñas et al., 2016).

The functional bridge between upregulated dopaminergic activity and the positive symptoms of psychosis is provided by the concept of *aberrant salience* (Kapur, 2003; Kapur et al., 2005). Because dopamine encodes the salience and novelty of stimuli, a dramatic upregulation of DA synthesis (which also increases the frequency of spontaneous dopaminergic spikes in the striatum) may generate the feeling that ordinary events, objects, and thoughts have suddenly become intensely meaningful and worthy of focused attention. Repeated episodes of sudden, unexplained salience build up to a sense of impending revelation—with intense emotions of excitement, anxiety, or fear—typical of the prodromal phase that precedes the onset of psychosis. From this perspective, delusional beliefs arise as attempts to make coherent sense of the overwhelming experience of aberrant salience. While extreme levels of aberrant salience can lead to a psychotic breakdown, low-level manifestations of the same processes have been associated with positive schizotypal traits in the nonclinical range and contribute to the link between schizotypy and creativity (Cicero et al., 2010). Both schizophrenic patients and people at high risk for psychosis show alterations in the connectivity of the *salience network*, a network of brain region involved in detecting and processing salient stimuli. The salience network is centered in the insula and includes the anterior cingulate cortex (ACC), OFC, and other subcortical structures (Wang, Ji et al., 2016).

From a computational perspective, the process underlying aberrant salience can be understood more precisely by treating the mind as a hierarchical predictive system based on Bayesian principles. In such a system, prior expectations are used to make predictions and updated when predictions fail—as when a certain action leads to an unexpected outcome. Prediction errors carry critical information for the system; for this reason, they are highly salient and are used to orient attention toward unexpected but significant stimuli. When errors cannot be corrected by adjusting the parameters of low-level mechanisms, they propagate upward in the control hierarchy and can affect the individual's perceptions and beliefs. There is considerable evidence that both dopamine and glutamate are implicated in encoding and relaying prediction errors in the brain. In a Bayesian framework, exaggerated dopaminergic activity blurs the distinction between relevant and irrelevant stimuli and generates a high rate of false prediction errors, which in turn amplify the salience of ordinary events and create a sense of strangeness and unpredictability. Delusions are formed later as error signals propagate upward, in an unsuccessful attempt to restore the system's predictive ability by altering existing beliefs (Corlett et al., 2009; Fletcher & Frith, 2009).

At the neuroendocrine level, psychotic conditions (both schizophrenia and BDs) are associated with elevated activity of the stress response system, especially in the sympathetic and HPA components. People at high risk for psychosis tend to have a hyperreactive HPA axis and a larger pituitary gland; patients undergoing their first psychotic episode often show a profile of elevated cortisol and blunted reactivity to specific stressors, likely as a result of decreased negative feedback by glucocorticoid receptors (Borges et al., 2013; Walker et al. 2008, 2013). Quite possibly, the blunted HPA reactivity of psychotic patients is a secondary consequence of their already high secretion of cortisol. Finally, schizophrenia is associated with altered profiles of immune functioning (including inflammatory activity), and several genes implicated in schizophrenia risk are also involved in immunological pathways (Haut et al., 2016; Kavanagh et al., 2015; Miller et al., 2011; Mørch et al., 2016). This is especially interesting in light of the bidirectional interplay between the immune system and the stress response system, and may contribute to explain the strong predictive association between early infections and increased risk for schizophrenia (more on this later).

Development and Course

Early indicators of schizophrenia risk can be observed already in the first year of life, chiefly in the domains of social behavior (lack of positive emotions, social withdrawal) and motor development (delays in walking, poor manual coordination; Caplan, 2016; Trotman et al., 2013). Mild psychotic-like experiences are a normal feature of cognitive development; in the general population, they peak between middle childhood and early adolescence (9–12 years) and typically subside with maturation without ever meeting the criterion for an SSD. Even people with a symptom profile that puts them at extremely high risk for schizophrenia may not develop the disorder for years (or at all); rates of transition to psychosis increase from about 20% within a 1-year interval to 65–80% within a 10-year interval (Fusar-Poli, Bonoldi et al., 2012; van Os et al., 2009). Schizotypal personality traits remain moderately stable during adolescence, begin to diminish in early adulthood, and continue to decrease throughout adulthood. Positive and disorganized traits show a steeper decline than negative ones, mirroring the age-related trajectory of dopaminergic function (Badcock & Dragović, 2006; Bora & Baysan Arabaci, 2009; Ericson et al., 2011; Khandaker et al., 2014).

The risk of schizophrenia is highest in young adulthood, with a peak around 20–25 years in men and 25–30 years in women. The somewhat earlier peak in men is consistent with a higher prevalence of negative symptoms, which tend to develop at a younger age compared with positive ones. The age of onset of schizophrenia follows a strong latitudinal gradient of increasingly earlier onset as one moves toward the equator (Shaner et al., 2007). While most cases of schizophrenia are diagnosed in adults, a small proportion arises in middle childhood or early adolescence, typically between 9 and 12 years of age ("childhood-onset" schizophrenia). Childhood-onset schizophrenia occurs more often in boys and is characterized by severe negative symptoms, marked reductions in cortical thickness and brain volume, and higher levels of mutation load and familial risk compared with the adult-onset variant (Asarnow, 2013; Caplan, 2016). Females are less at risk for childhood-onset psychosis but show a secondary, late-adulthood peak after menopause (45–60 years). Late-onset schizophrenia is strongly female-biased and usually involves persecutory hallucinations and delusions, with few or no negative symptoms. People who develop late-onset schizophrenia tend to have suspicious, reclusive personalities, low familial risk for psychosis, and good occupational and relational adjustment (Falkenburg & Tracy, 2014; Vahia et al., 2010; Wynn Owen & Castle, 1999). In total, the distribution of SSDs switches from strongly male-biased in middle childhood to strongly female-biased in late adulthood. Schizophrenia is a severe disorder, leading to lifelong impairment in personal and social life in about 50% of cases. Early onset and negative symptoms predict a poorer prognosis. In patients, both positive and negative symptoms diminish with age, although negative symptoms tend to be more persistent (Morgan et al., 2014; Savill et al., 2015; Trotman et al., 2013).

Risk Factors

Mutation load is a key factor in schizophrenia, with an important role for rare *copy number variations* (CNVs)—that is, variations in the number of copies of a certain DNA segment on a chromosome rather than in the sequence itself. Rare and de novo CNVs are more likely to be deleterious and are especially frequent in childhood-onset schizophrenia (Ahn et al., 2014; Caplan, 2016; Grozeva et al., 2010). As expected, advanced paternal age is associated with SSDs, although risk is also elevated in offspring of younger mothers and fathers (D'Onofrio et al., 2014; Merikangas et al., 2017). Strong negative selection on rare deleterious mutations may also partly account for the maintenance of common variants in closely linked genes on the same chromosomes, an effect known as *background selection* (Pardiñas et al., 2016).

In addition to mutations, a multitude of environmental factors contribute to increase the risk for schizophrenia and other SSDs. These include obstetrical complications (with a particularly strong effect of fetal hypoxia), maternal stress during pregnancy, fetal malnutrition, and prenatal infections (including those caused by *Toxoplasma*). Prenatal infections account for the peculiar seasonal pattern of SSDs, whereby people born in the winter and spring are at higher risk than those born in the summer and fall. Childhood infections that affect the brain and early neglect and abuse also increase the risk for psychosis. Later in life, stressful life events can trigger the onset of a psychotic episode in predisposed individuals. The same applies to psychoactive drugs that act on dopaminergic and glutamatergic pathways, including cocaine, cannabis, and other hallucinogens; note that people who are genetically predisposed to schizophrenia tend to make more use of these substances (Aas et al., 2018; Benros et al., 2012; Di Forti et al., 2007; Dreier et al., 2018; Giordano et al., 2015; Khandaker et al., 2014; Matheson et al., 2013; Trotman et al., 2013). Low socioeconomic status is associated with increased risk for schizophrenia, although this relation is likely confounded by the effect of IQ on education and income (Goldberg et al., 2011; Sariaslan et al., 2015). Schizophrenia rates are also elevated in people who were born or raised in urban environments and in first- and second-generation migrants, particularly from darker-skinned populations (mainly from Africa and the Caribbean; Cantor-Graae & Selten, 2005). Studies of latitudinal variation suggest that vitamin D deficiency is a likely risk factor for schizophrenia, and the available evidence supports this hypothesis (McGrath et al., 2010; Valipour et al., 2014). In total, the evidence is consistent with a pattern of G×E interaction between a genetic predisposition to SSDs—which is only partially determined by mutation load—and developmental stressors of various sorts. People at risk for schizophrenia seem to be more susceptible to a wide range of environmental factors, an effect that could be partly mediated by a hyperreactive stress response system.

EVOLUTIONARY MODELS

Schizophrenia presents researchers with an evolutionary paradox (van Dongen & Boomsma, 2013). The predisposition to schizophrenia is strongly heritable, and the disorder is clearly maladaptive at the individual level: compared with the rest of the population, the lifetime reproductive success of patients is about 50% in females and as low as 20% in males (Haukka et al., 2003; MacCabe et al., 2009; Power et al., 2013). Given this combination of low fertility and high heritability, alleles that increase the risk of schizophrenia should be rapidly eliminated by natural selection, and prevalence should drop to a very low rate determined by mutation–selection balance. However, this is not the case: schizophrenia is relatively common, with prevalence rates in the order of 1% (ranging from about 0.1% to 3% across countries; Kinney et al., 2009). While this is not an infrequent pattern in psychopathology, the so-called *schizophrenia paradox* is especially striking since schizophrenia is associated with the lowest fertility among common mental disorders (Keller & Miller, 2006; Power et al., 2013).

Partly for this reason, schizophrenia has attracted enormous interest from evolutionary scholars, who have advanced dozens of models and hypotheses over the decades (for a more complete overview, see Polimeni & Reiss, 2003; van Dongen & Boomsma, 2013). With few exceptions, schizophrenia and other SSDs are regarded as maladaptive conditions, and symptoms such as delusions and hallucinations are seen as the product of psychological and neurobiological dysfunctions. The main distinction in the evolutionary literature is between models that view the vulnerability to psychosis as a byproduct of the evolution of the human mind/brain, and models that postulate a fitness advantage in people who carry some predisposition to SSDs (e.g., schizotypal traits, risk-increasing alleles) but do not develop a clinically significant disorder. An especially influential model in the latter category maintains that schizotypy has evolved through sexual selection, likely as an amplifier trait (Nettle, 2001, 2006*a*; Shaner et al., 2004).

Another major advance in the evolutionary study of schizophrenia has been the *diametrical model* of autism and psychosis proposed by Crespi and Badcock (2008; Crespi et al., 2010). At the core of the model is the idea that psychosis spectrum disorders (including SSDs and BDs) and autism spectrum disorder (ASD) arise at the opposite ends of a continuum of cognitive specialization, ranging from extreme investment in mentalistic cognition (psychosis) to extreme investment in mechanistic cognition (autism). The model also synthesizes evidence that maternally and paternally expressed imprinted genes contribute in opposite ways to the risk of autism and psychosis, thus introducing intragenomic conflict as an additional factor in the evolution and development of these disorders. The diametrical model can be integrated with the sexual selection model and framed in a life history perspective, with schizotypal and autistic-like traits as specialized variants of fast and slow strategies (Del Giudice, 2014; Del Giudice et al., 2010, 2014*a*). An important but still unresolved issue in the diametrical model is the apparent overlap between some subtypes of SSDs and ASD—in particular between autistic symptoms in childhood and severe, early-onset schizophrenia.

Vulnerability to Psychosis as an Evolutionary Byproduct

Evolution in the cognitive niche has endowed our species with remarkable abilities such as language, abstract reasoning, and sophisticated mentalizing. These species-typical innovations have been accompanied by rapid changes in brain structure and functionality. While adaptations such as language are hugely beneficial, they are also likely to carry some costs. A number of authors have argued that vulnerability to psychosis is one of those costs—the price our species pays for its unique set of cognitive skills. From this perspective, there are no individual fitness benefits to psychosis proneness; vulnerability to schizophrenia and other psychoses is a general byproduct of our evolved design, and unfortunate combinations of genetic and environmental factors determine the onset of a full-fledged disorder in some individuals (McGuire & Troisi, 1998).

A paradigmatic example in this category is Horrobin's theory of schizophrenia (Horrobin, 1998, 2001; Horrobin et al., 1994). Horrobin developed a complex phylogenetic model of changes in brain chemistry during primate and human evolution, with a focus on the metabolism of lipids and its role in regulating neural function and brain connectivity. He speculated that changes in lipid metabolism enabled the creative explosion of technology, art, and religion that took place in the upper Paleolithic, around 40,000–50,000 years ago. According to the model, traits that have been subjected to strong, recent selection include creativity (especially of the artistic kind), religious ideation, and mentalizing skills that enable more effective social coordination and leadership—with the concomitant "dark side" of paranoia and suspiciousness toward out-group members. The risk of schizophrenia would be a side effect of these specifically human traits. While this model has substantial limitations (e.g., a narrow biochemical focus on lipids), it neatly illustrates the general idea of psychosis as a byproduct. Also, the adaptive traits identified by Horrobin as the evolutionary substrates for schizophrenia—artistic creativity, mentalizing/leadership, and religious imagination—continue to play a role in many of the more recent models.

Crow's Lateralization Model

An influential byproduct model of schizophrenia is the one developed by Crow (1990, 1997, 2000; Mitchell & Crow, 2005). According to Crow, schizophrenia arises from a failure to establish hemispheric dominance for language and other lateralized communicative abilities; this failure is further hypothesized to depend on a single genetic variant with major developmental effects. The resulting breakdown in the segregation of brain functions would impair the ability to distinguish between external and internal speech (hence auditory hallucinations) and cause a broad range of other social deficits. The main evidence in favor of this model comes from the increased frequency of mixed handedness and reduced brain asymmetry observed in schizophrenics. However, the same evidence can be interpreted as indicating a higher exposure to mutations and developmental stressors, coupled with a reduced ability to buffer perturbations through developmental canalization (Yeo et al., 1999). The idea that schizophrenia is caused (at least in part) by the accumulation of genetic and developmental disturbances is also consistent with the higher prevalence of minor physical anomalies and fluctuating asymmetry in schizophrenic patients. Most importantly, single-gene models of schizophrenia have been decisively falsified by the evidence from genomic association studies, which indicate the involvement of thousands of common and rare variants.

The Social Brain Theory of Psychosis

The *social brain theory* developed by Burns (2004, 2007, 2009) is arguably the most sophisticated and biologically plausible of current byproduct models. According to the theory, recent selection for increased mentalizing and social cognition in humans has led to a massive increase in the size and complexity of the cortical connections between the frontal, temporal, and parietal structures that constitute the "social brain." These structures include the DLPFC, OFC, ACC, amygdala, superior temporal sulcus (STS), and other temporal and parietal regions. Our species-typical pattern of connectivity is produced by changes in the timing of the developmental processes that regulate brain growth and maturation. However, the very complexity of the human social brain and the long time required to complete its maturation leave it vulnerable to dysfunctions caused by deleterious mutations and developmental insults, with a specific role for "toxic" aspects of the social environment such as chronic stress, urbanization, economic inequality, and migration. The resulting pattern of reduced fronto-temporal and fronto-parietal connectivity is viewed as the core neurobiological source of psychotic symptoms (including those of schizophrenia). In contrast with most other byproduct models, the social brain theory explicitly takes into account the role of mutations and environmental stressors, and can potentially explain systematic variations in schizophrenia risk across cultures and social groups.

More recent versions of the model have incorporated the concept of cliff-edged fitness functions (Burns, 2009; Nesse, 2004*b*). Traits such as exaggerated pruning of neural connections may enhance some cognitive skills when expressed at a moderate level (e.g., McGlashan & Hoffman, 2000); however, excessive expression of the same traits may overshoot the optimum and result in catastrophic, maladaptive failures of brain development. Such cliff-edged functions are more likely to be found in traits that have been subject to strong recent selection, without the time to evolve damage-limiting genetic variants. While Burns rejects the idea of an adaptive advantage for psychosis proneness, this aspect of the model does open the way to the possibility that moderate levels of schizotypy confer fitness benefits through enhanced mentalizing and/or creativity. The crucial problem is how to interpret the available evidence on the relations between schizotypy and fitness, as I discuss in detail in the next section.

Psychosis Proneness as an Adaptive Trait

With few exceptions, adaptive and byproduct theories to psychosis agree that most disorders in the spectrum are maladaptive conditions and that diagnosable psychotic symptoms reflect dysfunctional cognitive processes. However, adaptive models maintain that the predisposition to psychosis—or at least some of its components—confers a fitness advantage on its bearers, thus offsetting the severe reproductive costs of schizophrenia and other SSDs. In this perspective, then, schizophrenia can be framed as the individually maladaptive outcome of an adaptive trait. A classic example of this approach is the *balanced polymorphism model* by Huxley and colleagues (1964). These authors postulated the existence of a single genetic variant that would benefit heterozygote individuals by increasing their resistance to infections, allergies, and other immunological shocks, but cause schizophrenia in homozygotes (see Hoffer, 1994, for a polygenic version of this argument). They also speculated that schizophrenia might increase fertility in affected women, thus partly compensating for the dramatic decrease in men. This early model has been very influential in bringing schizophrenia under the evolutionary spotlight, even if its core assumptions have been falsified by later research.

Price and Stevens's Group-Splitting Model

Price and Stevens (1998, 1999; Stevens & Price, 2000) advanced the hypothesis that schizotypal traits promote charismatic/religious leadership, and play an adaptive role at the group level by favoring the splitting and dispersal of human communities (Chapter 1). Many aspects of positive schizotypy—magical thinking, paranoid ideation, and the tendency to form novel and unusual ideas and express them in idiosyncratic ways—can contribute to a compelling leader personality, often with religious or messianic overtones. According to Price and Stevens, schizotypal leaders act as catalyzers for the origin of new belief systems; if they are successful, the subgroups that form around them and their beliefs may eventually split from the original group and become new social entities.

This model postulates two kinds of benefits for schizotypal traits. On one level, schizotypy works as a high-risk strategy for the individual, with potentially high gains (becoming a charismatic leader) as well as losses (ostracism, schizophrenia). In some respects, schizotypy would be analogous to the adaptive *dispersal phenotypes* found in many other organisms, whereby some individuals develop an alternative morphological and/or behavioral profile that causes them to migrate away from the natal territory (e.g., swarming locusts). On another level, Price and Stevens suggested that, by increasing the rate of fission in human groups, schizotypy may have acted as a promoter and accelerator of group selection. Finally, the authors argued that modern social conditions (e.g., individualism, lack of close supportive relationships) may introduce an element of mismatch, increasing the risk that people with schizotypal personalities will develop a disorder instead of gaining status and influence in their groups.

Price and Stevens's model of schizotypy is speculative and mainly based on indirect anthropological evidence. Its dispersal/group selection component suffers from a lack of theoretical precision (how do potential group benefits interact with the individual fitness of schizotypal individuals?) and a dearth of empirical support. Also, the model does not explain the substantial role of deleterious mutations in the etiology of schizophrenia or the G×E interactions with risk factors as diverse as infections, perinatal complications, and migration. Despite these limitations, the model contains some important and potentially fertile ideas, particularly regarding the power of schizotypal personalities to inspire devoted following, group cohesion, and even religious enthusiasm under the right conditions. This view of schizotypy goes beyond the standard emphasis on creativity and merits systematic investigation. Moreover, evidence of social selection for schizotypy—for example through leader–follower dynamics—would be easy to integrate with the predictions of the sexual selection model (discussed next); indeed, the two types of selection often target the same traits, as many of the qualities that make an attractive sexual partner are also desirable in leaders and cooperation partners.

The Sexual Selection Model of Schizotypy

The sexual selection model of schizotypy was first proposed by Nettle (2001), who argued that the creativity associated with positive schizotypal traits can function as a sexually attractive display, leading to the evolution and maintenance of psychosis proneness through mate choice. The fitness advantages of schizotypy would be realized mainly through short-term mating, especially in men. Indeed, the evidence shows that positive (but not negative) schizotypy predicts unrestricted sociosexuality, reduced long-term mating orientation, and a higher number of sexual partners (Beaussart et al., 2012; Del Giudice et al., 2010, 2014*a*; Nettle & Clegg, 2006; Miller & Tal, 2007).

The model was later refined by Shaner and colleagues (2004), who suggested that sexual selection targets a set of traits involved in verbal courtship, including verbal/artistic creativity, emotional expressiveness, and mentalizing skills. In this revised formulation, schizotypy is not a target of sexual selection per se; rather, it works as an amplifier of those fitness indicators by increasing their sensitivity to individual condition. When schizotypal traits are expressed by individuals in good conditions (low mutation and parasite load, low developmental stress), they translate into enhanced creativity and mating success; in poor conditions, they increase the chances of mating failure and the risk of developing schizophrenia and other SSDs. According to this model, then, SSDs are maladaptive outcomes of an adaptive but risky mating strategy. Individual quality contributes to determine the balance between different facets of schizotypy—positive schizotypy likely represents the creative, "successful" manifestation of the strategy whereas negative schizotypy and disorganization may indicate low-level neurological dysfunction (Nettle, 2006*a*, 2006*b*). This interpretation is consistent with the association between a predominance of negative symptoms and poor prognosis in SSDs. Finally, the sexual selection model can potentially explain cross-cultural differences in the age of onset of schizophrenia, which should correlate systematically with differences in the timing of mating competition (as reflected, for example, in patterns of age at marriage; see Shaner et al., 2007).

A crucial but seldom appreciated feature of the sexual selection model is that it postulates at least two distinct, independent sources of genetic risk for schizophrenia and other SSDs (Figure 8.2). The first source comprises genetic variants that increase the expression of schizotypal traits (the amplifier). These variants are likely to be maintained through balancing selection and may affect the expression of schizotypy in various ways, for example by reducing canalization in brain development (Yeo et al., 1999). The second source comprises deleterious mutations whose effect is amplified by schizotypy, giving rise to epistatic (genotype–genotype) interactions. (Common genetic variants that decrease IQ may make a third independent contribution to schizophrenia risk.) The combination of high schizotypy and low mutation load (as well as low developmental stress) yields a fitness benefit through enhanced mating success, but the combination of high schizotypy, high mutation load, and/or developmental insults may cross the threshold for schizophrenia and result in a dramatic fitness loss, especially in men. The existence of two independent genetic sources of predisposition to psychosis is consistent with the finding that schizotypy is about 50% heritable, whereas the risk for schizophrenia reaches 80% heritability. People who develop SSDs are likely to carry many genetic variants of both types, whereas highly creative people with schizotypal personalities should mainly carry variants of the first type. Intriguingly, a recent genomic study found evidence of two distinct sets of common alleles associated with schizophrenia—one linked to bipolar disorder risk and higher educational attainment and another linked to low IQ and poor educational performance (Bansal et al., 2017). While partial, these findings are broadly compatible with the sexual selection model; as suggested by the authors of the study, they may also point to the existence of distinct subtypes of schizophrenia with different functional characteristics.

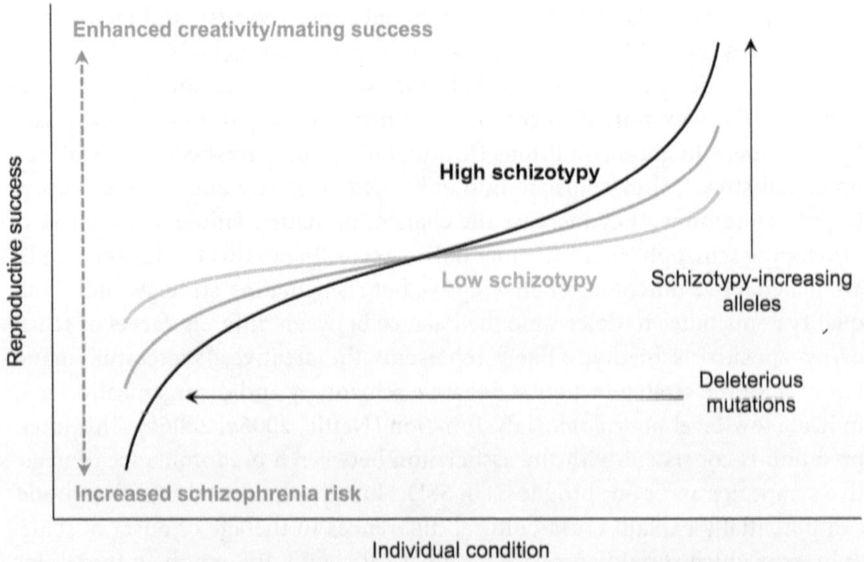

Figure 8.2. The sexual selection model of schizotypy. Schizotypy acts as an amplifier of individual condition, increasing the likelihood of developing exceptional creativity and mating success (when in good conditions) but also the risk of schizophrenia and reproductive failure (when in poor conditions). In this model, the genetic risk for schizophrenia reflects two distinct sources of variation with different evolutionary underpinnings: schizotypy-increasing alleles maintained by balancing selection and deleterious mutations that evolve under mutation-selection balance.

Fertility in Unaffected Relatives

The main criticism leveled against adaptive models of schizotypy is that studies of unaffected relatives show no evidence of increased fitness in the siblings and parents of schizophrenics. Many authors assume that, if the predisposition to psychosis is an adaptive trait, the unaffected close relatives of patients with SSDs should show a substantial increase in fertility—large enough to offset the fertility reduction seen in patients. In contrast with this prediction, studies show a small fertility decrease in the brothers of schizophrenics and only a slight increase in their sisters (similar results are found in studies of parents; Haukka et al., 2003; MacCabe et al., 2009; Power et al., 2013; Svensson et al., 2007; van Dongen & Boomsma, 2013).

These data have been used to reject the idea that psychosis proneness may be an adaptive trait (e.g., Burns, 2009; Doi et al., 2009; Power et al., 2013). However, this interpretation suffers from a fundamental problem. As it should be clear from the preceding discussion, the prediction of increased fitness in the relatives of schizophrenics depends on the assumption that genetic risk for psychosis is caused by a single source, as in the balanced polymorphism model by Huxley and colleagues (1964). But if the risk of psychosis depends on two independent genetic sources—one of which is mutation load—the prediction becomes one of *reduced* fertility in the close relatives of schizophrenics. This is because relatives are likely to share not only the patients' schizotypy-increasing alleles but also their deleterious mutations, in addition to various kinds of environmental stressors (Del Giudice, 2010).

In sum, the results of sibling studies are not nearly as decisive as often believed—they falsify simple adaptive models such as that by Huxley and colleagues but are consistent with the predictions of the sexual selection model. If the sexual selection model is correct, the proper comparison is not between SSD patients and their siblings, but between patients and people with similarly high schizotypy but low mutation load (see Figure 8.2). As noted in Chapter 5, an additional caveat in this type of research is the confounding effect of modern contraception; in populations with routine access to contraception, the past adaptiveness of a trait may be better reflected in measures of mating behavior than in realized fertility (Pérusse, 1993).

The Diametrical Model of Autism and Psychosis

Crespi and Badcock (2008) advanced an integrative model of autism and psychosis based on the idea of a fundamental tradeoff between mentalistic and mechanistic cognition. The diametrical model postulates a mentalistic–mechanistic continuum of individual variation, with elevated risk for psychosis at the hypermentalistic/hypomechanistic extreme and elevated risk for ASD at the hypermechanistic/hypomentalistic end (Figure 8.3). On this view, the marked mentalizing deficits observed in SSDs (e.g., low scores on theory of mind tests) do not reflect an inability to attribute mental states (as in autism), but rather a tendency to overattribute thoughts, emotions, and intentions to others and overinterpret their behavior, coupled with a relative lack of logical systemizing skills and—in the more severe disorders of the spectrum—frankly dysfunctional cognitive processes. For example, patients with paranoid symptoms tend to be acutely sensitive to emotional expressions and nonverbal cues but tend to interpret those cues in self-referential and often bizarre ways. The hypothesis of hyperactive mentalizing in SSDs has been gathering increasing empirical support over the years (e.g., Abu-Akel & Bailey, 2000; Abu-Akel et al., 2015; Brosnan et al., 2010; Ciaramidaro et al., 2015; Clemmensen et al., 2016; Frith, 2004; McCormick et al., 2012; Pflum et al., 2013; White et al., 2016). Psychosis spectrum disorders are also associated with indices of impaired mechanistic cognition, such as poor visuospatial skills (e.g., Zhai et al., 2011).

The diametrical relations between autism and psychosis are not limited to mentalistic and mechanistic cognition but also extend to patterns of growth and brain development. While the autism spectrum is generally marked by early overgrowth—high birth weight and length, large brain volume, and fast growth during childhood—psychosis is associated with reduced growth, especially during prenatal and early postnatal development (Byars et al., 2014; Crespi & Badcock, 2008). Together with data from epigenetic studies, these effects suggest that maternally and paternally expressed imprinted genes play opposite roles in

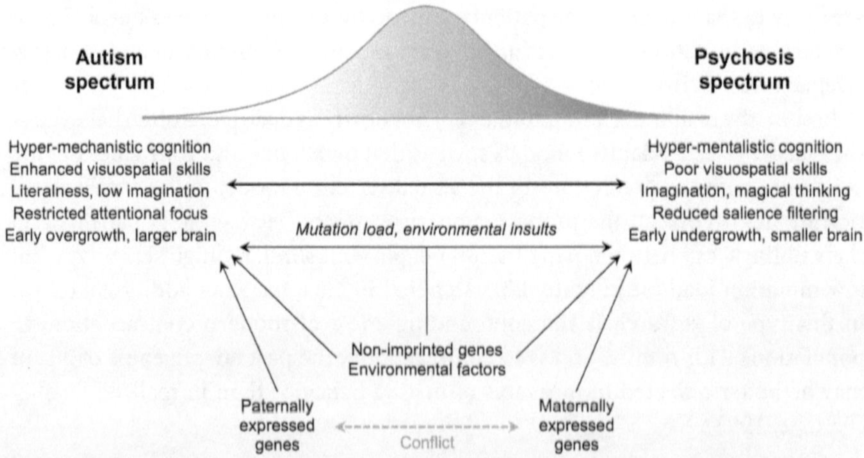

Figure 8.3. The diametrical model of autism and psychosis. Autism spectrum and psychosis spectrum disorders arise at opposite ends of a mechanistic-mentalistic continuum, and are associated with diametrical patterns of growth and cognition. Most people show "balanced" cognitive profiles and fall in the central region of the distribution. Maternally and paternally expressed imprinted genes tend to play opposite roles in the development of autism vs. psychosis; non-imprinted genes and environmental factors may either have directional effects, or increase the risk for disorders across the board (for example in the case of deleterious mutations, infections, disruptions of imprinting mechanisms).

the etiology of autism and psychosis. In particular, psychosis spectrum disorders seem to be associated with hyperexpression of maternally expressed genes (which tend to suppress early growth) and/or hypoexpression of paternally expressed genes (which promote fetal and infant growth at the expense of the mother). The conflict between maternal and paternal genes adds a layer of complexity to the evolution of these disorders. Mathematical models show that when maternal and paternal genes push the phenotype in opposite directions, they increase the risk of maladaptive outcomes by "decanalizing" trait development and amplifying the expression of extreme trait values in spite of the resulting fitness costs (Wilkins, 2011). Intragenomic conflict thus contributes to explain the schizophrenia paradox: at least in part, the severe fertility loss observed in schizophrenics may be a maladaptive byproduct of the adaptive but conflicting strategies of different sets of genes.

Other important diametrical effects are found in patterns of brain development. Schizophrenia is associated with cortical thinning, especially in prefrontal and temporal regions; autism is associated with increased cortical growth and thicker prefrontal areas (Baribeau & Anagnostou, 2013; Katz et al., 2016). When the same genes are involved in both SSDs and ASD, the two types of disorders tend to be associated with variants of opposite effect. For example, a mutation that upregulates a certain molecular pathway increases the risk of ASD, whereas a different mutation with downregulating effects increases that of SSDs; a higher number of CNVs in a variable region increases ASD risk, whereas a lower number increases SSD risk; and so on (see Crespi et al., 2010; Gilman et al., 2012; Kalkman, 2012).

That said, it is important to note that not *all* risk factors for autism and psychosis operate in a diametrical fashion (Figure 8.3). First, deleterious mutations that disrupt brain development are likely to increase the risk of dysfunction across the board, thus contributing to both SSDs and ASD (especially the more severe forms). The same applies to early developmental disturbances such as prenatal infections and perinatal complications. Second, the involvement of imprinted genes in ASD and SSDs means that disruptions of the cellular machinery that regulates imprinting may affect the risk for both types of disorders. While mutations in the imprinted genes themselves should have diametrical effects on autism and psychosis, mutations in the genetic pathways of imprinting mechanisms can be expected to increase the likelihood of imprinted-related disorders across the board. These considerations align with initial evidence that risk scores for autism and schizophrenia based on common genetic variants are only weakly correlated, if at all (Lee, Ripke et al., 2013; Vorstman et al., 2013).

Overlap Between Autism and Schizophrenia

According to the diametrical model, ASD and SSDs lie at opposite ends of a cognitive and developmental continuum. This proposition is fairly controversial; in the psychiatric literature, the extent and meaning of the diagnostic overlap between autism and schizophrenia have been hotly debated for decades (Chisholm et al., 2015; Crespi, 2011). There are obvious phenotypic similarities between autistic symptoms and the negative/disorganized symptoms of psychosis: notably, both involve deficits in communication and social interaction, speech and language problems, and lack of emotional responsivity. Likewise, autistic-like traits and negative schizotypy are positively correlated in the general population. Proponents of the diametrical model argue that these similarities are superficial and reflect very different underlying processes. For example, social anxiety in the autistic spectrum stems from a sense that other people are unpredictable and difficult to understand (mentalizing deficit), whereas in the schizophrenia spectrum it mainly originates from paranoid attributions of hidden hostility (hypermentalizing). Behavioral descriptions of symptoms fail to capture these crucial distinctions, and the same is true of standard personality questionnaires (Chisholm et al., 2015; Crespi, 2011; Del Giudice et al., 2010, 2014*a*).

A stronger challenge to the diametrical model comes from epidemiological studies, which have documented increased risk of ASD in schizophrenic patients and their relatives (and vice versa), as well as patterns of developmental continuity between autistic symptoms in childhood and psychotic symptoms in adolescence and adulthood (Cederlöf et al., 2016; Chisholm et al., 2015; Marín et al., 2018; Sullivan et al., 2012, 2013). These associations are likely inflated by the relatively high rate of misdiagnosis for these disorders: in particular, severe negative symptoms in childhood are often mistaken for autism, and idiosyncratic interests and preoccupations in autistic people are easy to misinterpret as psychotic delusions (Crespi, 2011; Van Schalkwyk et al., 2015). Still, the overlap is unlikely to be fully explained by problems with differential diagnosis. Based on the available literature, there seem to be two main sources of true co-occurrence between ASD and SSDs within families. First, mutation load is involved in both types of disorders. In addition to deleterious mutations that affect brain development, disruptions of imprinting mechanisms may contribute to increase the risk of both ASD and SSDs. Second, childhood-onset schizophrenia is specifically associated with higher genetic risk for autism and an early history of autistic symptoms (Ahn et al., 2016; Caplan, 2016). Childhood-onset schizophrenia is infrequent, strongly male-biased, and associated with a high rate of rare CNVs, suggesting an association with relatively severe forms of autism. Other indications of overlap come from studies of prenatal growth. While larger born babies are at increased risk of ASD and decreased risk of SSDs (as predicted by the diametric model), very small newborns are at higher risk for both types of disorders (Byars et al., 2014). In total, the evidence points to a small group of patients marked by high mutation load, prenatal undergrowth, and a confluence of autistic and psychotic symptoms in childhood. From the standpoint of the diametrical model, this group represents an important anomaly; understanding its characteristics should be a priority for evolutionary research in this area. In adults, the co-occurrence of autism and schizophrenia is very uncommon. A recent study of ASD patients with comorbid psychosis found that few patients had a diagnosis of schizophrenia. Instead, most of them showed "atypical" conditions marked by a prevalence of affective symptoms and relatively brief psychotic episodes, a profile closer to that of bipolar spectrum disorders (Larson et al., 2017).

The Diametrical Model in a Life History Perspective

The original version of the diametrical model offers a unified description of psychosis and ASD, but does not explain how selection maintains schizotypal and autistic-like traits beyond the general idea of a tradeoff between different cognitive skills. Crespi and Badcock (2008) speculated that the behavioral features associated with hyper- versus hypomentalistic traits in childhood may affect the cost of childrearing (e.g., by making children with mild schizotypal traits more susceptible to enculturation and thus less demanding for mothers). However, the evidence in this respect is extremely limited. Integrating the sexual selection model of schizophrenia with the diametrical model suggests a different set of tradeoffs: whereas schizotypal traits are mainly selected for in short-term mating, autistic-like traits may contribute to mating success in the context of long-term relationships and sustained parental investment, especially in men (Del Giudice et al., 2010; Chapter 10).

Even more broadly, a life history perspective suggests that schizotypal and autistic-like personalities represent specialized functional profiles within fast and slow strategies, as I discussed in Chapter 4. Consistent with this extended model, schizotypal and autistic-like traits show diametrical correlations with key life history markers such as impulsivity and sociosexuality (Del Giudice et al.,

2010, 2014*a*). Recasting the diametrical model within a life history framework also clarifies the opposite associations of SSDs and ASD with early brain and body growth, which is a key indicator of maternal investment in offspring quality (higher maternal investment and offspring growth in slow-spectrum ASD, lower investment and growth in fast-spectrum SSDs; see Petersen & Aarøe, 2015). Also consistent with this view, mathematical models of genomic imprinting show that paternal genes can specifically evolve to promote the development of autistic-like traits if the latter promote unselfish cooperation and/or increase the offspring's contribution to family resources, for example by delaying mating and reproduction. All these traits fit the functional profile of a slow strategy (Chapter 10; Del Giudice et al., 2010; Úbeda, 2008; Úbeda & Gardner, 2010).

Other Evolutionary Scenarios

While most evolutionary scholars regard schizophrenia as both maladaptive and dysfunctional, there are at least two notable exceptions. Polimeni and Reiss (2002) proposed that schizophrenia itself may be an adaptive strategy—a cognitive/behavioral specialization maintained by group selection, similar to the sterile castes of eusocial insects like ants and bees. According to these authors, psychotic symptoms are the basis for shamanic phenomena such as possession and communication with the dead; the hypothesized benefit is enhanced group cohesion through religious rituals. Within the taxonomy discussed in Chapter 5, this would place schizophrenia in the category of self-sacrificial adaptations. However, it is unclear whether the group selection scenario proposed by Polimeni and Reiss is evolutionarily plausible in human populations.

In their proposed revision of the social brain theory, Abed and Abbas (2011, 2014) argued that schizophrenia is not a universal byproduct of human evolution but a recent phenomenon—more precisely, the outcome of a mismatch between evolved psychological mechanisms and modern social conditions. According to their *out-group intolerance hypothesis*, paranoid symptoms reflect the hyperactivation of adaptive cognitive mechanisms that regulate relationships with out-group members. In traditional small-scale societies, people live mainly among kin and in-group members, and contacts with out-groups are rare and typically hostile. In modern societies, the loosening of kin relations and the extremely high frequency of out-group interactions may lead to hyperactivation of protective mechanisms in susceptible individuals. This mismatch hypothesis provides an elegant explanation of the risk-increasing effects of migration and urbanization, although it does not fit as well with other aspects of the epidemiology of SSDs. For example, the authors suggested that males should be especially sensitive to out-group threats (Abed & Abbas, 2014), but paranoid symptoms are more common in females. In addition to being speculative, the models by Polimeni and Reiss (2002) and Abed and Abbas (2011) are somewhat limited in scope; for example, they do not explain the origin of negative symptoms or account for the role of mutation load and reduced IQ. At the same time, they call attention to some important but too often neglected issues, such as the prominence of religious themes in psychosis and the specific challenges posed by extensive outgroup interactions in modern societies.

FSD CLASSIFICATION

As discussed in Chapter 4, the pattern of enhanced creativity, hypermentalizing, and unrestricted sociosexuality associated with positive schizotypy fits the broad contour of a fast life history strategy. Consistent with this interpretation, positive schizotypy also correlates with aggression, impulsivity, sensation seeking, and reduced concerns about social desirability. Impulsivity and high time discounting are common features of psychosis spectrum disorders, and a hostile-dominant interpersonal style is a stable correlate of paranoid symptoms (Del Giudice et al., 2014*a*; Fortgang et al. 2016; Horan et al., 2017; Podubinsky et al., 2012; Nederlof et al., 2012). Another life history–relevant trait associated with schizotypy and SPD is insecure romantic attachment. Attachment disorganization in infancy and childhood seems to be a common precursor of SSDs, especially in people with histories of trauma and abuse; early disorganization is consistent with the high anxiety and avoidance observed in adults with these disorders (Liotti & Gumley, 2008; Mikulincer & Shaver, 2016). Concerning the disgust system, there is evidence that positive schizotypy predicts lower levels of moral and sexual disgust (Del Giudice et al., 2014*b*).

The motivational and self-regulatory characteristics of schizotypy and SSDs are reflected at the level of broad personality traits. Schizotypal personalities are marked by high levels of neuroticism and low agreeableness, conscientiousness, and honesty-humility. Positive schizotypy is associated with elevated openness to experience, whereas negative schizotypy correlates with low openness and extraversion. In diagnosed patients, openness is elevated in SPD but reduced in schizophrenia (Asai et al., 2011; Ashton et al., 2012; Avia et al., 1995; Barrantes-Vidal et al., 2010; Camisa et al., 2005; Ohi et al., 2016; Ross et al., 2002; Samuel & Widiger, 2008). These findings support the idea that negative schizotypy captures low-level dysfunctional processes similar to those observed in schizophrenia. At the same time, the association with reduced openness and extraversion may be partly explained by the fact that measures of negative schizotypy are partially confounded with individual differences in autistic-like traits (Del Giudice et al., 2010, 2014*a*; Dinsdale et al., 2013; more on this in Chapter 10).

In addition to creativity, the cognitive profile of the schizophrenia spectrum is marked by a predominance of verbal over visuospatial ability. This is a robust finding in relatives of schizophrenic patients (Kravariti et al., 2006; Snitz et al., 2006; Zhai et al., 2011). Even in patients with low intelligence, verbal skills tend to be less strongly compromised than visuospatial ones; genetic risk scores for schizophrenia show negative correlations with genetic scores for the visuospatial component of IQ, but not with those for the visuospatial component (Hubbard et al., 2016).

Based on the behavioral and cognitive markers reviewed here, SSDs can be classified as F-type disorders linked to the seductive/creative profile. However, the existence of multiple subtypes within the schizophrenia spectrum—some of which seem to overlap with autism—suggests that there may be meaningful exceptions to the general pattern. The literature on puberty timing offers some intriguing if preliminary evidence. Two recent large studies found that early puberty is associated with schizotypy and psychotic experiences, consistent with a fast spectrum classification (Clemmensen et al., 2015; Smith-Woolley et al., 2017). In two smaller studies, positive schizotypy was associated with atypically early maturation, but also (to a lesser extent) with atypically *late* maturation. In contrast, negative schizotypy was associated with late maturation in males, but not in females (Gruzelier & Kaiser, 1996; Kaiser & Gruzelier 1999). As noted earlier, correlations with negative schizotypy in males are likely to be confounded by the effect of autistic-like traits. However, if findings of elevated schizotypy in late maturing people were replicated, they would point to some degree of functional heterogeneity within the schizophrenia spectrum. This is an important area for evolutionary research, and one where a life history approach may point to a deeper structure in what would otherwise be a confusing mass of empirical data.

Neurobiology

Dopamine and glutamate are the key neurotransmitters involved in the etiology of psychosis, but the role of serotonin (5-HT) has been investigated as well. Since serotonergic inputs inhibit DA release in mesolimbic pathways, it is reasonable to hypothesize that psychosis would be associated with downregulated serotonergic function (Kapur & Remington, 1996). The limited molecular evidence agrees with this prediction. Schizophrenia patients show reduced expression of the 5-HT_{2A} receptor, which suppresses dopaminergic activity and contributes to glutamatergic signaling; at the same time, they express high levels of the 5-HT_{1A} receptor, which is involved in the negative feedback loops that inhibit serotonin release (Selvaraj et al., 2014).

A number of studies have measured androgens in schizophrenic patients and people at high risk for psychosis. When testosterone levels are reduced in SSDs, the association seems to be largely driven by negative rather than positive symptoms. Also, epidemiological data indicate that psychosis risk in women is associated with polycystic ovarian syndrome (PCOS), a condition caused by excessive androgen levels (Cesta et al., 2016; Fernandez-Egea et al., 2011; Ko et al., 2007; Ramsey et al., 2013; Van Rijn et al., 2011). A recent meta-analysis found elevated DHEAS in schizophrenics and higher testosterone in first-episode patients; for chronic patients, testosterone levels seem to be higher in women but lower in men, possibly as a result of medication (Misiak et al., 2018). The available data on oxytocin (OT) are contradictory, partly because of the small size of most studies. There are reports of both elevated and reduced oxytocin in schizophrenia and both positive and negative correlations between OT levels and symptom severity. Attempts to treat psychotic symptoms with OT administration have yielded largely null results (Beckmann et al., 1985; Feifel et al., 2016; Jobst et al., 2014; Rubin et al., 2010, 2014; Strauss et al., 2015; Tseng et al., 2014; Williams & Bürkner, 2017). On the whole, the evidence seems to favor a positive association between oxytocinergic function and psychosis risk (Crespi, 2016*a*; Crespi & Hurd, 2015), but there is still no definite consensus in the literature. In contrast, neuroimaging studies generally find increased activation and connectivity of the default mode network in patients and their relatives, consistent with a profile of hypermentalistic cognition and self-absorption (Haut et al., 2016; Whitfield-Gabrieli & Ford, 2012). There is also initial evidence that schizophrenic patients show elevated levels of insulin-like growth factor 1 (IGF-1), an intriguing finding from a life history perspective (Palomino et al., 2013; see Chapter 4).

In summary, SSDs are associated with low serotonergic and high dopaminergic function, as well as hyperactivity of the stress response system. While the evidence on oxytocin and sex hormones is mixed the schizophrenia spectrum is characterized by a reliable pattern of reduced DLPFC activation and high default network activity/connectivity. These neurobiological findings are consistent with an F-type classification and match the hypothesized features of the creative/seductive profile.

9

The Bipolar Spectrum

OVERVIEW

Mania

The central feature of bipolar disorders (BDs) is *mania*, a state of abnormally high energy and activity coupled with persistently elevated, expansive, or irritable mood. Typical features of manic states include inflated self-esteem, exaggerated talkativeness, "racing thoughts" and flight of ideas, distractibility, and increased energy and goal-directed activity (e.g., starting multiple new projects at once). However, excitement and joy can easily turn into frustration and anger, especially if others fail to respond as desired or to share the person's enthusiasm. Mania is often associated with an increase in libido and sexual promiscuity, and may lead to risky and potentially damaging activities such as spending sprees, foolish money-making plans, dangerous driving, or gambling (American Psychiatric Association, 2013).

At the level of psychological mechanisms, mania reflects hyperactivation of the behavioral approach system (BAS) and exaggerated sensitivity to rewards (both "wanting" and "liking"). This general activation state amplifies approach motivation in a number of more specific domains—chiefly status, mating, play, and curiosity. The acquisition system also seems to be involved in several types of manic behaviors, from gambling to risky financial investments. Positive emotional reactivity is a core feature of manic states; more specifically, status- and achievement-related emotions such as pride and ambition are more strongly activated than prosocial, affiliative emotions such as compassion and trust (Ashok et al., 2017; Durbin et al., 2009; Gruber, 2011; Johnson, Leedom et al., 2012; Johnson, Carver et al., 2012; Meyer & Hoffmann, 2005; Nusslock et al., 2014).

In bipolar disorders, phases of mania typically alternate with periods of depression, although one high-intensity manic episode is sufficient for a diagnosis even without a history of depression (see later discussion). Moreover, patients may experience *mixed episodes* in which manic features (e.g., hyperactivity, restlessness) coexist with depressive thoughts and dejected feelings. The rate of cycling between mania and depression is extremely variable between people, from a few days to more than a year; rapid cycling predicts worse prognosis and a lower chance of remission and recovery. While adverse and stressful life events predict the onset of depression, the risk of mania is increased by *positive* events, especially those involving personal success and goal achievement. About 10–20% of women experience moderate mania after giving birth. Sleep deprivation and disruption of daily routines—which are more likely during periods of increased activity—also contribute to trigger mania in predisposed individuals; additionally, manic symptoms tend to follow a seasonal pattern with a peak in the spring and a trough in the fall (American Psychiatric Association, 2013; Cassidy & Carroll, 2002; Jamison, 1993; Miklowitz & Johnson, 2013, 2014; Simonsen et al., 2011). Both mania and depression can be accompanied by psychotic symptoms—the most common in the case of mania are grandiose delusions, sometimes mixed with persecutory and paranoid themes (e.g., powerful enemies jealous of the patient's success and special abilities; Knowles et al., 2011).

The Bipolar Spectrum

Hypomanic Traits

Like the schizophrenia spectrum, the spectrum of bipolar phenomena ranges all the way from normal personality traits to severe psychotic symptoms. The broad dimension of personality underlying the risk for bipolar disorders is usually labeled *hypomania*. Hypomanic traits have two main facets: a facet of mood volatility (*cyclothymia*) that is strongly linked to neuroticism, and a facet of excitement and vitality (*hyperthymia*) that overlaps with extraversion and openness. Finer distinctions within hypomania distinguish mood volatility from irritability, and social vitality from excitement (positive emotionality, cheerful mood); however, the social vitality facet overlaps almost completely with extraversion and is a poor predictor of manic symptoms (Schalet et al., 2011; Siedor et al., 2016; Stanton et al., 2016; Stringaris et al., 2011; Vazquez & Gonda, 2013; Watson & Naragon-Gainey, 2014).

Hypomanic traits are moderately correlated with positive schizotypy. Like positive schizotypy, hypomania is a robust predictor of artistic and verbal creativity, especially in combination with high intelligence. In addition to stimulating rich and unusual associations, hypomanic traits increase ideation fluency, allowing people to generate thoughts and ideas at a faster pace. Artists tend to be above average in hypomania, and creativity—both artistic and scientific—is elevated in the relatives of BD patients (Baas et al., 2016; Furnham et al., 2008; Jamison, 1993; Kyaga, 2015; Rawlings & Locarnini, 2008; Srivastava et al., 2010; Vellante et al., 2011). The evidence indicates that creativity is enhanced in hypomanic personalities and people with mild manic symptoms, but not in those experiencing full-blown manic episodes (Miklowitz & Johnson, 2013).

Bipolar Disorders

The DSM identifies three main types of bipolar disorders. Bipolar disorder I (BD-I) is defined by at least one manic episode lasting 1 week or more, with or without depression. Bipolar disorder II (BD-II) requires at least one episode of major depression (MDD) and one "hypomanic" episode; that is, a manic phase of at least 4 days without psychotic features and not severe enough to cause marked impairment. The symptom profile of BD-II is tilted toward depression; BD-II tends to be more chronic than BD-I, with more severe depressive episodes, more anxiety/irritability, and higher risk for suicide. When manic and depressive symptoms persist for 2 or more years without reaching the criteria for a manic episode (for BD-I) or MDD (for BD-II), the DSM diagnosis is of "cyclothymic disorder." It is not infrequent for bipolar symptoms to worsen over time, and 15–50% of people with cyclothymic disorder eventually meet the diagnostic criteria for BD-I or BD-II.

While the DSM classifies bipolar spectrum disorders based on the severity of manic and depressive symptoms, empirical studies of symptom clusters indicate the existence of four main prototypes of BD, each associated with a specific constellation of behavioral traits. The first type is characterized by pure manic symptoms, with high levels of excitement and euphoria but few or no psychotic symptoms. This cluster of "pure" bipolar symptoms shows the smallest overlap with the rest of the psychosis spectrum. The second type combines high-intensity mania and hyperthymic traits with severe psychosis, shows the highest family comorbidity with schizophrenia spectrum disorders (SSDs), and shares some of the same specific risk factors (e.g., migration). The remaining two types are both associated with moderate levels of psychotic symptoms. The third type (more common in women) is marked by intense depression and high risk of suicide. The fourth (more common in men) is characterized by severe mania with both hyperthymia and irritability, high levels of anger and hostility, antisocial behavior, risk-taking, and an especially strong association with substance use (Alda, 2004; Azorin et al., 2008; Sato et al., 2002).

Another important axis of differentiation within the bipolar spectrum is that of cognitive ability. On the whole, BDs are associated with below-average IQ (though not as low as in schizophrenia), but also above-average academic performance and educational attainment, at least in some studies (Bansal et al., 2017; Hagenaars et al., 2016; MacCabe et al., 2010; Tempelaar et al., 2017; Vreeker et al., 2016). These general findings mask a striking degree of heterogeneity. A subgroup of BD patients shows intact cognitive ability and *enhanced* social cognition; others show mild deficits in executive functions and verbal learning/memory; and others still suffer from global cognitive impairment, similar to schizophrenic patients. A crucial difference between these subgroups is the presence and severity of psychotic symptoms, which predict lower performance in verbal memory and tests of executive function (both reliable indicators of general intelligence). Executive functions are especially compromised in patients with elevated hyperthymia, which often show severe psychotic symptoms and/or antisocial behaviors. In contrast, manic symptoms without delusions and hallucinations are associated with higher premorbid IQ and better cognitive functioning (Bora et al., 2009; Burdick et al., 2014; Glahn & Burdick, 2011; Martínez-Arán et al., 2008; Smith, Anderson et al., 2015; Xu et al., 2014). Performance on mentalizing tests is usually impaired in BDs, particularly during acute manic episodes (Bora et al., 2016). However, researchers in this area have not tested the possibility that reduced performance may be explained by hyperactive mentalizing, as in the case of schizophrenia (Chapter 8).

The predisposition to disorders in the bipolar spectrum is highly heritable, with 80–90% of the variance explained by additive genetic factors and no shared environmental effects. Many of the common variants that contribute to the risk for BDs also contribute to that for SSDs. Some alleles are specifically linked to BDs and have been found to increase the frequency of manic symptoms in schizophrenia, but not that of positive and negative symptoms (Edvardsen et al., 2008; Knopik et al., 2017; Lee, Ripke et al., 2013; Lo et al., 2017; Ruderfer et al., 2014).

The ratio of males to females is approximately balanced for BD-I, whereas females are more at risk for BD-II and conditions with rapid cycling. Childhood-onset BDs are more common in boys; in contrast, women are overrepresented in late-onset bipolar conditions. However, mania in later life is often unrelated to familial risk for bipolar conditions and may have a completely different etiology (American Psychiatric Association, 2013; Hulvershorn & Nurnberger, 2014). The bipolar spectrum has a wide network of comorbidity that includes SSDs, defense activation conditions (generalized anxiety disorder [GAD], social anxiety disorder [SAD], panic disorder), as well as attention-deficit/hyperactivity disorder (ADHD), conduct disorder (CD), oppositional defiant disorder (ODD), substance use, and eating disorders. The comorbidity with ADHD and conduct disorders is especially high for childhood-onset BDs (up to 60–90%); symmetrically, ADHD symptoms in childhood increase the risk of BDs in adulthood (Blader & Carlson, 2013; Klimes-Dougan et al., 2016; McElroy et al., 2006, 2011; Meyer et al., 2004; Miklowitz & Johnson, 2013; Song et al., 2015). Personality disorders are very common, especially borderline personality disorder (BPD) and obsessive-compulsive personality disorder (OCPD) (Brieger et al., 2003; Fornaro et al., 2016; Grant et al., 2004). Finally, there is a nontrivial degree of comorbidity between BDs and autism, as I discuss in more detail later.

Neurobiological Correlates

The brain correlates of BDs include gray matter loss and reduced connectivity, though in a much attenuated form compared with schizophrenia. In addition, neuroimaging studies have documented a pattern of amygdala hyperactivity coupled with reduced functional connectivity between the amygdala and prefrontal areas. The volume of the amygdala is smaller than average in children and adolescents with BD, but larger than average in adult patients—probably reflecting a developmental trajectory of progressive enlargement over time (Ellison-Wright & Bullmore, 2010; Klimes-Dougan et al., 2016; Miklowitz & Johnson, 2013, 2014).

Predictably, manic and depressive states in BDs have distinct neurobiological correlates. Mania is strongly associated with increased dopaminergic activity in mesolimbic pathways, consistent with upregulated BAS activity. Dopaminergic hyperactivity is accompanied by higher norepinephrine levels in the brain and by a decrease in central acetylcholine (ACh). In contrast, there is evidence that ACh signaling in the brain is elevated during depressive episodes. High glutamate levels have also been documented in both children and adults with BD. The findings on serotonin levels in bipolar patients are highly inconsistent; a possibility is that serotonergic signaling is enhanced in depression and inhibited in mania, but there are not enough data to conclusively test this hypothesis (Ashok et al., 2017; Berk et al., 2007; Klimes-Dougan et al., 2016; Mahmood & Silverstone, 2001; Miklowitz & Johnson, 2014; Miller et al., 2016; van Enkhuizen et al., 2015; Walderhaug et al., 2011).

As discussed in Chapter 8, psychosis is associated with increased activation of the stress response system, especially in the HPA and sympathetic components. This also applies to bipolar disorders with psychotic features. In addition, depressive episodes in BDs are often characterized by a distinctive pattern of neuroendocrine and affective symptoms known as *melancholia*. Melancholia is a physiological state of sustained HPA hyperactivity, accompanied by overwhelming feelings of apprehension and gloom with ruminative thoughts that typically center on themes of illness, impending danger, guilt, and worthlessness. Melancholic patients show psychomotor disturbances (either retardation or agitation) and vegetative signs of reduced sleep, appetite, and libido. The neurobiological mechanisms underlying melancholia include elevated cortisol, reduced negative feedback on the HPA axis, and hyperactivation of the amygdala. Heart rate is also elevated, suggesting a combination of increased sympathetic and decreased parasympathetic activity. Melancholic symptoms are much more common in bipolar than unipolar depression and are strongly associated with psychotic symptoms in depression and BDs, but not in schizophrenia (Kemp et al., 2014; Parker et al., 2000, 2015; Shorter & Fink, 2010; Taylor & Fink, 2008; more on this in Chapter 14). Alterations of inflammatory processes are also involved in BDs, although to a lesser extent than in SSDs (Mørch et al., 2016).

Development and Course

Bipolar symptoms are fairly common in childhood and adolescence, but very few children meet the threshold for a diagnosable disorder. In fact, only about 5% of BD diagnoses are made before 12 years of age; childhood-onset forms of BD are especially severe and show the lowest recovery rates. The main childhood precursors of BDs are emotional reactivity, irritability, fearfulness, anxiety, and sleep problems (Blader & Carlson, 2013; Hulvershorn & Nurnberger, 2014; Klimes-Dougan et al., 2016). The age of onset of bipolar conditions is intrinsically difficult to pinpoint; to illustrate, consider a person who undergoes mild depressive episodes between age 16 and 19, followed by a more severe depression at 20 and a manic episode at 22. A BD diagnosis can be made at age 22, but when did the disorder really start? The fuzzy timeline of BDs is amplified by the fact that depressive symptoms tend to begin a few years earlier than manic symptoms, leading to considerable diagnostic ambiguity. Despite these difficulties, it is clear that BDs arise most frequently in adolescence and young adulthood; the mean age of onset is around 18 years for BD-I and 25 years for BD-II. As in schizophrenia, the distribution of BDs switches from male-biased in childhood to female-biased in late adulthood (American Psychiatric Association, 2013; Hulvershorn & Nurnberger, 2014; Miklowitz & Johnson, 2013).

While disorders in the bipolar spectrum can be severely impairing, a majority of BD patients show virtually complete remission in the periods between episodes. A high remission rate was recorded even in the 19th and early 20th centuries, before the introduction of effective pharmacological treatments in the 1950s (Alvarez Ariza et al., 2009). With age, depressive episodes tend to become longer and more frequent, consistent with a decrease in dopaminergic function. While the course of BDs is often chronic in psychiatric patients, community studies suggest that many people who would meet diagnostic criteria in adolescence or early adulthood undergo remission as they enter the third decade of life (Blader & Carlson, 2013; Cicero et al., 2009).

Risk Factors

As summarized in Figure 8.1, disorders in the bipolar spectrum are typically characterized by better cognitive functionality than those in the schizophrenia spectrum. Accordingly, the role of rare copy number variations (CNVs) is much smaller in the etiology of BDs compared with SSDs (Green et al., 2016; Grozeva et al., 2010). Similarly, prenatal and obstetrical complications are only weakly associated with the risk of BDs, with the exception of the more severe childhood-onset forms. While prematurity is a predictor of BDs, it does not necessarily imply a dysregulation of fetal development and is consistent with a pattern of reduced physiological investment by the mother (Chapter 8; Blader & Carlson, 2013; Hulvershorn & Nurnberger, 2014). The risk of BDs is elevated in offspring of older fathers, consistent with a role of mutation load; again, this pattern is considerably stronger in childhood-onset BDs, though not as strong as in schizophrenia. In addition, risk is somewhat elevated in children of teenage fathers and significantly so in those of older mothers (Byars et al., 2014; D'Onofrio et al., 2014; Frans et al., 2008). These effects are not readily explained in genetic terms but have intriguing implications when viewed from a life history perspective (more on this later).

While there are findings of associations with early stress and negative family relations, the epidemiological evidence is less consistent than in SSDs. For example, BD patients report a somewhat higher frequency of sexual abuse than nonclinical controls, but lower than patients with other mental disorders such as schizophrenia or depression (Maniglio, 2013). The data on socioeconomic status are also contradictory: epidemiological studies have documented associations with both higher and lower SES, possibly owing to the fact that different subtypes of the disorder show opposite relations with socioeconomic factors. Finally, the prevalence of BDs is elevated in high-income countries and in more individualistic, socially egalitarian cultures (Eid et al., 2013; Johnson & Johnson, 2014; Merikangas & Pato, 2009; Merikangas et al., 2011).

EVOLUTIONARY MODELS

Compared with the rich literature on schizophrenia, there has been relatively little evolutionary work on the bipolar spectrum. Virtually all models postulate some adaptive advantage for hypomanic traits or even bipolar symptoms in the clinical range. The idea that at least some conditions in the spectrum represent adaptive strategies is consistent with data showing a comparatively small fertility reduction in BD patients as a whole (the relative reproductive success is about 85% in females and 75% in males, compared with 50% and 20% in schizophrenia), as well as enhanced fertility in the patients' siblings and in young adults with the disorder (Jacobson, 2016; Power et al., 2013). Given the striking range of functionality that exists within the spectrum—including intelligence, mutation load, and recovery rates—it is natural to hypothesize a similarly large variation in the adaptive potential of bipolar symptoms.

Many authors have stressed the connection between manic symptoms and the dominance behaviors typical of high-ranking individuals (Gardner, 1982; Gilbert et al., 2007; Stevens & Price, 2000). However, the potential benefits of mania likely extend to prestige competition, mating and courtship (Akiskal & Akiskal, 2005), and even parental investment. Indeed, the existence of multiple distinct subtypes of BDs suggests that the bipolar spectrum may be quite heterogeneous from a functional standpoint. Accordingly, the diametrical model of autism and psychosis does not fully account for the epidemiology of bipolar disorders, which—in contrast with schizophrenia—show a relatively high comorbidity with autism. A life history perspective offers some new insights into the functional heterogeneity of BDs, which is not adequately addressed by existing evolutionary models.

Bipolar Symptoms as Status and Mating Behaviors

The first detailed analysis of bipolar symptoms as status-related behaviors was presented by Gardner (1982). Gardner noted the many analogies between the behavior of manic patients and that of high-ranking individuals in humans and other animals. In particular, the communicative pattern observed in mania—high energy, expansive body posture, fast and assertive speech—can be thought of as a highly canalized psychological state that is triggered by winning in dominance contests and is designed to signal one's superior social rank. Symmetrically, the communicative pattern associated with depression shows strong analogies with defeat and submission behaviors in low-ranking individuals (see Chapter 14; Annen et al., 2012). Gardner hypothesized that manic and depressive psychological states are not disordered in and of themselves; however, people with a predisposition to BDs have an especially low threshold for activating those states in response to external triggers and are insensitive to the stimuli that usually terminate them. As a result, predisposed people quickly enter into manic and/or depressive states and remain "locked" in those states for abnormally long stretches of time.

The idea that mania and depression reflect the winning and losing "programs" of the dominance system has been reprised and extended by others over the years (Gilbert et al., 2007; Johnson, Leedom et al., 2012; Stevens & Price, 2000; Wilson & Price, 2006). Akiskal and Akiskal (2005) took a broader view of the potential benefits of hypomanic traits and argued that hyperthymia does not only promote social dominance but also leadership (a prediction confirmed by Kyaga et al., 2015), exploration, territoriality, and courtship. They also suggested that cyclothymia specifically increases the pursuit of sexual and romantic opportunities, and that the creativity associated with cyclothymic traits facilitates seduction and enhances sexual attractiveness. On this view, the adaptive benefits of hypomanic traits would be maximal for people with milder forms of BDs and their relatives; however, Akiskal and Akiskal speculated that even extreme mania in some individuals may benefit group survival when human groups are faced with new, unexpected challenges. This group selection argument is potentially problematic; also problematic is the fact that the authors subscribed to the classic hypothesis (now decisively falsified) that bipolar risk depends on a small number of genes of major effect (Wilson, 1998).

The evolutionary models I just discussed rightly point to dominance and mating as key motivational aspects of mania. However, they take a narrow view of dominance and fail to fully acknowledge the implications of dual status hierarchies in our species. As discussed earlier, prestige competition can take many different forms, from political leadership to artistic and technical skills. Many behavioral features of hypomania—increased energy and self-esteem, goal-directedness, accelerated ideation—may help achieve mastery and success in technical domains in addition to artistic ones, especially when expressed at mild levels. Also, the excitement facet of hypomania is associated with *reduced* mating effort and sexual activity—a finding that does not match the standard evolutionary accounts (Schalet et al., 2011). Some people with hypomanic traits may primarily direct their energy and motivation toward nonsocial goals such as inventions, business ideas, and scientific research (e.g., Gartner, 2005). While this possibility has been largely neglected in past research, it dovetails with the role of dopamine and BAS activation in promoting industriousness and persistence in highly conscientious individuals (Chapter 3). Even more strikingly, the high frequency of hypomanic episodes in the postpartum period demonstrates how manic states can boost *parental* effort instead of mating effort. The motivational spectrum of mania clearly extends beyond dominance and mating, in line with the idea that BAS activation is a nonspecific regulatory process that can potentially support a wide range of motivations and goals, cooperative and affiliative as well as competitive (Krupić et al., 2016).

Bipolar Disorders and the Diametrical Model

According to the diametrical model of autism and psychosis presented in Chapter 8, bipolar disorders are part of the broader spectrum of psychosis. As such, they should share a profile of hypermentalistic and hypomechanistic cognition, early undergrowth, and overexpression of maternal genes (Crespi & Badcock, 2008). Overall, the evidence supports these predictions; for example, BD patients show impairments in visuospatial memory and a trend toward fetal undergrowth (Byars et al., 2014; Gallagher et al., 2015). However, the pattern is clearly less consistent than in schizophrenia and other SSDs. To begin, there is a relatively high comorbidity between autism and BDs (about 6–20% of patients with autism spectrum disorder [ASD] can be diagnosed with a bipolar spectrum condition), especially in patients with less severe cases of ASD and their relatives (Song et al., 2015; Vannucchi et al., 2014). Genetic risk scores for ASD and BDs are almost uncorrelated (less than .10), indicating that the genetic predisposition for the two types of disorder is transmitted independently in the population (Bulik-Sullivan et al., 2015; Lee, Ripke et al., 2013). However, the high comorbidity rate suggests a positive relation in a subgroup of BD patients and seems inconsistent with a fully diametrical model. The finding that BDs are more strongly associated with scientific than artistic professions in patients and their relatives also challenges the idea of reduced mechanistic skills in the bipolar spectrum (Kyaga et al., 2011, 2013). In addition, the association between fetal undergrowth and BD risk is weaker and less robust than in SSDs (Byars et al., 2014).

Taken together, these discordant findings suggest that BDs may contain a specific subtype characterized by little overlap with the psychosis spectrum and a stronger affinity to autism. As noted in a previous section, studies have identified a cluster of BD patients with little or no psychotic symptoms, high intelligence, and (most likely) low levels of mutation load. While there are no data on whether patients in this cluster also experience higher comorbidity with autism, the finding that comorbidity with BDs is especially common in the milder forms of ASD is at least consistent with a profile of high intelligence and low mutation load. In a life history framework, this would correspond to a distinction between two functional subtypes of BDs: a high-frequency, fast spectrum subtype associated with SSD risk and a low-frequency, slow spectrum subtype associated with ASD risk. In the next section I review additional evidence consistent with this hypothesis.

Other Evolutionary Scenarios

To conclude this section, it is worth mentioning the evolutionary model of bipolar disorders proposed by Sherman (2001, 2006, 2012). According to Sherman, disorders in the BD spectrum are adaptive strategies that evolved during the latest glacial period in response to a climatic pattern of long, severe winters and short summers. In the model, depression is an adaptation to winter that conserves energy and reduces social engagement, whereas mania is designed to promote concentrated activity in the spring/summer. Additionally, manic states would function as an "emergency reaction" in response to unexpected environmental challenges. Sherman explicitly argued that BDs evolved as adaptive strategies, even though they may have become maladaptive in modern environments due to evolutionary mismatches. A notable aspect of this model is the hypothesis that susceptibility alleles for BD originally evolved in Neandertal populations (who inhabited northern Europe between 300,000 and 30,000 years ago) and were transferred to *Homo sapiens* through intermixing during the late Pleistocene.

This model is highly speculative and fails to account for several important features of BDs, including their comorbidity with schizophrenia, the existence of mixed manic/depressive states, and sex differences in the symptoms and course of the disorder. Another problem with the idea that bipolar depression evolved as an adaptation for energy conservation is the high rate of melancholia in BDs: melancholic symptoms are marked by sustained activation of the HPA and sympathetic system, a physiological pattern with high metabolic costs. Across populations, the model predicts an epidemiological pattern of lower bipolar risk in people of African descent who carry fewer Neandertal-derived genes than do Europeans and Asians (Green, Krause et al., 2010); however, the available data offer little support to this prediction (Breslau et al., 2005; Delbello et al., 2001; Kessler et al., 2005; see Chapter 21). Despite these limitations, Sherman's model does provide an intriguing rationale for the marked seasonality of bipolar symptoms. More generally, the model highlights the key role of BAS activation/deactivation cycles in the allocation of energetic expenditures across the year, which might provide an evolutionarily ancient template for the regulation of other cyclical or time-limited activities such as courtship and childbearing.

FSD CLASSIFICATION

As anticipated earlier, the life history classification of bipolar conditions is complex and likely to involve multiple functional subtypes. On the whole, hypomanic traits and BDs are associated with fast traits such as impulsivity, risk-taking, sensation seeking, and narcissism (Akiskal & Akiskal, 2005; Durbin et al., 2009; Fortgang et al., 2016; Glahn & Burdick, 2011; Kwapil et al., 2011; Siedor et al., 2016; Stanton et al., 2016; Walsh et al., 2013). Offspring of BD patients are more likely to be sexually promiscuous and to have sex at an earlier age, consistent with a central role of mating effort in the bipolar phenotype (Nijjar et al., 2014). At the level of broad personality traits, hypomania correlates negatively with agreeableness and conscientiousness and positively with extraversion, openness, and neuroticism (Nelson & Rawlings, 2010; Siedor et al., 2016; Stanton et al., 2016; Walsh et al., 2012; Watson & Naragon-Gainey, 2014). Together with the data on creativity reviewed earlier and some evidence that manic symptoms are more strongly associated with verbal than visuospatial ability (Smith et al., 2015*b*), these findings argue for linking bipolar spectrum disorders to the seductive/creative profile of F-type psychopathology, together with schizophrenia and other SSDs. I proposed this classification for BDs in earlier versions of the life history framework (Del Giudice, 2014*b*, 2016*d*).

While an F-type classification is probably adequate for a majority of BD cases, a closer look at the evidence reveals a more complicated picture. To begin, different facets of hypomania show divergent patterns of correlation with life history markers. While cyclothymia is robustly associated with low agreeableness and conscientiousness, hyperthymia is not; moreover, the excitement facet predicts restricted sociosexuality and less engagement in risky behaviors (Schalet et al., 2011; Stanton et al., 2016; Watson & Naragon-Gainey, 2014). This suggests that a minority of hypomanic profiles (mainly characterized by hyperthymic traits) may be functionally related to the slow spectrum of psychopathology. Another indication of heterogeneity comes from the limited available data on puberty timing, which show higher levels of hypomanic traits in both early and late maturers (Graber et al., 1997). The risk of BDs is elevated in the offspring of teenage fathers (consistent with an F-type classification) but also in those of older mothers, which points to a functional association with delayed reproduction and slower life histories. Finally, autistic patients who also receive a diagnosis of psychosis typically show high levels of affective symptoms, consistent with a high comorbidity between BDs and ASD (Larson et al., 2017).

Based on this evidence, I tentatively propose to classify bipolar spectrum disorders into two subtypes: a high-frequency, fast spectrum subtype with strong links to schizophrenia (F-BDs) and a low-frequency, slow spectrum subtype with a bias toward ASD comorbidity (S-BDs). The slow spectrum subtype of BDs should be characterized by fewer psychotic symptoms and a lower rate of melancholia; also, depressive symptoms in this group of patients may be consistent with an energy conservation or "recovery" process that balances out the excess expenditure of manic episodes, as suggested by Sherman (2001). This provisional classification is intended as an initial step toward a better evolutionary understanding of bipolar pathology; more research will be needed to evaluate its merits and validate the putative subtypes proposed here.

Neurobiology

The neurobiology of BDs is still poorly understood, and there is no firm consensus on the role of serotonin in bipolar symptoms. A possibility is that different BD subtypes are associated with different patterns of serotonergic activity, but there is virtually no evidence bearing on this hypothesis. There have been initial reports of elevated oxytocin levels in bipolar patients, whose pattern of default network activity shows both similarities and differences with that of schizophrenics (Alonso-Lana et al., 2016; Calhoun et al., 2012; Dinsdale & Crespi, 2017; Öngür et al.,

2010; Turan et al., 2013). In addition, there is evidence that insulin-like growth factor 1 (IGF-1) is elevated in bipolar patients (Kim et al., 2013; Palomino et al., 2013; Scola & Andreazza, 2015). These findings are broadly consistent with the hypothesized features of the seductive/creative profile, but it is important to stress that they are based on very small samples. Other small studies have suggested that patients with mania have higher testosterone than schizophrenics (Ozcan & Banoglu, 2003); however, the findings about androgens in schizophrenia are less than straightforward, and some evidence suggests that reduced testosterone may be associated with negative but not positive symptoms (Chapter 8). In conclusion, the available data are not robust enough to support or contradict the proposed FSD classification and are still too coarse to permit the identification of functional subtypes based on neurobiological markers.

10

The Autism Spectrum

OVERVIEW

The Autism Triad

Disorders in the autism spectrum are defined by three clusters of symptoms collectively known as the "autism triad": impairments in social interaction, impairments in communication, and restricted/repetitive behaviors and interests. Social impairments include lack of emotional reciprocity and sharing, difficulties in understanding others' mental states, and problems in using and reading nonverbal behavior (e.g., gaze, facial expressions, body posture). Communicative impairments may range from delays or even complete failures of language acquisition to subtler disturbances in conversational behavior (e.g., turn-taking), stereotyped or idiosyncratic use of words, and difficulties with nonliteral speech (e.g., irony, sarcasm, metaphors). Similarly, restricted/repetitive behaviors range from severe symptoms such as stereotyped movements and inflexible routines to milder patterns of preference for sameness, narrow interests, and restricted focus on specific activities. Sensory symptoms are also very common and involve both hyper- and hyporeactivity to sensory inputs—for example, extreme sensitivity to sudden noises or bright lights, insensitivity to pain, or heightened perception of odors. Hyperreactivity can trigger episodes of sensory overload, especially when the person is faced with intense, confusing, or unpredictable stimuli. Sensory symptoms are grouped with restricted/repetitive behaviors in the standard diagnostic criteria for autism (American Psychiatric Association, 2013; Bernier & Dawson, 2016; Faja & Dawson, 2013).

In contrast with the classic view of a unitary autistic syndrome, the three components of the triad are only weakly correlated with one another, both at the phenotypic level (correlations between dimensions range from .10 to .40) and at the genotypic one (more than half of the genetic variance of each dimension is unique to that dimension; Happé & Ronald, 2008; Happé et al., 2006; Ronald et al., 2011). As a result, patients in the autism spectrum show widely variable combinations of symptoms. For example, about 25% of autistic patients lack even basic linguistic abilities, but another 25% possess elaborate syntactic skills and a rich vocabulary, even though they may still have trouble with nonliteral speech and conversational norms. The variability of symptoms is compounded by an extremely broad range of cognitive ability, spanning from severe intellectual disability to markedly above-average intelligence (Bernier & Dawson, 2016; Jones, Gliga et al., 2014). For all these reasons, the autism spectrum is best regarded as a heterogeneous collection of conditions with similar manifestations in behavior but different etiologies, correlates, and risk factors. As I detail in this chapter, differences in cognitive ability are especially important, as they point to deeper functional distinctions within this diagnostic category.

The Autism Spectrum

Autistic-Like Traits

Autistic symptoms can be viewed as extreme manifestations of cognitive and behavioral traits that are continuously distributed in the general population (Chapter 4; Baron-Cohen et al., 2001). Autistic-like traits—sometimes referred to as the "broader autism phenotype"—include poor social and mind-reading skills, difficulties in communication (e.g., making and getting jokes, keeping conversations going), restricted imagination in fictional contexts (e.g., reading fiction, pretend play), preferences for sameness and routines, strong and narrowly focused interests, and heightened attention to details and patterns. As with autistic symptoms, the various facets of autistic-like traits are only moderately correlated with one another. Autistic-like traits are consistently higher in males than in females (about 0.4 SD) and are 50–60% heritable, with no contribution from the shared environment (Hoekstra et al., 2007; Ruzich, Allison, Smith et al., 2015).

The cognitive profile of people high in autistic-like traits is shifted toward a male-typical prototype of enhanced mechanistic skills—including visuospatial abilities—and reduced mentalization and mind-reading (in Baron-Cohen's terminology, high *systemizing* and low *empathizing*). This observation is the basis for the theory of autism spectrum conditions as manifestations of an "extreme male brain" (Baron-Cohen, 2002, 2003). Autistic symptoms are also linked to a logical, deliberative style of reasoning and decision-making, as contrasted with an intuitive and emotion-based style (Brosnan et al., 2014; De Martino et al., 2008; South et al., 2014). Autistic-like traits are especially elevated in scientists and people working in technical fields; in children, restricted/repetitive behaviors and interests are specifically associated with the development of unusual talents in mathematics, music, and other specialized skills (Austin, 2005; Grinter et al., 2009; Happé & Vital, 2009; Ruthsatz & Urbach, 2012; Ruzich, Allison, Chakrabarti et al., 2015; Wheelwright et al., 2006).

As anticipated in Chapter 8, measuring autistic-like traits can be problematic because the content of standard autism questionnaires overlaps significantly with that of the questionnaires for negative schizotypy. The overlap is especially strong for items that describe interpersonal difficulties such as isolation, social anxiety, and communication problems, which—despite the superficial similarities—may occur for very different reasons in people with autistic-like and schizotypal symptoms. Unfortunately, studies in this area typically fail to control for schizotypy, with few exceptions (Dinsdale et al., 2013; Del Giudice et al., 2010, 2014*a*). For this reason, findings on the broader correlates of autistic-like traits must be interpreted with some caution.

Autism Spectrum Disorder

When autistic symptoms are severe enough to cause significant impairment in daily life, a person may be diagnosed with autism spectrum disorder (ASD). The latest edition of the *Diagnostic and Statistical Manual* (DSM-5) employs the ASD label for all the conditions in the spectrum. Severity is coded on three levels (from "requiring support" to "requiring very substantial support"), and there are additional specifiers for the presence of intellectual disability and/or language impairment. The unified category of ASD collapses previous diagnostic distinctions between low-functioning autism and high-functioning autism or "Asperger's syndrome," a mild variant characterized by intact language development and normal or even above-average IQ. This change in the criteria for ASD was the biggest move toward a dimensional model of psychopathology in the transition from the DSM-IV to the DSM-5; ironically, though, autism is among the few mental disorders that seem to fit a partially taxonic model instead of a fully dimensional one (Coghill & Sonuga-Barke, 2012; Haslam et al., 2012). Brain connectivity data also support a mixture of dimensional variation and qualitative differences within the spectrum (Elton et al., 2016).

Intellectual disability is present in about 40% of people with ASD. Empirical analyses of symptom clusters usually identify at least one subgroup with preserved language skills and better overall functioning, as well as a variable number of other subgroups mainly distinguished by their level of severity (Bernier & Dawson, 2016; Georgiades et al., 2013; Kim et al., 2016). In general, ASD patients perform best in tasks involving visuospatial skills and abstract spatial reasoning (Dawson et al., 2007; Stevenson & Gernsbacher, 2013). Autistic symptoms are associated with reduced executive functioning, although this effect is likely to be partly explained by the lower general intelligence of ASD patients as a group. Performance is lowest in tasks involving flexibility/switching, which is unsurprising considering that restricted/repetitive behavior is a core dimension of autistic symptoms. However, inhibition is also compromised, particularly in low-IQ individuals (Geurts et al., 2014; Westwood et al., 2016). At the motivational level, autism spectrum conditions are marked by reduced affiliation and interest in social activities; while people with autism tend to have comparatively low sex drive and are more likely to self-identify as asexual, the mating and pair bonding systems are usually active, and many ASD patients report an intense desire for romantic love and long-term relationships (Bejerot & Eriksson, 2014; Chevallier, Kohls et al., 2012; Gilmour et al., 2012; Strunz et al., 2017).

The genetics of autism is complex, consistent with a high level of heterogeneity within the spectrum. The symptom dimensions of the autism triad are 60–75% heritable; the overall heritability of ASD is at least 75%, and it is still unclear whether shared environmental effects make a non-negligible contribution to autism risk (Robinson et al., 2012; Tick et al., 2016). The heritable component of ASD reflects a combination of common genetic variants and rare and de novo mutations, including rare copy number variations (CNVs). There is also initial evidence that epigenetic mutations and disruptions may contribute to the development of ASD. Many of the large-effect variants that have been identified involve genes that regulate neural plasticity and brain connectivity. Autism-linked genes tend to be highly expressed throughout the brain during prenatal development; however, there are indications that some genes in this cluster are expressed at later stages (including middle childhood and adolescence) in specific brain regions such as the amygdala, hippocampus, and striatum. Recent findings also implicate networks of genes that contribute to epigenetic regulation and to the development of sensory pathways. In about 5% of cases, autism is caused by specific chromosomal abnormalities, almost half of which are located on the X chromosome (Betancur & Coleman, 2013; Iossifov et al., 2015; Krishnan et al., 2016; Marshall et al., 2013; Wong et al., 2014).

There is considerable overlap between the deleterious mutations that increase ASD risk and those that cause intellectual disability. Accordingly, rare and de novo mutations play a larger role in severe cases of ASD with intellectual disability, particularly when patients come from families with no previous diagnoses of autism (low familial risk). The prevalence of deleterious mutations is also higher in females with ASD, who tend to develop more severe forms of the disorder. Conversely, mutation load plays a comparatively minor role in milder cases of autism with high IQ, which are substantially more common in males. In this high-functioning subgroup, autistic symptoms are mainly determined by common allelic variants distributed across many genes of small effect (Anney, 2013; Betancur & Coleman, 2013; Iossifov et al., 2014; Robinson et al., 2014; Ronemus et al., 2014). Relatives of ASD patients in this subgroup are likely to carry many of the same alleles; typically, at least some family members show high levels of autistic-like traits or even diagnosable conditions in the spectrum. Common genetic variants for autistic-like traits are unlikely to be dysfunctional, and indeed, genetic risk scores for ASD based on common alleles predict *higher* IQ and educational attainment in the general population (Clarke et al., 2016; Crespi, 2016*b*; Hagenaars et al., 2016; see also Nishiyama et al., 2009).

Consistent with the male-biased distribution of autistic-like traits, autistic disorders are more common in males, with an overall 4:1 ratio for ASD. The male-to-female ratio increases dramatically as symptoms become milder, from about 1:1 in severe syndromes caused by highly disruptive mutations to more than 10:1 in high-functioning cases with normal IQ (French et al., 2013; Marshall et al., 2013). Autism is highly comorbid with attention-deficit/hyperactivity disorder (ADHD) and shares some of the same genetic factors. Bipolar disorders, obsessive-compulsive disorder (OCD), and D-type conditions such as depression, generalized anxiety disorder (GAD), and phobias are also fairly common. Finally, sleep disruptions occur in about 50–80% of ASD patients (Bernier & Dawson, 2016; Leyfer et al., 2006; Musser et al., 2014).

Neurobiological Correlates

Many patients with autism show a trajectory of accelerated brain development in infancy and early childhood, as part of a generalized pattern of physical overgrowth that begins prenatally. This early growth trajectory tapers off during childhood, with the result that differences in head and brain size between patients and controls disappear by adolescence. Brain/head overgrowth is more pronounced in males with ASD than in females. A minority of cases show abnormally *small* head size—an atypical pattern associated with low IQ scores and intellectual disability. The volume of the amygdala follows a similar trajectory of initial overgrowth followed by gradual deceleration in childhood (Campbell et al., 2014; Green et al., 2015; McKeague et al., 2015; Stigler & McDougle, 2013). On average, patients with ASD have larger prefrontal lobes with thicker cortical areas but reduced gray matter in the anterior cingulate cortex (ACC), medial prefrontal cortex (MPFC), and temporal regions including the superior temporal sulcus (STS). Several regions of the cerebellum develop atypically; the cerebellum is involved in many of the cognitive functions that are particularly compromised in autism, including attention switching and action sequencing (Bernier & Dawson, 2016; Carlisi et al., 2017; Faja & Dawson, 2013; Katz et al., 2016; Stigler & McDougle, 2013).

Regarding neural connections, the typical pattern associated with ASD is one of enhanced short-range connectivity (e.g., white matter fibers that connect different regions of the same lobe) coupled with reduced long-range connectivity between distant brain areas. Consistent with this pattern, autism is associated with a smaller corpus callosum, indicating diminished connectivity between the left and right hemispheres (Baribeau & Anagostou, 2013; Bernier & Dawson, 2016; Markram & Markram, 2010; Stigler & McDougle, 2013). The default mode network—a key substrate of mentalizing—is less active in ASD and has been found to show reduced or atypical patterns of connectivity in a number of studies. In contrast, connectivity is intensified between the primary sensory areas and the thalamus (the main relay station for sensory input), suggesting enhanced processing of perceptual information (Cerliani et al., 2015; Jung et al., 2015; Stigler & McDougle, 2013; Whitfield-Gabrieli & Ford, 2012).

To date, studies of neurotransmitters and neuromodulators in autism have yielded few reliable conclusions. This partly depends on the small size of most studies; another likely reason is the remarkable heterogeneity that exists within the diagnostic category of ASD. There is reasonably solid evidence for a pattern of upregulated glutamate and downregulated GABA, consistent with the general idea that autism is associated with an increased ratio of excitation to inhibition in the modulation of cortical activity (Blatt, 2013; Coghlan et al., 2012; Naaijen et al., 2016; Rosenberg et al., 2015; Zheng et al., 2016). Interestingly, reduced GABAergic transmission is also one of the main neurobiological correlates of neuroticism (Chapter 6); this might help explain the high comorbidity between autism and D-type disorders such as depression and phobias. The hypothesis that reduced oxytocinergic activity may contribute to the etiology of autism has been explored in a number of studies; the findings are split between those showing lower oxytocin levels in autistic patients and those that find no reliable differences with controls. In principle, this pattern is consistent with a small or subtle effect of oxytocin on autistic symptoms, but more research is needed to reach a firm conclusion (Cochran et al., 2013; Guastella & Hickie, 2016; Husarova et al., 2016; Miller, Bales et al., 2013; Parker et al., 2014; Taurines et al., 2014; Zhang et al., 2016).

In line with the extreme male brain theory of autism, there is indirect evidence that exposure to high levels of androgens (including testosterone) during prenatal and early postnatal development increases both autistic-like traits and the risk for autism spectrum condition (Auyeung & Baron-Cohen, 2013; Auyeung et al., 2009; Cesta et al., 2016; Kosidou et al., 2016). However, studies using direct measurement of androgens in the amniotic fluid or umbilical cord blood are still few, and their results are somewhat inconsistent (Baron-Cohen et al., 2015; Crespi & Hurd, 2015; Geier et al., 2014; Jamnadass et al., 2015; Kung, Constaninescu et al., 2016; Kung, Spencer et al., 2016; Teatero & Netley, 2013). Interestingly, early brain overgrowth in ASD may be partly driven by elevated testosterone levels since males have larger brains than females on average (Chapter 3). There is also evidence of elevated inflammatory markers in ASD consistent with the finding that prenatal infections increase the risk for the disorder (Akintude et al., 2013).

Cognitive and Computational Models

The cognitive underpinnings of autistic symptoms are the subject of a rich and rapidly developing theoretical literature. According to the *weak central coherence model* (Happé & Frith, 2006), people with ASD have a bias toward local processing of information that makes it harder for them to engage in global processing and connect details into a bigger picture (e.g., Booth & Happé, 2016). While the weak coherence account regards increased local processing as a deficit, other models frame the local, detail-oriented cognitive style that characterizes autism as a potential advantage. From the perspective of the extreme male brain theory, Baron-Cohen and colleagues (2009) argued that a highly detail-oriented style can boost systemizing skills by focusing attention on the elements and regularities of the system one is interested in (an exaggeration of the male-typical cognitive profile of high systemizing and low empathizing). Similarly, the *enhanced perceptual functioning model* (Mottron et al., 2006) argues that the ability to process low-level perceptual information in relative autonomy from global, top-down influences confers a range of potential benefits, from improved pattern recognition to enhanced sensory acuity and perceptual discrimination. The downside is slower performance in tasks that require global perceptual processing (Van der

Hallen et al., 2015). According to the *intense world theory* of autism (Markram & Markram, 2010), most of the key features of autistic cognition—but also emotional symptoms such as anxiety and sensory overwhelming—can be traced to a pattern of hyperreactivity and hyperplasticity of local neural circuits coupled with attenuated long-range connections between more distant brain regions.

More recently, Bayesian computational approaches have started to yield new insights into the nature of autistic cognition. Pellicano and Burr (2012) were the first to argue that, in the autism spectrum, the balance between sensory information (bottom-up processing) and prior expectations (top-down processing) is shifted toward incoming sensory information. In other words, prior expectations are somehow attenuated or treated as less informative. Attenuated priors would explain the increased perceptual accuracy and lower susceptibility to illusions observed in ASD; however, they would also have cognitive costs, including problems with ambiguous situations (top-down expectations are extremely useful to resolve perceptual ambiguity), susceptibility to sensory overload, and diminished tolerance of unpredictable or unexpected stimuli.

The idea that autistic symptoms arise from anomalies in predictive Bayesian processes has been extended and refined by various theorists (Friston et al., 2013; Lawson et al., 2014; Palmer et al., 2017; Van de Cruys et al., 2014). In hierarchical prediction systems, bottom-up information is combined with top-down expectations, and the relative weight of the two sources is partly determined by their respective precision. To perform this weighting operation, higher level processes include "hyperpriors" about the likely precision of the information collected at the lower levels of the system. Attenuated priors in autism can be formalized more precisely by postulating that sensory information is implicitly treated as more precise than prior expectations. This is the computational basis for the concept of *aberrant precision*: incoming sensory inputs—which contain both useful information and noise—are given more weight relative to priors because of their high assumed precision. This is equivalent to stating that prediction errors are given an inflexibly high weight (Van de Cruys et al., 2014).

This simple but elegant hypothesis can explain local processing biases and weak central coherence: because of aberrant precision, global high-level predictions are discounted as the system tries to formulate overly precise explanations of noisy sensory inputs and resolve a steady stream of prediction errors. Likewise, repetitive behaviors and preferences for routine can be explained as attempts to maintain a sense of control by generating highly predictable inputs. Social stimuli and situations are especially complex and dynamic; to avoid confusion, people rely heavily on prior expectations to "fill in" the details of their partners' mental states and communicative intentions. There is evidence that people high in autistic-like traits systematically discount the weight of social information, a process that may be modulated by oxytocin (Lawson et al., 2014; Sevgi et al., 2016). In a further extension of this type of model, Palmer and colleagues (2017) proposed that autistic people lack the flexibility to adjust the weight of sensory inputs in a context-dependent fashion. A possible reason is that their hyperpriors predict an overly stable, unchanging external environment. On this view, repetitive behaviors help reduce the person's uncertainty about the environment at the expense of active, flexible exploration.

Development and Course

Autistic disorders develop in early childhood, with symptoms typically emerging around 2–3 years of age. However, it may take several years for the disorder to be identified and diagnosed, especially in the milder cases. The earliest precursors of autism can be already detected in the first 6 months of life and include weak synchrony in mother–infant interactions, reduced social engagement (smiling, vocalizations, looking at faces), and a higher interest in objects compared with social stimuli. Later in development, autistic symptoms manifest as impairments of joint attention (e.g., pointing, gaze following), lack of imitation, and reduced symbolic play with a repetitive or "mechanical" quality. Developmental regression is not uncommon: in at least 20% of children with ASD, social skills that were present in the first year of life disappear rapidly during the second year. The occurrence of regression indicates that—at least in a certain proportion of cases—the etiology of autism involves specific alterations of developmental processes and not simply a failure to develop basic abilities (American Psychiatric Association, 2013; Bernier & Dawson, 2016; Faja & Dawson, 2013; Sheldrick et al., 2017).

ASD is a lifelong condition for most patients; autistic-like traits are fairly stable across adulthood, with no clear tendency to decline with age (Ruzich, Allison et al., 2015). At the same time, there is evidence that social and communicative symptoms tend to improve somewhat over time, and a subgroup of children with ASD (between 3% and 25%) eventually outgrow the initial diagnosis. Remission is most likely in the milder forms of ASD without intellectual disability; high IQ scores, normal language development, and absence of other neurological and psychiatric disorders are the strongest predictors of improvement (Helt et al., 2008; Seltzer et al., 2004; Wu et al., 2016).

Risk Factors

As discussed earlier, deleterious mutations including chromosomal abnormalities and rare/de novo CNVs play a major role in severe autism with intellectual disability and a much smaller one in milder conditions with normal or high intelligence. Advancing paternal and maternal age both predict increased risk of autism, with larger effects in ASD with intellectual disability. Paternal age is a stronger risk factor in daughters, consistent with the higher mutation load of females with ASD. In contrast with schizophrenia and bipolar disorders, the risk of autism is not elevated in the offspring of younger parents (Idring et al., 2014; Lee & McGrath, 2015; Leonard et al., 2011; Sandin et al., 2013). Another interesting finding is that ASD risk increases with both shorter and longer intervals between successive pregnancies (Cheslack-Postava et al., 2011, 2014; Durkin et al., 2015; Zerbo et al., 2015). Short interpregnancy intervals have been associated with folate depletion in mothers, which is a well-known risk factor for neural abnormalities and intellectual disability; accordingly, shorter intervals specifically predict higher risk for severe autism but *not* for milder, high-functioning ASD. Conversely, longer intervals between pregnancies—which could be framed as indicators of slow life history strategies in parents—are uniquely associated with risk for high-functioning autism (Conde-Agudelo et al., 2016).

Prenatal infections, exposure to toxic chemicals such as lead and alcohol, and obstetrical complications all contribute to increase the likelihood of ASD. Prenatal exposure to selective serotonin reuptake inhibitors (SSRIs) also predicts increased autism risk, although the association is confounded by preexisting maternal psychopathology (Bernier & Dawson, 2016; Kobayashi et al., 2016; Man et al., 2015; Mandy & Lai, 2016). As mentioned in Chapter 6, studies of socioeconomic status and risk of ASD paint a fairly complex picture. For autism with intellectual disability, most studies suggest either a lack of association with SES or a somewhat higher incidence in disadvantaged families. For high-functioning autism with normal IQ, studies in the United States typically find elevated risk at higher SES levels, whereas international studies tend to find no correlations with socioeconomic variables. The positive association between SES and autism rates in the United States can be partly explained by better access to healthcare in high-income, educated parents. However, there is evidence that healthcare access does not fully account for this pattern (Delobel-Ayoub et al., 2015; DiGuiseppi et al., 2016; Durkin et al., 2010; Fujiwara, 2014; Hill et al., 2014; Leonard et al., 2011; Rai et al., 2012; Wu et al., 2016).

EVOLUTIONARY MODELS

The first attempts to explain autism from an evolutionary perspective were made by ethologists in the 1970s (e.g., Richer, 1978; Tinbergen & Tinbergen, 1972). Tinbergen and Tinbergen (1972) famously proposed that autistic symptoms can be understood as withdrawal reactions to the intense stress and fear caused by traumatic infantile experiences. Perhaps because of the obvious weaknesses of the early approaches—which mirrored the limited scientific understanding of autism at the time—evolutionary research on ASD remained stagnant until about 15 years ago, when a new wave of research put this disorder back under the spotlight. The discovery that specific cognitive abilities are enhanced in autism prompted some authors to speculate that at least some autistic-like traits are adaptive skills selected in the context of hunting, tool-making, or other specialized niches that opened up in recent human evolution (Baron-Cohen, 2003; Reser, 2011). Other researchers started to explore the possibility that autism risk in humans is a maladaptive byproduct of selection for other traits, such as visuospatial intelligence or prolonged brain development (Crespi, 2013, 2016*b*; Ploeger & Galis, 2011). Many insights from this literature can be integrated within the diametrical model of autism and psychosis (Crespi & Badcock, 2008) and have been recently framed in a life history perspective with the hypothesis that autistic-like traits represent a male-typical profile of slow strategies (Del Giudice, 2014*a*; Del Giudice et al., 2010, 2014*a*).

Autistic-Like Traits as Adaptive Skills

The accumulating evidence that some cognitive skills are enhanced in people on the autism spectrum (e.g., Falter et al., 2012; Samson et al., 2012) suggests that those skills may have been under positive selection in the evolutionary past. Baron-Cohen (2003) speculated that perceptual, visuospatial, and mechanistic abilities could have been selected for in the context of hunting and tool-making (two male-typical activities in ancestral humans). The focused, systematic accumulation of knowledge associated with autistic-like traits can be extremely useful in learning and perfecting a variety of skills, from tracking prey to manufacturing weapons and other hunting tools. Enhanced perceptual and visuospatial abilities are also likely to be assets in these domains. While this hypothesis is quite plausible, the evidence in its support is still limited. In particular, there are no empirical studies on the distribution and correlates of autistic-like traits in forager populations. It is also possible that selection on these traits has intensified following recent social and technological changes, including those brought about by agriculture and rising social stratification (Del Giudice et al., 2010; see also Spikins, 2009).

Reser (2011) took the idea of autistic-like traits as adaptations even further and went on to argue that reduced social engagement and a preference for solitary activities may have been adaptive in their own respect, by enabling a "solitary forager" strategy in ancestral humans. Specifically, Reser proposed that solitary foraging can be optimal under conditions of food scarcity. Among nonhuman apes, orangutans have adapted to environments with low food density by evolving a solitary lifestyle with extremely low rates of social interactions. In humans, autistic-like traits would support a specialized foraging strategy with analogies to that of orangutans. Reser's model is highly speculative and suffers from some important limitations. As acknowledged by the author, there is no reliable evidence of solitary foraging in our species, although this possibility has never been systematically investigated. The model also predicts that autistic-like traits should be associated with faster behavioral development as part of a trajectory of early autonomy and self-sufficiency; however, the evidence points in the opposite direction—namely, toward a link between autism and a delayed, overextended developmental schedule (Crespi, 2013; more on this later). Moreover, autistic children do not seem to perform well in foraging-inspired tasks, casting doubt on the effectiveness of the autistic phenotype as a specialized forager strategy (Pellicano et al., 2011).

According to both Baron-Cohen and Reser, autistic-like traits in the nonclinical range can be adaptive, but most diagnosable cases of ASD are frankly maladaptive instances of trait overexpression. Baron-Cohen (2006) specifically suggested that assortative mating between people high in autistic-like traits may increase the risk of maladaptive autistic conditions in their offspring. Indeed, autism shows high levels of assortative mating, with partner correlations in the vicinity of .50; consistent with Baron-Cohen's hypothesis, parents of children with ASD also tend to be similarly high in autistic symptoms (Duvekot et al., 2016; Nordsletten et al., 2016). Studies of assortative mating for autistic-like traits in the general population have yielded contradictory results, but they are based on comparatively small samples and suffer from the limitations of existing self-report questionnaires (Constantino & Todd, 2005; Hoekstra et al., 2007).

Byproduct Models

According to byproduct models, autistic traits and symptoms do not have an evolved function of their own, but represent undesirable side effects of positive selection for other adaptive traits such as intelligence or brain size. Based on initial evidence that common genetic variants that increase autism risk also correlate with higher intelligence, Ploeger and Galis (2011) speculated that ASD may arise as the occasional maladaptive result of epistatic (genotype–genotype) interactions between multiple intelligence-enhancing genes. In this scenario, there is a large pool of alleles that normally increase intelligence and have a positive net effect on fitness. However, when some of those alleles occur together in specific, unusual combinations, their interaction disrupts brain development and leads to the development of autism. From a similar perspective, Crespi (2016*b*) advanced a detailed model predicated on the idea that many autism-related genes enhance specific components of intelligence—notably visuospatial abilities, focused attention, and deliberative problem-solving. Because of their history of recent positive selection, these cognitive traits are highly genetically variable but also especially vulnerable to disruptions caused by genetic or epigenetic mutations. In this model, autism risk is associated with a cognitive profile of "high but imbalanced" intelligence, so that the person's overall performance is impaired even if some specific components of cognition are enhanced. Crespi's imbalanced intelligence model mainly applies to high-functioning cases with normal or high IQ; at the same time, it points to recent positive selection as a plausible explanation for the large role of mutations in severe autism.

In another paper, Crespi (2013) synthesized several lines of evidence indicating that many symptoms of autism represent delays or noncompletions of typical developmental trajectories. Repetitive behaviors and preferences for sameness and routine normally peak in early childhood and decline afterward, but remain elevated in autism; like autistic patients, children have poor shifting abilities and tend to process information with a bias toward local (rather than global) features; the prevalence of short-range over long-range connections observed in the brain of adults with autism is also a normative feature of early brain development; and so on. Together, these observations suggest that vulnerability to ASD may be the maladaptive outcome of selection for a trajectory of slower, prolonged cognitive development in humans. Adaptive evolutionary shifts in the timing and rate of developmental processes (*heterochronies*) have boosted our species' intelligence and learning potential but also made us vulnerable to disorders in the autism spectrum. Like the imbalanced intelligence model, the heterochrony hypothesis can accommodate two distinct sources of genetic risk—common variants in genes that regulate brain development and rare large-effect mutations that disrupt the same processes in the more severe cases.

The Diametrical Model

The diametrical model of autism and psychosis described in Chapter 8 (Crespi & Badcock, 2008) represents a major step toward an integrated understanding of autism spectrum conditions. Consistent with the model, empirical research has confirmed a pattern of enhanced mechanistic and reduced mentalistic cognition in ASD (e.g., Paganini & Gaido, 2013). While the diametrical model centers on the mentalistic–mechanistic tradeoff, it also provides a broader context for by-product models that link autism risk to specific cognitive profiles (e.g., enhanced visuospatial skills) and developmental patterns (e.g., delayed behavioral and neurological development; Crespi, 2013, 2016*b*).

Even if the bulk of the empirical evidence on ASD fits the predictions of the diametrical model, there are also some inconsistent findings that point to functional heterogeneity within the spectrum. Specifically, autism risk has been found to increase in babies who are larger at birth (consistent with the model) but also in very *small* newborns (Byars et al., 2014; Mandy & Lai, 2016). Moreover, ASD with intellectual disability is sometimes linked with *reduced* head/brain growth in infancy instead of overgrowth (Green et al., 2015). These findings suggest that the diametrical model explains the characteristics of high-functioning autism better than those of severe autism with intellectual disability. Additional inconsistencies in the developmental correlates of ASD may depend on the existence of a subgroup of patients with high mutation load and a combination of severe autistic symptoms and childhood-onset psychosis (Chapter 8).

Autistic-Like Traits in a Life History Perspective

According to the extended life history model presented in Chapter 4, autistic-like traits can be understood as a male-typical variant of slow strategy linked to the skilled/provisioning profile. In principle, the life history model is compatible with adaptive hypotheses that emphasize the cognitive advantages of the broader autism phenotype. It also accounts for the patterns of heterochrony described by Crespi (2013): a trajectory of prolonged cognitive and behavioral development fits well with a slow strategy devoted to the accumulation of embodied capital through specialized skills learning. As noted in Chapter 8, framing the diametrical model of autism and psychosis in a life history perspective offers a deeper functional explanation of early over- and undergrowth trajectories in autism and schizophrenia. Just as importantly, a life history approach broadens the model's original focus on mechanistic and mentalistic cognition to include a much larger set of motivational and developmental correlates.

In the general population, the correlates of autistic-like traits include muted sex drive and restricted sociosexuality, preserved or heightened interest in romantic relationships, and increased investment of time and resources in long-term partners—all traits that promote parental investment at the expense of mating effort (Del Giudice, 2014; Del Giudice et al., 2010, 2014*a*). In line with the life history model, both autistic-like traits and ASD have been correlated with delayed pubertal timing in girls (Hergüner & Hergüner, 2016; Ingudomnukul et al., 2007; Knickmeyer et al., 2006; Whitehouse et al., 2011). However, a recent large-scale study found nonlinear associations between autistic-like traits and puberty timing in both sexes; in contrast with earlier findings, there was also a correlation with earlier menarche in girls (Smith-Woolley et al., 2017). While nonlinear associations may reflect functional heterogeneity, one should note that the existing studies of puberty timing in nonclinical samples are weakened by the failure to control for the overlap between self-reported autistic-like traits, negative schizotypy, and other kinds of symptoms (see Ashwood et al., 2016; Nishiyama et al., 2014). Until these methodological issues are properly addressed, empirical results should be taken with caution regardless of their direction.

By delaying mating and reproduction, autistic-like traits should extend a person's contribution to the family resources and reduce the net investment demands placed on his or her parents. As a consequence of prolonged, multigeneration resource investment in our species, the life history strategy of an individual modulates the investment provided by the parents, not just in infancy but also in adolescence and (to some extent) adulthood. This indirect link with parental investment might explain why paternally expressed imprinted genes tend to increase the risk of autism (Crespi & Badcock, 2008). Mathematical models indicate that paternal genes expressed in the offspring should favor a larger contribution to shared family resources; and while paternal genes promote increased demands for investment early on (when offspring depend critically on maternal investment, typically during pregnancy and lactation), they are expected to favor *reduced* demands as children grow up and begin to require investment from both parents (see Del Giudice et al., 2010; Úbeda, 2008; Úbeda & Gardner, 2010). In sum, paternally expressed genes may benefit from accelerated physical growth in infancy and early childhood but delayed mating and reproduction in adulthood.

While the life history model stresses the potential benefits of autistic-like traits in the context of a skilled/provisioning strategy, it does not assume that autism spectrum conditions are necessarily adaptive. In fact, the diagnostic category of ASD is so broad that it probably covers the full range of adaptiveness, from socially undesirable but potentially adaptive strategies (e.g., milder cases of high-functioning autism) to clearly maladaptive and/or dysfunctional conditions. Maladaptive conditions in the autism spectrum may arise from the overexpression of potentially adaptive traits—a risk amplified by assortative mating and intragenomic conflict between maternal and paternal genes—but also from qualitative dysfunctions caused by deleterious mutations and environmental insults. The two causal pathways are not mutually exclusive: for example, even if high levels of autistic-like traits are not maladaptive per se, they may render people more vulnerable to the potentially disruptive effects of mutations, infections, and other disturbances.

Autism Subtypes

In earlier sections, I reviewed evidence indicating that the diagnostic category of ASD contains two distinct subtypes. The first subtype is functionally linked to autistic-like traits in the nonclinical range, which in turn are mainly transmitted by common polygenic variation. This subtype is strongly male-biased, typically associated with normal or high IQ, and characterized by early overgrowth and longer intervals between pregnancies. The risk of high-functioning ASD is comparatively less affected by parental age and may show a (weak) positive association with socioeconomic status. In a life history perspective, this subtype of ASD can be classified as a slow spectrum condition (S-ASD), as proposed in the original version of the life history framework (Del Giudice, 2014*a*). Including this subtype in the slow spectrum does not imply that all cases of ASD with normal/high IQ represent instances of adaptive strategies. Even within a general pattern of intact cognitive functioning, autistic symptoms may still reach biologically maladaptive levels if they hinder or prevent reproduction. Another possibility is that autistic symptoms in small to moderate amounts contribute to enhanced functionality (e.g., improved mechanistic abilities and perceptual skills) but begin to interfere with overall cognitive performance when they cross a certain threshold.

The second subtype of ASD (provisionally labeled as O-type ASD or O-ASD) is mainly caused by the deleterious effects of rare and de novo mutations and other chromosomal anomalies, arises independently of autistic-like traits in family members, and is associated with low IQ or intellectual disability. This more severe subtype occurs at similar rates in males and females, is sometimes characterized by reduced brain/head growth and shorter interpregnancy intervals, and is strongly influenced by parental age but mostly unrelated to socioeconomic variables. In total, O-ASD—which comprises a heterogeneous collection of harmful dysfunctions—does not seem to show any consistent association with broader life history correlates and can be tentatively placed outside the scope of the FSD model (see Figure 6.2).

As illustrated in Figure 10.1, the two ideal subtypes can be expected to have fuzzy boundaries and overlap to some extent. People who carry many common variants for autistic-like traits are not immune to deleterious mutations and, in fact, may be more vulnerable to their disruptive effects; as a consequence, some ASD cases are going to reflect a hybrid etiology with elements of both subtypes. The distinction between high-functioning autism with normal/high IQ and severe autism with intellectual disability can be used as a convenient but approximate indicator of the underlying distinction between S-ASD and O-ASD (Figure 10.1) but should not be reified or employed rigidly: not only is the correspondence between intellectual profiles and functional subtypes necessarily imperfect,

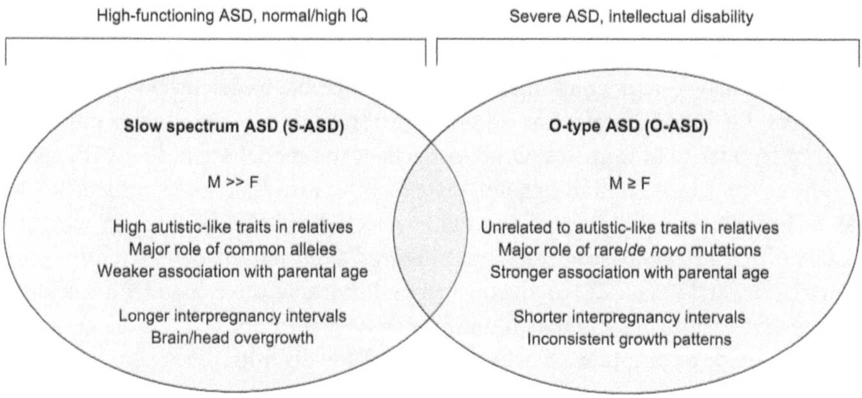

Figure 10.1. Two overlapping but functionally distinct subtypes of autism spectrum disorder (ASD). The key distinction is that between a slow spectrum subtype (S-ASD) with a strong functional link to autistic-like traits and a substantial contribution of common alleles, and an O-type variant with no connection to life history strategy and a major role of mutation load (O-ASD). This distinction is roughly approximated by that between high functioning ASD with normal/high IQ and severe ASD with intellectual disability.

but the subtypes themselves are not mutually exclusive and admit the possibility of hybrid cases.

Other Evolutionary Scenarios

As discussed in Chapter 8, Shaner and colleagues (2004) argued that schizophrenia is the dysfunctional extreme of a sexually selected fitness indicator and occurs when schizotypal traits are coupled with high mutation load and/or environmental insults. The same authors suggested that a similar scenario may explain the evolution of autism—but with a crucial difference: whereas sexual selection provides the context for schizophrenia, disorders in the autistic spectrum would arise as failures of a *parentally* selected indicator (Shaner et al., 2008). The key idea is that infants are under strong selection to display traits that solicit and maximize parental investment. These traits may be pleasant—as in the case of the exaggerated immature features that make infants "cute"—but also aversive or manipulative, as in the case of crying and tantrums. Shaner and colleagues conjectured that infants' level of "charm" depends on their sensitivity to social signals and the ability to express elaborate interpersonal behaviors designed to attract the parents' attention. In this scenario, ASD would then represent a catastrophic failure to develop such parentally selected behaviors following deleterious mutations or environmental insults.

While the model by Shaner and colleagues (2008) is intriguing, it has received little attention by researchers and is still in need of empirical testing. On the face of it, some of its predictions seem inconsistent with the available evidence.

For example, the authors argued that since male offspring are more physiologically costly for mothers, they should be under stronger selection for parentally selected displays—and, consequently, more vulnerable to deleterious mutations. However, the data indicate that ASD is more strongly associated with mutation load in females than in males. Other aspects of the model are in line with some recent counterintuitive findings: for instance, the idea that some autism-linked genes function as amplifiers of parentally selected traits might explain why the sisters of ASD patients seem to show *enhanced* attention to social stimuli in infancy (Chawarska et al., 2016). In conclusion, this model offers an unconventional perspective on autism, and may illuminate some features of severe ASD even if it fails to provide a comprehensive explanation of the disorder.

FSD CLASSIFICATION

The classification of a subtype of ASD as a slow spectrum condition (Figure 10.1) is supported by evidence that autistic-like traits correlate with S-type markers such as low impulsivity, restricted sociosexuality, and increased investment in long-term partners (as noted earlier, the findings on puberty timing are somewhat inconsistent). Moral and sexual disgust are also elevated in people with high autistic-like traits (Del Giudice et al., 2014*b*). In addition, there is evidence that autistic-like traits predict longer duration of romantic relationships even if they are associated with attachment insecurity, particularly avoidance (Gallitto & Leth-Steensen, 2015; Jobe & White, 2007; Lamport & Turner, 2014). A possibility discussed in Chapter 4 is that romantic avoidance may have multiple functional roles; specifically, elevated avoidance may indicate a general downregulation of mating motivations in high-autistic people.

Research on the broad personality correlates of autistic-like traits shows associations with higher neuroticism and lower extraversion, openness, and agreeableness (e.g., Austin, 2005; Del Giudice et al., 2014*a*; Gallitto & Leth-Steensen, 2015; Schwartzman et al., 2016). Again, one should keep in mind that self-report questionnaires for autistic-like traits are confounded with other dimensions of variation, including schizotypy and aspects of generalized anxiety (Ashwood et al., 2016; Nishiyama et al., 2014). This limits the interpretability of most personality studies. Taken at face value, the existing data are in agreement with the extended life history model. While agreeableness is a core marker of the prosocial/caregiving profile, I have argued that reduced empathy and social engagement play a functional role within the skilled/provisioning profile. There is converging evidence that lack of cognitive empathy and moderately low agreeableness do not prevent people with autistic symptoms from engaging in cooperation, reciprocity, and even altruism. In fact, the data suggest that people in the autistic spectrum take an alternative route to cooperation—one that depends more on shared norms and rules and less on emotional involvement. For example, high-functioning ASD patients are good at detecting cheaters who violate rules, and base their moral judgments on norm violation while ignoring emotional information about the cheating individuals. They also report normal affective responses to other people's suffering, even as they show deficits in cognitive empathy and mentalizing tasks (Brewer et al., 2015; Rogers et al., 2007; Rueda et al., 2015; Rutherford & Ray, 2009). Another strand of evidence shows that people with ASD are immune from reputation and audience effects—in other words, they do not alter their behaviors and opinions to make a good impression on others (Chevallier, Kohl et al., 2012; Chevallier, Molesworth, 2012; Izuma et al., 2011). Thanks to this unusual but straightforward social style, people high in autistic-like traits make trustworthy and reliable cooperation partners despite their relative lack of agreeableness (Frith & Frith, 2011; see also Allen et al., 2017).

The data on conscientiousness in the autism spectrum are less consistent and somewhat harder to interpret. Studies of personality in ASD patients have yielded contradictory results; in the general population, autistic-like traits have been associated with lower conscientiousness in some studies but not others. Moreover, attention to detail and repetitive/restricted behaviors are both associated with higher conscientiousness even in studies that find a negative correlation with autistic-like traits as a whole (Austin, 2005; Barger et al., 2016; Del Giudice et al., 2014*a*; Schwartzman et al., 2016; Strunz et al., 2015; Wakabayashi et al., 2006). As noted, a likely confound in many of these studies is the failure to control for negative schizotypy. Another problem with self-reports of conscientiousness is that people with unrealistically high standards for punctuality, precision, and orderliness may rate themselves as lower than average even if they are actually higher by objective standards. This methodological issue has been recognized in the literature on OCD (see Chapter 20), but similar concerns may plausibly apply to autistic-like traits and high-functioning ASD. More speculatively, individual differences in developmental timing might account for mixed findings on conscientiousness in autistic children. Among the Big Five, conscientiousness shows the strongest association with age: after a rapid increase between 15 and 20 years, conscientiousness scores keep rising at a more or less constant rate and do not plateau until the sixth decade of life (Soto et al., 2011). To the extent that autistic symptoms reflect a delayed and/or extended schedule of brain maturation (Crespi, 2013), the normative age-related increase in conscientiousness may occur more slowly even if the end point of the trajectory is higher than average. In other words, people with high-functioning autism may show comparatively low levels of conscientiousness in childhood, yet turn into conscientious adults as maturation proceeds.

Neurobiology

The tentative neurobiological markers of the skilled/provisioning profile discussed in Chapter 4 include upregulated serotonergic function, low oxytocinergic activity, and weaker activation of the default mode network. Earlier in this chapter, I discussed how the available evidence provides initial support for dampened default network activity and reduced oxytocin levels in the autism spectrum. There is also consistent evidence that serotonin is elevated in the blood of autistic patients, although the data on brain serotonin are still highly contradictory (Blatt, 2013; Muller et al., 2016). A few small studies have documented low insulin-like growth factor 1 (IGF-1) in autistic children, but there are also reports of elevated levels of the same hormone (Anlar et al., 2007; Mills et al., 2007; Neumeyer et al., 2013; Riikonen et al., 2006). In all, it is fair to say that the neurobiological literature on ASD contains few robust and consistent findings. To some extent, this state of things is not surprising—the autism spectrum is heterogeneous and includes distinct conditions with little functional overlap (Figure 10.1). Based on the typology I proposed in this chapter, one would predict that the putative neurobiological markers of the skilled/provisioning profile—such as high serotonin, low oxytocin—should be detected more reliably in high-functioning ASD patients with normal/high intelligence than in severe autism with intellectual disability.

11

Attention-Deficit/Hyperactivity Disorder

OVERVIEW

Attention-deficit/hyperactivity disorder (ADHD) is the diagnostic label for conditions marked by clinically significant levels of hyperactivity, impulsivity, and inattention. The dimension of hyperactivity/impulsivity comprises behaviors such as restlessness, fidgeting, inability to keep still, difficulty waiting one's turn, and frequently interrupting others. Inattention symptoms include poor sustained attention, distractibility, forgetfulness, wandering thoughts, and difficulty organizing tasks and activities. These two dimensions are moderately correlated with one another and continuously distributed in the general population. Taxometric studies indicate that clinical ADHD is the arbitrarily defined extreme of a distribution of symptoms rather than a qualitatively distinct category (American Psychiatric Association, 2013; Forster & Lavie, 2016; Nigg, 2013, 2016).

By definition, the symptoms of ADHD represent atypical patterns of self-regulation. Executive functions such as inhibition, shifting, and memory updating are generally reduced; this is especially apparent in real-world measures of impulsivity and distractibility. On average, people with ADHD show poor performance in laboratory tasks (about 0.4 to 0.7 SD below controls). However, there is also a subgroup of patients whose marked impairments in daily life are not matched by executive deficits in the laboratory (Barkley, 2012; Brown, 2013; Fair et al., 2012; Karalunas et al., 2014; McAuley et al., 2015; van Hulst et al., 2015; Wilcutt et al., 2005). In addition to executive functions, ADHD symptoms correlate with various traits at the interface between motivation and self-regulation—irritability, negative emotionality, elevated activation of the behavioral inhibition system (BIS), and aspects of behavioral approach system (BAS) activity such as high sensation seeking and low dependency on rewards (Heym et al., 2015; Rabinovitz et al., 2016). Reactive control processes are generally spared, in contrast with more proactive and deliberate forms of self-regulation (Nigg, 2016).

A crucial but sometimes neglected feature of ADHD is its striking association with low intelligence. On average, the IQ of patients diagnosed with ADHD is about 0.6 SD below that of controls—an even larger deficit than the one observed in schizophrenia. The negative correlation with intelligence is largely genetic and stronger for inattentive symptoms than for hyperactivity; as the severity of ADHD symptoms increases, patients are more likely to also suffer from intellectual disability, learning and motor impairments, and other cognitive deficits (Ahuja et al., 2013; Frazier et al., 2004; Kuntsi et al., 2004; Nigg, 2016; Wilcutt et al., 2012). Even though ADHD can be diagnosed in high-IQ individuals (Milioni et al., 2014), the overall pattern for this disorder is clearly one of reduced intellectual functioning. In view of the strong genetic correlation between ADHD symptoms and low intelligence, and the link between general intelligence (g) and laboratory tests of executive functions, it is reasonable to postulate that—at least in a subgroup of patients—ADHD symptoms arise from a generalized cognitive deficit rather than a specific impairment in self-regulation. While executive deficits in ADHD are not entirely explained by low intelligence (e.g., Martel et al., 2007; Wilcutt et al., 2005), intelligence is likely to play a major role in a sizable group of patients, particularly those with a profile of predominantly inattentive symptoms.

ADHD is widely recognized as a highly heterogeneous category in which multiple distinct conditions coexist because of their similar behavioral manifestations (Burns et al., 2014; Martel et al., 2010, 2011; Nigg, 2016). The DSM distinguishes between three presentations of ADHD—predominantly inattentive, predominantly hyperactive/impulsive, and combined—and three levels of symptom severity. While DSM presentations have some validity as descriptive summaries (e.g., comorbidity with conduct disorder [CD] and oppositional defiant disorder [ODD] is higher in the combined presentation), they do not add information beyond that already contained in dimensional symptom scores. Even more problematic is the fact that ADHD presentations are developmentally unstable, with an especially high rate of transition from the combined profile in early childhood to the inattentive profile in adolescence and adulthood (Barkley, 2016; Brown, 2013; Wilcutt et al., 2012; more on this later).

Within the inattentive presentation, it is possible to identify a particular configuration of symptoms labeled as "sluggish cognitive tempo" or, more recently, "concentration deficit disorder." This diagnostic category—presently not included in the DSM—describes a stable pattern of apathy, mind wandering, drowsiness, trouble staying alert, and general slowness and lack of initiative. Concentration deficits correlate with inattention but not hyperactivity and are associated with withdrawal, anxiety, and depression. Importantly, concentration deficit symptoms are only weakly associated with IQ and seem to be largely unrelated to executive functioning. This suggests a separate etiology for this condition, which may involve atypical processes of reactive control or even deficits in the regulation of general arousal (Barkley, 2015; Bauermeister et al., 2012; Becker & Langberg, 2013; Marshall et al., 2014; Nigg, 2016; Tamm et al., 2016).

The predisposition to ADHD is highly heritable (70–80%) and reflects a combination of common genetic variants and rare and de novo mutations. The contribution of rare copy number variations (CNVs) accounts for at least 10–15% of the total genetic risk. Interestingly, the common alleles that increase ADHD risk show moderate overlap with those associated with high extraversion (Ehli et al., 2012; Knopik et al., 2017; Lo et al., 2017; Martin et al., 2015; Nigg, 2016). There is also some evidence that ADHD symptoms are transmitted more strongly from the maternal side of the family, consistent with a role of imprinted genes (Goos et al., 2007). Males show a consistently higher risk for ADHD, with a ratio of about 2:1. Females are more likely to show high levels of inattentive symptoms, which in turn are more strongly associated with depression and anxiety than with antisocial and disruptive behaviors (American Psychiatric Association, 2013; Nigg, 2016). (In contrast, concentration deficits show only small sex differences in childhood and virtually no differences in adulthood; see Barkley, 2015.) The comorbidity network of ADHD is particularly wide and includes both autism and schizophrenia spectrum disorders, bipolar disorders, eating disorders, antisocial and conduct disorders, substance abuse, personality disorders (mainly borderline personality disorder [BPD], obsessive-compulsive personality disorder [OCPD], and narcissistic personality disorder [NPD]), and D-type conditions such as depression, generalized anxiety disorder (GAD), social anxiety disorder (SAD), and obsessive-compulsive disorder (OCD) (e.g., Burns et al., 2014; Cumyn et al., 2009; Hallerbäck et al., 2012; Matthies & Philipsen, 2014; Miller et al., 2007; Taylor et al., 2013; Yoshimasu et al., 2012).

Autism, Psychosis, and ADHD

ADHD shows an intricate pattern of phenotypic and genetic overlap with conditions in both the autism and the psychosis spectrum. As I argue in more detail later, this pattern offers important clues to the nature of functional subtypes within ADHD. In addition to high rates of comorbidity between ADHD, schizophrenia spectrum disorders (SSDs), and bipolar disorders (BDs), studies show that ADHD symptoms in childhood predict the later onset of both schizophrenia and BDs. The close relatives of ADHD patients are also at higher risk for psychosis (Brody, 2001; Chen et al., 2015; Dalsgaard et al., 2014; Greenwood et al., 2013; Hallerbäck et al., 2012; Keshavan et al., 2003; Larsson et al., 2013; Marangoni et al., 2015). The joint inheritance of ADHD and psychosis is partly explained by the effect of shared common variants, as shown by the small but reliable positive correlations between genetic risk scores for these disorders; some de novo mutations associated with both disorders have also been identified (Bulik-Sullivan et al., 2015; Hamshere et al., 2013; Thapar et al., 2016).

The link between ADHD and autism is less straightforward than the one with psychosis. On the one hand, there is substantial comorbidity between the two disorders and evidence of shared familial transmission. Genetic correlations estimated from twin studies are also sizable and positive (Hallerbäck et al., 2012; Musser et al., 2014; Polderman et al., 2013; Ronald et al., 2014). On the other hand—and in contrast with psychosis—genetic risk scores for ADHD and autism spectrum disorder (ASD) based on common alleles are *negatively* correlated (Bulik-Sullivan et al., 2015). This surprising finding suggests that the common genetic variants involved in ADHD mainly contribute to the risk of psychosis, whereas rare mutations of large effect contribute to increase risk for both autism and schizophrenia (and should be associated with a higher frequency of intellectual disability). Some of the common variants involved in ADHD may also decrease intelligence, consistent with the negative genetic correlation between ADHD and IQ and the positive one between IQ and common autism-linked alleles (Kuntsi et al., 2004; Chapter 10).

This interpretation of the genetic data fits well with evidence that people with comorbid ASD and ADHD have lower IQ and higher rates of intellectual disability than patients with ASD alone (Craig et al., 2015; Gadow, 2012; Joshi et al., 2014). Also, phenotypic and genetic correlations with autism are largest for inattention—which is more strongly correlated with intelligence—and smallest for hyperactivity. When combined ADHD symptoms co-occur with ASD, it is usually in severe cases with multiple types of autistic symptoms (Joshi et al., 2014; Leyfer et al., 2006; Polderman et al., 2013; Ronald et al., 2014). However, not all people with comorbid ASD and ADHD have intellectual disability, and the two diagnoses can coexist in high-functioning cases with normal intelligence. While there is relatively little information on this subgroup, there are indications that these patients may be characterized by high levels of perfectionism, restricted/repetitive behaviors, and low levels of executive flexibility/shifting (Mannion & Leader, 2014; Polderman et al., 2013; van der Meer et al., 2012; see also Martel et al., 2010 for evidence of a low-frequency variant of ADHD with perfectionistic features and mainly inattentive symptoms). Intriguingly, it has been suggested that low performance on shifting tasks in ADHD with comorbid autism reflect abnormal persistence and a difficulty in disengaging from the current task (i.e., insufficient shifting), whereas ADHD patients without ASD tend to be distracted by irrelevant features and find it difficult to purposefully shift their attention from one task to another (i.e., excessive shifting; Visser et al., 2016).

Neurobiological Correlates

In light of the associations with low IQ and psychosis just reviewed, it is unsurprising that ADHD has been linked to reduced brain volume and white matter integrity. Reduced integrity is especially apparent in fronto-parietal connections, which play a crucial role in supporting general intelligence. Another reliable correlate of ADHD is hypoactivation of the dorsolateral prefrontal cortex (DLPFC); similar hypoactivation patterns are seen in other brain networks involved in the regulation of attention (Cortese et al., 2012; Hart et al., 2013; Nigg, 2013, 2016; van Ewijk et al., 2012).

Apart from these general findings, the neurobiology of ADHD is still poorly understood. A classic hypothesis is that attention problems and hyperactivity are caused by deficits in the availability of mesolimbic dopamine (Sagvolden et al., 2005; Tripp & Wickens, 2009). This hypothesis was initially motivated by the finding that psychostimulants—which increase dopamine levels in the brain—alleviate

ADHD symptoms and promote concentration in patients. Much of the evidence supporting the hypodopaminergic hypothesis comes from investigations of candidate genes, but those findings have not been confirmed by large-scale genomic association studies. Moreover, stimulants have been found to have similar cognitive effects in nonclinical controls, and studies of dopaminergic signaling have yielded mixed results, some of which appear to indicate upregulated, rather than downregulated, dopaminergic function (del Campo et al., 2011; Gonon, 2009).

Adult patients with ADHD show attenuated responsivity to rewards in the ventral striatum, the central node of the mesolimbic dopaminergic system; this pattern is also puzzling because impulsivity in controls correlates with *increased* reward responsivity (Plichta & Scheres, 2014). This finding could be explained by the existence of a curvilinear relation between dopamine and impulsivity, by compensatory hyporesponsivity following chronic hyperresponsivity in childhood, or simply by the confounding effects of stimulant medications. In fact, elevated mesolimbic expression of the dopamine transporter (DAT) in ADHD—which should lead to lower synaptic availability of dopamine—seems to be a consequence of treatment with stimulants rather than an intrinsic feature of the disorder, as shown by the fact that unmedicated patients actually show lower DAT expression than controls (Fusar-Poli, Rubia et al., 2012). The possibility that mesolimbic dopamine may be upregulated in unmedicated ADHD is also plausible in light of the high comorbidity between ADHD and psychosis. Given the remarkable heterogeneity of ADHD, different subgroups of patients—for example those with psychotic versus autistic symptoms—may be characterized by different neurobiological profiles, which would contribute to explain the contradictory findings in the literature.

Recent computational models of ADHD have focused on *neural gain modulation*, a regulatory process that can potentially explain a wide range of inattention and hyperactivity symptoms. A high neural gain corresponds to a sharp cutoff between relevant and irrelevant stimuli in the response of neurons that encode salience and modulate attention. As gain decreases, neurons discriminate less strongly between relevant and irrelevant stimuli, and behavioral responses become more variable and less predictable. In other words, attenuated gain increases random variability in decision-making and promotes exploratory behavior, with the result that variations in neural gain shift the balance between exploration and exploitation (Hauser et al., 2016; see also Baird et al., 2000). Neural gain modulation involves both dopamine and norepinephrine; the available evidence indicates that attenuated gain is associated with reduced noradrenergic activity, whereas the role of dopamine is probably more complex (Aston-Jones & Cohen, 2005; Moore & Depue, 2016).

Development and Course

The symptoms of ADHD typically begin to manifest in early childhood; however, making a reliable diagnosis before 3–4 years of age is difficult because impulsive and hyperactive behaviors are normative in young children. With this caveat, epidemiological studies indicate that the onset of ADHD peaks between early and middle childhood. Children with diagnosable levels of ADHD symptoms in early childhood fall into two main categories. In a minority of cases, symptoms decline rapidly to nonclinical levels after the transition to middle childhood, resembling the childhood-limited trajectory of antisocial behavior described in Chapter 7. More often, however, symptoms remain elevated, although they tend to become milder toward the end of adolescence. Persistent ADHD trajectories predict higher levels of aggression and antisocial behavior. While impulsive/hyperactive symptoms predominate in the preschool years, inattention becomes more prominent across middle childhood; this developmental shift between different types of symptoms explains the high rate of transition from "combined" to "inattentive" presentations. When criteria are adjusted for age, more than half of children with ADHD may still have diagnosable levels of symptoms as young adults; even those who undergo remission continue to show impaired performance in laboratory tests of executive function (American Psychiatric Association, 2013; Barkley, 2016; Faraone et al., 2006; Kessler et al, 2005; McAuley et al., 2014; Nigg, 2013; Lahey et al., 2016; Sasser et al., 2016).

Risk Factors

As discussed earlier, deleterious mutations (including rare CNVs) make a substantial contribution to the risk of ADHD. Environmental risk factors include prenatal exposure to toxic chemicals (e.g., alcohol) and childhood maltreatment. There is strong evidence of associations with low birth weight, an effect that may be partly explained by faster life history strategies in mothers of children with ADHD. Consistent with this view, the risk of ADHD is significantly elevated in the offspring of younger mothers and fathers; when family-level effects are controlled for—which automatically controls for the parents' life history strategies—the data reveal a significant contribution of advancing paternal age, consistent with increasing mutation load (Capusan et al., 2016; Chudal et al., 2015; D'Onofrio et al., 2014; Nigg, 2013; Russell et al., 2014, 2015). Elevated ADHD risk is also associated with an individual or family history of autoimmune disorders (including type 1 diabetes), suggesting a potential role for immune-mediated neural damage (Nielsen et al., 2017).

Low socioeconomic status and economic hardship are robustly associated with a higher prevalence of ADHD (Cuffe et al., 2005; Russell et al., 2014, 2015), although the correlation is likely to be confounded by lower average intelligence in parents of affected children. Finally, ADHD risk is elevated in children of immigrants, especially those of African descent (Lehti et al., 2016). This epidemiological pattern parallels that of schizophrenia and provides additional evidence for the overlap between ADHD and psychosis.

EVOLUTIONARY MODELS

The evolutionary literature on ADHD is a small one. While a number of speculative hypotheses have been proposed over the years, they have generated almost no empirical research (Thagaard et al., 2016). This applies equally to models that regard ADHD as a currently or formerly adaptive strategy (Hartmann, 1993; Jensen et al., 1997; Shelley-Tremblay & Rosen, 1996; Williams & Taylor, 2006) and to those that argue that ADHD symptoms are harmful dysfunctions (Baird et al., 2000; Brody, 2001). Both sides of this debate have largely ignored the possibility of intermediate scenarios, for example involving maladaptive expression levels of potentially adaptive traits. Even more importantly, the evidence reviewed in this chapter clearly points to the existence of multiple subtypes within the diagnostic category of ADHD, and it is possible that different subtypes will require different evolutionary explanations.

ADHD as an Adaptive Strategy

Some authors have argued that ADHD symptoms are not dysfunctional per se and may have a positive adaptive value in certain environments or social niches. Specifically, Hartmann (1993) famously proposed that ADHD traits evolved in the context of hunting as they promote potentially beneficial traits such as rapid vigilance, exploration, and excitement seeking. In this model, the pathologization of ADHD is explained by the evolution of sedentary, persistent, routine-adapted "farmers" from ancestral populations of boredom-prone, flexible, and hypervigilant "hunters". People with ADHD would embody the ancient hunter strategy, which is no longer beneficial in a world dominated by farmers and their descendants. This hypothesis combines past adaptiveness with evolutionary mismatch in the present. In a similar vein, Shelley-Tremblay and Rosen (1996) speculated that ADHD traits may be adaptive as part of a "fighter" strategy in combination with aggressive and disruptive behaviors; alternatively, the same traits might contribute to attract maternal attention and thus increase infant and child survival. In another paper, Jensen and colleagues (1997) framed ADHD as a "response-ready" phenotype adapted to dangerous and resource-poor environments; those environments tend to favor impulsive decision-making and increase the benefits of hypervigilance to threats, rapid attentional scanning of the environment (inattention), and exploratory foraging (hyperactivity).

These adaptive hypotheses have been criticized on several counts. To begin, clinical manifestations of ADHD do not always match the behavioral effects postulated by the models. For example, the idea that inattention symptoms reflect hypervigilance is debatable, as people with ADHD often *ignore* danger and find themselves at higher risk for incidents of all kinds. Also, ADHD is often accompanied by deficits in motor coordination, which are likely to impair performance in a range of tasks, including hunting and fighting (Matejcek, 2003; Nigg,

2016). Children with ADHD tend to attract negative attention from parents and may be at higher risk for neglect and maltreatment, calling into question the idea that hyperactivity symptoms evolved to enhance parental investment. Similarly, the hunter–farmer model is inconsistent with the anthropological evidence that successful hunting in traditional societies requires considerable persistence, concentration, and planning (Shelley-Tremblay & Rosen, 1996; Williams & Taylor, 2006). While these arguments challenge simplistic assumptions about the selective pressures associated with hunting, some aspects of the hunter–farmer model are not implausible; as I discussed in Chapters 3 and 4, agriculture and its attending social changes have likely increased selection for traits such as self-control, lower time discounting, and tolerance for routine over the past few millennia.

Williams and Taylor (2006) employed evolutionary simulations to explore the idea that, instead of benefitting affected individuals, ADHD may be adaptive at the level of the group. They showed that, when faced with shifting environmental conditions, groups perform better—for example in collective foraging tasks—if they include a small proportion of individuals who employ random, unpredictable strategies. They further argued that ADHD implements such a random strategy, and speculated that this condition may have evolved for the benefit of groups even if it is detrimental for individual fitness. While the general idea of ADHD traits as high-exploration strategies fits with the insights of computational models, the group selection aspect of Williams and Taylor's model is unconvincing for two main reasons. First, the model does not provide a realistic account of the tradeoffs between individual and group fitness, the role of within-group relatedness, and other important features of the postulated social scenario. Second, evolutionary simulations based on the model seem to predict the evolution of higher levels of random exploration across the whole population, rather than very high levels concentrated in a few individuals (Williams & Taylor, 2006). This aspect of the results contradicts the authors' argument for clinical ADHD as an adaptive self-sacrificial strategy, although it might be consistent with other evolutionary scenarios.

ADHD as a Harmful Dysfunction

Critics of adaptive models have argued that ADHD symptoms are not evolved strategies but simply harmful dysfunctions of attention and self-regulation mechanisms (Baird et al., 2000; Brody, 2001; Matejcek, 2003). So far, the most detailed dysfunction model is the one advanced by Baird and colleagues (2000), who argued that ADHD is best understood as not just a disorder of self-regulation, but also (and primarily) a disorder of communication. In a nutshell, the authors argued for a bidirectional link between the evolution of language and social communication and that of executive functions. On the one hand, sophisticated communication demands high levels of self-regulation, particularly inhibition. On the other hand, internal speech and other forms of self-directed communication considerably broaden the range of regulatory strategies available to the individual, making it possible to verbally formulate and rehearse plans, praise or reproach oneself, and so on. According to Baird and colleagues, ADHD arises from the failure of the shared neural mechanisms that enable both self-regulation and effective communication. Like the other models discussed here, the one by Baird and colleagues is intriguing but has not been substantiated by empirical research. In general, proponents of dysfunction hypotheses rightly point to the negative real-world impact of many ADHD symptoms and their associations with impaired motor and cognitive performance. At the same time, they tend to embrace the simplistic view that impulsivity, risk-taking, and insensitivity to danger are by definition maladaptive (Baird et al., 2000; Brody, 2001; Matejcek, 2003).

Other Evolutionary Scenarios

As just summarized, the debate on the evolution of ADHD has pitted pure dysfunction models against speculations that clinical symptoms are manifestations of adaptive or formerly adaptive strategies. This black-and-white contrast neglects a variety of plausible alternatives, including the possibility that ADHD traits are adaptive at moderate levels (at least in some environments) but maladaptive and/or dysfunctional when they reach the threshold for a clinical diagnosis. This intermediate scenario is consistent with the taxometric evidence that clinical ADHD is the arbitrary extreme of a continuum of variation. Still, the role of mutation load in ADHD and the strong negative association with intelligence argue against a simple account in terms of excessive trait expression. Perhaps the fact that no single evolutionary model seems to account for all the features of ADHD should not surprise given the remarkable heterogeneity of this diagnostic category. As with other heterogeneous disorders, it may be more fruitful to look for functionally distinct subtypes, which in turn may fit different evolutionary scenarios. In the next section, I take a step in this direction from the perspective of the FSD model.

FSD CLASSIFICATION

There are good reasons to believe that the majority of ADHD cases are fast spectrum conditions that overlap with psychosis and antisocial/conduct disorders. The idea that ADHD symptoms reflect a fast life history strategy was first proposed by Frederick (2012). Indeed, ADHD in childhood predicts a range of fast spectrum traits such as risk-taking, precocious and promiscuous sexuality, early reproduction, and early mortality. ADHD symptoms have also been found to correlate with earlier puberty in girls, although there are some inconsistent findings (Barkley, 2016; Nigg, 2016; Ostojic & Miller, 2016; Smith-Woolley et al., 2017). Crucially, studies in which ADHD with conduct symptoms is distinguished from "pure" ADHD show that risk-taking, promiscuity, and early mortality are only associated with the comorbid form (Olazagasti et al., 2013; Sarver et al., 2014). Likewise, both hyperactivity and inattention symptoms correlate with low agreeableness and conscientiousness (as well as high neuroticism); however, correlations are much stronger in patients with a comorbid diagnosis of conduct problems, and there is evidence of multiple distinct personality profiles among children with ADHD (Gomez & Corr, 2014; Martel et al., 2010). Findings of associations with extraversion, sensation seeking, high time discounting, disorganized attachment in childhood, and romantic insecurity in adulthood should be interpreted in the same light (Demurie et al., 2012; Lo et al., 2017; Luman et al., 2005; Sizoo et al., 2009; Storebø et al., 2016; Thorell et al., 2012). No studies have specifically looked at ADHD with comorbid psychosis, but one can predict a similar pattern of results based on the evidence discussed in Chapters 8 and 9. In sum, ADHD most likely comprises a high-frequency fast spectrum subtype (F-ADHD) characterized by high levels of hyperactivity (especially in childhood); positive correlations with schizotypal, hypomanic, and/or psychopathic traits; comorbidity with antisocial disorders, SSDs, and BDs; and a major role of common alleles (Figure 11.1).

In the original version of the FSD model, I suggested that the fast spectrum variant of ADHD coexists with other subtypes that have different etiologies and functional characteristics (Del Giudice, 2014*b*). Most likely, one of those subtypes consists of "g-linked" conditions in which primarily inattentive symptoms and broadband deficits in executive functions arise as a manifestation of low general intelligence, largely independent of life history strategy. I tentatively label this subtype as O-type ADHD. Both common alleles and rare mutations contribute to individual differences in g and—by implication—to the risk for this subtype of ADHD. More speculatively, there is some evidence that ADHD also co-occurs with high-functioning autism characterized by normal or high intelligence; patients in this group tend to show restricted/repetitive behaviors, reduced flexibility/switching, and relatively high levels of perfectionism and conscientiousness

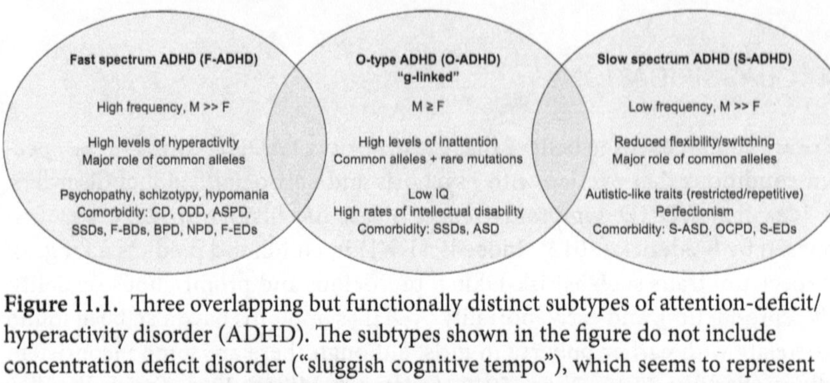

Figure 11.1. Three overlapping but functionally distinct subtypes of attention-deficit/hyperactivity disorder (ADHD). The subtypes shown in the figure do not include concentration deficit disorder ("sluggish cognitive tempo"), which seems to represent a separate category from ADHD. ASD = autism spectrum disorder. ASPD = antisocial personality disorder. BDs = bipolar disorders. BPD = borderline personality disorder. CD = conduct disorder. EDs = eating disorders. NPD = narcissistic personality disorder. OCPD = obsessive-compulsive personality disorder. ODD = oppositional-defiant disorder. SSDs = schizophrenia spectrum disorders.

(Del Giudice, 2014*b*; Martel et al., 2010; Polderman et al., 2013). This is consistent with the existence of a low-frequency, slow-spectrum ADHD subtype (S-ADHD) that overlaps with both ASD and OCPD (see Chapter 12).

If O-ADHD arises as a byproduct of low intelligence, it should be functionally unrelated to variation in life history strategies. At the same time, O-ADHD may co-occur with autism and schizophrenia when these disorders are accompanied by low IQ or intellectual disability. For this reason, the three putative subtypes of ADHD are expected to show some overlap, as illustrated in Figure 11.1. The co-occurrence of O-ADHD and ASD is a plausible explanation of the fact that severe autism is sometimes accompanied by multiple ADHD symptoms, with particularly high levels of inattention and impulsivity (Ronald et al., 2014).

Finally, some people diagnosed with ADHD according to DSM criteria are probably better described as suffering from concentration deficit disorder or "sluggish cognitive tempo". As noted earlier, this condition is somewhat distinct from ADHD, even if concentration deficit symptoms show moderate genetic correlations with inattention and hyperactivity (Moruzzi et al., 2014). So far, there are no indications that concentration deficit disorder may be functionally connected to individual differences in life history strategy. It seems clear that concentration deficits do not overlap with F-type ADHD, given their lack of association with either conduct or bipolar symptoms (Barkley, 2015); however, the available information on this condition is still too sketchy to warrant inclusion in the FSD model.

Neurobiology

Despite decades of intensive research on dopamine and norepinephrine in ADHD, the neurobiological underpinnings of this disorder are still unclear. Little reliable data exist on serotonergic and oxytocinergic function, although there are preliminary, small-sample reports of reduced oxytocin levels in the blood of children with ADHD (Sasaki et al., 2015). Increased activation of the default mode network has been reported in patients, but the evidence is still very limited (Cortese et al., 2012). Investigators have sought to identify characteristic patterns of stress physiology in ADHD; while some studies show a pattern of blunted HPA and parasympathetic reactivity (Pinto et al., 2016; Rash & Aguirre-Camacho, 2012), they do not control for the co-occurrence of antisocial and conduct symptoms. When comorbidity is taken into account, ADHD with CD/ODD is associated with blunted cortisol (one of the main neurobiological correlates of callous-unemotional traits); on the contrary, ADHD with anxiety disorders is associated with heightened HPA reactivity (Corominas et al., 2012). Hopefully, better subtyping of ADHD based on functional criteria (as in the FSD model) will help resolve these inconsistencies and suggest testable predictions; for example, reduced serotonergic function should be reliably associated with the fast spectrum subtype of ADHD but not with the S-type and O-type variants.

12

Personality Disorders

OVERVIEW

The categorization of personality disorders is one of the most problematic and contentious issues in psychiatry. Personality disorders are defined as pervasive, enduring, and inflexible patterns of dysfunctional behavior that can be linked to "pathological" configurations of personality traits. The taxonomy of personality disorders has undergone major changes with each new edition of the DSM, testifying to the fluid and ill-defined nature of this category. The DSM-IV (American Psychiatric Association, 2000) classified personality disorders into 10 discrete types, further grouped into three broad clusters: cluster A or *odd/eccentric* (paranoid, schizoid, schizotypal), cluster B or *dramatic/emotional* (antisocial, borderline, histrionic, narcissistic), and cluster C or *anxious/fearful* (avoidant, dependent, obsessive-compulsive). However, the validity of the DSM-IV taxonomy is questionable, since the boundaries of the three clusters are not reflected in patterns of comorbidity and genetic correlations; this problem is especially acute for disorders in clusters A and C.

The DSM-5 includes two separate models of personality disorders—the classic DSM-IV taxonomy and an alternative, hybrid model based on a mixture of dimensional personality traits and categorical types (American Psychiatric Association, 2013). The dimensional component of the alternative DSM-5 model includes five broad pathological traits (domains) with five facets each: *negative affectivity* (vs. emotional stability), *detachment* (vs. extraversion), *antagonism* (vs. agreeableness), *disinhibition* (vs. conscientiousness), and *psychoticism* (vs. lucidity). To a first approximation, the first four of these domains represent extreme versions of the corresponding Big Five factors—neuroticism, low extraversion, low agreeableness, and low conscientiousness. The psychoticism domain is a combination of positive and disorganized schizotypy (Chapter 8) and overlaps only in part with openness to experience (mainly with the imagination/aesthetics facets). Also, the antagonism domain is strongly and negatively correlated with the honesty-humility factor of the HEXACO model (Ashton et al., 2012; Griffin & Samuel, 2014; Krueger & Markon, 2014; Suzuki et al., 2015). A diagnosis of personality disorder may involve any combination of these pathological traits. On top of the dimensional system, the alternative DSM-5 model recognizes six distinctive configurations of traits and behaviors as discrete personality disorders: schizotypal (SPD), antisocial (ASPD), borderline (BPD), narcissistic (NPD), avoidant (APD), and obsessive-compulsive (OCPD).

Although the conditions classified as personality disorders are common and clinically significant, there are many reasons to doubt the validity of the category itself. In principle, the distinguishing features of personality disorders are stability across the lifespan, a strong association with personality traits, and—in the DSM-5—a dimensional rather than taxonic nature. In practice, however, none of these features is unique to personality disorders. To begin, taxometric studies have shown that most mental disorders—from conduct disorders to depression and bipolar disorders (BDs)—are best described by largely or fully dimensional models. Ironically, one of the few plausible exceptions to this general pattern is SPD, a personality disorder that is also part of the schizophrenia spectrum (Chapter 8). Second, personality disorders are not uniquely associated with personality variation. As documented throughout this book, most mental disorders show characteristic profiles of personality, including life history–related traits such as impulsivity, agreeableness, conscientiousness, and honesty-humility. Moreover, the range of personality traits regarded as pathological in the DSM is somewhat arbitrary; for example, the alternative DSM-5 model includes schizotypy (as "psychoticism") but not hypomanic or autistic-like traits, which are similarly distributed in the population. Based on the definition of a personality disorder, it is unclear why SPD is included in this category but mild autism is not. Third, the stability of personality disorders has been called into question by the findings of longitudinal studies: while the underlying personality profiles do not change much over time, the clinical symptoms of these disorders are surprisingly unstable, and many diagnosed individuals undergo remission within a few years. Like many other psychiatric conditions, personality disorders seem to involve a complex interplay of "trait" and "state" components with different temporal dynamics (Conway et al., 2017; Hopwood & Thomas, 2014; Skodol, 2014; Torvik et al., 2016). In conclusion, the boundaries of personality pathology are largely arbitrary; not coincidentally, both antisocial and schizotypal personality disorders are also included in other DSM categories.

Given the transitional state of the current classification system and the limited amount of research on dimensional personality diagnoses, in this chapter I focus on those disorders that are recognized in both the classic and alternative model of the DSM-5. Since ASPD and SPD have already been discussed in Chapters 7 and 8, here I will only consider four conditions: BPD, NPD, OCPD, and APD.

Borderline Personality Disorder

The central feature of BPD is a persistent and marked instability in affect, relationships, and self-image. People with this condition are hypersensitive to others' reactions and constantly worry about rejection and abandonment; their close relationships oscillate between extreme polarities of idealization and devaluation, overinvolvement and withdrawal. They tend to experience intense negative emotions and sudden emotional ups and downs, especially in social interactions; this affective instability is accompanied by chronic feelings of emptiness and psychological pain. About 75% of BPD patients experience dissociative states and paranoid thoughts under stress, and up to 50% develop transitory psychotic symptoms such as hallucinations and paranoid delusions. Impulsivity and risk-taking—including impulsive, promiscuous sexuality—are core features of BPD; suicide attempts and self-harm (e.g., cutting, burning) are also extremely common. In the DSM-5 personality model, BPD is marked by high levels of negative affectivity, antagonism, and disinhibition (American Psychiatric Association, 2013; Ebner-Priemer et al., 2015; Glaser et al., 2010; Hooley & St. Germain, 2013; Schroeder et al., 2013).

From a motivational standpoint, many borderline symptoms revolve around the attachment system and the closely related systems that regulate affiliation and pair bonding. In these patients, working models of attachment are often disorganized and feature a mix of contradictory and poorly integrated representations. This is reflected in romantic attachment styles, where extremely high anxiety coexists with elevated avoidance. The combination of anxiety and avoidance in borderline patients seems to derive from oscillations in the activation of the attachment system, with frequent shifts from preoccupation and fear of abandonment to withdrawal and distrust. These cycles of interpersonal rejection elicit shame and anger—two prominent emotions in BPD (Fonagy & Luyten, 2016; Mikulincer & Shaver, 2016).

On average, borderline symptoms are associated with lower IQ and poor academic performance. Laboratory tasks also indicate deficits in executive functions, which are probably explained by lower intelligence in BPD patients. Consistent with this view, patients perform best in tasks of flexibility/shifting, the dimension of executive functioning with the weakest link to general intelligence (Belsky D. W. et al., 2012; Coid, 1999; Hengartner et al., 2014; McClure et al., 2016; Melca et al., 2015; Ruocco, 2005). People with BPD tend to have high affective empathy; they are highly attuned to nonverbal behavior and very good at reading emotional expressions. At the same time, they perform poorly when using models of others' internal states (e.g., in perspective taking). In fact, there is evidence that BPD patients engage in hyperactive mentalizing, which likely contributes to a high frequency of paranoid thoughts and delusional experiences (Dinsdale & Crespi, 2013; Dinsdale et al., 2016; Fonagy & Luyten, 2016; Hengartner et al., 2014; Sharp et al., 2011). Mentalizing in BPD seems to be especially dependent on the person's motivational state; in particular, activation of the attachment system—and the corresponding disorganized representations—may provoke a shift toward rapid, automatic forms of mentalizing or even trigger sudden dissociative experiences (Fonagy & Luyten, 2016; Liotti, 2002; Liotti & Gilbert, 2011).

The predisposition to BPD is at least moderately genetic, with heritability estimates ranging between 40% and 70%. Nonshared environmental factors also play a sizable role (Amad et al., 2014; Belsky D. W. et al., 2012; Crowell et al.,

2013; Hopwood & Thomas, 2014; Hunt et al., 2015; Kendler et al., 2008; Torgersen et al., 2012). Traditionally, BPD is considered a female-typical condition, and clinical samples show a preponderance of females up to 3:1. However, community studies and recent clinical data suggest a more balanced ratio (Hooley & St. Germain, 2013; Oltmanns & Power, 2012). Common comorbidities include other personality disorders (mainly NPD, SPD, and ASPD), most D-type conditions (including depression, generalized anxiety disorder [GAD], phobias, and posttraumatic stress disorder [PTSD]), obsessive-compulsive disorder (OCD), bipolar disorders, attention-deficit/hyperactivity disorder (ADHD), and substance use. Comorbid eating disorders are more prevalent in females, whereas comorbid ASPD is more frequent in males (Grant et al., 2008; Hooley & St. Germain, 2013; Links et al., 2012; Silberschmidt et al., 2015). The overlap between borderline and bipolar disorders is particularly strong, both within individuals and within families. The risk of BDs in highest in women with BPD and is specifically predicted by affective and self-image instability. Tellingly, pharmacological treatments for rapid-cycling BDs also reduce borderline symptoms (Akiskal, 2004; Benazzi, 2006; Fornaro et al., 2016; MacKinnon & Pies, 2006; McDermid et al., 2015; Sjåstad et al., 2012). The moderate overlap between BPD and ASPD is largely due to shared genetic factors, which also contribute to explain the comorbidity with ADHD (Amad et al., 2014; Hunt et al., 2015; Kendler et al., 2008; Matthies & Philipsen, 2014; Reichborn-Kjennerud et al., 2015).

Development, Course, and Risk Factors

While BPD is usually diagnosed in young adults, borderline symptoms begin to develop in childhood and peak around puberty. The main developmental precursors of BPD are relational and physical aggression, emotional and interpersonal instability, and heightened sensitivity to shame. Self-harming behaviors may also emerge in childhood or early adolescence (Crowell et al., 2013; Fonagy & Luyten, 2016; Tackett et al., 2016; Vaillancourt et al., 2014). Some adolescents—mostly boys—show a combination of elevated borderline and callous-unemotional traits, which is a likely precursor of comorbid BPD and ASPD (Chabrol et al., 2012). After peaking in adolescence, borderline symptoms tend to decrease steadily throughout adulthood, consistent with the fact that BPD has very high rates of remission (up to 80–90% within 10 years; Reichborn-Kjennerud et al., 2015; Skodol, 2014).

Early stress seems to play an important role in the development of borderline symptoms, likely in interaction with genetic predispositions. Patients with BPD consistently report the highest levels of abuse, neglect, and trauma among the personality disorders. Overall, longitudinal studies support a causal role for harsh parenting, childhood maltreatment, and disorganized attachment relationships (Battle et al., 2004; Belsky D. W. et al., 2012; Crowell et al., 2013; Hooley & St. Germain, 2013; Liotti et al., 2000; Yen et al., 2002). Parents with BPD show high levels of hostile, insensitive, and unresponsive parenting (Laulik et al., 2013); this suggests that correlation between harsh parental behavior and BPD in offspring may be partly explained by shared genetic effects.

Narcissistic Personality Disorder

The defining feature of NPD is extreme narcissism, and people with this condition show clinically elevated levels of grandiosity, entitlement, and need for admiration. In the DSM-IV, the description of NPD centers around the patients' sense of self-importance or uniqueness (e.g., fantasies of unlimited success, power, or brilliance). In contrast, the DSM-5 stresses variability in self-esteem, which may vacillate between extremes depending on other people's responses. The intention is to capture the "vulnerable" aspects of narcissism, whereby overt grandiosity hides painful feelings of incompetence and insecurity. Both grandiose and vulnerable narcissism may lead to high, even unrealistic personal standards (perfectionism) and frequent feelings of envy. People with NPD are often arrogant and tend to build superficial relationships; while they are highly attuned to people's reactions to their own behavior, they find it difficult to empathize with the feelings and needs of others. In the alternative DSM-5 system, the grandiosity and attention seeking that characterize NPD are both facets of the broader antagonism trait. Vulnerable narcissism is strongly related to neuroticism/negative affectivity and is not specific to NPD—in fact, high levels of this trait are found in other personality disorders, such as BPD and SPD (American Psychiatric Association, 2013; Miller et al., 2013).

The diagnostic category of NPD is somewhat heterogeneous and may comprise a number of partially distinct variants. A large study identified three such variants: a *grandiose/malignant* subtype with high levels of entitlement, anger, hostility, and controlling and exploitative tendencies; a *high-functioning/exhibitionistic* subtype that combines entitlement with competitiveness, enjoyment of challenges, productive use of one's abilities, and an energetic and outgoing attitude; and a *fragile* subtype marked by depression, anxiety, hostility, envy, and fears of rejection and abandonment (Russ et al., 2008). The grandiose/malignant subtype is prone to externalizing behaviors and likely to show higher comorbidity with psychopathy/ASPD, while the fragile subtype may account for the overlap between NPD and other personality disorders such as BPD.

The motivational signature of NPD is dominated by a hyperactivated status system, although mating and sexual motives also play an important role. Hypersexuality is a common feature of this condition, and high levels of narcissism predict unrestricted sociosexuality and coercive and manipulative sexual behaviors in both sexes. People with NPD also tend to be sensitive to shame, though significantly less so than BPD patients (Blinkhorn et al., 2015; Jonason et al., 2009; Reise & Wright, 1996; Roepke & Vater, 2014; Schmitt et al., 2017). Based on the limited data available, cognition does not seem to be impaired in NPD, and there is some evidence that narcissistic traits correlate positively with IQ (Coid, 1999; Hengartner et al., 2014).

The heritability of NPD is rather high, with estimates of 70% or more in most studies (Roepke & Vater, 2014; Torgersen et al., 2012). Narcissistic traits show relatively small sex differences, mostly limited to facets of entitlement and desire for leadership and power (about 0.2–0.3 SD). Consistent with this pattern, the prevalence of NPD is somewhat higher in males, with a ratio of less than 2:1 (Coid, 1999; Grijalva, Newman et al., 2015; Roepke & Vater, 2014; Stinson et al., 2008; Torgersen et al., 2001). In addition to other personality disorders, NPD frequently co-occurs with bipolar disorders, substance use, ADHD, and various D-type conditions such as GAD, phobias, panic disorder, and PTSD (Cumyn et al., 2009; Miller et al., 2007; Stinson et al., 2008).

Development, Course, and Risk Factors

Narcissistic traits become manifest in middle childhood and peak with the transition to adolescence (Tackett et al., 2016; Thomaes & Brummelman, 2016). Like most personality disorders, NPD is usually diagnosed in young adulthood and its prevalence declines at older ages. The disorder has a moderate remission rate, even if the underlying personality traits tend to be fairly stable (Stinson et al., 2008; Roepke & Vater, 2014; Vater et al., 2014).

While NPD has a strong heritable component, there has been much speculation about the possible role of early experiences in the genesis of this condition. However, the evidence in this regard remains extremely limited. Studies of narcissistic traits have found correlations with overindulgent and permissive parenting during childhood, but also with recollections of harsh discipline and insecure parent–child relations (Thomaes & Brummelman, 2016). In all, there seem to be few consistent relations between family experiences and risk for NPD; moreover, none of the existing studies has attempted to control for genetic confounds between parents' behavior and offspring's personality.

Obsessive-Compulsive Personality Disorder

OCPD is a condition defined by a pervasive pattern of orderliness, perfectionism, and self-control. People with OCPD tend to have detailed and exacting standards, behave in an overly scrupulous and inflexible manner with regard to ethics and morality, and focus on work at the expense of leisure, friendships, and intimate relationships. Their preoccupation with details, rules, lists, and schedules may become so prominent that it interferes with the main point of the task; indeed, obsessive perfectionism can make it hard to actually complete tasks and projects. The cognitive and behavioral rigidity of people with this condition is reflected in their interpersonal style, which is often controlling and lacking in spontaneous emotional expression. Rigidity and need for control frequently lead to frustration and anger, which then have to be suppressed or restrained. Finally, OCPD patients can be extremely parsimonious—saving money without spending it and accumulating objects they have trouble discarding. The profile of OCPD in the alternative DSM-5 system is marked by extreme conscientiousness (the opposite of disinhibition) combined with facets of detachment and negative affectivity (American Psychiatric Association, 2013; Carter et al., 2016; Samuels & Costa, 2012; Steenkamp et al., 2015).

While the symptoms of OCPD are rooted in self-regulation and self-control, they also have significant motivational components. For example, orderliness is tightly linked to heightened disgust sensitivity (Haslam, 2011); research on OCPD has focused on pathogen and contamination stimuli, but moral and sexual disgust are also likely to be upregulated. The marked tendency of OCPD patients to experience shame and guilt (Schoenleber & Berenbaum, 2010, 2012) may stem from a number of possible motivational states (see Table 2.1), whereas thriftiness and hoarding point to a specific role of the acquisition system.

The risk of OCPD has a heritable component; estimates from the few available studies range from about 30% to more than 70% (Hopwood & Thomas, 2014; Kendler et al., 2008). The latter estimate is more plausible, given that conscientiousness itself is about 50% heritable. The sex distribution for this condition is approximately balanced, although some studies have found a somewhat higher prevalence in males (less than 2:1; Coid, 1999; Grant et al., 2004; Jackson & Burgess, 2000; Torgersen, 2001).

The comorbidity network of OCPD includes other personality disorders, especially in the DSM-IV cluster A (paranoid and schizoid), but also APD, NPD, and others (Diedrich & Voderholzer, 2015; Hummelen et al., 2008; Lenzenweger et al., 2007; Rossi et al., 2000). However, OCPD shows the lowest rates of comorbidity and the smallest genetic correlations with other personality disorders; shared genetic effects between OCPD and other personality conditions seem to operate mainly via neuroticism/negative emotionality (Kendler et al., 2008; Westen et al., 2003). Eating disorders—mainly with anorexic symptoms—are frequent in OCPD patients and their relatives; other commonly co-occurring conditions include GAD, social anxiety disorder (SAD), panic disorder, and OCD (De Reus & Emmelkamp, 2012; Samuels & Costa, 2012). The overlap between OCPD and OCD is especially interesting, considering that the two disorders are sometimes grouped into a unitary "obsessive-compulsive spectrum." While OCPD and OCD show small to moderate genetic correlations with one another, their comorbidity rates are relatively low (around 20–25%; De Reus & Emmelkamp, 2012; Taylor et al., 2011). When the two disorders co-occur, OCD symptoms tend to revolve around symmetry, ordering, hoarding, and cleaning; as I discuss in Chapter 20, this cluster of symptoms is characteristic of a slow spectrum subtype of OCD (Coles et al., 2008; Garyfallos et al., 2010; Gordon et al., 2013; Melca et al., 2015; Starcevic et al., 2013).

Development, Course, and Risk Factors

The epidemiology of OCPD shows a peak in the third decade of life—much later than other personality disorders—and an increase in prevalence throughout the fifth decade (Albert et al., 2004; Diedrich & Volderholzer, 2015; Grant et al., 2004; Samuels & Costa, 2012). OCPD symptoms remain fairly stable with age, and remission rates are lower than those of BPD and other personality conditions (Skodol, 2014; Tackett et al., 2016). Uniquely among personality disorders, the risk of OCPD increases at higher levels of income and education and is unrelated to indicators of early adversity such as neglect and abuse (Coid, 1999; Grant et al., 2004; Hengartner et al., 2013; Torgersen et al., 2001; Walsh et al., 2013). Obsessive-compulsive personality traits in childhood predict higher income and work success in adulthood (Ullrich et al., 2007); this suggests a bidirectional association between socioeconomic status and risk of OCPD, which may also reflect the effect of shared genetic factors. Finally, patients with OCPD report the lowest rates of trauma, maltreatment, and posttraumatic stress among the personality disorders (Battle et al., 2004; Yen et al., 2002).

Avoidant Personality Disorder

APD is characterized by a pattern of pervasive social inhibition, low self-esteem with intense feelings of inadequacy, and hypersensitivity to criticism and rejection. People with APD tend to avoid activities that involve interpersonal contact, are reluctant to get involved with people unless they are certain to be liked, and may struggle in intimate and sexual relationships for fear of shame and ridicule. In the alternative DSM-5 system, this configuration is captured by a combination of detachment and negative affectivity (American Psychiatric Association, 2013). The motivational signature of APD is a perceived or anticipated failure to reach status-related goals; patients form expectations of subjugation or social inferiority and experience frequent, intense feelings of shame (Carr & Francis, 2010; Schoenleber & Berenbaum, 2010).

Since most of its symptoms are manifestations of persistent social anxiety, it is unclear whether APD is merely a more severe version of SAD (Chapter 19) or even an alternative description of the same condition (Ledley et al., 2013; Sanislow et al., 2012). The phenotypic data are not decisive: while only 30–50% of patients with APD also qualify for a diagnosis of SAD, those who do have essentially the same symptom profile of those who do not, although in a more severe form. Moreover, medications that are effective to treat SAD also reduce APD symptoms (Reich, 2000; Sanislow et al., 2012). These findings demonstrate that the boundary between the two disorders is fuzzy, but they do not rule out the existence of meaningful differences. The evidence from twin studies suggests that SAD and APD may be best described as strongly overlapping conditions that reflect the same genetic factors, but largely distinct contributions from the (nonshared) environment. In other words, different types of experiences seem to interact with a common genetic predisposition to shift the resulting profile of symptoms toward either SAD or APD (Reichborn-Kjennerud et al., 2007; Torvik et al., 2016).

While the symptoms of APD are only 30–40% heritable, the underlying predisposition has a much higher heritability of about 70% (Hopwood & Thomas, 2014; Kendler et al., 2008; Reichborn-Kjennerud et al., 2007; Torvik et al., 2016). Females seem to develop APD somewhat more often than males, although the ratio is below 2:1 (Coid, 1999; Grant et al., 2004; Torgersen, 2001; Torvik et al., 2016). In addition to SAD and other D-type disorders, APD shows high comorbidity with OCD (which has both a defense activation and a slow spectrum subtype; see Chapter 20) and with other personality disorders, particularly OCPD and conditions in cluster A. There is also a nontrivial overlap with schizophrenia spectrum disorders, and negative symptoms of psychosis are often associated with marked social anxiety (Fogelson et al., 2007; Lenzenweger et al., 2007; Links et al., 2012; Westen et al., 2003).

Development, Course, and Risk Factors

The symptoms of APD begin to appear in childhood and intensify during adolescence and young adulthood. Unsurprisingly, shyness and inhibited temperament are important developmental precursors of APD; in addition, many patients report a history of unpopularity, loneliness, failure in social activities (e.g., sports), and victimization by peers. Parental overcontrol has also been correlated with risk of APD, but the association may be genetically confounded. The rate of maltreatment and trauma in APD is not especially high relative to other personality disorders, and the association with socioeconomic status is unclear. In total, peers seem to play a much larger role in the genesis of APD than the family environment; there is some evidence that experiences of success and achievement in middle childhood and adolescence predict better chances of remission (Battle et al., 2004; Ledley et al., 2013; Rettew et al., 2003; Skodol et al., 2007; Yen et al., 2002). In adults, APD has a moderate remission rate, although negative self-esteem tends to remain stable even in remitted patients. Social and occupational impairments show considerable inertia and often persist long after the symptoms have improved (Sanislow et al., 2012).

EVOLUTIONARY MODELS

Borderline Personality Disorder

McGuire and Troisi (1998) suggested that BPD and other personality disorders can be understood as failed attempts to implement adaptive behavioral strategies. While milder forms of borderline personality are potentially adaptive, BPD patients are hampered by suboptimal cognitive/behavioral processes—such as poor mentalizing and metacognitive skills—that lead to social impairments and maladaptive outcomes. This perspective is consistent with findings of lower intelligence in people with BPD. As noted in Chapter 6, low cognitive ability may contribute to the etiology of mental disorders in a number of ways—for example, by increasing the risk of maladaptive learning or by making it harder to stop vicious cycles during the onset of symptoms. High levels of negative affectivity (i.e., extreme neuroticism) in BPD are also consistent with a picture of reduced brain integrity and low-level dysfunction.

Brüne and colleagues (2010) were the first to explicitly argue that BPD represents the maladaptive extreme of a fast life history phenotype associated with risk-taking and short-term mating. This idea was later expanded by Brüne (2014, 2016; see also Del Giudice, 2014*b*), who reviewed evidence that BPD is associated with impulsivity, low agreeableness and conscientiousness, impaired cooperation in economic games, unrestricted sociosexuality, and reduced parental investment. Brüne argued that BPD is likely maladaptive, although milder versions of the same traits may be adaptive in the context of exploitative behavioral strategies.

As it turns out, the question of whether BPD as a diagnosable condition is adaptive or maladaptive is still unresolved. There are no reliable data on the fertility of patients with BPD; however, the main dimensions of borderline symptoms—impulsivity, antagonism, and negative emotionality—have been found to predict earlier reproduction and higher fertility (Vall et al., 2016). Another study found that "cluster B" traits (which include BPD but also NPD, ASPD, and histrionic personalities) correlate with increased mating and reproductive success, including higher fertility (Gutiérrez et al., 2013). These findings are consistent with the hypothesis that mild borderline traits can be adaptive, even in modern environments; intriguingly, they do not rule out the possibility that even clinically significant levels of the same traits may provide a net fitness benefit.

Narcissistic Personality Disorder

Evolutionary scholars have devoted almost no attention to NPD as a clinical condition, with the exception of McGuire and Troisi's brief suggestion that this disorder may represent the failure of a potentially successful social strategy (McGuire & Troisi, 1998). However, narcissism as a personality trait has been consistently linked to fast life history strategies, together with the other members of the dark triad (Chapter 4; Jonason et al., 2010, 2012, 2015; Schmitt et al., 2017). Antagonistic and cluster B symptoms (which include, but are not limited to, those of NPD) predict increased mating success and fertility (Vall et al., 2016); based on this limited evidence, NPD might turn out to be an adaptive strategy—though perhaps a risky one that sometimes ends in social rejection and reproductive failure. Alternatively, narcissistic disorders may result from overexpression of traits that are only adaptive in moderate amounts; for example, empirical studies indicate that leadership success is promoted by intermediate levels of narcissism but declines at the high end of the trait distribution (Grijalva, Harms et al., 2015).

Obsessive-Compulsive Personality Disorder

In a series of papers, Hertler (2014, 2015*a*, 2015*b*) presented an evolutionary scenario for OCPD, with some similarities to Sherman's model of bipolar disorders discussed in Chapter 9. Specifically, Hertler argued that OCPD may have evolved as an adaptive strategy in response to climatic stressors, seasonal fluctuations, and resource scarcity after Pleistocene migrations out of Africa brought humans to the colder regions of Europe and Asia. In Hertler's model, exaggerated conscientious traits promote constant preoccupation with survival tasks (e.g., foraging, shelter construction, food processing) and resource accumulation, even in the absence of immediate needs. This hypothesis has a certain plausibility, even if not all of its predictions are supported by the empirical evidence; for example, it is not the case that OCPD patients are low in agreeableness and openness to experience as postulated by the author (Samuel & Widiger, 2008; Tackett et al., 2016). Another limitation of the model is a narrow focus on Pleistocene conditions that neglects the possible advantages of obsessive-compulsive personality traits in agricultural societies. Hertler suggested that OCPD may have become mismatched to modern conditions that reward flexibility, adaptability, and cooperation in large groups—or, alternatively, that it may still be adaptive within some specialized niches, despite being devalued at the level of the broader society. The idea that OCPD is currently adaptive is corroborated by data showing that persistence/compulsivity symptoms predict higher income, upward social mobility, relationship stability, and more offspring (Vall et al., 2016). Moreover, cluster C traits (which include OCPD, APD, and other disorders) are systematically associated with academic and work success (Gutiérrez et al., 2013).

In a life history perspective, OCPD symptoms can be framed as manifestations of a slow strategy with characteristics of extreme conscientiousness (Del Giudice, 2014*a*; Hertler, 2016). The classification of OCPD as a slow spectrum condition is supported by its association with risk aversion and low time discounting (Leahy, 2002; Pinto et al., 2014). Interestingly, OCPD does not predict abnormal parenting behaviors, and patients report high levels of altruistic motivations and self-sacrifice (Carr & Francis, 2010; Johnson et al., 2006; Johnson, Cohen et al., 2008); this indicates that parental investment is not compromised and may even be enhanced in some respects (e.g., transfer of accumulated wealth and other resources). Despite the converging indications that OCPD traits have adaptive effects, they may promote fitness only up to a point (cliff-edged function); it is quite possible that the most severe forms of the disorder are maladaptive and/or genuinely dysfunctional.

Avoidant Personality Disorder

Social anxiety plays an important role in status competition as a behavioral defense against rejection and defeat. Intense social anxiety is especially adaptive for subordinate or unattractive individuals who need to avoid further status losses. However, excessive or misplaced anxiety may interfere with the acquisition of status and mates, and potentially lead to self-reinforcing circles of low self-esteem (Gilbert, 2001). To my knowledge, there have been no specific evolutionary analyses of APD; however, most of the evolutionary considerations that apply to SAD ("social phobia") remain valid for this disorder (see Chapter 19). As mentioned earlier, cluster C traits correlate with academic and work success; the same is true for symptoms of social subordination, which also predict later reproduction and a smaller number of offspring (Gutiérrez et al., 2013; Vall et al., 2016). In light of these limited data, it is difficult to draw any firm conclusions about the adaptiveness of APD. If APD develops in response to recurring perceptions of low social status and/or attractiveness, findings of reduced fertility in these patients might be explained by their lack of social success rather than by APD symptoms per se.

FSD CLASSIFICATION

The classification of BPD and NPD as fast spectrum conditions is relatively straightforward (Brüne, 2014, 2016; Del Giudice, 2014*b*). As noted in Chapter 4, narcissistic traits are linked to the seductive/creative profile of fast strategies; patients with NPD are low in agreeableness and the conscientiousness facets of perseverance and self-discipline, although they may score high in achievement striving (Samuel & Widiger, 2008; Stanton et al., 2016; Tackett et al., 2016). While narcissists have poor affective empathy, they possess normal or even enhanced cognitive empathy (Hengartner et al., 2014; Marissen et al., 2012; Nagler et al., 2014; Roepke & Vater, 2014; Wai & Tiliopoulos, 2012). In contrast, borderline symptoms are not clearly linked to a specific fast profile—they overlap with seductive/creative traits such as schizotypy and narcissism, but also with antagonistic/exploitative traits such as psychopathy and aggression. Some puzzling findings in this respect come from two studies in which self-reported borderline traits were negatively correlated with the HEXACO version of agreeableness, but not with honesty-humility (Hepp et al., 2014; Thielmann et al., 2014). This finding is surprising because BPD symptoms correlate with all the components of the dark triad—narcissism, Machiavellianism, and (secondary) psychopathy—which in turn are systematically associated with low honesty-humility (Chabrol et al., 2012; Hunt et al., 2015; Láng, 2015; Miller et al., 2010). Future research should address and resolve this inconsistency in the literature.

The neurobiological profile of BPD is not well understood. While the data support an involvement of dopaminergic and serotonergic pathways, the direction of the effects is unclear owing to the small size of the studies; so far, the available evidence points to downregulated serotonin and prefrontal (rather than mesolimbic) dopamine. Findings of reduced neural volume in the hippocampus, anterior cingulate cortex (ACC), and prefrontal regions are likely to be confounded by the frequent comorbidity with PTSD and depression. However, a pattern of smaller amygdala volume, increased amygdala reactivity, and reduced dorsolateral prefrontal cortex (DLPFC) activity seems to be characteristic of BPD patients (Crowell et al., 2013; Hooley & St. Germain, 2013; Schulze et al., 2016). Studies of stress physiology also paint a contradictory picture, with findings of both elevated and dampened activity in the HPA and sympathetic systems (e.g., Carrasco et al., 2007; Jogems-Kosterman et al., 2007; Lieb et al., 2004; Scott et al., 2013; Weinberg et al., 2009). In addition to small sample size, these inconsistent findings may reflect the wide comorbidity of BPD, which includes PTSD and depression alongside ASPD and psychosis. Finally, the few available studies seem to indicate low oxytocin levels in BPD and a mixed pattern of hyper- and hypoactivation in different regions of the default mode network (Amad et al., 2015; Jobst et al., 2016; Visintin et al., 2016). While these findings are preliminary, they converge with comorbidity data in suggesting that BPD does not fit the prototypical pattern of either the seductive/creative or the antisocial/exploitative profile.

At the other end of the fast–slow continuum, OCPD bears all the hallmarks of a slow spectrum disorder (Del Giudice, 2014*a*; Hertler, 2016). Patients with this condition report elevated anxiety in romantic relationships; however, those relationships tend to be long-lasting, indicating stability of the attachment bond (Mikulincer & Shaver, 2016; Vall et al., 2016). In line with a S-type classification, there is some evidence that children with elevated OCPD symptoms tend to have a slower pubertal development and lower levels of adrenal androgens; also, juvenile delinquents are *less* likely to develop OCPD than controls after demographic confounds are taken into account (Murray et al., 2016; Vaughn et al., 2015). Somewhat counterintuitively, OCPD traits are associated with higher affective empathy (Cain et al., 2015; Hengartner et al., 2014), and an initial study found increased connectivity in the default mode network of patients with OCDP (Coutinho et al., 2016).

In contrast with the other personality disorders reviewed in this section, the correlates of APD do not match the template of either an F-type or S-type condition. The avoidant personality can be understood as a combination of low self-esteem and chronic social anxiety. Consistent with this view, APD is associated with high neuroticism and low extraversion but is essentially unrelated to variation in agreeableness and conscientiousness (Samuels & Widiger, 2008). From the standpoint of the FSD model, APD is best regarded as a defense activation disorder in the fear cluster, together with SAD and other conditions such as phobias and panic disorder. I discuss these conditions in detail in Chapters 17–19.

13

Eating Disorders

OVERVIEW

Anorexia nervosa (AN) and bulimia nervosa (BN) are the most common and important conditions in the category of eating disorders (EDs). Bulimia is defined by recurrent binges—episodes of overeating accompanied by feelings of loss of control—followed by compensatory behaviors such as self-induced vomiting, use of laxatives, or intense exercise. Bulimic symptoms are driven by preoccupation with body weight, which is a major determinant of self-esteem in these patients. Bingeing–purging episodes must occur at least once a week to warrant a diagnosis of bulimia in the DSM, but they may occur several times a day in the most severe cases. When binges are not followed by compensatory behaviors, the DSM-5 prescribes the alternative diagnosis of binge-eating disorder (BED).

The main symptom of anorexia is significant loss of body weight following restriction of energy intake, coupled with intense fear of gaining weight and disturbances in body image (e.g., feeling overweight or too fat despite being abnormally thin). Body mass index (BMI) can be used as a rough index of severity, from mild (BMI ≥17) to extreme (BMI <15). Following the classic taxonomy of eating disorders, the DSM identifies two AN subtypes that correspond to different symptom presentations. In the binge–eating/purging subtype (AN-BP), weight loss is accompanied by binges and/or purging behaviors (e.g., vomiting, laxatives, enemas). In the restricting subtype (AN-R) there are no binges or purging, and weight loss is obtained solely through dieting, fasting, or exercise (American Psychiatric Association, 2013).

Both AN and BN are highly female-typical disorders, with ratios of 10:1 or more. Sex differences are attenuated in BED, whose female-to-male ratio may be as low as 2:1. In males, the risk for eating disorders is strongly associated with non-heterosexual orientations (Craighead et al., 2013; Feldman & Meyer, 2007; Lock & Kirz, 2013; Russell & Keel, 2002; Yean et al., 2013). The heritability of ED symptoms is about 50%, with a marked increase around puberty that points to a crucial role of sex hormones. Eating disorders are highly comorbid with bipolar disorders (BDs), schizophrenia, obsessive-compulsive disorder (OCD), depression, and other D-type disorders; other frequently co-occurring conditions are attention-deficit/hyperactivity disorder (ADHD) and personality disorders, most commonly borderline personality disorder (BPD, especially in bulimic and binge-eating/purging patients), avoidant personality disorder (APD), and obsessive-compulsive personality disorder (OCPD, especially in restricting patients). There are systematic patterns of shared familial transmission between OCD and EDs; in patients with both disorders, the onset of OCD usually precedes that of eating symptoms by a few years. Autism rates are also somewhat elevated in EDs (particularly anorexia). Finally, bulimic patients and anorexics in the binge-eating/purging subtype are at higher risk for posttraumatic stress disorder (PTSD) and substance use (Altman & Shankman, 2009; Coombs et al., 2011; Craighead et al., 2013; Duncan et al., 2017; Farstad et al., 2016; Halmi et al., 2003; Huke et al., 2013; McElroy et al., 2006, 2011; Westwood et al., 2016).

While bulimia, anorexia, and the two anorexic subtypes are usually treated as separate disorders, research has shown that different combinations of symptoms do not correspond to stable underlying conditions. In fact, many if not most patients move between diagnostic categories over time, not just between AN subtypes but also between AN and BN. Over the span of a few years, rates of diagnostic crossover range from about 15% from BN to AN-BP, to about 30% from AN to BN, to more than 50% between AN subtypes (Figure 13.1). The overall tendency is to progress from AN-R to AN-BP to BN: an initial phase of food restriction leads up to the onset of bingeing and purging, which is then followed by an increase in body weight. However, several other patterns are possible, and many patients switch back and forth between categories as their weight fluctuates and bingeing–purging symptoms intensify and subside (Eddy et al., 2008; Peat et al., 2009). On the whole, the distribution of EDs seems to fit a largely dimensional model. Taxometric studies suggest that BN and AN-BP may form a distinct taxon characterized by bingeing and purging, whereas the "pure" restricting symptoms of AN-R seem to lie on a continuum with normal variation in eating behavior (Gleaves et al., 2000; Luo et al., 2016; Williamson et al., 2005). In total, it is clear that standard diagnostic categories fail to capture the deeper structure of eating disorders, and should be regarded as nothing more than snapshots of a more complex dynamics. A better understanding of eating disorders and their symptoms can be gained by considering the nature of two self-reinforcing cycles that may be labeled the *self-starvation* and *bingeing–purging cycle* (Figure 13.1).

Self-Reinforcing Cycles in Eating Disorders

The Self-Starvation Cycle

The self-starvation cycle arises in predisposed individuals following an initial phase of food restriction and weight loss. Food restriction may be initially prompted by a variety of motives, from weight concerns and a desire for thinness to health-related or religious ideas (e.g., spiritual purity, ascetic self-denial). In fact, the cycle may even be started by *involuntary* weight loss due to physical illness (Figure 13.1). While fasting and exercise are initially aversive, they gradually

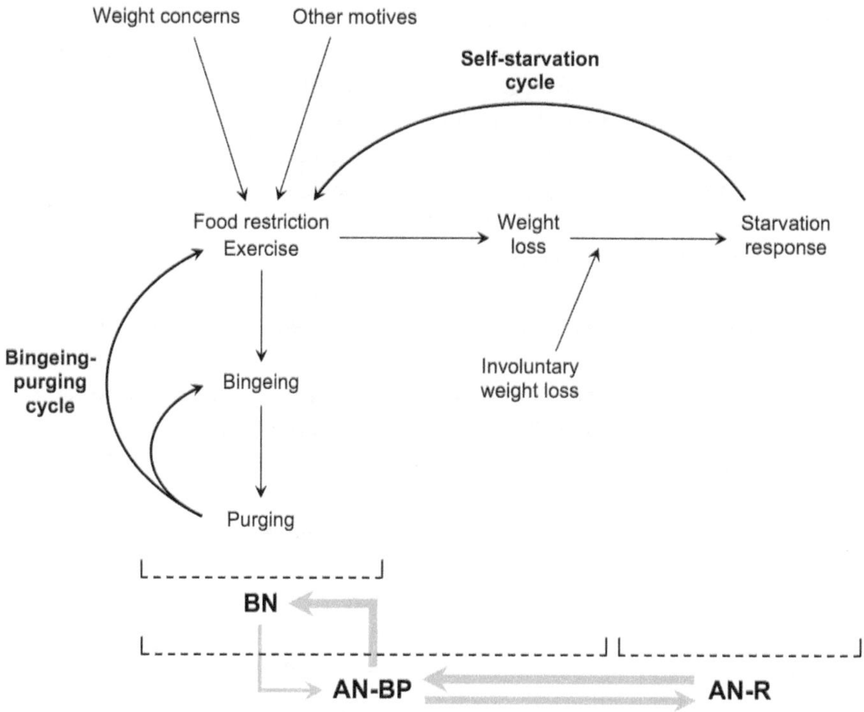

Figure 13.1. Self-reinforcing cycles in the etiology of eating disorders (EDs). The self-starvation cycle is crucially involved in anorexia nervosa and has been documented across time and cultures. The bingeing-purging cycle seems to occur only in modern, Westernized societies in response to weight concerns; this cycle underlies the symptoms of bulimia (BN) and the binge-eating/purging subtype of anorexia (AN-BP), but is not involved in the restricting subtype (AN-R). Gray arrows represent the probability of moving between diagnostic categories (thicker arrows = higher probabilities); the most common progression is from AN-R to AN-BP to BN, but many other patterns are possible, including back-and-forth transitions between AN-R and AN-BP or between AN-BP and BN.

become rewarding—even addictive—as the starvation response kicks in. At the same time, restricting behaviors that used to be deliberate become increasingly automatic, habitual, and difficult to interrupt (Dwyer et al., 2011; Guarda et al., 2015; Lock & Kirz, 2013; McGuire & Troisi 1998). The self-starvation cycle plays a crucial role in the onset of anorexia.

Increased physical activity is a key component of the starvation response in many animal species; in general, its function is to prompt exploration and extend the foraging range when food is scarce. This response is so ingrained that animals subjected to food restriction in conditions that allow physical activity (e.g., a running wheel) often starve themselves to death through strenuous exercise (Fessler, 2002; Guarda et al., 2015; Scheurink et al., 2010). In humans, pride is a powerful additional reward of self-starvation—achieving extraordinary levels of thinness and self-control makes many anorexic patients feel special and superior

(Allan & Goss, 2012). The starvation response also brings about some psychological changes that further contribute to reinforce the cycle. In particular, starvation dramatically interferes with executive flexibility/shifting, and patterns of behavior become increasingly rigid and inflexible. The balance between local and global processing is also shifted toward local details. This may contribute to common body image distortions in anorexia, as when patients focus obsessively on a specific body part (e.g., the neck or the hips) but perceive themselves as globally overweight (Pender et al., 2014; Westwood et al., 2016).

The self-starvation cycle has been documented across time and cultures, including non-Western ones. In modern Western societies, concerns with fat and thinness are the main reason for weight loss and probably explain the moderate rise of AN incidence across the second half of the 20th century. However, cases of self-starvation with spiritual and religious motivations have been common in Europe at least since the Middle Ages (and include several Catholic saints, most famously St. Catherine of Siena). In some Asian cultures, digestive discomfort is often cited as the initial reason for restricting food intake, but the resulting syndrome has essentially the same symptoms as anorexia in Western countries (Bell, 1985; Brumberg, 1989; Culbert et al., 2015; Keel & Klump, 2003). The DSM-5 criteria for anorexia include fear of gaining weight as a diagnostic requirement; for this reason, most historical and non-Western cases would not be diagnosed as AN within the current system. However, the present emphasis on thinness is likely a contingent sociohistorical fact and does not seem to represent a necessary feature of the disorder (Keel & Klump, 2003).

The Bingeing–Purging Cycle

Food restriction does not necessarily lead to self-starvation; in fact, a common effect of sustained weight loss is a tendency to binge whenever food is available (typically with feelings of automaticity and loss of control). Common triggers for binges include tempting food and excessive hunger, but also interpersonal stressors and strong emotions (Craighead et al., 2013; Polivy, 1996; Polivy et al., 1994). To compensate for impulsive overeating, some people start to adopt purging behaviors such as vomiting and laxative use. The combination of bingeing and purging may lead to the onset of a self-reinforcing cycle. Especially in the early stages of the cycle, bingeing and purging cause intense guilt, shame, and anxiety. Those negative emotions may then trigger more binges or prompt renewed attempts to restrict food, which ultimately end up strengthening the cycle. Bingeing and purging can be rewarding on a number of levels. On the one hand, these symptoms relieve anxiety, boredom, emptiness, and other negative feelings; on the other hand, they prevent stressful interactions with other people (e.g., staying home from school or work to binge), attract attention from family and friends, and may provide a way to communicate one's ill-defined psychological distress in concrete terms. Over time, the behavioral sequence of bingeing and purging becomes more automatic and less emotionally intense, but also harder to interrupt (Craighead et al., 2013; Pearson et al., 2014; Wedig & Nock, 2010).

In contrast with the universality and multiplicity of triggers of the self-starvation cycle, the bingeing–purging cycle that underlies BN and AN-BP has only been documented in modern, Westernized contexts and is virtually always motivated by weight concerns. A thinness ideal at the social and individual levels is not the only precondition for the bingeing–purging cycle: bingeing require easy access to large amounts of high-calorie food, and most purging methods are impractical without modern plumbing and sanitation. Together, these factors probably explain the lack of convincing cases of bulimia in absence of Western cultural influences and the dramatic rise of this disorder throughout the 20th century (Culbert et al., 2015; Keel & Klump, 2003).

At the individual level, impulsivity is a key predisposing factor to bingeing and purging (Craighead et al., 2014; Pearson et al., 2014). This explains why, on average, impulsivity and sensation seeking are higher in BN than AN patients and comparatively higher in AN-BP than in AN-R. Conversely, AN-R patients show the highest conscientiousness among the eating disorders (Cassin & von Ranson, 2005; Farstad et al., 2016; Ritschel et al., 2015). Given the high cross-over rates between diagnostic categories, these differences in personality cannot reflect stable differences between conditions. A more plausible interpretation is that preexisting differences in personality determine the likelihood of progressing through the various stages of the two cycles. For example, high conscientiousness and low impulsivity support the disciplined effort required to initiate the self-starvation cycle, while also making it easier to resist the impulse to binge after food deprivation.

Personality Subtypes

The fluidity of standard diagnostic categories for EDs has prompted the search for an alternative classification based on stable individual characteristics. Empirical studies of ED patients consistently identify three subtypes characterized by distinct personality and comorbidity profiles. The first subtype is usually labeled as *high-functioning*. Patients in this cluster have low rates of comorbidity with other mental disorders, a combination of comparatively low perfectionism and elevated self-esteem, high agreeableness and conscientiousness, and low neuroticism, anxiety, and depression. They tend to experience positive family relationships and few stressful life events, and are described by clinicians as likeable, empathetic, guilt-prone, and sensitive to others' needs. The second subtype is usually labeled as *overcontrolled* or *constricted*. These patients are high in both neuroticism and conscientiousness; they tend to be emotionally inhibited, low in self-esteem, and prone to depression and anxiety. The overcontrolled subtype shows the highest levels of perfectionism and obsessive-compulsive traits, as well as elevated comorbidity with OCPD, APD, social anxiety disorder (SAD), depression, and other D-type conditions. Finally, *undercontrolled* or *dysregulated* patients have a personality profile marked by impulsivity and sensation seeking, high neuroticism, and low agreeableness and conscientiousness. The undercontrolled subtype is associated with externalizing behaviors and stressful family environments; these patients show high rates of comorbidity with depression, PTSD, substance use, bipolar disorders, and cluster B personality disorders (including BPD, narcissistic personality disorder [NPD], and antisocial personality disorder [ASPD]) (American Psychiatric Association, 2013; Claes et al., 2006; Gillberg et al., 2007; Haynos et al., 2017; Hopwood et al., 2010; Thompson-Brenner & Westen, 2005; Thompson-Brenner et al., 2008; Turner et al., 2014; Westen & Harnden-Fischer, 2001; Wonderlich et al., 2005).

Despite their striking differences, the three personality subtypes just described are only weakly associated with specific ED symptoms, and all include patients with BN, AN-BP, and AN-R (though not in the same proportions). This is unsurprising if one considers the temporal instability of symptom-based diagnostic categories. The symptom constellations of the high-functioning and overcontrolled subtypes are very similar, although high-functioning patients are somewhat less likely to binge. Patients in the undercontrolled subtype have the highest specificity vis à vis DSM criteria: they show very high levels of bingeing–purging and are typically diagnosed with BN or AN-BP instead of AN-R (Claes et al., 2006; Hopwood et al., 2010; Thompson-Brenner et al., 2008; Turner et al., 2014; Westen & Harnden-Fischer, 2001).

Development and Course

The risk for eating dsorders peaks between adolescence and early adulthood, although eating symptoms may arise anytime from middle childhood to late adulthood. As a rule, earlier onset is associated with more severe symptoms and worse prognosis (Craighead et al., 2014; Lock & Kirz, 2013; Mitchell & Bulik, 2014). The pubertal surge of sex hormones plays a major role in the onset of eating symptoms in females, as shown by the fact that the heritability of EDs increases sharply at mid-puberty in girls, but not in boys. In particular, binge eating is strongly modulated by the interaction of estrogens and progesterone across the menstrual cycle, consistent with the role played by these hormones in the regulation of hunger and feeding (Chapter 2). Both the frequency of bingeing and its heritability peak after ovulation, in tandem with rising progesterone levels (Klump et al., 2014, 2015, 2016).

The developmental precursors of EDs include picky eating and refusal of food in childhood, followed by weight and shape concerns in adolescence. Excessive hunger and overeating in late childhood specifically predict the onset of binge eating. ADHD symptoms in childhood also greatly increase ED risk, mainly because impulsivity and low self-control promote overeating (Brewerton & Duncan, 2016; Fairweather-Schmidt & Wade, 2016; Rosenvinge & Petterson, 2015; Sonneville et al., 2015). The course of EDs is highly variable: recovery rates are about 50% for AN and 60% or more for BN, though patients may change diagnosis over time. Eating disorders carry a devastating mortality burden: a diagnosis of AN is associated with a sixfold increase in mortality, whereas BN predicts a twofold increase. Mortality in EDs is partly caused by the medical complications of starvation and bingeing–purging, but suicide risk is also elevated. Suicide accounts for about 20% of deaths in anorexic patients; unsurprisingly, the risk is higher in AN-BP than in AN-R (Arcelus et al., 2011; Pryor et al., 1996; Rosenvinge & Petterson, 2015).

Risk Factors

Eating disorders have been associated with a variety of family and socioeconomic factors, but the relations are not systematic and vary considerably across conditions and subtypes. On average, studies find that maltreatment, abuse, and stressful life events tend to increase the risk for EDs (particularly bulimia); however, research on personality subtypes shows that rates of early adversity are high in the undercontrolled subtype but low in the high-functioning subtype. Similarly, the overall correlation between socioeconomic status and ED risk is negative but inconsistent; more fine-grained studies show that bulimia may be somewhat more common in poor and disadvantaged families, whereas the risk of anorexia increases steadily at higher SES levels. In addition, EDs as a whole are much more common in urban than rural environments (Bulik et al., 2014; Gard & Freeman, 1996; Godart et al., 2013; Lindberg & Hjern, 2003; Martín et al., 2004; Mitchell & Bulik, 2014; Mitchinson & Hay, 2014; Swami, 2015).

Deleterious mutations and developmental disturbances do not seem to play a major role in eating symptoms, although there is some evidence that ED risk increases in the daughters of older fathers and is associated with prematurity and obstetric complications (Jacobi & Fittig, 2012; Racine et al., 2014). However, it is unclear whether these risk factors are specific to EDs or reflect their comorbidity with other disorders such as ADHD, autism, and psychosis. Body dissatisfaction, internalization of thinness ideals, and dieting (especially if unsuccessful) all predict the onset of EDs in adolescence and are treated as major risk factors in the literature. Alternatively, these putative risk factors may be interpreted as manifestations of the same processes that lead to the establishment of eating symptoms. Consistent with this view, weight concerns and internalized thinness ideals are about 50% heritable—about the same amount of genetic influence as ED symptoms themselves (Craighead et al., 2014; Culbert et al., 2015; Fairweather-Schmidt & Wade, 2016).

EVOLUTIONARY MODELS

Epidemiological data show that eating disorders predict dramatically increased mortality (2 to 6 times higher than controls) as well as reduced fertility (Power et al., 2013). The reproductive success of anorexic women is about 80% of the population average; figures are even lower for anorexic men (about 50%), possibly reflecting the high rate of homosexuality in these patients. This combination of outcomes strongly suggests a nonadaptive explanation for these conditions. While there have been initial speculations about an adaptive role for AN as a mate selection or fecundity regulation strategy (Crawford, 1989; Feierman, 1984), current evolutionary models regard EDs as either maladaptive outcomes of evolutionary mismatches or harmful dysfunctions in the mechanisms that regulate eating and starvation (see Li, Smith et al., 2014, for a review).

Some authors have focused specifically on the role of the evolved starvation response in the etiology of anorexic symptoms (Dwyer et al., 2011; Fessler, 2002; Guisinger, 2003). Proponents of the *reproduction suppression model* argue that eating disorders are maladaptive manifestations of adaptive mechanisms designed to regulate fecundity under stress (Salmon, Crawford, & Walters, 2008; Salmon, Crawford, Dane, & Zuberbier, 2008; Surbey, 1987), whereas the *sexual competition model* regards eating symptoms as maladaptive responses to heightened competition for physical attractiveness (Abed, 1998; Ferguson et al., 2011). Both reproductive suppression and sexual competition have been framed in a life history perspective and linked to women's life history strategies (Abed et al., 2012; Hill, Rodeheffer et al., 2013; Salmon et al., 2009); however, early work in this area failed to consider the existence of functional subtypes linked to different personality profiles. The functional heterogeneity of EDs was explicitly addressed in the original version of the life history framework (Del Giudice, 2014*a*, 2014*b*). As I discuss later, a broader life history approach is compatible with the sexual competition model but also accounts for the fact that ED symptoms may arise for reasons other than physical attractiveness (e.g., female competition for status, displays of moral purity).

Anorexia and the Starvation Response

Drawing on findings from the human and animal literature, Fessler (2002) argued that two seemingly paradoxical aspects of AN—excessive exercising in the context of energetic restriction and episodic impulsivity in the context of rigid self-restraint—are best understood as maladaptive manifestations of an evolved response to starvation. As noted earlier, motor hyperactivity can be adaptive in conditions of food scarcity because it promotes exploration and broadens the individual's foraging range. Impulsivity can also be adaptive under the "logic of scarcity," which favors a preference for small immediate rewards over long-term benefits. At the proximate level, impulsive behaviors are likely triggered by the drop in serotonin (5-HT) levels that follows starvation (the serotonin precursor tryptophan must be acquired from food). In anorexics, episodic impulsivity can prompt a wide range of problematic behaviors, from sudden anger outbursts and kleptomania to self-harm and suicide.

From a similar perspective, Dwyer and colleagues (2011) made a stronger dysfunction claim and hypothesized that anorexia arises from defective regulation of the starvation response. In some individuals, dysregulation may be caused by harmful mutations, while in others it may be induced by environmental stressors (e.g., excessive dieting). Dwyer and colleagues also made the case that insulin-like growth factor 1 (IGF-1, which shows reduced levels in anorexics) is a key node in an ancient, phylogenetically conserved molecular network that underlies the starvation response. These important contributions cast light on the mechanisms underlying the symptoms of anorexia. At the same time, they fail to account for the motivations that lead some people to initiate a physiological cycle of self-starvation and do not explain why EDs are so strongly concentrated in females. Progesterone and other sex hormones are clearly implicated in the modulation of hunger and binge eating, but their role in fasting and starvation has not been explored from an evolutionary standpoint.

The argument that anorexic symptoms arise from adaptive mechanisms was taken one step further by Guisinger (2003), who argued that all the core symptoms of AN—including food refusal and body image distortions—reflect an adaptive program designed to promote migration in conditions of famine (the "adapted to flee famine" hypothesis). This model is problematic in a number of ways. To begin, food refusal is potentially deadly and contributes to the very high mortality of anorexics. If the goal of the putative adaptive mechanism underlying AN is to flee food scarcity, it is unclear why patients should continue to refuse food when it becomes readily available (Li, Smith et al., 2014). Guisinger's speculative hypothesis on the origin of sex differences in AN is also unsatisfactory. According to this author, females have been historically more likely to marry outside the natal group and live with the husband's family (*patrilocality*); as a consequence, it would have been safer for them to travel far from home in search of food. However, not only is the exploration range in humans systematically larger in males, but the anthropological record shows that patterns of marital residence in foragers are quite flexible, in contrast with the traditional assumption of partilocality (Alvarez, 2004; Geary, 2010; Hill et al., 2011; Marlowe, 2004).

A recent study of genetic correlations yielded some new and fascinating insights into the interplay of adaptation and maladaptation in anorexia (Duncan et al., 2017). Using risk scores calculated from common alleles, the study found a pattern of genetic correlations between AN symptoms, low BMI and body fat, and multiple indicators of reduced insulin resistance and protective cholesterol metabolism. These findings are important for two reasons. First, they indicate that the same genetic factors that maintain normal variation in body size and shape also contribute to the risk of AN, a result consistent with the taxometric evidence of continuity between normal and disordered eating. Second, they suggest that selection for genetic variants that confer protection against some diseases (e.g., diabetes, heart conditions) may indirectly increase the risk of anorexia as a maladaptive byproduct.

The Reproductive Suppression Model

The reproductive suppression model of anorexia (Surbey, 1987) is based on the fact that female patients often undergo an interruption in ovulation and menstruation (*amenorrhea*). Surbey hypothesized that psychological stressors of various sorts may trigger temporary reproductive suppression in females (Chapter 4); amenorrhea would arise as an initial manifestation of this process and would then be reinforced by fasting and weight loss. In this model, AN is not adaptive per se; rather, it reflects the operation of adaptive mechanisms that regulate fecundity in times of stress, partly through changes in feeding patterns. The reproductive suppression model is based on plausible assumptions, even though fecundity can be regulated more directly by means that do not involve caloric restriction (e.g., changes in cortisol levels). That said, research has yet to find convincing empirical support for the model. There is some evidence that girls who perceive a lack of social support also show more dieting symptoms and feel less ready to become parents (Juda et al., 2004), but these findings do not demonstrate suppression at the physiological level and are compatible with a number of alternative theories. Other studies found that heightened perceptions of intrasexual competition and conflict predict eating symptoms and a desire for thinness (Salmon, Crawford, & Walters, 2008), but this pattern is equally consistent with the sexual competition model I discuss next. Another problematic finding from the standpoint of the reproductive suppression model is the higher incidence of AN in urban, high-SES contexts, which should prompt perceptions of better rather than worse reproductive prospects (Li, Smith et al., 2014). Still, reproductive suppression need not apply across the board and might only be involved in the etiology of specific ED subtypes; at present, this possibility remains untested.

The Sexual Competition Model

The sexual competition model of eating disorders (Abed, 1998) has two interlocking components. The first component is based on the universal male preference for a nubile "hourglass" body shape and the fact that women tend to accumulate body weight as they age, with the result that relative thinness is a reliable cue of youth and reproductive potential (Vaillancourt, 2013). The second component is specific to modern societies: as fertility declines and the age of reproduction shifts upward, women tend to retain an attractive nubile shape for longer, which increases the importance of thinness as an attractive display. At the same time, a number of converging trends contribute to intensify real and perceived mating competition among women, especially for long-term partners. Specifically, socially imposed monogamy reduces the number of available men; urban living dramatically increases the number of potential desirable competitors; and the media paint a visual landscape full of unrealistically thin, attractive women. The net outcome of these social changes is a process of runaway sexual competition that leads to an exaggerated desire for thinness in girls and women. Ironically, the process is largely driven by female intrasexual competition rather than direct male choice, and the resulting "ideal body" may be too thin to be maximally attractive to men. Runaway competition for thinness generates an evolutionary mismatch, which drives up the risk of maladaptive eating symptoms; in particular, Abed suggested that AN arises as a direct consequence of competition for thinness, whereas BN may stem from attempts to maintain a nubile body shape.

Ferguson and colleagues (2011) refined the model by stressing that modern social conditions specifically conspire to increase body dissatisfaction, which then contributes to increase the risk for EDs in predisposed women. In addition to the factors identified by Abed, they noted that, in affluent societies, women place less importance on resource provision by men, with the result that women compete for a smaller pool of physically attractive partners. The waning influence of parents on their daughters' marriage decisions would have a similar effect, by increasing the scope of female choice for physical attractiveness and the perceived intensity of sexual competition. Ferguson and colleagues also reviewed evidence that thin models in the media have comparatively small effects on body dissatisfaction, and mainly on women with preexisting weight concerns and/or high neuroticism. Instead, the largest and most consistent effects are those of mating competition in the peer network—that is, the number of attractive and available women in one's immediate social environment (for example, friends and colleagues).

The sexual competition model explains why urban living substantially increases ED risk and is consistent with the fact that thinness ideals across countries are better explained by economic affluence and urbanization than by Western cultural influences per se (Swami, 2015). Empirical studies consistently show that sexual competitiveness predicts higher ED symptoms and that cues of mating competition trigger food restriction, both in women and in gay men (Abed et al., 2012; Faer et al., 2005; Li et al., 2010; Li, Smith et al., 2014; Salmon, Crawford, & Walters, 2008). In a series of studies, Troop (2016; Troop et al., 2003, 2008, 2014) found that eating symptoms are more severe in women who perceive themselves as low in social status, experience social defeats, or show higher levels of shame and submissive behaviors. These data are broadly consistent with a sexual competition model, although social defeat and submission are also putative triggers of reproductive suppression.

Despite its remarkable empirical success, the sexual competition model still fails to capture the full spectrum of eating pathology. Historically, anorexic women do not seem to have been motivated by sexual attractiveness but rather by moral and spiritual concerns. As the historical record shows, ascetic self-starvation often brought women attention, fame, and even veneration by religious followers (Keel & Klump, 2003); while this pattern suggests a kind of morally tinged competition for status, it does not match the template of sexual competition for mates. Indeed, the social changes deemed responsible for the onset of runaway competition for thinness are all fairly recent, and cannot possibly account for the recurrence of anorexic syndromes through history. Contemporary data also show that while intrasexual competitiveness is the main predictor of eating symptoms across the board, status-oriented competitiveness may be uniquely associated with AN symptoms; this effect appears to be mediated by perfectionism, a pervasive correlate of EDs (Faer et al., 2005).

Eating Disorders in a Life History Perspective

The centrality of mating and reproductive effort in evolutionary models of EDs strongly suggests the existence of functional connections between eating symptoms and life history strategies. To begin, some studies have found correlations between ED behaviors and personality markers of fast strategies. The association is partly mediated by higher intrasexual competitiveness in women with faster strategies, consistent with the sexual competition model (Abed et al., 2012; Salmon et al., 2009). Other data offer preliminary support for the idea that cues of environmental danger may trigger divergent responses depending on early experiences; that is, promote food restriction in women exposed to low childhood stress (potentially as a form of reproductive suppression) but increase desire for food in those with stressful childhoods (possibly as a way to accumulate fat and maximize fecundity; Hill, Rodeheffer et al., 2013).

These initial studies have either treated eating disorders as a homogeneous category or distinguished between AN and BN symptoms, but have failed to consider the implications of personality subtypes within EDs. In the original version of the life history framework, I argued that the undercontrolled subtype represents a fast spectrum variant of EDs in which symptoms stem from intrasexual competition for short-term attractiveness. In contrast, both the high-functioning and overcontrolled subtypes are characterized by slow spectrum markers such as high conscientiousness and self-control (Del Giudice, 2014*a*, 2014*b*).

Of course, intrasexual competition for mates is not limited to fast strategies; weight concerns and body dissatisfaction can be powerful motives at both ends of the life history continuum. However, slow strategists mainly compete for long-term mates in committed relationships rather than short-term sexual partners. I suggested that this distinction contributes to differences in the rate of AN versus BN presentations between ED personality subtypes. Men with unrestricted sociosexuality and those who seek short-term sexual partners focus on body attractiveness and cues of fecundity (e.g., large breasts) at the expense of facial attractiveness (e.g., symmetric features) and cues of youth such as thinness. The latter are better indicators of future reproductive prospects and are more salient to men who look for long-term partners (Confer et al., 2010; Currie & Little, 2009; Lu & Chang, 2012; Zelazniewicz & Pawlowski, 2011). Moreover, cues of danger seem to shift men's preferences toward higher levels of body fat in women, in line with the hypothesis that people in unstable, unsafe contexts should value cues of current fecundity and survival ability in their partners (Pettijohn & Jungberg, 2004; Reeve et al., 2016). Based on these considerations, women at the slow end of the continuum should be more willing to become very thin—a powerful display of youth—even at the expense of other components of attractiveness. A stronger drive for thinness in the slow spectrum is consistent with the fact that the overcontrolled and high-functioning subtypes show lower rates of bulimia and higher rates of restricting anorexia than the undercontrolled subtype. While the life history classification presented in Del Giudice (2014*a*) focused on mating, the slow traits associated with overcontrolled and high-functioning subtypes also provide the motivational background for status competition based on moral purity and exceptional self-control.

Other Evolutionary Scenarios

With few exceptions (e.g., Dwyer et al., 2011), the evolutionary literature on eating disorders has paid little attention to the potential contribution of deleterious mutations and developmental insults such as obstetrical complications and early infections. While some studies have found normal or even higher IQ in anorexics, there is also evidence that AN is associated with brain atrophy, and it is still unclear whether the smaller brain volume in these patients is a consequence of chronic starvation or a premorbid risk factor (Bulik et al., 2014; Gillberg et al., 2007; Lopez et al., 2010). The possibility that low intelligence may be involved in the etiology of some ED subtypes—either by increasing the chance of maladaptive learning or through its effects on executive functioning—is worth considering more carefully in view of the sizable associations with ADHD and psychosis (see earlier discussion). Another unexplored idea is that parent–offspring conflict and parental manipulation may play a role in the onset of eating symptoms. In their own version of the reproductive suppression model, Voland and Voland (1989) speculated that wealthy, dominant parents might induce anorexia in daughters to delay or prevent their reproduction and shift all their resources toward sons. While this specific hypothesis lacks empirical support, it is possible that other types of evolutionary conflict (as, for example, intragenomic conflict between imprinted genes) may be involved in the regulation of eating, thus indirectly contributing to influence ED risk.

FSD CLASSIFICATION

In the FSD model, the classification of eating disorders is based on personality subtypes rather than symptoms or DSM categories, as shown in Figure 13.2. Fast spectrum EDs (F-EDs) correspond to the undercontrolled subtype, which is most commonly associated with BN and only rarely with AN-R. Slow spectrum eating disorders (S-EDs) fall into two distinct clusters. The high-functioning subtype bears the hallmarks of the prosocial/caregiving profile described in Chapter 4, including high agreeableness, empathy, and proneness to guilt and self-sacrifice. The overcontrolled subtype is more strongly associated with obsessive-compulsive and autistic-like traits, as well as high levels of neuroticism and inhibition. Anxiety, depression, and low self-esteem characterize this subtype, which seems to embody the pattern of social defeat described by Troop and colleagues (2003, 2008, 2014). If reproductive suppression is involved in the genesis of eating disorders, it is most likely in relation to this subtype (Del Giudice, 2014*a*). Another possibility is that—at least in some patients—the neurobiological changes that go hand

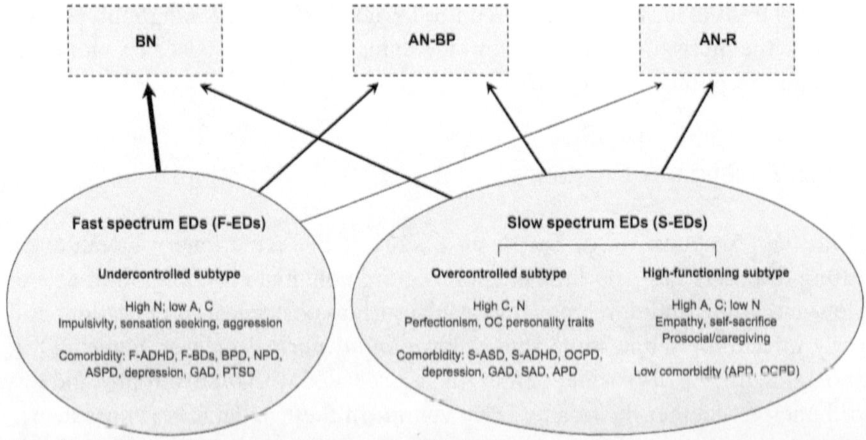

Figure 13.2. Eating disorders (EDs) in the FSD model. The undercontrolled personality subtype belongs to the fast spectrum, whereas overcontrolled and high-functioning subtypes are part of the slow spectrum. Furthermore, the high-functioning subtype is linked to the prosocial/caregiving profile within slow spectrum psychopathology. The distribution of specific categories (BN, AN-BP, and AN-R) differs between subtypes as indicated by the thickness of arrows; however, there is no one-to-one correspondence between functional subtypes and standard diagnostic distinctions. A = agreeableness. C = conscientiousness. N = neuroticism. ADHD = attention-deficit/hyperactivity disorder. AN-BP = anorexia nervosa, binge-eating/purging. AN-R = anorexia nervosa, restricting. APD = avoidant personality disorder. ASD = autism spectrum disorder. ASPD = antisocial personality disorder. BDs = bipolar disorders. BN = bulimia nervosa. BPD = borderline personality disorder. NPD = narcissistic personality disorder. OCPD = obsessive-compulsive personality disorder. PTSD = posttraumatic stress disorder. SAD = social anxiety disorder.

in hand with chronic starvation may produce a pattern of depression, anxiety, obsessive-compulsive cognitive rigidity, and reduced mentalizing (Bora & Köse, 2016; Gauthier et al., 2014; Pender et al., 2014). In other words, some anorexic patients would shift from the high-functioning to the overcontrolled subtype as a direct consequence of long-term starvation, rather than because of preexisting personality characteristics. Both the high-functioning and overcontrolled subtypes include more AN than BN patients, and together these two subtypes comprise the majority of AN-R cases (Claes et al., 2006; Hopwood et al., 2010; Westen & Harnden-Fischer, 2001).

While most of the available data on eating disorders are based on DSM categories rather than personality subtypes, they are consistent with the life history model I just described. Bulimia and binge eating are associated with anticipated menarche, early age at first sex, and higher sex drive (Jacobi & Fittig, 2012; Mendle, 2014; Mendle et al., 2007; Wiederman et al., 1996; Zehr et al., 2007). The data on puberty timing in anorexia are more equivocal, consistent with the idea that AN patients comprise a more even mixture of fast and slow spectrum subtypes (see Figure 13.2). Anorexics also score higher in measures of self-sacrifice and other-centeredness (Carter et al., 2012; Oldershaw et al., 2012). The differential association of AN and BN with socioeconomic variables also fits with the prediction that F-EDs (which include a high proportion of bulimic patients) should arise more frequently in disadvantaged environments, whereas S-EDs should be more common in higher socioeconomic strata.

Neurobiology

Neurobiological research on EDs has focused on standard diagnostic categories rather than personality subtypes; thus, findings in this area can be tied to the FSD model only indirectly. The most robust empirical pattern in the literature concerns serotonin. On average, serotonergic function is downregulated in both BN and AN patients but upregulated in recovered anorexics. Since starvation depletes tryptophan and consequently suppresses 5-HT signaling, reduced serotonin in acute anorexia is best understood as a state-dependent effect of malnutrition. Indeed, symptoms of depression, anxiety, and impulsivity in underweight anorexics seem to be partly explained by chronic serotonin depletion. Before starvation sets in, people at risk for developing AN symptoms probably have *elevated* serotonin levels (Bulik et al., 2014; Frank & Kaye, 2012; Gauthier et al., 2014). This pattern fits with the finding that, on average, impulsivity is higher in BN than AN and higher in AN-BP than AN-R. From the standpoint of the FSD model, the expected pattern is one of low premorbid serotonin in F-type EDs and elevated premorbid serotonin in S-type EDs. If the model in Figure 13.2 is accurate, differences in 5-HT function between life history subtypes should be stronger and more consistent than those between DSM categories. At the same time, anorexic patients—particularly those in the overcontrolled subtype—should show suppressed serotonergic activity in the acute phase of the disorder as a secondary effect of malnutrition.

Studies of dopaminergic function in eating disorders have been less conclusive, partly because of small sample size and partly because associations are confounded by the effects of starvation. In both AN and BN, large state-dependent alterations have been found in endogenous opioids, including β-endorphines (Bulik et al., 2014; Frank & Kaye, 2012). Because of its central role in the regulation of metabolism and energy allocation, the HPA axis is also deeply affected by starvation: the characteristic pattern associated with EDs is one of chronically elevated basal cortisol and blunted reactivity to stress. There is some evidence of reduced oxytocin—especially during acute anorexia—but recovered patients seem to show normal oxytocin levels (Culbert et al., 2016; Tortorella et al., 2014).

Androgens in EDs show an intriguing pattern: while anorexics tend to have low testosterone, there are indications that bulimia is associated with exposure to high levels of prenatal androgens. In addition, polycystic ovarian syndrome (PCOS, a condition caused by elevated androgens) has been associated with increased BN risk but decreased AN risk (Cesta et al., 2016; Culbert et al., 2016; Kothari et al., 2014). These findings fit with the data on the sexuality of anorexic and bulimic patients, and are broadly consistent with the idea that mating effort is increased in F-EDs but reduced in S-EDs. Still, it is possible that different subtypes within the slow spectrum may show different associations with androgen levels (e.g., higher levels in the overcontrolled subtype in association with ASD symptoms), net of the acute effects of starvation on androgen production and signaling.

14

Depression

OVERVIEW

Sadness and depression are universal emotional experiences. Depressive disorders are marked by severe, prolonged episodes of dejected mood and/or loss of interest and pleasure in activities that are normally rewarding (anhedonia). Depressed mood and anhedonia may be accompanied by distress symptoms such as feelings of worthlessness and guilt, recurrent thoughts of death and suicide, and a diminished ability to think or concentrate. Another important dimension of depression is that of *somatic symptoms*—alterations of appetite, sleep, libido, and arousal that are functionally connected to the activity of the stress response system. Somatic symptoms occur in two roughly specular versions. Melancholic or "typical" symptoms include decreased appetite and weight loss, insomnia, loss of libido, and psychomotor agitation or retardation (see Chapter 9). Melancholic symptoms usually worsen in the morning and are associated with overwhelming feelings of guilt, despair, dread, or emptiness. Atypical symptoms are less frequent and include increased appetite and weight gain, hypersomnia, and "leaden paralysis" (heavy, leaden feelings in the arms and/or legs). Patients with atypical symptoms tend to be highly sensitive to social rejection. Not infrequently, atypical symptoms occur without anhedonia; in this presentation, mood is reactive rather than flat and can improve in response to positive stimuli (American Psychiatric Association, 2013; Pae et al., 2009; Shorter & Fink, 2010). Taxometric studies indicate that affective/distress symptoms occur on a continuum that ranges from normal, everyday sadness to severe depression. In contrast, there is evidence that somatic symptoms may form a qualitatively distinct taxon with a specific neurobiological substrate (Ambrosini et al., 2002; Beach & Amir, 2003; Haslam et al., 2012; Liu, 2016; Van Loo et al., 2012).

Low self-esteem, a negative view of the world, and pessimistic expectations about the future constitute the "cognitive triad" of vulnerability to depression. These vulnerability factors can be framed as cognitive aspects of the broader trait of neuroticism—and indeed, neuroticism is the main personality correlate of depressive symptoms, particularly those of distress. In addition to high negative emotionality, low *positive* emotionality is a key predisposing factor for both depression and anxiety. The tendency to ruminate is another predictor of depression in response to stress. The defining features of rumination are a focus on the self (particularly one's failings) and repetitive thoughts about one's negative emotions and their causes. While ruminative thoughts are often realistic and accurate, they can generate self-reinforcing cycles that lead to increasingly dejected mood (Beck & Bredemeier, 2016; Hong & Cheung, 2015; Khazanov & Ruscio, 2016; Ritschel et al., 2013; Watson & Naragon-Gainey, 2014).

Depressed patients show a profile of dampened affective reactivity and pervasive negative biases in attention (increased focus on negative or self-threatening information) and memory (selective memory for negative events; Beck & Bredemeier, 2016; Bylsma et al., 2008; Kupferberg et al., 2016). Suppression of the behavioral approach system (BAS) is crucially involved in anhedonia, but the motivational substrates of depression are broader and include a variety of systems, from status and mating to affiliation and caregiving. In particular, shame and guilt—two powerful social emotions that cut across motivational domains—are consistently associated with the frequency and intensity of depressive symptoms (Kim et al., 2011; Kupferberg et al., 2016; O'Connor et al., 2002, 2007; Ritschel et al., 2013).

Many different types of stressful events can trigger a depressive episode. The most common are the loss of a relative or loved one, humiliation, social exclusion, romantic break-ups and rejections, loss of productivity (e.g., following an incident), and chronic stressors such as marital discord or financial difficulties (Beck & Bredemeier, 2016; Feliciano & Renn, 2014). While the initial episodes of depression are usually tied to specific triggering events, recurrent depressive bouts become more self-propelled and less dependent on context (*kindling*); also, experiencing repeated stressful events progressively lowers the threshold for a full-blown depressive response (*sensitization*). Recurrent depression episodes further increase neuroticism and reduce positive emotionality, partly because patients tend to avoid social interactions and become more isolated (Beck & Bredemeier, 2016; Khazanov & Ruscio, 2016; Ritschel et al., 2013; Rosenström et al., 2015; Rudenstine, 2014). On an abstract level, these phenomena can be understood as manifestations of psychological processes that update internal regulatory variables—variables that track the present and expected state of the environment (physical and social) and the person's ability to control the environment in order to gain fitness-promoting rewards. From this perspective, negative cognitive biases may not represent irrational distortions, but rather conditional adjustments of the individual's decision thresholds for responding to threats and rewards (Nesse, 2006; Nettle & Bateson, 2012).

Computational models of depression have begun to formalize these ideas in Bayesian terms by focusing on the expected reward rate; that is, the person's prior expectation about the probability of receiving rewards as a result of his or her future actions. This approach offers an elegant explanation of various depressive phenomena, especially those linked to anhedonia and pessimism. For example, negative attentional and memory biases may be explained by (explicit or implicit) beliefs that negative stimuli carry more information about the state of the environment than do positive ones. Increased processing of potential negative outcomes can trigger rumination and, ultimately, result in even more pessimistic priors (i.e., lower expected rewards). In turn, pessimistic priors promote inaction and motivational disengagement since the potential costs of one's action are not balanced by the expectation of rewards. To close the loop, inaction makes it more difficult to receive positive feedback and thus revise one's expectations, leading to the persistence of pessimistic expectations beyond the triggering event (Huys, Daw et al., 2015; see also Nettle & Bateson, 2012; Trimmer et al., 2013). Other computational models based on reinforcement learning suggest that depressed patients show a combination of reduced sensitivity to rewards with heightened aversion to losses. Depressed people also seem to perceive potential losses as closer in time and potential rewards as further away, which leads to paradoxical patterns of time discounting (e.g., high discounting of rewards in the near future but virtually no discounting of future losses; Chen, Takahashi et al., 2015).

Depressive Disorders

In the DSM-5, a diagnosis of major depressive disorder (MDD) requires depressed mood or anhedonia for at least 2 weeks and the presence of additional distress and/or somatic symptoms. Severely depressed patients with MDD may sometimes experience psychotic breaks with reality, such as delusions of guilt (e.g., having committed a terrible crime, being personally responsible for a catastrophe). The category of persistent depressive disorder (PDD, classically known as *dysthymia*) describes periods of chronic depressed mood that lasts for 2 years or longer. Depending on the number of symptoms they experience, PDD patients may or may not meet the more stringent criteria for MDD; however, persistent depression is globally more severe, with greater risk of suicide and higher levels of comorbidity (Klein & Black, 2013).

While the DSM embraces a unitary view of depression, its diagnostic criteria allow for a vast number of potential combinations, and two patients with MDD may easily have few or no symptoms in common (Fried & Nesse, 2015). To address heterogeneity within major depression, the DSM employs three levels of severity and several diagnostic specifiers ("with anxious distress," "with melancholic features," "with atypical features," and so on). Empirical analyses of symptoms clusters typically identify a mild subtype with predominantly low mood and distress symptoms, a severe subtype with melancholic symptoms in addition to distress and low mood, and a subtype marked by atypical symptoms. However, there is considerable variability across studies, which is expected given the dimensional nature of mood/distress symptoms and their heterogeneous manifestations (Carragher et al., 2009; Chen et al., 2000; Li, Aggen et al., 2014; Parker et al., 2015; Sullivan et al., 2002; Van Loo et al., 2012). The distinction between melancholic and atypical profiles is fairly stable across time, although there is a minority of patients who alternate between the two types of symptoms (Angst et al., 2007; Lamers et al., 2012).

The predisposition to depression is moderately heritable, around 40% in women and 30% in men. This genetic component largely reflects the effect of common variants, with only a minor contribution of rare and de novo mutations. Genetic factors seem to play a larger role in PDD compared with MDD; shared environmental factors account for a proportion of risk in children and adolescents, but not in adults. Heritability figures underscore the weight of the environment in the etiology of depression; consistent with the sensitization hypothesis, monozygotic twins become increasingly less similar in their threshold for depression as they move through adulthood (Flint & Kendler, 2014; Kendler & Halberstadt, 2013; Kendler et al., 2011; Klein & Black, 2013; Klein et al., 2013; Knopik et al., 2017). As I discuss in Chapter 15, the genetic determinants of depression are virtually the same as for generalized anxiety disorder (GAD) and overlap substantially (but not completely) with those of neuroticism and stress sensitivity (Hettema, 2008; Li et al., 2012; Mineka et al., 2014).

As is generally the case with D-type disorders, depression is more common in females, with an overall ratio of 1.5–2:1 (Feliciano & Renn, 2014; Nolen-Hoeksema & Hilt, 2009; Romans et al., 2007). This female-biased pattern is stronger for somatic depression and weaker (possibly even reversed) for depression without somatic symptoms. In particular, atypical profiles are 2–3 times more common in women than in men; patients who alternate between melancholic and atypical symptoms also tend to be females, with ratios of 5:1 or more (Angst et al., 2007; Baumeister & Parker, 2012; Carragher et al., 2009; Halbreich & Kahn, 2007; Pae et al., 2009; Rodgers et al., 2014, 2016; Silverstein, 2002). Sex differences in depression are partly mediated by sex differences in neuroticism and appear at puberty, around 13–14 years of age. Women are at higher risk for depression across cultures, with larger differences in more gender-egalitarian countries (the same pattern observed in personality traits; see Chapter 3; Goodwin & Gotlib, 2004; Hopcroft & Bradley, 2007; Hopcroft & McLaughlin, 2012; Klein et al., 2013; Twenge & Nolen-Hoelksema, 2002). Among the factors that increase depression risk in females are greater affiliation needs, higher sensitivity to interpersonal stressors and social rejection, and more engagement in ruminative coping (Hamilton et al., 2015; Kendler et al., 2005; Klein et al., 2013).

Depression is extremely common and co-occurs with all the other mental disorders. Comorbidity rates are especially high with other D-type conditions, in particular social anxiety disorder (SAD), avoidant personality disorder (APD), panic disorder, and GAD. Atypical symptom profiles are associated with higher rates of substance use and especially high risk of phobias, SAD, and APD. The strong association between atypical symptoms and social anxiety is not surprising, considering that rejection sensitivity is one of the hallmarks of atypical depression. Finally, PDD patients show higher rates of substance use than MDD patients, as well as a higher comorbidity with personality disorders such as borderline personality disorder (BPD) and APD (Angst et al., 2007; Kessler et al., 2014; Klein & Black, 2013; Langer & Rodebaugh, 2014; Mineka et al., 2014; Pae et al., 2009).

Neurobiological Correlates

Structural brain studies of depression have documented a loss of gray matter in most of the brain substrates of emotion and motivation, including the ventral prefrontal cortex (VMPFC and VLPFC) and the anterior cingulate cortex (ACC), amygdala, thalamus, hippocampus, and parahippocampal gyrus. This pattern seems to be more pronounced in patients with a history of early chronic stress, trauma, or abuse (Arnone et al., 2016; Ritschel et al., 2013; Roy & Campbell, 2013; Schmaal et al., 2017). Brain plasticity mechanisms are severely impaired in depression; patients with MDD show sizable deficits in attention, memory, and executive functioning that tend to persist even after remission. However, the correlation between premorbid IQ and risk for later onset of depression is small (less than −.10) and may be partly explained by the presence of mild depressive symptoms at the time of testing (Rock et al., 2014; Scult et al., 2017).

For some time, low serotonin (5-HT) has been regarded as the core neurobiological substrate of depression. However, the evidence that has accumulated over the years paints a more complex and potentially very different picture. Findings from various studies point to both increased and decreased serotonergic function in different areas of the brain; moreover, expression levels of the 5-HT transporter (which clears serotonin from the synapse) and receptor 5-HT_{1A} (which mediates negative feedback on serotonin release) are generally reduced—a pattern consistent with upregulated rather than downregulated serotoninergic signaling (Kambeitz & Howes, 2015; Nikolaus et al., 2012; Wang, Zhou et al., 2016). Accordingly, some authors have argued that depression may be associated with *elevated* brain serotonin, and that antidepressants that increase synaptic 5-HT levels may alleviate symptoms by triggering a delayed compensatory response that ultimately suppresses 5-HT release (Andrews & Thomson, 2009; Andrews et al., 2015). The high serotonin hypothesis of depression is consistent with the role of serotonin in promoting behavioral inhibition and risk aversion (Chapter 2); however, there is also evidence that reduced serotonergic function characterizes a subgroup of impulsive depressed patients at high risk for violent suicide (Ritschel et al., 2013). In total, serotonin may only play an indirect role in depression, and serotonergic activity in depressed patients may depend in large part on their preexisting personality profiles. Other neuromodulators seem to be involved in specific types of symptoms rather than depression in general. In particular, reduced dopaminergic signaling in mesolimbic circuits seems to correlate with anhedonia, and low levels of endogenous opioids have been associated with rejection sensitivity, which is especially high in patients with atypical symptoms (Gururajan et al., 2016; Kupferberg et al., 2016; Nikolaus et al., 2012; Ritschel et al., 2013).

In recent years, neurobiological research on depression has increasingly shifted from serotonin to GABA and glutamate. Reduced GABAergic function is consistently associated with various types of defense activation symptoms, from depression and anxiety to panic and posttraumatic stress (Gururajan et al., 2016; Kalueff

& Nutt, 2007; Möhler, 2012). The role of glutamate in depression is presently less clear, although several lines of evidence seem consistent with downregulated synaptic signaling (possibly coupled with increased negative feedback mediated by inhibitory N-methyl-D-aspartate [NMDA] receptors; Arnone et al., 2015; Gerhard et al., 2016; Krystal et al., 2013; Lener et al., 2016; Sanacora et al., 2012). Reduced glutamatergic function may work as a neurobiological bridge between depression and psychosis (see Chapter 8).

At the neuroendocrine level, the stress response system plays a prominent role in depression. The CRH receptor 1 has been linked to neuroticism in genomic studies, is expressed at higher levels in females, and plays a role in both depression and anxiety (Waters et al., 2015). More broadly, melancholic symptoms are characterized by sustained HPA axis activation, elevated CRH and cortisol levels, blunted cortisol reactivity, increased norepinephrine signaling, and a shift toward sympathetic autonomic control. Both cortisol levels and the intensity of melancholic symptoms peak early in the morning. In contrast, patients with atypical symptoms show low levels of CRH and norepinephrine but normative cortisol reactivity (Gold & Chrousos, 2002; Kemp et al., 2014; O'Keane et al., 2012; Pae et al., 2009; Shorter & Fink, 2010; Taylor & Fink, 2008). The evidence indicates that patients with alternating melancholic and atypical symptoms show a stress response pattern similar to that of "pure" melancholia; this suggests that shifting symptom profiles may reflect alternating phases of HPA activation/deactivation, as noted in Chapter 6. Intriguingly, rejection sensitivity seems to be a specific factor in the development of cyclical patterns of HPA activity (Stewart et al., 2007; Tops et al., 2008).

Sex hormones clearly participate in the etiology of depression, as underscored by the emergence of large sex differences at puberty; however, their exact role has been harder to pinpoint. In women, both high and low estrogen levels have been associated with depression risk. The available evidence points to a similar pattern for androgens in both sexes; for example, depressed and anxious women have lower testosterone (on average), but polycystic ovarian syndrome (PCOS) is associated with elevated androgens *and* increased depression risk (Cesta et al., 2016; Giltay et al., 2012; Johnson et al., 2013; Young & Korszun, 2010). It is quite possible that different types of symptoms may be linked to different hormonal patterns (e.g., Rodgers et al., 2015), but the evidence bearing on this hypothesis is still very limited.

To conclude this section it is important to consider the link between depression and inflammation. About a third of depressed patients show elevated inflammatory markers; cytokines that promote inflammation are also capable of inducing depressive symptoms, with stronger effects in women (Horowitz & Zunszain, 2015; Howren et al., 2009; Mills et al., 2013; Miller & Raison, 2016). A number of recent studies indicate that inflammation in depression may correlate specifically with atypical symptoms such as hypersomnia and increased appetite. The association seems to be partly explained by the higher body mass index (BMI) and obesity rate of patients with atypical profiles: fat deposition is a well-known promoter of inflammation, and adiposity-driven secretion of cytokines likely contributes to the well-documented bidirectional relation between obesity and atypical depression. Indeed, correlations between depressive symptoms and inflammatory markers are substantially attenuated once individual differences in BMI and obesity are accounted for (Capuron et al., 2017; Cassano et al., 2017; Duivis et al., 2013; Lamers et al., 2013, 2015; Rethorst et al., 2015; Rudolf et al., 2014). There is also initial evidence that gut microbes contribute to regulate inflammation and may have direct effects on brain functioning (including HPA activity) via hormonal signaling and activation of ascendant neural pathways. A number of researchers have suggested that gut microbes are involved in the etiology of depression and anxiety, although their exact role is still poorly understood (Foster & McVey Neufeld, 2013; Hayley et al., 2016).

Development and Course

The emotional and cognitive factors that predispose to depression (e.g., low self-esteem, negative cognitive biases) typically emerge in middle childhood and consolidate during adolescence. Irritability in childhood is an important precursor of anxiety and depression; in fact, depression in children is often marked by irritability rather than sadness (American Psychiatric Association, 2013; Hamilton et al., 2015; Savage et al., 2015). Anxiety and depression tend to predict one another across development: for example, childhood anxiety increases the risk of depression in adolescence, which in turn predicts higher anxiety in adulthood (Costello et al., 2011). In particular, social anxiety and SAD (which typically develop in middle childhood or adolescence) often initiate a trajectory toward later depression—first by increasing the risk of stressful experiences of social rejection, and second by reducing positive affect through isolation and avoidance (Jacobson & Newman, 2016; Langer & Rodebaugh, 2014).

The onset of depressive disorders peaks between adolescence and early adulthood; earlier age of onset predicts more severe symptoms, worse prognosis, and higher depression risk in close relatives. Consistent with a role of sex hormones in depression, puberty coincides with the emergence of new genetic risk factors in longitudinal studies (Feliciano & Renn, 2014; Klein & Black, 2013; Klein et al., 2013; Ritschel et al., 2013; Rudenstine, 2014). The typical course of MDD is time-limited (the average duration of an episode is about 6 months) but also recurrent; the probability of relapse increases after each new episode, consistent with a kindling effect. PDD is a chronic and often lifelong condition, with an average duration of 30 years (Feliciano & Renn, 2014).

Risk Factors

As already noted, mutation load plays a minor role in the etiology of depression and other defense activation disorders. Accordingly, paternal age is not associated with depressive symptoms. In contrast, advanced maternal age predicts higher rates of depression, anxiety, and posttraumatic stress (Flint & Kendler, 2014; Tearne et al., 2016). Prenatal stress may contribute to increase the risk of internalizing disorders; while there is some evidence for an effect of CRH exposure in utero, the data on maternal cortisol show little consistency (Howland et al., 2016; Zijlmans et al., 2015). Prenatal infections do not predict depression later in life, but a number of studies have linked chronic illness and inflammatory markers in childhood to increased depression risk in adulthood. It is still unclear whether these childhood effects are mediated by obesity; the possibility is consistent with findings that obesity in adolescence is a risk factor for depression, especially in girls (Du Preez et al., 2016).

Given the importance of stressful events and stress sensitization in the etiology of depressive symptoms, it is not surprising that adversity and low socioeconomic status are systematically associated with higher depression rates (Hopcroft & Bradley, 2007; Hopcroft & McLaughlin, 2012; Hudson, 2005; Lorant et al., 2003; Rudenstine, 2014). This association may be partly confounded by individual and family differences in intelligence; however, the effect is probably very small given the weak association between IQ and depression risk. Some data indicate that people who develop depression with somatic symptoms (melancholic and/or atypical) experience a higher rate of childhood adversity, including neglect and abuse (Li, Aggen et al., 2014; Sullivan et al., 2002). More broadly, stressful family relationships and insecure attachment in infancy and childhood contribute to increase the risk for both depression and anxiety across the life course. Insecure attachment relationships can influence the development of depressive symptoms in a number of ways—for example, by instilling feelings of unlovability or unworthiness, increasing one's sensitivity to real or perceived rejection, or promoting ineffective strategies for coping with stress (Klein et al., 2013; Madigan et al., 2013; Mikulincer & Shaver, 2016).

EVOLUTIONARY MODELS

There is little doubt that depressive symptoms serve a defensive function, but their target has turned out to be hard to define with precision. Starting with Price's *social rank theory* (Price, 1967), evolutionary scholars have proposed a variety of hypotheses about the triggers and adaptive value of depressed mood (for in-depth reviews, see Allen & Badcock, 2006; Durisko et al., 2015; Gilbert, 2006). Some models in this area are not specific to depression but represent general theories of positive and negative mood, framed as evolved decision-making strategies that maximize benefit–cost ratios in the face of uncertain rewards and threats (Nesse, 2000; Nettle, 2004; Nettle & Bateson, 2012; Trimmer et al., 2013).

Another family of models focuses more narrowly on social threats—loss, defeat, exclusion—and emphasizes the link between depression, submission, and risk avoidance (Bowlby, 1980; Gilbert, 1992, 2004; Price, 2007; Price & Sloman, 1987). All these models view depressed mood as an adaptive evolved response but regard clinical depression (of the kind that would be qualify for a MDD diagnosis) as a maladaptive and/or dysfunctional condition. However, the boundary between adaptive and maladaptive depression may not be so clear-cut. For example, Wakefield and colleagues have argued that some forms of MDD represent normal reactions to important losses, from the death of a loved one to the loss of a job. These authors identified a category of "uncomplicated" MDD with a relatively brief duration (up to 3 months) and no psychomotor retardation, feelings of worthlessness, or suicidal thoughts. The absence of such complicating symptoms predicts faster remission and low recurrence; conversely, their presence may be used to identify likely dysfunctional instances of depression (Wakefield & Schmitz, 2012, 2013*a*, 2013*b*; Wakefield et al., 2007).

Finally, some authors argue that severe, prolonged depression is an adaptation, in spite of its undeniable costs or even precisely *because* of them. Some adaptive models maintain that clinical depression works as an unconscious last-resort strategy of social bargaining; others suggest that rumination may be an evolved mechanism designed to solve complex social and nonsocial problems (Andrews & Thomson, 2009; Hagen, 2003; Watson & Andrews, 2002). From a different perspective, some authors have stressed the connections between depression and inflammation and argued that MDD has evolved as a costly defense against pathogens (Kinney & Tanaka, 2009; Raison & Miller, 2013*a*, 2013*b*). Adaptive theories of severe depression have aroused a great deal of skepticism. However, it is remarkable that, even though MDD is associated with increased mortality and other health and social costs, the reproductive success of patients is very close to the rest of the population (about 90% in men and 100% in women; Power et al., 2013). Despite their heuristic value and some initial empirical support, adaptive models are particularly difficult to test and remain largely speculative to this day.

General Models of Mood Regulation

This family of models is based on the notion that mood functions as a decision-making mechanism that regulates the individual's approach and avoidance tendencies, based on the likelihood of receiving rewards and punishments (Trimmer et al., 2013). This approach has obvious connections with reinforcement sensitivity theory and its emphasis on the role of behavioral inhibition and approach systems (BIS and BAS) in self-regulation (Chapter 2). Klinger (1975) originally theorized that, in order to conserve resources, low mood promotes motivational disengagement when the likely payoff of acting is not worth the cost. Elaborating on this model, Nesse (2000, 2006) argued that depressive feelings are adaptive in disengaging an organism from unattainable goals, and—more generally—conserving energy and resources when the expected reward rate is too low. On this view, clinical depression arises when unattainable goals are also perceived as vitally important and cannot be abandoned, leading to feelings of entrapment and hopelessness.

More recently, Nettle and Bateson (2012) presented a two-dimensional model of mood based on two independent decision thresholds—one for responding to punishments and one for responding to rewards. A low threshold for punishments results in anxiety and vigilance, whereas a high threshold for rewards translates into a depressed state characterized by anhedonia, pessimism, and fatigue. Specific events (e.g., gaining a valuable reward) evoke an immediate response but also induce a change in the individual's long-term expectations about the future, as instantiated in that individual's response thresholds. A key implication of this model is that cognitive "biases" such as pessimism are not necessarily maladaptive distortions; on the contrary, they are integral to the adaptive functioning of the decision-making system. This is consistent with experimental data showing that positive and negative emotionality affect the thresholds for detecting threats and rewards, and modulate the speed of decision-making in accordance with theoretical expectations (Paul et al., 2011).

Compared with similar computational approaches (e.g., Huys, Daw et al., 2015), these evolutionary models place more emphasis on the potential adaptive value of cognitive and affective biases. At the same time, attributing a functional role to biases makes it very difficult to discriminate between adaptive and maladaptive instances of depression. Authors working in this area typically draw the line at clinical depression or MDD, which they regard as virtually always dysfunctional. For example, Nettle (2004) argued that increasing levels of neuroticism bring both costs and benefits, leading to balancing selection on alleles that predispose to depression and anxiety disorders. If the net effect of neuroticism on fitness follows a cliff-edged function (a plausible scenario), a certain proportion of the population can be expected to express maladaptive levels of this trait and suffer from heightened vulnerability to severe depression (Nettle, 2004).

While general models of mood regulation offer some useful insights, they tend to be fairly abstract and only indirectly connected to the clinical phenomenology of depression. They are also limited in scope—while motivational disengagement and resource conservation may explain anhedonia and fatigue, they fall short of addressing the full complexity of depressive symptoms. In particular, existing models of mood have little to say on the possible function of melancholia and the relations among depressed affect, stress, and inflammation.

Depressed Mood as a Defense Against Social Threats

The models just reviewed treat rewards and punishments as broad, abstract categories of fitness-relevant stimuli. However, some of the most important contributions to fitness come from specific kinds of social relationships. Social threats and rewards are also unique in that they are mediated by complex patterns of signaling and communication (Gilbert, 2006). Social theories of depression focus on the role of depressed mood in the regulation of social interactions and pay special attention to its communicative implications. For example, Bowlby (1980) noted the analogies between depressive symptoms and evolved responses to separation from an attachment figure. In many species, when dependent offspring are separated from their caregiver they go through a predictable behavioral sequence, starting with an active phase of protest (crying, calling, restlessness) which—if separation persists—is followed by a passive phase of despair and inactivity. Despair functions to conserve resources and to minimize danger from predators and hostile conspecifics. From this perspective, depression is functionally analogous to the despair phase that follows social losses and persistent separations, such as the death of a loved one. Intriguingly, separation-induced despair also triggers inflammation and sickness behaviors, suggesting a functional link between depressive symptoms and immune functioning (Hennessy et al., 2009). While at least some types of social stressors activate the attachment and affiliation systems, most theorists have singled out dominance/status competition as the main motivational context for depression.

Social Competition Models

According to social competition models, depressed mood is an adaptive response to a perceived decline in the individual's social standing. While early contributions focused on rank in dominance hierarchies and the ethological concept of "resource holding power" (Price, 1967; Price & Sloman, 1987), the focus has since broadened to other aspects of status, including prestige, attractiveness, and other sources of "social attention holding power" (Gilbert, 1992, 2004; Price et al., 2007). In this perspective, depression is regarded as the expression of a defensive mechanism that triggers *involuntary* subordination following defeat or exclusion. The function of depressive states is to readjust the person to his or her new social position—first, by downregulating goal pursuit and reducing the motivation to compete and, second, by sending signals of submission and absence of threat to competitors. Stated otherwise, depressed mood works as an automatic de-escalation strategy; clinical depression ensues when de-escalation fails or, alternatively, when the person cannot accept subordination and defeat at a more conscious, deliberate level, thus setting off a dysfunctional cycle of increasingly severe symptoms. Modern social conditions may have exacerbated some aspects of social competition to the point of mismatch; possible candidate factors include life in large anonymous groups, rising inequality in status and wealth, and weakened family ties (Gilbert, 2006).

In accord with social competition models, there is considerable evidence linking depressive symptoms to subordination, submissiveness, and low perceived status. Events that involve humiliation are especially strong predictors of the onset of both MDD and anxiety symptoms (Dunn et al., 2012; Kendler et al. 2003; Siddaway et al., 2015; Sturman, 2011). In fact, social anxiety and depression can be regarded as two related manifestations of subordinate status: anxiety prompts vigilance toward social threats and challenges, whereas depression mediates disengagement and suppresses competition. This functional connection explains the strong comorbidity between depression and SAD (Langer & Rodebaugh, 2014; Sloman et al., 2006). Social competition models are also consistent with the fact that socioeconomic disadvantage is a strong risk factor for depression (Gilbert, 2006). However, there are other aspects of depression that are not well explained by these models. For example, suicidal thoughts—to the extent that they are not simply dysfunctional—are not easily understood as part of a submissive strategy (Hagen, 2011). Likewise, the role of somatic symptoms in these models is unclear, and social competition theorists have not addressed the particularly strong links among rejection sensitivity, social anxiety, and atypical depressive symptoms such as increased appetite and hypersomnia.

Some authors have sought to expand the social competition model beyond its original emphasis on status and defeat. O'Connor and colleagues noted that *winning* in social competition may also have psychological downsides. Specifically, the perception that one does not deserve to be happy or successful (especially in comparison with other, less fortunate family members) can trigger "survivor guilt," which has been associated with depressive symptoms (O'Connor et al., 2000, 2002, 2007). Others have attempted to integrate social competition with attachment theory. In attachment relationships, separation anxiety promotes reunion but also reconciliation with the caregiver; in the context of social hierarchies, anxiety may play a similar appeasement role with higher status individuals. On this view, anxious and depressive behaviors have complementary roles in conflict resolution. Developmentally, insecure attachment relationships with caregivers may amplify a person's sensitivity to rejection and preoccupation with status; conversely, secure attachment bonds may help people accept defeat and subordination in at least some domains, thus reducing the risk that depressed mood will escalate into a clinical syndrome (Gilbert, 2006; Price, 2003; Sloman, 2008; Sloman et al., 2006). Finally, there is evidence that attachment- versus competition-related stressors trigger somewhat different symptoms (an example of *situation–symptom congruence*; Keller & Nesse, 2005). The most robust finding so far is that social loss (e.g., death of a loved one, divorce) specifically predicts sadness and crying, whereas failure to reach an important goal is more strongly associated with fatigue and anhedonia (Keller & Nesse, 2005, 2006; Keller et al., 2007).

The Social Risk Hypothesis

The *social risk hypothesis* advanced by Allen and Badcock (2003) is an attempt to integrate previous models of depression within a more general framework. The central idea is that depressed mood is triggered by a perceived increase in the risk of being excluded from important relationships, with abandonment and ostracism as the ultimate threats. The concept of social risk is broadly construed to span various domains including attachment, affiliation, status, and power. Loss, defeat, entrapment, and failure at important goals can all be interpreted as warning cues that social exclusion has become more likely. According to this model, the overarching function of depression is to promote a risk-averse approach to social relations. More specifically, depressive symptoms serve two interlocking functions: on the one hand, they signal absence of threat and—at least when they are expressed with mild intensity—elicit support from kin and other close partners. On the other hand, they reduce the person's propensity toward high-risk investments (a version of motivational disengagement). Social risk aversion entails heightened vigilance to cues of threats and exclusion; this accounts for the frequent coexistence of depression, anxiety, and rejection sensitivity.

In a recent paper, Badcock and colleagues (2017) recast the social risk hypothesis in a Bayesian computational perspective based on the idea that the mind/brain works like a hierarchical predictive system (see Chapters 8 and 10). These authors speculated that depressed mood biases psychological processes toward risk-averse prior expectations when the social environment is perceived as hostile or unpredictable. Specifically, risk-averse priors can be implemented by increasing the weight assigned to prediction errors. Heightened reliance on prediction error increases vigilance and sensitivity to cues from the environment (as well as internal cues linked to inflammation and physiological stress) while simultaneously reducing the person's confidence in his or her predictions (rumination) and willingness to pursue rewards (anhedonia). When successful, these processes prompt the adaptive revision of one's beliefs and expectations; however, they can occasionally get stuck in vicious self-reinforcing cycles, leading to the onset of clinical depression.

The social risk hypothesis summarizes many key insights of previous models in an elegant and parsimonious way. However, it is not clear whether risk aversion can explain the whole spectrum of depressive symptoms. As discussed in Chapter 2, risk aversion is defined as a preference for sure, low-variance options over uncertain, high-variance ones. While anhedonia and pessimism reduce the willingness to take risks, they also seem to reduce the overall returns of behavior, not just its variance (Hagen, 2011). Indeed, models of mood regulation based on the expected rate of rewards can explain disengagement without invoking risk aversion (e.g., Huys, Daw et al., 2015). Understanding the role of risk sensitivity in the broader picture of mood and depression will require more computational work and more sophisticated models. Like most other theories, the social risk hypothesis does not offer a satisfactory account of suicidal ideation. Thoughts of suicide and self-harm seem to increase risk rather than decrease it, and are often associated with elevated impulsivity (Hagen, 2011). Another finding that is difficult to explain from the standpoint of risk aversion is the observation that depressed people behave less cooperatively and altruistically in economic games. This is puzzling since there are grounds to regard cooperation as a comparatively safe, risk-reducing option under most circumstances (Kupferberg et al., 2016; Pulcu et al., 2015; Surbey, 2011).

Clinical Depression as an Adaptation

Depression as Bargaining

Most evolutionary approaches to depression regard the disabling, even life-threatening aspects of MDD as prima facie evidence of maladaptation. In contrast with this view, Hagen (1999, 2002, 2003) suggested that clinical depression might have evolved as a last-resort bargaining strategy for individuals who find themselves trapped in conflicts of interest with other group members, to the extent that cooperation is no longer beneficial. Severely depressed individuals are incapacitated by their symptoms and become unable to cooperate with others and contribute to the welfare of the group, as if they were "going on strike." Importantly, depression as bargaining can only evolve in environments in which changing social partners is difficult or impossible, and cooperation can be enforced by punishment (thus making depression viable as an involuntary withdrawal of investment). Both of these conditions apply to small-scale societies in which kin-based organization, low population density, and intergroup conflicts severely restrict the range of potential cooperation partners. In this type of social context, clinical depression imposes severe costs on others while serving as a credible signal that cooperation is no longer viable for the affected individual. According to the bargaining model, suicidal thoughts represent the ultimate threat—that of permanent withdrawal from the social network. That depressed people sometimes commit suicide is viewed as the evolutionary cost that is required to keep the threat credible (and formidable).

In a similar vein, the *social navigation hypothesis* advanced by Watson and Andrews (2002) maintains that clinical depression is specifically triggered by complex multipartner social conflicts. Sometimes, people find themselves in situations where they would benefit from making drastic changes to their social arrangements; at the same time, they are prevented from doing so by other members of the group (relatives, partners, higher status individuals) who instead have more to gain from the status quo. When standard negotiation tactics fail, clinical depression allocates the person's cognitive resources to sustained rumination in the hope of finding a solution to the problem. In the meantime, depression sends an honest and credible signal of need and works as a passive strategy of "fitness extortion" that forces others to provide help, support, and concessions.

Models of depression as bargaining are as intriguing as they are speculative. In particular, there is still no convincing evidence that clinical depression brings about positive changes in the person's social niche (Hagen, 2011; Hagen & Thomson, 2004). To some extent, a lack of benefits from MDD could be attributed to mismatches with modern social conditions; indeed, ethnographic reports and preliminary data from traditional societies support the idea that small, highly interdependent groups maximize the bargaining power of depression (Hagen, 2003; Stieglitz, Schniter et al., 2015). To date, the best case for depression as bargaining comes from studies of postpartum depression (Hagen, 2002, 2003). The risk of postpartum depression is elevated in women who perceive a lack of social support and/or poor couple relationships, and there is evidence that relatives and partners significantly increase their own investment in the baby to make up for the mother's withdrawal. (For more discussion of adaptive vs. maladaptive models of postpartum depression and the possible role of evolutionary mismatches, see Hagen & Thornhill, 2017; Hahn-Holbrook & Haselton, 2014; Myers et al., 2016.)

Bargaining models potentially account for the common occurrence of suicidal thoughts and the selfish, self-interested behavior exhibited by depressed people in economic games (Kupferberg et al., 2016; Pulcu et al., 2015; Surbey, 2011). From the standpoint of bargaining, the fact that people tend to show negative reactions toward depressed patients is not surprising—ultimately, the function of the symptoms is to manipulate others and extort benefits against the best interest of social partners. As an analogy, one may consider infants' cries, which are also strongly aversive but reliably function as a means to obtain investment and attention from parents. At the same time, bargaining models fail to explain important phenomena such as stress sensitization and kindling (Hagen, 2011). Another problem with this approach is that depression can work as an effective bargaining tool only when it is severe and disabling; thus, bargaining can explain the function of clinical depression but not that of mild depressive symptoms. This is problematic given that mild and severe symptoms lie on a continuum (with the partial exception of somatic symptoms). It is possible that a complete account of the depressive spectrum will require a combination of concepts from social competition and bargaining models; however, no such integrated model exists at the moment.

The Analytical Rumination Hypothesis

Andrews and Thomson (2009) used the social navigation hypothesis as the springboard for an elaborate adaptive model of depressive rumination. According to the *analytical rumination hypothesis*, rumination is not a dysfunctional thought process but an evolved mechanism, specifically designed to analyze complex problems that resist solution but have crucial implications for fitness-relevant goals. Whereas positive mood favors a creative, global, and heuristic thinking style, rumination is repetitive, careful, analytical, and focused on details. In this model, melancholic symptoms of depression contribute to allocate cognitive effort to ruminative problem-solving by reducing the person's interest in other goals (anhedonia), directing energy to brain functions (HPA activation), and suppressing competing activities such as sleep and eating (insomnia, appetite loss). Anxiety and depression occur together when the person faces problems that, in addition to analysis, require vigilance to detect and anticipate future stressors. Melancholic symptoms overlap significantly with those of sickness behavior and starvation-induced depression, two ancient and evolutionarily conserved responses to physical threats. Both involve heightened HPA activity, anhedonia, weight loss, and suppression of sexual motivation; they also share a deeper functional similarity in that they promote the reallocation of limited resources to self-preservation (fighting infections, surviving starvation). Melancholic depression can be seen as a species-specific variant of the same general mechanism, designed to allocate energetic and cognitive resources to analytical problem-solving (Andrews & Durisko, 2017).

In addition to the intractable social problems emphasized by bargaining models, rumination can also be prompted by avoidable stressors that do not involve social conflicts of interest (e.g., financial loss, harm to a family member). Avoidable stressors trigger rumination with the goal of avoiding or preventing similar events in the future, mainly through sustained analysis of counterfactual scenarios (described as "brooding" in the clinical literature). The idea that rumination can have the goal of preventing avoidable harm in the future is consistent with the prominent role of guilt in depression. According to the analytical rumination hypothesis, defeat and status loss are depressogenic because they create new social problems and exacerbate existing ones. Women suffer higher rates of depression than men because their survival and reproduction depends more critically on the integrity of social networks (which provide help, protection, and resources). For this reason, they have a stronger evolved motivation to avoid social stressors, a lower tolerance for cues of social conflict, and more intense emotional responses when conflicts break out.

The analytical rumination hypothesis shares most of the strengths and weaknesses of bargaining models, including limited empirical support for its key propositions. There is some evidence that depressed mood increases cognitive accuracy and performance in reasoning tasks, but the strength and consistency of these effects is disputed. Unfortunately, the literature on cognitive performance is difficult to evaluate because, if rumination is designed to solve the particular problem that triggered the depressive episode, one should not expect it to increase cognitive performance across the board; on the contrary, the depressed patient's preoccupation with the object of rumination may well reduce the attentional and cognitive resources available for other tasks. There is initial evidence that disrupting rumination with distraction techniques enhances mood in the short term, but may end up lengthening the overall duration of the depressive episode (see Andrews & Thomson, 2009). However, clinical studies also indicate that techniques designed to prevent rumination can be quite effective in treating depression (e.g., Hagen et al., 2017; see Normann et al., 2014). What is still lacking is a convincing demonstration that depressive rumination is systematically beneficial in real-world situations. The hypothesis also fails to address the function of atypical symptoms such as hypersomnia and increased appetite, which—if anything—seem more likely to interfere with sustained rumination than to promote it.

Depression as Pathogen Defense

The analogies between depressive symptoms and sickness behaviors such as inactivity, loss of motivation, and decreased appetite have been noted for some time (Andrews & Durisko, 2017; Irwin & Miller, 2007). Kinney and Tanaka (2011) argued that clinical depression may contribute to the organism's response to infection by helping conserve energy and prioritize resources for the immune system. These authors speculated that depressive symptoms such as anhedonia and fatigue might play additional defensive roles, such as preventing exposure to new pathogens and reducing the risk of passing the infection on to relatives.

Raison and Miller (2013*a*, 2013*b*; Miller & Raison, 2016) took this idea one step further in their *pathogen–host defense hypothesis* of depression (PATHOS-D). The hypothesis maintains that depression is not just a behavioral complement to the organism's reaction against pathogens, but rather an integral component of the immune response that is largely mediated by cytokines and other immune-related molecules. On this view, social stressors such as defeat and separation do not directly trigger depression, but initially activate an inflammatory response to protect against potential wounds. In tandem with the stress response system, immune mediators then promote the onset of depressive symptoms as a form of sickness behavior (in part by modulating glutamatergic signaling in the brain). Because of the high prevalence of pathogen threats in the environment of evolutionary adaptedness (EEA) and the high potential hazards of infection, the immune system is likely to have evolved a proinflammatory bias consistent with the logic of the smoke detector principle. In developed countries, improved hygienic conditions and lack of exposure to previously common microorganisms ("old friends") have exacerbated this tendency and increased the prevalence of chronic, low-level inflammatory states. According to PATHOS-D, this evolutionary mismatch also contributes to increase the risk of clinical depression. It follows that, even though MDD originally evolved as an adaptive defense, it has become mostly maladaptive in modern sanitary conditions.

The link between depression and immunity is obviously important, and has been demonstrated in both modern societies and small-scale foragers (Stieglitz, Trumble et al., 2015). Future evolutionary models of depression should move beyond mood and stress-related symptoms to include immune responses and their potential adaptive function. At the same time, the role of inflammation in diagnosable conditions such as MDD is still poorly understood (see Del Giudice & Gangestad, 2018). As discussed earlier, chronic inflammation seems to be more common in patients with atypical symptoms—and, even then, there are indications that inflammation may arise as a downstream effect of fat deposition and obesity rather than as a direct function of depressive symptoms. Melancholic symptoms are not reliably linked to indicators of inflammation and may even be associated with *anti*-inflammatory processes (Del Giudice & Gangestad, 2018). Raison and Miller (2013*a*) themselves noted that the PATHOS-D hypothesis is unlikely to apply to all cases of depression and that pathogen defense may easily coexist with other adaptive functions (e.g., social competition or bargaining). All considered, the depression–immunity link is an exciting and promising research topic, but its implications for psychopathology are still far from clear.

FSD CLASSIFICATION

Although they differ in the specifics, virtually all the evolutionary models reviewed in this chapter agree on the defensive nature of depressive symptoms. In the current version of the FSD model, depression is included in the distress cluster of D-type disorders and may co-occur with both F-type and S-type conditions. As discussed in Chapter 6, depression and most other D-type conditions are expected to arise more often at the fast end of the continuum, partly as a function of higher exposure to threats and stressors. This would explain the finding that patients with MDD and PDD tend to be lower than average in conscientiousness, as well as the (comparatively small) negative correlations between depressive symptoms, conscientiousness, and agreeableness (Kotov et al., 2010; Watson & Naragon-Gainey, 2014). Depression and anxiety have been associated with early puberty in both sexes but also with late puberty in boys (Duncan et al., 2017; Mendle & Ferrero, 2012; Mendle et al., 2007).

On a more speculative note, a life history approach may be able to shed light on the many contradictory findings concerning the role of serotonin in depression. While low and high serotonin are usually treated as alternative neurobiological models of depression, they may actually identify different *subgroups* of depressed patients characterized by fast versus slow spectrum traits. This hypothesis is consistent with findings of low 5-HT in impulsive patients at risk for violent suicide. Other endocrine pathways may show similar patterns; for example, there is some evidence of elevated insulin-like growth factor 1 (IGF-1) in unmedicated and remitted MDD patients (Bot et al., 2016). While the link between IGF-1 and life history variation in humans is only tentative (Chapter 4), it is possible that different subgroups of patients may show different profiles of 5-HT and IGF-1 activity. If this hypothesis is correct, different neurobiological profiles should also be associated with different constellations of comorbidity and epidemiological risk (e.g., higher adversity in patients with low serotonin levels and elevated IGF-1). Looking at the correlates of depression through the lens of the FSD model may reveal a deeper structure behind the bewildering heterogeneity of this disorder (Fried & Nesse, 2015).

15

Generalized Anxiety Disorder

OVERVIEW

The DSM defines generalized anxiety disorder (GAD) as a chronic state of excessive, uncontrollable anxiety and worry about a number of different events and activities—from health, finances, and job responsibilities to small matters such as being late to an appointment. A duration of at least 6 months is required for a diagnosis. Stress-related symptoms in GAD include restlessness, fatigue, irritability, muscle tension, and sleep disturbances (American Psychiatric Association, 2013). The clinical category of GAD is rooted in that of "anxiety neurosis," which was classically described as a state of intense, free-floating anxiety with no particular object. However, current definitions downplay anxiety and emphasize the cognitive construct of *worry* as the core symptom of the disorder (Horwitz & Wakefield, 2012). Worry is conceptually similar to rumination, and the two types of symptoms correlate moderately with one another (about .50). The main difference is that rumination is self-centered and focused on past events, whereas worry is future-oriented; also, the goal of worry is to anticipate and prepare for potential threats rather than gain insight into one's current problems (Johnson et al., 2016; Mineka et al., 2014; Nolen-Hoeksema et al., 2008). The distinction between GAD and an anxious personality is somewhat fuzzy, and taxometric studies have found no evidence of a discrete boundary along the continuum of anxiety symptoms (Haslam et al., 2012). By definition, chronic worry reflects heightened activation of the behavioral inhibition system (BIS) and security system, whose function is to respond to potential threats with precautionary behaviors. Generalized anxiety symptoms are also associated with low positive emotionality, which may point to suppression of the behavioral approach system (BAS) (Khazanov & Ruscio, 2016; Woody & Szechtman, 2011).

Like depression, generalized anxiety is associated with attentional and memory biases toward threatening stimuli. Whereas moderate anxiety promotes heightened attention and difficulty disengaging from potential threats, clinical levels of worry may prompt attentional avoidance (Valentiner et al., 2014; Yiend et al., 2015). Patients with GAD systematically overestimate the probability that feared events will occur and exaggerate their likely consequences (catastrophizing). The use of worry as a coping strategy to deal with negative emotions may lead to spiraling cycles, in which the initial worry is compounded and amplified by "worry about worry"—the metacognitive concern that worry is uncontrollable and possibly dangerous to one's mental and physical health. Although worry about worry is not unique to GAD, it is especially pervasive in this condition (Horwitz & Wakefield, 2012; Newman & Llera, 2011; Rowa et al., 2013; Wells, 2000, 2005).

Generalized anxiety and depression are influenced by the same genetic factors, as reflected in a genetic correlation of 1.00 between GAD and major depressive disorder (MDD). About half of this association is explained by the shared effects of neuroticism. In contrast, the environmental determinants of the two disorders overlap only in part, with correlations between .20 and .60. This suggests that individual experiences shape a general predisposition to distress into specific configurations of symptoms; for example, MDD is uniquely associated with humiliation events, whereas GAD is more closely linked to experiences of danger. That said, depression and generalized anxiety often coexist—to the point that about 60% of patients with GAD also meet the diagnostic criteria for major depression (Hettema, 2008; Kendler et al., 2003; Knopik et al., 2017; Mineka et al., 2014). In addition to depression, GAD is highly comorbid with panic and social anxiety (social anxiety disorder [SAD] and avoidant personality disorder [APD]), but may co-occur with virtually any other type of psychopathology. Sex differences in GAD are somewhat less pronounced than in depression, with female-to-male ratios of about 1.5 to 2:1 (American Psychiatric Association, 2013; McLean & Anderson, 2009; McLean et al., 2011; Rowa et al., 2013; Valentiner et al., 2014).

Development and Course

The developmental precursors of anxiety are similar to those of depression (e.g., irritability in childhood). Compared with other conditions marked by fear and anxiety, GAD tends to be diagnosed later, with peak onset in young adulthood (around 20 years of age) and a broad window of risk that extends well into maturity. As a result, the mean age of onset for generalized anxiety is approximately 30 (Beesdo-Baum & Knappe, 2014; Rowa et al., 2013; Savage et al., 2015; Valentiner et al., 2014). The course of GAD is usually chronic, with many relapses and fluctuations over time. Episodes may last several months or even years, alternating with phases of temporary remission (Goodwin et al., 2014).

Risk Factors

Generalized anxiety and depression share most of their risk factors, including low socioeconomic status, insecure attachment relationships, chronic stress in early development—likely including prenatal exposure to maternal stress—and advanced maternal but not paternal age (Mikulincer & Shaver, 2016; Rowa et al., 2013; Tearne et al., 2016). New mothers are not only at risk for postpartum depression, but also show a spike in the risk for GAD, consistent with a strong functional connection between the two disorders (Wenzel et al., 2003). A specific risk factor for anxiety symptoms is loss of mobility due to injuries and disabilities, and GAD frequently co-occurs with various sorts of physical health problems (Bateson et al., 2011; Goodwin et al., 2014).

EVOLUTIONARY MODELS

Perhaps because anxiety and worry serve obvious defensive functions, GAD has received considerably less attention than depression in evolutionary psychopathology. Most evolutionary approaches have focused on social anxiety in the context of social competition and defeat (e.g., Langer & Rodebaugh, 2014; Sloman, 2008; Sloman et al., 2006). As an exception, Bateson and colleagues (2011) argued that the essence of GAD lies in a low detection threshold for threats and dangers, generalized across contexts and domains (see also Nettle & Bateson, 2012). While this account is probably too schematic and does not address the specific cognitive aspects of worry, it does capture an important feature of generalized anxiety. A low detection threshold and the attendant cognitive biases can be highly adaptive, especially for vulnerable individuals; in fact, actual and perceived vulnerability probably contributes to explain the association between anxiety symptoms and factors such as sex, socioeconomic disadvantage, physical illness, and reduced mobility (Bateson et al., 2011).

More generally, evolutionary cost–benefit analyses (e.g., the smoke detector principle) suggest that many "irrational" aspects of anxiety and fear may be design features rather than indicators of malfunction. For instance, automaticity and lack of top-down cognitive control are highly desirable features in a life-saving alarm system. Likewise, well-designed defenses often respond with disproportionate intensity to subtle cues of danger, and involve overgeneralization (e.g., becoming afraid of all snakes instead of just venomous ones) as a protection against potentially catastrophic errors of omission (false negatives). At the same time, even optimal learning processes sometimes produce maladaptive outcomes. In particular, the fact that anxiety triggers avoidance of contexts and situations perceived as threatening makes it difficult to revise incorrect beliefs about danger and unpredictability, and opens the way to self-reinforcing cycles that culminate in defense dysregulation (Meacham & Bergstrom, 2016).

For all these reasons, distinguishing between functional and dysfunctional mechanisms is especially difficult in the case of worry, anxiety, and fear (Horwitz & Wakefield, 2012). The data on survival and fertility in patients with anxiety disorders are also ambiguous. While moderate anxiety predicts lower mortality, clinical levels of anxiety symptoms are associated with a small mortality increase; however, this effect is largely explained by the comorbidity with depression (Bateson et al., 2011; Meier et al., 2016; Miloyan et al., 2016). Some data suggest that anxiety is associated with reduced fertility, but the effect may partly depend on sex (Jacobson, 2016). In addition to the usual caveats about fertility in modern societies (Chapters 4 and 5), these data raise difficult questions about the direction of causality: to the extent that anxiety symptoms are triggered by fitness-reducing factors such as stress, illness, and disability, correlations between anxiety and reduced survival or fertility may be spurious rather than causal.

FSD CLASSIFICATION

It is clear from the preceding discussion that GAD is a prototypical disorder of defense activation. Like depression, GAD is associated with elevated neuroticism and with neurobiological markers such as smaller hippocampus volume and downregulated GABAergic signaling (Kalueff & Nutt, 2007; Kotov et al., 2010; Möhler, 2012; Watson & Naragon-Gainey, 2014). In contrast with depression, patients with GAD show an enlarged amygdala, a structure that seems to play a specific role the detection of immediate and potential threats (Dunsmoor & Paz, 2015; Gray & McEwen, 2014; Rowa et al., 2013). There is evidence that anxiety symptoms (especially stress-related ones such as sleep disturbances and fatigue) correlate with higher levels of inflammatory cytokines and potentiated inflammatory responses to pathogens (Duivis et al., 2013; Vogelzangs et al., 2016). However, the functional links between anxiety and immunity are not well understood, and the caveats that apply to depression are also relevant here (see Del Giudice & Gangestad, 2018; Chapter 14). Generally speaking, D-type conditions occur more frequently in tandem with fast spectrum disorders; accordingly, generalized anxiety symptoms show weak negative correlations with conscientiousness and agreeableness (as well as with extraversion). At the same time, the personality profiles of patients with GAD are extremely variable and range from cold and dominant to warm, agreeable, and nonassertive (Kotov et al., 2010; Pincus et al., 2010; Watson & Naragon-Gainey, 2014). It has been suggested that worry may be functionally associated with slow life history strategies because it is intrinsically future-oriented (Fernandes et al., 2018). If so, GAD may co-occur with S-type conditions at higher rates than other defense activation disorders—a possibility that awaits rigorous empirical testing.

16

Posttraumatic Stress Disorder

OVERVIEW

Posttraumatic stress disorder (PTSD) is a label for the severe, prolonged response that some people develop after experiencing or witnessing a traumatic event. The DSM defines traumatic events as those involving actual or threatened death, serious injury, or sexual violence. Posttraumatic symptoms include intrusions ranging from recurrent dreams and involuntary memories to dissociative "flashbacks"; persistent avoidance of situations, thoughts, and feelings associated with the trauma; arousal symptoms such as hypervigilance, irritability with angry outbursts, sleep disturbances, and exaggerated startle response; and a range of cognitive/emotional alterations such as inability to remember important aspects of the trauma, persistent catastrophic beliefs (e.g., that no one can be trusted), and emotional numbing (e.g., estrangement, inability to feel positive emotions, loss of interest in significant activities). These symptoms may be accompanied by transitory psychotic experiences, usually in the form of paranoid ideas and auditory hallucinations (American Psychiatric Association, 2013).

It is important to note that all these symptoms are extremely common in the immediate aftermath of traumatic events. For example, 80–90% of the victims of sexual assault exhibit PTSD-like symptoms over the following days. In most people, however, symptoms subside within a couple of weeks, and only a minority meets the criteria for PTSD, which require a duration of at least 1 month. (Conditions that last for a shorter period of time can be diagnosed as "acute stress disorders.") For this reason, PTSD is best understood as a disorder of atypical recovery rather than one of atypical responding (Grubaugh, 2014; Resick et al., 2013).

Associative learning in the form of Pavlovian fear conditioning is widely thought to play a role in forming and maintaining posttraumatic symptoms. Consistent with this view, PTSD patients show reduced fear extinction in response to nonthreatening cues, are unable to inhibit fear in safe contexts, and overgeneralize fear reactions to a wide range of stimuli that may be only distantly related to the original trauma. Avoidance of threat-related thoughts and situations probably contributes to further exacerbate the disorder, as successful fear extinction requires exposing oneself to threatening conditioned cues in conditions of safety (Lissek & van Meurs, 2015; Mahan & Ressler, 2012; Zuj et al., 2016). Beyond simple associative learning, traumatic events sensitize the stress response system and amplify subsequent experiences of fear and anxiety. At the psychological level, severe trauma can painfully shatter a person's implicit beliefs that the world is a meaningful and predictable place, that other people can be trusted, and that he or she is worthy of love, competent, and in control (Cahill & Foa, 2007; Lissek & van Meurs, 2015; Resick et al., 2013). As I discuss later, these phenomena suggest that trauma may cause a radical, rapid revision of key internal regulatory variables. While fear and anxiety are central emotions in PTSD, patients experience many other types of negative feelings—chiefly disgust, shame, guilt, anger, and depression (Coyle et al., 2014; Power & Fyvie, 2013; Resick et al., 2013).

The heritability of PTSD is about 40%; as with depression, some evidence indicates that the contribution of genetic factors is higher in women, possibly as high as 70%. Crucially, exposure to traumatic events is also moderately heritable (50–60%) and shows an extremely strong genetic correlation with PTSD (about .90). Considering that most people do not develop PTSD after traumatic events, these data suggest that the same genetic predispositions increase both the likelihood of experiencing trauma *and* the intensity of the subsequent response (Afifi et al., 2010; Knopik et al., 2017; Sartor et al., 2012; Sheerin et al., 2017). Sex differences in the prevalence of PTSD increase in adolescence; the risk in women is 2–3 times higher than in men, despite the fact that women tend to experience fewer traumatic events (on average). Despite some inconsistent findings, the pattern of higher female risk for PTSD holds even in the military, especially following severe combat trauma (Crum-Cianflone & Jacobson, 2014; McLean et al., 2011; Nugent et al., 2014; Resick et al., 2013; Tolin & Foa, 2006; Trickey et al., 2012).

Comorbidity in PTSD is remarkably high: about 90% of patients receive at least another diagnosis, and up to 50% meet the criteria for at least three additional conditions. Depression, generalized anxiety disorder (GAD), substance use, and personality disorders are the most common co-occurrences. The deep connection with depression is underscored by a genetic correlation of .70–.80 between the two disorders. Having PTSD increases the future risk of depression and vice versa. The overlap between depression and PTSD is especially strong in women (Grubaugh, 2014; Najavits & Capezza, 2014; Resick et al., 2013). As noted earlier, psychotic symptoms are not uncommon in posttraumatic stress, especially when patients experience intrusions and hyperarousal. Accordingly, genetic scores for PTSD based on common alleles show a small but reliable correlation with those for schizophrenia and bipolar disorders (Alsawy et al., 2015; Sumner et al., 2016).

A number of empirical studies have identified "internalizing" and "externalizing" subtypes of PTSD based on their correlations with antisocial behavior, substance use, depression, and various types of personality disorders, in addition to a "simple" subtype with low levels of psychopathology (Forbes et al., 2010; Miller & Resick, 2007; Miller et al., 2003; Thomas et al., 2014; Wolf et al., 2012). However, these putative subtypes are not associated with different patterns of posttraumatic symptoms. A more parsimonious interpretation of the evidence is that PTSD co-occurs with a broad range of other disorders; the internalizing and externalizing subtypes identified in samples of PTSD patients may simply reflect the broader structure of comorbidity described by the transdiagnostic model (Chapter 6). While a recent study found some evidence of associations between specific combinations of posttraumatic symptoms and personality profiles (Contractor et al., 2016), the findings remain tentative and in need of replication.

Is PTSD a Valid Construct?

The diagnosis of PTSD was added to the DSM-III in 1980, under pressure from Vietnam veterans' advocacy groups and antiwar psychiatrists. Since then, the validity of PTSD as a clinical construct has been the object of endless controversies—scientific, political, and ethical (Horwitz & Wakefield, 2012; McNally, 2004; Shepard, 2004). While controversies persist, it has become apparent that there are several problems with the idea that PTSD is a specific syndrome that occurs in response to a specific class of traumatic events. To begin, people develop PTSD-like symptoms not only after trauma in the narrow sense (i.e., death or threat of death, serious injury, and sexual violence), but also in response to a much broader range of stressors. Examples are romantic breakups, divorce, financial problems, nonviolent death of a loved one, and even childbirth. Health complications and negative subjective experiences associated with childbirth (e.g., cesarean delivery, pain, lack of social support, infant complications) trigger postpartum PTSD in about 3% of women, often in tandem with postpartum depression (Ayers et al., 2016; Grekin & O'Hara, 2014). While the events listed in the DSM are more likely to induce PTSD than other stressors, their implied etiological specificity is not supported by the data. Moreover, taxometric studies indicate that posttraumatic stress has a dimensional structure, and attempts to identify discrete clusters of symptoms typically return subgroups that differ in severity rather than kind (Breslau et al., 2005; Grubaugh, 2014; Horwitz & Wakefield, 2012; Rosen & Lilienfeld, 2008; Steenkamp et al., 2012). Taken together, these lines of evidence strongly suggest that PTSD is not a specific response to trauma but the extreme version of a general emergency response to stress and threat.

The specificity of PTSD symptoms is also called into question by their strong overlap with those of anxiety and depression. For example, it is unclear to what extent "emotional numbing" can be differentiated from depressive anhedonia (Horwitz & Wakefield, 2012; Rosen & Lilienfeld, 2008). Other putative characteristics of PTSD, such as the presence of vivid, dissociated traumatic memories, have received equivocal support at best; potential indicators such as fragmentation and incoherence in narratives of the traumatic event do not occur reliably and may plausibly reflect hyperarousal rather than true dissociation (for a recent debate on this topic, see Brewin, 2016; Rubin, Berntsen et al., 2016; Rubin,

Deffler et al. 2016). Another problem with the concept of PTSD is the possibility of unintended iatrogenic effects. Critics have suggested that being diagnosed with PTSD—or even being sensitized to possible PTSD symptoms after an incident—may sometimes crystallize trauma by focusing the person's memory and identity on the traumatic event. The unintended result might be to stabilize the condition instead of allowing symptoms to decline naturally over time (Devilly et al., 2006; Horwitz & Wakefield, 2012). It is important to keep all these caveats in mind when approaching PTSD from an evolutionary perspective.

Neurobiological Correlates

Studies of brain structure in PTSD have found smaller volume in a number of emotion-related areas including the hippocampus, anterior cingulate cortex (ACC), and ventromedial prefrontal cortex (VMPFC). Smaller hippocampal size seems to precede the onset of the disorder and may represent a premorbid vulnerability factor. While the data on amygdala size are inconclusive, there is robust evidence of heightened amygdala reactivity. Hyperactivation of the amygdala is coupled with hypoactivation of the VMPFC, which among other things sends inhibitory projections to the amygdala (Campanella & Bremner, 2016; Gray & McEwen, 2014; Grubaugh, 2014; Kühn & Gallinat, 2013).

Unsurprisingly, the stress response system is involved in many posttraumatic symptoms, although the empirical findings are not always easy to interpret. The most reliable correlate of PTSD is increased sympathetic reactivity, and elevated heart rate following trauma increases the risk of developing the disorder (Bremner & Pearce, 2016; Morris et al., 2016; Resick et al., 2013). In contrast, there is no unique cortisol pattern associated with PTSD, although the HPA axis tends to show reduced sensitivity to negative feedback (mediated by the glucocorticoid receptor; Chapter 2). Cortisol tends to rise in the immediate aftermath of traumatic events and decline over time, possibly to lower than average levels. However, this pattern—which mirrors the trajectory of HPA adaptation to prolonged stress—seems to occur in people exposed to trauma regardless of whether or not they eventually develop PTSD (Klaassens et al., 2012; Morris et al., 2012, 2016; Steudte-Schmiedgen et al., 2016). Some data indicate altered opioid levels in PTSD patients—a plausible correlate considering that β-endorphin is released by the HPA axis under stress, and may mediate analgesia in traumatic events that involve physical harm (Bremner & Pearce, 2016).

As with other disorders of defense activation, PTSD symptoms are associated with reduced GABAergic signaling. Glutamate and other interacting molecules (e.g., brain-derived neurotrophic factor, BDNF) are also involved, although the available data are less univocal (Bremner & Pearce, 2016; Kalueff & Nutt, 2007; Mahan & Ressler, 2012; Möhler, 2012; Zuj et al., 2016). While only a few studies have investigated dopaminergic activity in PTSD, mesolimbic dopamine probably contributes to hyperarousal symptoms and to the brief psychotic states that sometimes occur after trauma. A role for dopamine in PTSD is also consistent with initial data showing increased coherence of the salience network (Bremner & Pearce, 2016; Campanella & Bremner, 2016; Resick et al., 2013).

Development and Course

Comparing PTSD rates at different ages is complicated by the fact that symptoms and diagnostic criteria are somewhat different for children and adults. In addition, the type and frequency of traumatic events varies dramatically across life stages and occupations (e.g., civilian vs. military). In general, the onset of PTSD peaks in adulthood; however, people who later develop PTSD often have a previous history of internalizing and/or externalizing symptoms in childhood. Patients with PTSD are at increased risk of suicide, above and beyond the contribution of depression and other comorbid conditions (American Psychiatric Association, 2013; Nugent et al., 2014).

Risk Factors

By definition, the most important immediate risk factor in PTSD is exposure to traumatic events, which in turn is partly influenced by genetic predispositions. Events that involve interpersonal and intentional violence or perceived death threats are especially strong predictors of posttraumatic stress. Lack of social support after the stressor further increases the likelihood of developing PTSD. Posttraumatic disorders are more prevalent in people with low education and socioeconomic status. While intelligence is seldom emphasized in the literature, there is solid evidence that a low IQ considerably increases the risk of PTSD. The effect of intelligence may partly confound that of SES, and likely contributes to explain the heritability of individual differences in exposure to dangerous, potentially traumatic situations (e.g., accidents; American Psychiatric Association, 2013; Malarbi et al., 2017; Nugent et al., 2014; Resick et al., 2013; Trickey et al., 2012). Like depression and anxiety, posttraumatic symptoms are somewhat more common in the offspring of older mothers (Tearne et al., 2016).

Insecure attachment and attachment-related stressors such as the loss of a parent in childhood are associated with elevated PTSD risk. A secure attachment style may make it easier to ask for and receive social support in the aftermath and—to some extent—buffer the impact of trauma on one's sense of safety and personal worth (Mikulincer & Shaver, 2016; Mikulincer et al., 2015; Nugent et al., 2014). At the level of learning mechanisms, researchers have identified some individual variables that predict future risk of PTSD; namely, slow fear extinction, reduced fear inhibition, response overgeneralization, and failure to habituate to negative stimuli (Lissek & van Meurs, 2015; Zuj et al., 2016). It is still unclear how these variables relate to broader personality traits; for example, response overgeneralization correlates with neuroticism and may indicate a more general intolerance of uncertainty and ambiguity (Lommen et al., 2010).

EVOLUTIONARY MODELS

The most detailed evolutionary treatment of PTSD is the *vigilance-defense model* developed by Cantor (2005, 2009; Cantor & Price, 2007). Cantor argued that posttraumatic symptoms are manifestations of adaptive defensive mechanisms—against predators, hostile conspecifics, and other types of threats—that we share with other mammals. Drawing on previous work by Marks (1987) and Blanchard and colleagues (1986), Cantor described an extended version of the standard "fight-flight-freeze" model in which threats may elicit six distinct types of defensive responses. These responses are arranged hierarchically and tend to follow a specific sequence: avoidance (avoiding situations and cues associated with potential threats), attentive immobility (the classic freeze), withdrawal/escape (flight), aggressive defense (fight), appeasement, and tonic immobility (Figure 16.1).

Appeasement is a defensive strategy specific to mammals that is rarely mentioned in discussions of fight-flight-freeze responses. When both withdrawal and aggression are impossible or unlikely to work, an endangered individual can use affiliation and submission displays—or even sexual offers—in the attempt to appease the aggressor (Cantor & Price, 2007). Tonic immobility is a last-resort response that is deployed when physical harm is inevitable, for example when the predator is about to strike. Tonic immobility is associated with dropping blood pressure, numbing, and analgesia (likely mediated by opioids); immobility may persist for minutes or even hours after the end of the threatening encounter. Both attentive and tonic immobility are controlled by brain nuclei in the periaqueductal gray (PAG), which in turn receive inputs from the amygdala and hypothalamus.

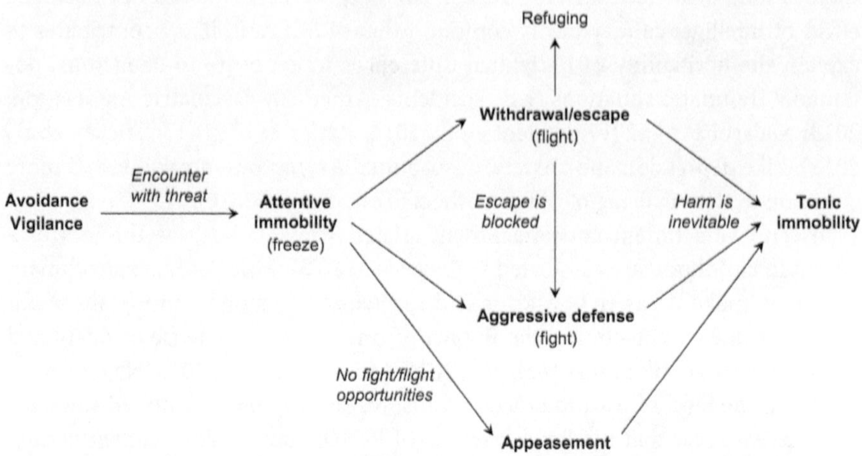

Figure 16.1. Defensive responses in mammals and their typical sequence of activation. When a threat is encountered, different behaviors can be triggered depending on contextual factors (e.g., opportunities for escape, strength of the aggressor). Tonic immobility is the last line of defense, deployed when all other strategies have failed and harm seems inevitable.

Freezing behaviors are potentiated by cortisol and inhibited by GABA (Hagenaars et al., 2014; Nijenhuis et al., 1998).

From the standpoint of the vigilance-defense model, PTSD symptoms can be explained as combinations of the specific defensive reactions depicted in Figure 16.1 and generalized hypervigilance. Thus, anger and irritability reflect the activation of aggressive defenses; intrusions are manifestations of enhanced memory for threats; and avoidance and overgeneralization can be understood as adaptive strategies designed to keep away from potentially dangerous situations. Hypervigilance is also linked to general perceptions of unpredictability and uncontrollability, particularly when a person has experienced loss of control during the traumatic event (Cantor, 2005). Consistent with this view, a symptom network analysis found that hypervigilance occupies a central place in PTSD, as quantified by the number and strength of connections with other symptoms (McNally et al., 2015). Also, a phylogenetic molecular study showed that more than 90% of the genomic sites that are differentially methylated in PTSD patients (a type of epigenetic modification that regulates gene expression) are not unique to humans but shared with other apes, suggesting the activation of an ancient, adaptive defensive system (Sipahi et al., 2014). Whether PTSD as a clinical condition is adaptive or maladaptive is an open question; the answer may depend on the intensity of symptoms and the specific contexts in which they arise (e.g., combat, sexual assault).

In a sense, the vigilance-defense model is a refinement of the general idea that PTSD is the extreme version of a normative response to stress and threat. For example, unpredictability and uncontrollability are key factors in the activation of the HPA axis (Chapter 2). However, the model offers some additional insights that are seldom emphasized in the literature. First, the model suggests that some typical behaviors in PTSD—reluctance to leave home, preference for familiar places—can be understood not simply as avoidance reactions but more specifically as manifestations of *refuging*. In animals, refuging is a component of withdrawal that goes beyond escape and involves return to a specific safe place (Figure 16.1). Another speculative but potentially important contribution is the proposal that defensive appeasement may play a crucial role in so-called *complex PTSD*. Complex PTSD is caused by prolonged trauma when the person is in a state of captivity under the control of the perpetrator; examples are hostage situations, kidnapping, torture, and domestic abuse. PTSD symptoms in these cases tend to be more persistent and generalized; moreover, they are associated with chronic guilt and shame, vulnerability to revictimization and self-harm, and idealization of the abuser (Herman, 1992). Cantor and Price (2007) argued that situations of traumatic entrapment leave appeasement as the only viable defense; the activation of appeasement mechanisms can explain otherwise puzzling features of complex PTSD (e.g., feelings of shame, idealization of the perpetrator) that closely resemble the so-called *Stockholm syndrome*. Finally, Cantor (2009) called attention to the potential role of tonic immobility in severe trauma. He noted that one-third to one-half of victims of rape and child sexual abuse report having experienced paralysis during victimization, and speculated that immobility during trauma may specifically predict the onset of numbing and avoidance symptoms.

Other Evolutionary Scenarios

From a life history perspective, traumatic experiences are especially interesting because of their potential impact on internal variables that track the safety and predictability of the environment. Traumatic events—especially those involving death threats and intentional violence—provide strong, direct evidence that the person is vulnerable to danger and unable to exert control in threatening situations. In principle, then, severe trauma might lead to a rapid revision of key regulatory variables followed by a shift toward faster life history strategies. There are indications in the literature that this may be the case. Cantor (2005) argued that the onset of PTSD is associated with an enduring motivational switch from affiliation and positive emotionality ("hedonic mode") to aggression and defensiveness ("agonic mode"). Similarly, attachment researchers have found longitudinal evidence that severe trauma followed by PTSD shifts attachment representations toward insecurity (Mikulincer & Shaver, 2016). The fact that risk-taking, sexual promiscuity, and a sense of foreshortened future are often reported as correlates of PTSD is also relevant in this context (Cantor & Price, 2007; Strom et al., 2012). It is possible that some types of trauma may mimic the effects of chronic developmental stress and trigger a rapid shift toward faster strategies, even in people who previously exhibited a slow life history profile.

FSD CLASSIFICATION

PTSD can be classified as a defense activation disorder that shares features with both the fear and distress clusters. Posttraumatic stress has the same personality profile of depression and GAD—namely, a strong positive correlation with neuroticism and smaller negative ones with conscientiousness, agreeableness, and extraversion (Kotov et al., 2010; Watson & Naragon-Gainey, 2014). There are two main reasons to expect a higher comorbidity between PTSD and disorders in the fast spectrum compared with those in the slow spectrum. As with depression and GAD, early life adversity and socioeconomic disadvantage increase the likelihood of trauma and may sensitize the stress response system, leading to stronger physiological responses to later traumatic events. In addition, it is possible that some types of severe trauma may cause a rapid shift in some aspects of the victim's life history strategy. If so, the comorbidity between PTSD and F-type disorders would partly reflect a specific causal pathway in which traumatic events trigger the onset of PTSD, which in turn increases the risk of F-type psychopathology later on. Properly testing this hypothesis would require longitudinal studies in which personality and psychopathology are assessed both before and after the traumatic event.

17

Specific Phobias

OVERVIEW

It is very common for people to be afraid of particular objects or situations, from snakes and spiders to flying and dental procedures. In many cases, the emotional intensity is out of proportion to the actual danger, and the fear is perceived as "irrational" and difficult to control. A diagnosis of specific phobia is made when the fear and anxiety associated with a particular target are persistent and severe enough to cause significant distress or interfere with the person's life. Patients actively avoid the phobic target and, if forced to endure it, respond with intense negative emotions—anxiety, fear, or even full-blown panic attacks (Chapter 18). This happens despite the fact that, in most cases, they are aware that their reaction is not justified by the actual danger posed by the feared object or situation. The DSM places phobias in the category of "anxiety disorders" together with generalized anxiety disorder (GAD), social anxiety disorder (SAD), panic, agoraphobia, and other less frequent conditions.

The definition of specific phobias is broad and potentially includes any number of unusual and bizarre fears. In practice, however, the overwhelming majority of phobias fall into four main categories. *Situational* phobias and those that relate to the *natural environment* are especially common and involve situations such as flying and driving or natural phenomena such as heights, water, thunderstorms/lightning, and the dark. Fear of heights is probably the single most common of all phobias. Fears of *animals* are somewhat less frequent; typical targets include snakes; small animals such as spiders, insects, and mice; or larger animals such as dogs. Finally, some people experience *blood-injection-injury* (BII) phobias, which are characterized by clinically significant distress about the sight or thought of blood, wounds, cuts, injections, or similar invasive medical procedure. While individual phobias are usually specific, they rarely occur in isolation: 75% of people with a specific phobia fear at least one additional object, and the average patient suffers from three different phobias (Adams et al., 2014; American Psychiatric Association, 2013; Valentiner et al., 2014).

From a motivational perspective, there are important distinctions within phobias that are not fully captured by the standard four-category taxonomy I just presented. Situational and natural environment phobias—the most common types—are dominated by fear and anxiety, which in turn indicate activation of the security and fear systems. Exposure to the phobic target is accompanied by strong sympathetic activation, consistent with a standard "flight" reaction. However, BII phobias and phobias of small animals such as spiders and insects show a strikingly different pattern. The main emotions associated with the target are aversion and *disgust* rather than fear; accordingly, exposure triggers automatic facial expressions of disgust and heightened parasympathetic activity (Adams et al., 2014; Page, 1994). Disgust reactions to blood, spiders, and other small animals are not just intense but also particularly resistant to extinction (Olatunji & Deacon, 2008; Olatunji et al., 2007, 2009).

Vasovagal fainting is a peculiar physiological response associated with BII phobias. When they are exposed to blood or cues of injections/injuries, many BII patients show a biphasic autonomic reaction. The initial phase is marked by sympathetic activation with accelerated heart rate, increased blood pressure, and vasoconstriction. This phase resembles the compensatory shock that normally follows a small hemorrhage. The initial sympathetic response is quickly followed by intense parasympathetic activation, leading to vasodilation, a sudden drop in heart rate and blood pressure, dizziness, and ultimately fainting. In most people without BII phobia, rapid vasovagal fainting is only triggered by severe hemorrhages and usually sets in after a person has lost about 30% of the blood volume (American Psychiatric Association, 2013; Diehl, 2005; Page, 1994). However, there may be a link between the reactions of BII patients and the episodes of nausea, dizziness, and fainting that sometimes occur at the sight of accidents with mutilated bodies or during medical procedures such as prostatic palpation, cervix dilation, or eye pressure tests (Marks, 1988). Although vasovagal reactions are very common in BII phobias, about 20% of patients with this condition have no history of fainting. This suggests heterogeneity within the BII category: some of these patients may show an emotional profile more similar to that of other phobias, with a central role of fear and anxiety instead of aversion/disgust (Page, 1994).

Both diagnosable phobias and irrational fears that do not reach clinical severity are moderately heritable; additive genetic factors account for about 40–50% of the variance in fears and about 30% in phobias. There is some evidence of a role for shared environmental factors, but only in situational phobias (Van Houtem et al., 2013). The risk of developing phobias is higher in females, with ratios of 2:1 or more. The largest sex differences occur in fears of the dark, thunderstorms and lightning, snakes, spiders, and small animals; the distribution by sex is more balanced for BII phobias, fear of heights, and fear of flying (Adams et al., 2014; Ajdacic-Gross et al., 2016; McLean et al., 2011; Valentiner et al., 2014). Phobias are very common and show high rates of co-occurrence with other D-type disorders—mainly panic, posttraumatic stress disorder (PTSD), SAD, avoidant personality disorder (APD), GAD, and depression (especially with atypical symptoms). Beyond the spectrum of defense activation, comorbidity is elevated in attention-deficit/hyperactivity disorder (ADHD), autism, bipolar disorders, and personality disorders including borderline personality disorder (BPD) and narcissistic personality disorder (NPD) (Adams et al., 2014; Chapters 9–12). There is also some evidence that, relative to other types of phobia, BII phobias in children and adolescents may be specifically associated with the development of antisocial/conduct disorders and ADHD (Kim et al., 2010).

Development and Course

Phobias typically develop in childhood or early adolescence; the median age of onset is between 7 and 11 years. However, the onset of fears often precedes that of clinical phobias by several years, and many patients report that they have had specific fears for as long as they can remember. Phobias involving animals, the natural environment, and BII develop earlier, usually in early childhood; situational phobias tend to arise later and peak during adolescence. The overall prevalence of phobias begins to drop after adolescence and keeps declining throughout adulthood. When they persist beyond childhood, phobias tend to be chronic and show low remission rates when untreated. Some types of fears seem to be less enduring than others: for example, animal phobias have somewhat higher rates of spontaneous remission than BII phobias (Adams et al., 2014; Ajdacic-Gross et al., 2016; American Psychiatric Association, 2013; Becker et al., 2007; Page, 1994; Goodwin et al., 2014; Kessler et al., 2005; Valentiner et al., 2014).

How Are Phobias Acquired?

The question of how phobias are acquired has sparked a long, fascinating, and still ongoing debate (see Adams et al., 2014; Coelho & Purkis, 2009). Classic accounts of phobias are based on associative learning. According to associative models, irrational fears are acquired either through Pavlovian conditioning (when a direct aversive experience becomes associated with the phobic target) or through socially mediated processes such as vicarious learning. For example, a child may develop a fear of thunderstorms after observing his mother's fearful reaction to thunder. While fear acquisition by direct or vicarious conditioning is easy to produce in the laboratory, the effects tend to be weak and transitory. Even more importantly, the majority of patients have no memory of specific conditioning events that may explain the origin of the phobia; when they report traumatic fear on their first exposure to the phobic object, the fear often seems to be caused by the object itself and not by a separate unconditioned stimulus (as would be required for Pavlovian learning). More sophisticated twin studies cast additional doubts on associative accounts, and show that even twins with the same phobia usually report different acquisition histories (Kendler et al., 2002; Poulton & Menzies, 2002). Even if autobiographical memories are subject to distortions and could miss a history of gradual, low-intensity conditioning, these data suggest that standard associative processes explain the onset of phobias only in a minority of cases.

An alternative to classic associative accounts comes from evolutionary models of *prepared learning*. As I discuss in more detail later, various authors have argued that organisms exposed to recurrent, potentially deadly threats over many generations should evolve a tendency to form rapid negative associations involving those threats. For evolutionary-relevant targets such as snakes, heights, and water, associative fear learning can be particularly fast—sometimes requiring a single negative experience—as well as strongly resistant to extinction (Mineka & Öhman, 2002; Öhman & Mineka, 2001; Rachman, 2002; Seligman, 1971). Even more radically, proponents of *nonassociative models* argue that phobias of evolutionary-relevant targets do not necessitate learning at all (Gray, 1987; Kennair, 2007; Menzies & Clarke, 1995). On this view, recurrent threats are genetically encoded: specific fears may emerge spontaneously during development, or are expressed when the person encounters the target in a state of arousal or anxiety (fear sensitization). The empirical evidence supports the idea that prepared learning and/or nonassociative sensitization are the most common pathways for fear acquisition. Classic conditioning seems to be responsible only for a relatively small proportion of phobias, particularly those with unusual or evolutionarily novel targets (Coelho & Purkis, 2009; Öhman, 2009; Poulton & Menzies, 2002).

Risk Factors

Beyond the predisposing role of nonspecific traits such as neuroticism and inhibited temperament in childhood (Adams et al., 2014; Kendler et al., 2002), there is little evidence that other factors reliably affect the risk of specific phobias. In particular, the prevalence of phobias is essentially unrelated to socioeconomic status; there is some evidence that family stress and physical abuse in childhood increase risk in adolescence and adulthood, with the exception of pure animal phobias (Ajdacic-Gross et al., 2016; Goodwin et al., 2014; Magee, 1999). A number of studies have found correlations with parental overprotection and intrusive parenting (Adams et al., 2014). These factors may plausibly play a role in the onset of phobias by limiting the child's exploration (including risky play; more on this later) and interfering with fear extinction. At the same time, the effect is unlikely to be entirely causal; at least in part, the combination of excessive worry in parents and fearfulness in their children may be explained by the influence of shared genetic factors.

EVOLUTIONARY MODELS

The targets of phobias are not randomly distributed; on the contrary, all the most common fears concern objects and situations that have been recurrent sources of danger in our evolutionary past. Some of those objects and situations still pose significant threats to survival (e.g., heights, water); many others have become exceedingly rare or considerably less dangerous, at least in urban environments (e.g., venomous snakes, thunderstorms). The fact that fears in the present tend to reflect ancient threats was already noted by Darwin (1877) and can be linked to the observation that people rarely become phobic of much deadlier objects such as guns, cars, or electric wires. Evolutionary models of phobias share the assumption that evolution has equipped us with a predisposition to fear certain targets more than others. In modern conditions, this evolved repertoire creates a high potential for mismatch, focusing defensive systems on negligible threats while downplaying some real and potentially lethal dangers (Horwitz & Wakefield, 2012; Marks & Nesse, 1994; McGuire & Troisi, 1998).

Preparedness Models

According to models of prepared learning, the mechanisms that mediate fear conditioning have become canalized throughout evolution to form rapid, intense, long-lasting associations with certain types of stimuli such as snakes, spiders, and heights (Marks, 1987; Rachman, 2002; Seligman, 1971). The adaptive reasoning behind this idea is that partial genetic encoding predisposes the organism to become fearful of recurrent threats but still requires the experience of concomitant signs of danger—a loud noise, an unpleasant tactile sensation, or a frightened facial expression. In principle, highly canalized conditioning could strike the optimal balance between the advantages of a rapid, potentially life-saving response and the flexibility of context-dependent learning.

Öhman and Mineka developed the most recent and elaborate version of the preparedness model. They also argued for the existence of an "evolved fear module" with characteristics of selectivity, automaticity, and encapsulation (Öhman, 2009; Öhman & Mineka, 2001; Mineka & Öhman, 2002). This model postulates that, after selective associations are formed, they generate a fear response with little voluntary control and without the need for conscious awareness of the stimulus (automaticity). When the fear response is activated, it runs its course regardless of the individual's beliefs and expectations—in other words, fear is impenetrable to deliberate cognitive control (encapsulation). Automaticity and encapsulation are adaptive features designed to speed up responding and prevent false negatives; together they explain the seemingly irrational and uncontrollable quality of phobias. In their work, Öhman and Mineka also proposed a specific brain network centered on the amygdala as the neural substrate of the fear module (Öhman & Mineka, 2001).

The predictions of preparedness models have been consistently supported in experimental studies. Evolutionary-relevant targets such as snakes and spiders are detected more quickly than other types of stimuli, especially against confusing or distracting visual backgrounds (New & German, 2015). In addition to capturing attention, evolutionary-relevant threats tend to produce faster and stronger fear conditioning, especially when they are paired with aversive stimuli that match the nature of the specific threat (e.g., when pictures of snakes are paired with a tactile shock instead of an unpleasant noise; Öhman & Mineka, 2001). The role of classic associative learning is probably limited to phobias for evolutionarily novel targets such as cars and dentists (Menzies & Harris, 1997). Importantly, some common phobias may recruit ancient evolved fears even if—strictly speaking—their targets are evolutionarily novel. For example, fear of flying may build on the more general fear of heights and falling, fear of dentists may be triggered by the sight of a sharp object close to one's head. and so on (Bracha, 2006; Marks & Nesse, 1994). While Öhman and Mineka's model has enjoyed considerable empirical success, it has also attracted some criticism. The main weakness of the model lies in its rigid conception of encapsulation; more recent studies have shown that cognitive factors can modulate extinction even for evolutionary-relevant stimuli. Also, later research has shown that the amygdala encodes salience for all sorts of motivationally relevant stimuli and is not as fear-specific as previously believed (Coelho & Purkis, 2009; Faucher & Blanchette, 2011; Mallan et al., 2013).

On the developmental side, evolutionary scholars have noted that prepared fears emerge at the age when they become adaptive. Fear of heights begins to manifest as soon as infants start crawling; fears of animals and monsters first appear when toddlers begin to move around more freely and explore their environment. In middle childhood, children become more autonomous and start helping with adult tasks; this is when fears of accidents and injuries become more pronounced (Boyer & Bergstrom, 2011; Marks, 1987). Children's fears are especially revealing as they seem to be based on universal, abstract "templates" for threatening objects: for example, nonexistent monsters are consistently imagined as lurking in the dark and having sharp teeth and claws (Boyer & Bergstrom, 2011).

Nonassociative Models

In preparedness models, associative learning—however rapid and canalized—retains a key role in the establishment of fears and phobias. Some authors have argued that learning in the strict sense may not be necessary and that evolved fears emerge spontaneously following an age-appropriate schedule. On this view, most fears manifest on the first encounter with the evolutionary-relevant target, with no need for independent cues of danger. However, a preexisting state of arousal or anxiety may sensitize the fear system and facilitate the consolidation of a phobic reaction. As a result, individuals who are higher in neuroticism and behavioral inhibition are also more likely to develop phobias (Gray, 1987; Menzies & Clarke, 1995). Other less obvious dimensions of individual differences may contribute as well; for example, there is evidence that the tendency to overestimate vertical distances in perceptual tasks predicts the intensity of fear of heights, not just in phobic patients but also in nonclinical controls (Jackson, 2009). Nonassociative models draw on the idea that, when facing potentially deadly threats, even a single learning episode can have catastrophic consequences. Boyer and Bergstrom (2011) noted that, in most cases, fear acquisition in childhood does not seem to depend on passive exposure to threatening stimuli. On the contrary, children spontaneously and actively search for specific threat cues in their environment, such as dark corners or traces of dangerous animals. This active process seems more consistent with genetically encoded templates than with associative learning.

Nonassociative models turn the classic account of phobias on its head. What is learned is not the fear—which is usually activated upon the first encounter with the target—but the *extinction* of fear, which brings about a sense of safety and control in presence of the target. In other words, phobias can be understood as failures of the normative process of fear extinction. In this vein, Sandseter and Kennair (2011) speculated that risky play is a crucial developmental mechanism by which children conquer their spontaneous fears. Risky play—for example involving heights, dangerous tools, or dangerous elements such as fire and water—combines controlled exposure to threats with positive emotions, heightened approach motivation, and a temporary suppression of anxiety. As children learn to cope effectively with various threats (and gain better coping skills as a result of physical and brain maturation), they gradually become less fearful and achieve a growing sense of mastery. According to these authors, not being able to engage in risky play may lead to protracted anxiety, even in individuals who have the mental and physical skills to cope effectively with danger. This hypothesis implicates a particular kind of mismatch in the origin of phobias: when risky play is prevented (for example by overprotective parents or risk-averse cultural norms), individuals may continue to avoid objects or situations that are no longer dangerous, with undesirable and potentially maladaptive consequences.

While prepared learning has been demonstrated in experimental situations, the biographical reports of phobic patients are generally more consistent with the nonassociative account (Kendler et al., 2002; Kennair, 2007; Menzies & Harris, 1997; Poulton & Menzies, 2002). Fears of heights and water show the strongest evidence of nonassociative origin (Bracha, 2006). However, distinguishing between sensitization and one-occasion learning can be extremely challenging, especially outside of the laboratory or when analyzing self-reported memories (Coelho & Purkis, 2009). It is probably reasonable to suggest that both types of processes are involved in the onset of common phobias (e.g., Öhman & Mineka, 2001); still, we do not know which pathway is the most prevalent in real-life situations and whether different types of evolved fears depend on somewhat different acquisition mechanisms.

Other Evolutionary Scenarios

The evolutionary models reviewed in this section deal primarily with the acquisition of fears. While this focus is appropriate for fear-inducing targets such as heights and snakes, it is inadequate to explain disgust-related phobias such as those for blood-injection-injury and small animals. As critics of prepared learning models have noted, most species of spiders are harmless to humans, and only 0.1% represent a significant threat (Faucher & Blanchette, 2011). The same argument applies even more strongly to insects, mice, and other animals in this category. Bracha (2006) speculated that phobias for insects and mice might have evolved as defenses against contagion, since these animals are common vectors of infectious diseases. While this hypothesis needs to be refined and tested, the idea that these phobias are functionally linked to avoidance of contamination is certainly consistent with the prominent role of aversion and disgust.

Disease avoidance may plausibly play a role in BII phobias as well, since blood is a powerful vector of contagion for a broad range of pathogens. Still, contamination risk alone does not explain the strong connection between BII phobia and vasovagal fainting. It is fair to say that fainting in BII phobias is very poorly understood from a biological standpoint. Bracha and colleagues (2005) proposed that fainting at the sight of blood or sharp objects may have helped women survive in ancestral wars by being taken captive instead of killed. This hypothesis is rather contrived, and data showing that women of reproductive age have a higher incidence of BII phobias than postmenopausal women (Bracha et al., 2007) are not sufficient to corroborate it. From another perspective, Diehl (2005) reviewed evidence that fainting after substantial blood loss facilitates clotting and increases survival, even in severely injured patients. He speculated that vasovagal fainting in BII patients may work as an anticipatory response to early indicators of potential blood loss. While this is an interesting suggestion, it is unclear whether the benefits of such a hair-trigger response are likely to outweigh its immediate costs. As noted by Marks (1988) three decades ago, we still know little about reactions to blood/injury cues in other animals. Of course, it is possible that vasovagal fainting is simply a dysfunction of the autonomic system, or the maladaptive extreme in a distribution of sensitivity to cues of potential injury (Marks, 1988; Page, 1994).

More generally, evolutionary research on phobias would greatly benefit from explicit mathematical models of fear acquisition. The principle that evolved fears combine genetically encoded (prior) information about recurrent threats with cues from the immediate environment—whether in the form of aversive cues or anxiety-driven sensitization—makes phobias an ideal target for Bayesian modeling. An evolutionary Bayesian approach might help elucidate the costs and benefits of associative versus nonassociative processes, evaluate their relative plausibility, and hopefully suggest critical empirical tests to distinguish between the two accounts.

Another promising direction for research is to focus on specific fears and explore the possibility of meaningful subtypes within the same descriptive category. For example, Bracha (2006) suggested that dentist phobias may actually comprise a mixture of three distinct conditions: an evolutionarily ancient, innate fear of drowning, a more recently evolved fear of sharp objects, and idiosyncratic fears acquired through conditioning during painful or traumatic dental procedures. The evolutionary hypotheses compiled by Bracha (2006) are not all plausible or well supported; however, the general point that different fears—or even different variants of the same fear—may have divergent evolutionary histories spanning different "time depths" is a valid and heuristically powerful one. Isbell's snake detection theory (Isbell, 2009) provides a striking illustration of this principle. Based on phylogenetic and comparative evidence, Isbell argued that primates have evolved specialized mechanisms for the rapid detection of snakes; even more generally, snake detection seems to have shaped several peculiar features of the primate visual system (e.g., Isbell & Etting, 2017; Van Le et al., 2013). In the primate lineage, snakes have been a major threat for at least 100 millions of years—initially as predators of the small-sized ancestors of present-day mammals, and later as venomous animals capable of injuring or killing even large apes. Consistent with the theory, different species of primates show different reactions to snakes depending on how long they coexisted with venomous species over evolutionary time. Moreover, human studies have found that pictures of snakes capture attention more effectively than most other stimuli, including spiders; notably, the effect seems to be especially pronounced in women (Öhman et al., 2012). These findings support the idea that snakes occupy a privileged place in the hierarchy of human fear targets and suggest that the neural and psychological substrates of snake phobias may differ in important ways from those involved in other common fears.

FSD CLASSIFICATION

Specific phobias are easily classified as defense activation disorders. In adults, elevated neuroticism is the main personality correlate of phobic symptoms (Adams et al., 2014; Kendler et al., 2002; Kotov et al., 2010). Like other D-type conditions, phobias are associated with hyperactivation of the amygdala. Another brain region that shows increased activation in patients is the insula, which is involved in the regulation of the autonomic system but also in the experience of disgust. In contrast, prefrontal areas tend to become *less* active during the presentation of phobic stimuli (Del Casale et al., 2012; Etkin & Wager, 2007). While most phobias can be regarded as part of the fear cluster together with panic, agoraphobia, and SAD/APD, small animal and BII phobias are primarily characterized by aversion and disgust, and may be best regarded as a distinct category within the broader family of defense activation disorders.

18

Panic and Agoraphobia

OVERVIEW

Panic attacks are dramatic episodes in which a surge of autonomic activity is accompanied by rapidly escalating levels of fear and distress. Within minutes, the person experiences a progression of increasingly alarming bodily symptoms—accelerated heart rate, palpitations, sweating, trembling or shaking, shortness of breath, nausea, dizziness, and sometimes fainting. These symptoms are accompanied by feelings of impending danger and an overwhelming urge to escape. Dissociative experiences are not uncommon during panic, and many patients experience fears of dying, losing control, or "going crazy." Panic attacks are often precipitated by particular events or situations, but can also occur unexpectedly without an obvious external trigger. About one-third of patients experience nocturnal attacks in which they suddenly wake up in a state of panic.

To properly frame the content of this chapter, it is crucial to distinguish between *panic* as an evolved defensive reaction, *panic attacks* as a common psychiatric symptom, and *panic disorder* as a chronic condition marked by recurrent panic attacks, worry, and distress. From a motivational standpoint, panic is a specific mode of operation of the fear system and can be understood as a defense against imminent, life-threatening danger. More specifically, panic is an extreme escape response marked by a combination of rapid sympathetic activation and parasympathetic withdrawal (Arch et al., 2013; Hamm et al., 2016; Nesse, 1987; Preter & Klein, 2008). In mammals, panic reactions can be triggered by a diverse range of threats—predator attacks, aggression by conspecifics, separation from parents, suffocation, and acute visceral pain. While anxiety, hypervigilance, and attentive immobility are deployed *before* actual contact with the source of threat, panic is specifically triggered when contact is imminent. The shift from anxiety and fear to panic is underlain by a rapid neurobiological switch between two distinct control systems. Anxiety and attentive freezing are controlled by a limbic network that includes the amygdala, hippocampus, anterior cingulate cortex (ACC), and ventromedial prefrontal cortex (VMPFC). In contrast, panic is mediated by specific nuclei in the periaqueductal gray (PAG), which in turn receive inputs from the hypothalamus and amygdala. During the panic response, activation of PAG nuclei is accompanied by inhibition of the amygdala (Canteras & Graeff, 2014; Hamm et al., 2016; Mobbs et al., 2007, 2009; Preter & Klein, 2008).

An important feature of panic attacks is their strong comorbidity with various physical health conditions—mainly cardiovascular, respiratory, and gastrointestinal diseases, diabetes, and pain-related disorders such as migraine and mastalgia (Goodwin et al., 2014; Preter & Klein, 2008, 2014; Schmidt et al., 2014). Poor physical health is a major predictor of panic attacks, and people with panic disorder are more at risk for developing future conditions. As noted earlier, panic can be triggered not only by external threats but also by introceptive cues of danger, such as acute chest pain and potential suffocation cues such as hypoxia (low blood oxygen), hypercapnia (high blood CO_2), or rising lactate concentrations. Suffocation detectors are present in various brain structures, including the hypothalamus and PAG; administering CO_2 or lactate to some patients directly triggers a panic attack. The bottom line is that, in a subgroup of patients, respiratory dysfunctions and/or a hypersensitive "suffocation alarm system" are critically involved in the etiology of panic (Klein, 1993; Preter & Klein, 2008).

In addition to respiratory dysfunctions and other physical conditions, a number of cognitive/behavioral variables have been linked to the risk of panic attacks. Some of those variables are not specific to panic—for example, patients with panic disorder tend to overgeneralize fear associations to nonthreatening stimuli, a feature shared with generalized anxiety disorder (GAD), posttraumatic stress disorder (PTSD), and other D-type conditions (Dunsmoor & Paz, 2015). Patients also tend to interpret bodily sensations in catastrophic ways; catastrophic appraisal further amplifies the initial sensations and may trigger a positive feedback loop, ending in a full-blown attack (Clark, 1986). Common responses to panic include cognitive avoidance and "safety behaviors"—carrying anxiolytic medications, bringing along a trusted person who can assist in case of an attack, and so on. These coping strategies attenuate symptoms in the short term; unfortunately, they also contribute to stabilize the disorder by preventing the extinction of conditioned fear to the places and situations that have been associated with panic (see Arch et al., 2013; Schmidt et al., 2014).

Panic Disorder

Panic is an extremely common symptom, and more than 80% of patients with anxiety-related conditions report having experienced at least one panic attack. A DSM diagnosis of panic disorder requires a history of recurrent, unexpected attacks (that is, at least some attacks must occur without obvious triggers) and a state of persistent worry about additional episodes. Indeed, "fear of fear" becomes the primary concern for many people with this disorder. Patients may become intensely concerned about physical or mental health risks (having a heart attack, going crazy), begin to avoid potential triggering situations, and become hypervigilant to subtle initial signs of panic, thus reinforcing a vicious cycle of anxiety and fear (American Psychiatric Association, 2013; Arch et al., 2013; Schmidt et al., 2014).

The heritability of panic disorder is 40–50%, a value that lies in the upper range for defense activation conditions (Arch et al., 2013; Hettema et al., 2001). This overall genetic predisposition reflects at least two distinct sources: one is nonspecific and shared with neuroticism, the other is specific to panic and underlies individual differences in the sensitivity to suffocation cues (e.g., CO_2 concentration; Battaglia et al., 2014). Starting from puberty, females are at higher risk than males for panic attacks. The overall female-to-male ratio for panic disorder is about 2:1, but the imbalance increases with increasing severity of the symptoms and is especially marked in panic disorder with agoraphobia (see next section). Comorbidity rates are high and span a wide range of conditions—mainly GAD, social anxiety disorder (SAD), and phobias but also depression, bipolar disorders (BDs), and personality disorders. Substance use (particularly alcohol) is also very common in patients with panic disorder, often as a self-medication strategy to control the symptoms (Arch et al., 2013; Goodwin et al., 2014; Schmidt et al., 2014).

Agoraphobia

Agoraphobia is defined by persistent fear or anxiety about open or confined spaces. The most common phobic situations are open spaces such as parking lots and bridges, enclosed spaces such as shops and theaters, public transportation, being in the middle of a crowd, or simply being outside of the home alone. These situations evoke anxious thoughts that escape will be difficult (or there will be no one to help) in case the patient happens to develop panic symptoms, fall, or get sick. To reach the threshold for a diagnosable phobia, the fear must be out of proportion to the plausible consequences of the event, and the patient must actively avoid phobic situations or—if absolutely necessary—endure them with intense distress (American Psychiatric Association, 2013).

Many patients with panic disorder develop agoraphobia as a secondary response to panic attacks. They begin to avoid situations similar to those associated with panic and end up increasingly restricting their movements as attacks recur. In these cases, the onset of agoraphobia can be explained as the result of fear conditioning to places, triggered by the perception of life-threatening danger that accompanies panic attacks (Klein, 1981; Nesse, 1987; Schmidt et al., 2014). While agoraphobia in clinical samples is almost always associated with panic, community studies indicate that agoraphobia without panic is not uncommon (e.g., Andrews & Slade, 2002). Some authors have that argued agoraphobia without panic does not arise from fear conditioning but from a specific, innate aversion to open spaces found in a minority of people (Bracha et al., 2006). Intriguingly, the link between agoraphobia and panic may run deeper than a simple associative learning account would suggest. As I discuss in more detail later, separation anxiety in childhood is a common precursor of panic attacks later in life; in some people, early experiences of perceived vulnerability and abandonment seem to pave the way for both panic and agoraphobia (Battaglia et al., 2014; Preter & Klein, 2008, 2014).

Neurobiological Correlates

The neurobiology of panic is complex and involves the interplay of multiple neural and endocrine systems. While panic is always accompanied by strong sympathetic activation, the data on HPA axis functioning are inconsistent, and there is some evidence that cortisol secretion is reduced during panic (Arch et al., 2013; Paul et al., 2014). Suppression of the HPA axis can be adaptive when the panic response is induced by suffocation cues: since cortisol increases oxygen consumption, HPA activation is counterproductive when the organism is struggling with oxygen shortage (Preter & Klein, 2014). The activity of panic circuits in the PAG is suppressed by inhibitory GABAergic neurons; accordingly, reduced GABAergic activity is a robust correlate of panic disorder (and many other D-type conditions). Progesterone stimulates GABA secretion, and the risk of panic attacks in women is highest in the days leading up to menstruation, when progesterone levels drop rapidly (Arch et al., 2013; Gururajan et al., 2016; Kalueff & Nutt, 2007; Lovick, 2014; Möhler, 2012). Endogenous opioids also inhibit panic, both by reducing separation distress (Chapter 2) and by directly suppressing the activity of suffocation detectors in the PAG. In all likelihood, the opioid system is a key neurobiological link between panic, agoraphobia, and pain-related conditions (Canteras & Graeff, 2014; Preter & Klein, 2008, 2014).

A great deal of neurobiological research on panic has focused on serotonin (5-HT). Animal studies have identified serotonergic projections to the PAG that inhibit fight–flight responses and suppress the activity of panic circuits. Antidepressants that target serotonergic function are effective in reducing panic attacks; moreover, lowering serotonin through pharmacological manipulations increases sensitivity to CO_2 and other panic-inducing molecules in at least some patients. Based on this evidence, the current consensus is that elevated serotonergic activity promotes anxiety but inhibits panic (Canteras & Graeff, 2014; Corchs et al., 2015; Hood et al., 2016; Paul et al., 2014). However, there are indications that the role of serotonin may be more complex. To begin, there are mounting doubts on whether the long-term effect of antidepressants is to increase or decrease brain 5-HT (Chapter 14). Some studies have found evidence that brain 5-HT is elevated in patients with panic disorder, and that panic attacks can be triggered by acute *increases* in serotonergic signaling. Moreover, molecules that induce panic often increase anxiety as well, which is inconsistent with a rigid view of anxiety and panic as functionally incompatible reactions (Bell & Nutt, 1998; Esler et al., 2007; Maron & Shlik, 2006). While the implications of these findings are still unclear, the association between panic and low serotonin may not be as robust as presently assumed—or, alternatively, it may apply only to a subset of patients, most likely those with hypersensitive suffocation detectors.

Development and Course

Panic disorder and agoraphobia are rare in childhood but increase in frequency after puberty. The onset of these disorders shows a first peak between late adolescence and early adulthood and a second one much later, around 40–50 years of age. Some of the developmental precursors of panic—such as shyness and inhibited temperament—are shared with other D-type disorders in the fear cluster. The connection with separation anxiety is more specific: children diagnosed with separation anxiety disorder are at higher risk for panic disorder later in life, and the two conditions are genetically correlated. Early separations and parental losses also predict the occurrence of headaches in adulthood, underscoring the link between panic and pain sensitivity. Consistent with the idea that opioids modulate the activity of panic circuits in the PAG, there is initial evidence of a G×E interaction in which the genetic hypersensitivity to CO_2 is amplified by early separations and other family stressors, leading to heightened risk of panic attacks (Battaglia et al., 2014; Beesdo-Baum & Knappe, 2014; Goodwin et al., 2014; Kossowsky et al., 2013; Preter & Kline, 2014; Roberson-Nay et al., 2012; Schmidt et al., 2014).

In most cases, patients with panic disorder remember an identifiable stressor at the time of the first attack. Not infrequently, the first attack occurs after the person has used alcohol or other drugs, either during acute intoxication or during withdrawal. This contributes to explain the high rate of co-occurrence between panic and substance use. Panic disorder is extremely debilitating, with cascading negative consequences on the person's social and occupational life. The outcomes are especially severe when panic is associated with agoraphobia. If untreated, panic disorder is usually chronic, with phases of waxing and waning but low rates of spontaneous recovery (American Psychiatric Association, 2013; Arch et al., 2013; Schmidt et al., 2014).

Risk Factors

To summarize the findings discussed in the previous sections, panic and agoraphobia are associated with early stress and adversity, with a specific role for separations and parental losses in childhood. In addition to psychosocial factors, various types of physical conditions can increase the risk of panic attacks. Respiratory diseases and smoking play an especially prominent role because of their impact on suffocation detectors. Finally, drug use in adolescence and adulthood contributes to trigger the onset of panic in a proportion of patients. All these risk factors seem to work in interaction with individual predispositions, including genetic differences in the sensitivity to introceptive alarm signals.

EVOLUTIONARY MODELS

A remarkable aspect of the neurobiological literature on panic is the degree to which it is informed by adaptive thinking. The idea that panic is an adaptive defense against immediate, life-threatening danger is widely accepted: both human and animal studies are grounded in a functional understanding of panic as a component of the fight–flight response (e.g., Hamm et al., 2016; Paul et al., 2014). While panic disorder as defined in the DSM is almost certainly dysfunctional (Kennair, 2007), panic attacks probably lie on a continuum of functionality and, in many instances, may be best understood as maladaptive outcomes (false alarms) of a sensitive but intact protective mechanism. The fact that patients with panic disorder experience higher mortality due to cardiovascular and other conditions (Schmidt et al., 2014) suggests that, even if chronic panic is not a useful response, the underlying mechanisms are sensitive to internal states that signal potential health threats.

While biological ideas are implicit in much of the literature, only a handful of authors have explicitly considered the nature of panic and agoraphobia from an evolutionary perspective (Bracha, 2006; Bracha et al., 2006; Nesse, 1987). These contributions do not change the basic picture but suggest some intriguing hypotheses that—if supported—could extend and refine existing models of panic. For example, Nesse (1987) speculated that human defensive systems have evolved to be especially sensitive to some types of situations, including open landscapes that offer no safe refuge and closed-in spaces with the potential for entrapment. Exposure to these situations should automatically lower the threshold for panic reactions, not only in patients but also in healthy individuals. Bracha (2006; Bracha et al., 2006) took this concept further and proposed that patients with simple agoraphobia (i.e., agoraphobia without a history of panic attacks) should be specifically sensitive to the absence of trees in the landscape; conversely, the presence of trees should have an anxiolytic effect on people with agoraphobic tendencies. This prediction is based on the idea that humans and their ancestors used trees as a major escape route from predators until their recent expansion into sparsely wooded habitats (e.g., the African savannah). Even without embracing the strong version of this hypothesis, there is no doubt that trees have been a source of refuge and hiding throughout most of our history. It is not implausible that trees (and, more generally, features of the landscape that suggest opportunities for retreat or escape) may have subtle anti-agoraphobic effects. An evolutionary perspective also contributes to explain the higher female prevalence of panic disorder and agoraphobia. On average, women are more physically vulnerable than men and less able to defend themselves against attacks. Accordingly, it is adaptive for them to be more sensitive to potential cues of vulnerability and entrapment, and display a lower threshold for the activation of escape behaviors (Nesse, 1987).

Other Evolutionary Scenarios

Somewhat paradoxically, panic has received little attention within evolutionary psychopathology compared with other defense activation conditions such as depression and specific phobias. However, existing models of panic and agoraphobia are still incomplete and could benefit from a deeper evolutionary analysis. To illustrate, Cantor (2005) pointed to the importance of refuging as a specific defensive strategy in the context of PTSD (Chapter 16). Refuging seems just as relevant to panic and agoraphobia—most patients perceive their home as a safe place and become increasingly reluctant to leave it—but it is not included in current models of these disorders. Agoraphobia also shows moderate assortative mating, with correlations between partners of .20–.30 (Nordsletten et al., 2016). Assortative mating for traits that predispose to agoraphobia likely contributes to increase the risk of maladaptive expression levels in the offspring.

Another limitation of existing models is the lack of a clear rationale for the serotonergic inhibition of suffocation-induced panic. The current understanding is that 5-HT simultaneously promotes attentive immobility (freezing) and inhibits escape (Paul et al., 2014). However, it remains unclear why it would be adaptive to specifically reduce one's sensitivity to suffocation cues during freezing. An intriguing and unexplored possibility is that attentive immobility may be associated with the reflexive interruption of breathing. By temporarily suppressing or slowing down respiration, animals can avoid acoustic detection by attackers and simultaneously improve their sensitivity to subtle noises. In this scenario, inhibition of suffocation detectors during freezing would play a highly specific adaptive role: to allow temporary respiratory suppression while preventing a self-induced panic response. If the serotonergic inhibition of panic turned out to be restricted to suffocation cues, a life history approach would suggest novel hypotheses on the etiology of panic in different subgroups of patients. For example, hypersensitivity to suffocation cues might be more common in patients who experience panic in conjunction with fast spectrum disorders, to the extent that the latter are associated with reduced serotonin levels.

FSD CLASSIFICATION

Panic and agoraphobia are clear-cut examples of defense activation disorders in the fear cluster. Like other D-type conditions, they are associated with elevated neuroticism and—to a smaller extent—with lower conscientiousness, agreeableness, and extraversion (Kotov et al., 2010; Watson & Naragon-Gainey, 2014). Together with some evidence of earlier menarche in girls who develop panic symptoms (Mendle et al., 2007), these data are consistent with the general idea that D-type conditions occur relatively more often at the fast end of the life history continuum.

19

Social Anxiety Disorder

OVERVIEW

Social anxiety disorder (SAD) or "social phobia" is marked by persistent fears and/or anxieties about social situations that expose the person to scrutiny by others. Social anxiety symptoms fall into three main dimensions: *social interaction* (e.g., meeting strangers, dating), *observation/close scrutiny* (e.g., eating in public, urinating in public restrooms), and *public performance* (public speaking, singing). About half of patients have social fears that generalize to many contexts, while the other half tend to be fearful of one specific type of situation. The single most common fear is that of public speaking or performing; accordingly, the DSM-5 recognizes a "performance only" subtype of SAD for patients whose anxiety is restricted to public speaking or other types of performance. Social anxiety is rooted in fears of rejection and negative evaluation—patients are afraid that others will think that they are stupid, anxious, weak, boring, or crazy. The fears experienced by SAD patients are clearly out of proportion to the plausible consequences of a mistake and strong enough to prompt chronic avoidance behaviors. When patients are forced to endure a threatening situation, they respond with fear and distress; common somatic symptoms of social anxiety include blushing, sweating, tremors, and "hot flushes" (American Psychiatric Association, 2013; Cox et al., 2008; Hofmann et al., 2014; Iza et al., 2014).

Taxometric and epidemiological studies show that social anxiety symptoms are arranged on a continuum of severity, with SAD patients at one extreme. These findings indicate that the diagnostic cutoff employed by the DSM is essentially arbitrary (Crome et al., 2010; Hetem et al., 2010; Ruscio & Meron, 2010). However, clinical social anxiety is not just an exaggerated version of shyness. People with SAD display some characteristic patterns of thought and behavior that give rise to self-reinforcing cycles and contribute to maintain the symptoms. Specifically, socially anxious patients harbor a deep sense of inadequacy and judge their own performance very harshly, even though they often have good social skills and do not actually make more mistakes than other people. They expect that others will judge them just as harshly and will focus on their mistakes and embarrassing bodily symptoms (blushing, sweating). When they are in social situations they fear, SAD patients become intensely focused on their own anxiety and on potential cues of rejection from others; as a result, they find it hard to pay attention to the positive feedback they receive. Their preoccupied, inhibited behavior may lead others to perceive them as strange or uninteresting, further reinforcing their sense of incompetence and prompting rumination and self-criticism. Avoidance of threatening situations interferes with fear extinction and prevents patients from experimenting with more effective coping strategies. In SAD patients, memories of frightening or humiliating social episodes often show the intrusive, repetitive quality associated with posttraumatic stress (Cremers & Roelofs, 2016; Hofmann et al., 2014; Ledley et al., 2013; Sloman et al., 2006).

The motivational signature of social anxiety is the perceived failure of status and affiliation goals, which triggers feelings of shame, embarrassment, exclusion, and defeat. Intriguingly, there is evidence that SAD patients also experience frequent anger but do not express or communicate it to others (Ledley et al., 2013). Suppressed anger may be interpreted as a symptom of involuntary subordination, in line with evolutionary models of social anxiety (see later discussion).

The heritability of SAD is about 30% in males and up to 50% in females. The genetic factors that predispose to SAD largely overlap with those underlying neuroticism and low extraversion (Cremers & Roelofs, 2016; Ledley et al., 2013; López-Solà et al., 2014). While females are somewhat more at risk of SAD than males, the female-to-male ratio for this condition is relatively balanced (less than 1.5:1). On average, women report more public speaking fears, whereas men tend to show more generalized symptoms (Hofmann et al., 2014; McLean et al., 2011; McNeil, 2010; Valentiner et al., 2014).

Social anxiety co-occurs with a broad range of mental disorders. Avoidant personality disorder (APD) overlaps substantially with SAD at the phenotypic and genetic levels, as discussed in Chapter 12. In addition to APD, the highest comorbidity rates occur with other defense activation disorders: specific phobias and depression (particularly with atypical symptoms), panic, agoraphobia, and generalized anxiety disorder (GAD), as well as with obsessive-compulsive disorder (OCD, which has both D-type and a S-type variants; see Chapter 20). SAD is also frequently comorbid with autism, psychosis, and eating disorders (Hofmann et al., 2014; Wenzel, 2010). There is evidence that SAD in middle childhood and adolescence predisposes to later depression by increasing the risk of social rejection and isolation. When depression and SAD occur together, they both tend to become more chronic, again suggesting a self-reinforcing cycle (Jacobson & Newman, 2016; Kessler et al., 2014; Langer & Rodebaugh, 2014; Pickard et al., 2017). The relation between SAD and psychosis is less straightforward. On the one hand, some patients with schizophrenia experience the diagnosis as a major blow to their social status, triggering social anxiety as a secondary condition (Birchwood et al., 2007). On the other hand, the onset of social anxiety not infrequently precedes that of paranoid delusions, and a large proportion of individuals at high risk for psychosis (but without a diagnosis of schizophrenia) meet the diagnostic criteria for SAD. In the psychosis spectrum, social anxiety may be a prodromal manifestation of paranoia or may even contribute to exacerbate the development of paranoid symptoms (Gajwani et al., 2013; Veras et al., 2015).

Substance use (typically alcohol) is very common in patients with SAD. The use of alcohol typically begins after the onset of social anxiety, consistent with a self-medication strategy (Hofmann et al., 2014; Ledley et al., 2013). Alcohol is a powerful anxiolytic; in SAD patients, drinking considerably reduces tension and facilitates positive social interactions. However, the price for these short-term benefits is the risk of escalation in the frequency and amount of drinking, which may worsen the anxiety symptoms in the long run (Battista et al., 2010; Bulley et al., 2016). In addition to self-medication, the high comorbidity with substance use is partly explained by the existence of a subgroup of SAD patients with high levels of impulsivity and risk-taking, who are strongly predisposed to use alcohol and other drugs (Nicholls et al., 2014).

Development and Course

The onset of SAD usually occurs between middle childhood and adolescence, when social competition intensifies and status and acceptance become pressing concerns. The main developmental precursors are inhibited temperament, shyness, and separation anxiety. While the onset of SAD can be gradual, about half of the patients remember a specific humiliating event that triggered the sudden onset of anxiety symptoms. Not infrequently, the affective experiences associated with the triggering event are similar to those reported by patients with posttraumatic stress symptoms. Peer victimization in childhood and adolescence are associated with higher risk of SAD; the evidence suggests a bidirectional relation in which social anxiety further increases victimization (American Psychiatric Association, 2013; Clauss & Blackford, 2012; Ledley et al., 2013; Ollendick & Hirshfeld-Becker, 2002; Valentiner et al., 2014).

The prevalence of SAD peaks around 20–25 years of age, then declines throughout adulthood. Symptoms also tend to become somewhat milder with advancing age. In diagnosed patients, the disorder tends to be chronic and persistent, with low rates of spontaneous remission (particularly in the generalized subtype); however, community studies show a higher rate of recovery than clinical samples (Goodwin et al., 2014; Hofmann et al., 2014; Kessler et al., 1998; Miloyan et al., 2014; Valentiner et al., 2014; Vriends et al., 2007). Unsurprisingly, a diagnosis of SAD is associated with a host of negative outcomes in the social, sexual, and occupational spheres—including fewer friends, lower chances of marrying, diminished work productivity, and high unemployment rates. Suicide risk is also elevated, especially when social anxiety coexists with depression (Hofmann et al., 2014; Langer & Rodebaugh, 2014; Lecrubier et al., 2000; Ledley et al., 2013).

Risk Factors

Epidemiological studies show a robust negative correlation between socioeconomic status and the prevalence of SAD. It is easy to see how low SES may exacerbate social anxiety by lowering one's perceived rank. Conversely, the lower work performance and higher unemployment rate of SAD patients inevitably contribute to reduce their income and occupational status (Bulley et al., 2016; Kessler et al., 1998; Patel et al., 2002). Parental overprotection, family conflict, and other relational stressors in childhood have been found to predict increased social anxiety later in life. Early difficulties with social and communication skills also increase the risk of SAD and contribute to its comorbidity with autism spectrum disorders (Ledley et al., 2013; Ollendick & Hirshfeld-Becker, 2002; Pickard et al., 2017).

EVOLUTIONARY MODELS

From an evolutionary perspective, social anxiety is linked to competition for status and acceptance. Socially anxious behaviors are functionally related to depression and implement a risk-averse strategy designed to prevent further status losses and exclusion from the group (Maner & Kenrick, 2010; Marks & Nesse, 1994). On this view, SAD represents the exaggerated version of the normal submissive response to potential risk of ostracism. Accordingly, current evolutionary models of SAD draw on the same conceptual framework of social competition models of depression (Chapter 14; Langer & Rodebaugh, 2014; Price, 2013; Sloman et al., 2006). The link with depression is well supported by the evidence. Depression and SAD are highly comorbid, and depressogenic perceptions of involuntary subordination and social defeat also predict social anxiety symptoms and submissive nonverbal behavior (Langer & Rodebaugh, 2014; Sturman, 2011). Some data indicate that SAD patients have low testosterone levels, consistent with defeat and subordination (Giltay et al., 2012).

The main limitation of standard evolutionary approaches is their incomplete account of the relations between SAD and psychosis. Evolutionary work on this topic has been motivated by the idea that receiving a diagnosis of schizophrenia is a threat to one's social status (Birchwood et al., 2006). As I noted earlier, however, social anxiety in the psychosis spectrum may be functionally connected to paranoid ideation at a deeper level. A better understanding of this connection may shed light on the evolutionary meaning of negative symptoms and on the possible role of social competition in the etiology of schizophrenia (Abed & Abbas, 2011, 2014).

Most evolutionary scholars argue that mild social anxiety is potentially adaptive, but regard SAD as a harmful dysfunction with damaging consequences for fitness. As it has been repeatedly noted in the literature, modern societies have a number of novel features that may induce evolutionary mismatches with our evolved status mechanisms—large anonymous groups, routine contact with strangers, marked socioeconomic inequality, and weakened ties with kin-based networks (Gilbert, 2006; Horwitz & Wakefield, 2012; Maner & Kenrick, 2010). In addition, Maner and Kenrick (2010) speculated that pathological levels of social anxiety may occasionally arise from unavoidable tradeoffs in the design of social defenses or as maladaptive levels of trait expression in people with extreme personality profiles (e.g., very high neuroticism and low extraversion). As with other types of anxiety, incorrect beliefs and expectations formed on the basis of early experience may become especially hard to revise because they prompt self-reinforcing avoidance behaviors (Meacham & Bergstrom, 2016). Interestingly, there is evidence of a certain degree of assortative mating for SAD, with correlations of .20–.30 between partners (Nordsletten et al., 2016).

Other Evolutionary Scenarios

Drawing an analogy with other phobias, Öhman and colleagues (1985) suggested that SAD may result from fear conditioning to social situations; specifically, rejecting or angry facial expressions may act as an evolutionary-relevant stimulus for the rapid acquisition of social fears. Indeed, a number of studies have shown that—similar to snakes and spiders—angry faces (particularly of adult males) trigger rapid detection and tend to produce strong fear conditioning (Mallan et al., 2013; Öhman, 2009; Öhman et al., 2012). However, it is still unclear whether this kind of prepared learning plays a role in the real-world etiology of SAD.

FSD CLASSIFICATION

According to the FSD taxonomy, SAD is a defense activation disorder in the fear cluster (together with APD, most specific phobias, panic, and agoraphobia). The combination of high neuroticism and low extraversion is the main personality correlate of social anxiety; in addition, SAD patients tend to have somewhat lower conscientiousness than controls when taken as a group (Kotov et al., 2010; Spinhoven et al., 2014). This negative association with conscientiousness might reflect the existence of a subgroup of socially anxious people with fast life history profiles characterized by impulsivity, risk-taking, and strong approach motivation (Nicholls et al., 2014).

Neurobiology

To a large extent, the neurobiology of SAD overlaps with that of specific phobias. The most robust brain correlate of social anxiety is hyperactivation of the amygdala and insula; neural activity is also increased in prefrontal regions and in the anterior cingulate cortex (ACC). Public speaking tasks stimulate a strong sympathetic and HPA response in many patients with SAD (Brühl et al., 2014; Cremers & Roelofs, 2016; Etkin & Wager, 2007); also, social anxiety in women has been associated with low progesterone levels in a number of studies (Duffy et al., 2017; Maner & Kenrick, 2010; Maner et al., 2010). There is some evidence that social anxiety is associated with upregulation of the default mode network (Cremers & Roelofs, 2016). While this activation pattern has been interpreted as evidence of the patients' self-focused absorption, the high comorbidity between SAD and psychotic symptoms might also contribute to explain the finding. The data concerning serotonin, dopamine, and oxytocin are still inconclusive, owing in part to the small size of the available studies (Cremers & Roelofs, 2016; Neumann & Slattery, 2016). From a life history perspective, one would expect these neurotransmitters to correlate more strongly with different personality and comorbidity profiles in SAD patients (e.g., reduced serotonergic signaling in impulsive patients; elevated oxytocin in psychosis spectrum patients) rather than with social anxiety per se.

20

Obsessive-Compulsive Disorder

OVERVIEW

Patients with obsessive-compulsive disorder (OCD) experience a distressing lack of control over their own thoughts and actions. *Obsessions* are intrusive, persistent, and recurrent mental contents—thoughts, images, impulses—that are experienced as unwanted and typically cause intense anxiety, discomfort, or disgust. For example, a person may start having persistent thoughts of being contaminated after touching a door handle in a public place, a perceived urge to harm his or her child, or intrusive sexual images perceived as immoral or revolting. Obsessions usually trigger *compulsions*, that is, repetitive behaviors (e.g., washing hands) or mental acts (e.g., praying, repeating words) through which the person tries to reduce distress or prevent a catastrophic outcome (contracting a disease, harming the child, and so on).

To qualify as OCD symptoms, compulsions must be clearly excessive or lack a realistic connection to the feared outcome. A patient may feel the need to wash his or her hands over and over again, or for a specific number of times; he or she may believe that anything that has been touched by "contaminated" hands is now also a source of contamination in an infinite chain of contagion. Patients may be more or less aware of the unrealistic, excessive quality of their compulsions. Not infrequently, the person's level of insight fluctuates dramatically—actions that feel compelling while they are being performed may look absurd in retrospect. OCD patients often try to resist compulsions, especially in the early stage of the disorder; with time, compulsive actions become increasingly automatic, and subjective resistance tends to dissipate. While performing compulsions, many patients report characteristic "not just right" experiences: in addition to anxiety (or even instead of it) they feel a sharp sense of uneasiness, dissatisfaction, or incompleteness until things look or feel exactly the right way.

Although a diagnosis of OCD only requires the presence of obsessions *or* compulsions, more than 95% of patients experience both kinds of symptoms. In the DSM-5, OCD is classified as part of a broader category of "obsessive-compulsive and related disorders," which also includes hoarding disorder, hair-pulling and skin-picking disorders, and other conditions. A tic-related subtype of OCD can be diagnosed when patients also have a history of tic disorder (American Psychiatric Association, 2013; Clark & del Palacio González, 2014; Neer & Ragsdale, 2014).

Obsessions and compulsions cluster into four main dimensions. The first dimension combines contamination obsessions and cleaning compulsions; these symptoms show especially strong correlations with sensitivity to disgust, particularly of the pathogen-related kind. The second dimension comprises taboo or "forbidden" thoughts and checking compulsions. The content of taboo obsessions can be aggressive (harming self or others), sexual (e.g., immoral or disgusting sexual acts; ego-dystonic doubts about one's sexual orientation), or religious (blasphemous thoughts). The third dimension combines symmetry obsessions and compulsions of counting, repeating, ordering, and arranging. These symptoms are often associated with a high frequency of tics and not just right experiences. Fourth and finally, OCD patients may engage in *hoarding*—a failure to discard worthless items such as old clothes, magazines and newspapers, letters, and bills. The majority of people with OCD show a mixture of symptoms from multiple dimensions, both concurrently and in different phases of the disorder (Berger & Anaki, 2014; Berle & Phillips, 2006; Bloch et al., 2008; Coles & Ravid, 2016; David et al., 2009; Del Giudice et al., 2014*b*; Mataix-Cols et al., 2005; Olatunji et al., 2014, 2015; Pertusa et al., 2008; Tolin et al., 2006). The limited taxometric evidence suggests that most OCD symptoms are dimensional and exist on a continuum from normative variation to severe psychopathology (Haslam et al., 2005; Olatunji et al., 2008). Taboo thoughts are a possible exception: the partially taxonic quality of these symptoms may depend on their association with positive schizotypy. Hoarding symptoms also show evidence of discontinuity, which may reflect the underlying distinction between OCD and hoarding disorder (see later discussion).

From a genetic standpoint, obsessive-compulsive symptoms are about 40% heritable with no shared environmental effects. There is evidence of a common genetic factor—moderately correlated with neuroticism—that contributes to OCD symptoms across the board. Among the four dimensions described earlier, hoarding shows the least genetic overlap with the common factor, having more than 50% of unique genetic variance (Bergin et al., 2014; Iervolino et al., 2011; López-Solà et al., 2014; Mataix-Cols et al., 2013; Taylor, 2011*a*; van Grootheest et al., 2008). In general, deleterious mutations and copy number variations (CNVs) do not seem to contribute significantly to the etiology of OCD; however, one study has identified a specific variable region of DNA that is associated with risk for OCD, autism, and schizophrenia (McGrath et al., 2014).

Sex differences in the prevalence of OCD are small and inconsistent. Although community studies find higher rates in females, diagnosed patients are somewhat more likely to be male, suggesting that males are at higher risk of developing severe forms of obsessions and compulsions. Males are also consistently overrepresented in early-onset OCD, especially when the onset is in early or middle childhood (Calamari et al., 2011; Fontenelle & Hasler, 2008; Ruscio et al., 2010; Taylor, 2011*b*). More subtly, there are systematic sex differences in the specific types of symptoms reported by patients. Females experience more contamination obsessions and cleaning compulsions than males, which is unsurprising given their higher sensitivity to pathogen disgust. Sexual/religious obsessions and checking compulsions are more frequent in males, whereas aggressive obsessions are not consistently associated with sex (de Mathis et al., 2011; Hasler et al., 2005; Labad et al., 2008; Torresan et al., 2013). As I discuss more in detail later, the fact that males are markedly less sensitive to sexual disgust than females but report *more* sexual obsessions suggests that pathogen and sexual disgust play different roles in the etiology of obsessive symptoms.

Comorbidity patterns in OCD are complex and heterogeneous. To begin, OCD shows strong comorbidity with all kinds of defense activation conditions, from depression and generalized anxiety disorder (GAD) to panic, phobias, social anxiety disorder (SAD), and avoidant personality disorder (APD). At the same time, OCD co-occurs with both autism and psychosis spectrum disorders, including schizophrenia spectrum disorders (SSDs) and bipolar disorders (BDs) (Calamari et al., 2011; Koyuncu et al., 2010; Meier, Petersen et al., 2014; Meier et al., 2015; Timpano et al., 2012). Patients with autism spectrum disorder (ASD) tend to have more comorbid tics and more symptoms of symmetry/ordering, hoarding, and thought neutralization. Network analyses indicate that the symptom constellation of OCD and that of ASD are bridged mainly by counting, repeating, and not just right experiences (Bejerot, 2007; Cadman et al., 2015; Ivarsson & Melin, 2008; Ruzzano et al., 2015; Stewart et al., 2016). People with psychosis spectrum disorders show a somewhat elevated frequency of sexual/aggressive and symmetry obsessions, as well as neutralization, ordering, and hoarding compulsions (Calamari et al., 2011; Melca et al., 2015; Poyurovsky, 2015). Finally, the rate of co-occurrence between OCD and obsessive-compulsive personality disorder (OCPD) is 20–25%; patients with both diagnoses usually report high levels of not-just-right experiences, symmetry obsessions, and ordering, cleaning, and hoarding compulsions (de Reus & Emmelkamp, 2012; Garyfallos et al., 2010; Gordon et al., 2013; Melca et al., 2015; Starcevic et al., 2013).

OCD Subtypes

Autogenous vs. Reactive Obsessions

The distinction between *autogenous* and *reactive* obsessions is based on the combination of three features: content, form, and triggering conditions (Lee & Kwon, 2003; Lee, Lee et al., 2005). The content of autogenous obsessions largely overlaps with that of taboo thoughts: disturbing and often bizarre mental contents of an aggressive, sexual, or blasphemous nature. Autogenous obsessions usually consist of images or urges that are distressing or anxiety-provoking in their own right. They have no apparent trigger in the immediate environment or are triggered by remote, bizarre associative links. Reactive obsessions concern more realistic fears of contamination, mistakes, accidents, and dirt/disarray. Reactive obsessions are triggered by cues of potential threats, and tend to take the form of doubts and apprehensions rather than urges and intrusive images. In reactive obsessions, anxiety is directed at the possible consequences of one's actions rather than at the obsession itself.

To summarize, reactive obsessions share many features of worry (and correlate with the use of worry as a coping strategy), whereas autogenous obsessions have a quasi-psychotic quality (Belloch et al., 2006; He et al., 2014; Lee, Lee et al., 2005). Indeed, the frequency of autogenous obsessions correlates with positive schizotypy and subtle indices of psychotic thought, as well as with lower levels of moral and sexual disgust and elevated hostility. Reactive obsessions are associated with both schizotypal and autistic-like traits and are predicted by higher levels of pathogen disgust (Brakoulias et al., 2013; Del Giudice et al., 2014*b*; Lee & Telch, 2005, 2010; Lee, Kim et al., 2005; Suhr et al., 2006). While pathogen disgust seems to play a straightforward role in increasing the frequency of contamination-related reactive obsessions, low levels of moral and sexual disgust could indicate a certain disinhibition in the generation of unusual and "taboo" ideas, which may then crystallize into full-blown autogenous obsessions.

Patients with OCD can be distinguished based on the type of their most distressing obsession, which tends to remain stable over time. Nevertheless, a sizable proportion of patients report both autogenous and reactive obsessions, and the two dimensions are positively correlated (Belloch et al., 2010; Besiroglu et al., 2007; Kennair, 2014). All in all, the autogenous–reactive distinction may be more useful to discriminate between types of symptoms than between groups of patients.

Harm Prevention vs. Not Just Right Experiences

In the majority of patients, OCD symptoms are accompanied by anxiety and/or disgust, which reflect the activation of the security and disgust systems. Compulsions are typically triggered by the perception of potential threats and directed at preventing catastrophic outcomes, whether external (contamination, accidents) or brought about by oneself (committing violence, sinning and going to hell). While standard accounts of OCD emphasize the role of harm prevention (or "harm avoidance"), some patients report symptoms that do not match this motivational template. In particular, symmetry obsessions and compulsions based on counting, repeating, ordering, and arranging are rarely accompanied by anxiety or disgust; instead, they are linked to feelings of discomfort, incompleteness, and imperfection. The underlying motivation is not to prevent harm but to get things "just right"; accordingly, compulsive rituals are not terminated by safety but by a sense of completion or perfection (Coles & Pietrefesa, 2008; Coles & Ravid, 2016; Radomsky & Rachman, 2004).

A considerable amount of evidence converges on the existence of a specific subgroup of patients characterized by a predominance of symmetry, repeating, and ordering symptoms that are primarily motivated by not just right feelings. These patients are likely to be males with early-onset OCD and perfectionistic traits, and show a pattern of high comorbidity with OCPD, autism, and tics. Hoarding and cleaning symptoms are also fairly common in these patients, possibly as a result of the parsimony, thriftiness, and cleanliness associated with OCPD (Bejerot et al.,

2014; de Mathis et al., 2006; do Rosario-Campos et al., 2005; Garyfallos et al., 2010; Gordon et al., 2013; Melca et al., 2015; Nakatani et al., 2011; Nestadt et al., 2009; Ruzzano et al., 2015; Starcevic et al., 2013; Taylor, 2011*b*).

It is important to note that not just right symptoms overlap only in part with the symmetry/ordering dimension of OCD. The reason is that symmetry obsessions and counting or ordering compulsions can also be motivated by harm prevention in patients with bizarre thoughts or magical thinking. For example, a patient may become convinced that the house will fall down if some objects are not arranged in a specific order, or that repeating an action a certain number of times will magically prevent the death of a loved one. In these cases, anxiety is usually present, and the symptoms do not cluster with not just right experiences as they usually do (Coles & Pietrefesa, 2008). This alternative pathway accounts for the fact that elevated symmetry/ordering symptoms are also found in OCD patients with psychosis spectrum conditions, who typically show a high frequency of autogenous obsessions (taboo thoughts).

OCD vs. Hoarding Disorder

Severe hoarding was traditionally regarded as a subtype of OCD, but with the DSM-5 it has been moved to a separate diagnostic category as *hoarding disorder*. There are very good reasons to treat hoarding without other obsessive-compulsive symptoms as a distinct condition. In contrast with OCD patients, hoarders show excessive acquisition (e.g., compulsive buying of unnecessary items), comparatively low levels of neuroticism and anxiety, and a profile of diffuse cognitive deficits—low IQ and academic achievement, slowness, inattention, and reduced executive functioning (including working memory). Unsurprisingly in light of these deficits, people with hoarding disorder tend to have extremely poor insight about their condition (Anholt et al., 2010; Grisham et al., 2005; Mataix-Cols et al., 2008; Pertusa et al., 2008, 2010; Tolin & Villavicencio, 2011; Woody et al., 2014). Hoarding symptoms show the lowest genetic correlations with other dimensions of OCD and seem to have partially distinct neural substrates (Iervolino et al., 2011; Nakao et al., 2014; Neer & Ragsdale, 2014). Of course, hoarding can be a genuine symptom of OCD when linked to an obsession: for example, a patient might have a compulsive need to read every page of a magazine before it can be discarded ("just right") or fear that something bad will happen if old bills are thrown away. In hoarding disorder, however, items are kept for intrinsic reasons—they are regarded as valuable, affectively significant, or potentially useful in the future (Pertusa et al., 2008, 2010). In the rest of this chapter, I will focus on OCD and will not discuss hoarding disorder any further.

Neurobiological Correlates

The core neurobiological substrate of OCD lies in the corticostriatal circuits that link frontal areas to the thalamus and subthalamic nucleus (STN) through the dorsal and ventral striatum (Gillan & Robbins, 2014; Neer & Ragsdale, 2014;

Woody & Szechtman, 2011). The main excitatory loop connects the orbitofrontal cortex (OFC) and ventromedial prefrontal cortex (VMPFC) to the striatum, the striatum to the thalamus, and the thalamus back to frontal areas. A parallel top-down inhibitory pathway goes from the dorsolateral prefrontal cortex (DLPFC) to the striatum to the STN, which is a central node for motor inhibition (Saxena et al., 1998). The dorsal striatum plays a key role in habit formation and in the control of goal-directed behavior; medial frontal areas such as the OFC and VMPFC deal with action selection. In addition, the ventrolateral prefrontal cortex (VLPFC) and anterior cingulate cortex (ACC) contribute to arbitrate between different modes of behavioral control (e.g., habitual "stimulus-response" associations vs. planned, goal-directed actions; Lee et al., 2014). While not part of the main corticostriatal loops, the insula is involved in the experience of disgust (Berle & Phillips, 2006).

Patients with OCD show reduced gray matter volume in the cortical areas that perform action selection and monitoring, including the ACC, medial prefrontal cortex (MPFC), VLPFC, and DLPFC. There is also evidence of low connectivity between the VLPFC and other cortical and subcortical regions. In contrast, the dorsal and ventral striatum are enlarged. Hyperactivation of the insula and VLPFC is coupled with reduced activation of the ACC and MPFC, consistent with a lack of top-down inhibitory control on striatal regions (Carlisi et al., 2017; Gruner et al., 2016; Norman et al., 2016). While the evidence is still limited, some data suggest that different types of symptoms (for example, aggressive vs. sexual/religious obsessions) may correspond to somewhat distinct activation patterns within these circuits (Nakao et al., 2014).

Studies of neurotransmitters in OCD are still limited in size and number, and so far have not yielded robust generalizations. In part, this may depend on the functional heterogeneity of OCD symptoms—for example, harm prevention is likely to have a different set of correlates than not just right experiences. Findings on GABA and glutamate have been mixed and inconsistent; glutamatergic signaling might be reduced in the ACC but elevated in the striatum and OFC (Naaijen et al., 2016; Simpson, Shungu et al., 2012; Wu, Hanna et al., 2012). Alterations in glutamate and GABA pathways may contribute to explain the overlap between OCD and psychosis. Animal and pharmacological studies converge in suggesting a role for dopamine and serotonin, although the empirical results are similarly mixed. Again, it is quite possible that different symptom subtypes have somewhat different neurobiological signatures (Szechtman et al., 2017).

Cognitive and Computational Models

According to standard cognitive theories of OCD, patients engage in dysfunctional interpretations of normal intrusive phenomena that are experienced by most people without causing significant distress. By interpreting harmless intrusions as unacceptable evidence that they are "mad, bad, or dangerous", OCD patients set in motion a self-reinforcing loop of obsessions and compulsions. Paradoxically, attempts to suppress distressing thoughts make them even more salient and persistent. At the same time, ruminations and worry about intrusions further increase anxiety and catastrophizing; the resulting negative mood reinforces the patients' feelings that something is wrong, prompting the repetition of compulsive behaviors (Davey et al., 2003; Rachman, 1997; Salkovskis, 1999).

Cognitive research on OCD has identified three main categories of beliefs that contribute to the etiology and maintenance of the symptoms (Calkins et al., 2013; Clark & del Palacio González, 2014; Neer & Ragsdale, 2014). The first is perfectionism/intolerance of uncertainty; this trait is particularly elevated in OCPD (Chapter 12) and may contribute to the onset of not just right experiences. The second is inflated responsibility, which in turn is linked to the propensity to experience guilt. A considerable amount of research has found correlations between guilt and obsessive-compulsive symptoms; moreover, inducing guilt in healthy participants increases obsessive-like doubts, not just right experiences, washing, and checking. In particular, "deontological" guilt (i.e., guilt about violating moral rules) seems to be an especially powerful trigger of OCD symptoms. Both perfectionism and inflated responsibility are elevated in patients with reactive obsessions (D'Olimpio & Mancini, 2014; Mancini & Gangemi, 2006; Mancini et al., 2008; Moulding et al., 2007; Shapiro & Stewart, 2011).

The third category comprises inflated beliefs about the importance of thoughts and the need to control them. The most important member of this category is *thought–action fusion*, the belief that thinking about an action or event is equivalent to carrying out that action, either in a moral sense (bad thoughts are just as reprehensible as bad actions) or because the thought will literally bring about a feared event (e.g., thinking that someone might die will cause the person to die). Beliefs about overimportance of thoughts and thought control are more frequent in highly religious people and mediate the observed association between religiosity and OCD. Thought–action fusion overlaps with magical thinking and is associated with religiosity, paranormal beliefs, and positive schizotypy. Most likely, thought–action fusion plays a significant role in the etiology of autogenous obsessions (Abramowitz et al., 2004; Brakoulias et al., 2013; Mauzay et al., 2016; Poyurovsky, 2015; Sica et al., 2002; Yorulmaz et al., 2009).

While the standard model of OCD works well as a first approximation, it needs to be amended in light of more recent findings on the factors that promote the onset of symptoms. To begin, perfectionism, inflated responsibility, and thought control are not unique to OCD—for example, beliefs about the need to control thoughts are also elevated in GAD patients. Conversely, other nonspecific dimensions of individual differences such as neuroticism and disgust sensitivity significantly increase the frequency of obsessive-compulsive symptoms. Most importantly, there is accumulating evidence that OCD patients actually experience more intrusions than do controls, as well as more bizarre and unusual contents. In addition, patients are less effective in suppressing neutral thoughts and not just distressing ones. Other studies show that experiencing a high frequency of taboo obsessions increases catastrophic interpretations more than the other way round (see Clark & del Palacio González, 2014; Cougle & Lee, 2014). In sum, people at risk for OCD may be especially vulnerable to intrusions and less able to control them. This vulnerability is plausibly linked to reduced executive functions: while OCD risk is largely unrelated to general intelligence, cognitive tasks show reduced inhibition, flexibility/shifting, and planning skills in patients (Abramovitch et al., 2013, 2015; Koenen et al., 2009; Snyder et al., 2015). It is easy to see how reduced inhibition and shifting may lead to difficulties in disengaging from obsessive thoughts and controlling compulsive urges. Indeed, poor executive inhibition is specifically associated with the frequency of autogenous obsessions (Ettelt et al., 2007; Lee & Telch, 2010; Lee et al., 2009).

From a computational and neurobiological perspective, there is robust evidence that OCD patients show a bias toward habitual learning as compared with goal-directed learning. The underlying cause of this bias is still unclear; possible options are impaired goal-directed learning, enhanced habitual learning, or—perhaps most plausibly—inflexible arbitration between different systems for learning and behavior control (which may also explain the patients' poor shifting performance in executive tasks). Also, negative emotional states such as anxiety and acute stress are known to bias cognitive processes toward habitual stimulus–response associations (Gillan & Robbins, 2014; Gruner et al., 2016). Whatever the exact reason, hyperactive habit formation may explain the rapid onset and consolidation of compulsive rituals in predisposed individuals. This perspective leads to a counterintuitive hypothesis: rather than compulsions being a response to obsessions, obsessions might arise as post-hoc attempts to explain compulsive urges ("I keep washing my hands, so I must be afraid of getting a disease"). The strong version of this hypothesis is unlikely given the evidence that OCD-like behaviors can be induced experimentally by triggering guilt; still, enhanced habit formation may make compulsive urges more difficult to resist and indirectly reinforce the development of obsessions (Gillan & Robbins, 2014).

Development and Course

The onset of OCD peaks in early adulthood, but a substantial minority of cases (about one-third) are diagnosed in childhood. The childhood-onset variant of OCD is much more common in males and tends to be more severe, with an especially high frequency of tics and symmetry, ordering, and religious symptoms. However, the content of obsessive-compulsive symptoms typically changes throughout childhood and adolescence, and, in most patients, it does not stabilize until adulthood. Changes in symptoms are mirrored by the emergence of new genetic factors at multiple developmental junctures, which may reflect the maturation of different motivational systems and self-regulatory mechanisms (do Rosario-Campos et al., 2005; Krebs et al., 2015; Mataix-Cols et al., 2008; Rettew et al., 1992; Rufer et al., 2005; Ruscio et al., 2010; Taylor, 2011*b*). In general, the onset of OCD is more gradual in males and more abrupt in females. Pregnancy and childbirth are times of heightened risk for the onset of OCD or the worsening of preexisting symptoms. While mothers are most likely to develop obsessions and compulsions around childbirth, there is some evidence that fathers can also be affected. The content of pregnancy and postpartum symptoms typically revolves around contamination, cleaning, checking, and thoughts of harming the infant; OCD-like phenomena of this kind are very common in new parents, although they normally remain at nonclinical levels (Abramowitz et al., 2003; Bogetto et al., 1999; Coelho et al., 2014). If untreated, the course of OCD tends to be chronic, with low remission rates (Neer & Ragsdale, 2014).

Risk Factors

Relatively little is known about the risk factors for OCD. Epidemiological studies find associations with childhood adversity, stress, and traumatic life events; however, these results are mostly based on retrospective self-reports and may be confounded by a number of individual and family variables. Similarly, correlations with parental rejection and overprotection may be partly explained by shared genetic influences. Several studies have investigated the prevalence of OCD in relation to socioeconomic status. The results are very mixed, with increased rates at both high and low levels of SES (Brander et al., 2016; Fontenelle & Hasler, 2008; Goodwin et al., 2014). As for parental age, the available data are inconclusive—in one study, OCD risk was higher in the offspring of older fathers; in another, it was higher in those of older mothers (Steinhausen et al., 2013; Wu, Liu et al., 2012).

EVOLUTIONARY MODELS

It is hard to overstate the biological significance of obsessions, compulsions, and the psychological mechanisms that produce them. On the one hand, compulsions bear striking similarities to various repetitive, ritualized behaviors observed in other animals—including self-grooming, food inspection and washing, and checking for predators (Rapoport, 1991). On the other hand, cultural rituals—which also share several features with OCD symptoms—perform a range of important functions in human societies, from group coordination in social and religious ceremonies to the transmission of knowledge between generations (Fiske & Haslam, 1997). Starting with the ethological model by Rapoport (1991) and continuing to this day, most evolutionary scholars have regarded OCD as a maladaptive condition. Specifically, obsessions and compulsions are thought to arise from the dysfunctional or inappropriate activation of evolved harm prevention mechanisms (Marks & Nesse, 1994).

OCD as a Disorder of Harm Prevention

Early evolutionary theories of OCD focused on overt behaviors such as washing and checking. Abed and de Pauw (1998) explicitly addressed the cognitive aspects of OCD and speculated that obsessive ruminations are produced by a specialized mechanism (a sort of "psychological immune system") that, when activated by cues of potential danger, automatically begins to generate a stream of hypothetical risk scenarios. By mentally simulating encounters with threats in a broad range of conditions, individuals can learn and refine prevention strategies without being exposed to actual danger. In a similar vein, Brüne (2006) stressed the importance of the metacognitive processes that allow people to represent and anticipate the future consequences of their actions and suggested that metacognitive deficits play a central role in the etiology of OCD. According to this model, OCD is analogous to a psychological autoimmune disease, in which an adaptive defense becomes hyperactive and ends up damaging the individual it should protect. For example, pregnancy and childbirth expose the infant and parents to a host of new dangers; while the subsequent upregulation of the parent's "psychological immunity" is generally adaptive, there is a risk that the system will overshoot and lead to the onset of OCD.

In a landmark contribution to this line of research, Szechtman and Woody (2004; Woody & Szechtman, 2011) detailed the logic of the *security system*, a motivational system designed to deal with potential threats that have a low probability of occurring but potentially catastrophic consequences (Chapter 2). To successfully avoid such threats, organisms must rely on subtle and indirect cues of danger; the optimal response is not fleeing or hiding, but increasing vigilance and actively probing the environment in search of further information. A peculiar feature of potential threats is that successful avoidance does not have visible effects—the feared event simply fails to occur. This lack of reliable feedback creates an intrinsic state of uncertainty and further reduces the organism's information about the true probability of the threat (Tooby & Cosmides, 2006). It also means that, when the security system is activated, there is no clear termination signal coming from the external environment. The "stop signal" that deactivates the system must then be generated internally, based on the correct execution of security-related behaviors (e.g., checking, washing, thought neutralization). The compulsive quality of adaptive precautionary behaviors is due to the fact that they are necessarily divorced from immediate goals and external indicators of success or failure.

Based on these considerations, Szechtman and Woody argued that OCD is a "pathology of stopping": the system becomes normally activated, but the stop signal that provides internal negative feedback and a sense of goal attainment—labeled *yedasentience* by these authors—is either attenuated or lacking. This idea has been supported in experimental studies (Hinds et al., 2012, 2015). OCD as a stopping disorder can be contrasted with GAD as a "pathology of starting," in which the security system becomes activated frequently and inappropriately (Chapter 15). The model advanced by Woody and Szechtman (2011) is complex and includes a detailed neurobiological account of the security system. In particular, these authors argued that corticostriatal circuits comprise two parallel pathways: a motivational pathway centered on the MPFC/OFC and a motor pathway that involves motor cortical areas and various regions within the striatum. Disconnection between the two pathways may underlie "pure obsessional" syndromes in which obsessions are not accompanied by behavioral compulsions.

The harm prevention model of OCD was further extended by Boyer and Liénard (2006). These authors advanced a general theory of ritualized behavior, from the development of routines in children to cultural rituals. The main idea is that ritualized behaviors arise from the joint action of a security motivational system (or *hazard-precaution system*) and a cognitive system for action parsing whose goal is to divide the flow of behavior into meaningful units. When the security system is activated by cues of danger, it triggers a search for appropriate action sequences in a special motor repertoire that contains evolved precautionary behaviors. At the same time, the parsing system begins to sequence behavior into smaller units and focus attention on the low-level properties of actions (e.g., washing hands in a particular sequence, avoiding "wrong" gestures). In the absence of a stop signal, doubts and not just right feelings prompt additional repetitions of the sequence, which may ultimately overload the working memory and bring about a temporary relief of anxiety.

The idea of an evolved repertoire of precautionary behaviors helps to make sense of the relatively narrow range of obsessive-compulsive themes across individuals and cultures. Boyer and Liénard identified four main categories of threats: contamination (triggered by disgust and followed by washing and cleaning), causing harm to offspring, causing social offence (e.g., taboo thoughts), and predators/intruders. They speculated that symmetry/ordering rituals may create structure in the environment, making it easier to detect intrusions by predators and hostile humans. While interesting, this hypothesis does not sit well with the fact that symmetry/ordering symptoms and not just right experiences often occur without significant anxiety and do not seem motivated by harm prevention (at least in a sizable subgroup of patients). Finally, Boyer and Liénard's theory integrates and extends previous work on the evolution of cultural rituals (Feygin et al., 2006; Fiske & Haslam, 1997), a fascinating aspect of the model that is beyond the scope of this chapter.

Figure 20.1 presents an integrative model of OCD as a disorder of harm prevention. The security system can be activated by a range of potential threats, both external (contamination, possible accidents) and internal (aggressive, sexual, blasphemous intrusions). In some cases, disgust (especially pathogen-related) provides the initial trigger for the security system. Even if evolutionary work on OCD has focused mainly on anxiety, disgust is clearly an important if understudied factor in the etiology of obsessive-compulsive symptoms (Berle & Phillips, 2006; Stein et al., 2001, 2016). The model in Figure 20.1 combines the basic structure of the evolutionary models reviewed in this section with some new insights into the role of habit formation; it also shows how various personality and cognitive traits can increase the risk of developing obsessions and/or compulsions by acting on different nodes of the causal sequence. While not just right experiences can arise in the context of harm prevention, this model does not account for symmetry/ordering symptoms that are *primarily* motivated by feelings of incompleteness and imperfection. In the next section, I argue for the existence of two distinct

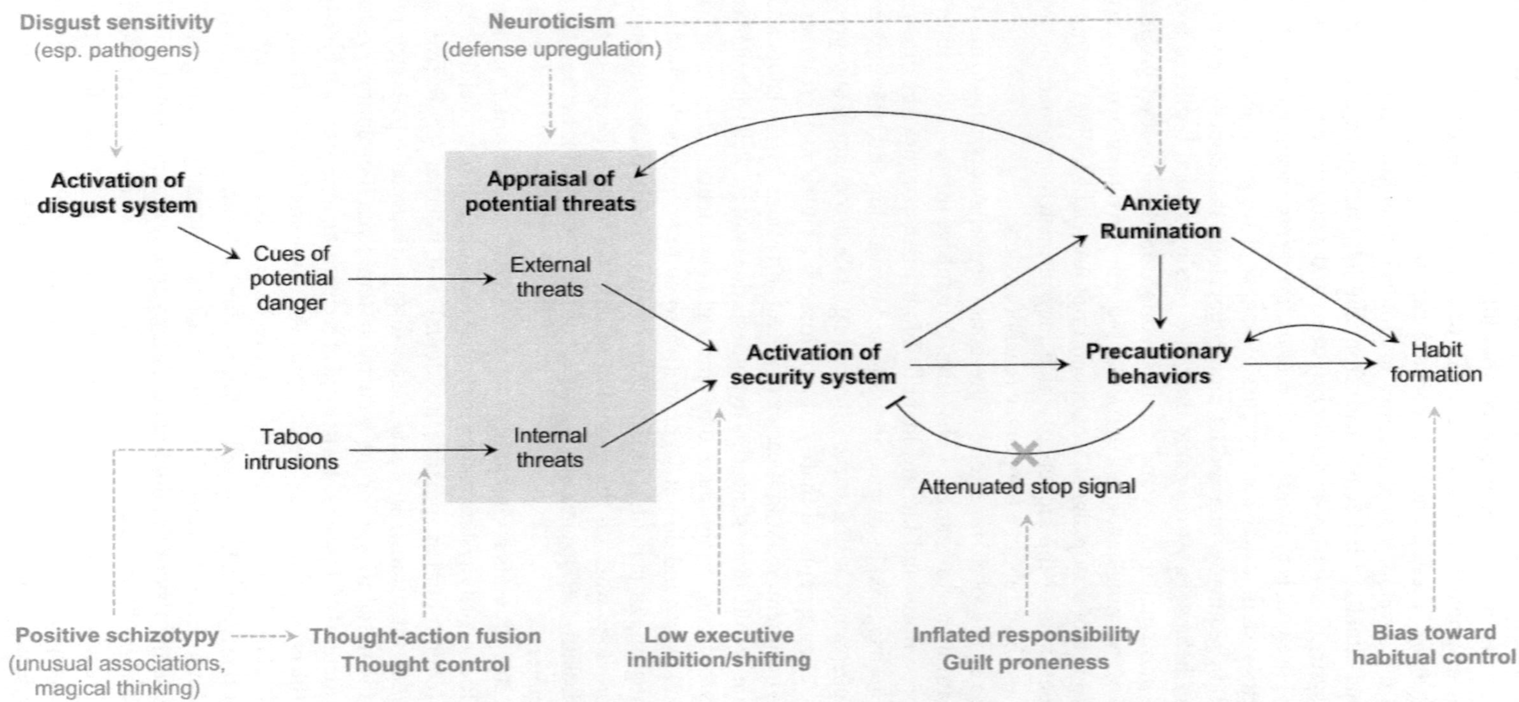

Figure 20.1. Integrative model of obsessive-compulsive disorder (OCD) as a harm prevention syndrome. Personality traits and cognitive factors that contribute to increase the risk of OCD are shown in gray.

subtypes of OCD: a defense activation disorder motivated by harm prevention and a slow spectrum subtype characterized by not just right experiences, symmetry/ordering symptoms, and marked overlap with OCPD and ASD.

Other Evolutionary Scenarios

A group selection hypothesis for the evolution of OCD was proposed by Polimeni and colleagues (2005). These authors speculated that OCD symptoms in a small proportion of the population may benefit the whole group, for example by increasing vigilance against predators (checking), preventing the spread of diseases (washing), and generally monitoring the environment (counting, ordering). At present, this hypothesis remains untested. As in other group selection scenarios, it is unclear whether (and how) inclusive fitness would promote obsessive-compulsive symptoms in a particular subset of individuals, even if those symptoms were beneficial to the group as a whole. The bizarre and unrealistic nature of many OCD symptoms is also a challenge for any adaptive explanation of this condition. At the same time, it is important to recognize that we know little about the effects of mild obsessive-compulsive traits on fitness-relevant outcomes such as survival, mating, and reproduction. For example, a preliminary but intriguing study by Glass (2012) found a small but positive correlation between obsessions and compulsions in a nonclinical sample and indicators of mating success.

FSD CLASSIFICATION

When the symptoms are motivated primarily by harm prevention, OCD can be classified as a defense activation disorder and identified with the label D-OCD. The main personality correlate of OCD is high neuroticism, although patients also report low extraversion and conscientiousness (Kotov et al., 2010; Pinto & Eisen, 2012). However, self-report data on low conscientiousness should be taken with a grain of salt, since many OCD patients have unrealistically high standards for cleanliness, punctuality, orderliness, and other indicators of conscientious behavior. In support of this interpretation, a study found negative correlations with conscientiousness only for observer-rated symptoms of hoarding and obsessive intrusions, but not for ordering, washing, or checking (Watson & Naragon-Gainey, 2014).

In addition to the defense activation subtype, there is a group of patients whose OCD symptoms are primarily motivated by not just right experiences, without significant levels of anxiety. As reviewed in the previous sections, this male-biased subtype is characterized by elevated perfectionism and overlaps with OCPD and the autism spectrum. These patients' symptoms typically center on symmetry, ordering, repeating, hoarding, and cleaning. From the standpoint of the autogenous–reactive distinction, obsessions in this subtype are mainly reactive.

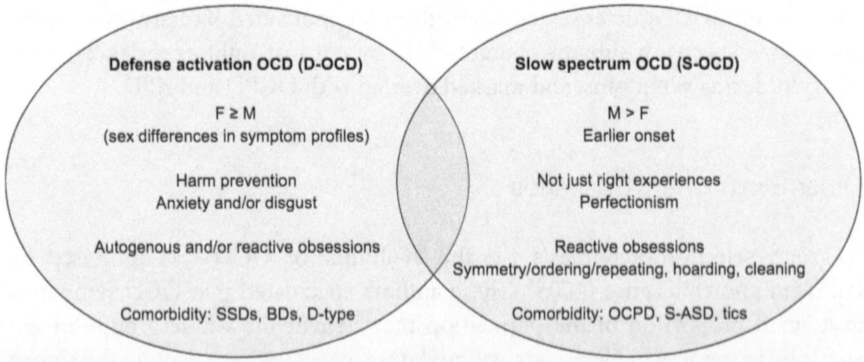

Figure 20.2. Two overlapping but functionally distinct subtypes of obsessive-compulsive disorder (OCD). ASD = autism spectrum disorder. ASPD = antisocial personality disorder. BDs = bipolar disorders. OCPD = obsessive-compulsive personality disorder. PTSD = posttraumatic stress disorder. SSDs = schizophrenia spectrum disorders.

Based on this symptom profile, I propose that this subtype can be classified as a slow spectrum condition (S-OCD). Of course, individual patients with S-OCD can also suffer from defense activation symptoms in the form of D-OCD, so the two subtypes are not mutually exclusive (Figure 20.2).

The distinction between D-OCD and S-OCD raises the question of whether it would make sense to identify an additional fast spectrum subtype of OCD characterized by positive schizotypy and taboo/autogenous obsessions, as I suggested in the original version of the life history framework (Del Giudice, 2014*a*, 2014*b*). While OCD overlaps significantly with the psychosis spectrum (see Figure 20.2), obsessions and compulsions in these patients seem to be motivated primarily by harm prevention and accompanied by intense anxiety and disgust—even if, in the case of taboo thoughts, the source of potential threats (e.g., committing blasphemy or immoral sexual acts) is internal rather than external. If this is the case, OCD syndromes with psychotic-like features may still be properly regarded as D-type disorders, even if the corresponding symptom profile is tilted toward autogenous obsessions and may involve a higher frequency of unusual/bizarre contents. This is why the current version of the FSD model does not include a fast spectrum subtype of OCD. Given the provisional nature of the model and the incomplete understanding of the links between schizotypy and OCD, it is possible that future research will call for additional distinctions within this diagnostic category.

PART IV

Conclusion

21

A Look at the Future

At the end of this journey, it is time to take stock of the field as it stands today and offer some thoughts about the future. The biological study of mental disorders is based on a set of basic principles shared with evolutionary medicine at large (Chapter 5). Among other things, those principles make it possible to draw fine-grained distinctions between different kinds of conditions, with a resolution and heuristic power unknown in other branches of psychopathology. Building on this foundation, researchers have advanced and tested a multitude of specific evolutionary models. As I documented in Part III of this book, the state of the art varies dramatically from one disorder to the next. For some disorders one finds theoretically sophisticated, empirically supported models that bridge the ultimate level of analysis with the proximate level of cognitive and neurobiological mechanisms. Examples of this kind include the harm prevention model of obsessive compulsive disorder (OCD) and the diametrical model of autism and psychosis. Other times, the available hypotheses are preliminary and largely untested, as in the case of attention-deficit/hyperactivity disorder (ADHD) or blood-injection-injury phobias. Research on depression perfectly illustrates both the dynamism of the discipline and its fragmented state, with many competing models—each with different strengths, weaknesses, and sources of evidence—but still little consensus and theoretical integration. In most cases, there are alternative evolutionary scenarios that remain to be tested and considerable scope for extending and refining the existing models.

The life history framework presented in Chapter 6 seeks to advance the discipline in a number of ways. To begin, it offers a principled way to integrate evolutionary models of mental disorders with broader patterns of individual and sex differences in personality, cognition, and (tentatively) neurobiology. A life history perspective also helps make sense of developmental trends in the onset and course of specific disorders, as well as patterns of risk and protective factors. Most importantly, the fast-slow-defense (FSD) model brings conceptual coherence to the classification of psychopathology, accounts for the large-scale structure of comorbidity, and provides the first biologically grounded alternative to transdiagnostic models based on empirically derived dimensions such as the internalizing, externalizing, and general psychopathology factors. These features make the life history framework a promising candidate as a unifying conceptual scheme for evolutionary psychopathology. At the same time, fleshing out the framework and properly testing all its components is going to require much additional work. Some of the functional categories I proposed in the previous chapters are still rather speculative—including the slow spectrum subtypes of bipolar disorders and OCD, the distinction between S-type and O-type autism, or the multiple variants of ADHD. Likewise, the extended model of life history strategies I sketched in Chapter 4 is tentative in several respects and most likely incomplete. While there are theoretical and empirical reasons to identify distinct psychological profiles within fast and slow strategies, this is only an initial step toward an exhaustive map of life history–related traits and their organization in our species.

The current version of the FSD model also leaves out entire categories of psychopathology that are promising targets for an evolutionary analysis. These include substance use disorders (Nesse & Berridge, 1997; Richardson et al., 2014, 2016; St. John-Smith et al., 2013; Sullivan et al., 2008; Vincke, 2016), dissociative disorders (Farina & Liotti, 2013), sexual dysfunctions (Apostolou, 2015), paraphilias, and gender dysphoria. Another fascinating and virtually unexplored topic is that of defense *inactivation* or d-type disorders—hypothetical conditions that primarily involve the suppression or downregulation of adaptive defenses. Evolutionary scholars have long argued that insufficient defenses are a likely source of pathology (Nesse, 1990); hopefully, the FSD model will stimulate research in this direction by bringing the issue of defense regulation into sharper relief.

In the rest of this concluding chapter, I consider three areas of further development for the discipline: proximate mechanisms, epidemiology, and development. These are all areas in which the evolutionary approach has not fully realized its potential; they are also ripe for major advances to be made in the near future.

MECHANISMS

In the end, the success of evolutionary psychopathology will depend on its ability to integrate the ultimate level of selection and adaptation with the proximate level of genetic, neurobiological, and computational processes. With some notable exceptions, existing evolutionary models of mental disorders have relatively little to say about proximate mechanisms. This is certainly true for the computational level of analysis: while some authors have examined disorders such as OCD and schizophrenia in light of information-processing problems (for example those involved in the detection of potential threats), few attempts have been made to formulate explicit computational models of the symptoms within an evolutionary framework (e.g., Badcock et al., 2017). Meanwhile, computational psychiatry is developing rapidly and achieving some impressive initial results, but so far with virtually no input from the evolutionary sciences. As a result, many computational models are formulated in highly abstract terms—typically involving an idealized decision maker facing generic rewards and punishments—and suffer from lack of consideration of the person's biological goals and motivations.

An evolutionary approach can make several important contributions to computational modeling. A partial list of useful insights would include (a) inclusive fitness is the ultimate currency of the payoffs of behavior, beyond immediate rewards and punishments; (b) psychological mechanisms are functionally specialized and motivated by domain-specific goals such as mating, survival, and status competition; (c) compromises and tradeoffs are ubiquitous, both between an individual's competing goals and between different components of fitness; (d) apparent computational biases may be adaptive rather than dysfunctional, especially when they are expressed in evolutionarily relevant ecological conditions; and (e) cognitive processes may serve specifically social functions, including communication and signaling (e.g., creativity in schizotypy as a possible mating display).

Conversely, a detailed consideration of information-processing mechanisms can illuminate and direct biological theorizing—for example by pointing to computational constraints on optimal behavior, or by identifying critical processing steps that may be especially vulnerable to dysregulation and dysfunction (Fawcett et al., 2015; McNamara & Houston, 2009; Trimmer & Houston, 2014). Integrating evolutionary and computational perspectives is not an easy task; even studying simple decision-making mechanisms raises thorny issues about the nature of heuristics and the optimal use of information (e.g., Castellano, 2015). Also, the relations between computational goals (e.g., efficiency, accuracy) and biological goals are likely to be complex in most realistic scenarios. Some authors make the strong simplifying assumption that predictive accuracy can be equated with fitness (e.g., Badcock et al., 2017). It is true that an organism's ability to predict is intimately linked to its potential for survival and reproduction; however, predictive accuracy is only part of the equation, and a complete model needs to explicitly consider the costs and benefits of behavior within the organism's ecology (Geisler & Diehl, 2003).

As I have noted in previous chapters, the empirical data on the neurobiology of mental disorders are patchy and often contradictory, especially with respect to central neurotransmitters/neuromodulators such as dopamine, serotonin, and glutamate. At a more basic level, our understanding on the functional role of key molecules such as oxytocin and testosterone is incomplete at best. Despite these limitations, there are promising examples of productive integration, as in models of OCD as a disorder of harm prevention (Boyer & Liénard, 2006; Woody & Szechtman, 2011). At a minimum, an evolutionary perspective offers a sophisticated taxonomy of motivational and regulatory systems, beyond the gaps and artificial distinctions that limit the validity of current neurobiologically inspired approaches such as the Research Domain Criteria (RDoC). Evolutionary models are also needed to successfully bridge the findings of animal research with those of human studies, given that different species face different constrains, tradeoffs, and ecological problems (e.g., Cantor, 2005; Szechtman et al., 2017). Of course, the domain of neurobiology is not restricted to neurotransmitters and hormones—it also includes structural aspects such as brain connectivity and neural integrity. On the whole, evolutionary scholars have paid little attention to the role of cognitive impairment, neural functionality, and intelligence in the etiology of mental disorders (Keller & Miller, 2006). This is a significant limitation, especially when studying conditions that are strongly linked to reduced cognitive ability, as for example schizophrenia and ADHD.

At present, our knowledge of the genetics of mental disorders includes a wealth of robust findings on patterns of heritability, genetic correlations, and the relative weight of rare mutations versus common variants. While this is all valuable information, we still know very little about the molecular underpinnings of psychopathology or even those of normal variation in personality and intelligence. (Unfortunately, the findings of candidate genes studies are still largely unreliable, for reasons discussed in Chapter 3.) This situation is destined to change rapidly as genomic databases become larger, richer, and more readily available. At the same time, advances in evolutionary genetics are making it easier to test hypotheses about the selective history of the genes that contribute to normal and pathological variation (e.g., Pardiñas et al., 2016). The prospects for evolutionary psychopathology are nothing short of thrilling. As higher quality data accumulate, researchers in the field will be able to adjust and constrain their theories based on indirect evidence of past selection. Even more importantly, some of the existing evolutionary models make interesting and detailed predictions about patterns of selection on different sets of genes—predictions that could inform future genomic research. For example, the sexual selection model of schizophrenia (Chapter 8) postulates at least two distinct sources of genetic risk: while rare and de novo mutations are overwhelmingly harmful and subject to negative selection, schizotypy-increasing alleles should be relatively common and evolve under balancing selection. (Common variants associated with lower IQ may represent a third independent source of risk.) The model also predicts a unique pattern of epistatic interaction, so that the same deleterious mutations should have a larger effect on schizophrenia risk when they occur in combination with schizotypy-increasing alleles. These unique predictions are theoretically interesting and could be tested using genomic data. At present, most studies in this area focus on distinguishing selective neutrality from positive selection or mutation–selection balance; balancing selection is rarely explored, partly because its genomic footprints are subtler and less straightforward than those of positive and negative selection and partly because theoretical models of balancing selection are still somewhat crude (Del Giudice, 2012*b*; Keller & Miller, 2006; Vitti et al., 2013).

In addition to genetic variation, epigenetic factors are likely to make significant contributions to psychopathology. Epigenetic mechanisms are especially interesting because they can mediate environmental effects on genetic expression in the individual (developmental plasticity), but also transmit those effects across multiple generations. In psychology and psychiatry, epigenetic processes are viewed almost exclusively through a proximate lens, with little or no consideration of their adaptive functions (e.g., Hill & Roth, 2016; Nestler et al., 2016). As a result, researchers may fail to appreciate the costs and benefits that underlie the evolution of various types of epigenetic mechanisms (Ledón-Rettig et al., 2013; Uller & Helanterä, 2013). For example, mathematical models suggest that epigenetic regulation of plasticity is more likely to evolve than faithful, multigenerational epigenetic inheritance unless the environment remains highly stable across generations (Furrow & Feldman, 2014; Herman et al., 2014). Beyond adaptive plasticity, epigenetic modifications are involved in genomic imprinting and other types of intragenomic conflict. So far, the diametrical model of autism and psychosis discussed in Chapter 8 is the only evolutionary model of psychopathology that makes explicit predictions about the role of epigenetic factors. There is enormous scope for innovative work in this area, and a growing biological literature that has yet to be tapped by those who study mental disorders.

EPIDEMIOLOGY

The interface between evolutionary psychopathology and epidemiology is an exceptionally fertile ground for new insights and discoveries. On the one hand, data on prevalence rates, risk factors, and other epidemiological variables can be used to indirectly test competing evolutionary models of specific conditions (e.g., Abed & Abbas, 2014). On the other hand, biological concepts help explain systematic patterns in the distribution of psychopathology, including seemingly paradoxical findings such as associations between higher socioeconomic status and increased risk for some disorders.

In this book, I have devoted a fair amount of space to review key epidemiological features of mental disorders—sex differences, developmental trajectories, risk and protective factors—and examine them from a life history perspective. While this approach has already yielded a number of valuable insights, the full potential of evolutionary epidemiology is far from being realized. The life history framework points to broad dimensions of the environment (such as harshness and unpredictability) and helps explain the age and sex distribution of major clusters of disorders (Chapter 6). However, the FSD model is only a first approximation: a finer grained analysis should focus on specific mechanisms—including motivational systems—and identify the environmental factors that modulate their function and/or increase the risk of dysfunction. For example, both sexual and status competition are intensified when people live in large, anonymous groups with little support from close kin. Migration to a different country can exacerbate these effects and trigger a host of defensive psychological processes (from depression to paranoia), especially when migration is associated with discrimination or transition to ethnic minority status. Other important contextual variables are the local sex ratio and the characteristics of the mating/marriage system (e.g., degree of polygyny, age at marriage, role of parents in mate choice). All these factors powerfully modulate the expression of mating, pair bonding, and status competition but have received very little attention in mainstream epidemiological research. Similar considerations apply to pathogen prevalence and the disgust system, or to resource availability and the acquisition system. With enough data on motivationally relevant dimensions of the environment, it should become possible to explain variation in the prevalence of specific conditions across time, places, and social contexts, above and beyond the general patterns predicted by the FSD model.

Population Differences and Deep Epidemiology

Implicit in the preceding paragraphs is the idea that environmental factors modulate the risk of psychopathology within an individual's lifetime through relatively short-term causal processes such as developmental plasticity, learning, or immediate responses to changes in the social and ecological context. Some of these effects can potentially reverberate through multiple generations via epigenetic inheritance, although the practical significance of this transmission channel is still unclear. However, there is no reason why persistent or recurrent environmental factors should not lead to changes in the frequency of the genetic variants that affect psychopathology, either directly or through their contributions to personality, behavior, and life history traits such as growth and sexual maturation. Over a sufficiently long timeframe, divergent selection pressures can be expected to lead to a certain amount of genetic differentiation across populations. The resulting effects may then persist through short-term ecological changes and migrations, and remain visible in societies whose members have different ancestries (Winegard et al., 2017). Of course, genetic differences do not act in isolation but rather interact with present ecological conditions—including a variety of social and economic factors—to yield observed patterns of variation at any given time. The study of evolved population differences in risk for disease could be labeled *deep epidemiology*, with analogy to the concept of *deep history* in evolutionary biology and anthropology (e.g., Shyrock & Smail, 2011; Vitt & Pianka, 2005).

For an example of how the short-term effects of ecological factors may blend into long-term selection pressures, consider the case of schizophrenia. Shaner and colleagues (2007) documented a latitudinal gradient in the age of onset of schizophrenia, with earlier onset in countries that are geographically closer to the Equator. These authors then reviewed a number of plausible explanatory factors, including higher pathogen load, earlier puberty and marriage, and higher rates of polygyny. Together, these factors converge on faster life histories and an earlier peak of mating competition, which—according to the sexual selection model—should lower the age of onset of schizophrenia. Crucially, variables such as pathogen load and polygyny are not transient but reflect persistent features of the physical and social environment, which makes it plausible to hypothesize a degree of genetic differentiation between populations that evolved at different latitudes.

In the United States, rates of schizophrenia and other schizophrenia spectrum disorders (SSDs) in blacks are systematically higher than those observed in whites (Bresnahan et al., 2007; Chavira et al., 2003; Delbello et al., 2001; Strakowski et al., 1996). The standard explanations offered in the literature are restricted to discrimination, poverty, and other evolutionarily recent social factors, to the exclusion of potential genetic contributions (e.g., Metzl, 2010). However, data from multiple countries (including but not limited to the United States) indicate that immigrants from Africa and the Caribbean and their offspring are at especially high risk for schizophrenia (Chapter 8); moreover, there is evidence that darker skin color—which correlates with ancestry from areas closer to the Equator—predicts schizophrenia risk across countries independent of latitude (Kinney et al., 2009). While these data are not conclusive, they suggest that genetic contributions to racial/ethnic differences in schizophrenia should not be ruled out. It bears stressing that genetic factors are only one component among many; for example, overall schizophrenia rates across countries increase farther *away* from the Equator, implicating additional variables such as seasonal infections and vitamin D deficiency. Moreover, the sexual selection model specifically predicts an interaction with individual condition, which includes developmental stressors and exposure to pathogens and may partly mediate the pathogenic effects of migration (Shaner et al., 2007). Evolutionary epidemiology is uniquely situated to make sense of these complex patterns, in which present conditions and the legacy of recent events interact with genetic inheritance from deep history.

The more general point is that persistent differences in socioecological conditions—including pathogen load, environmental unpredictability, and mating systems—can determine variable amounts of genetic divergence between populations. Furthermore, at least part of the observed differences between populations can be plausibly explained as variations along life history dimensions, with implications for the risk of F-spectrum versus S-spectrum disorders. This point needs to be qualified in two important ways. First, population differences in psychopathology risk do not necessarily map neatly onto standard racial/ethnic distinctions. While major racial groups (e.g., East Asians, sub-Saharan Africans) describe the large-scale structure of human ancestry to a first approximation, population differences can be parsed at various levels of resolution (Rosenberg et al., 2005; Wade, 2014). The ecological and genetic factors that contribute to increase risk for a given condition may well turn out to be specific to certain regional groups. Second and more important, life history variation between populations does not necessarily involve broad differences along the fast–slow continuum (as postulated by Rushton [1985, 2000]), but may be restricted to particular life history tradeoffs or specific behavioral profiles within fast and slow strategies. For example, rates of autism in the United States are systematically higher in whites compared with blacks (Hill et al., 2014; Mandell et al., 2009; Wu et al., 2016). Risk for SSDs and narcissistic traits are both higher in blacks (Bresnahan et al., 2007; Chavira et al., 2003; Delbello et al., 2001; Larson et al., 2015; Strakowski et al., 1996; Zeigler-Hill & Wallace, 2011); however, studies of conduct and antisocial disorders show a mixed and inconsistent picture, with little evidence of robust differences between the two groups (Angold et al., 2002; Breslau et al., 2006; Grant et al., 2004; Lahey et al., 2005; Vaughn et al., 2011, 2014). From the standpoint of the FSD model, these data suggest that black–white differences in psychopathology may not reflect global variation in fast versus slow strategies, but a more specific difference in the frequency of seductive/creative versus skilled/

provisioning profiles. Again, one should remember that observed population differences summarize the joint effect of multiple factors, from genetic and epigenetic variation to current socioeconomic conditions.

DEVELOPMENT

Developmental psychopathology is enjoying a remarkable phase of expansion and theoretical growth (Cicchetti, 2016). The discipline's initial commitment to *developmental systems theory* (DST) arguably contributed to prevent integration with evolutionary psychology in the first decades of its existence. A systems approach highlights several important issues, such as the bidirectional interplay between person and environment, the probabilistic rather than predetermined nature of developmental processes, the importance of plasticity, and the potential for nongenetic modes of inheritance. However, the more radical versions of DST—which are especially popular in developmental psychology—embrace a holistic philosophy with strong anti-Darwinian overtones and reject both adaptationist thinking and behavior genetics (e.g., Lerner, 2015; Overton, 2015; Witherington & Lickliter, 2017). Elsewhere, my colleagues and I have argued that the substantive issues highlighted by DST can be adequately framed within the framework of inclusive fitness ("soft" DST) and do not necessitate a rejection of mainstream evolutionary biology (Del Giudice & Ellis, 2016; see also Bjorklund, 2017; Bjorklund & Ellis, 2014; Robert et al., 2001).

As more developmental scientists break free from the strictures of radical DST, they will enjoy the opportunity to explore a full range of evolutionary insights and integrate them in their work. Just as developmental psychopathology has much to gain from a sophisticated biological approach, evolutionary psychopathology will benefit enormously from the contribution of developmentalists. Too often, evolutionary models of mental disorders focus narrowly on adult behavior, possibly owing to the field's emphasis on mating and reproduction. In this book, I strived to situate disorders within the broader context of human development, with the help of the life history framework and its intrinsically lifespan horizon. However, this initial attempt barely scratches the surface—the list of important questions at the intersection of evolution, development, and psychopathology is long and fascinating (e.g., Del Giudice & Ellis, 2016).

Developmental plasticity, genotype–environment (G×E) interactions, and epigenetics are at the forefront of current research in developmental psychopathology. As I noted earlier, epigenetic mechanisms are usually discussed from a proximate perspective, with little or no consideration of their evolved functions (Hill & Roth, 2016). In the case of G×E interactions, many researchers employ evolutionary theories of differential susceptibility (Chapter 3) to interpret and frame their empirical findings (see Grigorenko et al., 2016). However, there are many unanswered questions about the nature of differential susceptibility, and the field needs a sustained effort to address them in depth. For example, I recently presented a simple model of the evolution of different forms of genotype- and phenotype-environment interactions (Del Giudice, 2017). In contrast with standard assumptions in the literature, the model suggests that interactions involving differential susceptibility are more likely to have certain shapes instead of others. The results also underscore how the shape of interactions is of little help in distinguishing between underlying processes of vulnerability versus adaptive plasticity, again challenging common practices in the interpretation of data. We know even less about the conditions that may lead to the evolution of adaptive differences in plasticity and about the plausibility of different selection scenarios in humans (Frankenhuis et al., 2016).

An even deeper need for biological synthesis is apparent in the study of developmental plasticity and transitions between life stages. It is impossible to fully understand the logic of developmental transitions without a functional theory of the human life cycle. For example, adrenarche is starting to be regarded as an important sensitive period for the development of psychopathology; however, research in this area is largely atheoretical, which makes it hard to interpret the empirical findings and make testable predictions (Byrne et al., 2017). The concept of a developmental switch point could be extremely useful, especially coupled with a model of the specific biological functions of middle childhood (Del Giudice, 2014*c*; Hochberg, 2008, 2010). There is also a host of recent work on the evolution of sensitive periods, developmental trajectories, and variation in plasticity that leverages Bayesian principles to gain new insights and formulate empirical predictions (Fawcett & Frankenhuis, 2015; Stamps & Frankenhuis, 2016).

Even if studies of plasticity and person–environment interactions would benefit from deeper integration with evolutionary models, these topics are already well recognized in the mainstream and attract a lot of empirical effort. But the implications of an evolutionary approach do not end here. There are many other important issues that can only be approached from a biological perspective and could open up entirely new directions of research. A prime example is the role of evolutionary conflicts, both between family members (e.g., parent–offspring conflict) and within each individual's genome. Intragenomic conflicts—including, but not limited to, those between maternally and paternally expressed imprinted genes—may have a cascade of physiological and behavioral effects, with implications for both normal development and various types of mental disorders. The ramifications of parent–offspring conflict span multiple life stages, from prenatal stress to parent–child attachment to mate choice in adulthood (Del Giudice, 2014*d*; Schlomer et al., 2011). Even the development of plasticity in early life may turn into an opportunity for tension between parents and offspring, with as yet unexplored implications for the etiology of mental disorders (Del Giudice, 2015*c*). Traditionally, developmental psychology has tended to neglect or downplay the role of conflict and emphasize cooperation and altruism as desirable goals; evolutionary theory, on the other hand, is especially well-equipped to identify and describe the inevitable conflicts of interest that arise between biological actors. The end goal should be a realistic understanding of the interplay among altruism, cooperation, and conflict that characterizes human nature.

FINAL THOUGHTS

The future of evolutionary psychopathology is full of exciting opportunities. Whether the discipline will seize on them is going to depend on a number of factors. The most important is probably theoretical integration. What is needed is a set of organizing principles, flexible enough to accommodate a multiplicity of specific models and hypotheses, but also capable of explaining broad epidemiological and comorbidity patterns and supporting a biologically informed classification of disorders. In this book, I have argued that the life history framework can fulfill these needs. However, the success of evolutionary psychopathology will require more than a coherent conceptual framework. Evolutionary scholars should strive to connect their work on mental disorders to the normative study of individual and sex differences, not only in personality but also in intelligence and cognition; embrace behavior genetics, from classic twin studies to contemporary genomic research; and seek out new opportunities for collaboration with computational scientists in biology, psychology, and neuroscience. A vigorous effort to pursue these goals would propel the discipline forward, start a virtuous cycle of discovery, and—not least—attract a new generation of bright, creative researchers. Knowing that this book has helped to make it happen would be plenty of reward.

REFERENCES

Aas, M., Melle, I., Bettella, F., Djurovic, S., Le Hellard, S., Bjella, T., et al. (2018). Psychotic patients who used cannabis frequently before illness onset have higher genetic predisposition to schizophrenia than those who did not. *Psychological Medicine, 48*, 43–49.

Abed, R. T. (1998). The sexual competition hypothesis for eating disorders. *British Journal of Medical Psychology, 71*, 525–547.

Abed, R. T., & Abbas, M. J. (2011). A reformulation of the social brain theory for schizophrenia: The case for out-group intolerance. *Perspectives in Biology and Medicine, 54*, 132–151.

Abed, R. T., & Abbas, M. J. (2014). Can the new epidemiology of schizophrenia help elucidate its causation? *Irish Journal of Psychological Medicine, 31*, 1–5.

Abed, R. T., & de Pauw, K. W. (1998). An evolutionary hypothesis for obsessive-compulsive disorder: A psychological immune system? *Behavioural Neurology, 11*, 245–250.

Abed, R. T., Mehta, S., Figueredo, A. J., Aldridge, S., Balson, H., Meyer, C., et al. (2012). Eating disorders and intrasexual competition: Testing an evolutionary hypothesis among young women. *Scientific World Journal, 2012*, 290813.

Abramovitch, A., Abramowitz, J. S., & Mittelman, A. (2013). The neuropsychology of adult obsessive-compulsive disorder: A meta-analysis. *Clinical Psychology Review, 33*, 1163–1171.

Abramovitch, A., Abramowitz, J. S., Mittelman, A., Stark, A., Ramsey, K., & Geller, D. A. (2015). Research review: Neuropsychological test performance in pediatric obsessive-compulsive disorder: A meta-analysis. *Journal of Child Psychology & Psychiatry, 56*, 837–847.

Abramowitz, J. S., Deacon, B. J., Woods, C. M., & Tolin, D. F. (2004). Association between Protestant religiosity and obsessive-compulsive symptoms and cognitions. *Depression & Anxiety, 20*, 70–76.

Abramowitz, J. S., Schwartz, S. A., Moore, K. M., & Luenzmann, K. R. (2003). Obsessive-compulsive symptoms in pregnancy and the puerperium: A review of the literature. *Journal of Anxiety Disorders, 17*, 461–478.

Abrams, E. T., & Miller, E. M. (2011). The roles of the immune system in women's reproduction: Evolutionary constraints and life history trade-offs. *American Journal of Physical Anthropology, 146*, 134–154.

Abu-Akel, A. M., & Bailey, A. L. (2000). The possibility of different forms of theory of mind impairment in psychiatric and developmental disorders. *Psychological Medicine, 30*, 735–738.

Abu-Akel, A. M., Wood, S. J., Hansen, P. C., & Apperly, I. A. (2015). Perspective-taking abilities in the balance between autism tendencies and psychosis proneness. *Proceedings of the Royal Society of London B, 282*, 20150563.

Ackerman, P. L., & Heggestad, E. D. (1997). Intelligence, personality, and interests: Evidence for overlapping traits. *Psychological Bulletin, 121*, 219–245.

Adams, G. K., Watson, K. K., Pearson, J., & Platt, M. L. (2102). Neuroethology of decision making. In P. Hammerstein & J. R. Stevens (Eds.), *Evolution and the mechanisms of decision making* (pp. 81–96). Cambridge, MA: MIT Press.

Adams, T. G., Sawchuk, C. N., Cisler, J. M., Lohr, J. M., & Olatunji, B. O. (2014). Specific phobias. In P. Emmelkamp & T. Ehring (Eds.), *The Wiley handbook of anxiety disorders* (pp. 297–320). New York: Wiley.

Afifi, T. O., Asmundson, G. J., Taylor, S., & Jang, K. L. (2010). The role of genes and environment on trauma exposure and posttraumatic stress disorder symptoms: A review of twin studies. *Clinical Psychology Review, 30*, 101–112.

Agnew-Blais, J., & Seidman, L. J. (2014). Attention deficit/hyperactivity disorder over the life course. In K. C. Koenen, S. Rudenstine, E. Susser, & S. Galea (Eds.), *A life course approach to mental disorders* (pp. 156–164). Oxford: Oxford University Press.

Ahmed, A. O., Buckley, P. F., & Mabe, P. A. (2012). Latent structure of psychotic experiences in the general population. *Acta Psychiatrica Scandinavica, 125*, 54–65.

Ahn, K., An, S. S., Shugart, Y. Y., & Rapoport, J. L. (2016). Common polygenic variation and risk for childhood-onset schizophrenia. *Molecular Psychiatry, 21*, 94–96.

Ahn, K., Gotay, N., Andersen, T. M., Anvari, A. A., Gochman, P., Lee, Y., et al. (2014). High rate of disease-related copy number variations in childhood onset schizophrenia. *Molecular Psychiatry, 19*, 568–572.

Ahuja, A., Martin, J., Langley, K., & Thapar, A. (2013). Intellectual disability in children with attention deficit hyperactivity disorder. *Journal of Pediatrics, 163*, 890–895.

Aitken, S. J., Lyons, M., & Jonason, P. K. (2013). Dads or cads? Women's strategic decisions in the mating game. *Personality and Individual Differences, 55*, 118–122.

Ajdacic-Gross, V., Rodgers, S., Müller, M., Hengartner, M. P., Aleksandrowicz, A., Kawohl, W., et al. (2016). Pure animal phobia is more specific than other specific phobias: Epidemiological evidence from the Zurich Study, the ZInEP and the PsyCoLaus. *European Archives of Psychiatry and Clinical Neuroscience, 266*, 567–577.

Akintude, M. E., Heuer, L., & Van de Water, J. (2013). Immune abnormalities and autism spectrum disorders. In J. D. Buxbaum & P. R. Hof (Eds.), *The neuroscience of autism spectrum disorders* (pp. 233–248). Oxford: Academic Press.

Akiskal, H. S. (2004). Demystifying borderline personality: Critique of the concept and unorthodox reflections on its natural kinship with the bipolar spectrum. *Acta Psychiatrica Scandinavica, 110*, 401–407.

Akiskal, K. K., & Akiskal, H. S. (2005). The theoretical underpinnings of affective temperaments: Implications for evolutionary foundations of bipolar disorder and human nature. *Journal of Affective Disorders, 85*, 231–239.

Alba-Ferrara, L., & De Erausquin, G. A. (2013). What does anisotropy measure? Insights from increased and decreased anisotropy in selective fiber tracts in schizophrenia. *Frontiers in Integrative Neuroscience, 7*, 9.

Albert, U., Maina, G., Forner, F., & Bogetto, F. (2004). DSM-IV obsessive-compulsive personality disorder: Prevalence in patients with anxiety disorders and in healthy comparison subjects. *Comprehensive Psychiatry, 45*, 325–332.

Albertos, P., & Mareels, I. (2010). *Feedback and control for everyone*. Heidelberg, DE: Springer.

Alcock, J., Maley, C. C., & Aktipis, C. (2014). Is eating behavior manipulated by the gastrointestinal microbiota? Evolutionary pressures and potential mechanisms. *Bioessays, 36*, 940–949.

Alda, M. (2004). The phenotypic spectra of bipolar disorder. *European Neuropsychopharmacology, 14*, S94–S99.

Aleman, A., Kahn, R. S., & Selten, J. P. (2003). Sex differences in risk for schizophrenia: Evidence from meta-analysis. *Archives of General Psychiatry, 60*, 565–571.

Aleman, A., & Torres-Aleman, I. (2009). Circulating insulin-like growth factor I and cognitive function: Neuromodulation throughout the lifespan. *Progress in Neurobiology, 89*, 256–265.

Alexander, R. D. (1989). Evolution of the human psyche. In P. Mellars & C. Stringer (Eds.), *The human revolution: Behavioural and biological perspectives on the origins of modern humans* (pp. 455–513). Princeton, NJ: Princeton University Press.

Ali, F., & Chamorro-Premuzic, T. (2010). Investigating theory of mind deficits in non-clinical psychopathy and Machiavellianism. *Personality and Individual Differences, 49*, 169–174.

Alink, L. R., van IJzendoorn, M. H., Bakermans-Kranenburg, M. J., Mesman, J., Juffer, F., & Koot, H. M. (2008). Cortisol and externalizing behavior in children and adolescents: Mixed meta-analytic evidence for the inverse relation of basal cortisol and cortisol reactivity with externalizing behavior. *Developmental Psychobiology, 50*, 427–450.

Allan, S., & Goss, K. (2012). Shame and pride in eating disorders. In J. R. E. Fox & K. Goss (Eds.), *Eating and its disorders* (pp. 154–166). Chichester, UK: Wiley.

Allen, J. L., Briskman, J., Humayun, S., Dadds, M. R., & Scott, S. (2013). Heartless and cunning? Intelligence in adolescents with antisocial behavior and psychopathic traits. *Psychiatry Research, 210*, 1147–1153.

Allen, N. B., & Badcock, P. B. (2003). The social risk hypothesis of depressed mood: Evolutionary, psychosocial, and neurobiological perspectives. *Psychological Bulletin, 129*, 887–913.

Allen, N. B., & Badcock, P. B. (2006). Darwinian models of depression: A review of evolutionary accounts of mood and mood disorders. *Progress in Neuro-Psychopharmacology and Biological Psychiatry, 30*, 815–826.

Allen, T. A., & DeYoung, C. G. (2017). Personality neuroscience and the Five Factor Model. In T. A. Widiger (Ed.). *Oxford handbook of the Five Factor Model* (319–351). New York: Oxford University Press.

Allen, T. A., Rueter, A. R., Abram, S. V., Brown, J. S., & Deyoung, C. G. (2017). Personality and neural correlates of mentalizing ability. *European Journal of Personality, 31*, 599–613.

Allison, A. L., Peres, J. C., Boettger, C., Leonbacher, U., Hastings, P. D., & Shirtcliff, E. A. (2012). Fight, flight, or fall: Autonomic nervous system reactivity during skydiving. *Personality and Individual Differences, 53*, 218–223.

Alonso-Lana, S., Valentí, M., Romaguera, A., Sarri, C., Sarró, S., Rodríguez-Martínez, A., et al. (2016). Brain functional changes in first-degree relatives of patients with bipolar disorder: Evidence for default mode network dysfunction. *Psychological Medicine, 46*, 2513–2521.

Alsawy, S., Wood, L., Taylor, P. J., & Morrison, A. P. (2015). Psychotic experiences and PTSD: Exploring associations in a population survey. *Psychological Medicine, 45*, 2849–2859.

Al-Shawaf, L., Conroy-Beam, D., Asao, K., & Buss, D. M. (2016). Human emotions: An evolutionary psychological perspective. *Emotion Review, 8*, 173–186.

Al-Shawaf, L., Lewis, D. M. G., & Buss, D. M. (2015). Disgust and mating strategy. *Evolution & Human Behavior, 36*, 199–205.

Altman, S. E., & Shankman, S. A. (2009). What is the association between obsessive-compulsive disorder and eating disorders? *Clinical Psychology Review*, *29*, 638–646.

Alvarez, H. P. (2004). Residence groups among hunter-gatherers: A view of the claims and evidence for patrilocal bands. In B. Chapais & C. Berman (Eds.), *Kinship and Behavior in Primates* (pp. 420–442). Oxford: Oxford University Press.

Alvarez Ariza, M., Mateos Alvarez, R., & Berrios, G. E. (2009). A review of the natural course of bipolar disorders (manic-depressive psychosis) in the pre-drug era: Review of studies prior to 1950. *Journal of Affective Disorders*, *115*, 293–301.

Alvergne, A., Jokela, M., & Lummaa, V. (2010). Personality and reproductive success in a high-fertility human population. *Proceedings of the National Academy of Sciences USA*, *107*, 11745–11750.

Amad, A., Ramoz, N., Thomas, P., Jardri, R., & Gorwood, P. (2014). Genetics of borderline personality disorder: Systematic review and proposal of an integrative model. *Neuroscience & Biobehavioral Reviews*, *40*, 6–19.

Amad, A., Thomas, P., & Mercedes Perez-Rodriguez, M. (2015). Borderline personality disorder and Oxytocin: Review of clinical trials and future directions. *Current Pharmaceutical Design*, *21*, 3311–3316.

Ambrosini, P. J., Bennett, D. S., Cleland, C. M., & Haslam, N. (2002). Taxonicity of adolescent melancholia: A categorical or dimensional construct? *Journal of Psychiatric Research*, *36*, 247–256.

American Psychiatric Association (2000). *Diagnostic and Statistical Manual of mental disorders* (4th ed., text revision). Arlington, VA: APA.

American Psychiatric Association (2013). *Diagnostic and Statistical Manual of mental disorders* (5th ed.). Arlington, VA: APA.

Anderson, C., Hildreth, J. A. D., & Howland, L. (2015). Is the desire for status a fundamental human motive? A review of the empirical literature. *Psychological Bulletin*, *141*, 574–601.

Anderson, K. G. (2006). How well does paternity confidence match actual paternity? Evidence from worldwide nonpaternity rates. *Current Anthropology*, *47*, 513–520.

Anderson, M. L. (2010). Neural reuse: A fundamental organizational principle of the brain. *Behavioral and Brain Sciences*, *33*, 245–266.

Andersson, M., & Simmons, L. W. (2006). Sexual selection and mate choice. *Trends in Ecology and Evolution*, *21*, 296–302.

Andrews, G., & Slade, T. (2002). Agoraphobia without a history of panic disorder may be part of the panic disorder syndrome. *The Journal of Nervous & Mental Disease*, *190*, 624–630.

Andrews, P. W., Bharwani, A., Lee, K. R., Fox, M., & Thomson, J. A. (2015). Is serotonin an upper or a downer? The evolution of the serotonergic system and its role in depression and the antidepressant response. *Neuroscience & Biobehavioral Reviews*, *51*, 164–188.

Andrews, P. W., & Durisko, Z. (2017). The evolution of depressive phenotypes. In R. J. DeRubeis & D. R. Strunk (Eds.), *The Oxford handbook of mood disorders* (pp. 24–36). New York: Oxford University Press.

Andrews, P. W., & Thomson, J. A., Jr. (2009). The bright side of being blue: Depression as an adaptation for analyzing complex problems. *Psychological Review*, *116*, 620–654.

Angold, A., Erkanli, A., Farmer, E. M., Fairbank, J. A., Burns, B. J., Keeler, G., et al. (2002). Psychiatric disorder, impairment, and service use in rural African American and white youth. *Archives of General Psychiatry*, *59*, 893–901.

Angst, J., Gamma, A., Benazzi, F., Ajdacic, V., & Rössler, W. (2007). Melancholia and atypical depression in the Zurich study: Epidemiology, clinical characteristics, course, comorbidity and personality. *Acta Psychiatrica Scandinavica, 115*, 72–84.

Anholt, G. E., Cath, D. C., van Oppen, P., Eikelenboom, M., Smit, J. H., van Megen, H., et al. (2010). Autism and ADHD symptoms in patients with OCD: Are they associated with specific OC symptom dimensions or OC symptom severity? *Journal of Autism & Developmental Disorders, 40*, 580–589.

Anlar, B., Oktem, F., Bakkaloglu, B., Haliloglu, M., Oguz, H., Unal, F., et al. (2007). Urinary epidermal and insulin-like growth factor excretion in autistic children. *Neuropediatrics, 38*, 151–153.

Annen, S., Roser, P., & Brüne, M. (2012). Nonverbal behavior during clinical interviews: Similarities and dissimilarities among schizophrenia, mania, and depression. *The Journal of Nervous and Mental Disease, 200*, 26–32.

Anney, R. J. L. (2013). Common genetic variants in autism spectrum disorders. In J. D. Buxbaum & P. R. Hof (Eds.), *The neuroscience of autism spectrum disorders* (pp. 155–167). Oxford: Academic Press.

Apicella, C. L., Carré, J. M., & Dreber, A. (2015). Testosterone and economic risk taking: A review. *Adaptive Human Behavior and Physiology, 1*, 358–385.

Apostolou, M. (2007). Elements of parental choice: The evolution of parental preferences in relation to in-law selection. *Evolutionary Psychology, 5*, 70–83.

Apostolou, M. (2008*a*). Parent-offspring conflict over mating: The case of beauty. *Evolutionary Psychology, 6*, 303–315.

Apostolou, M. (2008*b*). Parent-offspring conflict over mating: The case of family background. *Evolutionary Psychology, 6*, 456–468.

Apostolou, M. (2010). Sexual selection under parental choice in agropastoral societies. *Evolution and Human Behavior, 31*, 39–47.

Apostolou, M. (2011). Parent-offspring conflict over mating: Testing the tradeoffs hypothesis. *Evolutionary Psychology, 9*, 470–495.

Apostolou, M. (2013). Interfamily conflict, reproductive success, and the evolution of male homosexuality. *Review of General Psychology, 17*, 288–296.

Apostolou, M. (2014). *Sexual selection under parental choice: The evolution of human mating behaviour*. Hove, UK: Psychology Press.

Apostolou, M. (2015). Sexual dysfunctions in men: An evolutionary perspective. *Evolutionary Psychological Science, 1*, 220–231.

Arcelus, J., Mitchell, A. J., Wales, J., & Nielsen, S. (2011). Mortality rates in patients with anorexia nervosa and other eating disorders: A meta-analysis of 36 studies. *Archives of General Psychiatry, 68*, 724–731.

Arch, J. J., Landy, L. N., & Craske, M. G. (2013). Panic disorder. In W. E. Craighead, D. J. Miklowitz, & L. W. Craighead (Eds.), *Psychopathology: History, diagnosis, and empirical foundations* (2nd ed., pp. 193–243). New York: Wiley.

Archer, J. (2009). Does sexual selection explain human sex differences in aggression? *Behavioral and Brain Sciences, 32*, 249–266.

Archer, J., & Mehdikhani, M. (2003). Variability among males in sexually selected attributes. *Review of General Psychology, 7*, 219–236.

Arnedo, J., Svrakic, D. M., del Val, C., Romero-Zaliz, R., Hernández-Cuervo, H., Fanous A. H., et al. (2015). Uncovering the hidden risk architecture of the schizophrenias: Confirmation in three independent genome-wide association studies. *American Journal of Psychiatry, 172*, 139–153.

Arnone, D., Job, D., Selvaraj, S., Abe, O., Amico, F., Cheng, Y., et al. (2016). Computational meta-analysis of statistical parametric maps in major depression. *Human Brain Mapping, 37*, 1393–1404.

Arnone, D., Mumuni, A. N., Jauhar, S., Condon, B., & Cavanagh, J. (2015). Indirect evidence of selective glial involvement in glutamate-based mechanisms of mood regulation in depression: Meta-analysis of absolute prefrontal neuro-metabolic concentrations. *European Neuropsychopharmacology, 25*, 1109–1117.

Aron, A. R. (2011). From reactive to proactive and selective control: Developing a richer model for stopping inappropriate responses. *Biological Psychiatry, 69*, e55–e68.

Arslan, R. C., & Penke, L. (2015*a*). Evolutionary genetics. In D. M. Buss (Ed.), *The handbook of evolutionary psychology* (2nd ed., pp. 1047–1066). New York: Wiley.

Arslan, R. C., & Penke, L. (2015*b*). Zeroing in on the genetics of intelligence. *Journal of Intelligence, 3*, 41–45.

Asai, T., Sugimori, E., Bando, N., & Tanno, Y. (2011). The hierarchic structure in schizotypy and the five-factor model of personality. *Psychiatry Research, 185*, 78–83.

Asarnow, R. F. (2013). Childhood schizophrenia. In T. P. Beauchaine & S. P. Hinshaw (Eds.), *Child and adolescent psychopathology* (2nd ed., pp. 685–714). Hoboken, NJ: Wiley.

Ashok, A. H., Marques, T. R., Jauhar, S., Nour, M. M., Goodwin, G. M., Young, A. H., et al. (2017). The dopamine hypothesis of bipolar affective disorder: The state of the art and implications for treatment. *Molecular Psychiatry, 22*, 666–679.

Ashton, M. C., & Lee, K. (2005). A defence of the lexical approach to the study of personality structure. *European Journal of Personality, 19*, 5–24.

Ashton, M. C., & Lee, K. (2008). The HEXACO model of personality structure and the importance of the H factor. *Social and Personality Psychology Compass, 2*, 1952–1962.

Ashton, M. C., Lee, K., de Vries, R. E., Hendrickse, J., & Born, M. P. (2012). The maladaptive personality traits of the Personality Inventory for DSM-5 (PID-5) in relation to the HEXACO personality factors and schizotypy/dissociation. *Journal of Personality Disorders, 26*, 641–659.

Ashton, M. C., Lee, K., Pozzebon, J. A., Visser, B. A., & Worth, N. C. (2010). Status-driven risk taking and the major dimensions of personality. *Journal of Research in Personality, 44*, 734–737.

Ashwood, K. L., Gillan, N., Horder, J., Hayward, H., Woodhouse, E., McEwen, F. S., et al. (2016). Predicting the diagnosis of autism in adults using the Autism-Spectrum Quotient (AQ) Questionnaire. *Psychological Medicine, 46*, 2595–2604.

Aston-Jones, G., & Cohen, J. D. (2005). An integrative theory of locus coeruleus-norepinephrine function: Adaptive gain and optimal performance. *Annual Review of Neuroscience, 28*, 403–450.

Atran, S. (1998). Folk biology and the anthropology of science: Cognitive universals and cultural particulars. *Behavioral and Brain Sciences, 21*, 547–569.

Aunger, R., & Curtis, V. (2013). The anatomy of motivation: An evolutionary-ecological approach. *Biological Theory, 8*, 49–63.

Austin, E. J. (2005). Personality correlates of the broader autism phenotype as assessed by the Autism Spectrum Quotient (AQ). *Personality and Individual Differences, 38*, 451–460.

Auyeung, B., & Baron-Cohen, S. (2013). Hormonal influences in typical development: Implications for autism. In J. D. Buxbaum & P. R. Hof (Eds.), *The neuroscience of autism spectrum disorders* (pp. 215–232). Oxford: Academic Press.

Auyeung, B., & Baron-Cohen, S., Ashwin, E., Knickmeyer, R., Taylor, K., & Hackett, G. (2009). Fetal testosterone and autistic traits. *British Journal of Psychology, 100*, 1–22.

Avia, M. D., Sanz, J., Sánchez-Bernardos, M. L., Martínez-Arias, M. R., Silva, F., & Graña, J. L. (1995). The five-factor model—II. Relations of the NEO-PI with other personality variables. *Personality and Individual Differences, 19*, 81–97.

Ayers, S., Bond, R., Bertullies, S., & Wijma, K. (2016). The aetiology of post-traumatic stress following childbirth: A meta-analysis and theoretical framework. *Psychological Medicine, 46*, 1121–1134.

Azorin, J. M., Kaladjian, A., Adida, M., Hantouche, E., Hameg, A., Lancrenon, S., et al. (2008). Toward the delineation of mania subtypes in the French National EPIMAN-II Mille Cohort. *European Archives of Psychiatry and Clinical Neuroscience, 258*, 497–504.

Baams, L., Overbeek, G., Dubas, J. S., & Van Aken, M. A. (2014). On early starters and late bloomers: The development of sexual behavior in adolescence across personality types. *Journal of Sex Research, 51*, 754–764.

Baas, M., Nijstad, B. A., Boot, N. C., & De Dreu, C. K. (2016). Mad genius revisited: Vulnerability to psychopathology, biobehavioral approach-avoidance, and creativity. *Psychological Bulletin, 142*, 668–692.

Badcock, J. C., & Dragović, M. (2006). Schizotypal personality in mature adults. *Personality and Individual Differences, 40*, 77–85.

Badcock, P. B., Davey, C. G., Whittle, S., Allen, N. B., & Friston, K. J. (2017). The depressed brain: An evolutionary systems theory. *Trends in Cognitive Sciences, 21*, 182–194.

Badcock, R. C. (2004). Mentalism and mechanism: The twin modes of human cognition. In C. Crawford & C. Salmon (Eds.), *Human nature and social values: Implications of evolutionary psychology for public policy* (pp. 99–116). Mahwah, NJ: Erlbaum.

Bagshaw, R., Gray, N. S., & Snowden, R. J. (2014). Executive function in psychopathy: The Tower of London, Brixton Spatial Anticipation and the Hayling Sentence Completion Tests. *Psychiatry Research, 220*, 483–489.

Bailey, D. H., & Geary, D. C. (2009). Hominid brain evolution: Testing climatic, ecological, and social competition models. *Human Nature, 20*, 67–79.

Bailey, D. H., Walker, R. S., Blomquist, G. E., Hill, K. R., Hurtado, A. M., & Geary, D. C. (2013). Heritability and fitness correlates of personality in the Ache, a natural-fertility population in Paraguay. *PLoS ONE, 8*, e59325.

Bailey, N. W., & Zuk, M. (2009). Same-sex sexual behavior and evolution. *Trends in Ecology & Evolution, 24*, 439–446.

Baird, J., Stevenson, J. C., & Williams, D. C. (2000). The evolution of ADHD: A disorder of communication? *Quarterly Review of Biology, 75*, 17–35.

Bakermans-Kranenburg, M. J., & van IJzendoorn, M. H. (2015). The hidden efficacy of interventions: Gene × environment experiments from a differential susceptibility perspective. *Annual Review of Psychology, 66*, 381–409.

Baldini, R. (2015). Harsh environments and "fast" human life histories: What does the theory say? *bioRxiv*, doi: 10.1101/014647.

Banai, B., & Pavela, I. (2015). Two-dimensional structure of the Sociosexual Orientation Inventory and its personality correlates. *Evolutionary Psychology, 13*, 1474704915604541.

Bandy, M. S. (2004). Fissioning, scalar stress, and social evolution in early village societies. *American Anthropologist, 106*, 322–333.

Bansal, R., Staib, L. H., Laine, A. F., Hao, X., Xu, D., Liu, J., et al. (2012). Anatomical brain images alone can accurately diagnose chronic neuropsychiatric illnesses. *PLoS ONE, 7*, e50698.

Bansal, V., Mitjans, M., Burik, C. A., Linner, R. K., Okbay, A., Rietveld, C. A., et al. (2017). GWAS results for educational attainment aid in identifying genetic heterogeneity of schizophrenia. *bioRxiv*, 114405.

Bar, M. (2007). The proactive brain: Using analogies and associations to generate predictions. *Trends in Cognitive Sciences, 11*, 280–289.

Barbaro, N., Boutwell, B. B., Barnes, J. C., & Shackelford, T. K. (2017*a*). Rethinking the transmission gap: What behavioral genetics and evolutionary psychology mean for attachment theory: A comment on Verhage et al. (2016). *Psychological Bulletin, 143*, 107–113.

Barbaro, N., Boutwell, B. B., Barnes, J. C., & Shackelford, T. K. (2017*b*). Genetic confounding of the relationship between father absence and age at menarche. *Evolution and Human Behavior, 38*, 357–365.

Barbey, A. K., Colom, R., Paul, E. J., & Grafman, J. (2014). Architecture of fluid intelligence and working memory revealed by lesion mapping. *Brain Structure and Function, 219*, 485–494.

Barger, B., Campbell, J., & Simmons, C. (2016). The five factor personality model in children with ASD during middle childhood. *Focus on Autism and Other Developmental Disabilities, 31*, 174–183.

Barger, N., Hanson, K. L., Teffer, K., Schenker-Ahmed, N. M., & Semendeferi, K. (2014). Evidence for evolutionary specialization in human limbic structures. *Frontiers in Human Neuroscience, 8*, 277.

Baribeau, D. A., & Anagnostou, E. (2013). A comparison of neuroimaging findings in childhood onset schizophrenia and autism spectrum disorder: A review of the literature. *Frontiers in Psychiatry, 4*, 175.

Barker, E. D., Oliver, B. R., & Maughan, B. (2010). Co-occurring problems of early onset persistent, childhood limited, and adolescent onset conduct problem youth. *Journal of Child Psychology and Psychiatry, 51*, 1217–1226.

Barkley, R. A. (2001). The executive functions and self-regulation: An evolutionary neuropsychological perspective. *Neuropsychology Review, 11*, 1–29.

Barkley, R. A. (2012). *Executive functions: What they are, how they work, and why they evolved*. New York: Guilford.

Barkley, R. A. (2015). Concentration deficit disorder (sluggish cognitive tempo). In R. A. Barkley (Ed.), *Attention deficit hyperactivity disorder: A handbook for diagnosis and treatment* (pp. 267–313). New York: Guilford.

Barkley, R. A. (2016). Recent longitudinal studies of childhood attention-deficit/hyperactivity disorder: Important themes and questions for further research. *Journal of Abnormal Psychology, 125*, 248–255.

Barlow, D. H., Ellard, K. K., Sauer-Zavala, S., Bullis, J. R., & Carl, J. R. (2014). The origins of neuroticism. *Perspectives on Psychological Science, 9*, 481–496.

Barlow, D. H., Sauer-Zavala, S., Carl, J. R., Bullis, J. R., & Ellard, K. K. (2014). The nature, diagnosis, and treatment of neuroticism: Back to the future. *Clinical Psychological Science, 2*, 344–365.

Barlow, D. P., & Bartolomei, M. S. (2014). Genomic imprinting in mammals. *Cold Spring Harbor Perspectives in Biology, 6*, a018382.

Baron-Cohen, S. (2002). The extreme male brain theory of autism. *Trends in Cognitive Sciences, 6*, 248–254.

Baron-Cohen, S. (2003). *The essential difference*. New York: Basic Books.

Baron-Cohen, S. (2006). The hyper-systemizing, assortative mating theory of autism. *Progress in Neuro-Psychopharmacology and Biological Psychiatry*, *30*, 865–872.

Baron-Cohen, S., Ashwin, E., Ashwin, C., Tavassoli, T., & Chakrabarti, B. (2009). Talent in autism: Hyper-systemizing, hyper-attention to detail and sensory hypersensitivity. *Philosophical Transactions of the Royal Society of London B: Biological Sciences*, *364*, 1377–1383.

Baron-Cohen, S., Auyeung, B., Nørgaard-Pedersen, B., Hougaard, D. M., Abdallah, M. W., Melgaard, L., et al. (2015). Elevated fetal steroidogenic activity in autism. *Molecular Psychiatry*, *20*, 369–376.

Baron-Cohen, S., Lombardo, M. V., Auyeung, B., Ashwin, E., Chakrabarti, B., & Knickmeyer, R. (2011). Why are autism spectrum conditions more prevalent in males? *PLoS Biology*, *9*, e1001081.

Baron-Cohen, S., Wheelwright, S., Skinner, R., Martin, J., & Clubley, E. (2001). The autism-spectrum quotient (AQ): Evidence from asperger syndrome/high-functioning autism, males and females, scientists and mathematicians. *Journal of Autism and Developmental Disorders*, *31*, 5–17.

Baror, S., & Bar, M. (2016). Associative activation and its relation to exploration and exploitation in the brain. *Psychological Science*, *27*, 776–789.

Barr, K. N., & Quinsey, V. L. (2004). Is psychopathy pathology or a life strategy? Implications for social policy. In C. Crawford & C. Salmon (Eds.), *Evolutionary psychology, public policy and personal decisions* (pp. 293–317). Mahwah, NJ: Erlbaum.

Barrantes-Vidal, N., Lewandowski, K. E., & Kwapil, T. R. (2010). Psychopathology, social adjustment and personality correlates of schizotypy clusters in a large nonclinical sample. *Schizophrenia Research*, *122*, 219–225.

Barrett, E. S., Tran, V., Thurston, S., Jasienska, G., Furberg, A. S., Ellison, P. T., et al. (2013). Marriage and motherhood are associated with lower testosterone concentrations in women. *Hormones and Behavior*, *63*, 72–79.

Barrett, H. C. (2015). *The shape of thought: How mental adaptations evolve*. New York: Oxford University Press.

Barrett, H. C., & Kurzban, R. (2006). Modularity in cognition: Framing the debate. *Psychological Review*, *113*, 628–647.

Bartels, M., van Weegen, F. I., van Beijsterveldt, C. E., Carlier, M., Polderman, T. J., Hoekstra, R. A., & Boomsma, D. I. (2012). The five factor model of personality and intelligence: A twin study on the relationship between the two constructs. *Personality and Individual Differences*, *53*, 368–373.

Basten, U., Hilger, K., & Fiebach, C. J. (2015). Where smart brains are different: A quantitative meta-analysis of functional and structural brain imaging studies on intelligence. *Intelligence*, *51*, 10–27.

Bateson, M., Brilot, B., & Nettle, D. (2011). Anxiety: An evolutionary approach. *Canadian Journal of Psychiatry*, *56*, 707–715.

Bateson, P., Gluckman, P., & Hanson, M. (2014). The biology of developmental plasticity and the Predictive Adaptive Response hypothesis. *Journal of Physiology*, *592*, 2357–2368.

Batey, M., & Furnham, A. (2008). The relationship between measures of creativity and schizotypy. *Personality and Individual Differences*, *45*, 816–821.

Battaglia, M., Ogliari, A., D'Amato, F., & Kinkead, R. (2014). Early-life risk factors for panic and separation anxiety disorder: Insights and outstanding questions arising from human and animal studies of CO2 sensitivity. *Neuroscience & Biobehavioral Reviews, 46*, 455–464.

Battista, S. R., Stewart, S. H., & Ham, L. S. (2010). A critical review of laboratory-based studies examining the relationships of social anxiety and alcohol intake. *Current Drug Abuse Reviews, 3*, 3–22.

Battle, C. L., Shea, M. T., Johnson, D. M., Zlotnick, C., Zanarini, M. C., Sanislow, C. A., et al. (2004). Childhood maltreatment associated with adult personality disorders: Findings from the Collaborative Longitudinal Personality Disorders Study. *Journal of Personality Disorders, 18*, 193–211.

Bauermeister, J. J., Barkley, R. A., Bauermeister, J. A., Martínez, J. V., & McBurnett, K. (2012). Validity of the sluggish cognitive tempo, inattention, and hyperactivity symptom dimensions: Neuropsychological and psychosocial correlates. *Journal of Abnormal Child Psychology, 40*, 683–697.

Baumeister, H., & Parker, G. (2012). Meta-review of depressive subtyping models. *Journal of Affective Disorders, 139*, 126–140.

Baxter, A. J., Brugha, T. S., Erskine, H. E., Scheurer, R. W., Vos, T., & Scott, J. G. (2015). The epidemiology and global burden of autism spectrum disorders. *Psychological Medicine, 45*, 601–613.

Beach, S. R., & Amir, N. (2003). Is depression taxonic, dimensional, or both? *Journal of Abnormal Psychology, 112*, 228.

Beauchaine, T. P., Neuhaus, E., Zalewski, M., Crowell, S. E., & Potapova, N. (2011). The effects of allostatic load on neural systems subserving motivation, mood regulation, and social affiliation. *Developmental Psychopathology, 23*, 975–999.

Beauchaine, T. P., & Thayer, J. F. (2015). Heart rate variability as a transdiagnostic biomarker of psychopathology. *International Journal of Psychophysiology, 98*, 338–350.

Beaussart, M. L., Kaufman, S. B., & Kaufman, J. C. (2012). Creative activity, personality, mental illness, and short-term mating success. *Journal of Creative Behavior, 46*, 151–167.

Bechhoefer, J. (2005). Feedback for physicists: A tutorial essay on control. *Reviews of Modern Physics, 77*, 783–836.

Beck, A. T., & Bredemeier, K. (2016). A unified model of depression: Integrating clinical, cognitive, biological, and evolutionary perspectives. *Clinical Psychological Science, 4*, 596–619.

Becker, E. S., Rinck, M., Türke, V., Kause, P., Goodwin, R., Neumer, S., et al. (2007). Epidemiology of specific phobia subtypes: Findings from the Dresden Mental Health Study. *European Psychiatry, 22*, 69–74.

Becker, S. P., & Langberg, J. M. (2013). Sluggish cognitive tempo among young adolescents with ADHD relations to mental health, academic, and social functioning. *Journal of Attention Disorders, 17*, 681–689.

Beckes, L., & Simpson, J. A. (2009). Attachment, reproduction, and life history trade-offs: A broader view of human mating. *Behavioral and Brain Sciences, 32*, 23–24.

Beckmann, H., Lang, R. E., & Gattaz, W. F. (1985). Vasopressin-oxytocin in cerebrospinal fluid of schizophrenic patients and normal controls. *Psychoneuroendocrinology, 10*, 187–191.

Beehner, J. C., & Lu, A. (2013). Reproductive suppression in female primates: A review. *Evolutionary Anthropology, 22*, 226–238.

Beesdo-Baum, K., & Knappe, S. (2014). Epidemiology and natural course. In P. Emmelkamp & T. Ehring (Eds.), *The Wiley handbook of anxiety disorders* (pp. 26–46). New York: Wiley.

Bejerot, S. (2007). An autistic dimension: A proposed subtype of obsessive-compulsive disorder. *Autism, 11*, 101–110.

Bejerot, S., & Eriksson, J. M. (2014). Sexuality and gender role in autism spectrum disorder: A case control study. *PLoS ONE, 9*, e87961.

Bejerot, S., Weizman, A., & Gross-Isseroff, R. (2014). Communality between obsessive compulsive disorder and autism spectrum disorders. In B. P. Vinood, R. P. Patel, & C. R. Martin (Eds.), *Comprehensive guide to autism* (pp. 671–692). New York: Springer.

Bell, C. J., & Nutt, D. J. (1998). Serotonin and panic. *British Journal of Psychiatry, 172*, 465–471.

Bell, R. M. (1985). *Holy anorexia*. Chicago: University of Chicago Press.

Belloch, A., Cabedo, E., Carrió, C., & Larsson, C. (2010). Cognitive therapy for autogenous and reactive obsessions: Clinical and cognitive outcomes at post-treatment and 1-year follow-up. *Journal of Anxiety Disorders, 24*, 573–580.

Belloch, A., Morillo Prats, C., & García-Soriano, G. (2006). Obsession subtypes: Relationships with obsessive-compulsive symptoms, dysfunctional beliefs and thought control strategies. *Revista de Psicopatología y Psicología Clinica, 11*, 65–78.

Belsky, D. W., Caspi, A., Arseneault, L., Bleidorn, W., Fonagy, P., Goodman, M., et al. (2012). Etiological features of borderline personality related characteristics in a birth cohort of 12-year-old children. *Development and Psychopathology, 24*, 251–265.

Belsky, J. (2012). The development of human reproductive strategies: Progress and prospects. *Current Directions in Psychological Science, 21*, 310–316.

Belsky, J., Bakermans-Kranenburg, M. J., & van IJzendoorn, M. H. (2007). For better and for worse: Differential susceptibility to environmental influences. *Current Directions in Psychological Science, 16*, 300–304.

Belsky, J., & Pluess, M. (2013). Beyond risk, resilience, and dysregulation: Phenotypic plasticity and human development. *Development and Psychopathology, 25*, 1243–1261.

Belsky, J., Ruttle, P. L., Boyce, W. T., Armstrong, J. M., & Essex, M. J. (2015). Early adversity, elevated stress physiology, accelerated sexual maturation, and poor health in females. *Developmental Psychology, 51*, 816–822.

Belsky, J., Schlomer, G. L., & Ellis, B. J. (2012). Beyond cumulative risk: Distinguishing harshness and unpredictability as determinants of parenting and early life history strategy. *Developmental Psychology, 48*, 662–673.

Belsky, J., Steinberg, L., & Draper, P. (1991). Childhood experience, interpersonal development, and reproductive strategy: An evolutionary theory of socialization. *Child Development, 62*, 647–670.

Benazzi, F. (2006). Borderline personality–bipolar spectrum relationship. *Progress in Neuro-Psychopharmacology and Biological Psychiatry, 30*, 68–74.

Benenson, J. F. (2013). The development of human female competition: Allies and adversaries. *Philosophical Transactions of the Royal Society of London B, 368*, 20130079.

Benenson, J. F. (2014). *Warriors and worriers: The survival of the sexes*. New York: Oxford University Press.

Benros, M. E., Mortensen, P. B., & Eaton, W. W. (2012). Autoimmune diseases and infections as risk factors for schizophrenia. *Annals of the New York Academy of Sciences, 1262*, 56–66.

Bereczkei, T. (2015). The manipulative skill: Cognitive devices and their neural correlates underlying Machiavellian's decision making. *Brain and Cognition, 99*, 24–31.

Berenbaum, S. A., & Beltz, A. M. (2011). Sexual differentiation of human behavior: Effects of prenatal and pubertal organizational hormones. *Frontiers in Neuroendocrinology, 32*, 183–200.

Berg, V., Lummaa, V., Lahdenperä, M., Rotkirch, A., & Jokela, M. (2014). Personality and long-term reproductive success measured by the number of grandchildren. *Evolution and Human Behavior*, *35*, 533–539.

Berger, U., & Anaki, D. (2014). The behavioral inhibition system (BIS) mediates major aspects of the relationship between disgust and OCD symptomology. *Journal of Obsessive-Compulsive & Related Disorders*, *3*, 249–256.

Berger-Tal, O., Nathan, J., Meron, E., & Saltz, D. (2014). The exploration–exploitation dilemma: A multidisciplinary framework. *PLoS ONE*, *9*, e95693.

Bergin, J., Verhulst, B., Aggen, S. H., Neale, M. C., Kendler, K. S., Bienvenu, O. J., et al. (2014). Obsessive compulsive symptom dimensions and neuroticism: An examination of shared genetic and environmental risk. *American Journal of Medical Genetics Part B: Neuropsychiatric Genetics*, *165*, 647–653.

Bergmüller, R., Schürch, R., & Hamilton, I. M. (2010). Evolutionary causes and consequences of consistent individual variation in cooperative behaviour. *Philosophical Transactions of the Royal Society of London B*, *365*, 2751–2764.

Berk, M., Dodd, S., Kauer-Sant'Anna, M., Malhi, G. S., Bourin, M., Kapczinski, F., et al. (2007). Dopamine dysregulation syndrome: Implications for a dopamine hypothesis of bipolar disorder. *Acta Psychiatrica Scandinavica*, *116*, 41–49.

Berle, D., & Phillips, E. S. (2006). Disgust and obsessive-compulsive disorder: An update. *Psychiatry*, *69*, 228–238.

Bernard, K., & Dozier, M. (2010). Examining infants' cortisol responses to laboratory tasks among children varying in attachment disorganization: Stress reactivity or return to baseline? *Developmental Psychology*, *46*, 1771–1778.

Bernier, R., & Dawson, G. (2016). Autism spectrum disorders. In D. Cicchetti (Ed.), *Developmental psychopathology: Vol. 3. Maladaptation and psychopathology* (3rd ed., pp. 81–115). New York: Wiley.

Berrigan, D., & Koella, J. C. (1994). The evolution of reaction norms: Simple models for age and size at maturity. *Journal of Evolutionary Biology*, *7*, 549–566.

Besiroglu, L., Uguz, F., Ozbebit, O., Guler, O., Cilli, A. S., & Askin, R. (2007). Longitudinal assessment of symptom and subtype categories in obsessive-compulsive disorder. *Depression & Anxiety*, *24*, 461–466.

Best, J. R., Miller, P. H., & Jones, L. L. (2009). Executive functions after age 5: Changes and correlates. *Developmental Review*, *29*, 180–200.

Betancur, C., & Coleman, M. (2013). Etiological heterogeneity in autism spectrum disorders: Role of rare variants. In J. D. Buxbaum & P. R. Hof (Eds.), *The neuroscience of autism spectrum disorders* (pp. 113–144). Oxford: Academic Press.

Betts, K. S., Williams, G. M., Najman, J. M., & Alati, R. (2015). The relationship between maternal depressive, anxious, and stress symptoms during pregnancy and adult offspring behavioral and emotional problems. *Depression and Anxiety*, *32*, 82–90.

Betzig, L. (2012). Means, variances, and ranges in reproductive success: Comparative evidence. *Evolution and Human Behavior*, *33*, 309–317.

Bezdjian, S., Baker, L. A., & Tuvblad, C. (2011). Genetic and environmental influences on impulsivity: A meta-analysis of twin, family and adoption studies. *Clinical Psychology Review*, *31*, 1209–1223.

Bielby, J., Mace, G. M., Bininda-Emonds, O. R. P., Cardillo, M., Gittleman, J. L., Jones, K. E., et al. (2007). The fast-slow continuum in mammalian life history: An empirical reevaluation. *The American Naturalist*, *169*, 748–757.

Bilderbeck, A. C., Brown, G. D., Read, J., Woolrich, M., Cowen, P. J., Behrens, et al. (2014). Serotonin and social norms tryptophan depletion impairs social comparison and leads to resource depletion in a multiplayer harvesting game. *Psychological Science, 25*, 1303–1313.

Birchwood, M., Trower, P., Brunet, K., Gilbert, P., Iqbal, Z., & Jackson, C. (2007). Social anxiety and the shame of psychosis: A study in first episode psychosis. *Behaviour Research & Therapy, 45*, 1025–1037.

Birdsell, J. B. (1973). A basic demographic unit. *Current Anthropology, 14*, 337–356.

Birkás, B., & Csathó, Á. (2015). Size the day: The time perspectives of the Dark Triad. *Personality and Individual Differences, 86*, 318–320.

Biro, F. M., Galvez, M. P., Greenspan, L. C., Succop, P. A., Vangeepuram, N., Pinney, S. M., et al. (2010). Pubertal assessment method and baseline characteristics in a mixed longitudinal study of girls. *Pediatrics, 126*, e583–e590.

Biro, P. A., & Stamps, J. A. (2010). Do consistent individual differences in metabolic rate promote consistent individual differences in behavior? *Trends in Ecology & Evolution, 25*, 653–659.

Bjorklund, D. F. (1997). The role of immaturity in human development. *Psychological Bulletin, 122*, 153–169.

Bjorklund, D. F. (2017). Prepared is not preformed: Commentary on Witherington and Lickliter. *Human Development, 59*, 235–241.

Bjorklund, D. F., & Causey, K. B. (2018). *Children's thinking: Cognitive development and individual differences* (6th ed.). Thousand Oaks, CA: Sage.

Bjorklund, D. F., & Ellis, B. J. (2014). Children, childhood, and development in evolutionary perspective. *Developmental Review, 34*, 225–264.

Bjorklund, D. F., Ellis, B. J., & Rosenberg, J. S. (2007). Evolved probabilistic cognitive mechanisms: An evolutionary approach to gene x environment x development interactions. *Advances in Child Development and Behavior, 35*, 1–39.

Bjørnebekk, A., Fjell, A. M., Walhovd, K. B., Grydeland, H., Torgersen, S., & Westlye, L. T. (2013). Neuronal correlates of the five factor model (FFM) of human personality: Multimodal imaging in a large healthy sample. *NeuroImage, 65*, 194–208.

Black, C. J., Figueredo, A. J., & Jacobs, W. J. (2017). Substance, history, and politics: An examination of the conceptual underpinnings of alternative approaches to the life history narrative. *Evolutionary Psychology*, 1474704916670402.

Blackwell, K. A., Chatham, C. H., Wiseheart, M., & Munakata, Y. (2014). A developmental window into trade-offs in executive function: The case of task switching versus response inhibition in 6-year-olds. *Neuropsychologia, 62*, 356–364.

Blader, J. C., & Carlson, G. A. (2013). Bipolar disorder. In T. P. Beauchaine & S. P. Hinshaw (Eds.), *Child and adolescent psychopathology* (2nd ed., pp. 613–648). Hoboken, NJ: Wiley.

Blair, R. J. (2005). Applying a cognitive neuroscience perspective to the disorder of psychopathy. *Development and Psychopathology, 17*, 865–891.

Blakemore, S.-J., Burnett, S., & Dahl, R. E. (2010). The role of puberty in the developing adolescent brain. *Human Brain Mapping, 31*, 926–933.

Blakemore, S.-J., & Mills, K. L. (2014). Is adolescence a sensitive period for sociocultural processing? *Annual Review of Psychology, 65*, 187–207.

Blakemore, S.-J., & Robbins, T. W. (2012). Decision-making in the adolescent brain. *Nature Neuroscience, 15*, 1184–1191.

Blanchard, R. (2008). Review and theory of handedness, birth order, and homosexuality in men. *Laterality, 13*, 51–70.

Blanchard, R. (2018). Fraternal birth order, family size, and male homosexuality: Meta-analysis of studies spanning 25 years. *Archives of Sexual Behavior, 47*, 1–15.

Blanchard, R. (2018). Response to commentaries: Meta-analysis of probability samples and other new evidence. *Archives of Aexual Behavior, 47*, 49–57.

Blanchard, R. J., Flannelly, K. J., & Blanchard, D. C. (1986). Defensive reactions of laboratory and wild Rattus norvegicus. *Journal of Comparative and Physiological Psychology, 100*, 101–107.

Bland, A. R., & Schaefer, A. (2012). Different varieties of uncertainty in human decision-making. *Frontiers in Neuroscience, 6*, 85.

Blatt, G. J. (2013). Inhibitory and excitatory systems in autism spectrum disorders. In J. D. Buxbaum & P. R. Hof (Eds.), *The neuroscience of autism spectrum disorders* (pp. 335–346). Oxford: Academic Press.

Bleidorn, W., Kandler, C., & Caspi, A. (2014). The behavioural genetics of personality development in adulthood—classic, contemporary, and future trends. *European Journal of Personality, 28*, 244–255.

Blinkhorn, V., Lyons, M., & Almond, L. (2015). The ultimate femme fatale? Narcissism predicts serious and aggressive sexually coercive behaviour in females. *Personality and Individual Differences, 87*, 219–223.

Bloch, M. H., Angeli Landeros-Weisenberger, M. D., Rosario, M. C., Pittenger, C., & Leckman, J. F. (2008). Meta-analysis of the symptom structure of obsessive-compulsive disorder. *American Journal of Psychiatry, 165*, 1532–1542.

Block, J. (2002). *Personality as an affect-processing system*. Mahwah, NJ: Erlbaum.

Block, J. H., & Block, J. (1980). The role of ego-control and ego-resiliency in the organization of behavior. In W. A. Collins (Ed.), *Minnesota Symposia on Child Psychology—Vol. 13* (pp. 39–101). Mahwah, NJ: Erlbaum.

Boccio, C. M., & Beaver, K. M. (2015). Psychopathic personality traits, intelligence, and economic success. *Journal of Forensic Psychiatry & Psychology, 26*, 551–569.

Boehm, C. (1999). *Hierarchy in the forest: The evolution of egalitarian behavior*. Cambridge, MA: Harvard University Press.

Bogaert, A. F., Skorska, M. N., Wang, C., Gabrie, J., MacNeil, A. J., Hoffarth, M. R., et al. (2017). Male homosexuality and maternal immune responsivity to the Y-linked protein NLGN4Y. *Proceedings of the National Academy of Sciences USA*, 201705895.

Bogetto, F., Venturello, S., Albert, U., Maina, G., & Ravizza, L. (1999). Gender-related clinical differences in obsessive-compulsive disorder. *European Psychiatry, 14*, 434–441.

Bogg, T., & Roberts, B. W. (2004). Conscientiousness and health-related behaviors: A meta-analysis of the leading behavioral contributors to mortality. *Psychological Bulletin, 130*, 887–919.

Bogin, B. (1997). Evolutionary hypotheses for human childhood. *Yearbook of Physical Anthropology, 40*, 63–89.

Bogin, B., & Smith, B. H. (1996). Evolution of the human life cycle. *American Journal of Human Biology, 8*, 703–716.

Boogert, N. J., Fawcett, T. W., & Lefebvre, L. (2011). Mate choice for cognitive traits: A review of the evidence in nonhuman vertebrates. *Behavioral Ecology, 22*, 447–459.

Book, A., Visser, B. A., & Volk, A. A. (2015). Unpacking "evil": Claiming the core of the Dark Triad. *Personality and Individual Differences, 73*, 29–38.

Booth, R. D., & Happé, F. G. (2016). Evidence of reduced global processing in autism spectrum disorder. *Journal of Autism and Developmental Disorders*. doi:10.1007/s10803-016-2724-6

Bora, E., Bartholomeusz, C., & Pantelis, C. (2016). Meta-analysis of Theory of Mind (ToM) impairment in bipolar disorder. *Psychological Medicine, 46*, 253–264.

Bora, E., & Baysan Arabaci, L. (2009). Effect of age and gender on schizotypal personality traits in the normal population. *Psychiatry and Clinical Neurosciences, 63*, 663–669.

Bora, E., & Köse, S. (2016). Meta-analysis of theory of mind in anorexia nervosa and bulimia nervosa: A specific İmpairment of cognitive perspective taking in anorexia nervosa? *International Journal of Eating Disorders, 49*, 739–740.

Bora, E., Yucel, M., & Pantelis, C. (2009). Cognitive endophenotypes of bipolar disorder: A meta-analysis of neuropsychological deficits in euthymic patients and their first-degree relatives. *Journal of Affective Disorders, 113*, 1–20.

Borgerhoff Mulder, M. (1987). On cultural and reproductive success: Kipsigis evidence. *American Anthropologist, 89*, 617–634.

Borgerhoff Mulder, M. (1989). Menarche, menopause and reproduction in the Kipsigis of Kenya. *Journal of Biosocial Science, 21*, 179–192.

Borgerhoff Mulder, M., & Beheim, B. A. (2011). Understanding the nature of wealth and its effects on human fitness. *Philosophical Transactions of the Royal Society of London B, 366*, 344–356.

Borgerhoff Mulder, M., Bowles, S., Hertz, T., Bell, A., Beise, J., Clark, G., et al. (2009). Intergenerational wealth transmission and the dynamics of inequality in small-scale societies. *Science, 326*, 682–688.

Borges, S., Gayer-Anderson, C., & Mondelli, V. (2013). A systematic review of the activity of the hypothalamic–pituitary–adrenal axis in first episode psychosis. *Psychoneuroendocrinology, 38*, 603–611.

Borowsky, I. W., Ireland, M., & Resnick, M. D. (2009). Health status and behavioral outcomes for youth who anticipate a high likelihood of early death. *Pediatrics, 124*, e81.

Borsboom, D., & Cramer, A. O. (2013). Network analysis: An integrative approach to the structure of psychopathology. *Annual Review of Clinical Psychology, 9*, 91–121.

Bos, P. A., Panksepp, J., Bluthé, R. M., & van Honk, J. (2012). Acute effects of steroid hormones and neuropeptides on human social–emotional behavior: A review of single administration studies. *Frontiers in Neuroendocrinology, 33*, 17–35.

Boschloo, L., van Borkulo, C. D., Rhemtulla, M., Keyes, K. M., Borsboom, D., & Schoevers, R. A. (2015). The network structure of symptoms of the Diagnostic and Statistical Manual of mental disorders. *PLoS ONE, 10*, e0137621.

Bot, M., Milaneschi, Y., Penninx, B. W., & Drent, M. L. (2016). Plasma insulin-like growth factor I levels are higher in depressive and anxiety disorders, but lower in antidepressant medication users. *Psychoneuroendocrinology, 68*, 148–155.

Bourdage, J. S., Lee, K., Ashton, M. C., & Perry, A. (2007). Big Five and HEXACO model personality correlates of sexuality. *Personality and Individual Differences, 43*, 1506–1516.

Bouret, S., & Sara, S. J. (2005). Network reset: A simplified overarching theory of locus coeruleus noradrenaline function. *Trends in Neurosciences, 28*, 574–582.

Bourke, A. F. G. (2011). *Principles of social evolution*. New York: Oxford University Press.

Boutwell, B. B., Barnes, J. C., Beaver, K. M., Haynes, R. D., Nedelec, J. L., & Gibson, C. L. (2015). A unified crime theory: The evolutionary taxonomy. *Aggression and Violent Behavior*, *25*, 343–353.

Boutwell, B. B., Barnes, J. C., Deaton, R., & Beaver, K. M. (2013). On the evolutionary origins of life-course persistent offending: A theoretical scaffold for Moffitt's developmental taxonomy. *Journal of Theoretical Biology*, *322*, 72–80.

Boutwell, B. B., Beaver, K. M., & Barnes, J. C. (2012). More alike than different: Assortative mating and antisocial propensity in adulthood. *Criminal Justice and Behavior*, *39*, 1240–1254.

Boutwell, B. B., Nedelec, J. L., Lewis, R. H., Barnes, J. C., & Beaver, K. M. (2015). A behavioral genetic test of the evolutionary taxonomy. *Evolutionary Psychological Science*, *1*, 241–250.

Bowlby, J. (1980). *Attachment and loss: Loss, sadness and depression* (Vol. 3). London: Hogarth Press.

Bowles, S. (2009). Did warfare among ancestral hunter-gatherers affect the evolution of human social behaviors? *Science*, *324*, 1293–1298.

Bowles, S., & Gintis, H. (2011). *A cooperative species: Human reciprocity and its evolution*. Princeton, NJ: Princeton University Press.

Boyce, W. T., & Ellis, B. J. (2005). Biological sensitivity to context: I. An evolutionary-developmental theory of the origins and functions of stress reactivity. *Development and Psychopathology*, *17*, 271–301.

Boyer, P., & Bergstrom, B. (2011). Threat-detection in child development: An evolutionary perspective. *Neuroscience & Biobehavioral Reviews*, *35*, 1034–1041.

Boyer, P., & Liénard, P. (2006). Precaution systems and ritualized behavior. *Behavioral and Brain Sciences*, *29*, 635–641.

Bracha, H. S. (2006). Human brain evolution and the "Neuroevolutionary Time-depth Principle": Implications for the reclassification of fear-circuitry-related traits in DSM-V and for studying resilience to warzone-related posttraumatic stress disorder. *Progress in Neuro-Psychopharmacology and Biological Psychiatry*, *30*, 827–853.

Bracha, H. S., Bienvenu, O. J., & Eaton, W. W. (2007). Testing the Paleolithic-human-warfare hypothesis of blood–injection phobia in the Baltimore ECA Follow-up Study—towards a more etiologically-based conceptualization for DSM-V. *Journal of Affective Disorders*, *97*, 1–4.

Bracha, H. S., Bracha, A. S., Williams, A. E., Ralston, T. C., & Matsukawa, J. M. (2005). The human fear-circuitry and fear-induced fainting in healthy individuals. *Clinical Autonomic Research*, *15*, 238–241.

Bracha, H. S., Lenze, S. M., & Shelton, J. (2006). Primary agoraphobia as a specific phobia. *British Journal of Psychiatry*, *189*, 470.

Braendle, C., Heyland, F., & Flatt, T. (2011). Integrating mechanistic and evolutionary analysis of life history variation. In T. Flatt & F. Heyland (Eds.), *Mechanisms of life history evolution. The genetics and physiology of life history traits and trade-offs* (pp. 3–10). New York: Oxford University Press.

Brakoulias, V., Starcevic, V., Berle, D., Milicevic, D., Moses, K., Hannan, A., et al. (2013). The characteristics of unacceptable/taboo thoughts in obsessive-compulsive disorder. *Comprehensive Psychiatry*, *54*, 750–757.

Brander, G., Pérez-Vigil, A., Larsson, H., & Mataix-Cols, D. (2016). Systematic review of environmental risk factors for obsessive-compulsive disorder: A proposed roadmap from association to causation. *Neuroscience & Biobehavioral Reviews*, *65*, 36–62.

Brase, G. L. (2006). Cues of parental investment as a factor in attractiveness. *Evolution and Human Behavior, 27*, 145–157.

Brase, G. L., & Brase, S. L. (2012). Emotional regulation of fertility decision making: What is the nature and structure of "baby fever"? *Emotion, 12*, 1141–1154.

Braver, T. S. (2012). The variable nature of cognitive control: A dual mechanisms framework. *Trends in Cognitive Sciences, 16*, 106–113.

Braver, T. S., Paxton, J. L., Locke, H. S., & Barch, D. M. (2009). Flexible neural mechanisms of cognitive control within human prefrontal cortex. *Proceedings of the National Academy of Sciences USA, 106*, 7351–7356.

Breedlove, S. M. (2017). Prenatal influences on human sexual orientation: Expectations versus data. *Archives of Sexual Behavior, 46*, 1583–1592.

Bremner, J. D., & Pearce, B. (2016). Neurotransmitter, neurohormonal, and neuropeptidal function in stress and PTSD. In J. D. Bremner (Ed.), *Posttraumatic stress disorder: From neurobiology to treatment* (pp. 181–232). Hoboken, NJ: Wiley.

Brennan, K. A., & Shaver, P. R. (1995). Dimensions of adult attachment, affect regulation, and romantic relationship functioning. *Personality and Social Psychology Bulletin, 21*, 267–283.

Breslau, J., Aguilar-Gaxiola, S., Kendler, K. S., Su, M., Williams, D., & Kessler, R. C. (2006). Specifying race-ethnic differences in risk for psychiatric disorder in a USA national sample. *Psychological Medicine, 36*, 57–68.

Breslau, N., Reboussin, B. A., Anthony, J. C., & Storr, C. L. (2005). The structure of posttraumatic stress disorder: Latent class analysis in 2 community samples. *Archives of General Psychiatry, 62*, 1343–1351.

Bresnahan, M., Begg, M. D., Brown, A., Schaefer, C., Sohler, N., Insel, B., et al. (2007). Race and risk of schizophrenia in a US birth cohort: Another example of health disparity? *International Journal of Epidemiology, 36*, 751–758.

Bretherton, I., & Munholland, K. A. (2008). Internal working models in attachment relationships. In J. Cassidy & P. R. Shaver (Eds.), *Handbook of attachment* (2nd ed., pp. 102–127). New York: Guilford.

Brewer, R., Marsh, A. A., Catmur, C., Cardinale, E. M., Stoycos, S., Cook, R., et al. (2015). The impact of autism spectrum disorder and alexithymia on judgments of moral acceptability. *Journal of Abnormal Psychology, 124*, 589.

Brewerton, T. D., & Duncan, A. E. (2016). Associations between attention deficit hyperactivity disorder and eating disorders by gender: Results from the national comorbidity survey replication. *European Eating Disorders Review, 24*, 536–540.

Brewin, C. R. (2016). Coherence, disorganization, and fragmentation in traumatic memory reconsidered: A response to Rubin et al. (2016). *Journal of Abnormal Psychology, 125*, 1011–1017.

Brezina, T., Tekin, E., & Topalli, V. (2009). "Might not be a tomorrow": A multimethods approach to anticipated early death and youth crime. *Criminology, 47*, 1091–1129.

Brieger, P., Ehrt, U., & Marneros, A. (2003). Frequency of comorbid personality disorders in bipolar and unipolar affective disorders. *Comprehensive Psychiatry, 44*, 28–34.

Briley, D. A., & Tucker-Drob, E. M. (2017). Comparing the developmental genetics of cognition and personality over the life span. *Journal of Personality, 85*, 51–64.

Brody, J. F. (2001). Evolutionary recasting: ADHD, mania and its variants. *Journal of Affective Disorders, 65*, 197–215.

Broerman, R. L., Ross, S. R., & Corr, P. J. (2014). Throwing more light on the dark side of psychopathy: An extension of previous findings for the revised Reinforcement Sensitivity Theory. *Personality and Individual Differences, 68*, 165–169.

Broesch, J., Barrett, H. C., & Henrich, J. (2014). Adaptive content biases in learning about animals across the life course. *Human Nature*, *25*, 181–199.

Brosens, J. J., Salker, M. S., Teklenburg, G., Nautiyal, J., Salter, S., Lucas, E. S., et al. (2014). Uterine selection of human embryos at implantation. *Scientific Reports*, *4*, 3894.

Brosnan, M., Ashwin, C., Walker, I., & Donaghue, J. (2010). Can an "Extreme Female Brain" be characterised in terms of psychosis? *Personality and Individual Differences*, *49*, 738–742.

Brosnan, M., Chapman, E., & Ashwin, C. (2014). Adolescents with autism spectrum disorder show a circumspect reasoning bias rather than 'jumping-to-conclusions'. *Journal of Autism and Developmental Disorders*, *44*, 513–520.

Brown, G. R., Laland, K. N., & Borgerhoff Mulder, M. (2009). Bateman's principles and human sex roles. *Trends in Ecology and Evolution*, *24*, 297–304.

Brown, J. H., Gillooly, J. F., Allen, A. P., Savage, V. M., & West, G. B. (2004). Toward a metabolic theory of ecology. *Ecology*, *85*, 1771–1789.

Brown, R. M., Brown, S. L., Johnson, A., Olsen, B., Melver, K., & Sullivan, M. (2009). Empirical support for an evolutionary model of self-destructive motivation. *Suicide and Life-Threatening Behavior*, *39*, 1–12.

Brown, S., Brown, R., & Preston, S. D. (2012). A Model of human caregiving motivation. In S. L. Brown, R. M. Brown, & L. A. Penner (Eds.), *Moving beyond self interest: Perspectives from evolutionary biology, neuroscience, and the social sciences* (pp. 75–88). New York: Oxford University Press.

Brown, T. E. (2013). *A new understanding of ADHD in children and adults: Executive function impairments*. New York: Routledge.

Broyd, S. J., Demanuele, C., Debener, S., Helps, S. K., James, C. J., & Sonuga-Barke, E. J. (2009). Default-mode brain dysfunction in mental disorders: A systematic review. *Neuroscience & Biobehavioral Reviews*, *33*, 279–296.

Bruckner, T. A., Saxton, K. B., Pearl, M., Currier, R., & Kharrazi, M. (2012). A test of maternal human chorionic gonadotropin during pregnancy as an adaptive filter of human gestations. *Proceedings of the Royal Society of London B*, *279*, 4604–4610.

Brühl, A. B., Delsignore, A., Komossa, K., & Weidt, S. (2014). Neuroimaging in social anxiety disorder: A meta-analytic review resulting in a new neurofunctional model. *Neuroscience & Biobehavioral Reviews*, *47*, 260–280.

Brumbach, B. H., Figueredo, A. J., & Ellis, B. J. (2009). Effects of harsh and unpredictable environments in adolescence on development of life history strategies. *Human Nature*, *20*, 25–51.

Brumberg, J. J. (1989). *Fasting girls: A history of anorexia nervosa*. New York: Plume.

Brüne, M. (2006). The evolutionary psychology of obsessive-compulsive disorder: The role of cognitive metarepresentation. *Perspectives in Biology & Medicine*, *49*, 317–329.

Brüne, M. (2014). Life history theory as organizing principle of psychiatric disorders: Implications and prospects exemplified by borderline personality disorder. *Psychological Inquiry*, *25*, 311–321.

Brüne, M. (2015). *Textbook of evolutionary psychiatry and psychosomatic medicine: The origins of psychopathology* (2nd ed.). Oxford: Oxford University Press.

Brüne, M. (2016). Borderline Personality DisorderL Why 'fast and furious'? *Evolution, Medicine, and Public Health*, *2016*, 52–66.

Brüne, M., Ghiassi, V., & Ribbert, H. (2010). Does borderline personality reflect the pathological extreme of an adaptive reproductive strategy? Insights and hypotheses from evolutionary life-history theory. *Clinical Neuropsychiatry*, *7*, 3–9.

Brunnlieb, C., Nave, G., Camerer, C. F., Schosser, S., Vogt, B., Münte, T. F., et al. (2016). Vasopressin increases human risky cooperative behavior. *Proceedings of the National Academy of Sciences USA, 113*, 2051–2056.

Bugental, D. B. (2000). Acquisition of the algorithms of social life: A domain-based approach. *Psychological Bulletin, 126*, 187–219.

Buizer-Voskamp, J. E., Laan, W., Staal, W. G., Hennekam, E. A., Aukes, M. F., Termorshuizen, F., et al. (2011). Paternal age and psychiatric disorders: Findings from a Dutch population registry. *Schizophrenia Research, 129*, 128–132.

Bulik, C. M., Trace, S. E., Kleiman, S. C., & Mazzeo, S. E. (2014). Feeding and eating disorders. In D. C. Beidel, B. C. Frueh, & M. Hersen (Eds.), *Adult psychopathology and diagnosis* (7th ed., pp. 473–522). New York: Wiley.

Bulik-Sullivan, B., Finucane, H. K., Anttila, V., Gusev, A., Day, F. R., Loh, P. R., et al. (2015). An atlas of genetic correlations across human diseases and traits. *Nature Genetics, 47*, 1236–1241.

Bulley, A., Miloyan, B., Brilot, B., Gullo, M. J., & Suddendorf, T. (2016). An evolutionary perspective on the co-occurrence of social anxiety disorder and alcohol use disorder. *Journal of Affective Disorders, 196*, 62–70.

Burdick, K. E., Russo, M., Frangou, S., Mahon, K., Braga, R. J., Shanahan, M., et al. (2014). Empirical evidence for discrete neurocognitive subgroups in bipolar disorder: Clinical implications. *Psychological Medicine, 44*, 3083–3096.

Burgaleta, M., Head, K., Álvarez-Linera, J., Martínez, K., Escorial, S., Haier, R., et al. (2012). Sex differences in brain volume are related to specific skills, not to general intelligence. *Intelligence, 40*, 60–68.

Burghardt, G. M. (2005). *The genesis of animal play*. Cambridge, MA: MIT Press.

Burns, G. L., Alves de Moura, M., Beauchaine, T. P., & McBurnett, K. (2014). Bifactor latent structure of ADHD/ODD symptoms: Predictions of dual-pathway/trait-impulsivity etiological models of ADHD. *Journal of Child Psychology and Psychiatry, 55*, 393–401.

Burns, J. K. (2004). An evolutionary theory of schizophrenia: Cortical connectivity, metarepresentation, and the social brain. *Behavioral and Brain Sciences, 27*, 831–855.

Burns, J. K. (2007). *The descent of madness: Evolutionary origins of psychosis and the social brain*. New York: Routledge.

Burns, J. K. (2009). Reconciling 'the new epidemiology' with an evolutionary genetic basis for schizophrenia. *Medical Hypotheses, 72*, 353–358.

Burt, A., & Trivers, L. R. (2006). *Genes in conflict: The biology of selfish genetic elements*. Cambridge, MA: Harvard University Press.

Burt, S. A. (2014). The shared environment as a key source of variability in child and adolescent psychopathology. *Journal of Child Psychology and Psychiatry, 55*, 304–312.

Burt, S. A., Klump, K. L., Gorman-Smith, D., & Neiderhiser, J. M. (2016). Neighborhood disadvantage alters the origins of children's nonaggressive conduct problems. *Clinical Psychological Science, 4*, 511–526.

Burton-Cheller, M. N., & Dunbar, R. I. M. (2014). Hamilton's rule predicts anticipated social support in humans. *Behavioral Ecology, 26*, 130–137.

Buss, D. M. (2000). *The dangerous passion: Why jealousy is as necessary as love and sex*. New York: Free Press.

Buss, D. M. (2003). *The evolution of desire: Strategies of human mating* (revised edition). New York: Basic Books.

Buss, D. M. (2011). Personality and the adaptive landscape: The role of individual differences in creating and solving social adaptive problems. In D. M. Buss & P. H.

Hawley (Eds.), *The evolution of personality and individual differences* (pp. 29–59). New York: Oxford University Press.

Buss, D. M. (2013). Sexual jealousy. *Psychological Topics, 22*, 155–182.

Buss, D. M. (Ed.). (2015). *The handbook of evolutionary psychology* (2nd ed.). New York: Wiley.

Buunk, A. P., Park, J. H., & Dubbs, S. L. (2008). Parent–offspring conflict in mate preferences. *Review of General Psychology, 12*, 47–62.

Byers, J. A., & Walker, C. (1995). Refining the motor training hypothesis for the evolution of play. *The American Naturalist, 146*, 25–40.

Byars, S. G., Stearns, S. C., & Boomsma, J. J. (2014). Opposite risk patterns for autism and schizophrenia are associated with normal variation in birth size: Phenotypic support for hypothesized diametric gene-dosage effects. *Proceedings of the Royal Society of London B, 281*, 20140604.

Bylsma, L. M., Morris, B. H., & Rottenberg, J. (2008). A meta-analysis of emotional reactivity in major depressive disorder. *Clinical Psychology Review, 28*, 676–691.

Byrd, A. L., Hawes, S. W., Loeber, R., & Pardini, D. A. (2016). Interpersonal callousness from childhood to adolescence: Developmental trajectories and early risk factors. *Journal of Clinical Child & Adolescent Psychology.* doi:10.1080/15374416.2016.1144190

Byrne, M. L., Whittle, S., Vijayakumar, N., Dennison, M., Simmons, J. G., & Allen, N. B. (2017). A systematic review of adrenarche as a sensitive period in neurobiological development and mental health. *Developmental Cognitive Neuroscience, 25*, 12–28.

Byrne, R. W. (2005). Social cognition: Imitation, imitation, imitation. *Current Biology, 15*, R489–R500.

Byrne, R. W., & Whiten, A. (1989). *Machiavellian intelligence: Social expertise and the evolution of intellect in monkeys, apes, and humans*. New York: Oxford University Press.

Byrnes, J. P., Miller, D. C., & Schafer, W. D. (1999). Gender differences in risk taking: A meta-analysis. *Psychological Bulletin, 125*, 367–383.

Cadman, T., Spain, D., Johnston, P., Russell, A., Mataix-Cols, D., Craig, M., et al. (2015). Obsessive-compulsive disorder in adults with high-functioning autism spectrum disorder: What does self-report with the OCI-R tell us? *Autism Research, 8*, 477–485.

Cahill, S. P., & Foa, E. B. (2007). Psychological theories of PTSD. In M. J. Friedman, T. M. Keane & P. A. Resick (Eds.), *Handbook of PTSD: Science and practice* (pp. 55–77). New York: Guilford.

Cain, N. M., Ansell, E. B., Simpson, H. B., & Pinto, A. (2015). Interpersonal functioning in obsessive-compulsive personality disorder. *Journal of Personality Assessment, 97*, 90–99.

Calamari, J. E., Chik, H. M., Pontarelli, N. K., & DeJong, B. L. (2011). Phenomenology and epidemiology of obsessive compulsive disorder. In G. Steketee (Ed.), *The Oxford handbook of obsessive compulsive and spectrum disorders* (pp. 11–47). New York: Oxford University Press.

Calhoun, V. D., Sui, J., Kiehl, K., Turner, J., Allen, E., & Pearlson, G. (2012). Exploring the psychosis functional connectome: Aberrant intrinsic networks in schizophrenia and bipolar disorder. *Frontiers in Psychiatry, 2*, 75.

Calkins, A. W., Berman, N. C., & Wilhelm, S. (2013). Recent advances in research on cognition and emotion in OCD: A review. *Current Psychiatry Reports, 15*, 357.

Camisa, K. M., Bockbrader, M. A., Lysaker, P., Rae, L. L., Brenner, C. A., & O'Donnell, B. F. (2005). Personality traits in schizophrenia and related personality disorders. *Psychiatry Research, 133*, 23–33.

Campanella, C., & Bremner, J. D. (2016). Neuroimaging of PTSD. In J. D. Bremner (Ed.), *Posttraumatic stress disorder: From neurobiology to treatment* (pp. 291–318). Hoboken, NJ: Wiley.

Campbell, A. (1999). Staying alive: Evolution, culture, and women's intrasexual aggression. *Behavioral and Brain Sciences, 22*, 203–252.

Campbell, A. (2004). Female competition: Causes, constraints, content, and contexts. *Journal of Sex Research, 41*, 16–26.

Campbell, B. C. (2006). Adrenarche and the evolution of human life history. *American Journal of Human Biology, 18*, 569–589.

Campbell, B. C. (2011). Adrenarche and middle childhood. *Human Nature, 22*, 327–349.

Campbell, D. J., Chang, J., & Chawarska, K. (2014). Early generalized overgrowth in autism spectrum disorder: Prevalence rates, gender effects, and clinical outcomes. *Journal of the American Academy of Child & Adolescent Psychiatry, 53*, 1063–1073.

Camperio Ciani, A., Cermelli, P., & Zanzotto, G. (2008). Sexually antagonistic selection in human male homosexuality. *PLoS ONE, 3*, e2282.

Camperio Ciani, A., & Pellizzari, E. (2012). Fecundity of paternal and maternal non-parental female relatives of homosexual and heterosexual men. *PLoS ONE, 7*, e51088.

Cannon, T. D. (2015). How schizophrenia develops: Cognitive and brain mechanisms underlying onset of psychosis. *Trends in Cognitive Sciences, 19*, 744–756.

Canteras, N. S., & Graeff, F. G. (2014). Executive and modulatory neural circuits of defensive reactions: Implications for panic disorder. *Neuroscience & Biobehavioral Reviews, 46*, 352–364.

Cantor, C. (2005). *Evolution and posttraumatic stress: Disorders of vigilance and defence.* Hove, UK: Routledge.

Cantor, C. (2009). Post-traumatic stress disorder: Evolutionary perspectives. *Australian and New Zealand Journal of Psychiatry, 43*, 1038–1048.

Cantor, C., & Price, J. (2007). Traumatic entrapment, appeasement and complex post-traumatic stress disorder: Evolutionary perspectives of hostage reactions, domestic abuse and the Stockholm syndrome. *Australian and New Zealand Journal of Psychiatry, 41*(5), 377–384.

Cantor-Graae, E., & Selten, J. P. (2005). Schizophrenia and migration: A meta-analysis and review. *American Journal of Psychiatry, 162*, 12–24.

Caplan, R. (2016). Childhood schizophrenia. In D. Cicchetti (Ed.), *Developmental psychopathology: Vol. 3. Maladaptation and psychopathology* (3rd ed., pp. 898–997). New York: Wiley.

Capuron, L., Lasselin, J., & Castanon, N. (2017). Role of adiposity-driven inflammation in depressive morbidity. *Neuropsychopharmacology, 42*, 115–128.

Capusan, A. J., Kuja-Halkola, R., Bendtsen, P., Viding, E., McCrory, E., Marteinsdottir, I., et al. (2016). Childhood maltreatment and attention deficit hyperactivity disorder symptoms in adults: A large twin study. *Psychological Medicine, 46*, 2637–2646.

Card, N. A., Stucky, B. D., Sawalani, G. M., & Little, T. D. (2008). Direct and indirect aggression during childhood and adolescence: A meta-analytic review of gender differences, intercorrelations, and relations to maladjustment. *Child Development, 79*, 1185–1229.

Careau, V., Montiglio, P. O., Garant, D., Pelletier, F., Speakman, J. R., Humphries, M. M., & Réale, D. (2015). Energy expenditure and personality in wild chipmunks. *Behavioral Ecology and Sociobiology, 69*, 653–661.

Carere, C., Caramaschi, D., & Fawcett, T. W. (2010). Covariation between personalities and individual differences in coping with stress: Converging evidence and hypotheses. *Current Zoology*, *56*, 728–740.

Carina Gillberg, I., Råstam, M., Wentz, E., & Gillberg, C. (2007). Cognitive and executive functions in anorexia nervosa ten years after onset of eating disorder. *Journal of Clinical and Experimental Neuropsychology*, *29*, 170–178.

Carlisi, C. O., Norman, L. J., Lukito, S. S., Radua, J., Mataix-Cols, D., & Rubia, K. (2017). Comparative multimodal meta-analysis of structural and functional brain abnormalities in autism spectrum disorder and obsessive-compulsive disorder. *Biological Psychiatry*, *82*, 83–102.

Carr, S. N., & Francis, A. J. (2010). Early maladaptive schemas and personality disorder symptoms: An examination in a non-clinical sample. *Psychology and Psychotherapy: Theory, Research and Practice*, *83*, 333–349.

Carragher, N., Adamson, G., Bunting, B., & McCann, S. (2009). Subtypes of depression in a nationally representative sample. *Journal of Affective Disorders*, *113*, 88–99.

Carragher, N., Krueger, R. F., Eaton, N. R., & Slade, T. (2015). Disorders without borders: Current and future directions in the meta-structure of mental disorders. *Social Psychiatry and Psychiatric Epidemiology*, *50*, 339–350.

Carragher, N., Teesson, M., Sunderland, M., Newton, N. C., Krueger, R. F., Conrod, P. J., et al. (2016). The structure of adolescent psychopathology: A symptom-level analysis. *Psychological Medicine*, *46*, 981–994.

Carrasco, J. L., Díaz-Marsá, M., Pastrana, J. I., Molina, R., Brotons, L., López-Ibor, M. I., et al. (2007). Hypothalamic–pituitary–adrenal axis response in borderline personality disorder without post-traumatic features. *British Journal of Psychiatry*, *190*, 357–358.

Carré, J. M., & Archer, J. (2018). Testosterone and human behavior: The role of individual and contextual variables. *Current Opinion in Psychology*, *19*, 149–153.

Carruthers, P. (2006). *The architecture of the mind*. New York: Oxford University Press.

Carruthers, P. (2009). How we know our own minds: The relationship between mindreading and metacognition. *Behavioral and Brain Sciences*, *32*, 121–182.

Carter, J. C., Kelly, A. C., & Norwood, S. J. (2012). Interpersonal problems in anorexia nervosa: Social inhibition as defining and detrimental. *Personality and Individual Differences*, *53*, 169–174.

Carter, N. T., Guan, L., Maples, J. L., Williamson, R. L., & Miller, J. D. (2016). The downsides of extreme conscientiousness for psychological well-being: The role of obsessive compulsive tendencies. *Journal of Personality*, *84*, 510–522.

Carver, C. S., Johnson, S. L., Joormann, J., & Scheier, M. F. (2015). An evolving view of the structure of self-regulation. In G. H. E. Gendolla, M. Tops, & S. Koole (Eds.), *Handbook of biobehavioral approaches to self-regulation* (pp. 9–24). New York: Springer.

Carver, C. S., Johnson, S. L., McCullough, M. E., Forster, D. E., & Joormann, J. (2014). Adulthood personality correlates of childhood adversity. *Frontiers in Psychology*, *5*, 1357.

Carver, C. S., Johnson, S. L., & Timpano, K. R. (2017). Toward a functional view of the p factor in psychopathology. *Clinical Psychological Science*. doi:10.1177/2167702617710037

Carver, C. S., & Scheier, M. F. (2011). Self-regulation of action and affect. In K. D. Vohs & R. F. Baumeister (Eds.), *Handbook of self-regulation: Research, theory, and applications* (2nd ed., pp. 3–21). New York: Guilford.

Casey, B. J., Jones, R. M., & Somerville, L. H. (2011). Braking and accelerating of the adolescent brain. *Journal of Research on Adolescence, 21*, 21–33.

Cashdan, E. (1995). Hormones, sex, and status in women. *Hormones and Behavior, 29*, 354–366.

Caspi, A., Houts, R. M., Belsky, D. W., Goldman-Mellor, S. J., Harrington, H., Israel, S., et al. (2014). The p-factor: One general psychopathology factor in the structure of psychiatric disorders? *Clinical Psychological Science, 2*, 119–127.

Cassano, P., Bui, E., Rogers, A. H., Walton, Z. E., Ross, R., Zeng, M., et al. (2017). Inflammatory cytokines in major depressive disorder: A case–control study. *Australian and New Zealand Journal of Psychiatry, 51*, 23–31.

Cassidy, F., & Carroll, B. J. (2002). Seasonal variation of mixed and pure episodes of bipolar disorder. *Journal of Affective Disorders, 68*, 25–31.

Cassidy, J. (2008). The nature of the child's ties. In J. Cassidy & P. R. Shaver (Eds.), *Handbook of attachment* (2nd ed., pp. 3–22). New York: Guilford.

Cassin, S. E., & von Ranson, K. M. (2005). Personality and eating disorders: A decade in review. *Clinical Psychology Review, 25*, 895–916.

Castellano, S. (2015). Bayes' rule and bias roles in the evolution of decision making. *Behavioral Ecology, 26*, 282–292.

Castellano, S., & Cermelli, P. (2010). Attractive amplifiers in sexual selection: Where efficacy meets honesty. *Evolutionary Ecology, 24*, 1187–1197.

Castellanos-Ryan, N., Brière, F. N., O'Leary-Barrett, M., Banaschewski, T., Bodke, A., Brimberg, U., et al. (2016). The structure of psychopathology in adolescence and its common personality and cognitive correlates. *Journal of Abnormal Psychology, 125*, 1039–1052.

Caudell, M. A., & Quinlan, R. J. (2012). Resource availability, mortality, and fertility: A path analytic approach to global life-history variation. *Human Biology, 84*, 101–125.

Cavanagh, J. F., & Frank, M. J. (2014). Frontal theta as a mechanism for cognitive control. *Trends in Cognitive Sciences, 18*, 414–421.

Cavanagh, J. F., Wiecki, T. V., Cohen, M. X., Figueroa, C. M., Samanta, J., Sherman, S. J., & Frank, M. J. (2011). Subthalamic nucleus stimulation reverses mediofrontal influence over decision threshold. *Nature Neuroscience, 14*, 1462–1467.

Cavazos-Rehg, P. A., Krauss, M. J., Spitznagel, E. L., Schootman, M., Bucholz, K. K., Peipert, J. F., et al. (2009). Age of sexual debut among US adolescents. *Contraception, 80*, 158–162.

Cederlöf, M., Pettersson, E., Sariaslan, A., Larsson, H., Östberg, P., Kelleher, I., et al. (2016). The association between childhood autistic traits and adolescent psychotic experiences is explained by general neuropsychiatric problems. *American Journal of Medical Genetics B, 171*, 153–159.

Cerliani, L., Mennes, M., Thomas, R. M., Di Martino, A., Thioux, M., & Keysers, C. (2015). Increased functional connectivity between subcortical and cortical resting-state networks in autism spectrum disorder. *JAMA Psychiatry, 72*, 767–777.

Černis, E., Vassos, E., Brébion, G., McKenna, P. J., Murray, R. M., David, A. S., et al. (2015). Schizophrenia patients with high intelligence: A clinically distinct sub-type of schizophrenia? *European Psychiatry, 30*, 628–632.

Cesta, C. E., Månsson, M., Palm, C., Lichtenstein, P., Iliadou, A. N., & Landén, M. (2016). Polycystic ovary syndrome and psychiatric disorders: Co-morbidity and heritability in a nationwide Swedish cohort. *Psychoneuroendocrinology, 73*, 196–203.

Chabris, C. F., Lee, J. J., Cesarini, D., Benjamin, D. J., & Laibson, D. I. (2015). The fourth law of behavior genetics. *Current Directions in Psychological Science, 24*, 304–312.

Chabrol, H., Valls, M., van Leeuwen, N., & Bui, E. (2012). Callous-unemotional and borderline traits in nonclinical adolescents: Personality profiles and relations to antisocial behaviors. *Personality and Individual Differences, 53*, 969–973.

Chandler, C. H., Ofria, C., & Dworkin, I. (2013). Runaway sexual selection leads to good genes. *Evolution, 67*, 110–119.

Chang, L., Connelly, B. S., & Geeza, A. A. (2012). Separating method factors and higher order traits of the Big Five: A meta-analytic multitrait–multimethod approach. *Journal of Personality and Social Psychology, 102*, 408–426.

Chapais, B. (2008). *Primeval kinship: How pair-bonding gave birth to human society*. Cambridge, MA: Harvard University Press.

Chapais, B. (2011). The evolutionary history of pair-bonding and parental collaboration. In C. A. Salmon & T. K. Shackelford (Eds.), *The Oxford handbook of evolutionary family psychology* (pp. 33–50). New York: Oxford University Press.

Chapman, B. P., & Goldberg, L. R. (2011). Replicability and 40-year predictive power of childhood ARC types. *Journal of Personality and Social Psychology, 101*, 593–606.

Chapman, H. A., Kim, D. A., Susskind, J. M., & Anderson, A. K. (2009). In bad taste: Evidence for the oral origins of moral disgust. *Science, 323*, 1222–1226.

Charlesworth, B. (1994). *Evolution in age-structured populations* (2nd ed.). New York: Cambridge University Press.

Charney, D. S., & Nestler, E. J. (Eds.) (2009). *Neurobiology of mental illness* (3rd ed). New York: Oxford University Press.

Chavira, D. A., Grilo, C. M., Shea, M. T., Yen, S., Gunderson, J. G., Morey, L. C., et al. (2003). Ethnicity and four personality disorders. *Comprehensive Psychiatry, 44*, 483–491.

Chawarska, K., Macari, S., Powell, K., DiNicola, L., & Shic, F. (2016). Enhanced social attention in female infant siblings at risk for autism. *Journal of the American Academy of Child & Adolescent Psychiatry, 55*, 188–195.

Chen, C., Takahashi, T., Nakagawa, S., Inoue, T., & Kusumi, I. (2015). Reinforcement learning in depression: A review of computational research. *Neuroscience & Biobehavioral Reviews, 55*, 247–267.

Chen, L. S., Eaton, W. W., Gallo, J. J., & Nestadt, G. (2000). Understanding the heterogeneity of depression through the triad of symptoms, course and risk factors: A longitudinal, population-based study. *Journal of Affective Disorders, 59*, 1–11.

Chen, M. H., Chen, Y. S., Hsu, J. W., Huang, K. L., Li, C. T., Lin, W. C., et al. (2015). Comorbidity of ADHD and subsequent bipolar disorder among adolescents and young adults with major depression: A nationwide longitudinal study. *Bipolar Disorders, 17*, 315–322.

Chen, P., & Vazsonyi, A. T. (2011). Future orientation, impulsivity, and problem behaviors: A longitudinal moderation model. *Developmental Psychology, 47*, 1633–1645.

Chen, X., Kuja-Halkola, R., Rahman, I., Arpegård, J., Viktorin, A., Karlsson, R., et al. (2015). Dominant genetic variation and missing heritability for human complex traits: Insights from twin versus genome-wide common SNP models. *American Journal of Human Genetics, 97*, 708–714.

Cheng, J. T., Tracy, J. L., & Henrich, J. (2010). Pride, personality, and the evolutionary foundations of human social status. *Evolution and Human Behavior, 31*, 334–347.

Cheslack-Postava, K., Liu, K., & Bearman, P. S. (2011). Closely spaced pregnancies are associated with increased odds of autism in California sibling births. *Pediatrics, 127*, 246–253.

Cheslack-Postava, K., Suominen, A., Jokiranta, E., Lehti, V., McKeague, I. W., Sourander, A., et al. (2014). Increased risk of autism spectrum disorders at short and long interpregnancy intervals in Finland. *Journal of the American Academy of Child & Adolescent Psychiatry, 53*, 1074–1081.

Chevallier, C., Kohls, G., Troiani, V., Brodkin, E. S., & Schultz, R. T. (2012). The social motivation theory of autism. *Trends in Cognitive Sciences, 16*, 231–239.

Chevallier, C., Molesworth, C., & Happé, F. (2012). Diminished social motivation negatively impacts reputation management: Autism spectrum disorders as a case in point. *PLoS ONE, 7*, e31107.

Chiappe, D., & MacDonald, K. (2005). The evolution of domain-general mechanisms in intelligence and learning. *Journal of General Psychology, 132*, 5–40.

Chisholm, J. S. (1993). Death, hope, and sex: Life-history theory and the development of reproductive strategies. *Current Anthropology, 34*, 1–24.

Chisholm, J. S. (1999*a*). *Death, hope, and sex: Steps to an evolutionary ecology of mind and morality*. Cambridge: Cambridge University Press.

Chisholm, J. S. (1999*b*). Attachment and time preference: Relations between early stress and sexual behavior in a sample of American university women. *Human Nature, 10*, 51–83.

Chisholm, J. S., Quinlivan, J. A., Petersen, R. W., & Coall, D. A. (2005). Early stress predicts age at menarche and first birth, adult attachment, and expected lifespan. *Human Nature, 16*, 233–265.

Chisholm, K., Lin, A., Abu-Akel, A., & Wood, S. J. (2015). The association between autism and schizophrenia spectrum disorders: A review of eight alternate models of co-occurrence. *Neuroscience & Biobehavioral Reviews, 55*, 173–183.

Chittka, L., Skorupski, P., & Raine, N. E. (2009). Speed– accuracy tradeoffs in animal decision making. *Trends in Ecology and Evolution, 24*, 400–407.

Christakis, N. A., & Fowler, J. H. (2014). Friendship and natural selection. *Proceedings of the National Academy of Sciences USA, 111*, 10796–10801.

Chudal, R., Joelsson, P., Gyllenberg, D., Lehti, V., Leivonen, S., Hinkka-Yli-Salomäki, S., et al. (2015). Parental age and the risk of Attention-Deficit/Hyperactivity Disorder: A nationwide, population-based cohort study. *Journal of the American Academy of Child & Adolescent Psychiatry, 54*, 487–494.

Chung, H. J., Weyandt, L. L., & Swentosky, A. (2014). The physiology of executive functioning. In S. Goldstein & G. A. Naglieri (Eds.), *Handbook of executive functioning* (pp. 13–28). New York: Springer.

Church, A. T., Alvarez, J. M., Mai, N. T., French, B. F., Katigbak, M. S., & Ortiz, F. A. (2011). Are cross-cultural comparisons of personality profiles meaningful? Differential item and facet functioning in the Revised NEO Personality Inventory. *Journal of Personality and Social Psychology, 101*, 1068–1089.

Ciaramidaro, A., Bölte, S., Schlitt, S., Hainz, D., Poustka, F., Weber, B., et al. (2015). Schizophrenia and autism as contrasting minds: Neural evidence for the hypo-hyper-intentionality hypothesis. *Schizophrenia Bulletin, 41*, 171–179.

Cicchetti, D. (2016). *Developmental psychopathology* (3rd ed.). New York: Wiley.

Cicero, D. C., Epler, A. J., & Sher, K. J. (2009). Are there developmentally limited forms of bipolar disorder? *Journal of Abnormal Psychology, 118*, 431–447.

Cicero, D. C., Kerns, J. G., & McCarthy, D. M. (2010). The Aberrant Salience Inventory: A new measure of psychosis proneness. *Psychological Assessment, 22*, 688–701.

Claes, L., Vandereycken, W., Luyten, P., Soenens, B., Pieters, G., & Vertommen, H. (2006). Personality prototypes in eating disorders based on the Big Five model. *Journal of Personality Disorders, 20*, 401–416.

Claridge, G. (1997). *Schizotypy: Implications for illness and health*. Oxford: Oxford University Press.

Clark, A. (2013). Whatever next? Predictive brains, situated agents, and the future of cognitive science. *Behavioral and Brain Sciences, 36*, 181–204.

Clark, D. A., & del Palacio González, A. (2014). Obsessive-compulsive disorder. In P. Emmelkamp & T. Ehring (Eds.), *The Wiley handbook of anxiety disorders* (pp. 233–253). New York: Wiley.

Clark, D. M. (1986). A cognitive approach to panic. *Behaviour Research and Therapy, 24*, 461–470.

Clarke, S., & Robertson, I. (2005). A meta-analytic review of the Big Five personality factors and accident involvement in occupational and non-occupational settings. *Journal of Occupational and Organizational Psychology, 78* 355–376.

Clarke, T. K., Lupton, M. K., Fernandez-Pujals, A. M., Starr, J., Davies, G., Cox, S., et al. (2016). Common polygenic risk for autism spectrum disorder (ASD) is associated with cognitive ability in the general population. *Molecular Psychiatry, 21*, 419–425.

Class, Q. A., Abel, K. M., Khashan, A. S., Rickert, M. E., Dalman, C., Larsson, H., et al. (2014). Offspring psychopathology following preconception, prenatal and postnatal maternal bereavement stress. *Psychological Medicine, 44*, 71–84.

Clauss, J. A., & Blackford, J. U. (2012). Behavioral inhibition and risk for developing social anxiety disorder: A meta-analytic study. *Journal of the American Academy of Child & Adolescent Psychiatry, 51*, 1066–1075.

Clegg, H., Nettle, D., & Miell, D. (2011). Status and mating success amongst visual artists. *Frontiers in Psychology, 2*, 310.

Clemmensen, L., van Os, J., Drukker, M., Munkholm, A., Rimvall, M. K., Væver, M., et al. (2016). Psychotic experiences and hyper-theory-of-mind in preadolescence–a birth cohort study. *Psychological Medicine, 46*, 87–101.

Clutton-Brock, T. H. (2007). Sexual selection in males and females. *Science, 318*, 1882–1885.

Clutton-Brock, T. H., & Huchard, E. (2013). Social competition and selection in males and females. *Philosophical Transactions of the Royal Society of London B, 368*, 20130074.

Cochran, D., Fallon, D., Hill, M., & Frazier, J. A. (2013). The role of oxytocin in psychiatric disorders: A review of biological and therapeutic research findings. *Harvard Review of Psychiatry, 21*, 219–247.

Cochran, G., & Harpending, H. (2009). *The 10,000 year explosion: How civilization accelerated human evolution*. New York: Basic Books.

Coelho, C. M., & Purkis, H. (2009). The origins of specific phobias: Influential theories and current perspectives. *Review of General Psychology, 13*, 335–348.

Coelho, F. M., Silva, R. A. D., Quevedo, L. D. Á., Souza, L. D., Pinheiro, K. A., & Pinheiro, R. T. (2014). Obsessive-compulsive disorder in fathers during pregnancy and postpartum. *Revista Brasileira de Psiquiatria, 36*, 271–273.

Coghill, D., & Sonuga-Barke, E. J. (2012). Categories versus dimensions in the classification and conceptualisation of child and adolescent mental disorder: Implications of recent empirical study. *Journal of Child Psychology and Psychiatry*, *53*, 469–489.

Coghlan, S., Horder, J., Inkster, B., Mendez, M. A., Murphy, D. G., & Nutt, D. J. (2012). GABA system dysfunction in autism and related disorders: From synapse to symptoms. *Neuroscience & Biobehavioral Reviews*, *36*, 2044–2055.

Coid, J., Yang, M., Tyrer, P., Roberts, A., & Ullrich, S. (2006). Prevalence and correlates of personality disorder in Great Britain. *British Journal of Psychiatry*, *188*, 423–431.

Coid, J. W. (1999). Aetiological risk factors for personality disorders. *British Journal of Psychiatry*, *174*, 530–538.

Cole, E. F., & Quinn, J. L. (2014). Shy birds play it safe: Personality in captivity predicts risk responsiveness during reproduction in the wild. *Biology Letters*, *10*, 20140178.

Coles, M. E., & Pietrefesa, A. S. (2008). Symmetry, ordering, and arranging. In J. S. Abramowitz, D. McKay, & S. Taylor (Eds.), *Obsessive-compulsive disorder: Subtypes and spectrum conditions* (pp. 36–52). New York: Elsevier.

Coles, M. E., Pinto, A., Mancebo, M. C., Rasmussen, S. A., & Eisen, J. L. (2008). OCD with comorbid OCPD: A subtype of OCD? *Journal of Psychiatric Research*, *42*, 289–296.

Coles, M. E., & Ravid, A. (2016). Clinical presentation of not-just right experiences (NJREs) in individuals with OCD: Characteristics and response to treatment. *Behaviour Research & Therapy*, *87*, 182–187.

Collins, T. J., & Gillath, O. (2012). Attachment, breakup strategies, and associated outcomes: The effects of security enhancement on the selection of breakup strategies. *Journal of Research in Personality*, *46*, 210–222.

Colom, R., Haier, R. J., Head, K., Álvarez-Linera, J., Quiroga, M. Á., Shih, P. C., et al. (2009). Gray matter correlates of fluid, crystallized, and spatial intelligence: Testing the P-FIT model. *Intelligence*, *37*, 124–135.

Combs, D. R., Mueser, K. T., & Drake, E. (2014). Schizophrenia. In D. C. Beidel, B. C. Frueh, & M. Hersen (Eds.), *Adult psychopathology and diagnosis* (7th ed., pp. 165–216). New York: Wiley.

Conde-Agudelo, A., Rosas-Bermudez, A., & Norton, M. H. (2016). Birth spacing and risk of autism and other neurodevelopmental disabilities: A systematic review. *Pediatrics*, *2016*, e20153482.

Confer, J. C., Perilloux, C., & Buss, D. M. (2010). More than just a pretty face: Men's priority shifts toward bodily attractiveness in short-term mating contexts. *Evolution and human Behavior*, *31*, 349–353.

Conroy-Beam, D., Buss, D. M., Pham, M. N., & Shackelford, T. K. (2015). How sexually dimorphic are human mate preferences? *Personality and Social Psychology Bulletin*, *41*, 1082–1093.

Constantinescu, M., & Hines, M. (2012). Relating prenatal testosterone exposure to postnatal behavior in typically developing children: Methods and findings. *Child Development Perspectives*, *6*, 407–413.

Constantino, J. N., & Todd, R. D. (2005). Intergenerational transmission of subthreshold autistic traits in the general population. *Biological Psychiatry*, *57*, 655–660.

Contractor, A. A., Armour, C., Shea, M. T., Mota, N., & Pietrzak, R. H. (2016). Latent profiles of DSM-5 PTSD symptoms and the "Big Five" personality traits. *Journal of Anxiety Disorders*, *37*, 10–20.

Conway, C. C., Hipwell, A. E., & Stepp, S. D. (2017). Seven-year course of borderline personality disorder features: Borderline pathology is as unstable as depression during adolescence. *Clinical Psychological Science*, *5*, 742–749.

Cook, T. B., Brenner, L. A., Cloninger, C. R., Langenberg, P., Igbide, A., Giegling, I., et al. (2015). "Latent" infection with *Toxoplasma gondii*: Association with trait aggression and impulsivity in healthy adults. *Journal of Psychiatric Research*, *60*, 87–94.

Cools, R. (2011). Dopaminergic control of the striatum for high-level cognition. *Current Opinion in Neurobiology*, *21*, 402–407.

Cools, R., Nakamura, K., & Daw, N. D. (2011). Serotonin and dopamine: Unifying affective, activational, and decision functions. *Neuropsychopharmacology*, *36*, 98–113.

Coombs, E., Brosnan, M., Bryant-Waugh, R., & Skevington, S. M. (2011). An investigation into the relationsgip between eating disorder psychopathology and autistic symptomatology in a non-clinical sample. *British Journal of Clinical Psychology*, *50*, 326–338.

Copeland, W. E., Adair, C. E., Smetanin, P., Stiff, D., Briante, C., Colman, I., et al. (2013). Diagnostic transitions from childhood to adolescence to early adulthood. *Journal of Child Psychology and Psychiatry*, *54*, 791–799.

Coppens, C. M., de Boer, S. F., & Koolhaas, J. M. (2010). Coping styles and behavioural flexibility: Towards underlying mechanisms. *Philosophical Transactions of the Royal Society of London B*, *365*, 4021–4028.

Copping, L. T., & Campbell, A. (2015). The environment and life history strategies: Neighborhood and individual-level models. *Evolution and Human Behavior*, *36*, 182–190.

Copping, L. T., Campbell, A., & Muncer, S. (2013*a*). Impulsivity, sensation seeking and reproductive behaviour: A life history perspective. *Personality and Individual Differences*, *54*, 908–912.

Copping, L. T., Campbell, A., & Muncer, S. (2013*b*). Violence, teenage pregnancy, and life history. *Human Nature*, *24*, 137–157.

Copping, L. T., Campbell, A., & Muncer, S. (2014*a*). Conceptualizing time preference: A life-history analysis. *Evolutionary Psychology*, *12*, 829–847.

Copping, L. T., Campbell, A., & Muncer, S. (2014*b*). Psychometrics and life history strategy: The structure and validity of the high K strategy scale. *Evolutionary Psychology*, *12*, 200–222.

Copping, L. T., Campbell, A., Muncer, S., & Richardson, G. B. (2017). The psychometric evaluation of human life histories: A reply to Figueredo, Cabeza de Baca, Black, Garcia, Fernandes, Wolf, and Woodley (2015). *Evolutionary Psychology*, 1474704916663727.

Corchs, F., Nutt, D. J., Hince, D. A., Davies, S. J., Bernik, M., & Hood, S. D. (2015). Evidence for serotonin function as a neurochemical difference between fear and anxiety disorders in humans? *Journal of Psychopharmacology*, *29*, 1061–1069.

Corlett, P. R., Frith, C. D., & Fletcher, P. C. (2009). From drugs to deprivation: A Bayesian framework for understanding models of psychosis. *Psychopharmacology*, *206*, 515–530.

Corominas, M., Ramos-Quiroga, J. A., Ferrer, M., Sáez-Francàs, N., Palomar, G., Bosch, R., et al. (2012). Cortisol responses in children and adults with attention deficit hyperactivity disorder (ADHD): A possible marker of inhibition deficits. *ADHD Attention Deficit and Hyperactivity Disorders*, *4*, 63–75.

Corr, P. J. (2013). Approach and avoidance behaviour: Multiple systems and their interactions. *Emotion Review*, *5*, 285–290.

Corr, P. J., DeYoung, C. G., & McNaughton, N. (2013). Motivation and personality: A neuropsychological perspective. *Social and Personality Psychology Compass, 7*, 158–175.

Cortese, S., Kelly, C., Chabernaud, C., Proal, E., Di Martino, A., Milham, M. P., et al. (2012). Toward systems neuroscience of ADHD: A meta-analysis of 55 fMRI studies. *American Journal of Psychiatry, 169*, 1038–1055.

Cortina, M., & Liotti, G. (2014). An evolutionary outlook on motivation: Implications for the clinical dialogue. *Psychoanalytic Inquiry, 34*, 864–899.

Cosmides, L., Barrett, H. C., & Tooby, J. (2010). Adaptive specializations, social exchange, and the evolution of human intelligence. *Proceedings of the National Academy of Sciences USA, 107*, 9007–9014.

Cosmides, L., & Tooby, J. (1999). Toward an evolutionary taxonomy of treatable conditions. *Journal of Abnormal Psychology, 108*, 453–464.

Cosmides, L., & Tooby, J. (2013). Evolutionary psychology: New perspectives on cognition and motivation. *Annual Review of Psychology, 64, 201–229.*

Cosmides, L., & Tooby, J. (2015). Adaptations for reasoning about social exchange. In D. M. Buss (Ed.), *The handbook of evolutionary psychology* (2nd ed., pp. 625–668). New York: Wiley.

Costa, P. T., Terracciano, A., & McCrae, R. R. (2001). Gender differences in personality traits across cultures: Robust and surprising findings. *Journal of Personality and Social Psychology, 81*, 322–331.

Costa, P. T. J., & McCrae, R. R. (1995). Domains and facets: Hierarchical personality assessment using the Revised NEO Personality Inventory. *Journal of Personality Assessment, 64*, 21–50.

Costello, E. J., Copeland, W., & Angold, A. (2011). Trends in psychopathology across the adolescent years: What changes when children become adolescents, and when adolescents become adults? *Journal of Child Psychology and Psychiatry, 52*, 1015–1025.

Costello, E. J., Mustillo, S., Erkanli, A., Keeler, G., & Angold, A. (2003). Prevalence and development of psychiatric disorders in childhood and adolescence. *Archives of General Psychiatry, 60*, 837–844.

Cougle, J. R., & Lee, H. J. (2014). Pathological and non-pathological features of obsessive-compulsive disorder: Revisiting basic assumptions of cognitive models. *Journal of Obsessive-Compulsive & Related Disorders, 3*, 12–20.

Coutinho, J., Goncalves, O. F., Soares, J. M., Marques, P., & Sampaio, A. (2016). Alterations of the default mode network connectivity in obsessive-compulsive personality disorder: A pilot study. *Psychiatry Research: Neuroimaging, 256*, 1–7.

Cox, B. J., Clara, I. P., Sareen, J., & Stein, M. B. (2008). The structure of feared social situations among individuals with a lifetime diagnosis of social anxiety disorder in two independent nationally representative mental health surveys. *Behaviour Research & Therapy, 46*, 477–486.

Coyle, E., Karatzias, T., Summers, A., & Power, M. (2014). Emotions and emotion regulation in survivors of childhood sexual abuse: The importance of "disgust" in traumatic stress and psychopathology. *European Journal of Psychotraumatology, 5*, 23306.

Craig, F., Lamanna, A. L., Margari, F., Matera, E., Simone, M., & Margari, L. (2015). Overlap between autism spectrum disorders and attention deficit hyperactivity disorder: Searching for distinctive/common clinical features. *Autism Research, 8*, 328–337.

Craighead, L. W., Martinez, M. A., & Klump, K. L. (2013). Bulimia nervosa and binge eating disorder. In W. E. Craighead, D. J. Miklowitz, & L. W. Craighead (Eds.), *Psychopathology: History, diagnosis, and empirical foundations* (2nd ed., pp. 445–481). New York: Wiley.

Cramer, A. O., Waldorp, L. J., van der Maas, H. L., & Borsboom, D. (2010*a*). Comorbidity: A network perspective. *Behavioral and Brain Sciences, 33*, 137–150.

Cramer, A. O., Waldorp, L. J., van der Maas, H. L., & Borsboom, D. (2010*b*). Complex realities require complex theories: Refining and extending the network approach to mental disorders. *Behavioral and Brain Sciences, 33*, 178–193.

Crawford, C. B. (1989). The theory of evolution: Of what value to psychology? *Journal of Comparative Psychology, 103*, 4–22.

Crawford, C. B., & Anderson, J. L. (1989). Sociobiology: An environmentalist discipline? *American Psychologist, 44*, 1449–1459.

Cremers, H. R., & Roelofs, K. (2016). Social anxiety disorder: A critical overview of neurocognitive research. *Wiley Interdisciplinary Reviews: Cognitive Science, 7*, 218–232.

Crespi, B. (2013). Developmental heterochrony and the evolution of autistic perception, cognition and behavior. *BMC Medicine, 11*, 119.

Crespi, B. J. (2000). The evolution of maladaptation. *Heredity, 84*, 623–629.

Crespi, B. J. (2010). The origins and evolution of genetic disease risk in modern humans. *Annals of the New York Academy of Sciences, 1206*, 80–109.

Crespi, B. J. (2011). One hundred years of insanity: Genomic, psychological, and evolutionary models of autism in relation to schizophrenia. In M. S. Ritsner (Ed.), *Handbook of schizophrenia spectrum disorders* (Vol. I., pp. 163–185). New York: Springer.

Crespi, B. J. (2016*a*). Oxytocin, testosterone, and human social cognition. *Biological Reviews, 91*, 390–408.

Crespi, B. J. (2016*b*). Autism as a disorder of high intelligence. *Frontiers in Neuroscience, 10*, 300.

Crespi, B., & Badcock, C. (2008). Psychosis and autism as diametrical disorders of the social brain. *Behavioral and Brain Sciences, 31*, 241–261.

Crespi, B. J., & Hurd, P. L. (2015). Genetically based correlates of serum oxytocin and testosterone in autism and schizotypy. *Personality and Individual Differences, 79*, 39–43.

Crespi, B., Stead, P., & Elliot, M. (2010). Comparative genomics of autism and schizophrenia. *Proceedings of the National Academy of Sciences USA, 107*, 1736–1741.

Crespi, E. J., Williams, T. D., Jessop, T. S., & Delehanty, B. (2013). Life history and the ecology of stress: How do glucocorticoid hormones influence life-history variation in animals? *Functional Ecology, 27*, 93–106.

Crockett, M. J., Siegel, J. Z., Kurth-Nelson, Z., Ousdal, O. T., Story, G., Frieband, C., et al. (2015). Dissociable effects of serotonin and dopamine on the valuation of harm in moral decision making. *Current Biology, 25*, 1852–1859.

Crome, E., Baillie, A., Slade, T., & Ruscio, A. M. (2010). Social phobia: Further evidence of dimensional structure. *Australian and New Zealand Journal of Psychiatry, 44*, 1012–1020.

Cronk, L. (1991). Wealth, status, and reproductive success among the Mukogodo of Kenya. *American Anthropologist, 93*, 345–360.

Cross, C. P., Copping, L. T., & Campbell, A. (2011). Sex differences in impulsivity: A meta- analysis. *Psychological Bulletin, 137*, 97–130.

Crow, T. J. (1990). Temporal lobe asymmetries as the key to the etiology of schizophrenia. *Schizophrenia Bulletin, 16*, 433–443.

Crow, T. J. (1997). Schizophrenia as failure of hemispheric dominance for language. *Trends in Neurosciences, 20*, 339–343.

Crow, T. J. (2000). Schizophrenia as the price that Homo sapiens pays for language: A resolution of the central paradox in the origin of the species. *Brain Research Reviews, 31*, 118–129.

Crowell, S. E., Kaufman, E. A., & Lenzenweger, M. F. (2013). The development of borderline personality and self-inflicted injury. In T. P. Beauchaine & S. P. Hinshaw (Eds.), *Child and adolescent psychopathology* (2nd ed., pp. 577–609). Hoboken, NJ: Wiley.

Crum-Cianflone, N. F., & Jacobson, I. (2014). Gender differences of postdeployment post-traumatic stress disorder among service members and veterans of the Iraq and Afghanistan conflicts. *Epidemiologic Reviews, 36*, 5–18.

Csibra, G., & Gergely, G. (2006). Social learning and social cognition: The case for pedagogy. In Y. Munakata & M. H. Johnson (Eds.), *Processes of change in brain and cognitive development: Vol. XXI. Attention and performance* (pp. 249–274). Oxford: Oxford University Press.

Cuffe, S. P., Moore, C. G., & McKeown, R. E. (2005). Prevalence and correlates of ADHD symptoms in the national health interview survey. *Journal of Attention Disorders, 9*, 392–401.

Culbert, K. M., Racine, S. E., & Klump, K. L. (2015). Research review: What we have learned about the causes of eating disorders–a synthesis of sociocultural, psychological, and biological research. *Journal of Child Psychology and Psychiatry, 56*, 1141–1164.

Culbert, K. M., Racine, S. E., & Klump, K. L. (2016). Hormonal factors and disturbances in eating disorders. *Current Psychiatry Reports, 18*, 1–16.

Cumyn, L., French, L., & Hechtman, L. (2009). Comorbidity in adults with attention-deficit hyperactivity disorder. *The Canadian Journal of Psychiatry, 54*, 673–683.

Currie, T. E., & Little, A. C. (2009). The relative importance of the face and body in judgments of human physical attractiveness. *Evolution and Human Behavior, 30*, 409–416.

Curry, O. S., Price, M. E., & Price, J. G. (2008). Patience is a virtue: Cooperative people have lower discount rates. *Personality and Individual Differences, 44*, 780–785.

Curtis, V. (2011). Why disgust matters. *Philosophical Transactions of the Royal Society of London B, 366*, 3478–3490.

Cuthbert, B. N., & Insel, T. R. (2013). Toward the future of psychiatric diagnosis: The seven pillars of RDoC. *BMC Medicine, 11*, 126.

Dadds, M. R., Moul, C., Cauchi, A., Dobson-Stone, C., Hawes, D. J., Brennan, J., et al. (2014). Methylation of the oxytocin receptor gene and oxytocin blood levels in the development of psychopathy. *Development and Psychopathology, 26*, 33–40.

Dalley, J. W., & Roiser, J. P. (2012). Dopamine, serotonin and impulsivity. *Neuroscience, 215*, 42–58.

Dalsgaard, S., Mortensen, P. B., Frydenberg, M., Maibing, C. M., Nordentoft, M., & Thomsen, P. H. (2014). Association between Attention-Deficit Hyperactivity Disorder in childhood and schizophrenia later in adulthood. *European Psychiatry, 29*, 259–263.

Dalwani, M. S., Tregellas, J. R., Andrews-Hanna, J. R., Mikulich-Gilbertson, S. K., Raymond, K. M., Banich, M. T., et al. (2014). Default mode network activity in male adolescents with conduct and substance use disorder. *Drug and Alcohol Dependence, 134*, 242–250.

Darwin, C. (1859). *On the origin of species by natural selection*. London: Murray.

Darwin, C. (1871). *On the descent of man, and selection in relation to sex*. London: Murray.

Darwin, C. (1877). A biographical sketch of an infant. *Mind, 2*, 285–294.

Davey, G. C. L., Field, A. P., & Startup, H. M. (2003). Obsessive-compulsive disorder with schizotypal personality disorder (Schizotypal OCD). In R. G. Menzies & P. de Silva (Eds.), *Obsessive-compulsive disorder: Theory, research and treatment* (pp. 63–76). Chichester, UK: Wiley.

David, B., Olatunji, B. O., Armstrong, T., Ciesielski, B. G., Bondy, C. L., & Broman-Fulks, J. (2009). Incremental specificity of disgust sensitivity in the prediction of obsessive-compulsive disorder symptoms: Cross-sectional and prospective approaches. *Journal of Behavior Therapy and Experimental Psychiatry, 40*, 533–543.

Davies, A. P. C., & Shackelford, T. K. (2008). Two human natures: How men and women evolved different psychologies. In C. Crawford & D. Krebs (Eds.), *Foundations of evolutionary psychology* (pp. 261–280). New York: Erlbaum.

Davies, S. E., Connelly, B. S., Ones, D. S., & Birkland, A. S. (2015). The General Factor of Personality: The "Big One," a self-evaluative trait, or a methodological gnat that won't go away? *Personality and Individual Differences, 81*, 13–22.

Davies, W., Lynn, P. M. Y., Relkovic, D., & Wilkinson, L. S. (2008). Imprinted genes and neuroendocrine function. *Frontiers in Neuroendocrinology, 29*, 413–427.

Daw, N. D., & Dayan, P. (2014). The algorithmic anatomy of model-based evaluation. *Philosophical Transactions of the Royal Society B, 369*, 20130478.

Daw, N. D., Niv, Y., & Dayan, P. (2005). Uncertainty-based competition between prefrontal and dorsolateral striatal systems for behavioral control. *Nature Neuroscience, 8*, 1704–1711.

Dawkins, R. (1976). *The selfish gene*. Oxford: Oxford University Press.

Dawson, M., Soulières, I., Gernsbacher, M. A., & Mottron, L. (2007). The level and nature of autistic intelligence. *Psychological Science, 18*, 657–662.

Day, T., & Bonduriansky, R. (2011). A unified approach to the evolutionary consequences of genetic and nongenetic inheritance. *The American Naturalist, 178*, e18–e36.

Dayan, P. (2102). Robust neural decision making. In P. Hammerstein & J. R. Stevens (Eds.), *Evolution and the mechanisms of decision making* (pp. 151–168). Cambridge, MA: MIT Press.

Dayan, P., & Daw, N. D. (2008). Decision theory, reinforcement learning, and the brain. *Cognitive, Affective, & Behavioral Neuroscience, 8*, 429–453.

Dean, A. C., Altstein, L. L., Berman, M. E., Constans, J. I., Sugar, C. A., & McCloskey, M. S. (2013). Secondary psychopathy, but not primary psychopathy, is associated with risky decision-making in noninstitutionalized young adults. *Personality and Individual Differences, 54*, 272–277.

Dean, L. G., Vale, G. L., Laland, K. N., Flynn, E., & Kendal, R. L. (2014). Human cumulative culture: A comparative perspective. *Biological Reviews, 89*, 284–301.

Deardorff, J., Gonzales, N. A., Christopher, F. S., Roosa, M. W., & Millsap, R. E. (2005). Early puberty and adolescent pregnancy: The influence of alcohol use. *Pediatrics, 116*, 1451–1456.

Deary, I. J., Penke, L., & Johnson, W. (2010). The neuroscience of human intelligence differences. *Nature Reviews Neuroscience, 11*, 201–211.

Debat, V., & David, P. (2001). Mapping phenotypes: Canalization, plasticity, and developmental stability. *Trends in Ecology and Evolution, 16*, 555–561.

DeBruine, L. M., Jones, B. C., Little, A. C., & Perrett, D. I. (2008). Social perception of facial resemblance in humans. *Archives of Sexual Behavior, 37*, 64–77.

de Catanzaro, D. (1991). Evolutionary limits to self-preservation. *Ethology and Sociobiology, 12*, 13–28.

de Catanzaro, D. (1995). Reproductive status, family interactions, and suicidal ideation: Surveys of the general public and high-risk groups. *Ethology and Sociobiology, 16*, 385–394.

Decety, J., Jackson, P. L., Sommerville, J. A., Chaminade, T., & Meltzoff, A. N. (2004). The neural bases of cooperation and competition: An fMRI investigation. *Neuroimage, 23*, 744–751.

Delbello, M. P., Lopez-Larson, M. P., Soutullo, C. A., & Strakowski, S. M. (2001). Effects of race on psychiatric diagnosis of hospitalized adolescents: A retrospective chart review. *Journal of Child and Adolescent Psychopharmacology, 11*, 95–103.

del Campo, N., Chamberlain, S. R., Sahakian, B. J., & Robbins, T. W. (2011). The roles of dopamine and noradrenaline in the pathophysiology and treatment of attention-deficit/hyperactivity disorder. *Biological Psychiatry, 69*, e145–e157.

Del Casale, A., Ferracuti, S., Rapinesi, C., Serata, D., Piccirilli, M., Savoja, V., et al. (2012). Functional neuroimaging in specific phobia. *Psychiatry Research: Neuroimaging, 202*, 181–197.

Del Giudice, M. (2009*a*). Sex, attachment, and the development of reproductive strategies. *Behavioral and Brain Sciences, 32*, 1–21.

Del Giudice, M. (2009*b*). On the real magnitude of psychological sex differences. *Evolutionary Psychology, 7*, 264–279.

Del Giudice, M. (2010). Reduced fertility in patients' families is consistent with the sexual selection model of schizophrenia and schizotypy. *PLoS ONE, 5*, e16040.

Del Giudice, M. (2011). Sex differences in romantic attachment: A meta-analysis. *Personality and Social Psychology Bulletin, 37*, 193–214.

Del Giudice, M. (2012*a*). Fetal programming by maternal stress: Insights from a conflict perspective. *Psychoneuroendocrinology, 37*, 1614–1629.

Del Giudice, M. (2012*b*). Sex ratio dynamics and fluctuating selection on personality. *Journal of Theoretical Biology, 297*, 48–60.

Del Giudice, M. (2013). Multivariate misgivings: Is *D* a valid measure of group and sex differences? *Evolutionary Psychology, 11*, 1067–1076.

Del Giudice, M. (2014*a*). An evolutionary life history framework for psychopathology. *Psychological Inquiry, 25*, 261–300.

Del Giudice, M. (2014*b*). A tower unto heaven: Toward an expanded framework for psychopathology. *Psychological Inquiry, 25*, 394–413.

Del Giudice, M. (2014*c*). Middle childhood: An evolutionary-developmental synthesis. *Child Development Perspectives, 8*, 193–200.

Del Giudice, M. (2014*d*). Early stress and human behavioral development: Emerging evolutionary perspectives. *Journal of Developmental Origins of Health and Disease, 5*, 270–280.

Del Giudice, M. (2015*a*). Self-regulation in an evolutionary perspective. In G. H. E. Gendolla, M. Tops, & S. Koole (Eds.), *Handbook of biobehavioral approaches to self-regulation* (pp. 25–42). New York: Springer.

Del Giudice, M. (2015*b*). Gender differences in personality and social behavior. In J. D. Wright (Ed.), *International encyclopedia of the social and behavioral sciences* (2nd ed., pp. 750–756). New York: Elsevier.

Del Giudice, M. (2015*c*). Plasticity as a developing trait: Exploring the implications. *Frontiers in Zoology, 12*, S4.

Del Giudice, M. (2015*d*). Attachment in middle childhood: An evolutionary-developmental perspective. *New Directions for Child and Adolescent Development, 148*, 15–30.

Del Giudice, M. (2016*a*). Sex differences in romantic attachment: A facet-level analysis. *Personality and Individual Differences, 88*, 125–128.

Del Giudice, M. (2016*b*). Differential susceptibility to the environment: Are developmental models compatible with the evidence from twin studies? *Developmental Psychology, 52*, 1330–1339.

Del Giudice, M. (2016*c*). The evolutionary future of psychopathology. *Current Opinion in Psychology, 7*, 44–50.

Del Giudice, M. (2016*d*). The life history model of psychopathology explains the structure of psychiatric disorders and the emergence of the p factor: A simulation study. *Clinical Psychological Science, 4*, 299–311.

Del Giudice, M. (2017). The evolution of interaction shape in differential susceptibility. *Child Development, 88*, 1897–1912.

Del Giudice, M., Angeleri, R., Brizio, A., & Elena, M. R. (2010). The evolution of autistic-like and schizotypal traits: A sexual selection hypothesis. *Frontiers in Psychology, 1*, 41.

Del Giudice, M., Angeleri, R., & Manera, V. (2009). The juvenile transition: A developmental switch point in human life history. *Developmental Review, 29*, 1–31.

Del Giudice, M., & Belsky, J. (2011). The development of life history strategies: Toward a multi-stage theory. In D. M. Buss & P. H. Hawley (Eds.), *The evolution of personality and individual differences.* (pp. 154–176). New York: Oxford University Press.

Del Giudice, M., Booth, T., & Irwing, P. (2012). The distance between Mars and Venus: Measuring global sex differences in personality. *PLoS ONE, 7*, e29265.

Del Giudice, M., & Ellis, B. J. (2016). Evolutionary foundations of developmental psychopathology. In D. Cicchetti (Ed.), *Developmental psychopathology: Vol. 2. Developmental neuroscience* (3rd ed., pp. 1–58). New York: Wiley.

Del Giudice, M., Ellis, B. J., & Shirtcliff, E. A. (2011). The Adaptive Calibration Model of stress responsivity. *Neuroscience & Biobehavioral Reviews, 35*, 1562–1592.

Del Giudice, M., & Gangestad, S. W. (2018). Rethinking IL-6 and CRP: Why they are more than inflammatory biomarkers, and why it matters. *Brain, Behavior and Immunity.*

Del Giudice, M., Gangestad, S. W., & Kaplan, H. S. (2015). Life history theory and evolutionary psychology. In D. M. Buss (Ed.), *The handbook of evolutionary psychology* (2nd ed., pp. 88–114). New York: Wiley.

Del Giudice, M., Klimczuk, A. C. E., Traficonte, D. M., & Maestripieri, D. (2014). Autistic-like and schizotypal traits in a life history perspective: Diametrical associations with impulsivity, sensation seeking, and sociosexual behavior. *Evolution & Human Behavior, 35*, 415–424.

Del Giudice, M., Zilioli, S., Kosel, F., & Watson, N. V. (2014). *Obsessing, fast and slow: A life history perspective on the structure of obsessive symptoms.* Presentation at the 26th Human Behavior and Evolution Society Conference, July 30–August 2, 2014, Natal, Brazil.

Delobel-Ayoub, M., Ehlinger, V., Klapouszczak, D., Maffre, T., Raynaud, J. P., Delpierre, C., et al. (2015). Socioeconomic disparities and prevalence of autism spectrum disorders and intellectual disability. *PLoS ONE, 10*, e0141964.

De Martino, B., Harrison, N. A., Knafo, S., Bird, G., & Dolan, R. J. (2008). Explaining enhanced logical consistency during decision making in autism. *Journal of Neuroscience, 28*, 10746–10750.

de Mathis, M. A., Diniz, J. B., do Rosário, M. C., Torres, A. R., Hoexter, M., Hasler, G., et al. (2006). What is the optimal way to subdivide obsessive-compulsive disorder? *CNS Spectrums, 11*, 762–779.

de Mathis, M. A. D., Alvarenga, P. D., Funaro, G., Torresan, R. C., Moraes, I., Torres, A. R., et al. (2011). Gender differences in obsessive-compulsive disorder: A literature review. *Revista Brasileira de Psiquiatria, 33*, 390–399.

Demurie, E., Roeyers, H., Baeyens, D., & Sonuga-Barke, E. (2012). Temporal discounting of monetary rewards in children and adolescents with ADHD and autism spectrum disorders. *Developmental Science, 15*, 791–800.

Denckla, M. B. (1996). A theory and model of executive function: A neuropsychological perspective. In G. R. Lyon & N. A. Krasnegor (Eds.), *Attention, memory, and executive function* (pp. 263–277). Baltimore, MD: Paul H. Brookes.

Denissen, J. J., & Penke, L. (2008). Motivational individual reaction norms underlying the Five-Factor model of personality: First steps towards a theory-based conceptual framework. *Journal of Research in Personality, 42*, 1285–1302.

Dennett, D. (1971). Intentional systems. *Journal of Philosophy, 68*, 87–106.

Dennett, D. (2009). Darwin's "strange inversion of reasoning". *Proceedings of the National Academy of Sciences USA, 106*, 10061–10065.

Dennett, D. C. (1995). *Darwin's dangerous idea: Evolution and the meanings of life.* New York: Simon & Schuster.

de Reus, R. J., & Emmelkamp, P. M. (2012). Obsessive–compulsive personality disorder: A review of current empirical findings. *Personality and Mental Health, 6*, 1–21.

de Ribera, O. S., Kavish, N., & Boutwell, B. (2017). On the relationship between psychopathy and general intelligence: A meta-analytic review. *bioRxiv*, 100693. doi:10.1101/100693

DeScioli, P., & Kurzban, R. (2013). A solution to the mysteries of morality. *Psychological Bulletin, 139*, 477–496.

Dessalles, J.-L. (2007). *Why we talk: The evolutionary origins of language.* New York: Oxford University Press.

Devaine, M., Hollard, G., & Daunizeau, J. (2014). Theory of mind: Did evolution fool us? *PLoS ONE, 9*, e87619.

Devilly, G. J., Gist, R., & Cotton, P. (2006). Ready! Fire! Aim! The status of psychological debriefing and therapeutic interventions: In the work place and after disasters. *Review of General Psychology, 10*, 318–345.

DeVoogd, T. J. (2004). Neural constraints on the complexity of avian song. *Brain, Behavior and Evolution, 63*, 221–232.

de Vries, R. E., Tybur, J. M., Pollet, T. V., & van Vugt, M. (2016). Evolution, situational affordances, and the HEXACO model of personality. *Evolution and Human Behavior, 37*, 407–421.

DeWitt, T. J., & Scheiner, S. M. (2004). *Phenotypic plasticity: Functional and conceptual approaches.* New York: Oxford University Press.

DeYoung, C. G. (2006). Higher-order factors of the Big Five in a multi-informant sample. *Journal of Personality and Social Psychology, 91*, 1138–1151.

DeYoung, C. G. (2010). Personality neuroscience and the biology of traits. *Social and Personality Psychology Compass, 4*, 1165–1180.

DeYoung, C. G. (2011). Impulsivity as a personality trait. In K. D. Vohs & R. F. Baumeister (Eds.), *Handbook of self-regulation* (2nd ed., pp. 485–504). New York: Guilford.

DeYoung, C. G. (2013). The neuromodulator of exploration: A unifying theory of the role of dopamine in personality. *Frontiers in Human Neuroscience, 7*, 762.

DeYoung, C. G. (2015). Cybernetic Big Five theory. *Journal of Research in Personality, 56*, 33–58.

DeYoung, C. G., & Gray, J. R. (2009). Personality neuroscience: Explaining individual differences in affect, behavior, and cognition. In P. J. Corr & G. Matthews (Eds.), *The Cambridge handbook of personality psychology* (pp. 323–346). Cambridge, MA: Cambridge University Press.

DeYoung, C. G., Peterson, J. B., & Higgins, D. M. (2002). Higher- order factors of the Big Five predict conformity: Are there neuroses of health? *Personality and Individual Differences, 33*, 533–552.

DeYoung, C. G., Quilty, L. C., & Peterson, J. B. (2007). Between facets and domains: 10 aspects of the Big Five. *Journal of Personality and Social Psychology, 93*, 880.

Diamond, A. (2013). Executive functions. *Annual Review of Psychology, 64*, 135–168.

Dick, D. M., Agrawal, A., Keller, M. C., Adkins, A., Aliev, F., Monroe, S., et al. (2015). Candidate gene–environment interaction research: Reflections and recommendations. *Perspectives on Psychological Science, 10*, 37–59.

Dickerson, S. S., & Kemeny, M. E. (2004). Acute stressors and cortisol responses: A theoretical integration and synthesis of laboratory research. *Psychological Bulletin, 130*, 355–391.

Dickman, S. J. (1990). Functional and dysfunctional impulsivity: Personality and cognitive correlates. *Journal of Personality and Social Psychology, 58*, 95–102.

Diedrich, A., & Voderholzer, U. (2015). Obsessive–compulsive personality disorder: A current review. *Current Psychiatry Reports, 17*, 1–10.

Diehl, R. R. (2005). Vasovagal syncope and Darwinian fitness. *Clinical Autonomic Research, 15*, 126–129.

Diflorio, A., & Jones, I. (2010). Is sex important? Gender differences in bipolar disorder. *International Review of Psychiatry, 22*, 437–452.

Di Forti, M., Lappin, J. M., & Murray, R. M. (2007). Risk factors for schizophrenia—all roads lead to dopamine. *European Neuropsychopharmacology, 17*, S101–S107.

Digman, J. M. (1997). Higher-order factors of the Big Five. *Journal of Personality and Social Psychology, 73*, 1246–1256.

DiGuiseppi, C. G., Daniels, J. L., Fallin, D. M., Rosenberg, S. A., Schieve, L. A., Thomas, K. C., et al. (2016). Demographic profile of families and children in the Study to Explore Early Development (SEED): Case-control study of autism spectrum disorder. *Disability and Health Journal, 9*, 544–551.

Dimaggio, G., Semerari, A., Carcione, A., Nicolò, G., & Procacci, M. (2007). *Psychotherapy of personality disorders: Metacognition, states of mind, and interpersonal cycles.* New York: Routledge.

Dinan, T. G., & Cryan, J. F. (2012). Regulation of the stress response by the gut microbiota: Implications for psychoneuroendocrinology. *Psychoneuroendocrinology, 37*, 1369–1378.

Dindo, L., & Fowles, D. (2011). Dual temperamental risk factors for psychopathic personality: Evidence from self-report and skin conductance. *Journal of Personality and Social Psychology, 100*, 557–566.

Dingemanse, N. J., & Réale, D. (2013). What is the evidence that natural selection maintains variation in animal personalities? In C. Carere & D. Maestripieri (Eds.), *Animal personalities: Behavior, physiology, and evolution* (pp. 201–220). Chicago: University of Chicago Press.

Dinn, W. M., & Harris, C. L. (2000). Neurocognitive function in antisocial personality disorder. *Psychiatry Research, 97*, 173–190.

Dinsdale, N., & Crespi, B. J. (2013). The borderline empathy paradox: Evidence and conceptual models for empathic enhancements in borderline personality disorder. *Journal of Personality Disorders, 27*, 172–195.

Dinsdale, N., Mokkonen, M., & Crespi, B. (2016). The "extreme female brain": Increased cognitive empathy as a dimension of psychopathology. *Evolution and Human Behavior, 37*, 323–336.

Dinsdale, N. L., & Crespi, B. J. (2017). Revisiting the wandering womb: Oxytocin in endometriosis and bipolar disorder. *Hormones and Behavior, 96*, 69–83.

Dinsdale, N. L., Hurd, P. L., Wakabayashi, A., Elliot, M., & Crespi, B. J. (2013). How are autism and schizotypy related? Evidence from a non-clinical population. *PLoS ONE, 8*, e63316.

Dishion, T. J., & Patterson, G. R. (2016). The development and ecology of antisocial behavior: Linking etiology, prevention, and treatment. In D. Cicchetti (Ed.), *Developmental psychopathology: Vol. 3. Maladaptation and psychopathology* (3rd ed., pp. 647–678). New York: Wiley.

Dixon, M. L., Andrews-Hanna, J. R., Spreng, R. N., Irving, Z. C., Mills, C., Girn, M., et al. (2017). Interactions between the default network and dorsal attention network vary across default subsystems, time, and cognitive states. *Neuroimage, 147*, 632–649.

Dochtermann, N. A., Schwab, T., & Sih, A. (2015). The contribution of additive genetic variation to personality variation: Heritability of personality. *Proceedings of the Royal Society of London B, 282*, 20142201.

Dodge, K. A. (1993). Social-cognitive mechanisms in the development of conduct disorder and depression. *Annual Review of Psychology, 44*, 559–584.

Dodge, K. A. (2006). Translational science in action: Hostile attributional style and the development of aggressive behavior problems. *Development and Psychopathology, 18*, 791–814.

Doherty, J. L., & Owen, M. J. (2014). Genomic insights into the overlap between psychiatric disorders: Implications for research and clinical practice. *Genome Medicine, 6*, 29.

Doi, N., Hoshi, Y., Itokawa, M., Usui, C., Yoshikawa, T., & Tachikawa, H. (2009). Persistence criteria for susceptibility genes for schizophrenia: A discussion from an evolutionary viewpoint. *PLoS ONE, 4*, e7799.

Dolan, M. (2012). The neuropsychology of prefrontal function in antisocial personality disordered offenders with varying degrees of psychopathy. *Psychological Medicine, 42*, 1715–1725.

Dolan, M., & Fullam, R. (2004). Theory of mind and mentalizing ability in antisocial personality disorders with and without psychopathy. *Psychological Medicine, 34*, 1093–1102.

D'Olimpio, F., & Mancini, F. (2014). Role of deontological guilt in obsessive-compulsive disorder–like checking and washing behaviors. *Clinical Psychological Science, 2*, 727–739.

Donaldson-Matasci, M. C., Bergstrom, C. T., & Lachmann, M. (2013). When unreliable cues are good enough. *The American Naturalist, 182*, 313–327.

D'Onofrio, B. M., Rickert, M. E., Frans, E., Kuja-Halkola, R., Almqvist, C., Sjölander, A., et al. (2014). Paternal age at childbearing and offspring psychiatric and academic morbidity. *JAMA Psychiatry, 71*, 432–438.

Dorn, L. D., Rose, S. R., Rotenstein, D., Susman, E. J., Huang, B., Loucks, T. L., et al. (2008). Differences in endocrine parameters and psychopathology in girls with premature adrenarche versus on-time adrenarche. *Journal of Pediatric Endocrinology and Metabolism, 21*, 439–448.

do Rosario-Campos, M. C., Leckman, J. F., Curi, M., Quatrano, S., Katsovitch, L., Miguel, E. C., et al. (2005). A family study of early-onset obsessiv-ecompulsive disorder. *American Journal of Medical Genetics Part B: Neuropsychiatric Genetics, 136*, 92–97.

Draper, P., & Harpending, H. (1982). Father absence and reproductive strategy: An evolutionary perspective. *Journal of Anthropological Research, 38*, 255–273.

Draper, P., & Harpending, H. (1988). A sociobiological perspective on the development of human reproductive strategies. In K. B. MacDonald (Ed.), *Sociobiological perspectives on human development* (pp. 340–372). New York: Springer.

Dreier, J. W., Berg-Beckhoff, G., Andersen, A. M. N., Susser, E., Nordentoft, M., & Strandberg-Larsen, K. (2018). Fever and infections during pregnancy and psychosis-like experiences in the offspring at age 11: A prospective study within the Danish National Birth Cohort. *Psychological Medicine, 48*, 426–436.

Dubbs, S. L., & Buunk, A. P. (2010). Parents just don't understand: Parent-offspring conflict over mate choice. *Evolutionary Psychology, 8*, 586–598.

Duckworth, A. L., & Kern, M. L. (2011). A meta-analysis of the convergent validity of self-control measures. *Journal of Research in Personality, 45*, 259–268.

Duffy, K. A., Harris, L. T., Chartrand, T. L., & Stanton, S. J. (2017). Women recovering from social rejection: The effect of the person and the situation on a hormonal mechanism of affiliation. *Psychoneuroendocrinology, 76*, 174–182.

Duivis, H. E., Vogelzangs, N., Kupper, N., de Jonge, P., & Penninx, B. W. (2013). Differential association of somatic and cognitive symptoms of depression and anxiety with inflammation: Findings from the Netherlands Study of Depression and Anxiety (NESDA). *Psychoneuroendocrinology, 38*, 1573–1585.

Dunbar, J., Sheeder, J., Lezotte, D., Dabelea, D., & Stevens-Simon, C. (2008). Age at menarche and first pregnancy among psychosocially at-risk adolescents. *American Journal of Public Health, 98*, 1822–1824.

Dunbar, R. I. M. (1993). Co-evolution of neocortex size, group size and language in humans. *Behavioral and Brain Sciences, 16*, 681–735.

Dunbar, R. I. M., & Shultz, S. (2007). Evolution in the social brain. *Science, 317*, 1344–1347.

Dunbar, R. I. M., & Shultz, S. (2010). Bondedness and sociality. *Behaviour, 147*, 775–803.

Duncan, L., Yilmaz, Z., Gaspar, H., Walters, R., Goldstein, J., Anttila, V., et al. (2017). Significant locus and metabolic genetic correlations revealed in genome-wide association study of anorexia nervosa. *American Journal of Psychiatry.* doi:10.1176/appi.ajp.2017.16121402

Duncan, L. E., Pollastri, A. R., & Smoller, J. W. (2014). Mind the gap: Why many geneticists and psychological scientists have discrepant views about gene–environment interaction (G×E) research. *American Psychologist, 69*, 249.

Dunkel, C. S., & Decker, M. (2010). Convergent validity of measures of life-history strategy. *Personality and Individual Differences, 48*, 681–684.

Dunkel, C. S., van der Linden, D., Beaver, K. M., & Woodley, M. A. (2014). Using a prison sample to assess the association between the general factor of personality and general intelligence. *Intelligence, 47*, 72–82.

Dunkel, C. S., van der Linden, D., Brown, N. A., & Mathes, E. W. (2016). Self-report based general factor of personality as socially-desirable responding, positive self-evaluation, and social-effectiveness. *Personality and Individual Differences, 92*, 143–147.

Dunn, J. C., Whelton, W. J., & Sharpe, D. (2012). Retreating to safety: Testing the social risk hypothesis model of depression. *Evolution and Human Behavior, 33*, 746–758.

Dunsmoor, J. E., & Paz, R. (2015). Fear generalization and anxiety: Behavioral and neural mechanisms. *Biological Psychiatry, 78*, 336–343.

Du Preez, A., Leveson, J., Zunszain, P. A., & Pariante, C. M. (2016). Inflammatory insults and mental health consequences: Does timing matter when it comes to depression? *Psychological Medicine, 46*, 2041–2057.

Durbin, C. E., Schalet, B. D., Hayden, E. P., Simpson, J., & Jordan, P. L. (2009). Hypomanic personality traits: A multi-method exploration of their association with normal and abnormal dimensions of personality. *Journal of Research in Personality, 43*, 898–905.

Durisko, Z., Mulsant, B. H., & Andrews, P. W. (2015). An adaptationist perspective on the etiology of depression. *Journal of Affective Disorders, 172*, 315–323.

Durkin, M. S., DuBois, L. A., & Maenner, M. J. (2015). Inter-pregnancy intervals and the risk of autism spectrum disorder: Results of a population-based study. *Journal of Autism and Developmental Disorders, 45*, 2056–2066.

Durkin, M. S., Maenner, M. J., Meaney, F. J., Levy, S. E., DiGuiseppi, C., Nicholas, J. S., et al. (2010). Socioeconomic inequality in the prevalence of autism spectrum disorder: Evidence from a US cross-sectional study. *PLoS ONE, 5*, e11551.

Durrant, R., & Ellis, B. J. (2003). Evolutionary psychology. In M. Gallagher & R. J. Nelson (Eds.), *Comprehensive handbook of psychology* (Vol. 3, pp. 1–33). New York: Wiley.

Durrant, R., & Ward, T. (2015). *Evolutionary criminology: Towards a comprehensive explanation of crime*. London: Academic Press.

Duvekot, J., Ende, J., Constantino, J. N., Verhulst, F. C., & Greaves-Lord, K. (2016). Symptoms of autism spectrum disorder and anxiety: Shared familial transmission and cross-assortative mating. *Journal of Child Psychology and Psychiatry, 57*, 759–769.

Dwyer, D. S., Horton, R. Y., & Aamodt, E. J. (2011). Role of the evolutionarily conserved starvation response in anorexia nervosa. *Molecular Psychiatry, 16*, 595–603.

Eastwick, P. W. (2009). Beyond the Pleistocene: Using phylogeny and constraint to inform the evolutionary psychology of human mating. *Psychological Bulletin, 135*, 794–821.

Eaton, N. R., Rodriguez-Seijas, C., Carragher, N., & Krueger, R. F. (2015). Transdiagnostic factors of psychopathology and substance use disorders: A review. *Social Psychiatry and Psychiatric Epidemiology, 50*, 171–182.

Ebner-Priemer, U. W., Houben, M., Santangelo, P., Kleindienst, N., Tuerlinckx, F., Oravecz, Z., et al. (2015). Unraveling affective dysregulation in borderline personality disorder: A theoretical model and empirical evidence. *Journal of Abnormal Psychology, 124*, 186–198.

Eddy, K. T., Dorer, D. J., Franko, D. L., Tahilani, K., Thompson-Brenner, H., & Herzog, D. B. (2008). Diagnostic crossover in anorexia nervosa and bulimia nervosa: Implications for DSM-V. *American Journal of Psychiatry, 165*, 245–250.

Edelstein, R. S., Wardecker, B. M., Chopik, W. J., Moors, A. C., Shipman, E. L., & Lin, N. J. (2015). Prenatal hormones in first-time expectant parents: Longitudinal changes and within-couple correlations. *American Journal of human Biology, 27*, 317–325.

Edvardsen, J., Torgersen, S., Røysamb, E., Lygren, S., Skre, I., Onstad, S., et al. (2008). Heritability of bipolar spectrum disorders. Unity or heterogeneity? *Journal of Affective Disorders, 106*, 229–240.

Edwards, A. C., Bacanu, S. A., Bigdeli, T. B., Moscati, A., & Kendler, K. S. (2016). Evaluating the dopamine hypothesis of schizophrenia in a large-scale genome-wide association study. *Schizophrenia Research, 176*, 136–140.

Edwards, R. C., & Hans, S. L. (2015). Infant risk factors associated with internalizing, externalizing, and co-occurring behavior problems in young children. *Developmental Psychology, 51*, 489–499.

Ehli, E. A., Abdellaoui, A., Hu, Y., Hottenga, J. J., Kattenberg, M., van Beijsterveldt, T., et al. (2012). De novo and inherited CNVs in MZ twin pairs selected for discordance and concordance on Attention Problems. *European Journal of Human Genetics, 20*, 1037–1043.

Eid, L., Heim, K., Doucette, S., McCloskey, S., Duffy, A., & Grof, P. (2013). Bipolar disorder and socioeconomic status: What is the nature of this relationship? *International Journal of Bipolar Disorders, 1*, 9.

Ein-Dor, T. (2015). Attachment dispositions and human defensive behavior. *Personality and Individual Differences, 81*, 112–116.

Ein-Dor, T., Mikulincer, M., & Shaver, P. R. (2011). Attachment insecurities and the processing of threat-related information: Studying the schemas involved in insecure people's coping strategies. *Journal of Personality and Social Psychology, 101*, 78–93.

Eisenegger, C., Haushofer, J., & Fehr, E. (2011). The role of testosterone in social interaction. *Trends in Cognitive Sciences, 15*, 263–271.

Elbert, T., Weierstall, R., & Schauer, M. (2010). Fascination violence: On mind and brain of man hunters. *European Archives of Psychiatry and Clinical Neuroscience, 260*, S100–S105.

Eliassen, S., Jørgensen, C., Mangel, M., & Giske, J. (2007). Exploration or exploitation: Life expectancy changes the value of learning in foraging strategies. *Oikos, 116*, 513–523.

Ellis, B. J. (2013). The hypothalamic–pituitary–gonadal axis: A switch-controlled, condition-sensitive system in the regulation of life history strategies. *Hormones and Behavior, 64*, 215–225.

Ellis, B. J., Boyce, W. T., Belsky, J., Bakermans-Kranenburg, M. J., & van IJzendoorn, M. H. (2011). Differential susceptibility to the environment: An evolutionary-neurodevelopmental theory. *Development and Psychopathology, 23*, 7–28.

Ellis, B. J., & Del Giudice, M. (2014). Beyond allostatic load: Rethinking the role of stress in regulating human development. *Development and Psychopathology, 26*, 1–20.

Ellis, B. J., Del Giudice, M., Dishion, T. J., Figueredo, A. J., Gray, P., Griskevicius, V., et al. (2012). The evolutionary basis of risky adolescent behavior: Implications for science, policy, and practice. *Developmental Psychology, 48*, 598–623.

Ellis, B. J., Del Giudice, M., & Shirtcliff, E. A. (2017). The Adaptive Calibration Model of stress responsivity: Concepts, findings, and implications for developmental psychopathology. In T. P. Beauchaine & S. P. Hinshaw (Eds.), *Child and adolescent psychopathology* (3rd ed., 237–276). New York: Wiley.

Ellis, B. J., & Essex, M. J. (2007). Family environments, adrenarche, and sexual maturation: A longitudinal test of a life history model. *Child Development, 78*, 1799–1817.

Ellis, B. J., Figueredo, A. J., Brumbach, B. H., & Schlomer, G. L. (2009). The impact of harsh versus unpredictable environments on the evolution and development of life history strategies. *Human Nature, 20*, 204–268.

Ellis, B. J., Shirtcliff, E. A., Boyce, W. T., Deardorff, J., & Essex, M. J. (2011). Quality of early family relationships and the timing and tempo of puberty: Effects depend on biological sensitivity to context. *Development and Psychopathology, 23*, 85–99.

Ellison, P. T. (2001). *On fertile ground: A natural history of human reproduction*. Cambridge, MA: Harvard University Press.

Ellison-Wright, I., & Bullmore, E. (2010). Anatomy of bipolar disorder and schizophrenia: A meta-analysis. *Schizophrenia Research, 117*, 1–12.

Else-Quest, N. M., Hyde, J. S., Goldsmith, H. H., & Van Hulle, C. A. (2006). Gender differences in temperament: A meta-analysis. *Psychological Bulletin, 132*, 33–72.

Elton, A., Di Martino, A., Hazlett, H. C., & Gao, W. (2016). Neural connectivity evidence for a categorical-dimensional hybrid model of autism spectrum disorder. *Biological Psychiatry, 80*, 120–128.

Enard, D., Messer, P. W., & Petrov, D. A. (2014). Genome-wide signals of positive selection in human evolution. *Genome Research, 24*, 885–895.

Engelmann, J. M., Herrmann, E., & Tomasello, M. (2015). Chimpanzees trust conspecifics to engage in low-cost reciprocity. *Proceedings of the Royal Society of London B, 282*, 20142803.

Engen, S., Lande, R., & Sæther, B. E. (2013). A quantitative genetic model of r-and K-selection in a fluctuating population. *The American Naturalist, 181*, 725–736.

Erdle, S., & Rushton, J. P. (2011). Does self-esteem or social desirability account for a general factor of personality (GFP) in the Big Five? *Personality and Individual Differences, 50*, 1152–1154.

Ericson, M., Tuvblad, C., Raine, A., Young-Wolff, K., & Baker, L. A. (2011). Heritability and longitudinal stability of schizotypal traits during adolescence. *Behavior Genetics, 41*, 499–511.

Ericsson, M., Lundholm, C., Fors, S., Aslan, A. K. D., Zavala, C., Reynolds, C. A., et al. (2017). Childhood social class and cognitive aging in the Swedish Adoption/Twin Study of Aging. *Proceedings of the National Academy of Sciences, 114*, 7001–7006.

Ermer, E., Cosmides, L., & Tooby, J. (2008). Relative status regulates risky decision making about resources in men: Evidence for the co-evolution of motivation and cognition. *Evolution and Human Behavior, 29*, 106–118.

Esch, T., & Stefano, G. B. (2005). The neurobiology of love. *Neuroendocrinology Letters, 26*, 175–192.

Esler, M., Lambert, E., Alvarenga, M., Socratous, F., Richards, J., Esler, M., et al. (2007). Increased brain serotonin turnover in panic disorder patients in the absence of a panic attack: Reduction by a selective serotonin reuptake inhibitor: Research Report. *Stress, 10*, 295–304.

Esperger, Z., & Bereczkei, T. (2012). Machiavellianism and spontaneous mentalization: One step ahead of others. *European Journal of Personality, 26*, 580–587.

Etkin, A., & Wager, T. D. (2007). Functional neuroimaging of anxiety: A meta-analysis of emotional processing in PTSD, social anxiety disorder, and specific phobia. *American Journal of Psychiatry, 164*, 1476–1488.

Ettelt, S., Ruhrmann, S., Barnow, S., Buthz, F., Hochrein, A., Meyer, K., et al. (2007). Impulsiveness in obsessive-compulsive disorder: Results from a family study. *Acta Psychiatrica Scandinavica, 115*, 41–47.

Evans, J. S. B. (2008). Dual-processing accounts of reasoning, judgment, and social cognition. *Annual Review of Psychology, 59*, 255–278.

Evans, J. S. B., & Stanovich, K. E. (2013). Dual-process theories of higher cognition: Advancing the debate. *Perspectives on Psychological Science, 8*, 223–241.

Faer, L. M., Hendriks, A., Abed, R. T., & Figueredo, A. J. (2005). The evolutionary psychology of eating disorders: Female competition for mates or for status? *Psychology and Psychotherapy: Theory, Research and Practice, 78*, 397–417.

Fair, D. A., Bathula, D., Nikolas, M. A., & Nigg, J. T. (2012). Distinct neuropsychological subgroups in typically developing youth inform heterogeneity in children with ADHD. *Proceedings of the National Academy of Sciences, 109*, 6769–6774.

Fairchild, G., van Goozen, S. H., Stollery, S. J., Aitken, M. R., Savage, J., Moore, S. C., et al. (2009). Decision making and executive function in male adolescents with early-onset or adolescence-onset conduct disorder and control subjects. *Biological Psychiatry, 66*, 162–168.

Fairweather-Schmidt, A. K., & Wade, T. D. (2016). Characterizing and predicting trajectories of disordered eating over adolescence. *Journal of Abnormal Psychology, 125*, 369–380.

Faja, S., & Dawson, G. (2013). Autism spectrum disorders. In T. P. Beauchaine & S. P. Hinshaw (Eds.), *Child and adolescent psychopathology* (2nd ed., pp. 649–684). Hoboken, NJ: Wiley.

Falkenburg, J., & Tracy, D. K. (2014). Sex and schizophrenia: A review of gender differences. *Psychosis, 6*, 61–69.

Falter, C. M., Elliott, M. A., & Bailey, A. J. (2012). Enhanced visual temporal resolution in autism spectrum disorders. *PLoS ONE, 7*, e32774.

Fanning, J. R., Berman, M. E., Guillot, C. R., Marsic, A., & McCloskey, M. S. (2014). Serotonin (5-HT) augmentation reduces provoked aggression associated with primary psychopathy traits. *Journal of Personality Disorders, 28*, 449–461.

Faraone, S. V., Biederman, J., & Mick, E. (2006). The age-dependent decline of attention deficit hyperactivity disorder: A meta-analysis of follow-up studies. *Psycholgical Medicine, 36*, 159–165.

Farina, B., & Liotti, G. (2013). Does a dissociative psychopathological dimension exist? A review on dissociative processes and symptoms in developmental trauma spectrum disorders. *Clinical Neuropsychiatry, 10*, 11–19.

Farstad, S. M., McGeown, L. M., & von Ranson, K. M. (2016). Eating disorders and personality, 2004–2016: A systematic review and meta-analysis. *Clinical Psychology Review, 46*, 91–105.

Faucher, L., & Blanchette, I. (2011). Fearing new dangers: Phobias and the cognitive complexity of human emotions. In P. R. Adriaens & A. De Block (Eds.), *Maladapting minds: Philosophy, psychiatry, and evolutionary theory* (pp. 35–64). Oxford: Oxford University Press.

Faulkner, P., & Deakin, J. W. (2014). The role of serotonin in reward, punishment and behavioural inhibition in humans: Insights from studies with acute tryptophan depletion. *Neuroscience & Biobehavioral Reviews, 46*, 365–378.

Fawcett, T. W., & Frankenhuis, W. E. (2015). Adaptive explanations for sensitive windows in development. *Frontiers in Zoology, 12, S*3.

Fawcett, T. W., Marshall, J. A., & Higginson, A. D. (2015). The evolution of mechanisms underlying behaviour. *Current Zoology, 61*, 221–225.

Fawcett, T. W., McNamara, J. M., & Houston, A. I. (2012). When is it adaptive to be patient? A general framework for evaluating delayed rewards. *Behavioural Processes, 89*, 128–136.

Fearon, R. M. P., & Belsky, J. (2011). Infant–mother attachment and the growth of externalizing problems across the primary-school years. *Journal of Child Psychology and Psychiatry, 52*, 782–791.

Feierman, J. R. (1984). Anorexia nervosa: A human female reproductive strategy? *International Journal of Primatology, 5*, 338.

Feifel, D., Shilling, P. D., & MacDonald, K. (2016). A review of oxytocin's effects on the positive, negative, and cognitive domains of schizophrenia. *Biological Psychiatry, 79*, 222–233.

Feil, R., & Fraga, M. F. (2012). Epigenetics and the environment: Emerging patterns and implications. *Nature Reviews Genetics, 13*, 97–109.

Feldman, M. B., & Meyer, I. H. (2007). Eating disorders in diverse lesbian, gay, and bisexual populations. *International Journal of Eating Disorders, 40*, 218–226.

Feldman, R. (2017). The neurobiology of human attachments. *Trends in Cognitive Sciences, 21*, 80–99.

Feliciano, L., & Renn, B. N. (2014). Mood disorders: Depressive disorders. In D. C. Beidel, B. C. Frueh, & M. Hersen (Eds.), *Adult psychopathology and diagnosis* (7th ed., pp. 253–298). New York: Wiley.

Ferdowsian, H. R., Durham, D. L., Johnson, C. M., Brüne, M., Kimwele, C., Kranendonk, G., et al. (2012). Signs of generalized anxiety and compulsive disorders in chimpanzees. *Journal of Veterinary Behavior: Clinical Applications and Research, 7*, 353–361.

Ferdowsian, H. R., Durham, D. L., Kimwele, C., Kranendonk, G., Otali, E., Akugizibwe, T., et al. (2011). Signs of mood and anxiety disorders in chimpanzees. *PLoS ONE, 6*, e19855.

Ferguson, C. J., Winegard, B., & Winegard, B. M. (2011). Who is the fairest one of all? How evolution guides peer and media influences on female body dissatisfaction. *Review of General Psychology, 15*, 11.

Fernandes, H. B. F., Lynn, R., & Hertler, S. (2018). Race differences in anxiety disorders, social anxiety and worry: An examination of the Differential-K theory in clinical psychology. *Mankind Quarterly, 58*, 466–500.

Fernandez-Egea, E., García-Rizo, C., Miller, B., Parellada, E., Justicia, A., Bernardo, M., et al. (2011). Testosterone in newly diagnosed, antipsychotic-naive men with nonaffective psychosis: A test of the accelerated aging hypothesis. *Psychosomatic Medicine, 73*, 643–647.

Fessler, D. M. (2002). Pseudoparadoxical impulsivity in restrictive anorexia nervosa: A consequence of the logic of scarcity. *International Journal of Eating Disorders, 31*, 376–388.

Feygin, D. L., Swain, J. E., & Leckman, J. F. (2006). The normalcy of neurosis: Evolutionary origins of obsessive-compulsive disorder and related behaviors. *Progress in Neuro-Psychopharmacology & Biological Psychiatry, 30*, 854–864.

Field, Y., Boyle, E. A., Telis, N., Gao, Z., Gaulton, K. J., Golan, D., et al. (2016). Detection of human adaptation during the past 2,000 years. *Science, 354*, 760–764.

Figueredo, A. J. (2007). *The Arizona Life History Battery*. Retrieved from http://www.u.arizona.edu/~ajf/alhb.html

Figueredo, A. J., & Jacobs, W. J. (2010). Aggression, risk-taking, and alternative life history strategies: The behavioral ecology of social deviance. In M. Frias-Armenta & V. Corral-Verdugo (Eds.), *Biopsychosocial perspectives on aggression* (pp. 3–27). Hauppauge, NY: Nova Science Publishers.

Figueredo, A. J., & Rushton, J. P. (2009). Evidence for shared genetic dominance between the general factor of personality, mental and physical health, and life history traits. *Twin Research and Human Genetics, 12*, 555–563.

Figueredo, A. J., Vásquez, G., Brumbach, B. H., & Schneider, S. M. R. (2004). The heritability of life history strategy: The K-factor, covitality, and personality. *Social Biology, 51*, 121–143.

Figueredo, A. J., Vásquez, G., Brumbach, B. H., & Schneider, S. M. R. (2007). The K-factor, covitality, and personality: A psychometric test of life history theory. *Human Nature, 18*, 47–73.

Figueredo, A. J., Vásquez, G., Brumbach, B. H., Schneider, S. M. R., Sefcek, J. A., Tal, I. R., et al. (2006). Consilience and Life History Theory: From genes to brain to reproductive strategy. *Developmental Review, 26*, 243–275.

Figueredo, A. J., Vásquez, G., Brumbach, B. H., Sefcek, J. A., Krisner, B. R., & Jacobs, W. J. (2005). The K-Factor: Individual differences in life-history strategy. *Personality and Individual Differences, 39*, 1349–1360.

Figueredo, A. J., Wolf, P. S. A., Gladden, P. R., Olderbak, S., Andrzejczak, D. J., & Jacobs, W. J. (2011). Ecological approaches to personality. In D. M. Buss & P. H. Hawley (Eds.), *The evolution of personality and individual differences* (pp. 210–241). New York: Oxford University Press.

Figueredo, A. J., Wolf, P. S., Olderbak, S. G., Gladden, P. R., Fernandes, H. B. F., Wenner, C., et al. (2014). A meta-analytic validation of the Mini-K short form of the Arizona Life History Battery. *Evolutionary Behavioral Sciences, 8*, 148–185.

Figueredo, A. J., Woodley, M. A., & Jacobs, W. J. (2015). The General Factor of Personality: A hierarchical life history model. In D. M. Buss (Ed.), *The handbook of evolutionary psychology* (2nd ed., pp. 943–967). New York: Wiley.

Finch, C. E., & Rose, M. R. (1995). Hormones and the physiological architecture of life history evolution. *Quarterly Review of Biology, 70*, 1–52.

Fischer, A. G., Jocham, G., & Ullsperger, M. (2015). Dual serotonergic signals: A key to understanding paradoxical effects? *Trends in Cognitive Sciences, 19*, 21–26.

Fischer, B., Taborsky, B., & Kokko, H. (2011). How to balance the offspring quality–quantity tradeoff when environmental cues are unreliable. *Oikos, 120*, 258–270.

Fischer, B., van Doorn, G. S., Dieckmann, U., & Taborsky, B. (2014). The evolution of age-dependent plasticity. *The American Naturalist, 183*, 108–125.

Fischer, J., Mikhael, J. G., Tenenbaum, J. B., & Kanwisher, N. (2016). Functional neuroanatomy of intuitive physical inference. *Proceedings of the National Academy of Sciences USA, 113*, E5072–E5081.

Fiske, A. P., & Haslam, N. (1997). Is obsessive-compulsive disorder a pathology of the human disposition to perform socially meaningful rituals? Evidence of similar content. *The Journal of Nervous & Mental Disease, 185*, 211–222.

Flegr, J. (2013). Influence of latent *Toxoplasma* infection on human personality, physiology and morphology: Pros and cons of the *Toxoplasma*–human model in studying the manipulation hypothesis. *Journal of Experimental Biology, 216*, 127–133.

Fleming, K. A., Heintzelman, S. J., & Bartholow, B. D. (2016). Specifying associations between conscientiousness and executive functioning: Mental set shifting, not prepotent response inhibition or working memory updating. *Journal of Personality, 84*, 348–360.

Fletcher, G. J. O., Simpson, J. A., Campbell, L., & Overall, N. C. (2015). Pair-Bonding, romantic love, and evolution: The curious case of *Homo sapiens*. *Perspectives on Psychological Science, 10*, 20–36.

Fletcher, P. C., & Frith, C. D. (2009). Perceiving is believing: A Bayesian approach to explaining the positive symptoms of schizophrenia. *Nature Reviews Neuroscience, 10*, 48–58.

Flinn, M. V. (2006). Evolution and ontogeny of the stress response to social challenges in the human child. *Developmental Review, 26*, 138–174.

Flinn, M. V., Geary, D. C., & Ward, C. V. (2005). Ecological dominance, social competition, and coalitionary arms races: Why humans evolved extraordinary intelligence. *Evolution and Human Behavior, 26*, 10–46.

Flinn, M. V., Nepomnaschy, P. A., Muehlenbein, M. P., & Ponzi, D. (2011). Evolutionary functions of early social modulation of hypothalamic–pituitary–adrenal axis development in humans. *Neuroscience & Biobehavioral Reviews, 35*, 1611–1629.

Flint, J., & Kendler, K. S. (2014). The genetics of major depression. *Neuron, 81*, 484–503.

Floresco, S. B. (2015). The nucleus accumbens: An interface between cognition, emotion, and action. *Annual Review of Psychology, 66*, 25–52.

Fogelson, D. L., Nuechterlein, K. H., Asarnow, R. A., Payne, D. L., Subotnik, K. L., Jacobson, K. C., et al. (2007). Avoidant personality disorder is a separable schizophrenia-spectrum personality disorder even when controlling for the presence of paranoid and schizotypal personality disorders: The UCLA family study. *Schizophrenia Research, 91*, 192–199.

Foldes, H. J., Duehr, E. E., & Ones, D. S. (2008). Group differences in personality: Meta-analyses comparing five US racial groups. *Personnel Psychology, 61*, 579–616.

Fonagy, P., & Luyten, P. (2016). A multilevel perspective on the development of borderline personality disorder. In D. Cicchetti (Ed.), *Developmental psychopathology: Vol. 3. Maladaptation and psychopathology* (3rd ed., pp. 726–792). New York: Wiley.

Fontenelle, L. F., & Hasler, G. (2008). The analytical epidemiology of obsessive-compulsive disorder: Risk factors and correlates. *Progress in Neuro-Psychopharmacology and Biological Psychiatry, 32*, 1–15.

Forbes, D., Elhai, J. D., Miller, M. W., & Creamer, M. (2010). Internalizing and externalizing classes in posttraumatic stress disorder: A latent class analysis. *Journal of Traumatic Stress, 23*, 340–349.

Forbes, E. E., & Dahl, R. E. (2010). Pubertal development and behavior: Hormonal activation of social and motivational tendencies. *Brain and Cognition, 72*, 66–72.

Forbes, L. S. (1997). The evolutionary biology of spontaneous abortion in humans. *Trends in Ecology and Evolution, 12*, 446–450.

Forbes, M. K., Tackett, J. L., Markon, K. E., & Krueger, R. F. (2016). Beyond comorbidity: Toward a dimensional and hierarchical approach to understanding psychopathology across the life span. *Development and Psychopathology, 28*, 971–986.

Forbes, M. K., Wright, A. G. C., Markon, K. E., & Krueger, R. F. (2017). Evidence that psychopathology symptom networks have limited replicability. *Journal of Abnormal Psychology, 126*, 969–988.

Fornaro, M., Orsolini, L., Marini, S., De Berardis, D., Perna, G., Valchera, A., et al. (2016). The prevalence and predictors of bipolar and borderline personality disorders comorbidity: Systematic review and meta-analysis. *Journal of Affective Disorders, 195*, 105–118.

Fornito, A., Harrison, B. J., Goodby, E., Dean, A., Ooi, C., Nathan, P. J., et al. (2013). Functional dysconnectivity of corticostriatal circuitry as a risk phenotype for psychosis. *JAMA Psychiatry, 70*, 1143–1151.

Forster, S., & Lavie, N. (2016). Establishing the attention-distractibility trait. *Psychological Science, 27*, 203–212.

Fortgang, R. G., Hultman, C. M., van Erp, T. G. M., & Cannon, T. D. (2016). Multidimensional assessment of impulsivity in schizophrenia, bipolar disorder, and major depressive disorder: Testing for shared endophenotypes. *Psychological Medicine, 46*, 1497–1507.

Foster, J. A., & McVey Neufeld, K. A. (2013). Gut–brain axis: How the microbiome influences anxiety and depression. *Trends in Neurosciences, 36*, 305–312.

Foster, K. R., & Kokko, H. (2009). The evolution of superstitious and superstition-like behaviour. *Proceedings of the Royal Society of London B, 276*, 31–37.

Fouts, H. N., Hewlett, B. S., & Lamb, M. E. (2005). Parent–offspring weaning conflicts among the Bofi farmers and foragers in central Africa. *Current Anthropology, 46*, 29–50.

Fowles, D. C., & Dindo, L. (2006). A dual-deficit model of psychopathy. In C. J. Patrick (Ed.), *Handbook of psychopathy* (pp. 14–34). New York: Guilford.

Fox, C. R., & Tannenbaum, D. (2011). The elusive search for stable risk preferences. *Frontiers in Psychology, 2*, 298.

Fox, R. (2004). Sects and evolution. *Society, 41*, 36–46.

Fraley, R. C., Roisman, G. I., Booth-LaForce, C., Owen, M. T., & Holland, A. S. (2013). Interpersonal and genetic origins of adult attachment styles: A longitudinal study from infancy to early adulthood. *Journal of Personality and Social Psychology, 104*, 817–838.

Francioli, L. C., Polak, P. P., Koren, A., Menelaou, A., Chun, S., Renkens, I., et al. (2015). Genome-wide patterns and properties of de novo mutations in humans. *Nature Genetics, 47*, 822–826.

Frank, G. K., & Kaye, W. H. (2012). Current status of functional imaging in eating disorders. *International Journal of Eating Disorders, 45*, 723–736.

Frank, M. J., Cohen, M. X., & Sanfey, A. G. (2009). Multiple systems in decision making: A neurocomputational perspective. *Current Directions in Psychological Science, 18*, 73–77.

Frankenhuis, W. E., & Del Giudice, M. (2012). When do adaptive developmental mechanisms yield maladaptive outcomes? *Developmental Psychology, 48*, 628–642.

Frankenhuis, W. E., & Panchanathan, K. (2011). Balancing sampling and specialization: An adaptationist model of incremental development. *Proceedings of the Royal Society of London B, 278*, 3558–3565.

Frankenhuis, W. E., Panchanathan, K., & Belsky, J. (2016). A mathematical model of the evolution of individual differences in developmental plasticity arising through parental bet-hedging. *Developmental Science, 19*, 251–274.

Frans, E. M., Sandin, S., Reichenberg, A., Lichtenstein, P., Långström, N., & Hultman, C. M. (2008). Advancing paternal age and bipolar disorder. *Archives of General Psychiatry, 65*, 1034–1040.

Franz, M., & Matthews, L. J. (2010). Social enhancement can create adaptive, arbitrary and maladaptive cultural traditions. *Proceedings of the Royal Society of London B, 277*, 3363–3372.

Frazier, T. W., Demaree, H. A., & Youngstrom, E. A. (2004). Meta-analysis of intellectual and neuropsychological test performance in attention-deficit/hyperactivity disorder. *Neuropsychology, 18*, 543–555.

Frederick, M. J. (2012). Birth weight predicts scores on the ADHD self-report scale and attitudes towards casual sex in college men: A short-term life history strategy? *Evolutionary Psychology, 10*, 342–351.

Freeman, S. M., Clewett, D. V., Bennett, C. M., Kiehl, K. A., Gazzaniga, M. S., & Miller, M. B. (2015). The posteromedial region of the default mode network shows attenuated task-induced deactivation in psychopathic prisoners. *Neuropsychology, 29*, 493–500.

French, L. R., Bertone, A., Hyde, K. L., & Fombonne, E. (2013). Epidemiology of autism spectrum disorders. In J. D. Buxbaum & P. R. Hof (Eds.), *The neuroscience of autism spectrum disorders* (pp. 3–24). Oxford: Academic Press.

Frey, R., Pedroni, A., Mata, R., Rieskamp, J., & Hertwig, R. (2017). Risk preference shares the psychometric structure of major psychological traits. *Science Advances, 3*, e1701381.

Fried, E. I., & Nesse, R. M. (2015). Depression is not a consistent syndrome: An investigation of unique symptom patterns in the STAR* D study. *Journal of Affective Disorders, 172*, 96–102.

Friedman, N. P., Miyake, A., Young, S. E., DeFries, J. C., Corley, R. P., & Hewitt, J. K. (2008). Individual differences in executive functions are almost entirely genetic in origin. *Journal of Experimental Psychology: General, 137*, 201–225.

Frisell, T., Pawitan, Y., Långström, N., & Lichtenstein, P. (2012). Heritability, assortative mating and gender differences in violent crime: Results from a total population sample using twin, adoption, and sibling models. *Behavior Genetics, 42*, 3–18.

Friston, K., Schwartenbeck, P., FitzGerald, T., Moutoussis, M., Behrens, T., & Dolan, R. J. (2014). The anatomy of choice: Dopamine and decision-making. *Philosophical Transactions of the Royal Society B, 369*, 20130481.

Friston, K. J., Lawson, R., & Frith, C. D. (2013). On hyperpriors and hypopriors: Comment on Pellicano and Burr. *Trends in Cognitive Science, 17*, 1.

Frith, C. D. (2004). Schizophrenia and theory of mind. *Psychological Medicine, 34*, 385–389.

Frith, U., & Frith, C. (2010). The social brain: Allowing humans to boldly go where no other species has been. *Philosophical Transactions of the Royal Society of London B, 365*, 165–176.

Frith, U., & Frith, C. (2011). Reputation management: In autism, generosity is its own reward. *Current Biology, 21*, R994–R995.

Frost, P. (2011). Human nature or human natures? *Futures, 43*, 740–748.

Frost, P., & Harpending, H. C. (2015). Western Europe, state formation, and genetic pacification. *Evolutionary Psychology, 13*, 230–243.

Fu, W., O'Connor, T. D., Kang, H. M., Abecasis, G., Leal, S. M., Gabriel, S., et al. (2013). Analysis of 6,515 exomes reveals the recent origin of most human protein-coding variants. *Nature, 493*, 216–270.

Fujiwara, T. (2014). Socioeconomic status and the risk of suspected autism spectrum disorders among 18-month-old toddlers in Japan: A population-based study. *Journal of Autism and Developmental Disorders, 44*, 1323–1331.

Furmark, T. (2002). Social phobia: Overview of community surveys. *Acta Psychiatrica Scandinavica, 105*, 84–93.

Furnham, A., Batey, M., Anand, K., & Manfield, J. (2008). Personality, hypomania, intelligence and creativity. *Personality and Individual Differences, 44*, 1060–1069.

Furnham, A., Richards, S. C., & Paulhus, D. L. (2013). The Dark Triad of personality: A 10 year review. *Social and Personality Psychology Compass, 7*, 199–216.

Furrow, R. E., & Feldman, M. W. (2014). Genetic variation and the evolution of epigenetic regulation. *Evolution, 68*, 673–683.

Fusar-Poli, P., Bonoldi, I., Yung, A. R., Borgwardt, S., Kempton, M. J., Valmaggia, L., et al. (2012). Predicting psychosis: Meta-analysis of transition outcomes in individuals at high clinical risk. *Archives of General Psychiatry, 69*, 220–229.

Fusar-Poli, P., Rubia, K., Rossi, G., Sartori, G., & Balottin, U. (2012). Striatal dopamine transporter alterations in ADHD: Pathophysiology or adaptation to psychostimulants? A meta-analysis. *American Journal of Psychiatry, 169*, 264–272.

Futuyma, D. J. (2017). *Evolution* (4th ed.). Sunderland, MA: Sinauer.

Gadow, K. D. (2012). Schizophrenia spectrum and attention-deficit/hyperactivity disorder symptoms in autism spectrum disorder and controls. *Journal of the American Academy of Child & Adolescent Psychiatry, 51*, 1076–1084.

Gajwani, R., Patterson, P., & Birchwood, M. (2013). Attachment: Developmental pathways to affective dysregulation in young people at ultra-high risk of developing psychosis. *British Journal of Clinical Psychology, 52*, 424–437.

Gallagher, P., Gray, J. M., & Kessels, R. P. (2015). Fractionation of visuo-spatial memory processes in bipolar depression: A cognitive scaffolding account. *Psychological Medicine, 45*, 545–558.

Gallitto, E., & Leth-Steensen, C. (2015). Autistic traits and adult attachment styles. *Personality and Individual Differences, 79*, 63–67.

Gangestad, S. W. (2011). Evolutionary processes explaining the genetic variance in personality: An exploration of scenarios. In D. M. Buss & P. H. Hawley (Eds.), *The evolution of personality and individual differences* (pp. 338–375). New York: Oxford University Press.

Gangestad, S. W. (2016). An evolutionary perspective on oxytocin and its behavioral effects. *Current Opinion in Psychology, 7*, 115–119.

Gangestad, S. W., Caldwell Hooper, A. E., & Eaton, M. (2012). On the function of placental corticotropin-releasing hormone: A role in maternal-fetal conflicts over blood glucose concentrations. *Biological Reviews, 87*, 856–873.

Gangestad, S. W., & Scheyd, G. J. (2005). The evolution of human physical attractiveness. *Annual Review of Anthropology, 34*, 523–548.

Gangestad, S. W., & Simpson, J. A. (2000). The evolution of human mating: Trade-offs and strategic pluralism. *Behavioral and Brain Sciences, 23*, 573–644.

Gao, Y., & Raine, A. (2010). Successful and unsuccessful psychopaths: A neurobiological model. *Behavioral Sciences & the Law, 28*, 194–210.

Gard, M. C., & Freeman, C. P. (1996). The dismantling of a myth: A review of eating disorders and socioeconomic status. *International Journal of Eating Disorders, 20*, 1–12.

Gardner, R. (1982). Mechanisms in manic-depressive disorder: An evolutionary model. *Archives of General Psychiatry, 39*, 1436–1441.

Gartner, J. D. (2005). *The hypomanic edge: The link between (a little) craziness and (a lot of) success in America.* New York: Simon & Schuster.

Garyfallos, G., Katsigiannopoulos, K., Adamopoulou, A., Papazisis, G., Karastergiou, A., & Bozikas, V. P. (2010). Comorbidity of obsessive-compulsive disorder with obsessive-compulsive personality disorder: Does it imply a specific subtype of obsessive-compulsive disorder? *Psychiatry Research, 177*, 156–160.

Gatzke-Kopp, L. M. (2011). The canary in the coalmine: The sensitivity of mesolimbic dopamine to environmental adversity during development. *Neuroscience & Biobehavioral Reviews, 35*, 794–803.

Gaughan, E. T., Miller, J. D., & Lynam, D. R. (2012). Examining the utility of general models of personality in the study of psychopathy: A comparison of the HEXACO-PI-R and NEO PI-R. *Journal of Personality Disorders, 26*, 513–523.

Gauthier, C., Hassler, C., Mattar, L., Launay, J. M., Callebert, J., Steiger, H., et al. (2014). Symptoms of depression and anxiety in anorexia nervosa: Links with plasma tryptophan and serotonin metabolism. *Psychoneuroendocrinology, 39*, 170–178.

Gaydosh, L., Belsky, D. W., Domingue, B. W., Boardman, J. D., & Harris, K. M. (2017). Father absence and accelerated reproductive development. *bioRxiv*, 123711.

Geary, D. C. (2002). Sexual selection and human life history. *Advances in Child Development and Behavior, 30*, 41–101.

Geary, D. C. (2005). Evolution of paternal investment. In D. Buss (Ed.), *The handbook of evolutionary psychology* (pp. 483–505). Hoboken, NJ: Wiley.

Geary, D. C. (2010). *Male, female: The evolution of human sex differences* (2nd ed). Washington, DC: APA Press.

Geary, D. C. (2015). *Evolution of vulnerability: Implications for sex differences in health and development*. San Diego, CA: Academic Press.

Geary, D. C., Byrd-Craven, J., Hoard, M. K., Vigil, J., & Numtee, C. (2003). Evolution and development of boys' social behavior. *Developmental Review, 23*, 444–470.

Geary, D. C., Winegard, B., & Winegard, B. (2014). Reflections on the evolution of human sex differences: Social selection and the evolution of competition among women. In V. A. Weekes-Shackelford & T. K. Shackelford (Eds.), *Evolutionary perspectives on human sexual psychology and behavior* (pp. 393–412). New York: Springer.

Geier, M., Kern, J. K., King, P. G., Sykes, L., & Geier, D. A. (2014). Treatment of elevated male hormones in autism. In V. B. Patel, V. R. Preedy, & C. R. Martin (Eds.), *Comprehensive guide to autism* (pp. 1313–1331). New York: Springer.

Geisler, W. S., & Diehl, R. L. (2003). A Bayesian approach to the evolution of perceptual and cognitive systems. *Cognitive Science, 27*, 379–402.

Gentzler, A. L., & Kerns, K. A. (2004). Associations between insecure attachment and sexual experiences. *Personal Relationships, 11*, 249–265.

Georgiades, S., Szatmari, P., Boyle, M., Hanna, S., Duku, E., Zwaigenbaum, L., et al. (2013). Investigating phenotypic heterogeneity in children with autism spectrum disorder: A factor mixture modeling approach. *Journal of Child Psychology and Psychiatry, 54*, 206–215.

Gerhard, D. M., Wohleb, E. S., & Duman, R. S. (2016). Emerging treatment mechanisms for depression: Focus on glutamate and synaptic plasticity. *Drug Discovery Today, 21*, 454–464.

Gerish, B., & Antebi, A. (2011). Molecular basis of life history regulation in *C. elegans* and other organisms. In T. Flatt & F. Heyland (Eds.), *Mechanisms of life history evolution: The genetics and physiology of life history traits and trade-offs* (pp. 284–298). New York: Oxford University Press.

Gervais, M. M., Kline, M., Ludmer, M., George, R., & Manson, J. H. (2013). The strategy of psychopathy: Primary psychopathic traits predict defection on low-value relationships. *Proceedings of the Royal Society of London B*, *280*, 20122773.

Gettler, L. T. (2014). Applying socioendocrinology to evolutionary models: Fatherhood and physiology. *Evolutionary Anthropology*, *23*, 146–160.

Geurts, H. M., Bergh, S. F., & Ruzzano, L. (2014). Prepotent response inhibition and interference control in autism spectrum disorders: Two meta-analyses. *Autism Research*, *7*, 407–420.

Gigerenzer, G. (2008). Why heuristics work. *Perspectives on Psychological Science*, *3*, 20–29.

Gigerenzer, G., & Brighton, H. (2009). *Homo heuristicus:* Why biased minds make better inferences. *Topics in Cognitive Science*, *1*, 107–143.

Gignac, G. E., & Bates, T. C. (2017). Brain volume and intelligence: The moderating role of intelligence measurement quality. *Intelligence*, *64*, 18–29.

Gilbert, P. (1992). *Depression: The evolution of powerlessness*. Hove, UK: Psychology Press.

Gilbert, P. (1995). Biopsychosocial approaches and evolutionary theory as aids to integration in clinical psychology and psychotherapy. *Clinical Psychology and Psychotherapy*, *2*, 135–156.

Gilbert, P. (2001). Evolution and social anxiety: The role of attraction, social competition, and social hierarchies. *Psychiatric Clinics of North America*, *24*, 723–751.

Gilbert, P. (2002). Evolutionary approaches to psychopathology and cognitive therapy. *Journal of Cognitive Psychotherapy*, *16*, 263–294.

Gilbert, P. (2004). Depression: A biopsychosocial, integrative and evolutionary approach. In M. Power (Ed.), *Mood disorders: A handbook of science and practice* (pp. 99–142). Chichester, UK: Wiley.

Gilbert, P. (2006). Evolution and depression: Issues and implications. *Psychological Medicine*, *36*, 287–297.

Gilbert, P. (2015). An evolutionary approach to emotion in mental health with a focus on affiliative emotions. *Emotion Review*, *7*, 230–237.

Gilbert, P., & Bailey, K. G. (2000). *Genes on the couch: Explorations in evolutionary psychotherapy*. London: Routledge.

Gilbert, P., McEwan, K., Hay, J., Irons, C., & Cheung, M. (2007). Social rank and attachment in people with a bipolar disorder. *Clinical Psychology & Psychotherapy*, *14*, 48–53.

Gillan, C. M., & Robbins, T. W. (2014). Goal-directed learning and obsessive-compulsive disorder. *Philosophical Transactions of the Royal Society B*, *369*, 20130475.

Gillath, O., & Schachner, D. A. (2006). How do sexuality and attachment interrelate? Goals, motives, and strategies. In M. Mikulincer & G. S. Goodman (Eds.) *Dynamics of romantic love: Attachment, caregiving, and sex* (pp. 337–355). New York: Guilford.

Gillberg, I. C., Råstam, M., Wentz, E., & Gillberg, C. (2007). Cognitive and executive functions in anorexia nervosa ten years after onset of eating disorder. *Journal of Clinical and Experimental Neuropsychology*, *29*, 170–178.

Gilman, S. R., Chang, J., Xu, B., Bawa, T. S., Gogos, J. A., Karayiorgou, M., & Vitkup, D. (2012). Diverse types of genetic variation converge on functional gene networks involved in schizophrenia. *Nature Neuroscience*, *15*, 1723–1728.

Gilmour, L., Schalomon, P. M., & Smith, V. (2012). Sexuality in a community based sample of adults with autism spectrum disorder. *Research in Autism Spectrum Disorders*, *6*, 313–318.

Giltay, E. J., Enter, D., Zitman, F. G., Penninx, B. W., van Pelt, J., Spinhoven, P., et al. (2012). Salivary testosterone: Associations with depression, anxiety disorders, and antidepressant use in a large cohort study. *Journal of Psychosomatic Research, 72*, 205–213.

Giordano, G. N., Ohlsson, H., Sundquist, K., Sundquist, J., & Kendler, K. S. (2015). The association between cannabis abuse and subsequent schizophrenia: A Swedish national co-relative control study. *Psychological Medicine, 45*, 407–414.

Giuliano, F., & Clement, P. (2005). Neuroanatomy and physiology of ejaculation. *Annual Review of Sex Research, 16*, 190–216.

Glahn, D. C., & Burdick, K. E. (2011). Clinical endophenotypes for bipolar disorder. In H. K. Manji & C. A. Zarate, Jr. (Eds.), *Behavioral neurobiology of bipolar disorder and its treatment* (pp. 51–68). New York: Springer.

Gläscher, J., Tranel, D., Paul, L. K., Rudrauf, D., Rorden, C., Hornaday, A., et al. (2009). Lesion mapping of cognitive abilities linked to intelligence. *Neuron, 61*, 681–691.

Glaser, J. P., Van Os, J., Thewissen, V., & Myin-Germeys, I. (2010). Psychotic reactivity in borderline personality disorder. *Acta Psychiatrica Scandinavica, 121*, 125–134.

Glass, D. J. (2012). *Factor structure of OCD: Toward an evolutionary neuro-cognitive model of obsessive-compulsive disorder* (Unpublished thesis). State Univeristy of New York at New Paltz.

Gleaves, D. H., Lowe, M. R., Green, B. A., Cororve, M. B., & Williams, T. L. (2000). Do anorexia and bulimia nervosa occur on a continuum? A taxometric analysis. *Behavior Therapy, 31*, 195–219.

Glenn, A. L., Kurzban, R., & Raine, A. (2011). Evolutionary theory and psychopathy. *Aggression and Violent Behavior, 16*, 371–380.

Glover, V. (2011). Prenatal stress and the origins of psychopathology: An evolutionary perspective. *Journal of Child Psychology and Psychiatry, 52*, 356–367.

Gluckman, P. D., Beedle, A. S., Buklijas, T., Low, F. M., & Hanson, M. A. (2016). *Principles of evolutionary medicine* (2nd ed.). Oxford: Oxford University Press.

Gluckman, P. D., Hanson, M. A., & Spencer, H. G. (2005). Predictive adaptive responses and human evolution. *Trends in Ecology & Evolution, 20*, 527–533.

Gluckman, P. D., Low, F. M., Buklijas, T., Hanson, M. A., & Beedle, A. S. (2011). How evolutionary principles improve the understanding of human health and disease. *Evolutionary Applications, 4*, 249–263.

Gnambs, T. (2013). The elusive general factor of personality: The acquaintance effect. *European Journal of Personality, 27*, 507–520.

Godart, N. T., Legleye, S., Huas, C., Coté, S. M., Choquet, M., Falissard, B., et al. (2013). Epidemiology of anorexia nervosa in a French community-based sample of 39,542 adolescents. *Open Journal of Epidemiology, 3*, 53–61.

Goekoop, R., & Goekoop, J. G. (2014). A network view on psychiatric disorders: Network clusters of symptoms as elementary syndromes of psychopathology. *PLoS ONE, 9*, e112734.

Gold, P. W., & Chrousos, G. P. (2002). Organization of the stress system and its dysregulation in melancholic and atypical depression: High vs low CRH/NE states. *Molecular Psychiatry, 7*, 254–275.

Goldberg, S., Fruchter, E., Davidson, M., Reichenberg, A., Yoffe, R., & Weiser, M. (2011). The relationship between risk of hospitalization for schizophrenia, SES, and cognitive functioning. *Schizophrenia Bulletin, 37*, 664–670.

Goldstein, S., & Naglieri, G. A. (Eds.) (2014). *Handbook of executive functioning.* New York: Springer.

Gomez, R., & Corr, P. J. (2014). ADHD and personality: A meta-analytic review. *Clinical Psychology Review, 34,* 376–388.

Gómez-Robles, A., Hopkins, W. D., & Sherwood, C. C. (2014). Modular structure facilitates mosaic evolution of the brain in chimpanzees and humans. *Nature Communications, 5,* 4469.

Gonon, F. (2009). The dopaminergic hypothesis of attention-deficit/hyperactivity disorder needs re-examining. *Trends in Neurosciences, 32,* 2–8.

Goodnight, C. (2013). On multilevel selection and kin selection: Contextual analysis meets direct fitness. *Evolution, 67,* 1539–1548.

Goodwin, R. D., Beesdo-Baum, K., Knappe, S., & Stein, D. J. (2014). Life course epidemiology of anxiety disorders. In K. C. Koenen, S. Rudenstine, E. Susser, & S. Galea (Eds.), *A life course approach to mental disorders* (pp. 97–110). Oxford: Oxford University Press.

Goodwin, R. D., & Gotlib, I. H. (2004). Gender differences in depression: The role of personality factors. *Psychiatry Research, 126,* 135–142.

Goos, L. M., Ezzatian, P., & Schachar, R. (2007). Parent-of-origin effects in attention-deficit hyperactivity disorder. *Psychiatry Research, 149,* 1–9.

Gopnik, A., & Bonawitz, E. (2015). Bayesian models of child development. *Wiley Interdisciplinary Reviews: Cognitive Science, 6,* 75–86.

Gordon, O. M., Salkovskis, P. M., Oldfield, V. B., & Carter, N. (2013). The association between obsessive compulsive disorder and obsessive compulsive personality disorder: Prevalence and clinical presentation. *British Journal of Clinical Psychology, 52,* 300–315.

Gottfredson, L. S. (2002). g: Highly general and highly practical. In R. J. Sternberg & E. L. Grigorenko (Eds.), *The general factor of intelligence: How general is it?* (pp. 331–380). Mahwah, NJ: Erlbaum.

Gottfredson, L. S. (2004). Intelligence: Is it the epidemiologists' elusive "fundamental cause" of social class inequalities in health? *Journal of Personality and Social Psychology, 86,* 174–199.

Gottfredson, L. S. (2011). Intelligence and social inequality: Why the biological link? In T. Chamorro-Premuzic, A. Furnham, & S. von Stumm (Eds.), *The Wiley-Blackwell handbook of individual differences* (pp. 538–576). New York: Wiley.

Gottlieb, J., Oudeyer, P. Y., Lopes, M., & Baranes, A. (2013). Information-seeking, curiosity, and attention: Computational and neural mechanisms. *Trends in Cognitive Sciences, 17,* 585–593.

Graber, J. A., Lewinsohn, P. M., Seeley, J. R., & Brooks-Gunn, J. (1997). Is psychopathology associated with the timing of pubertal development? *Journal of the American Academy of Child & Adolescent Psychiatry, 36,* 1768–1776.

Graeff, F. G. (2004). Serotonin, the periaqueductal gray and panic. *Neuroscience & Biobehavioral Reviews, 28,* 239–259.

Grafen, A. (1985). A geometric view of relatedness. *Oxford Surveys in Evolutionary Biology, 2,* 28–90.

Grafen, A. (1999). Formal Darwinism, the individual-as-maximizing-agent analogy and bet- hedging. *Proceedings of the Royal Society of London B, 266,* 799–803.

Grafen, A. (2006). Optimisation of inclusive fitness. *Journal of Theoretical Biology, 238,* 541–563.

Grafen, A. (2009). Formalizing Darwinism and inclusive fitness theory. *Philosophical Transactions of the Royal Society B, 364*, 3135–3141.

Grant, B. E., Hasin, D. S., Stinson, F. S., Dawson, D. A., Chou, S. P., Ruan, W. J., et al. (2004). Prevalence, correlates, and disability of personality disorders in the United States: Results from the National Epidemiological Survey on alcohol and related conditions. *Journal of Clinical Psychiatry, 65*, 948–958.

Grant, B. F., Chou, S. P., Goldstein, R. B., Huang, B., Stinson, F. S., Saha, T. D., et al. (2008). Prevalence, correlates, disability, and comorbidity of DSM-IV borderline personality disorder: Results from the Wave 2 National Epidemiologic Survey on Alcohol and Related Conditions. *Journal of Clinical Psychiatry, 69*, 533–545.

Gray, J., & McEwen, B. (2014). Neuroendocrinology and neurotransmitters. In P. Emmelkamp & T. Ehring (Eds.), *The Wiley handbook of anxiety disorders* (pp. 254–273). New York: Wiley.

Gray, J. A. (1987). The *psychology of fear and stress* (2nd ed.). New York: McGraw-Hill.

Gray, J. A., & McNaughton, N. (2000). *The neuropsychology of anxiety* (2nd ed.). New York: Oxford University Press.

Gray, P. (2011). The special value of children's age-mixed play. *American Journal of Play, 3*, 500–522.

Grazioplene, R. G., Chavez, R. S., Rustichini, A., & DeYoung, C. G. (2016). White matter correlates of psychosis-linked traits support continuity between personality and psychopathology. *Journal of Abnormal Psychology, 125*, 1135–1145.

Green, C., Dissanayake, C., & Loesch, D. (2015). A review of physical growth in children and adolescents with Autism Spectrum Disorder. *Developmental Review, 36*, 156–178.

Green, E. K., Rees, E., Walters, J. T. R., Smith, K. G., Forty, L., Grozeva, D., et al. (2016). Copy number variation in bipolar disorder. *Molecular Psychiatry, 21*, 89–93.

Green, J. G., McLaughlin, K. A., Berglund, P. A., Gruber, M. J., Sampson, N. A., Zaslavsky, A. M., et al. (2010). Childhood adversities and adult psychiatric disorders in the national comorbidity survey replication I: Associations with first onset of DSM-IV disorders. *Archives of General Psychiatry, 67*, 113–123.

Green, L., & Myerson, J. (1996). Exponential versus hyperbolic discounting of delayed outcomes: Risk and waiting time. *American Zoologist, 36*, 496–505.

Green, R. E., Krause, J., Briggs, A. W., Maricic, T., Stenzel, U., Kircher, M., et al. (2010). A draft sequence of the Neandertal genome. *Science, 328*, 710–722.

Greengross, G., & Miller, G. (2011). Humor ability reveals intelligence, predicts mating success, and is higher in males. *Intelligence, 39*, 188–192.

Greenwood, T. A., Joo, E. J., Shekhtman, T., Sadovnick, A. D., Remick, R. A., Keck, P. E., et al. (2013). Association of dopamine transporter gene variants with childhood ADHD features in bipolar disorder. *American Journal of Medical Genetics Part B: Neuropsychiatric Genetics, 162*, 137–145.

Gregg, C., Zhang, J., Weissbourd, B., Luo, S., Schroth, G. P., Haig, D., et al. (2010). High-resolution analysis of parent-of-origin allelic expression in the mouse brain. *Science, 329*, 643–648.

Greif, M. L., Kemler Nelson, D. G., Keil, F. C., & Gutierrez, F. (2006). What do children want to know about animals and artifacts? Domain-specific requests for information. *Psychological Science, 17*, 455–459.

Greiling, H., & Buss, D. M. (2000). Women's sexual strategies: The hidden dimension of short-term extra-pair mating. *Personality and Individual Differences, 28*, 929–963.

Grekin, R., & O'Hara, M. W. (2014). Prevalence and risk factors of postpartum posttraumatic stress disorder: A meta-analysis. *Clinical Psychology Review, 34,* 389–401.

Grey, K. R., Poggi Davis, E., Sandman, C. A., & Glynn, L. M. (2013). Human milk cortisol is associated with infant temperament. *Psychoneuroendocrinology, 38,* 1178–1185.

Griffin, S. A., & Samuel, D. B. (2014). A closer look at the lower-order structure of the Personality Inventory for DSM-5: Comparison with the Five-Factor Model. *Personality Disorders: Theory, Research, and Treatment, 5,* 406–412.

Griffith, J. W., Zinbarg, R. E., Craske, M. G., Mineka, S., Rose, R. D., Waters, A. M., et al. (2010). Neuroticism as a common dimension in the internalizing disorders. *Psychological Medicine, 40,* 1125–1136.

Grigorenko, E. L., Bick, J., Campbell, D. J., Lewine, G., Abrams, J., Nguyen, V., et al. (2016). The trilogy of G×E: Conceptualization, operationalization, and application. In D. Cicchetti (Ed.), *Developmental psychopathology: Vol. 2. Developmental neuroscience* (3rd ed., pp. 287–338). New York: Wiley.

Grijalva, E., Harms, P. D., Newman, D. A., Gaddis, B. H., & Fraley, R. C. (2015). Narcissism and leadership: A meta-analytic review of linear and nonlinear relationships. *Personnel Psychology, 68,* 1–47.

Grijalva, E., Newman, D. A., Tay, L., Donnellan, M. B., Harms, P. D., Robins, R. W., et al. (2015). Gender differences in narcissism: A meta-analytic review. *Psychological Bulletin, 141,* 261–310.

Grillot, R. L., Simmons, Z. L., Lukaszewski, A. W., & Roney, J. R. (2014). Hormonal and morphological predictors of women's body attractiveness. *Evolution and Human Behavior, 35,* 176–183.

Grinter, E. J., Van Beek, P. L., Maybery, M. T., & Badcock, D. R. (2009). Brief report: Visuospatial analysis and self-rated autistic-like traits. *Journal of Autism and Developmental Disorders, 39,* 670–677.

Grisham, J. R., Brown, T. A., Liverant, G. I., & Campbell-Sills, L. (2005). The distinctiveness of compulsive hoarding from obsessive-compulsive disorder. *Journal of Anxiety Disorders, 19,* 767–779.

Griskevicius, V., Delton, A. W., Robertson, T. E., & Tybur, J. M. (2011). Environmental contingency in life history strategies: The influence of mortality and socioeconomic status on reproductive timing. *Journal of Personality and Social Psychology, 100,* 241–254.

Griskevicius, V., Tybur, J. M., Sundie, J. M., Cialdini, R. B., Miller, G. F., & Kenrick, D. T. (2007). Blatant benevolence and conspicuous consumption: When romantic motives elicit strategic costly signals. *Journal of Personality and Social Psychology, 93,* 85–102.

Groh, A. M., Roisman, G. I., van IJzendoorn, M. H., Bakermans-Kranenburg, M. J., & Fearon, R. (2012). The significance of insecure and disorganized attachment for children's internalizing symptoms: A meta-analytic study. *Child Development, 83,* 591–610.

Grossman, S. R., Andersen, K. G., Shlyakhter, I., Tabrizi, S., Winnicki, S., Yen, A., et al. (2013). Identifying recent adaptations in large-scale genomic data. *Cell, 152,* 703–713.

Grozeva, D., Kirov, G., Ivanov, D., Jones, I. R., Jones, L., Green, E. K., et al. (2010). Rare copy number variants: A point of rarity in genetic risk for bipolar disorder and schizophrenia. *Archives of General Psychiatry, 67,* 318–327.

Grubaugh, A. L. (2014). Trauma and stressor-related disorders. In D. C. Beidel, B. C. Frueh, & M. Hersen (Eds.), *Adult psychopathology and diagnosis* (7th ed., pp. 387–406). New York: Wiley.

Gruber, J. (2011). A review and synthesis of positive emotion and reward disturbance in bipolar disorder. *Clinical Psychology & Psychotherapy, 18*, 356–365.

Gruner, P., Anticevic, A., Lee, D., & Pittenger, C. (2016). Arbitration between action strategies in obsessive-compulsive disorder. *The Neuroscientist, 22*, 188–198.

Gruzelier, J. H., & Kaiser, J. (1996). Syndromes of schizotypy and timing of puberty. *Schizophrenia Research, 21*, 183–194.

Guarda, A. S., Schreyer, C. C., Boersma, G. J., Tamashiro, K. L., & Moran, T. H. (2015). Anorexia nervosa as a motivated behavior: Relevance of anxiety, stress, fear and learning. *Physiology and Behavior, 152*, 466–472.

Guastella, A. J., & Hickie, I. B. (2016). Oxytocin treatment, circuitry, and autism: A critical review of the literature placing oxytocin into the autism context. *Biological Psychiatry, 79*, 234–242.

Guidano, V. F., & Liotti, G. (1983). *Cognitive processeas and emotional disorders.* New York: Guilford.

Guisinger, S. (2003). Adapted to flee famine: Adding an evolutionary perspective on anorexia nervosa. *Psychological Review, 110*, 745–761.

Gunnar, M., & Quevedo, K. (2007). The neurobiology of stress and development. *Annual Review of Psychology, 58*, 145–173.

Gururajan, A., Clarke, G., Dinan, T. G., & Cryan, J. F. (2016). Molecular biomarkers of depression. *Neuroscience & Biobehavioral Reviews, 64*, 101–133.

Gurven, M., & Kaplan, H. (2009). Beyond the grandmother hypothesis: Evolutionary models of human longevity. In J. Sokolovsky (Ed.), *The cultural context of aging* (pp. 53–66). Westport, CT: Praeger.

Gurven, M., von Rueden, C., Massenkoff, M., Kaplan, H., & Lero Vie, M. (2013). How universal is the Big Five? Testing the five-factor model of personality variation among forager-farmers in the Bolivian Amazon. *Journal of Personality and Social Psychology, 104*, 354–370.

Gurven, M., von Rueden, C., Stieglitz, J., Kaplan, H., & Rodriguez, D. E. (2014). The evolutionary fitness of personality traits in a small-scale subsistence society. *Evolution and Human Behavior, 35*, 17–25.

Gutiérrez, F., Gárriz, M., Peri, J. M., Ferraz, L., Sol, D., Navarro, J. B., et al. (2013). Fitness costs and benefits of personality disorder traits. *Evolution and Human Behavior, 34*, 41–48.

Hagen, E. H. (1999). The functions of postpartum depression. *Evolution and Human Behavior, 20*, 325–359.

Hagen, E. H. (2002). Depression as bargaining: The case postpartum. *Evolution and Human Behavior, 23*, 323–336.

Hagen, E. H. (2003). The bargaining model of depression. In P. Hammerstein (Ed.), *Genetic and cultural evolution of cooperation* (pp. 95–123). Cambridge, MA: MIT Press.

Hagen, E. H. (2011). Evolutionary theories of depression: A critical review. *The Canadian Journal of Psychiatry, 56*, 716–726.

Hagen, E. H., & Thomson, J. A. (2004). Social navigation hypothesis of depression revisited. *Journal of Affective Disorders, 83*, 285–286.

Hagen, E. H., & Thornhill, R. (2017). Testing the psychological pain hypothesis for postnatal depression: Reproductive success versus evidence of design. *Evolution, Medicine, and Public Health, 2017*, 17–23.

Hagen, R., Hjemdal, O., Solem, S., Kennair, L. E. O., Nordahl, H. M., Fisher, P., et al. (2017). Metacognitive therapy for depression in adults: A waiting list randomized controlled trial with six months follow-up. *Frontiers in Psychology, 8*, 31.

Hagenaars, M. A., Oitzl, M., & Roelofs, K. (2014). Updating freeze: Aligning animal and human research. *Neuroscience & Biobehavioral Reviews, 47*, 165–176.

Hagenaars, S. P., Harris, S. E., Davies, G., Hill, W. D., Liewald, D. C., Ritchie, S. J., et al. (2016). Shared genetic aetiology between cognitive functions and physical and mental health in UK Biobank (N= 112 151) and 24 GWAS consortia. *Molecular Psychiatry, 21*, 1624–1632.

Hahn-Holbrook, J., & Haselton, M. (2014). Is postpartum depression a disease of modern civilization? *Current Directions in Psychological Science, 23*, 395–400.

Haidt, J. (2007). The new synthesis in moral psychology. *Science, 316*, 998–1002.

Haidt, J., & Kesebir, S. (2010). Morality. In S. Fiske, D. Gilbert, & G. Lindzey (Eds.), *Handbook of social psychology* (5th ed., pp. 797–832). Hoboken, NJ: Wiley.

Haig, D. (1993). Genetic conflicts in human pregnancy. *Quarterly Review of Biology, 68*, 495–532.

Haig, D. (1997). Parental antagonism, relatedness asymmetries and genomic imprinting. *Proceedings of the Royal Society of London B, 264*, 1657–1662.

Haig, D. (2000). The kinship theory of genomic imprinting. *Annual Review of Ecology and Systematics, 31*, 9–32.

Haig, D. (2010). Fertile soil or no man's land: Cooperation and conflict in the placental bed. In R. Pijnenborg, I. Brosens, & R. Romero (Eds.), *Placental bed disorders: Basic science and its translation to obstetrics* (pp. 165–173). Cambridge: Cambridge University Press.

Haig, D. (2014). Genetic dissent and individual compromise. *Biology and Philosophy, 29*, 233–239.

Halbreich, U., & Kahn, L. S. (2007). Atypical depression, somatic depression and anxious depression in women: Are they gender-preferred phenotypes? *Journal of Affective Disorders, 102*, 245–258.

Hall, M. L., van Asten, T., Katsis, A. C., Dingemanse, N. J., Magrath, M. J., & Mulder, R. A. (2015). Animal personality and pace-of-life syndromes: Do fast-exploring fairy-wrens die young? *Frontiers in Ecology and Evolution, 3*, 28.

Hallerbäck, M. U., Lugnegård, T., & Gillberg, C. (2012). ADHD and nicotine use in schizophrenia and Asperger syndrome: A controlled study. *Journal of Attention Disorders*, 1087054712439099.

Hallmayer, J. F., Kalaydjieva, L., Badcock, J., Dragović, M., Howell, S., Michie, P. T., et al. (2005). Genetic evidence for a distinct subtype of schizophrenia characterized by pervasive cognitive deficit. *The American Journal of Human Genetics, 77*, 468–476.

Halmi, K. A., Sunday, S. R., Klump, K. L., Strober, M., Leckman, J. F., Fichter, M., et al. (2003). Obsessions and compulsions in anorexia nervosa subtypes. *International Journal of Eating Disorders, 33*, 308–319.

Halpern, D. F., Benbow, C. P., Geary, D. C., Gur, R. C., Hyde, J. S., & Gernsbacher, M. A. (2007). The science of sex differences in science and mathematics. *Psychological Science in the Public Interest, 8*, 1–51.

Haltigan, J. D., Roisman, G. I., Susman, E. J., Barnett-Walker, K., & Monahan, K. C. (2011). Elevated trajectories of externalizing problems are associated with lower awakening cortisol levels in midadolescence. *Developmental Psychology, 47*, 472–478.

Hamilton, J. L., Stange, J. P., Abramson, L. Y., & Alloy, L. B. (2015). Stress and the development of cognitive vulnerabilities to depression explain sex differences in depressive symptoms during adolescence. *Clinical Psychological Science, 3*, 702–714.

Hamilton, W. D. (1964). The genetical evolution of social behavior. *Journal of Theoretical Biology, 7*, 1–52.

Hamm, A. O., Richter, J., Pané-Farré, C., Westphal, D., Wittchen, H. U., Vossbeck-Elsebusch, A. N., et al. (2016). Panic disorder with agoraphobia from a behavioral neuroscience perspective: Applying the research principles formulated by the Research Domain Criteria (RDoC) initiative. *Psychophysiology, 53*, 312–322.

Hammen, C. (2005). Stress and depression. *Annual Review of Clinical Psychology, 1*, 293–319.

Hamshere, M. L., Stergiakouli, E., Langley, K., Martin, J., Holmans, P., Kent, L., et al. (2013). Shared polygenic contribution between childhood attention-deficit hyperactivity disorder and adult schizophrenia. *British Journal of Psychiatry, 203*, 107–111.

Happé, F., & Frith, U. (2006). The weak coherence account: Detail-focused cognitive style in autism spectrum disorders. *Journal of Autism and Developmental Disorders, 36*, 5–25.

Happé, F., & Ronald, A. (2008). The "fractionable autism triad": A review of evidence from behavioural, genetic, cognitive and neural research. *Neuropsychology Review, 18*, 287–304.

Happé, F., Ronald, A., & Plomin, R. (2006). Time to give up on a single explanation for autism. *Nature Neuroscience, 9*, 1218–1220.

Happé, F., & Vital, P. (2009). What aspects of autism predispose to talent? *Philosophical Transactions of the Royal Society B: Biological Sciences, 364*, 1369–1375.

Harmon-Jones, E., & Harmon-Jones, C. (2015). Neural foundations of motivational orientations. In G. H. E. Gendolla, M. Tops, & S. Koole (Eds.), *Handbook of biobehavioral approaches to self-regulation* (pp. 175–187). New York: Springer.

Harpending, H. C., & Draper, P. (1988). Antisocial behavior and the other side of cultural evolution. In T. E. Moffitt & S. A. Mednick (Eds.), *Biological contributions to crime causation* (pp. 110–125). Boston, MA: Nijhoff.

Harpending, H. C., Draper, P., & Pennington, R. (1990). Cultural evolution, parental care, and mortality. In A. C. Swedlund & G. J. Armelagos (Eds.), *Disease in Populations in Transition* (pp. 251–65). New York: Gergin and Garvey.

Harpending, H. C., & Sobus, J. (1987). Sociopathy as an adaptation. *Ethology and Sociobiology, 8*, 63–72.

Harris, G. T., Rice, M. E., Hilton, N. Z., Lalumiere, M. L., & Quinsey, V. L. (2007). Coercive and precocious sexuality as a fundamental aspect of psychopathy. *Journal of Personality Disorders, 21*, 1–27.

Harris, G. T., Rice, M. E., & Lalumière, M. (2001). Criminal violence: The roles of psychopathy, neurodevelopmental insults, and antisocial parenting. *Criminal Justice and Behavior, 28*, 402–426.

Harris, J. A., Rushton, J. P., Hampson, E., & Jackson, D. N. (1996). Salivary testosterone and self-report aggressive and pro-social personality characteristics in men and women. *Aggressive Behavior, 22*, 321–331.

Hart, C. M., & Van Vugt, M. (2006). From fault line to group fission: Understanding membership changes in small groups. *Personality and Social Psychology Bulletin, 32*, 392–404.

Hart, H., Radua, J., Nakao, T., Mataix-Cols, D., & Rubia, K. (2013). Meta-analysis of functional magnetic resonance imaging studies of inhibition and attention in attention-deficit/hyperactivity disorder: Exploring task-specific, stimulant medication, and age effects. *Journal of the American Medical Association Psychiatry, 70*, 185–198.

Hartmann, T. (1993). *Attention deficit disorder: A different perspective*. Lancaster, UK: Underwood-Miller.

Haslam, N. (2011). The return of the anal character. *Review of General Psychology, 15*, 351–360.

Haslam, N., Holland, E., & Kuppens, P. (2012). Categories versus dimensions in personality and psychopathology: A quantitative review of taxometric research. *Psychological Medicine, 42*, 903–920.

Haslam, N., Williams, B. J., Kyrios, M., McKay, D., & Taylor, S. (2005). Subtyping obsessive-compulsive disorder: A taxometric analysis. *Behavior Therapy, 36*, 381–391.

Hasler, G., LaSalle-Ricci, V. H., Ronquillo, J. G., Crawley, S. A., Cochran, L. W., Kazuba, D., et al. (2005). Obsessive–compulsive disorder symptom dimensions show specific relationships to psychiatric comorbidity. *Psychiatry Research, 135*, 121–132.

Hasson, O. (1990). The role of amplifiers in sexual selection: An integration of the amplifying and Fisherian mechanisms. *Evolutionary Ecology, 4*, 277–289.

Hau, M., & Wingfield, J. C. (2011). Hormonally regulated trade-offs: Evolutionary variability and phenotypic plasticity in testosterone signaling pathways. In T. Flatt & F. Heyland (Eds.), *Mechanisms of life history evolution: The genetics and physiology of life history traits and trade-offs* (pp. 349–362). New York: Oxford University Press.

Haubold, A., Peterson, B. S., & Bansal, R. (2012). Annual research review: Progress in using brain morphometry as a clinical tool for diagnosing psychiatric disorders. *Journal of Child Psychology and Psychiatry, 53*, 519–535.

Haukka, J., Suvisaari, J., & Lönnqvist, J. (2003). Fertility of patients with schizophrenia, their siblings, and the general population: A cohort study from 1950 to 1959 in Finland. *American Journal of Psychiatry, 160*, 460–463.

Hauser, T. U., Fiore, V. G., Moutoussis, M., & Dolan, R. J. (2016). Computational psychiatry of ADHD: Neural gain impairments across marrian levels of analysis. *Trends in Neurosciences, 39*, 63–73.

Haut, K. M., Schvarcz, A., Cannon, T. D., & Bearden, C. E. (2016). Neurodevelopmental theories of schizophrenia: Twenty-first century perspectives. In D. Cicchetti (Ed.), *Developmental psychopathology: Vol. 2. Developmental neuroscience* (3rd ed., pp. 885–930). New York: Wiley.

Hawes, D. J., Brennan, J., & Dadds, M. R. (2009). Cortisol, callous-unemotional traits, and pathways to antisocial behavior. *Current Opinion in Psychiatry, 22*, 357–362.

Hawks, J., Wang, E. T., Cochran, G. M., Harpending, H. C., & Moyzis, R. K. (2007). Recent acceleration of human adaptive evolution. *Proceedings of the National Academy of Sciences USA, 104*, 20753–20758.

Hawley, P. H. (2014*a*). Ontogeny and social dominance: A developmental view of human power patterns. *Evolutionary Psychology, 12*, 318–342.

Hawley, P. H. (2014*b*). The duality of human nature: Coercion and prosociality in youths' hierarchy ascension and social success. *Current Directions in Psychological Science, 23*, 433–438.

Haydon, A. A., Herring, A. H., Prinstein, M. J., & Halpern, C. T. (2012). Beyond age at first sex: Patterns of emerging sexual behavior in adolescence and young adulthood. *Journal of Adolescent Health, 50*, 456–463.

Hayley, S., Audet, M. C., & Anisman, H. (2016). Inflammation and the microbiome: Implications for depressive disorders. *Current Opinion in Pharmacology, 29*, 42–46.

Haynos, A. F., Pearson, C. M., Utzinger, L. M., Wonderlich, S. A., Crosby, R. D., Mitchell, J. E., et al. (2017). Empirically derived personality subtyping for predicting clinical symptoms and treatment response in bulimia nervosa. *International Journal of Eating Disorders, 50*, 506–514.

Haysom, H. J., Mitchem, D. G., Lee, A. J., Wright, M. J., Martin, N. G., Keller, M. C., et al. (2015). A test of the facultative calibration/reactive heritability model of extraversion. *Evolution and Human Behavior, 36*, 414–419.

Hayward, A. D., Nenko, I., & Lummaa, V. (2015). Early-life reproduction is associated with increased mortality risk but enhanced lifetime fitness in pre-industrial humans. *Proceedings of the Royal Society of London B, 282*, 20143053.

He, L., Ewing, J., Shaw, A. M., Wang, J., & Chasson, G. S. (2014). A cross-sectional investigation of autogenous and reactive obsessions and associated cognitive and symptom correlates in China. *International Journal of Clinical and Health Psychology, 14*, 93–101.

Helt, M., Kelley, E., Kinsbourne, M., Pandey, J., Boorstein, H., Herbert, M., et al. (2008). Can children with autism recover? If so, how? *Neuropsychology Review, 18*, 339–366.

Henderson, A. J. Z., Bartholomew, K., & Dutton, D. G. (1997). He loves me, he loves me not: Attachment and separation resolution of abused women. *Journal of Family Violence, 12*, 169–191.

Hengartner, M. P., Ajdacic-Gross, V., Rodgers, S., Müller, M., Haker, H., & Rössler, W. (2014). Fluid intelligence and empathy in association with personality disorder trait-scores: Exploring the link. *European Archives of Psychiatry and Clinical Neuroscience, 264*, 441–448.

Hengartner, M. P., Ajdacic-Gross, V., Rodgers, S., Müller, M., & Rössler, W. (2013). Childhood adversity in association with personality disorder dimensions: New findings in an old debate. *European Psychiatry, 28*, 476–482.

Hengartner, M. P., Ajdacic-Gross, V., Wyss, C., Angst, J., & Rössler, W. (2016). Relationship between personality and psychopathology in a longitudinal community study: A test of the predisposition model. *Psychological Medicine, 46*, 1693–1705.

Hennessy, M. B., Schiml-Webb, P. A., & Deak, T. (2009). Separation, sickness, and depression: A new perspective on an old animal model. *Current Directions in Psychological Science, 18*, 227–231.

Henrich, J., Boyd, R., & Richerson, P. J. (2012). The puzzle of monogamous marriage. *Philosophical Transactions of the Royal Society of London B, 367*, 657–669.

Henrich, J., Ensminger, J., McElrath, R., Barr, A., Barrett, C., Bolyanatz, A., et al. (2010). Markets, religion, community size, and the evolution of fairness and punishment. *Science, 327*, 1480–1484.

Henrich, J., & Gil-White, F. J. (2001). The evolution of prestige: Freely conferred deference as a mechanism for enhancing the benefits of cultural transmission. *Evolution and Human Behavior, 22*, 165–196.

Hepp, J., Hilbig, B. E., Moshagen, M., Zettler, I., Schmahl, C., & Niedtfeld, I. (2014). Active versus reactive cooperativeness in borderline psychopathology: A dissection based on the HEXACO model of personality. *Personality and Individual Differences, 56*, 19–23.

Hergüner, A., & Hergüner, S. (2016). Association between age at menarche and autistic traits in Turkish university students. *American Journal of Human Biology, 28*, 44–47.

Herman, J. L. (1992). Complex PTSD: A syndrome in survivors of prolonged and repeated trauma. *Journal of Traumatic Stress, 5*, 377–391.

Herman, J. J., Spencer, H. G., Donohue, K., & Sultan, S. E. (2014). How stable 'should' epigenetic modifications be? Insights from adaptive plasticity and bet hedging. *Evolution, 68*, 632–643.

Hernández Blasi, C., & Bjorklund, D. F. (2003). Evolutionary developmental psychology: A new tool for better understanding human ontogeny. *Human Development, 46*, 259–281.

Hertler, S. C. (2014). The continuum of conscientiousness: The antagonistic interests among obsessive and antisocial personalities. *Polish Psychological Bulletin, 45*, 52–63.

Hertler, S. C. (2015*a*). Migration load, ecological opportunity, and obsessive-compulsive personality disorder etiology: Obsessive character as an adaptation to seasonality. *Evolutionary Psychological Science, 1*, 52–67.

Hertler, S. C. (2015*b*). Obsessive compulsive personality disorder as an adaptive anachronism: The operation of phylogenetic inertia upon obsessive populations in western modernity. *Psihologijske Teme, 24*, 207–232.

Hertler, S. C. (2016). The biology of obsessive-compulsive personality disorder symptomatology: Identifying an extremely K-selected life history variant. *Evolutionary Psychological Science, 2*, 1–15.

Hetem, L. A. B., Ferrari, M. C. F., Trzesniak, C., Martín-Santos, R., Borduqui, T., de Lima Osório, F., et al. (2010). Social anxiety disorder: What are we losing with the current diagnostic criteria? *Acta Psychiatrica Scandinavica, 121*, 216–226.

Hettema, J. M. (2008). What is the genetic relationship between anxiety and depression? *American journal of Medical Genetics C, 148*, 140–146.

Hettema, J. M., Neale, M. C., & Kendler, K. S. (2001). A review and meta-analysis of the genetic epidemiology of anxiety disorders. *American Journal of Psychiatry, 158*, 1568–1578.

Heyes, C. (2014). Submentalizing: I am not really reading your mind. *Perspectives on Psychological Science, 9*, 131–143.

Heym, N., Kantini, E., Checkley, H. L., & Cassaday, H. J. (2015). Gray's revised Reinforcement Sensitivity Theory in relation to attention-deficit/hyperactivity and Tourette-like behaviors in the general population. *Personality and Individual Differences, 78*, 24–28.

Hill, A. K., Hunt, J., Welling, L. L. M., Cárdenas, R. A., Rotella, M. A., Wheatley, J. R., et al. (2013). Quantifying the strength and form of sexual selection on men's traits. *Evolution and Human Behavior, 34*, 334–341.

Hill, A. P., Zuckerman, K., & Fombonne, E. (2014). Epidemiology of autism spectrum disorders. In F. R. Volkmar, R. Paul, S. J. Rogers, & K. A. Pelphrey (Eds.), *Handbook of autism and pervasive developmental disorders* (4th ed., pp. 57–96). New York: Wiley.

Hill, K., & Kaplan, H. (1999). Life history traits in humans: Theory and empirical studies. *Annual Review of Anthropology, 28*, 397–430.

Hill, K., & Roth, T. L. (2016). Epigenetic mechanisms in the development of behavior. In D. Cicchetti (Ed.), *Developmental psychopathology: Vol. 2. Developmental neuroscience* (3rd ed., pp. 416–441). New York: Wiley.

Hill, K. R., Walker, R. S., Božičević, M., Eder, J., Headland, T., Hewlett, B., et al. (2011). Co-residence patterns in hunter-gatherer societies show unique human social structure. *Science, 331*, 1286–1289.

Hill, S. E., Rodeheffer, C. D., DelPriore, D. J., & Butterfield, M. E. (2013). Ecological contingencies in women's calorie regulation psychology: A life history approach. *Journal of Experimental Social Psychology, 49*, 888–897.

Hill, S. K., Reilly, J. L., Keefe, R. S., Gold, J. M., Bishop, J. R., Gershon, E. S., et al. (2013). Neuropsychological impairments in schizophrenia and psychotic bipolar disorder: Findings from the Bipolar-Schizophrenia Network on Intermediate Phenotypes (B-SNIP) study. *American Journal of Psychiatry, 170*, 1275–1284.

Hill, W. D., Arslan, R. C., Xia, C., Luciano, M., Amador, C., Navarro, P., et al. (2018). Genomic analysis of family data reveals additional genetic effects on intelligence and personality. *Molecular Psychiatry*. doi:10.1038/s41380-017-0005-1.

Hill, W. D., Weiss, A., McIntosh, A. M., Gale, C. R., & Deary, I. J. (2017). Genetic contribution to two factors of neuroticism is associated with affluence, better health, and longer life. *bioRxiv*, 146787.

Hinds, A. L., Woody, E. Z., Schmidt, L. A., Van Ameringen, M., & Szechtman, H. (2015). In the wake of a possible mistake: Security motivation, checking behavior, and OCD. *Journal of Behavior Therapy & Experimental Psychiatry, 49*, 133–140.

Hinds, A. L., Woody, E. Z., Van Ameringen, M., Schmidt, L. A., & Szechtman, H. (2012). When too much is not enough: Obsessive-compulsive disorder as a pathology of stopping, rather than starting. *PLoS ONE, 7*, e30586.

Hines, M. (2011). Gender development and the human brain. *Annual Review of Neuroscience, 34*, 69–88.

Hirschberg, A. L. (2012). Sex hormones, appetite and eating behaviour in women. *Maturitas, 71*, 248–256.

Hirstein, W., & Ramachandran, V. S. (1997). Capgras syndrome: A novel probe for understanding the neural representation of the identity and familiarity of persons. *Proceedings of the Royal Society of London B, 264*, 437–444.

Hochberg, Z. (2008). Juvenility in the context of life history theory. *Archives of Disease in Childhood, 93*, 534–539.

Hochberg, Z. (2010). Evo-devo of child growth III: Premature juvenility as an evolutionary trade-off. *Hormone Research in Paediatrics, 73*, 430–437.

Hochberg, Z., & Albertsson-Wikland, K. (2008). Evo-devo of infantile and childhood growth. *Pediatric Research, 64*, 2–7.

Hoekstra, R. A., Bartels, M., Verweij, C. J., & Boomsma, D. I. (2007). Heritability of autistic traits in the general population. *Archives of Pediatrics & Adolescent Medicine, 161*, 372–377.

Hoekstra, R. A., Happé, F., Baron-Cohen, S., & Ronald, A. (2010). Limited genetic covariance between autistic traits and intelligence: Findings from a longitudinal twin study. *American Journal of Medical Genetics B, 153*, 994–1007.

Hoffer, A. (1994). Schizophrenia: An evolutionary defence against severe stress. *Journal of Orthomolecular Medicine, 9*, 205–221.

Hofmann, S. G. (2014). Toward a cognitive-behavioral classification system for mental disorders. *Behavior Therapy, 45*, 576–587.

Hofmann, S. G., Aka, B. T., Piquer, A. (2014). Social anxiety disorder. In P. Emmelkamp & T. Ehring (Eds.), *The Wiley handbook of anxiety disorders* (pp. 378–423). New York: Wiley.

Hofmann, W., Schmeichel, B. J., & Baddeley, A. D. (2012). Executive functions and self-regulation. *Trends in Cognitive Sciences, 16*, 174–180.

Holmes, A. J., Lee, P. H., Hollinshead, M. O., Bakst, L., Roffman, J. L., Smoller, J. W., et al. (2012). Individual differences in amygdala-medial prefrontal anatomy link negative affect, impaired social functioning, and polygenic depression risk. *Journal of Neuroscience, 32*, 18087–18100.

Holtzman, N. S., & Strube, M. J. (2013). Above and beyond short-term mating, long-term mating is uniquely tied to human personality. *Evolutionary Psychology, 11*, 1101–1129.

Hone, L. S. E., Hurwitz, W., & Lieberman, D. (2015). Sex differences in preferences for humor: A replication, modification, and extension. *Evolutionary Psychology, 13*, 167–181.

Hönekopp, J., & Watson, S. (2011). Meta-analysis of the relationship between digit-ratio 2D: 4D and aggression. *Personality and Individual Differences, 51*, 381–386.

Hong, R. Y., & Cheung, M. W. L. (2015). The structure of cognitive vulnerabilities to depression and anxiety: Evidence for a common core etiologic process based on a meta-analytic review. *Clinical Psychological Science, 3*, 892–912.

Hood, S. D., Bell, C. J., Argyropoulos, S. V., & Nutt, D. J. (2016). Don't panic. A guide to tryptophan depletion with disorder-specific anxiety provocation. *Journal of Psychopharmacology, 30*, 1137–1140.

Hooley, J. M, & St. Germain, S. A. (2013). Borderline personality disorder. In W. E. Craighead, D. J. Miklowitz, & L. W. Craighead (Eds.), *Psychopathology: History, diagnosis, and empirical foundations* (2nd ed., pp. 511–549). New York: Wiley.

Hooper, P. L., Gurven, M., Winking, J., & Kaplan, H. S. (2015). Inclusive fitness and differential productivity across the life course determine intergenerational transfers in a small-scale human society. *Proceedings of the Royal Society of London B, 282*, 20142808.

Hopcroft, R. L., & Bradley, D. B. (2007). The sex difference in depression across 29 countries. *Social Forces, 85*, 1483–1507.

Hopcroft, R. L., & McLaughlin, J. (2012). Why is the sex gap in feelings of depression wider in high gender equity countries? The effect of children on the psychological well-being of men and women. *Social Science Research, 41*, 501–513.

Hopwood, C. J., Ansell, E. B., Fehon, D. C., & Grilo, C. M. (2010). Personality heterogeneity in female adolescent inpatients with features of eating disorders. *Comprehensive Psychiatry, 51*, 585–591.

Hopwood, C. J., & Thomas, K. M. (2014). Personality disorders. In D. Beidel & B. Freuh (Eds.), *Adult psychopathology and diagnosis* (7th ed., pp. 739–774). New York: Wiley.

Horan, W. P., Johnson, M. W., & Green, M. F. (2017). Altered experiential, but not hypothetical, delay discounting in schizophrenia. *Journal of Abnormal Psychology, 126*, 301–311.

Horowitz, M. A., & Zunszain, P. A. (2015). Neuroimmune and neuroendocrine abnormalities in depression: Two sides of the same coin. *Annals of the New York Academy of Sciences, 1351*, 68–79.

Horrobin, D. F. (1998). Schizophrenia: The illness that made us human. *Medical Hypotheses, 50*, 269–288.

Horrobin, D. F. (2001). *The madness of Adam and Eve: How schizophrenia shaped humanity*. Ealing, UK: Bantam.

Horrobin, D. F., Glen, A. I. M., & Vaddadi, K. (1994). The membrane hypothesis of schizophrenia. *Schizophrenia Research, 13*, 195–207.

Horwitz, A. V., & Wakefield, J. C. (2012). *All we have to fear: Psychiatry's transformation of natural anxieties into mental disorders*. New York: Oxford University Press.

Houston, A. I. (2010). Evolutionary models of metabolism, behaviour and personality. *Philosophical Transactions of the Royal Society B, 365*, 3969–3975.

Hovey, D., Lindstedt, M., Zettergren, A., Jonsson, L., Johansson, A., Melke, J., et al. (2016). Antisocial behavior and polymorphisms in the oxytocin receptor gene: Findings in two independent samples. *Molecular Psychiatry, 21*, 983–988.

Howes, C., & Spieker, S. (2008). Attachment relationships in the context of multiple caregivers. In J. Cassidy & P. R. Shaver (Eds.), *Handbook of attachment* (2nd ed., pp. 317–332). New York: Guilford.

Howes, O. D., Kambeitz, J., Kim, E., Stahl, D., Slifstein, M., Abi-Dargham, A., et al. (2012). The nature of dopamine dysfunction in schizophrenia and what this means for treatment: Meta-analysis of imaging studies. *Archives of General Psychiatry, 69*, 776–786.

Howes, O. D., & Kapur, S. (2009). The dopamine hypothesis of schizophrenia: Version III—the final common pathway. *Schizophrenia Bulletin, 35*, 549–562.

Howland, M. A., Sandman, C. A., Glynn, L. M., Crippen, C., & Davis, E. P. (2016). Fetal exposure to placental corticotropin-releasing hormone is associated with child self-reported internalizing symptoms. *Psychoneuroendocrinology, 67*, 10–17.

Howren, M. B., Lamkin, D. M., & Suls, J. (2009). Associations of depression with C-reactive protein, IL-1, and IL-6: A meta-analysis. *Psychosomatic Medicine, 71*, 171–186.

Hrdy S. B. (1999). *Mother Nature: Maternal instincts and how they shape the human species*. New York: Ballantine.

Hrdy, S. B. (2005). Comes the child before the man: How cooperative breeding and prolonged postweaning dependence shaped human potentials. In M. E. Lamb & B. S. Hewlett (Eds.), *Hunter-gatherer childhoods: Evolutionary, developmental, and cultural perspectives* (pp. 65–91). Chicago: Aldine.

Hubbard, L., Tansey, K. E., Rai, D., Jones, P., Ripke, S., Chambert, K. D., et al. (2016). Evidence of common genetic overlap between schizophrenia and cognition. *Schizophrenia Bulletin, 42*, 832–842.

Hublin, J. J., Ben-Ncer, A., Bailey, S. E., Freidline, S. E., Neubauer, S., Skinner, M. M., et al. (2017). New fossils from Jebel Irhoud, Morocco and the pan-African origin of *Homo sapiens*. *Nature, 546*, 289–292.

Hudson, C. G. (2005). Socioeconomic status and mental illness: Tests of the social causation and selection hypotheses. *American Journal of Orthopsychiatry, 75*, 3–18.

Huey, S. J., Jr., & Weisz, J. R. (1997). Ego control, ego resiliency, and the five-factor model as predictors of behavioral and emotional problems in clinic-referred children and adolescents. *Journal of Abnormal Psychology, 106*, 404–415.

Hughes, K. A., Moore, R. A., Morris, P. H., & Corr, P. J. (2012). Throwing light on the dark side of personality: Reinforcement sensitivity theory and primary/secondary psychopathy in a student population. *Personality and Individual Differences, 52*, 532–536.

Huke, V., Turk, J., Saeidi, S., Kent, A., & Morgan, J. (2013). Autism spectrum disorders in eating disorder populations: A systematic review. *European Eating Disorders Review, 21*, 345–351.

Hulvershorn, L., & Nurnberger, J., Jr. (2014). Bipolar disorder. In K. C. Koenen, S. Rudenstine, E. Susser, & S. Galea (Eds.), *A life course approach to mental disorders* (pp. 76–87). Oxford: Oxford University Press.

Hummelen, B., Wilberg, T., Pedersen, G., & Karterud, S. (2008). The quality of the DSM-IV obsessive-compulsive personality disorder construct as a prototype category. *The Journal of Nervous and Mental Disease, 196*, 446–455.

Hunt, E. (2011). *Human intelligence*. New York: Cambridge University Press.

Hunt, E., Bornovalova, M. A., & Patrick, C. J. (2015). Genetic and environmental overlap between borderline personality disorder traits and psychopathy: Evidence for promotive effects of factor 2 and protective effects of factor 1. *Psychological Medicine, 45*, 1471–1481.

Hunt, J., & Hodgson, D. (2010). What is fitness, and how do we measure it? In D. F. Westneat & C. W. Fox (Eds.), *Evolutionary behavioral ecology* (pp. 46–70). New York: Oxford University Press.

Hurlemann, R., Patin, A., Onur, O. A., Cohen, M. X., Baumgartner, T., Metzler, S., et al. (2010). Oxytocin enhances amygdala-dependent, socially reinforced learning and emotional empathy in humans. *Journal of Neuroscience, 30*, 4999–5007.

Hurly, A. T. (2003). The twin threshold model: Risk-intermediate foraging by rufous hummingbirds, *Selasphorus rufus*. *Animal Behaviour, 66*, 751–761.

Husarova, V. M., Lakatosova, S., Pivovarciova, A., Babinska, K., Bakos, J., Durdiakova, J., et al. (2016). Plasma oxytocin in children with autism and its correlations with behavioral parameters in children and parents. *Psychiatry Investigation, 13*, 174–183.

Huxley, J., Mayr, E., Osmond, H., & Hoffer, A. (1964). Schizophrenia as a genetic morphism. *Nature, 204*, 220–221.

Huys, Q. J., Daw, N. D., & Dayan, P. (2015). Depression: A decision-theoretic analysis. *Annual Review of Neuroscience, 38*, 1–23.

Huys, Q. J., Guitart-Masip, M., Dolan, R. J., & Dayan, P. (2015). Decision-theoretic psychiatry. *Clinical Psychological Science, 3*, 400–421.

Idring, S., Magnusson, C., Lundberg, M., Ek, M., Rai, D., Svensson, A. C., et al. (2014). Parental age and the risk of autism spectrum disorders: Findings from a Swedish population-based cohort. *International Journal of Epidemiology, 43*, 107–115.

Iervolino, A. C., Rijsdijk, F. V., Cherkas, L., Fullana, M. A., & Mataix-Cols, D. (2011). A multivariate twin study of obsessive-compulsive symptom dimensions. *Archives of General Psychiatry, 68*, 637–644.

Ingudomnukul, E., Baron-Cohen, S., Wheelwright, S., & Knickmeyer, R. (2007). Elevated rates of testosterone-related disorders in women with autism spectrum conditions. *Hormones and Behavior, 51*, 597–604.

Insel, T., Cuthbert, B., Garvey, M., Heinssen, R., Pine, D. S., Quinn, K., et al. (2010). Research domain criteria (RDoC): Toward a new classification framework for research on mental disorders. *American Journal of Psychiatry, 167*, 748–751.

Iossifov, I., Levy, D., Allen, J., Ye, K., Ronemus, M., Lee, et al. (2015). Low load for disruptive mutations in autism genes and their biased transmission. *Proceedings of the National Academy of Sciences, 112*, E5600–E5607.

Iossifov, I., O'Roak, B. J., Sanders, S. J., Ronemus, M., Krumm, N., Levy, D., et al. (2014). The contribution of de novo coding mutations to autism spectrum disorder. *Nature, 515*, 216–221.

Iredale, W., Van Vugt, M., & Dunbar, R. I. M. (2008). Showing off in humans: Male generosity as a mating signal. *Evolutionary Psychology, 6*, 386–392.

Irwin, M. R., & Miller, A. H. (2007). Depressive disorders and immunity: 20 years of progress and discovery. *Brain, Behavior, and Immunity, 21*, 374–383.

Isbell, L. A. (2009). *The fruit, the tree, and the serpent: Why we see so well*. Cambridge, MA: Harvard University Press.

Isbell, L. A., & Etting, S. F. (2017). Scales drive detection, attention, and memory of snakes in wild vervet monkeys (*Chlorocebus pygerythrus*). *Primates, 58*, 121–129.

Isen, J. D., McGue, M. K., & Iacono, W. G. (2015). Aggressive-antisocial boys develop into physically strong young men. *Psychological Science, 26*, 444–455.

Ivarsson, T., & Melin, K. (2008). Autism spectrum traits in children and adolescents with obsessive-compulsive disorder (OCD). *Journal of Anxiety Disorders, 22*, 969–978.

Iza, M., Wall, M. M., Heimberg, R. G., Rodebaugh, T. L., Schneier, F. R., Liu, S. M., et al. (2014). Latent structure of social fears and social anxiety disorders. *Psychological Medicine, 44*, 361–370.

Izuma, K., Matsumoto, K., Camerer, C. F., & Adolphs, R. (2011). Insensitivity to social reputation in autism. *Proceedings of the National Academy of Sciences, 108*, 17302–17307.

Jack, A. I., Dawson, A. J., Begany, K. L., Leckie, R. L., Barry, K. P., Ciccia, A. H., et al. (2013). fMRI reveals reciprocal inhibition between social and physical cognitive domains. *NeuroImage, 66*, 385–401.

Jackson, H. J., & Burgess, P. M. (2000). Personality disorders in the community: A report from the Australian National Survey of Mental Health and Wellbeing. *Social Psychiatry and Psychiatric Epidemiology, 35*, 531–538.

Jackson, J. J., & Kirkpatrick, L. A. (2007). The structure and measurement of human mating strategies: Toward a multidimensional model of sociosexuality. *Evolution and Human Behavior, 28*, 382–391.

Jackson, J. J., Connolly, J. J., Garrison, S. M., Leveille, M. M., & Connolly, S. L. (2015). Your friends know how long you will live: A 75-year study of peer-rated personality traits. *Psychological Science, 26*, 335–340.

Jackson, R. E. (2009). Individual differences in distance perception. *Proceedings of the Royal Society of London B*, 2009.004.

Jacobi, C., & Fittig, E. (2012). Psychosocial risk factors for eating disorders. In W. S. Agras (Ed.), *The Oxford handbook of eating disorders* (pp. 123–136). New York: Oxford University Press.

Jacobs, R. A., & Kruschke, J. K. (2011). Bayesian learning theory applied to human cognition. *Wiley Interdisciplinary Reviews: Cognitive Science, 2*, 8–21.

Jacobson, N. C. (2016). Current evolutionary adaptiveness of psychiatric disorders: Fertility rates, parent-child relationship quality, and psychiatric disorders across the lifespan. *Journal of Abnormal Psychology, 125*, 824–839.

Jacobson, N. C., & Newman, M. G. (2016). Perceptions of close and group relationships mediate the relationship between anxiety and depression over a decade later. *Depression & Anxiety, 33*, 66–74.

Jaeggi, A. V., De Groot, E., Stevens, J. M., & Van Schaik, C. P. (2013). Mechanisms of reciprocity in primates: Testing for short-term contingency of grooming and food sharing in bonobos and chimpanzees. *Evolution and Human Behavior, 34*, 69–77.

Jaeggi, A. V., & Gurven, M. (2013). Reciprocity explains food sharing in humans and other primates independent of kin selection and tolerated scrounging: A phylogenetic meta-analysis. *Proceedings of the Royal Society of London B, 280*, 20131615.

Jaffee, S. R. (2016). Quantitative and molecular behavior genetic studies of gene-environment correlation. In D. Cicchetti (Ed.), *Developmental psychopathology: Vol. 2. Developmental neuroscience* (3rd ed., pp. 242–286). New York: Wiley.

Jaffee, S. R., Caspi, A., Moffitt, T. E., Polo-Tomas, M., Price, T. S., & Taylor, A. (2004). The limits of child effects: Evidence for genetically mediated child effects on corporal punishment but not on physical maltreatment. *Developmental Psychology, 40*, 1047–1058.

James, J., & Ellis, B. J. (2013). The development of human reproductive strategies: Toward an integration of life history and sexual selection models. In J. A. Simpson & L. Campbell (Eds.), *The Oxford handbook of close relationships* (pp. 771–794). New York: Oxford University Press.

Jamison, K. R. (1993). *Touched with fire: Manic-depressive illness and the artistic temperament*. New York: Free Press.

Jamnadass, E. S., Keelan, J. A., Hollier, L. P., Hickey, M., Maybery, M. T., & Whitehouse, A. J. (2015). The perinatal androgen to estrogen ratio and autistic-like traits in the general population: A longitudinal pregnancy cohort study. *Journal of Neurodevelopmental Disorders, 7*, 17.

Jang, S. A., Smith, S. W., & Levine, T. R. (2002). To stay or to leave? The role of attachment styles in communication patterns and potential termination of romantic relationships following discovery of deception. *Communication Monographs, 69*, 236–52.

Janicke, T., Häderer, I. K., Lajeunesse, M. J., & Anthes, N. (2016). Darwinian sex roles confirmed across the animal kingdom. *Science Advances, 2*, e1500983.

Jennings, W. G., & Reingle, J. M. (2012). On the number and shape of developmental/life-course violence, aggression, and delinquency trajectories: A state-of-the-art review. *Journal of Criminal Justice, 40*, 472–489.

Jennings, W. G., Rocque, M., Fox, B. H., Piquero, A. R., & Farrington, D. P. (2016). Can they recover? An assessment of adult adjustment problems among males in the abstainer, recovery, life-course persistent, and adolescence-limited pathways followed up to age 56 in the Cambridge Study in Delinquent Development. *Development and Psychopathology, 28*, 537–549.

Jensen, A. R. (1998). *The g factor: The science of mental ability*. Westport, CT: Praeger.

Jensen, P. S., Mrazek, D., Knapp, P. K., Steinberg, L., Pfeffer, C., Schowalter, J., et al. (1997). Evolution and revolution in child psychiatry: ADHD as a disorder of adaptation. *Journal of the American Academy of Child & Adolescent Psychiatry, 36*, 1672–1681.

Jeschke, J. M., Gabriel, W., & Kokko, H. (2008). r-Strategist/K-Strategists. In S. E. Jørgensen & B. D. Fath (Eds.), *Encyclopedia of ecology* (Vol. 4, pp. 3113–3122). Oxford: Elsevier.

Jeschke, J. M., & Kokko, H. (2009). The roles of body size and phylogeny in fast and slow life histories. *Evolutionary Ecology, 23*, 867–878.

Jiang, J., Heller, K., & Egner, T. (2014). Bayesian modeling of flexible cognitive control. *Neuroscience & Biobehavioral Reviews, 46*, 30–43.

Jobe, L. E., & White, S. W. (2007). Loneliness, social relationships, and a broader autism phenotype in college students. *Personality and Individual Differences, 42*, 1479–1489.

Jobling, M. A., Hurles, M., & Tyler-Smith, C. (2004). *Human evolutionary genetics: Origins, peoples & diseases*. New York: Garland.

Jobst, A., Dehning, S., Ruf, S., Notz, T., Buchheim, A., Henning-Fast, K., et al. (2014). Oxytocin and vasopressin levels are decreased in the plasma of male schizophrenia patients. *Acta Neuropsychiatrica, 26*, 347–355.

Jobst, A., Padberg, F., Mauer, M. C., Daltrozzo, T., Bauriedl-Schmidt, C., Sabass, L., et al. (2016). Lower oxytocin plasma levels in borderline patients with unresolved attachment representations. *Frontiers in Human Neuroscience, 10*, 1–11.

Jogems-Kosterman, B. J., De Knijff, D. W., Kusters, R., & van Hoof, J. J. (2007). Basal cortisol and DHEA levels in women with borderline personality disorder. *Journal of Psychiatric Research, 41*, 1019–1026.

Johnson, D. P., Rhee, S. H., Friedman, N. P., Corley, R. P., Munn-Chernoff, M. A., Hewitt, J. K., et al. (2016). A twin study examining rumination as a transdiagnostic correlate of psychopathology. *Clinical Psychological Science, 4*, 971–987.

Johnson, J. G., Cohen, P., Kasen, S., & Brook, J. (2008). Psychiatric disorders in adolescence and early adulthood and risk for child-rearing difficulties during middle adulthood. *Journal of Family Issues, 29*, 210–233.

Johnson, J. G., Cohen, P., Kasen, S., Ehrensaft, M. K., & Crawford, T. N. (2006). Associations of parental personality disorders and axis I disorders with child rearing behavior. *Psychiatry, 69*, 336–350.

Johnson, J. M., Nachtigall, L. B., & Stern, T. A. (2013). The effect of testosterone levels on mood in men: A review. *Psychosomatics, 54*, 509–514.

Johnson, K. R., & Johnson, S. L. (2014). Cross-national prevalence and cultural correlates of bipolar I disorder. *Social Psychiatry and Psychiatric Epidemiology, 49*, 1111–1117.

Johnson, R. T., Burk, J. A., & Kirkpatrick, L. A. (2007). Dominance and prestige as differential predictors of aggression and testosterone levels in men. *Evolution and Human Behavior, 28*, 345–351.

Johnson, S. L., Carver, C. S., & Gotlib, I. H. (2012). Elevated ambitions for fame among persons diagnosed with bipolar I disorder. *Journal of Abnormal Psychology, 121*, 602–609.

Johnson, S. L., Leedom, L. J., & Muhtadie, L. (2012). The dominance behavioral system and psychopathology: Evidence from self-report, observational, and biological studies. *Psychological Bulletin, 138*, 692–743.

Johnson, W., & Bouchard, T. J. (2005). The structure of human intelligence: It is verbal, perceptual, and image rotation (VPR), not fluid and crystallized. *Intelligence, 33*, 393–416.

Johnson, W., & Bouchard, T. J. (2007). Sex differences in mental abilities: g masks the dimensions on which they lie. *Intelligence, 35*, 23–39.

Johnson, W., Carothers, A., & Deary, I. J. (2008*a*). Sex differences in variability in general intelligence: A new look at the old question. *Perspectives on Psychological Science, 3*, 518–531.

Johnson, W., Jung, R. E., Colom, R., & Haier, R. J. (2008*b*). Cognitive abilities independent of IQ correlate with regional brain structure. *Intelligence, 36*, 18–28.

Johnson, W., Penke, L., & Spinath, F. M. (2011). Heritability in the era of molecular genetics: Some thoughts for understanding genetic influences on behavioural traits. *European Journal of Personality, 25*, 254–266.

Johnson-Laird, P. N., & Oatley, K. (1992). Basic emotions, rationality, and folk theory. *Cognition & Emotion, 6*, 201–223.

Jokela, M. (2012). Birth-cohort effects in the association between personality and fertility. *Psychological Science, 23*, 835–841.

Jokela, M., Alvergne, A., Pollet, T. V., & Lummaa, V. (2011). Reproductive behavior and personality traits of the Five Factor Model. *European Journal of Personality, 25*, 487–500.

Jokela, M., Batty, G. D., Nyberg, S. T., Virtanen, M., Nabi, H., Singh-Manoux, A., et al. (2013). Personality and all-cause mortality: Individual-participant meta-analysis of 3,947 deaths in 76,150 adults. *American Journal of Epidemiology, 178*, 667–675.

Jonason, P. K., Duineveld, J. J., & Middleton, J. P. (2015). Pathology, pseudopathology, and the Dark Triad of personality. *Personality and Individual Differences, 78*, 43–47.

Jonason, P. K., Kaufman, S. B., Webster, G. D., & Geher, G. (2013). What lies beneath the dark triad dirty dozen: Varied relations with the Big Five. *Individual Differences Research, 11*, 81–90.

Jonason, P. K., Koenig, B. L., & Tost, J. (2010). Living a fast life: The Dark Triad and life history theory. *Human Nature, 21*, 428–442.

Jonason, P. K., Li, N. P., Webster, G. D., & Schmitt, D. P. (2009). The dark triad: Facilitating a short-term mating strategy in men. *European Journal of Personality, 23*, 5–18.

Jonason, P. K., Webster, G. D., Schmitt, D. P., Li, N. P., & Crysel, L. (2012). The antihero in popular culture: Life history theory and the dark triad personality traits. *Review of General Psychology, 16*, 192–199.

Jones, D. N., & Figueredo, A. J. (2013). The core of darkness: Uncovering the heart of the Dark Triad. *European Journal of Personality, 27*, 521–531.

Jones, E. J. H., Gliga, T., Bedford, R., Charman, T., & Johnson, M. H. (2014). Developmental pathways to autism: A review of prospective studies of infants at risk. *Neuroscience & Biobehavioral Reviews, 39*, 1–33.

Jones, J. H. (2009). The force of selection on the human life cycle. *Evolution and Human Behavior, 30*, 305–314.

Jones, J. H. (2015). Resource transfers and life history evolution. *Annual Review of Anthropology, 44*, 513–531.

Jones, J. H., & Bird, R. B. (2014). The marginal valuation of fertility. *Evolution and Human Behavior, 35*, 65–71.

Jones, O. R., Scheuerlein, A., Salguero-Gómez, R., Camarda, C. G., Schaible, R., Casper, B. B., et al. (2014). Diversity of ageing across the tree of life. *Nature, 505*, 169–173.

Jones, P. A. (2012). Functions of DNA methylation: Islands, start sites, gene bodies and beyond. *Nature Reviews Genetics, 13*, 484–492.

Jones, S. E., Miller, J. D., & Lynam, D. R. (2011). Personality, antisocial behavior, and aggression: A meta-analytic review. *Journal of Criminal Justice, 39*, 329–337.

Joshi, G., Faraone, S. V., Wozniak, J., Tarko, L., Fried, R., Galdo, M., et al. (2014). Symptom profile of ADHD in youth with high-functioning autism spectrum disorder: A comparative study in psychiatrically referred populations. *Journal of Attention Disorders*, 1087054714543368.

Juda, M. N., Campbell, L., & Crawford, C. B. (2004). Dieting symptomatology in women and perceptions of social support: An evolutionary approach. *Evolution and Human Behavior, 25*, 200–208.

Jung, M., Mody, M., Saito, D. N., Tomoda, A., Okazawa, H., Wada, Y., & Kosaka, H. (2015). Sex differences in the default mode network with regard to autism spectrum traits: A resting state fMRI Study. *PloS ONE, 10*, e0143126.

Jung, R. E., Grazioplene, R., Caprihan, A., Chavez, R. S., & Haier, R. J. (2010). White matter integrity, creativity, and psychopathology: Disentangling constructs with diffusion tensor imaging. *PLoS ONE, 5*, e9818.

Jung, R. E., & Haier, R. J. (2007). The Parieto-Frontal Integration Theory (P-FIT) of intelligence: Converging neuroimaging evidence. *Behavioral and Brain Sciences, 30*, 135–154.

Juster, R. P., Bizik, G., Picard, M., Arsenault-lapierre, G., Sindi, S., Trepanier, L., et al. (2011). A transdisciplinary perspective of chronic stress in relation to psychopathology throughout life span development. *Development and Psychopathology, 23*, 725–776.

Kacelnik, A. (2102). Putting mechanisms into behavioral ecology. In P. Hammerstein & J. R. Stevens (Eds.), *Evolution and the mechanisms of decision making* (pp. 21–38). Cambridge, MA: MIT Press.

Kacelnik, A., & Bateson, M. (1997). Risk-sensitivity: Crossroads for theories of decision-making. *Trends in Cognitive Sciences, 1*, 304–309.

Kahn, J. A., Kaplowitz, R. A., Goodman, E., & Emans, S. J. (2002). The association between impulsiveness and sexual risk behaviors in adolescent and young adult women. *Journal of Adolescent Health, 30*, 229–232.

Kaiser, J., & Gruzelier, J. H. (1999). Timing of puberty and syndromes of schizotypy: A replication. *International Journal of Psychophysiology, 34*, 237–247.

Kalick, S. M., Zebrowitz, L. A., Langlois, J. H., & Johnson, R. M. (1998). Does human facial attractiveness honestly advertise health? Longitudinal data on an evolutionary question. *Psychological Science, 9*, 8–13.

Kalkman, H. O. (2012). Potential opposite roles of the extracellular signal-regulated kinase (ERK) pathway in autism spectrum and bipolar disorders. *Neuroscience & Biobehavioral Reviews, 36*, 2206–2213.

Kalueff, A. V., & Nutt, D. J. (2007). Role of GABA in anxiety and depression. *Depression and Anxiety, 24*, 495–517.

Kambeitz, J. P., & Howes, O. D. (2015). The serotonin transporter in depression: Meta-analysis of in vivo and post mortem findings and implications for understanding and treating depression. *Journal of Affective Disorders, 186*, 358–366.

Kanwisher, N. (2010). Functional specificity in the human brain: A window into the functional architecture of the mind. *Proceedings of the National Academy of Sciences USA, 107*, 11163–11170.

Kaplan, H. S. (1996). A theory of fertility and parental investment in traditional and modern human societies. *Yearbook of Physical Anthropology, 39*, 91–135.

Kaplan, H. S., Gurven, M., & Lancaster, J. B. (2007). Brain evolution and the human adaptive complex: An ecological and social theory. In S. W. Gangestad & J. A. Simpson (Eds.), *The evolution of mind: Fundamental questions and controversies* (pp. 269–279), New York: Guilford.

Kaplan, H. S., Hill, K., Lancaster, J. B., & Hurtado, A. M. (2000). A theory of human life history evolution: Diet, intelligence, and longevity. *Evolutionary Anthropology, 9*, 156–185.

Kaplan, H. S., Hooper, P. L., & Gurven, M. (2009). The evolutionary and ecological roots of human social organization. *Philosophical Transactions of the Royal Society B, 364*, 3289–3299.

Kaplan, H. S., & Robson, A. J. (2009). We age because we grow. *Proceedings of the Royal Society of London B, 276*, 1837–1844.

Kapur, S. (2003). Psychosis as a state of aberrant salience: A framework linking biology, phenomenology, and pharmacology in schizophrenia. *American Journal of Psychiatry, 160*, 13–23.

Kapur, S., Mizrahi, R., & Li, M. (2005). From dopamine to salience to psychosis: Linking biology, pharmacology and phenomenology of psychosis. *Schizophrenia Research, 79*, 59–68.

Kapur, S., & Remington, G. (1996). Serotonin-dopamine interaction and its relevance to schizophrenia. *American Journal of Psychiatry, 153*, 466–476.

Karalunas, S. L., Fair, D., Musser, E. D., Aykes, K., Iyer, S. P., & Nigg, J. T. (2014). Subtyping attention-deficit/hyperactivity disorder using temperament dimensions: Toward biologically based nosologic criteria. *JAMA Psychiatry, 71*, 1015–1024.

Kardum, I., Hudek-Knezevic, J., Schmitt, D. P., & Covic, M. (2017). Assortative mating for Dark Triad: Evidence of positive, initial, and active assortment. *Personal Relationships, 24*, 75–83.

Katz, J., d'Albis, M. A., Boisgontier, J., Poupon, C., Mangin, J. F., Guevara, P., et al. (2016). Similar white matter but opposite grey matter changes in schizophrenia and high-functioning autism. *Acta Psychiatrica Scandinavica, 134*, 31–39.

Kaufman, S. B., & Paul, E. S. (2014). Creativity and schizophrenia spectrum disorders across the arts and sciences. *Frontiers in Psychology, 5*, 1145.

Kavanagh, D. H., Tansey, K. E., O'donovan, M. C., & Owen, M. J. (2015). Schizophrenia genetics: Emerging themes for a complex disorder. *Molecular Psychiatry, 20*, 72–76.

Kayser, A. S., Mitchell, J. M., Weinstein, D., & Frank, M. J. (2014). Dopamine, locus of control, and the exploration-exploitation tradeoff. *Neuropsychopharmacology, 40*, 454–462.

Keagy, J., Savard, J.-F., & Borgia, G. (2012). Cognitive ability and the evolution of multiple behavioral display traits. *Behavioral Ecology, 23*, 448–456.

Keel, P. K., & Klump, K. L. (2003). Are eating disorders culture-bound syndromes? Implications for conceptualizing their etiology. *Psychological Bulletin, 129*, 747–769.

Keeley, L. H. (1996). *War before civilization: The myth of the peaceful savage*. New York: Oxford University Press.

Kell, H. J., Lubinski, D., Benbow, C. P., & Steiger, J. H. (2013). Creativity and technical innovation spatial ability's unique role. *Psychological Science, 24*, 1831–1836.

Keller, M. C., & Miller, G. (2006). Resolving the paradox of common, harmful, heritable mental disorders: Which evolutionary genetic models work best? *Behavioral and Brain Sciences, 29*, 385–452.

Keller, M. C., Neale, M. C., & Kendler, K. S. (2007). Association of different adverse life events with distinct patterns of depressive symptoms. *American Journal of Psychiatry, 164*, 1521–1529.

Keller, M. C., & Nesse, R. M. (2005). Is low mood an adaptation? Evidence for subtypes with symptoms that match precipitants. *Journal of Affective Disorders, 86*, 27–35.

Keller, M. C., & Nesse, R. M. (2006). The evolutionary significance of depressive symptoms: Different adverse situations lead to different depressive symptom patterns. *Journal of Personality and Social Psychology, 91*, 316–330.

Keltner, D., Haidt, J., & Shiota, L. (2006). Social functionalism and the evolution of emotions. In M. Schaller, D. Kenrick, & J. Simpson (Eds.), *Evolution and social psychology* (pp. 115–142). New York: Psychology Press.

Kemp, A. H., Quintana, D. S., Quinn, C. R., Hopkinson, P., & Harris, A. W. (2014). Major depressive disorder with melancholia displays robust alterations in resting state heart rate and its variability: Implications for future morbidity and mortality. *Frontiers in Psychology, 5*, 1387.

Kendler, K. S., Aggen, S. H., Czajkowski, N., Røysamb, E., Tambs, K., Torgersen, S., et al. (2008). The structure of genetic and environmental risk factors for DSM-IV personality disorders: A multivariate twin study. *Archives of General Psychiatry, 65,* 1438–1446.

Kendler, K. S., Aggen, S. H., & Patrick, C. J. (2012). A multivariate twin study of the DSM-IV criteria for antisocial personality disorder. *Biological Psychiatry, 71,* 247–253.

Kendler, K. S., Eaves, L. J., Loken, E. K., Pedersen, N. L., Middeldorp, C. M., Reynolds, C., et al. (2011). The impact of environmental experiences on symptoms of anxiety and depression across the life span. *Psychological Science, 22,* 1343–1352.

Kendler, K. S., & Gardner, C. O. (2016). Depressive vulnerability, stressful life events and episode onset of major depression: A longitudinal model. *Psychological Medicine, 46,* 1865–1874.

Kendler, K. S., & Halberstadt, L. J. (2013). The road not taken: Life experiences in monozygotic twin pairs discordant for major depression. *Molecular Psychiatry, 18,* 975–984.

Kendler, K. S., Hettema, J. M., Butera, F., Gardner, C. O., & Prescott, C. A. (2003). Life event dimensions of loss, humiliation, entrapment, and danger in the prediction of onsets of major depression and generalized anxiety. *Archives of General Psychiatry, 60,* 789–796.

Kendler, K. S., Kuhn, J., & Prescott, C. A. (2004). The interrelationship of neuroticism, sex, and stressful life events in the prediction of episodes of major depression. *American Journal of Psychiatry, 161,* 631–636.

Kendler, K. S., Myers, J., & Prescott, C. A. (2002). The etiology of phobias: An evaluation of the stress-diathesis model. *Archives of General Psychiatry, 59,* 242–248.

Kendler, K. S., Myers, J., & Prescott, C. A. (2005). Sex differences in the relationship between social support and risk for major depression: A longitudinal study of opposite-sex twin pairs. *American Journal of Psychiatry, 162,* 250–256.

Kennair, L. E. O. (2003). Evolutionary psychology and psychopathology. *Current Opinion in Psychiatry, 16,* 691–699.

Kennair, L. E. O. (2007). Fear and fitness revisited. *Evolutionary Psychology, 5,* 105–117.

Kennair, L. E. O. (2010). Climbing Mount Impossible: An important book written too early. *Evolutionary Psychology, 8,* 297–302.

Kennair, L. E. O. (2011). The problem of defining psychopathology and challenges to evolutionary psychology theory. In D. M. Buss & P. H. Hawley (Eds.), *The evolution of personality and individual differences* (pp. 451–479). New York: Oxford University Press.

Kennair, L. E. O. (2014). Evolutionary psychopathology and life history: A clinician's perspective. *Psychological Inquiry, 25,* 346–351.

Kennis, M., Rademaker, A. R., & Geuze, E. (2013). Neural correlates of personality: An integrative review. *Neuroscience & Biobehavioral Reviews, 37,* 73–95.

Kenrick, D. T., Griskevicius, V., Neuberg, S. L., & Schaller, M. (2010). Renovating the pyramid of needs: Contemporary extensions built upon ancient foundations. *Perspectives on Psychological Science, 5,* 292–314.

Kenrick, D. T., & Keefe, R. C. (1992). Age preferences in mates reflect sex differences in human reproductive strategies. *Behavioral and Brain Sciences, 15,* 75–133.

Keramati, M., Dezfouli, A., & Piray, P. (2011). Speed/accuracy trade-off between the habitual and the goal-directed processes. *PLoS Computational Biology, 7,* e1002055.

Keshavan, M. S., Sujata, M., Mehra, A., Montrose, D. M., & Sweeney, J. A. (2003). Psychosis proneness and ADHD in young relatives of schizophrenia patients. *Schizophrenia Research, 59,* 85–92.

Kessler, R. C., Berglund, P., Demler, O., Jin, R., Merikangas, K. R., & Walters, E. E. (2005). Lifetime prevalence and age-of-onset distributions of DSM-IV disorders in the National Comorbidity Survey Replication. *Archives of General Psychiatry, 62*, 593–602.

Kessler, R. C., Scott, K. M., Shahly, V., & Zaslavsky, A. M. (2014). The big picture. In C. S. Richards & M. W. O'Hara (Eds.), *The Oxford handbook of depression and comorbidity* (pp. 599–614). New York: Oxford University Press.

Kessler, R. C., Stein, M. B., & Berglund, P. (1998). Social phobia subtypes in the National Comorbidity Survey. *American Journal of Psychiatry, 155*, 613–619.

Khalife, N., Glover, V., Taanila, A., Ebeling, H., Järvelin, M. R., & Rodriguez, A. (2013). Prenatal glucocorticoid treatment and later mental health in children and adolescents. *PloS ONE, 8*, e81394.

Khandaker, G. M., Barnett, J. H., White, I. R., & Jones, P. B. (2011). A quantitative meta-analysis of population-based studies of premorbid intelligence and schizophrenia. *Schizophrenia Research, 132*, 220–227.

Khandaker, G. M., Clarke, M., Cannon, M., & Jones, P. B. (2014). Schizophrenia and related psychosis. In K. C. Koenen, S. Rudenstine, E. Susser, & S. Galea (Eds.), *A life course approach to mental disorders* (pp. 61–75). Oxford: Oxford University Press.

Khazanov, G. K., & Ruscio, A. M. (2016). Is low positive emotionality a specific risk factor for depression? A meta-analysis of longitudinal studies. *Psychological Bulletin, 142*, 991–1015.

Kim, S., Thibodeau, R., & Jorgensen, R. S. (2011). Shame, guilt, and depressive symptoms: A meta-analytic review. *Psychological Bulletin, 137*, 68–96.

Kim, S. H., Macari, S., Koller, J., & Chawarska, K. (2016). Examining the phenotypic heterogeneity of early autism spectrum disorder: Subtypes and short-term outcomes. *Journal of Child Psychology and Psychiatry, 57*, 93–102.

Kim, S. J., Kim, B. N., Cho, S. C., Kim, J. W., Shin, M. S., Yoo, H. J., et al. (2010). The prevalence of specific phobia and associated co-morbid features in children and adolescents. *Journal of Anxiety Disorders, 24*, 629–634.

Kim, Y. K., Na, K. S., Hwang, J. A., Yoon, H. K., Lee, H. J., Hahn, S. W., et al. (2013). High insulin-like growth factor-1 in patients with bipolar I disorder: A trait marker? *Journal of Affective Disorders, 151*, 738–743.

Kinney, D. K., & Tanaka, M. (2009). An evolutionary hypothesis of depression and its symptoms, adaptive value, and risk factors. *The Journal of Nervous and Mental Disease, 197*, 561–567.

Kinney, D. K., Teixeira, P., Hsu, D., Napoleon, S. C., Crowley, D. J., Miller, A., et al. (2009). Relation of schizophrenia prevalence to latitude, climate, fish consumption, infant mortality, and skin color: A role for prenatal vitamin d deficiency and infections? *Schizophrenia Bulletin, 35*, 582–595.

Kirkwood, T. B. L. (1990). The disposable soma theory of aging. In D. E. Harrison (Ed.), *Genetic effects on aging II* (pp. 9–19). Caldwell, NJ: Telford.

Klaassens, E. R., Giltay, E. J., Cuijpers, P., van Veen, T., & Zitman, F. G. (2012). Adulthood trauma and HPA-axis functioning in healthy subjects and PTSD patients: A meta-analysis. *Psychoneuroendocrinology, 37*, 317–331.

Klasios, J. (2013). Cognitive traits as sexually selected fitness indicators. *Review of General Psychology, 17*, 428–442.

Klein, D. F. (1981). Anxiety reconceptualized. In D. F. Klein & J. Rabkin (Eds.), *Anxiety: New research and changing concepts* (pp. 235–261). New York: Raven.

Klein, D. F. (1993). False suffocation alarms, spontaneous panics, and related conditions: An integrative hypothesis. *Archives of General Psychiatry, 50*, 306–317.

Klein, D. N., & Black, S. R. (2013). Persistent depressive disorder: Dysthymia and chronic depression. In W. E. Craighead, D. J. Miklowitz, & L. W. Craighead (Eds.), *Psychopathology: History, diagnosis, and empirical foundations* (2nd ed., pp. 334–363). New York: Wiley.

Klein, D. N., Kujawa, A. J., Black, S. R., Pennock, A. T. (2013). Depressive disorders. In T. P. Beauchaine & S. P. Hinshaw (Eds.), *Child and adolescent psychopathology* (2nd ed., pp. 543–575). Hoboken, NJ: Wiley.

Klimes-Dougan, B., Kenndy, K. P., & Cullen, K. R. (2016). Bipolar disorder from a developmental psychopathology perspective: Focusing on phenomenology, etiology, and neurobiology. In D. Cicchetti (Ed.), *Developmental psychopathology: Vol. 3. Maladaptation and psychopathology* (3rd ed., pp. 898–949). New York: Wiley.

Klinger, E. (1975). Consequences of commitment to and disengagement from incentives. *Psychological Review, 82*, 1–25.

Klump, K. L., Hildebrandt, B. A., O'Connor, S. M., Keel, P. K., Neale, M., Sisk, C. L., et al. (2015). Changes in genetic risk for emotional eating across the menstrual cycle: A longitudinal study. *Psychological Medicine, 45*, 3227–3237.

Klump, K. L., O'Connor, S. M., Hildebrandt, B. A., Keel, P. K., Neale, M., Sisk, C. L., et al. (2016). Differential effects of estrogen and progesterone on genetic and environmental risk for emotional eating in women. *Clinical Psychological Science*, 2167702616641637.

Klump, K. L., Racine, S. E., Hildebrandt, B., Burt, S. A., Neale, M., Sisk, C. L., et al. (2014). Influences of ovarian hormones on dysregulated eating: A comparison of associations in women with versus women without binge episodes. *Clinical Psychological Science, 2*, 545–559.

Knickmeyer, R. C., Wheelwright, S., Hoekstra, R., & Baron-Cohen, S. (2006). Age of menarche in females with autism spectrum conditions. *Developmental Medicine & Child Neurology, 48*, 1007–1008.

Knoch, D., & Nash, K. (2015). Self-control in social decision making: A neurobiological perspective. In G. H. E. Gendolla, M. Tops, & S. Koole (Eds.), *Handbook of biobehavioral approaches to self-regulation* (pp. 221–234). New York: Springer.

Knopik, V. S., Neiderhiser, J. M., DeFries, J. C., & Plomin, R. (2017). *Behavioral genetics* (7th ed.). New York: Worth.

Knowles, R., McCarthy-Jones, S., & Rowse, G. (2011). Grandiose delusions: A review and theoretical integration of cognitive and affective perspectives. *Clinical Psychology Review, 31*, 684–696.

Ko, Y. H., Jung, S. W., Joe, S. H., Lee, C. H., Jung, H. G., Jung, I. K., et al. (2007). Association between serum testosterone levels and the severity of negative symptoms in male patients with chronic schizophrenia. *Psychoneuroendocrinology, 32*, 385–391.

Kobak, R., & Madsen, S. (2008). Disruptions in attachment bonds. In J. Cassidy & P. R. Shaver (Eds.), *Handbook of attachment* (2nd ed., pp. 23–47). New York: Guilford.

Kobayashi, T., Matsuyama, T., Takeuchi, M., & Ito, S. (2016). Autism spectrum disorder and prenatal exposure to selective serotonin reuptake inhibitors: A systematic review and meta-analysis. *Reproductive Toxicology, 65*, 170–178.

Koenen, K. C., Moffitt, T. E., Roberts, A. L., Martin, L. T., Kubzansky, L., Harrington, H., et al. (2009). Childhood IQ and adult mental disorders: A test of the cognitive reserve hypothesis. *American Journal of Psychiatry, 166*, 50–57.

Koenen, K. C., Rudenstine, S., Susser, E. & Galea S. (Eds.) (2014). *A life course approach to mental disorders*. Oxford: Oxford University Press.

Kokko, H., Brooks, R., McNamara, J. M., & Houston, A. I. (2002). The sexual selection continuum. *Proceedings of the Royal Society of London B, 269*, 1331–1340.

Kokko, H., & Jennions, M. (2008). Parental investment, sexual selection and sex ratios. *Journal of Evolutionary Biology, 21*, 919–948.

Koolhaas, J. M., Korte, S. M., De Boer, S. F., Van Der Vegt, B. J., Van Reenen, C. G., Hopster, H., et al. (1999). Coping styles in animals: Current status in behavior and stress-physiology. *Neuroscience & Biobehavioral Reviews, 23*, 925–935.

Korte, S. M., Koolhaas, J. M., Wingfield, J. C., & McEwen, B. S. (2005). The Darwinian concept of stress: Benefits of allostasis and costs of allostatic load and the trade-offs in health and disease. *Neuroscience and Biobehavioral Reviews, 29*, 3–38.

Kosidou, K., Dalman, C., Widman, L., Arver, S., Lee, B. K., Magnusson, C., et al. (2016). Maternal polycystic ovary syndrome and the risk of autism spectrum disorders in the offspring: A population-based nationwide study in Sweden. *Molecular Psychiatry, 21*, 1441–1448.

Kossowsky, J., Pfaltz, M. C., Schneider, S., Taeymans, J., Locher, C., & Gaab, J. (2013). The separation anxiety hypothesis of panic disorder revisited: A meta-analysis. *American Journal of Psychiatry, 170*, 768–781.

Koster, J. (2011). Hypothetical rankings of prospective husbands for female kin in low-land Nicaragua: Consensus analysis indicates high agreement and associations with wealth and hunting skill. *Evolution and Human Behavior, 32*, 356–363.

Kothari, R., Gafton, J., Treasure, J., & Micali, N. (2014). 2D: 4D Ratio in children at familial high-risk for eating disorders: The role of prenatal testosterone exposure. *American Journal of Human Biology, 26*, 176–182.

Kotov, R., Chang, S. W., Fochtmann, L. J., Mojtabai, R., Carlson, G. A., Sedler, M. A., et al. (2011). Schizophrenia in the internalizing-externalizing framework: A third dimension? *Schizophrenia Bulletin, 37*, 1168–1178.

Kotov, R., Gamez, W., Schmidt, F., & Watson, D. (2010). Linking "big" personality traits to anxiety, depressive, and substance use disorders: A meta-analysis. *Psychological Bulletin, 136*, 768–821.

Kotov, R., Krueger, R. F., Watson, D., Achenbach, T. M., Althoff, R. R., Bagby, R. M., et al. (2017). The Hierarchical Taxonomy of Psychopathology (HiTOP): A dimensional alternative to traditional nosologies. *Journal of Abnormal Psychology, 126*, 454–477.

Koyuncu, A., Tükel, R., Özyıldırım, İ., Meteris, H., & Yazıcı, O. (2010). Impact of obsessive-compulsive disorder comorbidity on the sociodemographic and clinical features of patients with bipolar disorder. *Comprehensive Psychiatry, 51*, 293–297.

Kramer, K. L. (2010). Cooperative breeding and its significance to the demographic success of humans. *Annual Review of Anthropology, 39*, 417–436.

Kramer, K. L. (2011). The evolution of human parental care and recruitment of juvenile help. *Trends in Ecology and Evolution, 26*, 533–540.

Kramer, P., & Bressan, P. (2015). Humans as superorganisms: How microbes, viruses, imprinted genes, and other selfish entities shape our behavior. *Perspectives on Psychological Science, 10*, 464–481.

Kravariti, E., Toulopoulou, T., Mapua-Filbey, F., Schulze, K., Walshe, M., Sham, P., et al. (2006). Intellectual asymmetry and genetic liability in first-degree relatives of probands with schizophrenia. *British Journal of Psychiatry, 188*, 186–187.

Krebs, G., Waszczuk, M. A., Zavos, H. M. S., Bolton, D., & Eley, T. C. (2015). Genetic and environmental influences on obsessive-compulsive behaviour across development: A longitudinal twin study. *Psychological Medicine, 45*, 1539–1549.

Krishnan, A., Zhang, R., Yao, V., Theesfeld, C. L., Wong, A. K., Tadych, A., et al. (2016). Genome-wide prediction and functional characterization of the genetic basis of autism spectrum disorder. *Nature Neuroscience, 19*, 1454–1462.

Krueger, R. F., & Markon, K. E. (2006). Reinterpreting comorbidity: A model-based approach to understanding and classifying psychopathology. *Annual Review of Clinical Psychology, 2*, 111–133.

Krueger, R. F., & Markon, K. E. (2014). The role of the DSM-5 personality trait model in moving toward a quantitative and empirically based approach to classifying personality and psychopathology. *Annual Review of Clinical Psychology, 10*, 477–501.

Krueger, R. F., & Tackett, J. L. (2006). *Personality and psychopathology*. New York: Guilford.

Kruesi, M., & Schowalter, J. (2006). Conduct disorder and evolutionary biology. In P. S. Jensen, P. Knapp, & D. A. Mrazek (Eds.), *Toward a new diagnostic system for child psychopathology: Moving beyond the DSM* (pp. 111–130). New York: Guilford.

Kruger, D. J., Reischl, T., & Zimmerman, M. A. (2008). Time perspective as a mechanism for functional developmental adaptation. *Journal of Social, Evolutionary, and Cultural Psychology, 2*, 1–22.

Kruger, D. J., Wang, X. T., & Wilke, A. (2007). Towards the development of an evolutionarily valid domain-specific risk-taking scale. *Evolutionary Psychology, 5*, 555–568.

Krüger, T. H., Haake, P., Chereath, D., Knapp, W., Janssen, O. E., Exton, M. S., et al. (2003). Specificity of the neuroendocrine response to orgasm during sexual arousal in men. *Journal of Endocrinology, 177*, 57–64.

Krupić, D., Gračanin, A., & Corr, P. J. (2016). The evolution of the Behavioural Approach System (BAS): Cooperative and competitive resource acquisition strategies. *Personality and Individual Differences, 94*, 223–227.

Krupp, D. B., Sewall, L. A., Lalumière, M. L., Sheriff, C., & Harris, G. T. (2012). Nepotistic patterns of violent psychopathy: Evidence for adaptation? *Frontiers in Psychology, 3*, 305.

Krupp, D. B., Sewall, L. A., Lalumière, M. L., Sheriff, C., & Harris, G. T. (2013). Psychopathy, adaptation, and disorder. *Frontiers in Psychology, 4*, 139.

Krystal, J. H., Sanacora, G., & Duman, R. S. (2013). Rapid-acting glutamatergic antidepressants: The path to ketamine and beyond. *Biological Psychiatry, 73*, 1133–1141.

Kühn, S., & Gallinat, J. (2013). Gray matter correlates of posttraumatic stress disorder: A quantitative meta-analysis. *Biological Psychiatry, 73*, 70–74.

Kuijper, B., Pen, I., & Weissing, F. J. (2012). A guide to sexual selection theory. *Annual Review of Ecology, Evolution and Systematics, 43*, 287–311.

Kung, K. T., Constantinescu, M., Browne, W. V., Noorderhaven, R. M., & Hines, M. (2016). No relationship between early postnatal testosterone concentrations and autistic traits in 18 to 30-month-old children. *Molecular Autism, 7*, 15.

Kung, K. T., Spencer, D., Pasterski, V., Neufeld, S., Glover, V., O'Connor, T. G., et al. (2016). No relationship between prenatal androgen exposure and autistic traits: Convergent evidence from studies of children with congenital adrenal hyperplasia and of amniotic testosterone concentrations in typically developing children. *Journal of Child Psychology and Psychiatry*, *57*, 1455–1462.

Kuntsi, J., Eley, T. C., Taylor, A., Hughes, C., Asherson, P., Caspi, A., & Moffitt, T. E. (2004). Co-occurrence of ADHD and low IQ has genetic origins. *American Journal of Medical Genetics Part B: Neuropsychiatric Genetics*, *124*, 41–47.

Kuntsi, J., Eley, T. C., Taylor, A., Hughes, C., Asherson, P., Caspi, A., et al. (2004). Co-occurrence of ADHD and low IQ has genetic origins. *American Journal of Medical Genetics B*, *124*, 41–47.

Kupferberg, A., Bicks, L., & Hasler, G. (2016). Social functioning in major depressive disorder. *Neuroscience and Biobehavioral Reviews*, *69*, 313–332.

Kurzban, R., & Houser, D. (2005). Experiments investigating cooperative types in humans: A complement to evolutionary theory and simulations. *Proceedings of the National Academy of Sciences USA*, *102*, 1803–1807.

Kuzawa, C. W., & Bragg, J. M. (2012). Plasticity in human life history strategy. *Current Anthropology*, *53*, S369–S382.

Kuzawa, C. W., Chugani, H. T., Grossman, L. I., Lipovich, L., Muzik, O., Hof, P. R., et al. (2014). Metabolic costs and evolutionary implications of human brain development. *Proceedings of the national Academy of Sciences USA*, *111*, 13010–13015.

Kuznar, L. A. (2002). Evolutionary applications of risk sensitivity models to socially stratified species: Comparison of sigmoid, concave, and linear functions. *Evolution and Human Behavior*, *23*, 265–280.

Kwapil, T. R., Barrantes-Vidal, N., Armistead, M. S., Hope, G. A., Brown, L. H., Silvia, P. J., et al. (2011). The expression of bipolar spectrum psychopathology in daily life. *Journal of Affective Disorders*, *130*, 166–170.

Kyaga, S. (2015). *Creativity and mental illness: The mad genius in question*. New York: Palgrave.

Kyaga, S., Landén, M., Boman, M., Hultman, C. M., Långström, N., & Lichtenstein, P. (2013). Mental illness, suicide and creativity: 40-year prospective total population study. *Journal of Psychiatric Research*, *47*, 83–90.

Kyaga, S., Lichtenstein, P., Boman, M., Hultman, C., Långström, N., & Landén, M. (2011). Creativity and mental disorder: Family study of 300,000 people with severe mental disorder. *British Journal of Psychiatry*, *199*, 373–379.

Kyaga, S., Lichtenstein, P., Boman, M., & Landén, M. (2015). Bipolar disorder and leadership: A total population study. *Acta Psychiatrica Scandinavica*, *131*, 111–119.

Labad, J., Menchon, J. M., Alonso, P., Segalas, C., Jimenez, S., Jaurrieta, N., et al. (2008). Gender differences in obsessive-compulsive symptom dimensions. *Depression and Anxiety*, *25*, 832–838.

La Cerra, M. M. (1994). *Evolved mate preferences in women: Psychological adaptations for assessing a man's willingness to invest inn offspring* (Unpublished doctoral dissertation). University of California, Santa Barbara.

Laceulle, O. M., O'Donnell, K., Glover, V., O'Connor, T. G., Ormel, J., Van Aken, M. A., et al. (2014). Stressful events and psychological difficulties: Testing alternative candidates for sensitivity. *European Child & Adolescent Psychiatry*, *23*, 103–113.

Laceulle, O. M., Vollebergh, W. A., & Ormel, J. (2015). The structure of psychopathology in adolescence: Replication of a general psychopathology factor in the TRAILS study. *Clinical Psychological Science*, *3*, 850–860.

Lahey, B. B., Lee, S. S., Sibley, M. H., Applegate, B., Molina, B. S., & Pelham, W. E. (2016). Predictors of adolescent outcomes among 4–6-year-old children with attention-deficit/hyperactivity disorder. *Journal of Abnormal Psychology, 125*, 168–181.

Lahey, B. B., Loeber, R., Burke, J. D., & Applegate, B. (2005). Predicting future antisocial personality disorder in males from a clinical assessment in childhood. *Journal of Consulting and Clinical Psychology, 73*, 389.

Lahey, B. B., Rathouz, P. J., Keenan, K., Stepp, S. D., Loeber, R., & Hipwell, A. E. (2015). Criterion validity of the general factor of psychopathology in a prospective study of girls. *Journal of Child Psychology and Psychiatry, 56*, 415–422.

Lahey, B. B., Van Hulle, C. A., Singh, A. L., Waldman, I. D., & Rathouz, P. J. (2011). Higher-order genetic and environmental structure of prevalent forms of child and adolescent psychopathology. *Archives of General Psychiatry, 68*, 181–189.

Lahey, B. B., & Waldman, I. D. (2003). A developmental propensity model of the origins of conduct problems during childhood and adolescence. In B. B. Lahey, T. E. Moffitt, & A. Caspi (Eds.), *Causes of conduct disorder and juvenile delinquency* (pp. 76–117). New York: Guilford.

Lahey, B. B., Zald, D. H., Hakes, J. K., Krueger, R. F., & Rathouz, P. J. (2014). Patterns of heterotypic continuity associated with the cross-sectional correlational structure of prevalent mental disorders in adults. *JAMA Psychiatry, 71*, 989–996.

Laing, S. V., Fernyhough, C., Turner, M., & Freeston, M. H. (2009). Fear, worry, and ritualistic behaviour in childhood: Developmental trends and interrelations. *Infant and Child Development, 18*, 351–366.

Lalumière, M. L., Harris, G. T., & Rice, M. E. (2001). Psychopathy and developmental instability. *Evolution and Human Behavior, 22*, 75–92.

Lam, D. D., Garfield, A. S., Marston, O. J., Shaw, J., & Heisler, L. K. (2010). Brain serotonin system in the coordination of food intake and body weight. *Pharmacology Biochemistry and Behavior, 97*, 84–91.

Lamers, F., Beekman, A. T. F., Van Hemert, A. M., Schoevers, R. A., & Penninx, B. W. J. H. (2016). Six-year longitudinal course and outcomes of subtypes of depression. *British Journal of Psychiatry, 208*, 62–68.

Lamers, F., Rhebergen, D., Merikangas, K. R., De Jonge, P., Beekman, A. T. F., & Penninx, B. W. J. H. (2012). Stability and transitions of depressive subtypes over a 2-year follow-up. *Psychological Medicine, 42*, 2083–2093.

Lamers, F., Vogelzangs, N., Merikangas, K. R., De Jonge, P., Beekman, A. T. F., & Penninx, B. W. J. H. (2013). Evidence for a differential role of HPA-axis function, inflammation and metabolic syndrome in melancholic versus atypical depression. *Molecular Psychiatry, 18*, 692–699.

Lamport, D., & Turner, L. A. (2014). Romantic attachment, empathy, and the broader autism phenotype among college students. *The Journal of Genetic Psychology, 175*, 202–213.

Lancaster, L. T., & Sinervo, B. (2011). Epistatic social and endocrine networks and the evolution of life history trade-offs and plasticity. In T. Flatt & F. Heyland (Eds.), *Mechanisms of life history evolution. The genetics and physiology of life history traits and trade-offs* (pp. 329–348). New York: Oxford University Press.

Lande, R., Engen, S., & Sæther, B. E. (2009). An evolutionary maximum principle for density-dependent population dynamics in a fluctuating environment. *Philosophical Transactions of the Royal Society B, 364*, 1511–1518.

Láng, A. (2015). Borderline personality organization predicts Machiavellian interpersonal tactics. *Personality and Individual Differences, 80*, 28–31.

Lange, A., & Dukas, R. (2009). Bayesian approximations and extensions: Optimal decisions for small brains and possibly big ones too. *Journal of Theoretical Biology, 259*, 503–516.

Langer, J. K., & Rodebaugh, T. L. (2014). Comorbidity of social anxiety disorder and depression. In C. S. Richards & M. W. O'Hara (Eds.), *The Oxford handbook of depression and comorbidity* (pp. 111–128). New York: Oxford University Press.

Larson, F. V., Lai, M. C., Wagner, A. P., Baron-Cohen, S., Holland, A. J., & MRC AIMS Consortium. (2015). Testing the 'Extreme Female Brain' theory of psychosis in adults with autism spectrum disorder with or without co-morbid psychosis. *PloS ONE, 10*, e0128102.

Larson, F. V., Wagner, A. P., Jones, P. B., Tantam, D., Lai, M. C., Baron-Cohen, S., et al. (2017). Psychosis in autism: Comparison of the features of both conditions in a dually affected cohort. *British Journal of Psychiatry, 210*, 269–275.

Larsson, H., Rydén, E., Boman, M., Långström, N., Lichtenstein, P., & Landén, M. (2013). Risk of bipolar disorder and schizophrenia in relatives of people with attention-deficit hyperactivity disorder. *British Journal of Psychiatry, 203*, 103–106.

Larsson, H., Sariaslan, A., Långström, N., D'Onofrio, B., & Lichtenstein, P. (2014). Family income in early childhood and subsequent attention deficit/hyperactivity disorder: A quasi-experimental study. *Journal of Child Psychology and Psychiatry, 55*, 428–435.

Laulik, S., Chou, S., Browne, K. D., & Allam, J. (2013). The link between personality disorder and parenting behaviors: A systematic review. *Aggression and Violent Behavior, 18*, 644–655.

Larmuseau, M. H. D., Matthijs, K., & Wenseleers, T. (2016). Cuckolded fathers rare in human populations. *Trends in Ecology and Evolution, 31*, 327–329.

Lawson, D. W., Alvergne, A., & Gibson, M. A. (2012). The life-history trade-off between fertility and child survival. *Proceedings of the Royal Society of London B, 279*, 4755–4764.

Lawson, D. W., & Borgerhoff Mulder, M. (2016). The offspring quantity–quality trade-off and human fertility variation. *Philosophical Transactions of the Royal Society B, 371*, 20150145.

Lawson, E. A., Marengi, D. A., DeSanti, R. L., Holmes, T. M., Schoenfeld, D. A., & Tolley, C. J. (2015). Oxytocin decreases caloric intake in men. *Obesity, 23*, 950–956.

Lawson, R. P., Rees, G., & Friston, K. J. (2014). An aberrant precision account of autism. *Frontiers in Human Neuroscience, 8*, 302.

Leahy, R. L. (2002). Decision making and personality disorders. *Journal of Cognitive Psychotherapy, 16*, 209–225.

Lecrubier, Y., Wittchen, H. U., Faravelli, C., Bobes, J., Patel, A., & Knapp, M. (2000). A European perspective on social anxiety disorder. *European Psychiatry, 15*, 5–16.

Ledley, D. R., Erwin, B. A., Morrison, A. S., & Heimberg, R. G. (2013). Social anxiety disorder. In W. E. Craighead, D. J. Miklowitz, & L. W. Craighead (Eds.), *Psychopathology: History, diagnosis, and empirical foundations* (2nd ed., pp. 147–192). New York: Wiley.

Ledón-Rettig, C. C., Richards, C. L., & Martin, L. B. (2013). Epigenetics for behavioral ecologists. *Behavioral Ecology, 24*, 311–324.

Lee, A. J., & Zietsch, B. P. (2011). Experimental evidence that women's mate preferences are directly influenced by cues of pathogen prevalence and resource scarcity. *Biology Letters, 7*, 892–895.

Lee, B. K., & McGrath, J. J. (2015). Advancing parental age and autism: Multifactorial pathways. *Trends in Molecular Medicine, 21*, 118–125.

Lee, H. J., Kim, Z. S., & Kwon, S. M. (2005). Thought disorder in patients with obsessive-compulsive disorder. *Journal of Clinical Psychology, 61*, 401–413.

Lee, H. J., & Kwon, S. M. (2003). Two different types of obsession: Autogenous obsessions and reactive obsessions. *Behaviour Research & Therapy, 41*, 11–29.

Lee, H. J., Lee, S. H., Kim, H. S., Kwon, S. M., & Telch, M. J. (2005). A comparison of autogenous/reactive obsessions and worry in a nonclinical population: A test of the continuum hypothesis. *Behaviour Research & Therapy, 43*, 999–1010.

Lee, H. J., & Telch, M. J. (2005). Autogenous/reactive obsessions and their relationship with OCD symptoms and schizotypal personality features. *Journal of Anxiety Disorders, 19*, 793–805.

Lee, H. J., & Telch, M. J. (2010). Differences in latent inhibition as a function of the autogenous–reactive OCD subtype. *Behaviour Research & Therapy, 48*, 571–579.

Lee, H. J., Yost, B. P., & Telch, M. J. (2009). Differential performance on the go/no-go task as a function of the autogenous-reactive taxonomy of obsessions: Findings from a non-treatment seeking sample. *Behaviour Research & Therapy, 47*, 294–300.

Lee, J. J. (2009). The role of a general cognitive factor in the evolution of human intelligence. In S. M. Platek & T. K. Shackelford (Eds.), *Foundations in evolutionary cognitive neuroscience* (pp. 57–96). Cambridge, MA: Cambridge University Press.

Lee, K., & Ashton, M. C. (2012). *The H factor of personality*. Waterloo, CA: Wilfrid Laurier University Press.

Lee, K., Ashton, M. C., Wiltshire, J., Bourdage, J. S., Visser, B. A., & Gallucci, A. (2013). Sex, power, and money: Prediction from the Dark Triad and Honesty–Humility. *European Journal of Personality, 27*, 169–184.

Lee, S. H., Ripke, S., Neale, B. M., Faraone, S. V., Purcell, S. M., Perlis, R. H., et al. (2013). Genetic relationship between five psychiatric disorders estimated from genome-wide SNPs. *Nature Genetics, 45*, 984–994.

Lee, S. W., Shimojo, S., & O'Doherty, J. P. (2014). Neural computations underlying arbitration between model-based and model-free learning. *Neuron, 81*, 687–699.

Le Galliard, J. F., Paquet, M., Cisel, M., & Montes-Poloni, L. (2013). Personality and the pace-of-life syndrome: Variation and selection on exploration, metabolism and locomotor performances. *Functional Ecology, 27*, 136–144.

Lehti, V., Chudal, R., Suominen, A., Gissler, M., & Sourander, A. (2016). Association between immigrant background and ADHD: A nationwide population-based case-control study. *Journal of Child Psychology and Psychiatryi, 57*, 967–975.

Lener, M. S., Niciu, M. J., Ballard, E. D., Park, M., Park, L. T., Nugent, A. C., et al. (2016). Glutamate and gamma-aminobutyric acid systems in the pathophysiology of major depression and antidepressant response to ketamine. *Biological Psychiatry, 81*, 886–897.

Lenzenweger, M. F. (2010). *Schizotypy and schizophrenia: The view from experimental psychopathology*. New York: Guilford.

Lenzenweger, M. F., Lane, M. C., Loranger, A. W., & Kessler, R. C. (2007). DSM-IV personality disorders in the National Comorbidity Survey Replication. *Biological Psychiatry, 62*, 553–564.

Leonard, H., Glasson, E., Nassar, N., Whitehouse, A., Bebbington, A., Bourke, J., et al. (2011). Autism and intellectual disability are differentially related to sociodemographic background at birth. *PLoS ONE, 6*, e17875.

Lerner, R. M. (2015). Eliminating genetic reductionism from developmental science. *Research in Human Development, 12*, 178–188.

LeVay, S. (2017). *Gay, straight and the reason why: The science of sexual orientation* (2nd ed.). New York: Oxford University Press.

Levy, T., Bloch, Y., Bar-Maisels, M., Gat-Yablonski, G., Djalovski, A., Borodkin, K., et al. (2015). Salivary oxytocin in adolescents with conduct problems and callous-unemotional traits. *European Child & Adolescent Psychiatry, 24*, 1543–1551.

Lewandowski, K. E., Sperry, S. H., Cohen, B. M., & Öngür, D. (2014). Cognitive variability in psychotic disorders: A cross-diagnostic cluster analysis. *Psychological Medicine, 44*, 3239–3248.

Leyfer, O. T., Folstein, S. E., Bacalman, S., Davis, N. O., Dinh, E., Morgan, J., et al. (2006). Comorbid psychiatric disorders in children with autism: Interview development and rates of disorders. *Journal of Autism and Developmental Disorders, 36*, 849–861.

Li, N. P., Smith, A. R., Griskevicius, V., Cason, M. J., & Bryan, A. (2010). Intrasexual competition and eating restriction in heterosexual and homosexual individuals. *Evolution and Human Behavior, 31*, 365–372.

Li, N. P., Smith, A. R., Yong, J. C., & Brown, T. A. (2014). Intrasexual competition and other theories of eating restriction. In V. A. Weekes-Shackelford & T. K. Shackelford (Eds.), *Evolutionary perspectives on human sexual psychology and behavior* (pp. 323–346). New York: Springer.

Li, X., McGue, M., & Gottesman, I. I. (2012). Two sources of genetic liability to depression: Interpreting the relationship between stress sensitivity and depression under a multifactorial polygenic model. *Behavior Genetics, 42*, 268–277.

Li, Y., Aggen, S., Shi, S., Gao, J., Tao, M., Zhang, K., et al. (2014). Subtypes of major depression: Latent class analysis in depressed Han Chinese women. *Psychological Medicine, 44*, 3275–3288.

Lieb, K., Rexhausen, J. E., Kahl, K. G., Schweiger, U., Philipsen, A., Hellhammer, D. H., et al. (2004). Increased diurnal salivary cortisol in women with borderline personality disorder. *Journal of Psychiatric Research, 38*, 559–565.

Lieberman, D., Tooby, J., & Cosmides, L. (2007). The architecture of human kin detection. *Nature, 445*, 727–731.

Lienard, P. (2011). Life stages and risk-avoidance: Status-and context-sensitivity in precaution systems. *Neuroscience & Biobehavioral Reviews, 35*, 1067–1074.

Lilienfeld, S. O., Francis Smith, S., & Watts, A. L. (2013). Issues in diagnosis: Conceptual issues and controversies. In W. E. Craighead, D. J. Miklowitz, & L. W. Craighead (Eds.), *Psychopathology: History, diagnosis, and empirical foundations* (2nd ed., pp. 1–35). New York: Wiley.

Lilienfeld, S. O., Latzman, R. D., Watts, A. L., Smith, S. F., & Dutton, K. (2014). Correlates of psychopathic personality traits in everyday life: Results from a large community survey. *Frontiers in Psychology, 5*, 740.

Lilienfeld, S. O., & Marino, L. (1999). Essentialism revisited: Evolutionary theory and the concept of mental disorder. *Journal of Abnormal Psychology, 108*, 400–411.

Lilienfeld, S. O., Waldman, I. D., Landfield, K., Watts, A. L., Rubenzer, S., & Faschingbauer, T. R. (2012). Fearless dominance and the US presidency: Implications of psychopathic personality traits for successful and unsuccessful political leadership. *Journal of Personality and Social Psychology, 103*, 489–505.

Lilienfeld, S. O., Watts, A. L., & Francis Smith, S. F. (2015). Successful psychopathy: A scientific status report. *Current Directions in Psychological Science, 24*, 298–303.

Lilienfeld, S. O., Watts, A. L., Francis Smith, S., Berg, J. M., & Latzman, R. D. (2015). Psychopathy deconstructed and reconstructed: Identifying and assembling the personality building blocks of Cleckley's chimera. *Journal of Personality, 83*, 593–610.

Lindberg, L., & Hjern, A. (2003). Risk factors for anorexia nervosa: A national cohort study. *International Journal of Eating Disorders, 34*, 397–408.

Lindová, J., Příplatová, L., & Flegr, J. (2012). Higher extraversion and lower conscientiousness in humans infected with *Toxoplasma*. *European Journal of Personality, 26*, 285–291.

Lindquist, K. A., Wager, T. D., Kober, H., Bliss-Moreau, E., & Barrett, L. F. (2012). The brain basis of emotion: A meta-analytic review. *Behavioral and Brain Sciences, 35*, 121–143.

Links, P. S., Ansari, J. Y., Fazalullasha, F., & Shah, R. (2012). The Relationship of personality disorders and Axis I clinical disorders. In T. A. Widiger (Ed.), *The Oxford handbook of personality disorders* (237–259). New York: Oxford University Press.

Liotti, G. (2002). The inner schema of borderline states and its correction during psychotherapy: A cognitive-evolutionary approach. *Journal of Cognitive Psychotherapy, 16*, 349–366.

Liotti, G., & Gilbert, P. (2011). Mentalizing, motivation, and social mentalities: Theoretical considerations and implications for psychotherapy. *Psychology and Psychotherapy: Theory, Research and Practice, 84*, 9–25.

Liotti, G., & Gumley, A. (2008). An attachment perspective on schizophrenia: The role of disorganized attachment, dissociation and mentalization. In A. Moskowitz, I. Schäfer, & M. J. Dorahy (Eds.), *Psychosis, trauma and dissociation: Emerging perspectives on severe psychopathology* (pp. 117–133). New York: Wiley.

Liotti, G., Pasquini, P., & Cirrincione, R. (2000). Predictive factors for borderline personality disorder: Patients' early traumatic experiences and losses suffered by the attachment figure. *Acta Psychiatrica Scandinavica, 102*, 282–289.

Lippa, R. A. (2005). Sexual orientation and personality. *Annual Review of Sex Research, 16*, 119–153.

Lippa, R. A. (2008). Sex differences and sexual orientation differences in personality: Findings from the BBC Internet survey. *Archives of Sexual Behavior, 37*, 173–187.

Lippa, R. A. (2009). Sex differences in sex drive, sociosexuality, and height across 53 nations: Testing evolutionary and social structural theories. *Archives of Sexual Behavior, 38*, 631–651.

Lippa, R. A. (2010). Gender differences in personality and interests: When, where, and why? *Social and Personality Psychology Compass, 4*, 1098–1110.

Lissek, S., & van Meurs, B. (2015). Learning models of PTSD: Theoretical accounts and psychobiological evidence. *International Journal of Psychophysiology, 98*, 594–605.

Little, A. C., Connely, J., Feinberg, D. R., Jones, B. C., & Roberts, S. C. (2011). Human preference for masculinity differs according to context in faces, bodies, voices, and smell. *Behavioral Ecology, 22*, 862–868.

Liu, R. T. (2016). Taxometric evidence of a dimensional latent structure for depression in an epidemiological sample of children and adolescents. *Psychological Medicine, 46*, 1265–1275.

Lo, M. T., Hinds, D. A., Tung, J. Y., Franz, C., Fan, C. C., Wang, Y., et al. (2017). Genome-wide analyses for personality traits identify six genomic loci and show correlations with psychiatric disorders. *Nature Genetics, 49*, 152–156.

LoBue, V., & Rakison, D. H. (2013). What we fear most: Developmental advantage for threat-relevant stimuli. *Developmental Review, 33*, 285–303.

Lock, J., & Kirz, N. (2013). Anorexia nervosa. In W. E. Craighead, D. J. Miklowitz, & L. W. Craighead (Eds.), *Psychopathology: History, diagnosis, and empirical foundations* (2nd ed., pp. 482–510). New York: Wiley.

Locke, J. L., & Bogin, B. (2006). Language and life history: A new perspective on the development and evolution of human language. *Behavioral and Brain Sciences, 29*, 259–280.

Loehlin, J. C., Bartels, M., Boomsma, D. I., Bratko, D., Martin, N. G., Nichols, R. C., et al. (2015). Is there a genetic correlation between general factors of intelligence and personality? *Twin Research and Human Genetics, 18*, 234–242.

Loewenstein, G. (1994) The psychology of curiosity: A review and reinterpretation. *Psychological Bulletin, 116*, 75–98

Lommen, M. J., Engelhard, I. M., & van den Hout, M. A. (2010). Neuroticism and avoidance of ambiguous stimuli: Better safe than sorry? *Personality and Individual Differences, 49*(8), 1001–1006.

Lopez, C., Stahl, D., & Tchanturia, K. (2010). Estimated intelligence quotient in anorexia nervosa: A systematic review and meta-analysis of the literature. *Annals of General Psychiatry, 9*, 40.

López Herráez, D., Bauchet, M., Tang, K., Theunert, C., Pugach, I., Li, J., et al. (2009). Genetic variation and recent positive selection in worldwide human populations: Evidence from nearly 1 million SNPs. *PLoS ONE, 4*, e7888.

López-Solà, C., Fontenelle, L. F., Alonso, P., Cuadras, D., Foley, D. L., Pantelis, C., et al. (2014). Prevalence and heritability of obsessive-compulsive spectrum and anxiety disorder symptoms: A survey of the Australian Twin Registry. *American Journal of Medical Genetics Part B: Neuropsychiatric Genetics, 165*, 314–325.

Lorant, V., Deliège, D., Eaton, W., Robert, A., Philippot, P., & Ansseau, M. (2003). Socioeconomic inequalities in depression: A meta-analysis. *American Journal of Epidemiology, 157*, 98–112.

Lorber, M. F. (2004). Psychophysiology of aggression, psychopathy, and conduct problems: A meta-analysis. *Psychological Bulletin, 130*, 531–552.

Lorber, M. F., Del Vecchio, T., & Slep, A. M. S. (2015). The emergence and evolution of infant externalizing behavior. *Development and Psychopathology, 27*, 663–680.

Lovallo, W. R., & Sollers, J. J. (2007). Autonomic nervous system. In J. Fink (Ed.), *Encyclopedia of stress* (2nd ed., pp. 282–289). San Diego, CA: Academic Press.

Lovick, T. A. (2014). Sex determinants of experimental panic attacks. *Neuroscience & Biobehavioral Reviews, 46*, 465–471.

Lu, F. M., Zhou, J. S., Zhang, J., Xiang, Y. T., Zhang, J., Liu, Q., et al. (2015). Functional connectivity estimated from resting-state fMRI reveals selective alterations in male adolescents with pure conduct disorder. *PLoS ONE, 10*, e0145668.

Lu, H. J., & Chang, L. (2012). Automatic attention towards face or body as a function of mating motivation. *Evolutionary Psychology, 10*, 120–135.

Lu, Q., & Bourrat, P. (2017). The evolutionary gene and the extended evolutionary synthesis. *British Journal for the Philosophy of Science*. doi:10.1093/bjps/axw035

Lucas, R. E., Deiner, E., Grob, A., Suh, E. M., & Shao, L., 2000. Cross-cultural evidence for the fundamental features of extraversion. *Journal of Personality and Social Psychology, 79*, 452–468.

Lukaszewski, A. W. (2015). Parental support during childhood predicts life history-related personality variation and social status in young adults. *Evolutionary Psychological Science, 1*, 131–140.

Lukaszewski, A. W., Gurven, M., von Rueden, C. R., & Schmitt, D. P. (2017). What explains personality covariation? A test of the socioecological complexity hypothesis. *Social Psychological and Personality Science, 18*, 943–952.

Lukaszewski, A. W., Larson, C. M., Gildersleeve, K. A., Roney, J. R., & Haselton, M. G. (2014). Condition-dependent calibration of men's uncommitted mating orientation: evidence from multiple samples. *Evolution and Human Behavior, 35*, 319–326.

Lukaszewski, A. W., & Roney, J. R. (2010). Kind toward whom? Mate preferences for personality traits are target specific. *Evolution and Human Behavior, 31*, 29–38.

Lukaszewski, A. W., & Roney, J. R. (2011). The origins of extraversion: Joint effects of facultative calibration and genetic polymorphism. *Personality and Social Psychology Bulletin, 37*, 409–421.

Lukaszewski, A. W., & von Rueden, C. R. (2015). The extraversion continuum in evolutionary perspective: A review of recent theory and evidence. *Personality and Individual Differences, 77*, 186–192.

Luman, M., Oosterlaan, J., & Sergeant, J. A. (2005). The impact of reinforcement contingencies on AD/HD: A review and theoretical appraisal. *Clinical Psychology Review, 25*, 183–213.

Luo, X., Donnellan, M. B., Burt, S. A., & Klump, K. L. (2016). The dimensional nature of eating pathology: Evidence from a direct comparison of categorical, dimensional, and hybrid models. *Journal of Abnormal Psychology, 125*, 715–726.

Luttbeg, B., & Sih, A. (2010). Risk, resources and state-dependent adaptive behavioural syndromes. *Philosophical Transactions of the Royal Society of London B, 365*, 3977–3990.

Lyon, B. E., & Montgomerie, R. (2012). Sexual selection is a form of social selection. *Philosophical Transactions of the Royal Society of London B, 367*, 2266–2273.

Lyons, M., Caldwell, T., & Shultz, S. (2010). Mind-reading and manipulation: Is Machiavellianism related to theory of mind? *Journal of Evolutionary Psychology, 8*, 261–274.

Lyons-Ruth, K., & Jacobvitz, D. (2008). Attachment disorganization. In J. Cassidy & P. R. Shaver (Eds.), *Handbook of attachment* (2nd ed., pp. 666–697). New York: Guilford.

MacArthur, R. H., & Wilson, E. O. (1967). *The theory of island biogeography*. Princeton, NJ: Princeton University Press.

MacCabe, J. H., Koupil, I., & Leon, D. A. (2009). Lifetime reproductive output over two generations in patients with psychosis and their unaffected siblings: The Uppsala

1915–1929 Birth Cohort Multigenerational Study. *Psychological Medicine, 39*, 1667–1676.

MacCabe, J. H., Lambe, M. P., Cnattingius, S., Sham, P. C., David, A. S., Reichenberg, A., et al. (2010). Excellent school performance at age 16 and risk of adult bipolar disorder: National cohort study. *British Journal of Psychiatry, 196*, 109–115.

MacDonald, K. (1995*a*). The Establishment and maintenance of socially imposed monogamy in Western Europe. *Politics and the Life Sciences, 14*, 3–23.

MacDonald, K. (1997). Life history theory and human reproductive behavior: Environmental/contextual influences and heritable variation. *Human Nature, 8*, 327–359.

MacDonald, K. B. (1995*b*). Evolution, the 5-factor model, and levels of personality. *Journal of Personality, 63*, 525–567.

Machin, A. J., & Dunbar, R. I. (2011). The brain opioid theory of social attachment: A review of the evidence. *Behaviour, 148*, 985–1025.

Mack, T. D., Hackney, A. A., & Pyle, M. (2011). The relationship between psychopathic traits and attachment behavior in a non-clinical population. *Personality and Individual Differences, 51*, 584–588.

MacKinnon, D. F., & Pies, R. (2006). Affective instability as rapid cycling: Theoretical and clinical implications for borderline personality and bipolar spectrum disorders. *Bipolar Disorders, 8*, 1–14.

MacMillan, J., & Kofoed, L. (1984). Sociobiology and antisocial personality disorder. *Journal of Nervous and Mental Disorders, 172*, 1177–1180.

Madigan, S., Atkinson, L., Laurin, K., & Benoit, D. (2013). Attachment and internalizing behavior in early childhood: A meta-analysis. *Developmental Psychology, 49*, 672–689.

Madsen, E. A., Tunney, R. J., Fieldman, G., Plotkin, H. C., Dunbar, R. I. M., Richardson, J.-M., et al. (2007). Kinship and altruism: A cross-cultural experimental study. *British Journal of Psychology, 98*, 339–359.

Magee, W. J. (1999). Effects of negative life experiences on phobia onset. *Social Psychiatry & Psychiatric Epidemiology, 34*, 343–351.

Mahan, A. L., & Ressler, K. J. (2012). Fear conditioning, synaptic plasticity and the amygdala: Implications for posttraumatic stress disorder. *Trends in Neurosciences, 35*, 24–35.

Mahmood, T., & Silverstone, T. (2001). Serotonin and bipolar disorder. *Journal of Affective Disorders, 66*, 1–11.

Maia, T. V., & Frank, M. J. (2017). An integrative perspective on the role of dopamine in schizophrenia. *Biological Psychiatry, 81*, 52–66.

Major, J. T., Johnson, W., & Deary, I. J. (2012). Comparing models of intelligence in Project TALENT: The VPR model fits better than the CHC and extended Gf–Gc models. *Intelligence, 40*, 543–559.

Malarbi, S., Abu-Rayya, H. M., Muscara, F., & Stargatt, R. (2017). Neuropsychological functioning of childhood trauma and post-traumatic stress disorder: A meta-analysis. *Neuroscience & Biobehavioral Reviews, 72*, 68–86.

Malaspina, D., Gilman, C., & Kranz, T. M. (2015). Paternal age and mental health of offspring. *Fertility and Sterility, 103*, 1392–1396.

Mallan, K. M., Lipp, O. V., & Cochrane, B. (2013). Slithering snakes, angry men and out-group members: What and whom are we evolved to fear? *Cognition and Emotion, 27*, 1168–1180.

Man, K. K., Tong, H. H., Wong, L. Y., Chan, E. W., Simonoff, E., & Wong, I. C. (2015). Exposure to selective serotonin reuptake inhibitors during pregnancy and risk of autism spectrum disorder in children: A systematic review and meta-analysis of observational studies. *Neuroscience & Biobehavioral Reviews, 49*, 82–89.

Mancini, F., & Gangemi, A. (2006). The role of responsibility and fear of guilt in hypothesis-testing. *Journal of Behavior Therapy & Experimental Psychiatry, 37*, 333–346.

Mancini, F., Gangemi, A., Perdighe, C., & Marini, C. (2008). Not just right experience: Is it influenced by feelings of guilt? *Journal of Behavior Therapy & Experimental Psychiatry, 39*, 162–176.

Mandell, D. S., Wiggins, L. D., Carpenter, L. A., Daniels, J., DiGuiseppi, C., Durkin, M. S., et al. (2009). Racial/ethnic disparities in the identification of children with autism spectrum disorders. *American Journal of Public Health, 99*, 493–498.

Mandy, W., & Lai, M. C. (2016). Annual Research Review: The role of the environment in the developmental psychopathology of autism spectrum condition. *Journal of Child Psychology and Psychiatry, 57*, 271–292.

Maner, J. K., & Kenrick, D. T. (2010). When adaptations go awry: Functional and dysfunctional aspects of social anxiety. *Social Issues & Policy Review, 4*, 111–142.

Maner, J. K., Miller, S. L., Schmidt, N. B., & Eckel, L. A. (2010). The endocrinology of exclusion rejection elicits motivationally tuned changes in progesterone. *Psychological Science, 21*, 581–588.

Maniglio, R. (2013). Prevalence of child sexual abuse among adults and youths with bipolar disorder: a systematic review. *Clinical Psychology Review, 33*, 561–573.

Mannion, A., & Leader, G. (2014). Attention-deficit/hyperactivity disorder (AD/HD) in autism spectrum disorder. *Research in Autism Spectrum Disorders, 8*, 432–439.

Manson, J. H. (2015). Life history strategy and the HEXACO personality dimensions. *Evolutionary Psychology, 13*, 48–66.

Manson, J. H. (2017). Are extraversion and openness indicators of a slow life history strategy? *Evolution and Human Behavior, 38*, 552–560.

Manuck, S. B., & McCaffery, J. M. (2014). Gene-environment interaction. *Annual Review of Psychology, 65*, 41–70.

Manuck, S. B., Kaplan, J. R., & Lotrich, F. E. (2006). Brain serotonin and aggressive disposition in humans and nonhuman primates. In R. J. Nelson (Ed.), *Biology of aggression* (pp. 65–113). New York: Oxford.

Marangoni, C., De Chiara, L., & Faedda, G. L. (2015). Bipolar disorder and ADHD: Comorbidity and diagnostic distinctions. *Current Psychiatry Reports, 17*, 1–9.

Marazziti, D., Dell'Osso, B., Baroni, S., Mungai, F., Catena, M., Rucci, P., et al. (2006). A relationship between oxytocin and anxiety of romantic attachment. *Clinical Practice and Epidemiology in Mental Health, 2*, 28.

Marceau, K., Ruttle, P. L., Shirtcliff, E. A., Essex, M. J., & Susman, E. J. (2015). Developmental and contextual considerations for adrenal and gonadal hormone functioning during adolescence: Implications for adolescent mental health. *Developmental Psychobiology, 57*, 742–768.

Marín, J. L., Rodríguez-Franco, M. A., Chugani, V. M., Maganto, M. M., Villoria, E. D., & Bedia, R. C. (2018). Prevalence of schizophrenia spectrum disorders in average-IQ adults with autism spectrum disorders: A meta-analysis. *Journal of Autism and Developmental Disorders*, *48*, 239–250.

Marissen, M. A., Deen, M. L., & Franken, I. H. (2012). Disturbed emotion recognition in patients with narcissistic personality disorder. *Psychiatry Research*, *198*, 269–273.

Markey, P. M., & Markey, C. N. (2007). The interpersonal meaning of sexual promiscuity. *Journal of Research in Personality*, *41*, 1199–1212.

Markram, K., & Markram, H. (2010). The intense world theory—a unifying theory of the neurobiology of autism. *Frontiers in Human Neuroscience*, *4*, 224.

Marks, I. (1988). Blood-injury phobia: A review. *The American Journal of Psychiatry*, *145*, 1207–1213.

Marks, I. M. (1987). *Fears, phobias, and rituals*. New York: Oxford University Press.

Marks, I. M., & Nesse, R. M. (1994). Fear and fitness: An evolutionary analysis of anxiety disorders. *Ethology and Sociobiology*, *15*, 247–261.

Marlowe, F. (2004). Marital residence among foragers. *Current Anthropology*, *45*, 277–284.

Marlowe, F. W. (2003). The mating system of foragers in the Standard Cross-Cultural Sample. *Cross-Cultural Research*, *37*, 282–306.

Marlowe, F. W. (2005). Hunter-gatherers and human evolution. *Evolutionary Anthropology*, *14*, 54–67.

Marlowe, F. W., Berbesque, J. C., Barr, A., Barrett, C., Bolyanatz, A., Cardenas, J. C., et al. (2008). More 'altruistic' punishment in larger societies. *Proceedings of the Royal Society of London B*, *275*, 587–590.

Maron, E., & Shlik, J. (2006). Serotonin function in panic disorder: Important, but why? *Neuropsychopharmacology*, *31*, 1–11.

Marshall, C. R., Lionel, A. C., & Scherer, S. W. (2013). Copy number variation in autism spectrum disorders. In J. D. Buxbaum & P. R. Hof (Eds.), *The neuroscience of autism spectrum disorders* (pp. 145–154). Oxford: Academic Press.

Marshall, J. A. R. (2011). Group selection and kin selection: Formally equivalent approaches. *Trends in Ecology and Evolution*, *26*, 325–332.

Marshall, S. A., Evans, S. W., Eiraldi, R. B., Becker, S. P., & Power, T. J. (2014). Social and academic impairment in youth with ADHD, predominately inattentive type and sluggish cognitive tempo. *Journal of Abnormal Child Psychology*, *42*, 77–90.

Martel, M., Nikolas, M., & Nigg, J. T. (2007). Executive function in adolescents with ADHD. *Journal of the American Academy of Child & Adolescent Psychiatry*, *46*, 1437–1444.

Martel, M. M. (2013). Sexual selection and sex differences in the prevalence of childhood externalizing and adolescent internalizing disorders. *Psychological Bulletin*, *139*, 1221–1259.

Martel, M. M. (2014). Application of an integrated evolutionary psychological framework to psychopathology. *Psychological Inquiry*, *25*, 352–354.

Martel, M. M., Goth-Owens, T., Martinez-Torteya, C., & Nigg, J. T. (2010). A person-centered personality approach to heterogeneity in attention-deficit/hyperactivity disorder (ADHD). *Journal of Abnormal Psychology*, *119*, 186–196.

Martel, M. M., Roberts, B., Gremillion, M., Von Eye, A., & Nigg, J. T. (2011). External validation of bifactor model of ADHD: Explaining heterogeneity in psychiatric comorbidity, cognitive control, and personality trait profiles within DSM-IV ADHD. *Journal of Abnormal Child Psychology*, *39*, 1111–1123.

Martin, A. R., Ruiz, J. N., Nieto, J. M., Jiménez, L. E., & De Haro, A. C. (2004). Epidemiological study of the influence of family and socioeconomic status in disorders of eating behaviour. *European Journal of Clinical Nutrition*, *58*, 846–852.

Martin, J., O'Donovan, M. C., Thapar, A., Langley, K., & Williams, N. (2015). The relative contribution of common and rare genetic variants to ADHD. *Translational Psychiatry*, *5*, e506.

Martin, L. R., Friedman, H. S., & Schwartz, J. E. (2007). Personality and mortality risk across the life span: The importance of conscientiousness as a biopsychosocial attribute. *Health Psychology*, *26*, 428–436.

Martínez-Arán, A., Torrent, C., Tabares-Seisdedos, R., Salamero, M., Daban, C., Balanza-Martinez, V., et al. (2008). Neurocognitive impairment in bipolar patients with and without history of psychosis. *Journal of Clinical Psychiatry*, *69*, 233–239.

Marvin, R. S., & Britner, P. A. (2008). Normative development. In J. Cassidy & P. R. Shaver (Eds.), *Handbook of attachment* (2nd ed., pp. 269–294). New York: Guilford.

Mason, O. J., Mort, H., & Woo, J. (2015). Investigating psychotic traits in poets. *Psychological Medicine*, *45*, 667–669.

Mata, R., Josef, A. K., & Hertwig, R. (2016). Propensity for risk taking across the life span and around the globe. Psychological Science, *27*, 231–243.

Mataix-Cols, D., Boman, M., Monzani, B., Rück, C., Serlachius, E., Långström, N., et al. (2013). Population-based, multigenerational family clustering study of obsessive-compulsive disorder. *JAMA Psychiatry*, *70*, 709–717.

Mataix-Cols, D., do Rosario-Campos, M. C., & Leckman, J. F. (2005). A multidimensional model of obsessive-compulsive disorder. *American Journal of Psychiatry*, *162*, 228–238.

Mataix-Cols, D., Nakatani, E., Micali, N., & Heyman, I. (2008). Structure of obsessive-compulsive symptoms in pediatric OCD. *Journal of the American Academy of Child & Adolescent Psychiatry*, *47*, 773–778.

Matejcek, Z. (2003). Is ADHD adaptive or non-adaptive behavior? *Neuroendocrinology Letters*, *24*, 148–150.

Matheson, S. L., Shepherd, A. M., Pinchbeck, R. M., Laurens, K. R., & Carr, V. J. (2013). Childhood adversity in schizophrenia: A systematic meta-analysis. *Psychological Medicine*, *43*, 225–238.

Mathot, K. J., & Frankenhuis, W. E. (2018). Models of pace-of-life syndromes (POLS): a systematic review. *Behavioral Ecology and Sociobiology*, *72*, 41.

Mathys, C., Daunizeau, J., Friston, K. J., & Stephan, K. E. (2011). A Bayesian foundation for individual learning under uncertainty. *Frontiers in Human Neuroscience*, *5*, 39.

Matthies, S. D., & Philipsen, A. (2014). Common ground in attention deficit hyperactivity disorder (ADHD) and borderline personality disorder (BPD)–Review of recent findings. *Borderline Personality Disorder and Emotion Dysregulation*, *1*, 1–13.

Mauzay, D., Spradlin, A., & Cuttler, C. (2016). Devils, witches, and psychics: The role of thought-action fusion in the relationships between obsessive-compulsive features, religiosity, and paranormal beliefs. *Journal of Obsessive-Compulsive & Related Disorders*, *11*, 113–120.

Mayr, E. (1963). *Animal species and evolution*. Cambridge, MA: Harvard University Press.

Mazur, A., & Booth, A. (1998). Testosterone and dominance in men. *Behavioral and Brain Sciences*, *21*, 353–363.

McAdams, T., Rowe, R., Rijsdijk, F., Maughan, B., & Eley, T. C. (2011). The covariation of antisocial behavior and substance use in adolescence: A behavioral genetic perspective. *Journal of Research on Adolescence*, *22*, 100–112.

McAndrew, F. T., & Perilloux, C. (2012). Is self-sacrificial competitive altruism primarily a male activity? *Evolutionary Psychology*, *10*, 50–65.

McAuley, T., Crosbie, J., Charach, A., & Schachar, R. (2014). The persistence of cognitive deficits in remitted and unremitted ADHD: A case for the state-independence of response inhibition. *Journal of Child Psychology and Psychiatry*, *55*, 292–300.

McClure, G., Hawes, D. J., & Dadds, M. R. (2016). Borderline personality disorder and neuropsychological measures of executive function: A systematic review. *Personality and Mental Health*, *10*, 43–57.

McCormick, L. M., Brumm, M. C., Beadle, J. N., Paradiso, S., Yamada, T., & Andreasen, N. (2012). Mirror neuron function, psychosis, and empathy in schizophrenia. *Psychiatry Research: Neuroimaging*, *201*, 233–239.

McCrae, R. R., & Costa, P. T. (2003). *Personality in adulthood: A five-factor theory perspective* (2nd ed.). New York: Guilford.

McCullough, M. E., Pedersen, E. J., Schroder, J. M., Tabak, B. A., & Carver, C. S. (2013). Harsh childhood environmental characteristics predict exploitation and retaliation in humans. *Proceedings of the Royal Society of London B*, *280*, 20122104.

McDermid, J., Sareen, J., El-Gabalawy, R., Pagura, J., Spiwak, R., & Enns, M. W. (2015). Co-morbidity of bipolar disorder and borderline personality disorder: Findings from the National Epidemiologic Survey on Alcohol and Related Conditions. *Comprehensive Psychiatry*, *58*, 18–28.

McDonald, D. B. (1993). Demographic consequences of sexual selection in the long-tailed manakin. *Behavioral Ecology*, *4*, 297–309.

McElroy, S. L., Frye, M. A., Hellemann, G., Altshuler, L., Leverich, G. S., Suppes, T., et al. (2011). Prevalence and correlates of eating disorders in 875 patients with bipolar disorder. *Journal of Affective Disorders*, *128*, 191–198.

McElroy, S. L., Kotwal, R., & Keck, P. E. (2006). Comorbidity of eating disorders with bipolar disorder and treatment implications. *Bipolar Disorders*, *8*, 686–695.

McFeeters, D., Boyda, D., & Siobhan, O. (2015). Patterns of stressful life events: Distinguishing suicide ideators from suicide attempters. *Journal of Affective Disorders*, *175*, 192–198.

McGlashan, T. H., & Hoffman, R. E. (2000). Schizophrenia as a disorder of developmentally reduced synaptic connectivity. *Archives of General Psychiatry*, *57*, 637–648.

McGrath, J., Saha, S., Chant, D., & Welham, J. (2008). Schizophrenia: A concise overview of incidence, prevalence, and mortality. *Epidemiologic Reviews*, *30*, 67–76.

McGrath, J. J., Burne, T. H., Féron, F., Mackay-Sim, A., & Eyles, D. W. (2010). Developmental vitamin D deficiency and risk of schizophrenia: A 10-year update. *Schizophrenia Bulletin*, *36*, 1073–1078.

McGrath, L. M., Yu, D., Marshall, C., Davis, L. K., Thiruvahindrapuram, B., Li, B., et al. (2014). Copy number variation in obsessive-compulsive disorder and tourette syndrome: A cross-disorder study. *Journal of the American Academy of Child & Adolescent Psychiatry*, *53*, 910–919.

McGuire, M. T., & Troisi, A. (1998). *Darwinian psychiatry*. New York: Oxford University Press.

McKeague, I. W., Brown, A. S., Bao, Y., Hinkka-Yli-Salomäki, S., Huttunen, J., & Sourander, A. (2015). Autism with intellectual disability related to dynamics of head circumference growth during early infancy. *Biological Psychiatry*, *77*, 833–840.

McLaughlin, K. A., Sheridan, M. A., Tibu, F., Fox, N. A., Zeanah, C. H., & Nelson, C. A. (2015). Causal effects of the early caregiving environment on development of stress response systems in children. *Proceedings of the National Academy of Sciences USA*, *112*, 5637–5642.

McLean, C. P., & Anderson, E. R. (2009). Brave men and timid women? A review of the gender differences in fear and anxiety. *Clinical Psychology Review*, *29*, 496–505.

McLean, C. P., Asnaani, A., Litz, B. T., & Hofmann, S. G. (2011). Gender differences in anxiety disorders: Prevalence, course of illness, comorbidity and burden of illness. *Journal of Psychiatric Research*, *45*, 1027–1035.

McMahon, S. D., Grant, K. E., Compas, B. E., Thurm, A. E., & Ey, S. (2003). Stress and psychopathology in children and adolescents: Is there evidence of specificity? *Journal of Child Psychology and Psychiatry*, *44*, 107–133.

McNally, L., & Jackson, A. L. (2013). Cooperation creates selection for tactical deception. *Proceedings of the Royal Society of London B*, *280*, 20130699.

McNally, R. J. (2004). Conceptual problems with the DSM-IV criteria for posttraumatic stress disorder. In G. M. Rosen (Ed.), *Posttraumatic stress disorder: Issues and controversies* (pp. 1–14). Chichester, UK: Wiley.

McNally, R. J. (2016). Can network analysis transform psychopathology? *Behaviour Research and Therapy*, *86*, 95–104.

McNally, R. J., Robinaugh, D. J., Wu, G. W., Wang, L., Deserno, M. K., & Borsboom, D. (2015). Mental disorders as causal systems a network approach to posttraumatic stress disorder. *Clinical Psychological Science*, *3*, 836–849.

McNamara, J. M., & Houston, A. I. (2009). Integrating function and mechanism. *Trends in Ecology & Evolution*, *24*, 670–675.

McNeil, D. (2010). Evolution of terminology and constructs in social anxiety and its disorders. In S. G. Hofmann & P. M. Dibartolo (Eds.), *Social anxiety: Clinical, developmental, and social perspectives* (2nd ed., pp. 3–23). London: Elsevier.

Meacham, F., & Bergstrom, C. T. (2016). Adaptive behavior can produce maladaptive anxiety due to individual differences in experience. *Evolution, Medicine, and Public Health*, *2016*, 270–285.

Mealey, L. (1995). The sociobiology of sociopathy: An integrated evolutionary model. *Behavioral and Brain Sciences*, *18*, 523–541.

Meaney, M. J. (2010). Epigenetics and the biological definition of gene × environment interactions. *Child Development*, *81*, 41–79.

Meehl, P. E. (1962). Schizotaxia, schizotypy, schizophrenia. *American Psychologist*, *17*, 827–838.

Meier, M. H., Caspi, A., Reichenberg, A., Keefe, R. S., Fisher, H. L., Harrington, H., et al. (2014). Neuropsychological decline in schizophrenia from the premorbid to the postonset period: Evidence from a population-representative longitudinal study. *American Journal of Psychiatry*, *171*, 91–101.

Meier, S. M., Mattheisen, M., Mors, O., Mortensen, P. B., Laursen, T. M., & Penninx, B. W. (2016). Increased mortality among people with anxiety disorders: Total population study. *British Journal of Psychiatry*, *209*, 216–221.

Meier, S. M., Petersen, L., Pedersen, M. G., Arendt, M. C., Nielsen, P. R., Mattheisen, M., et al. (2014). Obsessive-compulsive disorder as a risk factor for schizophrenia: A nationwide study. *JAMA Psychiatry*, *71*, 1215–1221.

Meier, S. M., Petersen, L., Schendel, D. E., Mattheisen, M., Mortensen, P. B., & Mors, O. (2015). Obsessive-compulsive disorder and autism spectrum disorders: Longitudinal and offspring risk. *PloS ONE, 10*, e0141703.

Meij, J. J., Van Bodegom, D., Ziem, J. B., Amankwa, J., Polderman, A. M., Kirkwood, T. B. L., et al. (2009). Quality-quantity trade-off of human offspring under adverse environmental conditions. *Journal of Evolutionary Biology, 22*, 1014–1023.

Meisenberg, G., & Woodley, M. A. (2013). Global behavioral variation: A test of differential-K. *Personality and Individual Differences, 55*, 273–278.

Melca, I. A., Yücel, M., Mendlowicz, M. V., de Oliveira-Souza, R., & Fontenelle, L. F. (2015). The correlates of obsessive-compulsive, schizotypal, and borderline personality disorders in obsessive-compulsive disorder. *Journal of Anxiety Disorders, 33*, 15–24.

Mellentin, A. I., Dervisevic, A., Stenager, E., Pilegaard, M., & Kirk, U. (2015). Seeing enemies? A systematic review of anger bias in the perception of facial expressions among anger-prone and aggressive populations. *Aggression and Violent Behavior, 25*, 373–383.

Mendle, J. (2014). Why puberty matters for psychopathology. *Child Development Perspectives, 8*, 218–222.

Mendle, J., & Ferrero, J. (2012). Detrimental psychological outcomes associated with pubertal timing in adolescent boys. *Developmental Review, 32*, 49–66.

Mendle, J., Leve, L. D., Van Ryzin, M., Natsuaki, M. N., & Ge, X. (2011). Associations between early life stress, child maltreatment, and pubertal development among girls in foster care. *Journal of Research on Adolescence, 21*, 871–880.

Mendle, J., Turkheimer, E., & Emery, R. E. (2007). Detrimental psychological outcomes associated with early pubertal timing in adolescent girls. *Developmental Review, 27*, 151–171.

Menzies, R. G., & Clarke, J. C. (1995). The etiology of phobias: A nonassociative account. *Clinical Psychology Review, 15*, 23–48.

Menzies, R. G., & Harris, L. M. (1997). Mode of onset in evolutionary-relevant and evolutionary-neutral phobias: Evidence from a clinical sample. *Depression and Anxiety, 5*, 134–136.

Merikangas, A. K., Calkins, M. E., Bilker, W. B., Moore, T. M., Gur, R. C., & Gur, R. E. (2017). Parental age and offspring psychopathology in the Philadelphia Neurodevelopmental Cohort. *Journal of the American Academy of Child & Adolescent Psychiatry, 56*, 391–400.

Merikangas, K. R., Jin, R., He, J. P., Kessler, R. C., Lee, S., Sampson, N. A., et al. (2011). Prevalence and correlates of bipolar spectrum disorder in the world mental health survey initiative. *Archives of General Psychiatry, 68*, 241–251.

Merikangas, K. R., & Pato, M. (2009). Recent developments in the epidemiology of bipolar disorder in adults and children: Magnitude, correlates, and future directions. *Clinical Psychology: Science and Practice, 16*, 121–133.

Metzl, J. M. (2010). *The protest psychosis: How schizophrenia became a Black disease.* Boston, MA: Beacon Press.

Meunier, D., Lambiotte, R., & Bullmore, E. T. (2010). Modular and hierarchically modular organization of brain networks. *Frontiers in Neuroscience, 4*, 200.

Meyer, S. E., Carlson, G. A., Wiggs, E. A., Martinez, P. E., Ronsaville, D. S., Klimes-Dougan, B., et al. (2004). A prospective study of the association among impaired executive functioning, childhood attentional problems, and the development of bipolar disorder. *Development and Psychopathology, 16*, 461–476.

Meyer, T. D., & Hofmann, B. U. (2005). Assessing the dysregulation of the behavioral activation system: The hypomanic personality scale and the BIS–BAS scales. *Journal of Personality Assessment, 85*, 318–324.

Miczek, K. A., & Fish, E. W. (2006). Monoamines, GABA, glutamate, and aggression. In R. J. Nelson (Ed.), *Biology of aggression* (pp. 114–149). New York: Oxford.

Migeon, B. R. (2007). Why females are mosaics, X-chromosome inactivation, and sex differences in disease. *Gender Medicine, 4*, 97–105.

Miklowitz, D. J., & Johnson, S. L. (2013). Bipolar disorder. In W. E. Craighead, D. J. Miklowitz, & L. W. Craighead (Eds.), *Psychopathology: History, diagnosis, and empirical foundations* (2nd ed., pp. 364–402). New York: Wiley.

Miklowitz, D. J., & Johnson, S. L. (2014). Bipolar and related disorders. In D. C. Beidel, B. C. Frueh, & M. Hersen (Eds.), *Adult psychopathology and diagnosis* (7th ed.) (pp. 217–252). New York: Wiley.

Mikulincer, M., & Shaver, P. R. (2016). *Attachment in adulthood: Structure, dynamics, and change* (2nd ed.). New York: Guilford.

Mikulincer, M., Shaver, P. R., & Pereg, D. (2003). Attachment theory and affect regulation: The dynamics, development, and cognitive consequences of attachment-related strategies. *Motivation and Emotion, 27*, 77–102.

Mikulincer, M., Shaver, P. R., & Solomon, Z. (2015). An attachment perspective on traumatic and post- traumatic reactions. In M. P. Safir, H. S. Wallach, & S. Rizzo (Eds.), *Future directions in post-traumatic stress disorder: Prevention, diagnosis, and treatment* (pp. 79–96). New York: Springer Press.

Milioni, A. L. V., Chaim, T. M., Cavallet, M., de Oliveira, N. M., Annes, M., dos Santos, B., et al. (2014). High IQ may "mask" the diagnosis of ADHD by compensating for deficits in executive functions in treatment-naïve adults with ADHD. *Journal of Attention Disorders*, 1087054714554933.

Miller, A. H., & Raison, C. L. (2016). The role of inflammation in depression: From evolutionary imperative to modern treatment target. *Nature Reviews Immunology, 16*, 22–34.

Miller, B. J., Buckley, P., Seabolt, W., Mellor, A., & Kirkpatrick, B. (2011). Meta-analysis of cytokine alterations in schizophrenia: Clinical status and antipsychotic effects. *Biological Psychiatry, 70*, 663–671.

Miller, G. E., Chen, E., & Parker, K. J. (2011). Psychological stress in childhood and susceptibility to the chronic diseases of aging: Moving toward a model of behavioral and biological mechanisms. *Psychological Bulletin, 137*, 959–997.

Miller, G. E., Chen, E., & Zhou, E. S. (2007). If it goes up, must it come down? Chronic stress and the hypothalamic-pituitary-adrenocortical axis in humans. *Psychological Bulletin, 133*, 25–45.

Miller, G. F. (1999). Sexual selection for cultural displays. In R. Dunbar, C. Knight, & C. Power (Eds.), *The evolution of culture* (pp. 71–91). Edinburgh, SCT: Edinburgh University Press.

Miller, Miller, G. F. (2000). *The mating mind*. New York: Anchor Books.

Miller, G. F. (2007). Sexual selection for moral virtues. *Quarterly Review of Biology, 82*, 97–125.

Miller, G. F. (2011). Are pleiotropic mutations and Holocene selective sweeps the only evolutionary-genetic processes left for explaining heritable variation in human psychological traits? In D. M. Buss & P. H. Hawley (Eds.), *The evolution of personality and individual differences* (pp. 376–399). New York: Oxford University Press.

Miller, G. F., & Tal, I. R. (2007). Schizotypy versus openness and intelligence as predictors of creativity. *Schizophrenia Research, 93*, 317–324.

Miller, J. D., Dir, A., Gentile, B., Wilson, L., Pryor, L. R., & Campbell, W. K. (2010). Searching for a vulnerable dark triad: Comparing factor 2 psychopathy, vulnerable narcissism, and borderline personality disorder. *Journal of Personality, 78*, 1529–1564.

Miller, J. D., Gentile, B., Wilson, L., & Campbell, W. K. (2013). Grandiose and vulnerable narcissism and the DSM–5 pathological personality trait model. *Journal of Personality Assessment, 95*, 284–290.

Miller, J. M., Everett, B. A., Oquendo, M. A., Ogden, R. T., Mann, J. J., & Parsey, R. V. (2016). Positron emission tomography quantification of serotonin transporter binding in medication-free bipolar disorder. *Synapse, 70*, 24–32.

Miller, M., Bales, K. L., Taylor, S. L., Yoon, J., Hostetler, C. M., Carter, C. S., et al. (2013). Oxytocin and vasopressin in children and adolescents with autism spectrum disorders: Sex differences and associations with symptoms. *Autism Research, 6*, 91–102.

Miller, M. W., Greif, J. L., & Smith, A. A. (2003). Multidimensional Personality Questionnaire profiles of veterans with traumatic combat exposure: Externalizing and internalizing subtypes. *Psychological Assessment, 15*, 205–215.

Miller, M. W., & Resick, P. A. (2007). Internalizing and externalizing subtypes in female sexual assault survivors: Implications for the understanding of complex PTSD. *Behavior Therapy, 38*, 58–71.

Miller, T. W., Nigg, J. T., & Faraone, S. V. (2007). Axis I and II comorbidity in adults with ADHD. *Journal of Abnormal Psychology, 116*, 519–528.

Mills, J. L., Hediger, M. L., Molloy, C. A., Chrousos, G. P., Manning-Courtney, P., Yu, K. F., et al. (2007). Elevated levels of growth-related hormones in autism and autism spectrum disorder. *Clinical Endocrinology, 67*, 230–237.

Mills, N. T., Scott, J. G., Wray, N. R., Cohen-Woods, S., & Baune, B. T. (2013). Research review: The role of cytokines in depression in adolescents: A systematic review. *Journal of Child Psychology and Psychiatry, 54*, 816–835.

Mills-Koonce, W. R., Wagner, N. J., Willoughby, M. T., Stifter, C., Blair, C., & Granger, D. A. (2015). Greater fear reactivity and psychophysiological hyperactivity among infants with later conduct problems and callous-unemotional traits. *Journal of Child Psychology and Psychiatry, 56*, 147–154.

Miloyan, B., Bulley, A., Bandeen-Roche, K., Eaton, W. W., & Gonçalves-Bradley, D. C. (2016). Anxiety disorders and all-cause mortality: Systematic review and meta-analysis. *Social Psychiatry and Psychiatric Epidemiology, 51*, 1467–1475.

Miloyan, B., Bulley, A., Pachana, N. A., & Byrne, G. J. (2014). Social Phobia symptoms across the adult lifespan. *Journal of Affective Disorders, 168*, 86–90.

Mincic, A. M. (2015). Neuroanatomical correlates of negative emotionality-related traits: A systematic review and meta-analysis. *Neuropsychologia, 77*, 97–118.

Mineka, S., Anand, D., & Sumner, J. A. (2014). Important issues in understanding comorbidity between generalized anxiety disorder and major depressive disorder. In C. S. Richards & M. W. O'Hara (Eds.), *The Oxford handbook of depression and comorbidity* (pp. 129–147). New York: Oxford University Press.

Mineka, S., & Öhman, A. (2002). Phobias and preparedness: The selective, automatic, and encapsulated nature of fear. *Biological Psychiatry, 52*, 927–937.

Minsky, M. (1988). *Society of mind*. New York: Simon & Schuster.

Mishra, S. (2014). Decision-making under risk: Integrating perspectives from biology, economics, and psychology. *Personality and Social Psychology Review*, *18*, 280–307.

Misiak, B., Frydecka, D., Loska, O., Moustafa, A. A., Samochowiec, J., Kasznia, J., et al. (2018). Testosterone, DHEA and DHEA-S in patients with schizophrenia: A systematic review and meta-analysis. *Psychoneuroendocrinology*, *89*, 92–102.

Mitchell, K. S., & Bulik, C. M. (2014). Life course epidemiology of eating disorders. In K. C. Koenen, S. Rudenstine, E. Susser, & S. Galea (Eds.), *A life course approach to mental disorders* (pp. 148–155). Oxford: Oxford University Press.

Mitchell, R. L., & Crow, T. J. (2005). Right hemisphere language functions and schizophrenia: The forgotten hemisphere? *Brain*, *128*, 963–978.

Mitchell, R. H., & Goldstein, B. I. (2014). Inflammation in children and adolescents with neuropsychiatric disorders: A systematic review. *Journal of the American Academy of Child & Adolescent Psychiatry*, *53*, 274–296.

Mitchell-Olds, T., Willis, J. H., & Goldstein, D. B. (2007). Which evolutionary processes influence natural genetic variation for phenotypic traits? *Nature Reviews Genetics*, *8*, 845–856.

Mitchison, D., & Hay, P. (2014). The epidemiology of eating disorders: Genetic, environmental, and societal factors. *Clinical Epidemiology*, *6*, 89–97.

Mittal, C., & Griskevicius, V. (2014). Sense of control under uncertainty depends on people's childhood environment: A life history theory approach. *Journal of Personality and Social Psychology*, *107*, 621–637.

Mittal, C., Griskevicius, V., Simpson, J. A., Sung, S., & Young, E. S. (2015). Cognitive adaptations to stressful environments: When childhood adversity enhances adult executive function. *Journal of Personality and Social Psychology*, *109*, 604–621.

Miyake, A., & Friedman, N. P. (2012). The nature and organization of individual differences in executive functions four general conclusions. *Current Directions in Psychological Science*, *21*, 8–14.

Mobbs, D., Marchant, J. L., Hassabis, D., Seymour, B., Tan, G., Gray, M., et al. (2009). From threat to fear: The neural organization of defensive fear systems in humans. *Journal of Neuroscience*, *29*, 12236–12243.

Mobbs, D., Petrovic, P., Marchant, J. L., Hassabis, D., Weiskopf, N., Seymour, B., et al. (2007). When fear is near: Threat imminence elicits prefrontal-periaqueductal gray shifts in humans. *Science*, *317*, 1079–1083.

Moffitt, T. E. (1993). Adolescence-limited and life-course-persistent antisocial behavior: A developmental taxonomy. *Psychological Review*, *100*, 674–701.

Moffitt, T. E. (2003). Life-course-persistent and adolescence-limited antisocial behavior: A 10-year research review and a research agenda. In B. B. Lahey, T. E. Moffitt, & A. Caspi (Eds.), *Causes of conduct disorder and juvenile delinquency* (pp. 49–75). New York: Guilford.

Moffitt, T. E., & Caspi, A. (2005). Life-course persistent and adolescence-limited antisocial males: Longitudinal followup to adulthood. In D. M. Stoff & E. J. Susman (Eds.), *Developmental psychobiology of aggression* (pp. 161–186). Cambridge: Cambridge University Press.

Moffitt, T. E., Caspi, A., Harrington, H., & Milne, B. J. (2002). Males on the life-course-persistent and adolescence-limited antisocial pathways: Follow-up at age 26 years. *Development and Psychopathology*, *14*, 179–207.

Möhler, H. (2012). The GABA system in anxiety and depression and its therapeutic potential. *Neuropharmacology, 62*, 42–53.

Mokkonen, M., Koskela, E., Mappes, T., & Mills, S. C. (2016). Evolutionary conflict between maternal and paternal interests: Integration with evolutionary endocrinology. *Integrative and Comparative Biology, 56*, 146–158.

Montiglio, P. O., Ferrari, C., & Réale, D. (2013). Social niche specialization under constraints: Personality, social interactions and environmental heterogeneity. *Philosophical Transactions of the Royal Society B, 368*, 20120343.

Moore, S. R., & Depue, R. A. (2016). Neurobehavioral foundations of environmental reactivity. *Psychological Bulletin, 142*, 107–164.

Mørch, R. H., Dieset, I., Færden, A., Hope, S., Aas, M., Nerhus, M., et al. (2016). Inflammatory evidence for the psychosis continuum model. *Psychoneuroendocrinology, 67*, 189–197.

Morgan, A. B., & Lilienfeld, S. O. (2000). A meta-analytic review of the relation between antisocial behavior and neuropsychological measures of executive function. *Clinical Psychology Review, 20*, 113–136.

Morgan, C., Lappin, J., Heslin, M., Donoghue, K., Lomas, B., Reininghaus, U., et al. (2014). Reappraising the long-term course and outcome of psychotic disorders: The AESOP-10 study. *Psychological Medicine, 44*, 2713–2726.

Morris, M. C., Compas, B. E., & Garber, J. (2012). Relations among posttraumatic stress disorder, comorbid major depression, and HPA function: A systematic review and meta-analysis. *Clinical Psychology Review, 32*, 301–315.

Morris, M. C., Hellman, N., Abelson, J. L., & Rao, U. (2016). Cortisol, heart rate, and blood pressure as early markers of PTSD risk: A systematic review and meta-analysis. *Clinical Psychology Review, 49*, 79–91.

Morris, M. L. (2016). Vocational interests in the United States: Sex, age, ethnicity, and year effects. *Journal of Counseling Psychology, 63*, 604–615.

Moruzzi, S., Rijsdijk, F., & Battaglia, M. (2014). A twin study of the relationships among inattention, hyperactivity/impulsivity and sluggish cognitive tempo problems. *Journal of Abnormal Child Psychology, 42*, 63–75.

Mottron, L., Dawson, M., Soulieres, I., Hubert, B., & Burack, J. (2006). Enhanced perceptual functioning in autism: An update, and eight principles of autistic perception. *Journal of Autism and Developmental Disorders, 36*, 27–43.

Mõttus, R., Allik, J., & Realo, A. (2010). An attempt to validate national mean scores of Conscientiousness: No necessarily paradoxical findings. *Journal of Research in Personality, 44*, 630–640.

Moul, C., Dobson-Stone, C., Brennan, J., Hawes, D., & Dadds, M. (2013). An exploration of the serotonin system in antisocial boys with high levels of callous-unemotional traits. *PLoS ONE, 8*, e56619.

Moulding, R., Kyrios, M., Doron, G., & Nedeljkovic, M. (2007). Autogenous and reactive obsessions: Further evidence for a two-factor model of obsessions. *Journal of Anxiety Disorders, 21*, 677–690.

Muller, C. L., Anacker, A. M. J., & Veenstra-VanderWeele, J. (2016). The serotonin system in autism spectrum disorder: From biomarker to animal models. *Neuroscience, 321*, 24–41.

Mullins-Sweatt, S. N., Glover, N. G., Derefinko, K. J., Miller, J. D., & Widiger, T. A. (2010). The search for the successful psychopath. *Journal of Research in Personality, 44*, 554–558.

Munafò, M. R., & Flint, J. (2011). Dissecting the genetic architecture of human personality. *Trends in Cognitive Sciences, 15*, 395–400.

Muncer, S. J. (2011). The general factor of personality: Evaluating the evidence from meta-analysis, confirmatory factor analysis and evolutionary theory. *Personality and Individual Differences, 51*, 775–778.

Mundy, L. K., Romaniuk, H., Canterford, L., Hearps, S., Viner, R. M., Bayer, J. K., et al. (2016). Adrenarche and the emotional and behavioral problems of late childhood. *Journal of Adolescent Health, 57*, 608–616.

Muris, P., Merckelbach, H., Otgaar, H., & Meijer, E. (2017). The malevolent side of human nature: A meta-analysis and critical review of the literature on the Dark Triad (Narcissism, Machiavellianism, and Psychopathy). *Perspectives on Psychological Science, 12*, 183–204.

Murray, C. R., Simmons, J. G., Allen, N. B., Byrne, M. L., Mundy, L. K., Seal, M. L., et al. (2016). Associations between dehydroepiandrosterone (DHEA) levels, pituitary volume, and social anxiety in children. *Psychoneuroendocrinology, 64*, 31–39.

Musek, J. (2007). A general factor of personality: Evidence for the Big One in the five-factor model. *Journal of Research in Personality, 41*, 1213–1233.

Musser, E. D., Hawkey, E., Kachan-Liu, S. S., Lees, P., Roullet, J. B., Goddard, K., et al. (2014). Shared familial transmission of autism spectrum and attention-deficit/hyperactivity disorders. *Journal of Child Psychology and Psychiatry, 55*, 819–827.

Myers, S., Burger, O., & Johns, S. E. (2016). Postnatal depression and reproductive success in modern, low-fertility contexts. *Evolution, Medicine, and Public Health, 2016*, 71–84.

Naaijen, J., Zwiers, M. P., Amiri, H., Williams, S. C., Durston, S., Oranje, B., et al. (2016). Fronto-striatal glutamate in autism spectrum disorder and obsessive compulsive disorder. *Neuropsychopharmacology*. doi:10.1038/npp.2016.260

Nagasako, E. M., Oaklander, A. L., & Dworkin, R. H. (2003). Congenital insensitivity to pain: An update. *Pain, 101*, 213–219.

Nagler, U. K., Reiter, K. J., Furtner, M. R., & Rauthmann, J. F. (2014). Is there a "dark intelligence"? Emotional intelligence is used by dark personalities to emotionally manipulate others. *Personality and Individual Differences, 65*, 47–52.

Najavits, L. M., & Capezza, N. M. (2014). Depression and posttraumatic stress disorder comorbidity. In C. S. Richards & M. W. O'Hara (Eds.), *The Oxford handbook of depression and comorbidity* (pp. 100–110). New York: Oxford University Press.

Nakao, T., Okada, K., & Kanba, S. (2014). Neurobiological model of obsessive-compulsive disorder: Evidence from recent neuropsychological and neuroimaging findings. *Psychiatry & Clinical Neurosciences, 68*, 587–605.

Nakatani, E., Krebs, G., Micali, N., Turner, C., Heyman, I., & Mataix-Cols, D. (2011). Children with very early onset obsessive-compulsive disorder: Clinical features and treatment outcome. *Journal of Child Psychology and Psychiatry, 52*, 1261–1268.

National Institute of Mental Health (2018). *RDoC matrix*. Retrieved on February 1, 2018 from https://www.nimh.nih.gov/research-priorities/rdoc/constructs/rdoc-matrix.shtml.

Neale, M. C., & Kendler, K. S. (1995). Models of comorbidity for multifactorial disorders. *American Journal of Human Genetics, 57*, 935–953.

Nedelec, J. L., & Beaver, K. M. (2014). Physical attractiveness as a phenotypic marker of health: An assessment using a nationally representative sample of American adults. *Evolution and Human Behavior, 35*, 456–463.

Nederlof, A. F., Muris, P., & Hovens, J. E. (2012). Psychotic-like experiences and aggressive behavior in a non-clinical sample. *Personality and Individual Differences, 53*, 33–37.

Neer, S. M., & Ragsdale, K. A. (2014). Obsessive-compulsive and related disorders. In D. Beidel & B. Freuh (Eds.), *Adult psychopathology and diagnosis* (7th ed., pp. 355–386). New York: Wiley.

Negriff, S., & Susman, E. J. (2011). Pubertal timing, depression, and externalizing problems: A framework, review, and examination of gender differences. *Journal of Research on Adolescence, 21*, 717–746.

Nelson, B., & Rawlings, D. (2010). Relating schizotypy and personality to the phenomenology of creativity. *Schizophrenia Bulletin, 36*, 388–399.

Nelson, M. T., Seal, M. L., Pantelis, C., & Phillips, L. J. (2013). Evidence of a dimensional relationship between schizotypy and schizophrenia: A systematic review. *Neuroscience & Biobehavioral Reviews, 37*, 317–327.

Nesse, R. (2000). Is depression an adaptation? *Archives of General Psychiatry, 57*, 14–20.

Nesse, R. M. (1987). An evolutionary perspective on panic disorder and agoraphobia. *Ethology and Sociobiology, 8*, 73–83.

Nesse, R. M. (1990). Evolutionary explanations of emotions. *Human Nature, 1*, 261–289.

Nesse, R. M. (2001*a*). The smoke detector principle. *Annals of the New York Academy of Sciences, 935*, 75–85.

Nesse, R. M. (2001*b*). On the difficulty of defining disease: A Darwinian perspective. *Medicine, Health Care and Philosophy, 4*, 37–46.

Nesse, R. M. (2004*a*). Natural selection and the elusiveness of happiness. *Philosophical Transactions of the Royal Society of London B, 359*, 1333–1347.

Nesse, R. M. (2004*b*). Cliff-edged fitness functions and the persistence of schizophrenia. *Behavioral and Brain Sciences, 27*, 862–863.

Nesse, R. M. (2005*a*). Natural selection and the regulation of defenses: A signal detection analysis of the smoke detector principle. *Evolution and Human Behavior, 26*, 88–105.

Nesse, R. M. (2005*b*). Maladaptation and natural selection. *The Quarterly Review of Biology, 80*, 62–70.

Nesse, R. M. (2006). Evolutionary explanations of mood and mood disorders. In D. J. Stein, D. J. Kupfur, & A. F. Schatzberg (Eds.), *American Psychiatric Publishing textbook of mood disorders* (pp. 159–175). Arlington, VA: American Psychiatric Publishing.

Nesse, R. M. (2007). Runaway social selection for displays of partner value and altruism. *Biological Theory, 2*, 143–155.

Nesse, R. M. (2011). Ten questions for evolutionary studies of disease vulnerability. *Evolutionary Applications, 4*, 264–277.

Nesse, R. M. (2015). Evolutionary psychology and mental health. In D. M. Buss (Ed.), *The handbook of evolutionary psychology* (2nd ed., pp. 1007–1026). Hoboken, NJ: Wiley.

Nesse, R. M., & Berridge, K. C. (1997). Psychoactive drug use in evolutionary perspective. *Science, 278*, 63–66.

Nesse, R. M., & Ellsworth, P. C. (2009). Evolution, emotions, and emotional disorders. *American Psychologist, 64*, 129–139.

Nesse, R. M., & Jackson, E. D. (2006). Evolution: Psychiatric nosology's missing biological foundation. *Clinical Neuropsychiatry, 3*, 121–131.

Nestadt, G., Di, C. Z., Riddle, M. A., Grados, M. A., Greenberg, B. D., Fyer, A. J., et al. (2009). Obsessive–compulsive disorder: Subclassification based on co-morbidity. *Psychological Medicine*, *39*, 1491–1501.

Nestler, E. J., Peña, C. J., Kundakovic, M., Mitchell, A., & Akbarian, S. (2016). Epigenetic basis of mental illness. *The Neuroscientist*, *22*, 447–463.

Nettle, D. (2001). *Strong imagination: Madness, creativity and human nature*. New York: Oxford University Press.

Nettle, D. (2004). Evolutionary origins of depression: A review and reformulation. *Journal of Affective Disorders*, *81*, 91–102.

Nettle, D. (2006*a*). Reconciling the mutation-selection balance model with the schizotypy-creativity connection. *Behavioral and Brain Sciences*, *29*, 418.

Nettle, D. (2006*b*). Schizotypy and mental health amongst poets, visual artists, and mathematicians. *Journal of Research in Personality*, *40*, 876–890.

Nettle, D. (2009*a*). Beyond nature versus culture: Cultural variation as an evolved characteristic. *Journal of the Royal Anthropological Institute*, *15*, 223–240.

Nettle, D. (2009*b*). Ecological influences on human behavioural diversity: A review of recent findings. *Trends in Ecology and Evolution*, *24*, 618–624.

Nettle, D. (2009*c*). *Evolution and genetics for psychology*. Oxford: Oxford University Press.

Nettle, D. (2011*a*). Evolutionary perspectives on the Five Factor model of personality. In D. M. Buss & P. H. Hawley (Eds.), *The evolution of personality and individual differences* (pp. 5–28). New York: Oxford University Press.

Nettle, D. (2011*b*). Flexibility in reproductive timing in human females: Integrating ultimate and proximate explanations. *Philosophical Transactions of the Royal Society B*, *366*, 357–365.

Nettle, D., & Bateson, M. (2012). The evolutionary origins of mood and its disorders. *Current Biology*, *22*, R712–R721.

Nettle, D., & Bateson, M. (2015). Adaptive developmental plasticity: What is it, how can we recognize it and when can it evolve? *Proceedings of the Royal Society of London B*, *282*, 20151005.

Nettle, D., & Clegg, H. (2006). Schizotypy, creativity and mating success in humans. *Proceedings of the Royal Society of London B*, *273*, 611–615.

Nettle, D., Coall, D. A., & Dickins, T. E. (2011). Early-life conditions and age at first pregnancy in British women. *Proceedings of the Royal Society of London B*, *278*, 1721–1727.

Nettle, D., Dickins, T. E., Coall, D. A., & de Mornay Davies, P. (2013). Patterns of physical and psychological development in future teenage mothers. *Evolution, Medicine, and Public Health*, *2013*, 187–196.

Nettle, D., & Pollet, T. V. (2008). Natural selection on male wealth in humans. *The American Naturalist*, *172*, 658–666.

Neumann, A., Pappa, I., Lahey, B. B., Verhulst, F. C., Medina-Gomez, C., Jaddoe, V. W., et al. (2016). Single nucleotide polymorphism heritability of a general psychopathology factor in children. *Journal of the American Academy of Child and Adolescent Psychiatry*, *55*, 1038–1045.

Neumann, I. D., & Slattery, D. A. (2016). Oxytocin in general anxiety and social fear: A translational approach. *Biological Psychiatry*, *79*, 213–221.

Neumeyer, A. M., Gates, A., Ferrone, C., Lee, H., & Misra, M. (2013). Bone density in peripubertal boys with autism spectrum disorders. *Journal of Autism and Developmental Disorders*, *43*, 1623–1629.

New, J. J., & German, T. C. (2015). Spiders at the cocktail party: An ancestral threat that surmounts inattentional blindness. *Evolution and Human Behavior, 36*, 165–173.

Newbury-Helps, J., Feigenbaum, J., & Fonagy, P. (2017). Offenders with antisocial personality disorder display more impairments in mentalizing. *Journal of Personality Disorders, 31*, 232–255.

Newman, M. G., & Llera, S. J. (2011). A novel theory of experiential avoidance in generalized anxiety disorder: A review and synthesis of research supporting a contrast avoidance model of worry. *Clinical Psychology Review, 31*, 371–382.

Nicholls, J., Staiger, P. K., Williams, J. S., Richardson, B., & Kambouropoulos, N. (2014). When social anxiety co-occurs with substance use: Does an impulsive social anxiety subtype explain this unexpected relationship? *Psychiatry Research, 220*, 909–914.

Nielsen, P. R., Benros, M. E., & Dalsgaard, S. (2017). Associations between autoimmune diseases and Attention-Deficit/Hyperactivity Disorder: A nationwide study. *Journal of the American Academy of Child and Adolescent Psychiatry, 56*, 234–240.

Nigg, J. (2013). Attention-deficit/hyperactivity disorder. In T. P. Beauchaine & S. P. Hinshaw (Eds.), *Child and adolescent psychopathology* (2nd ed., pp. 377–410). Hoboken, NJ: Wiley.

Nigg, J. (2016). Attention and impulsivity. In D. Cicchetti (Ed.), *Developmental psychopathology: Vol. 3. Maladaptation and psychopathology* (3rd ed., pp. 591–646). New York: Wiley.

Nijenhuis, E. R., Vanderlinden, J., & Spinhoven, P. (1998). Animal defensive reactions as a model for trauma-induced dissociative reactions. *Journal of Traumatic Stress, 11*, 243–260.

Nijjar, R., Ellenbogen, M. A., & Hodgins, S. (2014). Personality, coping, risky behavior, and mental disorders in the offspring of parents with bipolar disorder: A comprehensive psychosocial assessment. *Journal of Affective Disorders, 166*, 315–323.

Nikolaus, S., Hautzel, H., Heinzel, A., & Müller, H. W. (2012). Key players in major and bipolar depression—A retrospective analysis of in vivo imaging studies. *Behavioural Brain Research, 232*, 358–390.

Nishiyama, T., Suzuki, M., Adachi, K., Sumi, S., Okada, K., Kishino, H., et al. (2014). Comprehensive comparison of self-administered questionnaires for measuring quantitative autistic traits in adults. *Journal of Autism and Developmental Disorders, 44*, 993–1007.

Nishiyama, T., Taniai, H., Miyachi, T., Ozaki, K., Tomita, M., & Sumi, S. (2009). Genetic correlation between autistic traits and IQ in a population-based sample of twins with autism spectrum disorders (ASDs). *Journal of Human Genetics, 54*, 56–61.

Noftle, E. E., & Shaver, P. R. (2006). Attachment dimensions and the big five personality traits: Associations and comparative ability to predict relationship quality. *Journal of Research in Personality, 40*, 179–208.

Nolen-Hoeksema, S., & Hilt, L. M. (2009). Gender differences in depression. In I. H. Gotlib & C. L. Hammen (Eds.), *Handbook of depression* (2nd ed., pp. 386–404). New York: Guilford.

Nolen-Hoeksema, S., Wisco, B. E., & Lyubomirsky, S. (2008). Rethinking rumination. *Perspectives on Psychological Science, 3*, 400–424.

Noordhof, A., Krueger, R. F., Ormel, J., Oldehinkel, A. J., & Hartman, C. A. (2015). Integrating autism-related symptoms into the dimensional internalizing and externalizing model of psychopathology: The TRAILS Study. *Journal of Abnormal Child Psychology, 43*, 577–587.

Nordsletten, A. E., Larsson, H., Crowley, J. J., Almqvist, C., Lichtenstein, P., & Mataix-Cols, D. (2016). Patterns of nonrandom mating within and across 11 major psychiatric disorders. *JAMA Psychiatry, 73*, 354–361.

Norenzayan, A., & Shariff, A. F. (2008). The origin and evolution of religious prosociality. *Science, 322*, 58–62.

Norenzayan, A., Shariff, A. F., Willard, A. K., Slingerland, E., Gervais, W. M., McNamara, R. A., et al. (2016). The cultural evolution of prosocial religions. *Behavioral and Brain Sciences, 39*, e1.

Norman, L. J., Carlisi, C., Lukito, S., Hart, H., Mataix-Cols, D., Radua, J., et al. (2016). Structural and functional brain abnormalities in attention-deficit/hyperactivity disorder and obsessive-compulsive disorder: A comparative meta-analysis. *JAMA Psychiatry, 73*, 815–825.

Normann, N., Emmerik, A. A., & Morina, N. (2014). The efficacy of metacognitive therapy for anxiety and depression: A meta-analytic review. *Depression and Anxiety, 31*, 402–411.

Norton, P. J., & Paulus, D. J. (2016). Toward a unified treatment for emotional disorders: Update on the science and practice. *Behavior Therapy, 47*, 854–868.

Nugent, N. R., Brown, R., Stratton, K., & Amstadter, A. B. (2014). Life course epidemiology of anxiety disorders. In K. C. Koenen, S. Rudenstine, E. Susser, & S. Galea (Eds.), *A life course approach to mental disorders* (pp. 111–132). Oxford: Oxford University Press.

Nusslock, R., Young, C. B., & Damme, K. S. (2014). Elevated reward-related neural activation as a unique biological marker of bipolar disorder: Assessment and treatment implications. *Behaviour Research and Therapy, 62*, 74–87.

Oakley, B., Knafo, A., Madhavan, G., & Wilson, D. S. (Eds.). (2012). *Pathological altruism*. New York: Oxford University Press.

O'Boyle, E. H., Forsyth, D. R., Banks, G. C., Story, P. A., & White, C. D. (2015). A meta-analytic test of redundancy and relative importance of the Dark Triad and Five-Factor Model of personality. *Journal of Personality, 83*, 644–664.

O'Connor, L. E., Berry, J., Lewis, T., Mulherin, K., & Crisostomo, P. S. (2007). Empathy and depression: The moral system on overdrive. In T. F. D. Farrow & P. W. R. Woodruff (Eds.), *Empathy and mental illness* (pp. 58–62). New York: Cambridge University Press.

O'Connor, L. E., Berry, J. W., Weiss, J., & Gilbert, P. (2002). Guilt, fear, submission, and empathy in depression. *Journal of Affective Disorders, 71*, 19–27.

O'Connor, L. E., Berry, J. W., Weiss, J., Schweitzer, D., & Sevier, M. (2000). Survivor guilt, submissive behaviour and evolutionary theory: The down-side of winning in social comparison. *British Journal of Medical Psychology, 73*, 519–530.

O'Keane, V., Frodl, T., & Dinan, T. G. (2012). A review of atypical depression in relation to the course of depression and changes in HPA axis organization. *Psychoneuroendocrinology, 37*, 1589–1599.

Ogilvie, J. M., Stewart, A. L., Chan, R. C., & Shum, D. H. (2011). Neuropsychological measures of executive function and antisocial behavior: A meta-analysis. *Criminology, 49*, 1063–1107.

Ohi, K., Shimada, T., Nitta, Y., Kihara, H., Okubo, H., Uehara, T., et al. (2016). The Five-Factor Model personality traits in schizophrenia: A meta-analysis. *Psychiatry Research*, *240*, 34–41.

Öhman, A. (2009). Of snakes and faces: An evolutionary perspective on the psychology of fear. *Scandinavian Journal of Psychology*, *50*, 543–552.

Öhman, A., Dimberg, U., & Öst, L.-G. (1985). Animal and social phobias: Biological constraints on learned fear responses. In S. Reiss & R. R. Bootzin (Eds.), *Theoretical issues in behavior therapy* (pp. 123–178). Orlando, FL: Academic Press.

Öhman, A., & Mineka, S. (2001). Fears, phobias, and preparedness: Toward an evolved module of fear and fear learning. *Psychological Review*, *108*, 483.

Öhman, A., Soares, S. C., Juth, P., Lindström, B., & Esteves, F. (2012). Evolutionary derived modulations of attention to two common fear stimuli: Serpents and hostile humans. *Journal of Cognitive Psychology*, *24*, 17–32.

Olatunji, B. O., & Deacon, B. (2008). Specificity of disgust sensitivity in the prediction of fear and disgust responding to a brief spider exposure. *Journal of Anxiety Disorders*, *22*, 328–336.

Olatunji, B. O., Ebesutani, C., Haidt, J., & Sawchuk, C. N. (2014). Specificity of disgust domains in the prediction of contamination anxiety and avoidance: A multimodal examination. *Behavior Therapy*, *45*, 469–481.

Olatunji, B. O., Ebesutani, C., & Kim, E. H. (2015). Examination of a bifactor model of the Three Domains of Disgust Scale: Specificity in relation to obsessive-compulsive symptoms. *Psychological Assessment*, *27*, 102.

Olatunji, B. O., Smits, J. A., Connolly, K., Willems, J., & Lohr, J. M. (2007). Examination of the decline in fear and disgust during exposure to threat-relevant stimuli in blood-injection- injury phobia. *Journal of Anxiety Disorders*, *21*, 445–455.

Olatunji, B. O., Williams, B. J., Haslam, N., Abramowitz, J. S., & Tolin, D. F. (2008). The latent structure of obsessive-compulsive symptoms: A taxometric study. *Depression and Anxiety*, *25*, 956–968.

Olatunji, B. O., Wolitzky-Taylor, K. B., Ciesielski, B. G., Armstrong, T., Etzel, E. N., & David, B. (2009). Fear and disgust processing during repeated exposure to threat-relevant stimuli in spider phobia. *Behaviour Research and Therapy*, *47*, 671–679.

Olazagasti, M. A. R., Klein, R. G., Mannuzza, S., Belsky, E. R., Hutchison, J. A., Lashua-Shriftman, E. C., et al. (2013). Does childhood attention-deficit/hyperactivity disorder predict risk-taking and medical illnesses in adulthood? *Journal of the American Academy of Child & Adolescent Psychiatry*, *52*, 153–162.

Olderbak, S., Gladden, P., Wolf, P. S. A., & Figueredo, A. J. (2014). Comparison of life history strategy measures. *Personality and Individual Differences*, *58*, 82–88.

Oldershaw, A., DeJong, H., Hambrook, D., Broadbent, H., Tchanturia, K., Treasure, J., et al. (2012). Emotional processing following recovery from anorexia nervosa. *European Eating Disorders Review*, *20*, 502–509.

Ollendick, T. H., & Hirshfeld-Becker, D. R. (2002). The developmental psychopathology of social anxiety disorder. *Biological Psychiatry*, *51*, 44–58.

Oltmanns, T. F., & Powers, A. D. (2012). Gender and personality disorders. In T. A. Widiger (Ed.), *The Oxford handbook of personality disorders* (206–218). New York: Oxford University Press.

Öngür, D., Lundy, M., Greenhouse, I., Shinn, A. K., Menon, V., Cohen, B. M., et al. (2010). Default mode network abnormalities in bipolar disorder and schizophrenia. *Psychiatry Research: Neuroimaging*, *183*, 59–68.

Oppenheim, R. W. (1981). Ontogenetic adaptations and retrogressive processes in the development of the nervous system and behavior. In K. J. Connolly & H. F. R. Prechtl (Eds.), *Maturation and development: Biological and psychological perspectives* (pp. 73–108). Philadelphia, PA: International Medical Publications.

Ormel, J., Bastiaansen, A., Riese, H., Bos, E. H., Servaas, M., Ellenbogen, M., et al. (2013). The biological and psychological basis of neuroticism: Current status and future directions. *Neuroscience & Biobehavioral Reviews, 37*, 59–72.

Orzeck, T., & Lung, E. (2005). Big-five personality differences of cheaters and non-cheaters. *Current Psychology, 24*, 274–286.

Ostojic, D., & Miller, C. J. (2016). Association between pubertal onset and symptoms of ADHD in female university students. *Journal of Attention Disorders, 20*, 782–791. doi:10.1177/1087054714535249

Ottaviani, C., Mancini, F., Petrocchi, N., Medea, B., & Couyoumdjian, A. (2013). Autonomic correlates of physical and moral disgust. *International Journal of Psychophysiology, 89*, 57–62.

Overton, W. F. (2015). Processes, relations, and relational-developmental-systems. In R. M. Lerner (Ed.), *Handbook of child psychology and developmental science: Vol. 1. Theory and method* (pp. 9–62). Hoboken, NJ: Wiley.

Ozcan, D. D. M. E., & Banoglu, R. (2003). Gonadal hormones in schizophrenia and mood disorders. *European Archives of Psychiatry and Clinical Neuroscience, 253*, 193–196.

Pae, C. U., Tharwani, H., Marks, D. M., Masand, P. S., & Patkar, A. A. (2009). Atypical depression: A comprehensive review. *CNS Drugs, 23*, 1023–1037.

Paganini, C., & Gaido, D. (2013). Perception in autism: An interactive global research between folk psychology and folk physics. *Journal of Social, Evolutionary, and Cultural Psychology, 7*, 175–195.

Page, A. C. (1994). Blood-injury phobia. *Clinical Psychology Review, 14*, 443–461.

Palmer, C. J., Lawson, R. P., & Hohwy, J. (2017). Bayesian approaches to autism: Towards volatility, action, and behavior. *Psychological Bulletin, 143*, 521–542.

Palomino, A., González-Pinto, A., Martinez-Cengotitabengoa, M., de Azua, S. R., Alberich, S., Mosquera, F., et al. (2013). Relationship between negative symptoms and plasma levels of insulin-like growth factor 1 in first-episode schizophrenia and bipolar disorder patients. *Progress in Neuro-Psychopharmacology and Biological Psychiatry, 44*, 29–33.

Panksepp, J. (1998). *Affective neuroscience: The foundations of human and animal emotions*. New York: Oxford University Press.

Panksepp, J. (2011). Cross-species affective neuroscience decoding of the primal affective experiences of humans and related animals. *PLoS ONE, 6*, e21236.

Pardiñas, A. F., Holmans, P., Pocklington, A. J., Escott-Price, V., Ripke, S., Carrera, N., et al. (2016). Common schizophrenia alleles are enriched in mutation-intolerant genes and maintained by background selection. *bioRxiv*, 068593. doi:10.1101/068593

Pardini, D. A., Fite, P. J., & Burke, J. D. (2008). Bidirectional associations between parenting practices and conduct problems in boys from childhood to adolescence: The moderating effect of age and African-American ethnicity. *Journal of Abnormal Child Psychology, 36*, 647–662.

Parent, A.-S., Teilmann, G., Juul, A., Skakkebaek, N. E., Toppari, J., & Bourguignon, J.-P. (2003). The timing of normal puberty and the age limits of sexual precocity: Variations around the world, secular trends, and changes after migration. *Endocrine Reviews, 24*, 668–693.

Paris, J., & Phillips, J. (2013). *Making the DSM-5: Concepts and controversies*. New York: Springer.

Parker, G., McClure, G., & Paterson, A. (2015). Melancholia and catatonia: Disorders or specifiers? *Current Psychiatry Reports, 17*, 536.

Parker, G., Roy, K., Wilhelm, K., Mitchell, P., & Hadzi-Pavlovic, D. (2000). The nature of bipolar depression: Implications for the definition of melancholia. *Journal of Affective Disorders, 59*, 217–224.

Parker, K. J., Garner, J. P., Libove, R. A., Hyde, S. A., Hornbeak, K. B., Carson, D. S., et al. (2014). Plasma oxytocin concentrations and OXTR polymorphisms predict social impairments in children with and without autism spectrum disorder. *Proceedings of the National Academy of Sciences, 111*, 12258–12263.

Parkinson, C., & Wheatley, T. (2015). The repurposed social brain. *Trends in Cognitive Sciences, 19*, 133–141.

Patalay, P., Fonagy, P., Deighton, J., Belsky, J., Vostanis, P., & Wolpert, M. (2015). A general psychopathology factor in early adolescence. *British Journal of Psychiatry, 207*, 15–22.

Patel, A., Knapp, M., Henderson, J., & Baldwin, D. (2002). The economic consequences of social phobia. *Journal of Affective Disorders, 68*, 221–233.

Patrick, C. J., & Bernat, E. M. (2006). The construct of emotion as a bridge between personality and psychopathology. In R. F. Krueger & J. L. Tackett (Eds.), *Personality and psychopathology* (pp. 174–209). New York: Guilford.

Patrick, S. C., & Browning, L. E. (2011). Exploration behaviour is not associated with chick provisioning in great tits. *PLoS ONE, 6*, e26383–e26383.

Patrick, S. C., Chapman, J. R., Dugdale, H. L., Quinn, J. L., & Sheldon, B. C. (2012). Promiscuity, paternity and personality in the great tit. *Proceedings of the Royal Society of London B, 279*, 1724–1730.

Patten, M. M., Ross, L., Curley, J. P., Queller, D. C., Bonduriansky, R., & Wolf, J. B. (2014). The evolution of genomic imprinting: Theories, predictions and empirical tests. *Heredity, 113*, 119–128.

Patterson, P. H. (2011). *Infectious behavior: Brain-immune connections in autism, schizophrenia, and depression*. Cambridge, MA: MIT Press.

Paul, E. D., Johnson, P. L., Shekhar, A., & Lowry, C. A. (2014). The Deakin/Graeff hypothesis: Focus on serotonergic inhibition of panic. *Neuroscience & Biobehavioral Reviews, 46*, 379–396.

Paul, E. S., Cuthill, I., Kuroso, G., Norton, V., Woodgate, J., & Mendl, M. (2011). Mood and the speed of decisions about anticipated resources and hazards. *Evolution and Human Behavior, 32*, 21–28.

Paulhus, D. L. (2014). Toward a taxonomy of dark personalities. *Current Directions in Psychological Science, 23*, 421–426.

Pearl, S. B., & Norton, P. J. (2017). Transdiagnostic versus diagnosis specific cognitive behavioural therapies for anxiety: A meta-analysis. *Journal of Anxiety Disorders, 46*, 11–24.

Pearson, C. M., Riley, E. N., Davis, H. A., & Smith, G. T. (2014). Research review: Two pathways toward impulsive action: An integrative risk model for bulimic behavior in youth. *Journal of Child Psychology and Psychiatry, 55*, 852–864.

Peat, C., Mitchell, J. E., Hoek, H. W., & Wonderlich, S. A. (2009). Validity and utility of subtyping anorexia nervosa. *International Journal of Eating Disorders, 42*, 590–594.

Pellegrini, A. D. (2013). Play. In P. Zelazo (Ed.), *Oxford handbook of developmental psychology* (pp. 276–299). New York: Oxford University Press.

Pellicano, E., & Burr, D. (2012). When the world becomes 'too real': A Bayesian explanation of autistic perception. *Trends in Cognitive Sciences, 16*, 504–510.

Pellicano, E., Smith, A. D., Cristino, F., Hood, B. M., Briscoe, J., & Gilchrist, I. D. (2011). Children with autism are neither systematic nor optimal foragers. *Proceedings of the National Academy of Sciences, 108*, 421–426.

Pelt, D. H., van der Linden, D., Dunkel, C. S., & Born, M. P. (2017). The general factor of personality and job performance: Revisiting previous meta-analyses. *International Journal of Selection and Assessment, 25*, 333–346.

Pender, S., Gilbert, S. J., & Serpell, L. (2014). The neuropsychology of starvation: Set-shifting and central coherence in a fasted nonclinical sample. *PloS ONE, 9*, e110743.

Penke, L. (2011). Bridging the gap between modern evolutionary psychology and the study of individual differences. In D. M. Buss & P. H. Hawley (Eds.), *The evolution of personality and individual differences* (pp. 243–297). New York: Oxford University Press.

Penke, L., Denissen, J. J. A., & Miller, G. F. (2007). The evolutionary genetics of personality. *European Journal of Personality, 21*, 549–587.

Penke, L., & Jokela, M. (2016). The evolutionary genetics of personality revisited. *Current Opinion in Psychology, 7*, 104–109.

Penke, L., Maniega, S. M., Bastin, M. E., Hernandez, M. V., Murray, C., Royle, N. A., et al. (2012). Brain white matter tract integrity as a neural foundation for general intelligence. *Molecular Psychiatry, 17*, 1026–1030.

Pepper, G. V., & Nettle, D. (2014). Out of control mortality matters: The effect of perceived uncontrollable mortality risk on a health-related decision. *PeerJ, 2*, e459.

Perilloux, C., Cloud, J. M., & Buss, D. M. (2013). Women's physical attractiveness and short-term mating strategies. *Personality and Individual Differences, 54*, 490–495.

Perilloux, C., Fleischman, D. S., & Buss, D. M. (2011). Meet the parents: Parent-offspring convergence and divergence in mate preferences. *Personality and Individual Differences, 50*, 253–258.

Pertusa, A., Frost, R. O., & Mataix-Cols, D. (2010). When hoarding is a symptom of OCD: A case series and implications for DSM-V. *Behaviour Research & Therapy, 48*, 1012–1020.

Pertusa, A., Fullana, M. A., Singh, S., Alonso, P., Menchón, J. M., & Mataix-Cols, D. (2008). Compulsive hoarding: OCD symptom, distinct clinical syndrome, or both? *American Journal of Psychiatry, 165*, 1289–1298.

Pérusse, D. (1993). Cultural and reproductive success in industrial societies: Testing the relationship at the proximate and ultimate levels. *Behavioral and Brain Sciences, 16*, 267–283.

Pessiglione, M., & Lebreton, M. (2015). From the reward circuit to the valuation system: How the brain motivates behavior. In G. H. E. Gendolla, M. Tops, & S. Koole (Eds.), *Handbook of biobehavioral approaches to self-regulation* (pp. 157–174). New York: Springer.

Peters, J., & Büchel, C. (2011). The neural mechanisms of inter-temporal decision-making: Understanding variability. *Trends in Cognitive Sciences, 15*, 227–239.

Peters, M., Manning, J. T., & Reimers, S. (2007). The effects of sex, sexual orientation, and digit ratio (2D: 4D) on mental rotation performance. *Archives of Sexual Behavior, 36*, 251–260.

Petersen, M. B., & Aarøe, L. (2015). Birth weight and social trust in adulthood: Evidence for early calibration of social cognition. *Psychological Science, 26*, 1681–1692.

Pettijohn, T. F., & Jungeberg, B. J. (2004). Playboy playmate curves: Changes in facial and body feature preferences across social and economic conditions. *Personality and Social Psychology Bulletin, 30*, 1186–1197.

Peyrot, W. J., Robinson, M. R., Penninx, B. W. J. H., & Wray, N. R. (2016). Exploring boundaries for the genetic consequences of assortative mating for psychiatric traits. *JAMA Psychiatry, 73*, 1189–1195.

Pfaus, J. G. (2009). Pathways of sexual desire. *Journal of Sexual Medicine, 6*, 1506–1533.

Pflum, M. J., Gooding, D. C., & White, H. J. (2013). Hint, hint: Theory of mind performance in schizotypal individuals. *Journal of Nervous and Mental Disease, 201*, 394–399.

Philippi, T., & Seger, J. (1989). Hedging one's evolutionary bets, revisited. *Trends in Ecology and Evolution, 4*, 41–44.

Pianka, E. R. (1970). On r- and K-selection. *American Naturalist, 104*, 592–596.

Piccinini, G., & Scarantino, A. (2011). Information processing, computation, and cognition. *Journal of Biological Physics, 37*, 1–38.

Pickard, H., Rijsdijk, F., Happé, F., & Mandy, W. (2017). Are social and communication difficulties a risk factor for the development of social anxiety? *Journal of the American Academy of Child & Adolescent Psychiatry, 56*, 344–351.

Pietromonaco, P. R., & Powers, S. I. (2015). Attachment and health-related physiological stress processes. *Current Opinion in Psychology, 1*, 34–39.

Pietschnig, J., Penke, L., Wicherts, J. M., Zeiler, M., & Voracek, M. (2015). Meta-analysis of associations between human brain volume and intelligence differences: How strong are they and what do they mean? *Neuroscience and Biobehavioral Reviews, 57*, 411–432.

Pigliucci, M. (2005). Evolution of phenotypic plasticity: Where are we going now? *Trends in Ecology and Evolution, 20*, 481–486.

Pincus, A. L., Lukowitsky, M. R., & Wright, A. G. C. (2010). The interpersonal nexus of personality and psychopathology. In T. Millon, R. F. Krueger, & E. Simonsen (Eds.), *Contemporary directions in psychopathology: Scientific foundations of the DSM-V and ICD-11* (pp. 523–552). New York: Guilford.

Pinker, S. (1994). *The language instinct: How the mind creates language*. New York: Harper Collins.

Pinker, S. (2010). The cognitive niche: Coevolution of intelligence, sociality, and language. *Proceedings of the National Academy of Sciences USA, 107*, 8993–8999.

Pinto, A., & Eisen, J. L. (2012). Personality features of OCD and spectrum conditions. In G. Steketee (Ed.), *The Oxford hand-book of obsessive compulsive and spectrum disorders* (pp. 189–208). Oxford: Oxford University Press.

Pinto, A., Steinglass, J. E., Greene, A. L., Weber, E. U., & Simpson, H. B. (2014). Capacity to delay reward differentiates obsessive-compulsive disorder and obsessive-compulsive personality disorder. *Biological Psychiatry, 75*, 653–659.

Pinto, R., Rijsdijk, F., Ouellet-Morin, I., Asherson, P., McLoughlin, G., & Kuntsi, J. (2016). The aetiological association between the dynamics of cortisol productivity and ADHD. *Journal of Neural Transmission, 123*, 991–1000.

Placek, C. D., & Quinlan, R. J. (2012). Adolescent fertility and risky environments: A population-level perspective across the lifespan. *Proceedings of the Royal Society of London B, 279,* 20121022.

Plichta, M. M., & Scheres, A. (2014). Ventral–striatal responsiveness during reward anticipation in ADHD and its relation to trait impulsivity in the healthy population: A meta-analytic review of the fMRI literature. *Neuroscience & Biobehavioral Reviews, 38,* 125–134.

Ploeger, A., & Galis, F. (2011). Evolutionary approaches to autism: An overview and integration. *McGill Journal of Medicine, 13,* 38–43.

Plomin, R., & Deary, I. J. (2015). Genetics and intelligence differences: Five special findings. *Molecular Psychiatry, 20,* 98–108.

Plomin, R., & von Stumm, S. (2018). The new genetics of intelligence. *Nature Reviews Genetics, 19,* 148–159.

Pluess, M. (2015). Individual differences in environmental sensitivity. *Child Development Perspectives, 9,* 138–143.

Pluess, M., & Belsky, J. (2013). Vantage sensitivity: Individual differences in response to positive experiences. *Psychological Bulletin, 139,* 901–916.

Podubinski, T., Daffern, M., & Lee, S. (2012). A prospective examination of the stability of hostile-dominance and its relationship to paranoia over a one-year follow-up. *Personality and Individual Differences, 52,* 586–590.

Polderman, T. J., Benyamin, B., de Leeuw, C. A., Sullivan, P. F., van Bochoven, A., Visscher, P. M., et al. (2015). Meta-analysis of the heritability of human traits based on fifty years of twin studies. *Nature Genetics, 47,* 702–709.

Polderman, T. J. C., Hoekstra, R. A., Vinkhuyzen, A. A. E., Sullivan, P. F., van der Sluis, S., & Posthuma, D. (2013). Attentional switching forms a genetic link between attention problems and autistic traits in adults. *Psychological Medicine, 43,* 1985–1996.

Polimanti, R., & Gelernter, J. (2017). Widespread signatures of positive selection in common risk alleles associated to autism spectrum disorder. *PLoS Genetics, 13,* e1006618.

Polimeni, J., & Reiss, J. P. (2002). How shamanism and group selection may reveal the origins of schizophrenia. *Medical Hypotheses, 58,* 244–248.

Polimeni, J., & Reiss, J. P. (2003). Evolutionary perspectives on schizophrenia. *Canadian Journal of Psychiatry, 48,* 34–39.

Polimeni, J., Reiss, J. P., & Sareen, J. (2005). Could obsessive-compulsive disorder have originated as a group-selected adaptive trait in traditional societies? *Medical Hypotheses, 65,* 655–664.

Polivy, J. (1996). Psychological consequences of food restriction. *Journal of the American Dietetic Association, 96,* 589–592.

Polivy, J., Zeitlin, S. B., Herman, P. C., & Beal, A. L. (1994). Food restriction and binge eating: A study of former prisoners of war. *Journal of Abnormal Psychology, 103,* 409–411.

Porges, S. W. (2001). The polyvagal theory: Phylogenetic substrates of a social nervous system. *International Journal of Psychophysiology, 42,* 123–146.

Porges, S. W. (2007). The polyvagal perspective. *Biological Psychology, 74,* 116–143.

Posada, G., Lu, T., Trumbell, J., Kaloustian, G., Trudel, M., Plata, S. J., et al. (2013). Is the secure base phenomenon evident here, there, and anywhere? A cross-cultural study of child behavior and experts' definitions. *Child Development, 84,* 1896–1905.

Potter, A. I., & Nestor, P. G. (2010). IQ subtypes in schizophrenia: Distinct symptom and neuropsychological profiles. *Journal of Nervous and Mental Disease, 198,* 580–585.

Poulin, R. (2010). Parasite manipulation of host behavior: An update and frequently asked questions. *Advances in the Study of Behavior, 41*, 151–186.

Poulton, R., & Menzies, R. G. (2002). Non-associative fear acquisition: A review of the evidence from retrospective and longitudinal research. *Behaviour Research and Therapy, 40*, 127–149.

Power, M. J., & Fyvie, C. (2013). The role of emotion in PTSD: Two preliminary studies. *Behavioural & Cognitive Psychotherapy, 41*, 162–172.

Power, R. A., Kyaga, S., Uher, R., MacCabe, J. H., Långström, N., Landen, M., et al. (2013). Fecundity of patients with schizophrenia, autism, bipolar disorder, depression, anorexia nervosa, or substance abuse vs. their unaffected siblings. *JAMA Psychiatry, 70*, 22–30.

Powers, S., & Lehmann, L. (2014). An evolutionary model explaining the Neolithic transition from egalitarianism to leadership and despotism. *Proceedings of the Royal Society of London B, 281*, 20141349.

Poyurovsky, M. (2015). Obsessive-compulsive disorder with schizotypal personality disorder (Schizotypal OCD). In L. De Haan, F. Schirmbeck, & M. Zink (Eds.), *Obsessive-compulsive symptoms in schizophrenia* (pp. 63–76). Cham, CH: Springer.

Preston, S. D. (2014). Hoarding in animals: The argument for a homology. In R. O. Frost & G. Steketee (Eds.), *The Oxford handbook of hoarding and acquiring* (pp. 187–205). New York: Oxford University Press.

Preston, S. D., & Vickers, B. D. (2014). The psychology of acquisitiveness. In S. D. Preston, M. L. Kringelbach, & B. Knutson (Eds.), *The interdisciplinary science of consumption* (pp. 127–146). Cambridge, MA: MIT Press.

Preter, M., & Klein, D. F. (2008). Panic, suffocation false alarms, separation anxiety and endogenous opioids. *Progress in Neuro-Psychopharmacology and Biological Psychiatry, 32*, 603–612.

Preter, M., & Klein, D. F. (2014). Lifelong opioidergic vulnerability through early life separation: A recent extension of the false suffocation alarm theory of panic disorder. *Neuroscience & Biobehavioral Reviews, 46*, 345–351.

Price, D. H. (2007). Buying a piece of anthropology. *Anthropology Today, 23*, 17–22.

Price, J. (1967). The dominance hierarchy and the evolution of mental illness. *Lancet, 290*, 243–246.

Price, J. S. (2003). Evolutionary aspects of anxiety disorders. *Dialogues in Clinical Neuroscience, 5*, 223–236.

Price, J. S. (2013). An evolutionary perspective on anxiety and anxiety disorders. In F. Durbano (Ed.), *New insights into anxiety disorders* (pp. 3–20). Rijeka, HR: InTech.

Price, J. S., Gardner, R., Wilson, D. R., Sloman, L., Rohde, P., & Erickson, M. (2007). Territory, rank and mental health: The history of an idea. *Evolutionary Psychology, 5*, 531–554.

Price, J. S., & Sloman, L. (1987). Depression as yielding behavior: An animal model based on Schjelderup-Ebbe's pecking order. *Ethology and Sociobiology, 8*, 85–98.

Price, J. S., & Stevens, A. (1998). The human male socialization strategy set: Cooperation, defection, individualism, and schizotypy. *Evolution and Human Behavior, 19*, 57–70.

Price, J. S., & Stevens, A. (1999). An evolutionary approach to psychiatric disorders: Group-splitting and schizophrenia. In D. Rosen & M. Luebbert (Eds.), *Evolution of the psyche* (pp. 196–207). Westport, CT: Greenwood.

Promislow, D. E., & Harvey, P. H. (1990). Living fast and dying young: A comparative analysis of life-history variation among mammals. *Journal of Zoology, 220*, 417–437.

Pronk, T. M., Karremans, J. C., & Wigboldus, D. H. (2011). How can you resist? Executive control helps romantically involved individuals to stay faithful. *Journal of Personality and Social Psychology, 100*, 827–837.

Pryor, T., Wiederman, M. W., & McGilley, B. (1996). Clinical correlates of anorexia nervosa subtypes. *International Journal of Eating Disorders, 19*, 371–379.

Pulcu, E., Thomas, E. J., Trotter, P. D., McFarquhar, M., Juhász, G., Sahakian, B. J., et al. (2015). Social-economical decision making in current and remitted major depression. *Psychological Medicine, 45*, 1301–1313.

Puts, D. A. (2010). Beauty and the beast: Mechanisms of sexual selection in humans. *Evolution and Human Behavior, 31*, 157–175.

Quinlan, R. J. (2008). Human pair-bonds: Evolutionary functions, ecological variation, and adaptive development. *Evolutionary Anthropology, 17*, 227–238.

Quinlan, R. J. (2010). Extrinsic mortality effects on reproductive strategies in a Caribbean community. *Human Nature, 21*, 124–139.

Quinlan, R. J., & Quinlan, M. B. (2007). Evolutionary ecology of human pair-bonds: Cross-Cultural tests of alternative hypotheses. *Cross-Cultural Research, 41*, 149–169.

Quintelier, K. J., Ishii, K., Weeden, J., Kurzban, R., & Braeckman, J. (2013). Individual differences in reproductive strategy are related to views about recreational drug use in Belgium, the Netherlands, and Japan. *Human Nature, 24*, 196–217.

Quirk, K., Owen, J., Shuck, B., Fincham, F. D., Knopp, K., & Rhoades, G. (2016). Breaking bad: Commitment uncertainty, alternative monitoring, and relationship termination in young adults. *Journal of Couple & Relationship Therapy, 15*, 61–74.

Rabinovitz, B. B., O'Neill, S., Rajendran, K., & Halperin, J. M. (2016). Temperament, executive control, and attention-deficit/hyperactivity disorder across early development. *Journal of Abnormal Psychology, 125*, 196–206.

Rachman, S. (1997). A cognitive theory of obsessions. *Behaviour Research & Therapy, 35*, 793–802.

Rachman S. (2002). Fears born and bred: Non-associative fear acquisition. *Behaviour Research and Therapy, 40*, 121–208.

Racine, S. E., Culbert, K. M., Burt, S. A., & Klump, K. L. (2014). Advanced paternal age at birth: Phenotypic and etiologic associations with eating pathology in offspring. *Psychological Medicine, 44*, 1029–1041.

Radomsky, A. S., & Rachman, S. (2004). Symmetry, ordering and arranging compulsive behaviour. *Behaviour Research & Therapy, 42*, 893–913.

Rahman, Q. (2005). The neurodevelopment of human sexual orientation. *Neuroscience & Biobehavioral Reviews, 29*, 1057–1066.

Rai, D., Lewis, G., Lundberg, M., Araya, R., Svensson, A., Dalman, C., et al. (2012). Parental socioeconomic status and risk of offspring autism spectrum disorders in a Swedish population-based study. *Journal of the American Academy of Child & Adolescent Psychiatry, 51*, 467–476.

Raine, A. (1992). Sex differences in schizotypal personality in a nonclinical population. *Journal of Abnormal Psychology, 101*, 361–364.

Raine, A., Dodge, K., Loeber, R., Gatzke-Kopp, L., Lynam, D., Reynolds, C., et al. (2006). The reactive–proactive aggression questionnaire: Differential correlates of reactive and proactive aggression in adolescent boys. *Aggressive Behavior, 32*, 159–171.

Raison, C. L., & Miller, A. H. (2013*a*). The evolutionary significance of depression in Pathogen Host Defense (PATHOS-D). *Molecular Psychiatry, 18*, 15–37.

Raison, C. L., & Miller, A. H. (2013*b*). Malaise, melancholia and madness: The evolutionary legacy of an inflammatory bias. *Brain, Behavior, and Immunity, 31*, 1–8.

Ramos, E. J., Meguid, M. M., Campos, A. C., & Coelho, J. C. (2005). Neuropeptide Y, α-melanocyte-stimulating hormone, and monoamines in food intake regulation. *Nutrition, 21*, 269–279.

Ramsey, J. M., Schwarz, E., Guest, P. C., van Beveren, N. J., Leweke, F. M., Rothermundt, M., et al. (2013). Distinct molecular phenotypes in male and female schizophrenia patients. *PLoS ONE, 8*, e78729.

Rapoport, J. L. (1991). Recent advances in obsessive-compulsive disorder. *Neuropsychopharmacology, 5*, 1–10.

Räsänen, S., Pakaslahti, A., Syvälahti, E., Jones, P., & Isohanni, M. (2000). Sex differences in schizophrenia: A review. *Nordic Journal of Psychiatry, 54*, 37–45.

Rash, J. A., & Aguirre-Camacho, A. (2012). Attention-deficit hyperactivity disorder and cardiac vagal control: A systematic review. *ADHD Attention Deficit and Hyperactivity Disorders, 4*, 167–177.

Rawlings, D., & Locarnini, A. (2008). Dimensional schizotypy, autism, and unusual word associations in artists and scientists. *Journal of Research in Personality, 42*, 465–471.

Réale, D., Garant, D., Humphries, M. M., Bergeron, P., Careau, V., & Montiglio, P. O. (2010). Personality and the emergence of the pace-of-life syndrome concept at the population level. *Philosophical Transactions of the Royal Society B, 365*, 4051–4063.

Reeve, S. D., Kelly, K. M., & Welling, L. L. (2016). Transitory environmental threat alters sexually dimorphic mate preferences and sexual strategy. *Evolutionary Psychological Science, 2*, 101–113.

Reich, J. (2000). The relationship of social phobia to avoidant personality disorder: A proposal to reclassify avoidant personality disorder based on clinical empirical findings. *European Psychiatry, 15*, 151–159.

Reichborn-Kjennerud, T., Czajkowski, N., Torgersen, S., Neale, M. C., Ørstavik, R. E., Tambs, K., et al. (2007). The relationship between avoidant personality disorder and social phobia: A population-based twin study. *American Journal of Psychiatry, 164*, 1722–1728.

Reichborn-Kjennerud, T., Czajkowski, N., Ystrøm, E., Ørstavik, R., Aggen, S. H., Tambs, K., et al. (2015). A longitudinal twin study of borderline and antisocial personality disorder traits in early to middle adulthood. *Psychological Medicine, 45*, 3121–3131.

Reise, S. P., & Wright, T. M. (1996). Personality traits, cluster B personality disorders, and sociosexuality. *Journal of Research in Personality, 30*, 128–136.

Rentfrow, P. J., Gosling, S. D., & Potter, J. (2008). A theory of the emergence, persistence, and expression of geographic variation in psychological characteristics. *Perspectives on Psychological Science, 3*, 339–369.

Reser, J. E. (2011). Conceptualizing the autism spectrum in terms of natural selection and behavioral ecology: The solitary forager hypothesis. *Evolutionary Psychology, 9*, 207–238.

Resick, P. A., Monson, C. M., & Rizvi, S. L. (2013). Posttraumatic stress disorder. In W. E. Craighead, D. J. Miklowitz, & L. W. Craighead (Eds.), *Psychopathology: History, diagnosis, and empirical foundations* (2nd ed., pp. 244–284). New York: Wiley.

Rethorst, C. D., Greer, T. L., Toups, M. S. P., Bernstein, I., Carmody, T. J., & Trivedi, M. H. (2015). IL-1β and BDNF are associated with improvement in hypersomnia but not insomnia following exercise in major depressive disorder. *Translational Psychiatry, 5*, e611.

Rettew, D. C., Swedo, S. E., Leonard, H. L., Lenane, M. C., & Rapoport, J. L. (1992). Obsessions and compulsions across time in 79 children and adolescents with obsessive-compulsive disorder. *Journal of the American Academy of Child & Adolescent Psychiatry, 31*, 1050–1056.

Rettew, D. C., Zanarini, M. C., Yen, S., Grilo, C. M., Skodol, A. E., Shea, M. T., et al. (2003). Childhood antecedents of avoidant personality disorder: A retrospective study. *Journal of the American Academy of Child & Adolescent Psychiatry, 42*, 1122–1130.

Revelle, W., & Wilt, J. (2013). The General Factor of Personality: A general critique. *Journal of Research in Personality, 47*, 493–504.

Reznick, D., Nunney, L., & Tessier, A. (2000). Big houses, big cars, superfleas and the costs of reproduction. *Trends in Ecology and Evolution, 15*, 421–425.

Richardson, G. B., Chen, C. C., Dai, C. L., Hardesty, P. H., & Swoboda, C. M. (2014). Life history strategy and young adult substance use. *Evolutionary Psychology, 12*, 932–957.

Richardson, G. B., Dai, C. L., Chen, C. C., Nedelec, J. L., Swoboda, C. M., & Chen, W. W. (2016). Adolescent life history strategy in the intergenerational transmission and developmental stability of substance use. *Journal of Drug Issues, 46*, 102–121.

Richardson, G. B., Sanning, B. K., Lai, M. H. C., Copping, L. T., Hardesty, P. H., & Kruger, D. J. (2017). On the psychometric study of human life history strategies: State of the science and evidence of two independent dimensions *Evolutionary Psychology*, 1474704916666840.

Richer, J. (1978). The partial noncommunication of culture to autistic children: An application of human ethology. In M. Rutter & E. Schopler (Eds.), *Autism: A reappraisal of concepts and treatment* (pp. 47–61). New York: Springer.

Richerson, P. J., & Boyd, R. (2005). *Not by genes alone: How culture transformed human evolution*. Chicago: University of Chicago Press.

Rickard, I. J., Frankenhuis, W. E., & Nettle, D. (2014). Why are childhood family factors associated with timing of maturation? A role for internal state. *Perspectives on Psychological Science, 9*, 3–15.

Riikonen, R., Makkonen, I., Vanhala, R., Turpeinen, U., Kuikka, J., & Kokki, H. (2006). Cerebrospinal fluid insulin-like growth factors IGF-1 and IGF-2 in infantile autism. *Developmental Medicine & Child Neurology, 48*, 751–755.

Rilling, J. K. (2011). The neurobiology of cooperation and altruism. In R. W. Sussman & C. R. Cloninger (Eds.), *Origins of altruism and cooperation* (pp. 295–306). New York: Springer.

Rinaudo, P., & Wang, E. (2012). Fetal programming and metabolic syndrome. *Annual Review of Physiology, 74*, 107–130.

Ritchie, S. J., Booth, T., Valdés Hernández, M. d. C., Corley, J., Muñoz Maniega, S., Gow, A. J., et al. (2015). Beyond a bigger brain: Multivariable structural brain imaging and intelligence. *Intelligence, 51*, 47–56.

Ritchie, S. J., Cox, S. R., Shen, X., Lombardo, M. V., Reus, L. M., Alloza, C., et al. (2017). Sex differences in the adult human brain: Evidence from 5,216 UK Biobank participants. *bioRxiv*, 123729.

Ritschel, F., King, J. A., Geisler, D., Flohr, L., Neidel, F., Boehm, I., et al. (2015). Temporal delay discounting in acutely ill and weight-recovered patients with anorexia nervosa. *Psychological Medicine, 45*, 1229–1239.

Ritschel, L. A., Gillespie, C. F., Arnarson, E. Ö., & Craighead, W. E. (2013). Major depressive disorder. In W. E. Craighead, D. J. Miklowitz, & L. W. Craighead (Eds.),

Psychopathology: History, diagnosis, and empirical foundations (2nd ed., pp. 285–333). New York: Wiley.

Ritter, K., Dziobek, I., Preißler, S., Rüter, A., Vater, A., Fydrich, T., et al. (2011). Lack of empathy in patients with narcissistic personality disorder. *Psychiatry Research, 187*, 241–247.

Roberson-Nay, R., Eaves, L. J., Hettema, J. M., Kendler, K. S., & Silberg, J. L. (2012). Childhood separation anxiety disorder and adult onset panic attacks share a common genetic diathesis. *Depression and Anxiety, 29*, 320–327.

Robert, J. S., Hall, B. K., & Olson, W. M. (2001). Bridging the gap between developmental systems theory and evolutionary developmental biology. *BioEssays, 23*, 954–962.

Roberts, B. W., Luo, J., Briley, D. A., Chow, P. I., Su, R., & Hill, P. L. (2017). A systematic review of personality trait change through intervention. *Psychological Bulletin, 143*, 117–141.

Robinson, E. B., Koenen, K. C., McCormick, M. C., Munir, K., Hallett, V., Happé, F., et al. (2012). A multivariate twin study of autistic traits in 12-year-olds: Testing the fractionable autism triad hypothesis. *Behavior Genetics, 42*, 245–255.

Robinson, E. B., Samocha, K. E., Kosmicki, J. A., McGrath, L., Neale, B. M., Perlis, R. H., et al. (2014). Autism spectrum disorder severity reflects the average contribution of de novo and familial influences. *Proceedings of the National Academy of Sciences, 111*, 15161–15165.

Rock, P. L., Roiser, J. P., Riedel, W. J., & Blackwell, A. D. (2014). Cognitive impairment in depression: A systematic review and meta-analysis. *Psychological Medicine, 44*, 2029.

Rodgers, S., Ajdacic-Gross, V., Müller, M., Hengartner, M. P., Holtforth, M. G., Angst, J., et al. (2014). The role of sex on stability and change of depression symptom subtypes over 20 years: A latent transition analysis. *European Archives of Psychiatry and Clinical Neuroscience, 264*, 577–588.

Rodgers, S., Grosse Holtforth, M., Hengartner, M. P., Müller, M., Aleksandrowicz, A. A., Rössler, W., et al. (2015). Serum testosterone levels and symptom-based depression subtypes in men. *Frontiers in Psychiatry, 6*, 61.

Rodgers, S., Vandeleur, C. L., Ajdacic-Gross, V., Aleksandrowicz, A. A., Strippoli, M. P. F., Castelao, E., et al. (2016). Tracing the associations between sex, the atypical and the combined atypical-melancholic depression subtypes: A path analysis. *Journal of Affective Disorders, 190*, 807–818.

Rodriguez-Seijas, C., Eaton, N. R., & Krueger, R. F. (2015). How transdiagnostic factors of personality and psychopathology can inform clinical assessment and intervention. *Journal of Personality Assessment, 97*, 425–435.

Roe, K., & Murphy, D. (2011). Function, dysfunction, and adaptation? In P. R. Adriaens & A. De Block (Eds.), *Maladapting minds: Philosophy, psychiatry, and evolutionary theory* (pp. 216–237). Oxford: Oxford University Press.

Roepke, S., & Vater, A. (2014). Narcissistic personality disorder: An integrative review of recent empirical data and current definitions. *Current Psychiatry Reports, 16*, 445.

Roff, D. A. (2002). *Life history evolution*. Sunderland, MA: Sinauer.

Rogers, K., Dziobek, I., Hassenstab, J., Wolf, O. T., & Convit, A. (2007). Who cares? Revisiting empathy in Asperger syndrome. *Journal of Autism and Developmental Disorders, 37*, 709–715.

Rogers, R. D. (2011). The roles of dopamine and serotonin in decision making: Evidence from pharmacological experiments in humans. *Neuropsychopharmacology, 36*, 114–132.

Romans, S. E., Tyas, J., Cohen, M. M., & Silverstone, T. (2007). Gender differences in the symptoms of major depressive disorder. *The Journal of Nervous and Mental Disease, 195*, 905–911.

Romeo, R. D. (2003). Puberty: A period of both organizational and activational effects of steroid hormones on neurobehavioural development. *Journal of Neuroendocrinology, 15*, 1185–1192.

Romer, D., Betancourt, L. M., Brodsky, N. L., Giannetta, J. M., Yang, W., & Hurt, H. (2011). Does adolescent risk taking imply weak executive function? A prospective study of relations between working memory performance, impulsivity, and risk taking in early adolescence. *Developmental Science, 14*, 1119–1133.

Ronald, A., Happé, F., Hughes, C., & Plomin, R. (2005). Nice and nasty theory of mind in preschool children: Nature and nurture. *Social Development, 14*, 664–684.

Ronald, A., Larsson, H., Anckarsäter, H., & Lichtenstein, P. (2011). A twin study of autism symptoms in Sweden. *Molecular Psychiatry, 16*, 1039–1047.

Ronald, A., Larsson, H., Anckarsäter, H., & Lichtenstein, P. (2014). Symptoms of autism and ADHD: A Swedish twin study examining their overlap. *Journal of Abnormal Psychology, 123*, 440–451.

Ronemus, M., Iossifov, I., Levy, D., & Wigler, M. (2014). The role of de novo mutations in the genetics of autism spectrum disorders. *Nature Reviews Genetics, 15*, 133–141.

Roney, J. R., & Gettler, L. T. (2015). The role of testosterone in human romantic relationships. *Current Opinion in Psychology, 1*, 81–86.

Roney, J. R., Lukaszewski, A. W., & Simmons, Z. L. (2007). Rapid endocrine responses of young men to social interactions with young women. *Hormones and Behavior, 52*, 326–333.

Roney, J. R., & Simmons, Z. L. (2013). Hormonal predictors of sexual motivation in natural menstrual cycles. *Hormones and Behavior, 63*, 636–645.

Roose, A., Bijttebier, P., Claes, L., & Lilienfeld, S. O. (2011). Psychopathic traits in adolescence: Associations with the revised Reinforcement Sensitivity Theory systems. *Personality and Individual Differences, 50*, 201–205.

Rosen, G. M., & Lilienfeld, S. O. (2008). Posttraumatic stress disorder: An empirical evaluation of core assumptions. *Clinical Psychology Review, 28*, 837–868.

Rosenberg, A., Patterson, J. S., & Angelaki, D. E. (2015). A computational perspective on autism. *Proceedings of the National Academy of Sciences, 112*, 9158–9165.

Rosenberg, N. A., Mahajan, S., Ramachandran, S., Zhao, C., Pritchard, J. K., & Feldman, M. W. (2005). Clines, clusters, and the effect of study design on the inference of human population structure. *PLoS Genetics, 1*, e70.

Rosenström, T., Jylhä, P., Pulkki-Råback, L., Holma, M., Raitakari, O. T., Isometsä, E., et al. (2015). Long-term personality changes and predictive adaptive responses after depressive episodes. *Evolution and Human Behavior, 36*, 337–344.

Rosenvinge, J. H., & Pettersen, G. (2015). Epidemiology of eating disorders part II: An update with a special reference to the DSM-5. *Advances in Eating Disorders: Theory, Research and Practice, 3*, 198–220.

Ross, S. R., Lutz, C. J., & Bailley, S. E. (2002). Positive and negative symptoms of schizotypy and the five-factor model: A domain and facet level analysis. *Journal of Personality Assessment, 79*, 53–72.

Rossi, A., Marinangeli, M. G., Butti, G., Kalyvoka, A., & Petruzzi, C. (2000). Pattern of comorbidity among anxious and odd personality disorders: The case of obsessive-compulsive personality disorder. *CNS Spectrums, 5*, 23–26.

Rotkirch, A. (2007). "All that she wants is a(nother) baby"? Longing for children as a fertility incentive of growing importance. *Journal of Evolutionary Psychology, 5*, 89–104.

Rotkirch, A., Basten, S., Väisänen, H., & Jokela, M. (2011). Baby longing and men's reproductive motivation. *Vienna Yearbook of Population Research, 9*, 283–306.

Rowa, K., Hood, H. K., & Antony, M. M. (2013). Generalized anxiety disorder. In W. E. Craighead, D. J. Miklowitz, & L. W. Craighead (Eds.), *Psychopathology: History, diagnosis, and empirical foundations* (2nd ed., pp. 108–146). New York: Wiley.

Rowe, D. C. (2002). On genetic variation in menarche and age at first sexual intercourse: A critique of the Belsky–Draper hypothesis. *Evolution and Human Behavior, 1*, 1–8.

Roy, A., & Campbell, M. K. (2013). A unifying framework for depression: Bridging the major biological and psychosocial theories through stress. *Clinical & Investigative Medicine, 36*, 170–190.

Rozin, P. (1990). Development in the food domain. *Developmental Psychology, 26*, 555–562.

Rozin, P., Haidt, J., & McCauley, C. R. (2008). Disgust. In M. Lewis, J. M. Haviland-Jones, & L. F. Barrett (Eds.), *Handbook of emotions* (3rd ed., pp. 757–776). New York: Guilford.

Rubin, D. C., Berntsen, D., Ogle, C. M., Deffler, S. A., & Beckham, J. C. (2016). Scientific evidence versus outdated beliefs: A response to Brewin (2016). *Journal of Abnormal Psychology, 125*, 1018–1021.

Rubin, D. C., Deffler, S. A., Ogle, C. M., Dowell, N. M., Graesser, A. C., & Beckham, J. C. (2016). Participant, rater, and computer measures of coherence in posttraumatic stress disorder. *Journal of Abnormal Psychology, 125*, 11–25.

Rubin, L. H., Carter, C. S., Bishop, J. R., Pournajafi-Nazarloo, H., Drogos, L. L., Hill, S. K., et al. (2014). Reduced levels of vasopressin and reduced behavioral modulation of oxytocin in psychotic disorders. *Schizophrenia Bulletin, 40*, 1374–1384.

Rubin, L. H., Carter, C. S., Drogos, L., Pournajafi-Nazarloo, H., Sweeney, J. A., & Maki, P. M. (2010). Peripheral oxytocin is associated with reduced symptom severity in schizophrenia. *Schizophrenia Research, 124*, 13–21.

Rudenstine, S. (2014). Applying a life course perspective to depression. In K. C. Koenen, S. Rudenstine, E. Susser, & S. Galea (Eds.), *A life course approach to mental disorders* (pp. 88–96). Oxford: Oxford University Press.

Ruderfer, D. M., Fanous, A. H., Ripke, S., McQuillin, A., Amdur, R. L., Gejman, P. V., et al. (2014). Polygenic dissection of diagnosis and clinical dimensions of bipolar disorder and schizophrenia. *Molecular Psychiatry, 19*, 1017–1024.

Rudolf, S., Greggersen, W., Kahl, K. G., Hüppe, M., & Schweiger, U. (2014). Elevated IL-6 levels in patients with atypical depression but not in patients with typical depression. *Psychiatry Research, 217*, 34–38.

Rueda, P., Fernández-Berrocal, P., & Baron-Cohen, S. (2015). Dissociation between cognitive and affective empathy in youth with Asperger Syndrome. *European Journal of Developmental Psychology, 12*, 85–98.

Rufer, M., Grothusen, A., Maß, R., Peter, H., & Hand, I. (2005). Temporal stability of symptom dimensions in adult patients with obsessive-compulsive disorder. *Journal of Affective Disorders, 88*, 99–102.

Ruocco, A. C. (2005). The neuropsychology of borderline personality disorder: A meta-analysis and review. *Psychiatry Research, 137*, 191–202.

Ruscio, A. M., & Meron, A. (2010). The latent structure of social anxiety disorder: Consequences of shifting to a dimensional diagnosis. *Journal of Abnormal Psychology, 119*, 662–671.

Ruscio, A. M., Stein, D. J., Chiu, W. T., & Kessler, R. C. (2010). The epidemiology of obsessive-compulsive disorder in the National Comorbidity Survey Replication. *Molecular Psychiatry, 15*, 53–63.

Rushton, J. P. (1985). Differential K theory: The sociobiology of individual and group differences. *Personality and Individual Differences, 6*, 441–452.

Rushton, J. P. (1987). An evolutionary theory of health, longevity, and personality: Sociobiology and r/K reproductive strategies. *Psychological Reports, 60*, 539–549.

Rushton, J. P. (2000). *Race, evolution, and behavior: A life history perspective* (2nd abridged ed.). Port Huron, MI: Charles Darwin Research Institute.

Rushton, J. P. (2012). The general factor of personality: A reply to Muncer. *Personality and Individual Differences, 52*, 236–239.

Rushton, J. P., & Irwing, P. (2009). A general factor of personality in 16 sets of the Big Five, the Guilford–Zimmerman Temperment Survey, the California Psychological Inventory, and the Temperament and Character Inventory. *Personality and Individual Differences, 47*, 558–564.

Russ, E., Shedler, J., Bradley, R., & Westen, D. (2008). Refining the construct of narcissistic personality disorder: Diagnostic criteria and subtypes. *American Journal of Psychiatry, 165*, 1473–1481.

Russell, A. E., Ford, T., & Russell, G. (2015). Socioeconomic associations with ADHD: Findings from a mediation analysis. *PloS one, 10*, e0128248.

Russell, C. J., & Keel, P. K. (2002). Homosexuality as a specific risk factor for eating disorders in men. *International Journal of Eating Disorders, 31*(3), 300–306.

Russell, G., Ford, T., Rosenberg, R., & Kelly, S. (2014). The association of attention deficit hyperactivity disorder with socioeconomic disadvantage: Alternative explanations and evidence. *Journal of Child Psychology and Psychiatry, 55*, 436–445.

Rutherford, M. D., & Ray, D. (2009). Cheater detection is preserved in autism spectrum disorders. *Journal of Social, Evolutionary, and Cultural Psychology, 3*, 105.

Ruthsatz, J., & Urbach, J. B. (2012). Child prodigy: A novel cognitive profile places elevated general intelligence, exceptional working memory and attention to detail at the root of prodigiousness. *Intelligence, 40*, 419–426.

Rutter, M., Moffitt, T. E., & Caspi, A. (2006). Gene–environment interplay and psychopathology: Multiple varieties but real effects. *Journal of Child Psychology and Psychiatry, 47*, 226–261.

Ruzich, E., Allison, C., Chakrabarti, B., Smith, P., Musto, H., Ring, H., et al. (2015). Sex and STEM occupation predict Autism-Spectrum Quotient (AQ) scores in half a million people. *PLoS ONE, 10*, e0141229.

Ruzich, E., Allison, C., Smith, P., Watson, P., Auyeung, B., Ring, H., et al. (2015). Measuring autistic traits in the general population: A systematic review of the Autism-Spectrum Quotient (AQ) in a nonclinical population sample of 6,900 typical adult males and females. *Molecular Autism, 6*, 2.

Ruzzano, L., Borsboom, D., & Geurts, H. M. (2015). Repetitive behaviors in autism and obsessive-compulsive disorder: New perspectives from a network analysis. *Journal of Autism and Developmental Disorders, 45*, 192–202.

Sadeh, A., Guterman, H., Gersani, M., & Ovadia, O. (2009). Plastic bet-hedging in an amphicarpic annual: An integrated strategy under variable conditions. *Evolutionary Ecology*, *23*, 373–388.

Sæther, B.-E. (1987). The influence of body weight on the covariation between reproductive traits in European birds. *Oikos*, *48*, 79–88.

Sagvolden, T., Johansen, E. B., Aase, H., & Russell, V. A. (2005). A dynamic developmental theory of attention-deficit/hyperactivity disorder (ADHD) predominantly hyperactive/impulsive and combined subtypes. *Behavioral and Brain Sciences*, *28*, 397–418.

Salkovskis, P. M. (1999). Understanding and treating obsessive-compulsive disorder. *Behaviour Research & Therapy*, *37*, S29–S52.

Salmon, C., Crawford, C. B., & Walters, S. (2008). Anorexic behavior, female competition and stress: Developing the female competition stress test. *Evolutionary Psychology*, *6*, 147470490800600112.

Salmon, C., Crawford, C., Dane, L., & Zuberbier, O. (2008). Ancestral mechanisms in modern environments. *Human Nature*, *19*, 103–117.

Salmon, C., Figueredo, A. J., & Woodburn, L. (2009). Life history strategy and disordered eating behavior. *Evolutionary Psychology*, *7*, 585–600.

Salonia, A., Giraldi, A., Chivers, M. L., Georgiadis, J. R., Levin, R., Maravilla, K. R., & McCarthy, M. M. (2010). Physiology of women's sexual function: Basic knowledge and new findings. *Journal of Sexual Medicine*, *7*, 2637–2660.

Salvatore, J. E., Aliev, F., Bucholz, K., Agrawal, A., Hesselbrock, V., Hesselbrock, M., et al. (2015). Polygenic risk for externalizing disorders gene-by-development and gene-by-environment effects in adolescents and young adults. *Clinical Psychological Science*, *3*, 189–201.

Samson, F., Mottron, L., Soulieres, I., & Zeffiro, T. A. (2012). Enhanced visual functioning in autism: An ALE meta-analysis. *Human Brain Mapping*, *33*, 1553–1581.

Samuel, D. B., & Widiger, T. A. (2008). A meta-analytic review of the relationships between the five-factor model and DSM-IV-TR personality disorders: A facet level analysis. *Clinical Psychology Review*, *28*, 1326–1342.

Samuels, J., & Costa, P. T. (2012). Obsessive-compulsive personality disorder. In T. A. Widiger (Ed.), *The Oxford handbook of personality disorders* (pp. 566–581). New York: Oxford University Press.

Sanacora, G., Treccani, G., & Popoli, M. (2012). Towards a glutamate hypothesis of depression: An emerging frontier of neuropsychopharmacology for mood disorders. *Neuropharmacology*, *62*, 63–77.

Sanborn, A. N., & Chater, N. (2016). Bayesian brains without probabilities. *Trends in Cognitive Sciences*, *20*, 883–893.

Sanchez, R., Parkin, J. C., Chen, J. Y., & Gray, P. B. (2009). Oxytocin, vasopressin, and human social behavior. In P. T. Ellison & P. B. Gray (Eds.), *Endocrinology of social relationships* (pp. 319–339). Cambridge, MA: Harvard University Press.

Sandin, S., Kolevzon, A., Levine, S. Z., Hultman, C. M., & Reichenberg, A. (2013). Parental and perinatal risk factors for autism: Epidemiological findings and potential mechanisms. In J. D. Buxbaum & P. R. Hof (Eds.), *The neuroscience of autism spectrum disorders* (pp. 195–202). Oxford: Academic press.

Sandler, D. P., Wilcox, A. J., & Horney, L. F. (1984). Age at menarche and subsequent reproductive events. *American Journal of Epidemiology*, *119*, 765–774.

Sandseter, E. B. H., & Kennair, L. E. O. (2011). Children's risky play from an evolutionary perspective: The anti-phobic effects of thrilling experiences. *Evolutionary Psychology*, *9*, 147470491100900212.

Sani, F. (2008). Schism in groups: A social psychological account. *Social and Personality Psychology Compass*, *2*, 718–732.

Sanislow, C. A., Bartolini, E. E., & Zoloth, E. C. (2012). Avoidant personality disorder. In V. S. Ramachandran (Ed.), *Encyclopedia of human behavior* (2nd ed., pp. 257–266). San Diego, CA: Academic Press.

Sanislow, C. A., Pine, D. S., Quinn, K. J., Kozak, M. J., Garvey, M. A., Heinssen, R. K., et al. (2010). Developing constructs for psychopathology research: Research domain criteria. *Journal of Abnormal Psychology*, *119*, 631–639.

Sariaslan, A., Långström, N., D'Onofrio, B., Hallqvist, J., Franck, J., & Lichtenstein, P. (2013). The impact of neighbourhood deprivation on adolescent violent criminality and substance misuse: A longitudinal, quasi-experimental study of the total Swedish population. *International Journal of Epidemiology*, *42*, 1057–1066.

Sariaslan, A., Larsson, H., D'Onofrio, B., Långström, N., Fazel, S., & Lichtenstein, P. (2015). Does population density and neighborhood deprivation predict schizophrenia? A nationwide Swedish family-based study of 2.4 million individuals. *Schizophrenia Bulletin*, *41*, 494–502.

Sartor, C. E., Grant, J. D., Lynskey, M. T., McCutcheon, V. V., Waldron, M., Statham, D. J., et al. (2012). Common heritable contributions to low-risk trauma, high-risk trauma, posttraumatic stress disorder, and major depression. *Archives of General Psychiatry*, *69*, 293–299.

Sarver, D. E., McCart, M. R., Sheidow, A. J., & Letourneau, E. J. (2014). ADHD and risky sexual behavior in adolescents: Conduct problems and substance use as mediators of risk. *Journal of Child Psychology and Psychiatry*, *55*, 1345–1353.

Sasaki, T., Hashimoto, K., Oda, Y., Ishima, T., Kurata, T., Takahashi, J., et al. (2015). Decreased levels of serum oxytocin in pediatric patients with attention deficit/hyperactivity disorder. *Psychiatry Research*, *228*, 746–751.

Sasser, T. R., Kalvin, C. B., & Bierman, K. L. (2016). Developmental trajectories of clinically significant attention-deficit/hyperactivity disorder (ADHD) symptoms from grade 3 through 12 in a high-risk sample: Predictors and outcomes. *Journal of Abnormal Psychology*, *125*, 207–219.

Sato, T., Bottlender, R., Kleindienst, N., & Moller, H. J. (2002). Syndromes and phenomenological subtypes underlying acute mania: A factor analytic study of 576 manic patients. *American Journal of Psychiatry*, *159*, 968–974.

Saucier, G. (2009). What are the most important dimensions of personality? Evidence from studies of descriptors in diverse languages. *Social and Personality Psychology Compass*, *3*, 620–637.

Saucier, G., Thalmayer, A. G., Payne, D. L., Carlson, R., Sanogo, L., Ole-Kotikash, L., et al. (2014). A basic bivariate structure of personality attributes evident across nine languages. *Journal of Personality*, *82*, 1–14.

Savage, J., Verhulst, B., Copeland, W., Althoff, R. R., Lichtenstein, P., & Roberson-Nay, R. (2015). A genetically informed study of the longitudinal relation between irritability and anxious/depressed symptoms. *Journal of the American Academy of Child & Adolescent Psychiatry*, *54*, 377–384.

Savage, V. M., Gillooly, J. F., Brown, J. H., West, G. B., & Charnov, E. L. (2004). Effects of body size and temperature on population growth. *The American Naturalist, 163*, 429–441.

Savard, C., Brassard, A., Lussier, Y., & Sabourin, S. (2015). Subclinical psychopathic traits and romantic attachment in community couples: A dyadic approach. *Personality and Individual Differences, 72*, 128–134.

Savill, M., Banks, C., Khanom, H., & Priebe, S. (2015). Do negative symptoms of schizophrenia change over time? A meta-analysis of longitudinal data. *Psychological Medicine, 45*, 1613–1627.

Saxena, S., Brody, A. L., Schwartz, J. M., & Baxter, L. R. (1998). Neuroimaging and frontal-subcortical circuitry in obsessive-compulsive disorder. *The British Journal of Psychiatry, 173*, 26–37.

Scelza, B. A. (2011). Female choice and extrapair paternity in a traditional human population. *Biology Letters, 7*, 889–891.

Schaafsma, S. M., Pfaff, D. W., Spunt, R. P., & Adolphs, R. (2015). Deconstructing and reconstructing theory of mind. *Trends in Cognitive Sciences, 19*, 65–72.

Schalet, B. D., Durbin, C. E., & Revelle, W. (2011). Multidimensional structure of the Hypomanic Personality Scale. *Psychological Assessment, 23*, 504–522.

Schalkwyk, L. C., Meaburn, E. L., Smith, R., Dempster, E. L., Jeffries, A. R., Davies, M. N., et al. (2010). Allelic skewing of DNA methylation is widespread across the genome. *American Journal of Human Genetics, 86*, 196–212.

Scheidel, W. (2009). A peculiar institution? Greco-Roman monogamy in global context. *History of the Family, 14*, 280–291.

Scheurink, A. J., Boersma, G. J., Nergårdh, R., & Södersten, P. (2010). Neurobiology of hyperactivity and reward: Agreeable restlessness in anorexia nervosa. *Physiology and Behavior, 100*, 490–495.

Schlagenhauf, F., Rapp, M. A., Huys, Q. J., Beck, A., Wüstenberg, T., Deserno, L., et al. (2013). Ventral striatal prediction error signaling is associated with dopamine synthesis capacity and fluid intelligence. *Human Brain Mapping, 34*, 1490–1499.

Schlichting, C. D., & Pigliucci, M. (1998). *Phenotypic evolution: A reaction norm perspective*. Sunderland, MA: Sinauer.

Schlomer, G. L., & Cleveland, H. H. (2014). Life history theory in psychopathology: More than an elegant heuristic? *Psychological Inquiry, 25*, 363–368.

Schlomer, G. L., Del Giudice, M., & Ellis, B. J. (2011). Parent-offspring conflict theory: An evolutionary framework for understanding conflict within human families. *Psychological Review, 118*, 496–521.

Schlomer, G. L., Ellis, B. J., & Garber, J. (2010). Mother–child conflict and sibling relatedness: A test of hypotheses from parent–offspring conflict theory. *Journal of Research on Adolescence, 20*, 287–306.

Schmaal, L., Hibar, D. P., Sämann, P. G., Hall, G. B., Baune, B. T., Jahanshad, N., et al. (2017). Cortical abnormalities in adults and adolescents with major depression based on brain scans from 20 cohorts worldwide in the ENIGMA Major Depressive Disorder Working Group. *Molecular Psychiatry, 22*, 900–909.

Schmidt, N. B., Korte, K. J., Norr, A. M., Keough, M. E., & Timpano, K. R. (2014). Panic disorder and agoraphobia. In P. Emmelkamp & T. Ehring (Eds.), *The Wiley handbook of anxiety disorders* (pp. 321–356). New York: Wiley.

Schmitt, D. P. (2005). Sociosexuality from Argentina to Zimbabwe: A 48-nation study of sex, culture, and strategies of human mating. *Behavioral and Brain Sciences, 28*, 247–275.

Schmitt, D. P. (2007). Sexual strategies across sexual orientations: How personality traits and culture relate to sociosexuality among gays, lesbians, bisexuals, and heterosexuals. *Journal of Psychology & Human Sexuality, 18*, 183–214.

Schmitt, D. P. (2012). When the difference is in the details: A critique of Zentner and Mitura (2012). "Stepping out of the caveman's shadow: Nations' gender gap predicts degree of sex differentiation in mate preferences". *Evolutionary Psychology, 10*, 720–726.

Schmitt, D. P. (2015*a*). Fundamentals of human mating strategies. In D. M. Buss (Ed.), *The handbook of evolutionary psychology* (2nd ed., pp. 294–316). Hoboken, NJ: Wiley.

Schmitt, D. P. (2015*b*). The evolution of culturally-variable sex differences: Men and women are not always different, but when they are. . . it appears not to result from patriarchy or sex role socialization. In T. C. Shackelford & R. D. Hansen (Eds.), *The evolution of sexuality* (pp. 221–256). New York: Springer.

Schmitt, D. P., Alcalay, L., Allensworth, M., Allik, J., Ault, L., Austers, I., Bennett, K. L., et al. (2003). Are men universally more dismissing than women? Gender differences in romantic attachment across 62 cultural regions. *Personal Relationships, 10*, 307–331.

Schmitt, D. P., Alcalay, L., Allik, J., Alves, I. C. B., Anderson, C. A., Angelini, A. L., et al. (2017). Narcissism and the strategic pursuit of short-term mating: Universal links across 11 world regions of the International Sexuality Description Project-2. *Psychological Topics, 26*, 89–137.

Schmitt, D. P., & Buss, D. M. (2000). Sexual dimensions of person description: Beyond or subsumed by the Big Five? *Journal of Research in Personality, 34*, 141–177.

Schmitt, D. P., & International Sexuality Description Project. (2003). Universal sex differences in the desire for sexual variety: Tests from 52 nations, 6 continents, and 13 islands. *Journal of Personality and Social Psychology, 85*, 85–104.

Schmitt, D. P., & Pilcher, J. J. (2004). Evaluating evidence of psychological adaptation: How do we know one when we see one? *Psychological Science, 15*, 643–649.

Schmitt, D. P., & Shackelford, T. K. (2008). Big five traits related to short-term mating: From personality to promiscuity across 46 nations. *Evolutionary Psychology, 6*, 246–282.

Schoenleber, M., & Berenbaum, H. (2010). Shame aversion and shame-proneness in Cluster C personality disorders. *Journal of Abnormal Psychology, 119*, 197–205.

Schoenleber, M., & Berenbaum, H. (2012). Aversion and proneness to shame in self-and informant-reported personality disorder symptoms. *Personality Disorders: Theory, Research, and Treatment, 3*, 294–304.

Schönenberg, M., & Jusyte, A. (2014). Investigation of the hostile attribution bias toward ambiguous facial cues in antisocial violent offenders. *European Archives of Psychiatry and Clinical Neuroscience, 264*, 61–69.

Schrider, D. R., & Kern, A. D. (2017). Soft sweeps are the dominant mode of adaptation in the human genome. *Molecular Biology and Evolution*. doi:10.1093/molbev/msx154

Schroeder, K., Fisher, H. L., & Schäfer, I. (2013). Psychotic symptoms in patients with borderline personality disorder: Prevalence and clinical management. *Current Opinion in Psychiatry, 26*, 113–119.

Schulze, L., Schmahl, C., & Niedtfeld, I. (2016). Neural correlates of disturbed emotion processing in borderline personality disorder: A multimodal meta-analysis. *Biological Psychiatry*, *79*, 97–106.

Schwartzman, B. C., Wood, J. J., & Kapp, S. K. (2016). Can the five factor model of personality account for the variability of autism symptom expression? Multivariate approaches to behavioral phenotyping in adult autism spectrum disorder. *Journal of Autism and Developmental Disorders*, *46*, 253–272.

Scola, G., & Andreazza, A. C. (2015). The role of neurotrophins in bipolar disorder. *Progress in Neuro-Psychopharmacology and Biological Psychiatry*, *56*, 122–128.

Scott, L. N., Levy, K. N., & Granger, D. A. (2013). Biobehavioral reactivity to social evaluative stress in women with borderline personality disorder. *Personality Disorders: Theory, Research, and Treatment*, *4*, 91–100.

Scott-Phillips, T. C., Dickins, T. E., & West, S. A. (2011). Evolutionary theory and the ultimate- proximate distinction in the human behavioral sciences. *Perspectives on Psychological Science*, *6*, 38–47.

Scult, M. A., Paulli, A. R., Mazure, E. S., Moffitt, T. E., Hariri, A. R., & Strauman, T. J. (2017). The association between cognitive function and subsequent depression: A systematic review and meta-analysis. *Psychological Medicine*, *47*, 1–17.

Seara-Cardoso, A., & Viding, E. (2015). Functional neuroscience of psychopathic personality in adults. *Journal of Personality*, *83*, 723–737.

Seery, M. D. (2011). Resilience: A silver lining to experiencing adverse life events? *Current Directions in Psychological Science*, *20*, 390–394.

Seery, M. D., Holman, E. A., & Silver, R. C. (2010). Whatever does not kill us: Cumulative lifetime adversity, vulnerability, and resilience. *Journal of Personality and Social Psychology*, *99*, 1025–1041.

Seery, M. D., Leo, R. J., Lupien, S. P., Kondrak, C. L., & Almonte, J. L. (2013). An upside to adversity? Moderate cumulative lifetime adversity is associated with resilient responses in the face of controlled stressors. *Psychological Science*, *24*, 1181–1189.

Segarra, P., Poy, R., López, R., & Moltó, J. (2014). Characterizing Carver and White's BIS/BAS subscales using the Five Factor Model of personality. *Personality and Individual Differences*, *61*, 18–23.

Seligman, M. E. (1971). Phobias and preparedness. *Behavior Therapy*, *2*, 307–320.

Seltzer, M. M., Shattuck, P., Abbeduto, L., & Greenberg, J. S. (2004). Trajectory of development in adolescents and adults with autism. *Mental Retardation and Developmental Disabilities Research Reviews*, *10*, 234–247.

Selvaraj, S., Arnone, D., Cappai, A., & Howes, O. (2014). Alterations in the serotonin system in schizophrenia: A systematic review and meta-analysis of postmortem and molecular imaging studies. *Neuroscience & Biobehavioral Reviews*, *45*, 233–245.

Sentse, M., Kretschmer, T., Haan, A., & Prinzie, P. (2017). Conduct problem trajectories between age 4 and 17 and their association with behavioral adjustment in emerging adulthood. *Journal of Youth and Adolescence*, *46*, 1633–1642.

Servaas, M. N., van der Velde, J., Costafreda, S. G., Horton, P., Ormel, J., Riese, H., et al. (2013). Neuroticism and the brain: A quantitative meta-analysis of neuroimaging studies investigating emotion processing. *Neuroscience & Biobehavioral Reviews*, *37*, 1518–1529.

Sesardic, N. (2005). *Making sense of heritability*. Cambridge, MA: Cambridge University Press.

Sevgi, M., Diaconescu, A. O., Tittgemeyer, M., & Schilbach, L. (2016). Social bayes: Using Bayesian modeling to study autistic trait–related differences in social cognition. *Biological Psychiatry*, *80*, 112–119.

Seyfarth, R. M., & Cheney, D. L. (2012). The evolutionary origins of friendship. *Annual Review of Psychology, 63*, 153–177.

Shackelford, T. K., Schmitt, D. P., & Buss, D. M. (2005). Universal dimensions of human mate preferences. *Personality and Individual Differences, 39*, 447–458.

Shaner, A., Miller, G., & Mintz, J. (2007). Evidence of a latitudinal gradient in the age at onset of schizophrenia. *Schizophrenia Research, 94*, 58–63.

Shaner, A., Miller, G., & Mintz, J. (2008). Autism as the low-fitness extreme of a parentally selected fitness indicator. *Human Nature, 19*, 389–413.

Shaner, A., Miller, G. F., & Mintz, J. (2004). Schizophrenia as one extreme of a sexually selected fitness indicator. *Schizophrenia Research, 70*, 101–109.

Shapiro, L. J., & Evelyn Stewart, S. (2011). Pathological guilt: A persistent yet overlooked treatment factor in obsessive-compulsive disorder. *Annals of Clinical Psychiatry, 23*, 63–70.

Sharp, C. (2008). Theory of Mind and conduct problems in children: Deficits in reading the "emotions of the eyes". *Cognition and Emotion, 22*, 1149–1158.

Sharp, C., Ha, C., Michonski, J., Venta, A., & Carbone, C. (2012). Borderline personality disorder in adolescents: Evidence in support of the Childhood Interview for DSM-IV Borderline Personality Disorder in a sample of adolescent inpatients. *Comprehensive Psychiatry, 53*, 765–774.

Sharp, C., Pane, H., Ha, C., Venta, A., Patel, A. B., Sturek, J., et al. (2011). Theory of mind and emotion regulation difficulties in adolescents with borderline traits. *Journal of the American Academy of Child & Adolescent Psychiatry, 50*, 563–573.

Shaw, D. S., Gilliom, M., Ingoldsby, E. M., & Nagin, D. (2003). Trajectories leading to school-age conduct problems. *Developmental Psychology, 39*, 189–200.

Sheerin, C. M., Lind, M. J., Bountress, K. E., Nugent, N. R., & Amstadter, A. B. (2017). The genetics and epigenetics of PTSD: Overview, recent advances, and future directions. *Current Opinion in Psychology, 14*, 5–11.

Sheldrick, R. C., Maye, M. P., & Carter, A. S. (2017). Age at first identification of autism spectrum disorder: An analysis of two US surveys. *Journal of the American Academy of Child & Adolescent Psychiatry, 56*, 313–320.

Shelley-Tremblay, J. F., & Rosen, L. A. (1996). Attention deficit hyperactivity disorder: An evolutionary perspective. *The Journal of Genetic Psychology, 157*, 443–453.

Shepard, B. (2004). Risk factors and PTSD: A historian's perspective. In G. M. Rosen (Ed.), *Posttraumatic stress disorder: Issues and controversies* (pp. 39–62). Chichester, UK: Wiley.

Sheppard, P., Pearce, M. S., & Sear, R. (2016). How does childhood socioeconomic hardship affect reproductive strategy? Pathways of development. *American Journal of Human Biology, 28*, 356–363.

Sherman, J. A. (2001). Evolutionary Origin of Bipolar Disorder (EOBD). *Psycoloquy, 12*, 1–24.

Sherman, J. A. (2006). Bipolar disorder evolved as an adaptation to severe climate. *Behavioral and Brain Sciences, 29*, 421–422.

Sherman, J. A. (2012). Evolutionary origin of bipolar disorder-revised: EOBD-R. *Medical Hypotheses, 78*, 113–122.

Sherman, P. W., & Flaxman, S. M. (2002). Nausea and vomiting of pregnancy in an evolutionary perspective. *American Journal of Obstetrics and Gynecology, 186*, s190–s197.

Sherman, R. A., Figueredo, A. J., & Funder, D. C. (2013). The behavioral correlates of overall and distinctive life history strategy. *Journal of Personality and Social Psychology, 105*, 873–888.

Shorter, E., & Fink, M. (2010). *Endocrine psychiatry: Solving the riddle of melancholia*. New York: Oxford University Press.

Shudo, E., Haccou, P., & Iwasa, Y. (2003). Optimal choice between feedforward and feedback control in gene expression to cope with unpredictable danger. *Journal of Theoretical Biology, 223*, 149–160.

Shyrock, A., & Smail, D. L. (Eds.). (2011). *Deep history: The architecture of past and present*. Berkeley, CA: University of California Press.

Sica, C., Novara, C., & Sanavio, E. (2002). Religiousness and obsessive-compulsive cognitions and symptoms in an Italian population. *Behaviour Research & Therapy, 40*, 813–823.

Siddaway, A. P., Taylor, P. J., Wood, A. M., & Schulz, J. (2015). A meta-analysis of perceptions of defeat and entrapment in depression, anxiety problems, posttraumatic stress disorder, and suicidality. *Journal of Affective Disorders, 184*, 149–159.

Siedor, L., Maples-Keller, J. L., Miller, J. D., & Campbell, W. K. (2016). Narcissism and hypomania revisited: A test of the similarities and differences in their empirical networks. *Current Psychology, 35*, 244–254.

Sih, A., & Del Giudice, M. (2012). Linking behavioural syndromes and cognition: A behavioural ecology perspective. *Philosophical Transactions of the Royal Society of London B, 367*, 2762–2772.

Silberschmidt, A., Lee, S., Zanarini, M., & Schulz, S. C. (2015). Gender differences in borderline personality disorder: Results from a multinational, clinical trial sample. *Journal of Personality Disorders, 29*, 828–838.

Silverstein, B. (2002). Gender differences in the prevalence of somatic versus pure depression: Aa replication. *American Journal of Psychiatry, 159*, 1051–1052.

Silvia, P. J., Kaufman, J. C., Reiter-Palmon, R., & Wigert, B. (2011). Cantankerous creativity: Honesty–humility, agreeableness, and the HEXACO structure of creative achievement. *Personality and Individual Differences, 51*, 687–689.

Simonsen, H., Shand, A. J., Scott, N. W., & Eagles, J. M. (2011). Seasonal symptoms in bipolar and primary care patients. *Journal of Affective Disorders, 132*, 200–208.

Simonton, D. K. (1999). *Origins of genius: Darwinian perspectives on creativity*. New York: Oxford University Press.

Simonton, D. K. (2014). The mad (creative) genius: What do we know after a century of historiometric research? In J. C. Kaufman (Ed.), *Creativity and mental illness* (pp. 25–41). Cambridge: Cambridge University Press.

Simpson, H. B., Shungu, D. C., Bender, J., Mao, X., Xu, X., Slifstein, M., & Kegeles, L. S. (2012). Investigation of cortical glutamate–glutamine and γ-aminobutyric acid in obsessive-compulsive disorder by proton magnetic resonance spectroscopy. *Neuropsychopharmacology, 37*, 2684–2692.

Simpson, J. A., & Gangestad, S. W. (1991). Individual differences in sociosexuality: Evidence for convergent and discriminant validity. *Journal of Personality and Social Psychology, 60*, 870–883.

Simpson, J. A., Griskevicius, V., Kuo, S. I., Sung, S., & Collins, W. A. (2012). Evolution, stress, and sensitive periods: The influence of unpredictability in early versus late childhood on sex and risky behavior. *Developmental Psychology, 48*, 674–686.

Simpson, J. A., Wilson, C. L., & Winterheld, H. A. (2004). Sociosexuality and romantic relationships. In J. H. Harvey, A. Wenzel, & S. Sprecher (Eds.), *Handbook of sexuality in close relationships* (pp. 87–112). Mahwah, NJ: Erlbaum.

Sinervo, B., Clobert, J., Miles, D. B., McAdam, A., & Lancaster, L. T. (2008). The role of pleiotropy vs signaller–receiver gene epistasis in life history trade-offs: Dissecting the genomic architecture of organismal design in social systems. *Heredity, 101*, 197–211.

Sipahi, L., Uddin, M., Hou, Z. C., Aiello, A. E., Koenen, K. C., Galea, S., et al. (2014). Ancient evolutionary origins of epigenetic regulation associated with posttraumatic stress disorder. *Frontiers in Human Neuroscience, 8*, 284.

Sizoo, B., van den Brink, W., van Eenige, M. G., & van der Gaag, R. J. (2009). Personality characteristics of adults with autism spectrum disorders or attention deficit hyperactivity disorder with and without substance use disorders. *The Journal of Nervous and Mental Disease, 197*, 450–454.

Sjåstad, H. N., Gråwe, R. W., & Egeland, J. (2012). Affective disorders among patients with borderline personality disorder. *PloS ONE, 7*, e50930.

Skirbekk, V., & Blekesaune, M. (2014). Personality traits increasingly important for male fertility: Evidence from Norway. *European Journal of Personality, 28*, 521–529.

Skodol, A. E. (2014). Borderline, schizotypal, avoidant, obsessive-compulsive, and other personality disorders. In K. C. Karestan, S. Rudenstine, E. Susser, & S. Galea (Eds.), *A life course approach to mental disorders* (pp. 174–181). Oxford: Oxford University Press.

Skodol, A. E., Bender, D. S., Pagano, M. E., Shea, M. T., Yen, S., Sanislow, C. A., et al. (2007). Positive childhood experiences: Resilience and recovery from personality disorder in early adulthood. *The Journal of Clinical Psychiatry, 68*, 1102–1108.

Slade, T. (2007). The descriptive epidemiology of internalizing and externalizing psychiatric dimensions. *Social Psychiatry and Psychiatric Epidemiology, 42*, 554–560.

Slagt, M., Semon Dubas, J., Deković, M., & van Aken, M. A. G. (2016). Differences in sensitivity to parenting depending on child temperament: A meta-analysis. *Psychological Bulletin, 142*, 1068–1110.

Slaughter, V., Imuta, K., Peterson, C. C., & Henry, J. D. (2015). Meta-analysis of theory of mind and peer popularity in the preschool and early school years. *Child Development, 86*, 1159–1174.

Sloman, L. (2008). A new comprehensive evolutionary model of depression and anxiety. *Journal of Affective Disorders, 106*, 219–228.

Sloman, L., Farvolden, P., Gilbert, P., & Price, J. (2006). The interactive functioning of anxiety and depression in agonistic encounters and reconciliation. *Journal of Affective Disorders, 90*, 93–99.

Smallwood, P. D. (1996). An introduction to risk sensitivity: The use of Jensen's inequality to clarify evolutionary arguments of adaptation and constraint. *American Zoologist, 36*, 392–401.

Smith, D. J., Anderson, J., Zammit, S., Meyer, T. D., Pell, J. P., & Mackay, D. (2015). Childhood IQ and risk of bipolar disorder in adulthood: Prospective birth cohort study. *British Journal of Psychiatry Open, 1*, 74–80.

Smith, D. J., Escott-Price, V., Davies, G., Bailey, M. E., Conde, L. C., Ward, J., et al. (2015). Genome-wide analysis of over 106,000 individuals identifies 9 neuroticism-associated loci. *bioRxiv*, 032417.

Smith-Woolley, E., Rimfeld, K., & Plomin, R. (2017). Weak associations between pubertal development and psychiatric and behavioral problems. *Translational Psychiatry, 7*, e1098.

Snitz, B. E., Macdonald, A. W., & Carter, C. S. (2006). Cognitive deficits in unaffected first-degree relatives of schizophrenia patients: A meta-analytic review of putative endophenotypes. *Schizophrenia Bulletin, 32*, 179–194.

Snyder, H. R., & Hankin, B. L. (2016). Spiraling out of control: Stress generation and subsequent rumination mediate the link between poorer cognitive control and internalizing psychopathology. *Clinical Psychological Science*, *4*, 1047–1064.

Snyder, H. R., Kaiser, R. H., Warren, S. L., & Heller, W. (2015). Obsessive-compulsive disorder is associated with broad impairments in executive function: A meta-analysis. *Clinical Psychological Science*, *3*, 301–330.

Snyder, J., Cramer, A., Afrank, J., & Patterson, G. R. (2005). The contributions of ineffective discipline and parental hostile attributions of child misbehavior to the development of conduct problems at home and school. *Developmental Psychology*, *41*, 30–41.

Sober, E., & Wilson, D. S. (1998). *Unto others: The evolution and psychology of unselfish behavior*. Cambridge, MA: Harvard University Press.

Soderstrom, H., Blennow, K., Manhem, A., & Forsman, A. (2001). 5-HIAA as a negative and HVA as a positive predictor of psychopathy. *Journal of Neural Transmission*, *108*, 869–878.

Soderstrom, H., Blennow, K., Sjodin, A. K., & Forsman, A. (2003). New evidence for an association between the CSF HVA: 5-HIAA ratio and psychopathic traits. *Journal of Neurology, Neurosurgery & Psychiatry*, *74*, 918–921.

Song, J., Bergen, S. E., Kuja-Halkola, R., Larsson, H., Landén, M., & Lichtenstein, P. (2015). Bipolar disorder and its relation to major psychiatric disorders: A family-based study in the Swedish population. *Bipolar Disorders*, *17*, 184–193.

Sonneville, K. R., Calzo, J. P., Horton, N. J., Field, A. E., Crosby, R. D., Solmi, F., et al. (2015). Childhood hyperactivity/inattention and eating disturbances predict binge eating in adolescence. *Psychological Medicine*, *45*, 2511–2520.

Soto, C. J., John, O. P., Gosling, S. D., & Potter, J. (2011). Age differences in personality traits from 10 to 65: Big Five domains and facets in a large cross-sectional sample. *Journal of Personality and Social Psychology*, *100*, 330–348.

South, M., Chamberlain, P. D., Wigham, S., Newton, T., Le Couteur, A., McConachie, H., et al. (2014). Enhanced decision making and risk avoidance in high-functioning autism spectrum disorder. *Neuropsychology*, *28*, 222–228.

Spain, S. L., Pedroso, I., Kadeva, N., Miller, M. B., Iacono, W. G., McGue, M., et al. (2016). A genome-wide analysis of putative functional and exonic variation associated with extremely high intelligence. *Molecular Psychiatry*, *21*, 1145–1151.

Sparks, A. M., Fessler, D. M. T., Chan, K. Q., Ashokkumar, A., & Holbrook, C. (2018). Disgust as a mechanism for decision making under risk: Illuminating sex differences and individual risk-taking correlates of disgust propensity. *Emotion*. doi:10.1037/emo0000389

Sperber, D. (1994). The modularity of thought and the epidemiology of representations. In L. A. Hirschfeld & S. A. Gelman (Eds.), *Mapping the mind: Domain specificity in cognition and culture* (pp. 39–67). New York: Cambridge University Press.

Spikins, P. (2009). Autism, the integrations of "difference" and the origins of modern human behaviour. *Cambridge Archaeological Journal*, *19*, 179–201.

Spinhoven, P., Elzinga, B. M., van Hemert, A. M., de Rooij, M., & Penninx, B. W. (2014). A longitudinal study of facets of extraversion in depression and social anxiety. *Personality & Individual Differences*, *71*, 39–44.

Spinka, M., Newberry, R. C., & Bekoff, M. (2001). Mammalian play: Training for the unexpected. *Quarterly Review of Biology*, *76*, 141–168.

Spironelli, C., Segrè, D., Stegagno, L., & Angrilli, A. (2014). Intelligence and psychopathy: A correlational study on insane female offenders. *Psychological Medicine*, *44*, 111–116.

Srivastava, S., Childers, M. E., Baek, J. H., Strong, C. M., Hill, S. J., Warsett, K. S., et al. (2010). Toward interaction of affective and cognitive contributors to creativity in bipolar disorders: A controlled study. *Journal of Affective Disorders, 125*, 27–34.

Stamps, J. A. (2007). Growth-mortality tradeoffs and "personality traits" in animals. *Ecology Letters, 10*, 355–363.

Stamps, J. A., & Frankenhuis, W. E. (2016). Bayesian models of development. *Trends in Ecology & Evolution, 31*, 260–268.

Stanton, K., Daly, E., Stasik-O'Brien, S. M., Ellickson-Larew, S., Clark, L. A., & Watson, D. (2016). An integrative analysis of the narcissistic personality inventory and the hypomanic personality scale: Implications for construct validity. *Assessment*. doi:10.1177/1073191115625801

Starcevic, V., Berle, D., Brakoulias, V., Sammut, P., Moses, K., Milicevic, D., et al. (2013). Obsessive–compulsive personality disorder co-occurring with obsessive-compulsive disorder: Conceptual and clinical implications. *Australian and New Zealand Journal of Psychiatry, 47*, 65–73.

Starrfelt, J., & Kokko, H. (2012). Bet-hedging—a triple trade-off between means, variances and correlations. *Biological Reviews, 85*, 742–755.

Stearns, S. C. (1992). *The evolution of life histories*. Oxford: Oxford University Press.

Stearns, S. C., & Medzhitov, R. (2016). *Evolutionary medicine*. Sunderland, MA: Sinauer.

Stearns, S. C., Nesse, R. M., Govindaraju, D. R., & Ellison, P. T. (2010). Evolutionary perspectives on health and medicine. *Proceedings of the National Academy of Sciences USA, 107*, 1691–1695.

Steenkamp, M. M., Nickerson, A., Maguen, S., Dickstein, B. D., Nash, W. P., & Litz, B. T. (2012). Latent classes of PTSD symptoms in Vietnam veterans. *Behavior Modification, 36*, 857–874.

Steenkamp, M. M., Suvak, M. K., Dickstein, B. D., Shea, M. T., & Litz, B. T. (2015). Emotional functioning in obsessive-compulsive personality disorder: Comparison to borderline personality disorder and healthy controls. *Journal of Personality Disorders, 29*, 794–808.

Stefanou, C., & McCabe, M. P. (2012). Adult attachment and sexual functioning: A review of past research. *Journal of Sexual Medicine, 9*, 2499–2507.

Stein, D. J., Hermesh, H., Eilam, D., Segalas, C., Zohar, J., Menchon, J., et al. (2016). Human compulsivity: A perspective from evolutionary medicine. *European Neuropsychopharmacology, 26*, 869–876.

Stein, D. J., Liu, Y., Shapira, N. A., & Goodman, W. K. (2001). The psychobiology of obsessive-compulsive disorder: How important is the role of disgust? *Current Psychiatry Reports, 3*, 281–287.

Steinberg, L., Albert, D., Cauffman, E., Banich, M., Graham, S., & Woolard, J. (2008). Age differences in sensation seeking and impulsivity as indexed by behavior and self-report: Evidence for a dual systems model. *Developmental Psychology, 44*, 1764–1778.

Steinhausen, H. C., Bisgaard, C., Munk-Jørgensen, P., & Helenius, D. (2013). Family aggregation and risk factors of obsessive-compulsive disorders in a nationwide three-generation study. *Depression and Anxiety, 30*, 1177–1184.

Stephens, D. W., Kerr, B., & Fernández-Juricic, E. (2004). Impulsiveness without discounting: The ecological rationality hypothesis. *Proceedings of the Royal Society of London B, 271*, 2459–2465.

Sterling, P., & Eyer, J. (1988). Allostasis: A new paradigm to explain arousal pathology. In S. Fisher & J. Reason (Eds.), *Handbook of life stress, cognition, and health* (pp. 629–650). Oxford: Oxford University Press.

Steudte-Schmiedgen, S., Kirschbaum, C., Alexander, N., & Stalder, T. (2016). An integrative model linking traumatization, cortisol dysregulation and posttraumatic stress disorder: Insight from recent hair cortisol findings. *Neuroscience & Biobehavioral Reviews*, *69*, 124–135.

Stevens, A., & Price, J. (2000). *Evolutionary psychiatry: A new beginning* (2nd ed.). New York: Routledge.

Stevenson, J. L., & Gernsbacher, M. A. (2013). Abstract spatial reasoning as an autistic strength. *PloS ONE*, *8*, e59329.

Stewart, E., Cancilliere, M. K., Freeman, J., Wellen, B., Garcia, A., Sapyta, J., et al. (2016). Elevated autism spectrum disorder traits in young children with OCD. *Child Psychiatry & Human Development*, *47*, 993–1001.

Stewart, J. G., & Harkness, K. L. (2015). The interpersonal toxicity of excessive reassurance-seeking: Evidence from a longitudinal study of romantic relationships. *Journal of Social and Clinical Psychology*, *34*, 392–410.

Stewart, J. W., McGrath, P. J., Quitkin, F. M., & Klein, D. F. (2007). Atypical depression: Current status and relevance to melancholia. *Acta Psychiatrica Scandinavica*, *115*, 58–71.

Stewart-Williams, S. (2007). Altruism among kin vs. nonkin: Effects of cost of help and reciprocal exchange. *Evolution and Human Behavior*, *28*, 193–198.

Stewart-Williams, S., & Thomas, A. G. (2013). The ape that thought it was a peacock: Does evolutionary psychology exaggerate human sex differences? *Psychological Inquiry*, *24*, 137–168.

Stieglitz, J., Schniter, E., von Rueden, C., Kaplan, H., & Gurven, M. (2015). Functional disability and social conflict increase risk of depression in older adulthood among Bolivian forager-farmers. *Journals of Gerontology B*, *70*, 948–956.

Stieglitz, J., Trumble, B. C., Thompson, M. E., Blackwell, A. D., Kaplan, H., & Gurven, M. (2015). Depression as sickness behavior? A test of the host defense hypothesis in a high pathogen population. *Brain, Behavior, and Immunity*, *49*, 130–139.

Stigler, K. A., & McDougle, C. J. (2013). Structural and functional MRI studies of autism spectrum disorders. In J. D. Buxbaum & P. R. Hof (Eds.), *The neuroscience of autism spectrum disorders* (pp. 251–266). Oxford: Academic Press.

Stinso, F. S., Dawson, D. A., Goldstein, R. B., Chou, S. P., Huang, B., Smith, S. M., et al. (2008). Prevalence, correlates, disability, and comorbidity of DSM-IV narcissistic personality disorder: Results from the wave 2 national epidemiologic survey on alcohol and related conditions. *Journal of Clinical Psychiatry*, *69*, 1033–1045.

Stinson, F. S., Dawson, D. A., Goldstein, R. B., Chou, S. P., Huang, B., Smith, S. M., et al. (2008). Prevalence, correlates, disability, and comorbidity of DSM-IV narcissistic personality disorder: Results from the wave 2 national epidemiologic survey on alcohol and related conditions. *The Journal of Clinical Psychiatry*, *69*, 1033–1045.

Stiver, K. A., & Alonzo, S. H. (2009). Parental and mating effort: Is there necessarily a trade- off? *Ethology*, *115*, 1101–1126.

St. John-Smith, P., McQueen, D., Edwards, L., & Schifano, F. (2013). Classical and novel psychoactive substances: Rethinking drug misuse from an evolutionary psychiatric perspective. *Human Psychopharmacology: Clinical & Experimental*, *28*, 394–401.

Stoneham, A. C., & Coughtrey, A. E. (2009). The role of schizotypy and creativity in a group problem-solving task. *Personality and Individual Differences, 46*, 827–831.

Storebø, O. J., Rasmussen, P. D., & Simonsen, E. (2016). Association between insecure attachment and ADHD: Environmental mediating factors. *Journal of Attention Disorders, 20*, 187–196.

Strakowski, S. M., Flaum, M., Amador, X., Bracha, H. S., Pandurangi, A. K., Robinson, D., et al. (1996). Racial differences in the diagnosis of psychosis. *Schizophrenia Research, 21*, 117–124.

Strauss, G. P., Keller, W. R., Koenig, J. I., Gold, J. M., Ossenfort, K. L., & Buchanan, R. W. (2015). Plasma oxytocin levels predict olfactory identification and negative symptoms in individuals with schizophrenia. *Schizophrenia Research, 162*, 57–61.

Stringaris, A., Stahl, D., Santosh, P., & Goodman, R. (2011). Dimensions and latent classes of episodic mania-like symptoms in youth: An empirical enquiry. *Journal of Abnormal Child Psychology, 39*, 925–937.

Strom, T. Q., Leskela, J., James, L. M., Thuras, P. D., Voller, E., Weigel, R., et al. (2012). An exploratory examination of risk-taking behavior and PTSD symptom severity in a veteran sample. *Military Medicine, 177*, 390–396.

Strunz, S., Schermuck, C., Ballerstein, S., Ahlers, C. J., Dziobek, I., & Roepke, S. (2017). Romantic relationships and relationship satisfaction among adults with Asperger syndrome and high-functioning autism. *Journal of Clinical Psychology, 73*, 113–125.

Strunz, S., Westphal, L., Ritter, K., Heuser, I., Dziobek, I., & Roepke, S. (2015). Personality pathology of adults with autism spectrum disorder without accompanying intellectual impairment in comparison to adults with personality disorders. *Journal of Autism and Developmental Disorders, 45*, 4026–4038.

Sturman, E. D. (2011). Involuntary subordination and its relation to personality, mood, and submissive behavior. *Psychological Assessment, 23*, 262–276.

Sugden, K., Moffitt, T. E., Pinto, L., Poulton, R., Williams, B. S., & Caspi, A. (2016). Is *Toxoplasma gondii* infection related to brain and behavior impairments in humans? Evidence from a population-representative birth cohort. *PLoS ONE, 11*, e0148435.

Suhr, J. A., Spitznagel, M. B., & Gunstad, J. (2006). An obsessive-compulsive subtype of schizotypy: Evidence from a nonclinical sample. *The Journal of Nervous & Mental Disease, 194*, 884–886.

Sullivan, P. F., Magnusson, C., Reichenberg, A., Boman, M., Dalman, C., Davidson, M., et al. (2012). Family history of schizophrenia and bipolar disorder as risk factors for autism. *Archives of General Psychiatry, 69*, 1099–1103.

Sullivan, P. F., Prescott, C. A., & Kendler, K. S. (2002). The subtypes of major depression in a twin registry. *Journal of Affective Disorders, 68*, 273–284.

Sullivan, R. J., Hagen, E. H., & Hammerstein, P. (2008). Revealing the paradox of drug reward in human evolution. *Proceedings of the Royal Society of London B: Biological Sciences, 275*, 1231–1241.

Sullivan, R. M., Brake, W. G. (2003). What the rodent prefrontal cortex can teach us about attention-deficit/hyperactivity disorder: The critical role of early developmental events on prefrontal function. *Behavioural Brain Research, 146*, 43–55.

Sullivan, S., Rai, D., Golding, J., Zammit, S., & Steer, C. (2013). The association between autism spectrum disorder and psychotic experiences in the Avon longitudinal study of parents and children (ALSPAC) birth cohort. *Journal of the American Academy of Child & Adolescent Psychiatry, 52*, 806–814.

Sumner, J. A., Duncan, L., Ratanatharathorn, A., Roberts, A. L., & Koenen, K. C. (2016). PTSD has shared polygenic contributions with bipolar disorder and schizophrenia in women. *Psychological Medicine, 46*, 669–671.

Sun, S. S., Schubert, C. M., Chumlea, W. C., Roche, A. F., Kulin, H. E., Lee, P. A., et al. (2002). National estimates of the timing of sexual maturation and racial differences among US children. *Pediatrics, 110*, 911–919.

Sundie, J. M., Kenrick, D. T., Griskevicius, V., Tybur, J. M., Vohs, K. D., & Beal, D. J. (2011). Peacocks, Porsches, and Thorstein Veblen: Conspicuous consumption as a sexual signaling system. *Journal of Personality and Social Psychology, 100*, 664–680.

Sung, S., Simpson, J. A., Griskevicius, V., Sally, I., Kuo, C., Schlomer, G. L., & Belsky, J. (2016). Secure infant-mother attachment buffers the effect of early-life stress on age of menarche. *Psychological Science, 27*, 667–674.

Surbey, M. K. (1987). Anorexia nervosa, amenorrhea, and adaptation. *Ethology and Sociobiology, 8*, 47–61.

Surbey, M. K. (2011). Adaptive significance of low levels of self-deception and cooperation in depression. *Evolution and Human Behavior, 32*, 29–40.

Susman, E. J. (2006). Psychobiology of persistent antisocial behavior: Stress, early vulnerabilities and the attenuation hypothesis. *Neuroscience & Biobehavioral Reviews, 30*, 376–389.

Suzuki, T., Samuel, D. B., Pahlen, S., & Krueger, R. F. (2015). DSM-5 alternative personality disorder model traits as maladaptive extreme variants of the five-factor model: An item-response theory analysis. *Journal of Abnormal Psychology, 124*, 343–354.

Svanbäck, R., Pineda-Krch, M., & Doebeli, M. (2009). Fluctuating population dynamics promotes the evolution of phenotypic plasticity. *The American Naturalist, 174*, 176–189.

Svardal, H., Rueffler, C., & Hermisson, J. (2011). Comparing environmental and genetic variance as adaptive response to fluctuating selection. *Evolution, 65*, 2492–2513.

Svensson, A. C., Lichtenstein, P., Sandin, S., & Hultman, C. M. (2007). Fertility of first-degree relatives of patients with schizophrenia: A three generation perspective. *Schizophrenia Research, 91*, 238–245.

Swami, V. (2015). Cultural influences on body size ideals. *European Psychologist, 20*, 44–51.

Swanson, E. M., & Dantzer, B. (2014). Insulin-like growth factor-1 is associated with life-history variation across Mammalia. *Proceedings of the Royal Society of London B, 281*, 20132458.

Szechtman, H., Ahmari, S. E., Beninger, R. J., Eilam, D., Harvey, B. H., Edemann-Callesen, H., et al. (2017). Obsessive-compulsive disorder: Insights from animal models. *Neuroscience & Biobehavioral Reviews, 76*, 254–279.

Szechtman, H., & Woody, E. (2004). Obsessive-compulsive disorder as a disturbance of security motivation. *Psychological Review, 111*, 111–127.

Szepsenwol, O., Griskevicius, V., Simpson, J. A., Young, E. S., Fleck, C., & Jones, R. E. (2017). The effect of predictable early childhood environments on sociosexuality in early adulthood. *Evolutionary Behavioral Sciences, 11*, 131–145.

Sznycer, D., Cosmides, L., & Tooby, J. (2017). Adaptationism carves emotions at their functional joints. *Psychological inquiry, 28*, 56–62.

Taborsky, M., & Brockmann, H. J. (2010). Alternative reproductive tactics and life history phenotypes. In P. Kappeler (Ed.), *Animal behaviour: Evolution and mechanisms* (537–586). New York: Springer.

Tackett, J. L., Herzhoff, K., Balsis, S., & Cooper, L. (2016). Toward a unifying perspective on personality pathology across the life span. In D. Cicchetti (Ed.), *Developmental psychopathology: Vol. 3. Maladaptation and psychopathology* (3rd ed., pp. 1039–1078). New York: Wiley.

Tamm, L., Garner, A. A., Loren, R. E. A., Epstein, J. N., Vaughn, A. J., Ciesielski, H. A., & Becker, S. P. (2016). Slow sluggish cognitive tempo symptoms are associated with poorer academic performance in children with ADHD. *Psychiatry Research*, *242*, 251–259.

Taurines, R., Schwenck, C., Lyttwin, B., Schecklmann, M., Jans, T., Reefschläger, L., et al. (2014). Oxytocin plasma concentrations in children and adolescents with autism spectrum disorder: Correlation with autistic symptomatology. *ADHD Attention Deficit and Hyperactivity Disorders*, *6*, 231–239.

Taylor, J., Allan, N., Mikolajewski, A. J., & Hart, S. A. (2013). Common genetic and nonshared environmental factors contribute to the association between socioemotional dispositions and the externalizing factor in children. *Journal of Child Psychology and Psychiatry*, *54*, 67–76.

Taylor, M. A., & Fink, M. (2008). Restoring melancholia in the classification of mood disorders. *Journal of Affective Disorders*, *105*, 1–14.

Taylor, S. (2011*a*). Etiology of obsessions and compulsions: A meta-analysis and narrative review of twin studies. *Clinical Psychology Review*, *31*, 1361–1372.

Taylor, S. (2011*b*). Early versus late onset obsessive-compulsive disorder: Evidence for distinct subtypes. *Clinical Psychology Review*, *31*, 1083–1100.

Taylor, S., Asmundson, G. J., & Jang, K. L. (2011). Etiology of obsessive-compulsive symptoms and obsessive-compulsive personality traits: Common genes, mostly different environments. *Depression and Anxiety*, *28*, 863–869.

Tearne, J. E., Robinson, M., Jacoby, P., Allen, K. L., Cunningham, N. K., Li, J., & McLean, N. J. (2016). Older maternal age is associated with depression, anxiety, and stress symptoms in young adult female offspring. *Journal of Abnormal Psychology*, *125*, 1–10.

Teatero, M. L., & Netley, C. (2013). A critical review of the research on the extreme male brain theory and digit ratio (2D: 4D). *Journal of Autism and Developmental Disorders*, *43*, 2664–2676.

Tempelaar, W. M., Termorshuizen, F., MacCabe, J. H., Boks, M. P. M., & Kahn, R. S. (2017). Educational achievement in psychiatric patients and their siblings: A register-based study in 30 000 individuals in The Netherlands. *Psychological Medicine*, *47*, 776–784.

Tempelhof, T. C., & Allen, J. S. (2008). Partner-specific investment strategies: Similarities and differences in couples and associations with sociosexual orientation and attachment dimensions. *Personality and Individual Differences*, *45*, 41–48.

Thagaard, M. S., Faraone, S. V., Sonuga-Barke, E. J., & Østergaard, S. D. (2016). Empirical tests of natural selection-based evolutionary accounts of ADHD: A systematic review. *Acta Neuropsychiatrica*, *28*, 249–256.

Thapar, A., Martin, J., Mick, E., Vásquez, A. A., Langley, K., Scherer, S. W., et al. (2016). Psychiatric gene discoveries shape evidence on ADHD's biology. *Molecular Psychiatry*, *21*, 1202–1207.

Thielmann, I., Hilbig, B. E., & Niedtfeld, I. (2014). Willing to give but not to forgive: Borderline personality features and cooperative behavior. *Journal of Personality Disorders*, *28*, 778–795.

Thomaes, S., & Brummelman, E. (2016). Narcissism. In D. Cicchetti (Ed.), *Developmental psychopathology: Vol. 3. Maladaptation and psychopathology* (3rd ed., pp. 679–725). New York: Wiley.

Thomas, K. M., Hopwood, C. J., Donnellan, M. B., Wright, A. G., Sanislow, C. A., McDevitt-Murphy, M. E., et al. (2014). Personality heterogeneity in PTSD: Distinct temperament and interpersonal typologies. *Psychological Assessment*, *26*, 23–34.

Thompson-Brenner, H., Eddy, K. T., Satir, D. A., Boisseau, C. L., & Westen, D. (2008). Personality subtypes in adolescents with eating disorders: Validation of a classification approach. *Journal of Child Psychology and Psychiatry*, *49*, 170–180.

Thompson-Brenner, H., & Westen, D. (2005). Personality subtypes in eating disorders: Validation of a classification in a naturalistic sample. *British Journal of Psychiatry*, *186*, 516–524.

Thorell, L. B., Rydell, A. M., & Bohlin, G. (2012). Parent–child attachment and executive functioning in relation to ADHD symptoms in middle childhood. *Attachment and Human Development*, *14*, 517–532.

Thornhill, R., & Gangestad, S. W. (2008). *The evolutionary biology of human female sexuality*. New York: Oxford University Press.

Tick, B., Bolton, P., Happé, F., Rutter, M., & Rijsdijk, F. (2016). Heritability of autism spectrum disorders: A meta-analysis of twin studies. *Journal of Child Psychology and Psychiatry*, *57*, 585–595.

Timpano, K. R., Rubenstein, L. M., & Murphy, D. L. (2012). Phenomenological features and clinical impact of affective disorders in OCD: A focus on the bipolar disorder and OCD connection. *Depression & Anxiety*, *29*, 226–233.

Tinbergen, E. A., & Tinbergen, N. (1972). Early childhood autism: An ethological approach. *Advances in Ethology, 10*.

Tinbergen, N. (1963). On the aims and methods of ethology. *Zeitschrift für Tierpsychologie*, *20*, 410–433.

Tither, J. M., & Ellis, B. J. (2008). Impact of fathers on daughters' age at menarche: A genetically and environmentally controlled sibling study. *Developmental Psychology*, *44*, 1409–1420.

Tognetti, A., Berticat, C., Raymond, M., & Faurie, C. (2012). Sexual selection of human cooperative behaviour: An experimental study in rural Senegal. *PLoS ONE*, *7*, e44403.

Tolin, D. F., & Foa, E. B. (2006). Sex differences in trauma and posttraumatic stress disorder: A quantitative review of 25 years of research. *Psychological Bulletin*, *132*, 959–992.

Tolin, D. F., & Villavicencio, A. (2011). Inattention, but not OCD, predicts the core features of hoarding disorder. *Behaviour Research & Therapy*, *49*, 120–125.

Tolin, D. F., Woods, C. M., & Abramowitz, J. S. (2006). Disgust sensitivity and obsessive-compulsive symptoms in a non-clinical sample. *Journal of Behavior Therapy & Experimental Psychiatry*, *37*, 30–40.

Tomasello, M. (2009). *Why we cooperate*. Cambridge, MA: MIT Press.

Tooby, J., & Cosmides, L. (1990). The past explains the present: Emotional adaptations and the structure of ancestral environments. *Ethology and Sociobiology*, *11*, 375–424.

Tooby, J., & Cosmides, L. (1992). The psychological foundations of culture. In J. Barkow, L. Cosmides, & J. Tooby (Eds.), *The adapted mind: Evolutionary psychology and the generation of culture*. New York: Oxford University Press.

Tooby, J., & Cosmides, L. (2006). The evolved architecture of hazard management: Risk detection reasoning and the motivational computation of threat magnitudes. *Behavioral & Brain Sciences*, *29*, 631–633.

Tooby, J., & Cosmides, L. (2008). The evolutionary psychology of the emotions and their relationship to internal regulatory variables. In M. Lewis, J. M. Haviland-Jones, & L. F. Barrett (Eds.), *Handbook of emotions* (3rd Ed., pp. 114–137). New York: Guilford.

Tooby, J., & Cosmides, L. (2010). Groups in mind: The coalitional roots of war and morality. In H. Høgh-Olesen (Ed.), *Human morality and sociality: Evolutionary and comparative perspectives* (pp. 191–234). New York: Palgrave Macmillan.

Tooby, J., & Cosmides, L. (2015). The theoretical foundations of evolutionary psychology. In D. M. Buss (Ed.), *The handbook of evolutionary psychology, Vol 1: Foundations* (2nd ed.) (pp. 3–87). New York, NY: Wiley.

Tooby, J., Cosmides, L., Sell, A., Lieberman, D., & Sznycer, D. (2008). Internal regulatory variables and the design of human motivation: A computational and evolutionary approach. In A. J. Elliot (Ed.), *Handbook of approach and avoidance motivation* (pp. 252–271). New York: Taylor & Francis.

Tooby, J., & DeVore, I. (1987). The reconstruction of hominid evolution through strategic modeling. In W. G. Kinzey (Ed.), *The evolution of human behavior: Primate models* (pp. 183–237) Albany, NY: SUNY Press.

Tops, M., Boksem, M. A., Luu, P., & Tucker, D. (2010). Brain substrates of behavioral programs associated with self-regulation. *Frontiers in Psychology, 1*, 152.

Tops, M., Riese, H., Oldehinkel, A. J., Rijsdijk, F. V., & Ormel, J. (2008). Rejection sensitivity relates to hypocortisolism and depressed mood state in young women. *Psychoneuroendocrinology, 33*, 551–559.

Torgersen, S., Kringlen, E., & Cramer, V. (2001). The prevalence of personality disorders in a community sample. *Archives of General Psychiatry, 58*, 590–596.

Torgersen, S., Myers, J., Reichborn-Kjennerud, T., Røysamb, E., Kubarych, T. S., & Kendler, K. S. (2012). The heritability of Cluster B personality disorders assessed both by personal interview and questionnaire. *Journal of Personality Disorders, 26*, 848–866.

Toronchuk, J. A., & Ellis, G. F. (2013). Affective neuronal selection: The nature of the primordial emotion systems. *Frontiers in Psychology, 3*, 589.

Torresan, R. C., Ramos-Cerqueiraa, A. T., Shavitt, R. G., Conceicao do Rosario, M., de Mathis, M. A., Miguel, E. C., et al. (2013). Symptom dimensions, clinical course and comorbidity in men and women with obsessive-compulsive disorder. *Psychiatry Research, 209*, 186–195.

Tortorella, A., Brambilla, F., Fabrazzo, M., Volpe, U., Monteleone, A. M., Mastromo, D., et al. (2014). Central and peripheral peptides regulating eating behaviour and energy homeostasis in anorexia nervosa and bulimia nervosa: A literature review. *European Eating Disorders Review, 22*, 307–320.

Torvik, F. A., Welander-Vatn, A., Ystrom, E., Knudsen, G. P., Czajkowski, N., Kendler, K. S., et al. (2016). Longitudinal associations between social anxiety disorder and avoidant personality disorder: A twin study. *Journal of Abnormal Psychology, 125*, 114–124.

Towne, B., Czerwinski, S. A., Demerath, E. W., Blangero, J., Roche, A. F., & Siervogel, R. M. (2005). Heritability of age at menarche in girls from the Fels Longitudinal Study. *American Journal of Physical Anthropology, 128*, 210–219.

Trickey, D., Siddaway, A. P., Meiser-Stedman, R., Serpell, L., & Field, A. P. (2012). A meta-analysis of risk factors for post-traumatic stress disorder in children and adolescents. *Clinical Psychology Review, 32*, 122–138.

Trimmer, P. C., & Houston, A. I. (2014). An evolutionary perspective on information processing. *Topics in Cognitive Science, 6*, 312–330.

Trimmer, P. C., Houston, A. I., Marshall, J. A. R., Bogacz, R., Paul, E. S., Mendl, M. T., et al. (2008). Mammalian choices: Combining fast-but-inaccurate and slow-but-accurate decision-making systems. *Proceedings of the Royal Society of London B, 275*, 2353–2361.

Trimmer, P. C., Paul, E. S., Mendl, M. T., McNamara, J. M., & Houston, A. I. (2013). On the evolution and optimality of mood states. *Behavioral Sciences, 3*, 501–521.

Tripp, G., & Wickens, J. R. (2009). Neurobiology of ADHD. *Neuropharmacology, 57*, 579–589.

Trivers, R. L. (1971). The evolution of reciprocal altruism. *Quarterly Review of Biology, 46*, 35–57.

Trivers, R. L. (1972). Parental investment and sexual selection. In B. Campbell (Ed.), *Sexual selection and the descent of man 1871–1971* (pp. 136–179). Chicago: Aldine.

Trivers, R. L. (1974). Parent-offspring conflict. *American Zoologist, 14*, 249–264.

Troisi, A. (2015). The evolutionary diagnosis of mental disorder. *WIREs Cognitive Science, 6*, 323–331.

Troisi, A., & McGuire, M. T. (2002). Darwinian psychiatry and the concept of mental disorder. *Neuroendocrinology Letters, 23*, 31–38.

Troop, N. A. (2016). Social rank, rank-related life events and eating pathology. *European Eating Disorders Review, 24*, 75–77.

Troop, N. A., Allan, S., Serpell, L., & Treasure, J. L. (2008). Shame in women with a history of eating disorders. *European Eating Disorders Review, 16*, 480–488.

Troop, N. A., Allan, S., Treasure, J. L., & Katzman, M. (2003). Social comparison and submissive behaviour in eating disorder patients. *Psychology and Psychotherapy: Theory, Research and Practice, 76*, 237–249.

Troop, N. A., Andrews, L., Hiskey, S., & Treasure, J. L. (2014). Social rank and symptom change in eating disorders: A 6-month longitudinal study. *Clinical Psychology and Psychotherapy, 21*, 115–122.

Trotman, H. D., Mittal, V. A., Tessner, K. D., & Walker, E. F. (2013). Schizophrenia and the psychosis spectrum. In W. E. Craighead, D. J. Miklowitz, & L. W. Craighead (Eds.), *Psychopathology: History, diagnosis, and empirical foundations* (2nd ed., pp. 403–444). New York: Wiley.

Trzaskowski, M., Harlaar, N., Arden, R., Krapohl, E., Rimfeld, K., McMillan, A., et al. (2014). Genetic influence on family socioeconomic status and children's intelligence. *Intelligence, 42*, 83–88.

Tseng, H. C., Chi, M. H., Lee, L. T., Tsai, H. C., Lee, I. H., Chen, K. C., et al. (2014). Sex-specific associations between plasma oxytocin levels and schizotypal personality features in healthy individuals. *Journal of Psychiatric Research, 51*, 37–41.

Turan, T., Uysal, C., Asdemir, A., & Kılıç, E. (2013). May oxytocin be a trait marker for bipolar disorder? *Psychoneuroendocrinology, 38*, 2890–2896.

Turkheimer, E., Pettersson, E., & Horn, E. E. (2014). A phenotypic null hypothesis for the genetics of personality. *Annual Review of Psychology, 65*, 515–540.

Turner, B. J., Claes, L., Wilderjans, T. F., Pauwels, E., Dierckx, E., Chapman, A. L., et al. (2014). Personality profiles in eating disorders: Further evidence of the clinical utility of examining subtypes based on temperament. *Psychiatry Research, 219*, 157–165.

Twenge, J. M., & Nolen-Hoeksema, S. (2002). Age, gender, race, socioeconomic status, and birth cohort difference on the children's depression inventory: A meta-analysis. *Journal of Abnormal Psychology, 111*, 578–588.

Tybur, J. M., Bryan, A. D., Lieberman, D., Hooper, A. E. C., & Merriman, L. A. (2011). Sex differences and sex similarities in disgust sensitivity. *Personality and Individual Differences, 51*, 343–348.

Tybur, J. M., & de Vries, R. E. (2013). Disgust sensitivity and the HEXACO model of personality. *Personality and Individual Differences, 55*, 660–665.

Tybur, J. M., & Gangestad, S. W. (2011). Mate preferences and infectious disease: Theoretical considerations and evidence in humans. *Philosophical Transactions of the Royal Society of London B, 366*, 3375–3388.

Tybur, J. M., Inbar, Y., Güler, E., & Molho, C. (2015). Is the relationship between pathogen avoidance and ideological conservatism explained by sexual strategies? *Evolution and Human Behavior, 36*, 489–497.

Tybur, J. M., Lieberman, D., & Griskevicius, V. (2009). Microbes, mating, and morality: Individual differences in three functional domains of disgust. *Journal of Personality and Social Psychology, 97*, 103.

Tybur, J. M., Lieberman, D., Kurzban, R., & DeScioli, P. (2013). Disgust: Evolved function and structure. *Psychological Review, 120*, 65–84.

Úbeda, F. (2008). Evolution of genomic imprinting with biparental care: Implications for Prader-Willi and Angelman syndromes. *PLoS Biology, 6*, e208.

Úbeda, F., & Gardner, A. (2010). A model for genomic imprinting in the social brain: Juveniles. *Evolution, 64*, 2587–2600.

Úbeda, F., & Gardner, A. (2011). A model for genomic imprinting in the social brain: Adults. *Evolution, 65*, 462–475.

Úbeda, F., & Gardner, A. (2012). A model for genomic imprinting in the social brain: Elders. *Evolution, 66*, 1567–1581.

Úbeda, F., & Haig, D. (2003). Dividing the child. *Genetica, 117*, 103–110.

Udry, J. R., & Cliquet, R. L. (1982). A cross-cultural examination of the relationship between ages at menarche, marriage, and first birth. *Demography, 19*, 53–63.

Uller, T., & Helanterä, H. (2013). Non-genetic inheritance in evolutionary theory: A primer. *Non-Genetic Inheritance, 1*, 27–32.

Ullrich, S., Farrington, D. P., & Coid, J. W. (2007). Dimensions of DSM-IV personality disorders and life-success. *Journal of Personality Disorders, 21*, 657–663.

Urfer-Parnas, A., Mortensen, E. L., Saebye, D., & Parnas, J. (2010). Pre-morbid IQ in mental disorders: A Danish draft-board study of 7486 psychiatric patients. *Psychological Medicine, 40*, 547–556.

Vachon, D. D., Lynam, D. R., Widiger, T. A., Miller, J. D., McCrae, R. R., & Costa, P. T. (2013). Basic traits predict the prevalence of personality disorder across the life span: The example of psychopathy. *Psychological Science, 24*, 698–705.

Vahia, I. V., Palmer, B. W., Depp, C., Fellows, I., Golshan, S., Kraemer, H. C., et al. (2010). Is late-onset schizophrenia a subtype of schizophrenia? *Acta Psychiatrica Scandinavica, 122*, 414–426.

Vaillancourt, T. (2013). Do human females use indirect aggression as an intrasexual competition strategy? *Philosophical Transactions of the Royal Society B, 368*, 20130080.

Vaillancourt, T., Brittain, H. L., McDougall, P., Krygsman, A., Boylan, K., Duku, E., et al. (2014). Predicting borderline personality disorder symptoms in adolescents from childhood physical and relational aggression, depression, and attention-deficit/hyperactivity disorder. *Development & Psychopathology*, *26*, 817–830.

Valentiner, D. P., Fergus, T. A., Behar, E., & Conybeare, D. J. (2014). Anxiety disorders. In D. C. Beidel, B. C. Frueh, & M. Hersen (Eds.), *Adult psychopathology and diagnosis* (7th ed., pp. 299–354). New York: Wiley.

Valipour, G., Saneei, P., & Esmaillzadeh, A. (2014). Serum vitamin D levels in relation to schizophrenia: A systematic review and meta-analysis of observational studies. *Journal of Clinical Endocrinology & Metabolism*, *99*, 3863–3872.

Vall, G., Gutiérrez, F., Peri, J. M., Gárriz, M., Baillés, E., Garrido, J. M., et al. (2016). Seven dimensions of personality pathology are under sexual selection in modern Spain. *Evolution and Human Behavior*, *37*, 169–178.

van Anders, S. M., Goldey, K. L., & Kuo, P. X. (2011). The steroid/peptide theory of social bonds: Integrating testosterone and peptide responses for classifying social behavioral contexts. *Psychoneuroendocrinology*, *36*, 1265–1275.

Van de Cruys, S., Evers, K., Van der Hallen, R., Van Eylen, L., Boets, B., de-Wit, L., et al. (2014). Precise minds in uncertain worlds: Predictive coding in autism. *Psychological Review*, *121*, 649–675.

van den Berg, P., Fawcett, T. W., Buunk, A. P., & Weissing, F. J. (2013). The evolution of parent–offspring conflict over mate choice. *Evolution and Human Behavior*, *34*, 405–411.

Van der Hallen, R., Evers, K., Brewaeys, K., Van den Noortgate, W., & Wagemans, J. (2015). Global processing takes time: A meta-analysis on local–global visual processing in ASD. *Psychological Bulletin*, *141*, 549–573.

VanderLaan, D. P., Ren, Z., & Vasey, P. L. (2013). Male androphilia in the ancestral environment: An ethnological analysis. *Human Nature*, *24*, 375–401.

van der Linden, D., Pekaar, K. A., Bakker, A. B., Schermer, J. A., Vernon, P. A., Dunkel, C. S., et al. (2017). Overlap between the general factor of personality and emotional intelligence: A meta-analysis. *Psychological Bulletin*, *143*, 36–52.

van der Linden, D., te Nijenhuis, J., & Bakker, A. B. (2010). The General Factor of Personality: A meta-analysis and a criterion-related validity study. *Journal of Research in Personality*, *44*, 315–327.

van der Meer, J. M., Oerlemans, A. M., van Steijn, D. J., Lappenschaar, M. G., de Sonneville, L. M., Buitelaar, J. K., et al. (2012). Are autism spectrum disorder and attention-deficit/hyperactivity disorder different manifestations of one overarching disorder? Cognitive and symptom evidence from a clinical and population-based sample. *Journal of the American Academy of Child & Adolescent Psychiatry*, *51*, 1160–1172.

van Dongen, J., & Boomsma, D. I. (2013). The evolutionary paradox and the missing heritability of schizophrenia. *American Journal of Medical Genetics B*, *162*, 122–136.

van Doorn, G. S., Wolf, M., Leimar, O., & Weissing, F. J. 2009 Animal personalities and the divergence of life histories. In M. Wolf (Ed.), *Adaptive individual differences*. PhD thesis, University of Groningen, The Netherlands. http://dissertations.ub.rug.nl/science/2009/m.wolf/.

van Enkhuizen, J., Janowsky, D. S., Olivier, B., Minassian, A., Perry, W., Young, J. W., et al. (2015). The catecholaminergic-cholinergic balance hypothesis of bipolar disorder revisited. *European Journal of Pharmacology*, *753*, 114–126.

van Ewijk, H., Heslenfeld, D. J., Zwiers, M. P., Buitelaar, J. K., & Oosterlaan, J. (2012). Diffusion tensor imaging in attention deficit/hyperactivity disorder: A systematic review and meta-analysis. *Neuroscience and Biobehavioral Reviews*, *36*, 1093–1106.

van Goozen, S. H., Fairchild, G., Snoek, H., & Harold, G. T. (2007). The evidence for a neurobiological model of childhood antisocial behavior. *Psychological Bulletin, 133*, 149–182.

van Grootheest, D. S., Boomsma, D. I., Hettema, J. M., & Kendler, K. S. (2008). Heritability of obsessive-compulsive symptom dimensions. *American Journal of Medical Genetics B, 147*, 473–478.

Van Houtem, C. M. H. H., Laine, M. L., Boomsma, D. I., Ligthart, L., Van Wijk, A. J., & De Jongh, A. (2013). A review and meta-analysis of the heritability of specific phobia subtypes and corresponding fears. *Journal of Anxiety Disorders, 27*, 379–388.

Van Hulst, B. M., De Zeeuw, P., & Durston, S. (2015). Distinct neuropsychological profiles within ADHD: A latent class analysis of cognitive control, reward sensitivity and timing. *Psychological Medicine, 45*, 735–745.

van Ijzendoorn, M. H., & Bakermans-Kranenburg, M. J. (2015). Genetic differential susceptibility on trial: Meta-analytic support from randomized controlled experiments. *Development and Psychopathology, 27*, 151–162.

van Ijzendoorn, M. H., Belsky, J., & Bakermans-Krananburg, M. J. (2012). Serotonin transporter genotype 5HTTLPR as a marker of differential susceptibility? A meta-analysis of child and adolescent gene-by-environment studies. *Translational Psychiatry, 2*, e147.

van Ijzendoorn, M. H., Schuengel, C., & Bakermans–Kranenburg, M. J. (1999). Disorganized attachment in early childhood: Meta-analysis of precursors, concomitants, and sequelae. *Development and Psychopathology, 11*, 225–250.

Van Le, Q., Isbell, L. A., Matsumoto, J., Nguyen, M., Hori, E., Maior, R. S., et al. (2013). Pulvinar neurons reveal neurobiological evidence of past selection for rapid detection of snakes. *Proceedings of the National Academy of Sciences USA, 110*, 19000–19005.

Van Loo, H. M., De Jonge, P., Romeijn, J. W., Kessler, R. C., & Schoevers, R. A. (2012). Data-driven subtypes of major depressive disorder: A systematic review. *BMC Medicine, 10*, 156.

Vannucchi, G., Masi, G., Toni, C., Dell, L., Erfurth, A., & Perugi, G. (2014). Bipolar disorder in adults with Asperger' s Syndrome: A systematic review. *Journal of Affective Disorders, 168*, 151–160.

van Os, J., Linscott, R. J., Myin-Germeys, I., Delespaul, P., & Krabbendam, L. (2009). A systematic review and meta-analysis of the psychosis continuum: Evidence for a psychosis proneness–persistence–impairment model of psychotic disorder. *Psychological Medicine, 39*, 179–195.

Van Rijn, S., Aleman, A., De Sonneville, L., Sprong, M., Ziermans, T., Schothorst, P., et al. (2011). Neuroendocrine markers of high risk for psychosis: Salivary testosterone in adolescent boys with prodromal symptoms. *Psychological Medicine, 41*, 1815–1822.

van Schaik, C. P., Isler, K., & Burkart, J. M. (2012). Explaining brain size variation: From social to cultural brain. *Trends in Cognitive Sciences, 16*, 277–284.

Van Schalkwyk, G. I., Peluso, F., Qayyum, Z., McPartland, J. C., & Volkmar, F. R. (2015). Varieties of misdiagnosis in ASD: An illustrative case series. *Journal of Autism and Developmental Disorders, 45*, 911–918.

van Schouwenburg, M., Aarts, E., & Cools, R. 2010. Dopaminergic modulation of cognitive control: Distinct roles for the prefrontal cortex and the basal ganglia. *Current Pharmaceutical Design, 16*, 2026–2032.

Vater, A., Ritter, K., Strunz, S., Ronningstam, E. F., Renneberg, B., & Roepke, S. (2014). Stability of narcissistic personality disorder: Tracking categorical and dimensional rating systems over a two-year period. *Personality Disorders: Theory, Research, and Treatment, 5*, 305–313.

Vaughn, M. G., DeLisi, M., Gunter, T., Fu, Q., Beaver, K. M., Perron, B. E., et al. (2011). The severe 5%: A latent class analysis of the externalizing behavior spectrum in the United States. *Journal of Criminal Justice*, *39*, 75–80.

Vaughn, M. G., Salas-Wright, C. P., DeLisi, M., & Maynard, B. R. (2014). Violence and externalizing behavior among youth in the United States: Is there a severe 5%? *Youth Violence & Juvenile Justice*, *12*, 3–21.

Vaughn, M. G., Salas-Wright, C. P., DeLisi, M., Maynard, B. R., & Boutwell, B. (2015). Prevalence and correlates of psychiatric disorders among former juvenile detainees in the United States. *Comprehensive Psychiatry*, *59*, 107–116.

Vazquez, G. H., & Gonda, X. (2013). Affective temperaments and mood disorders: A review of current knowledge. *Current Psychiatry Reviews*, *9*, 21–32.

Veenstra, R., Lindenberg, S., Verhulst, F. C., & Ormel, J. (2009). Childhood-limited versus persistent antisocial behavior: Why do some recover and others do not? The TRAILS study. *Journal of Early Adolescence*, *29*, 718–742.

Vellante, M., Zucca, G., Preti, A., Sisti, D., Rocchi, M. B. L., Akiskal, K. K., et al. (2011). Creativity and affective temperaments in non-clinical professional artists: An empirical psychometric investigation. *Journal of Affective Disorders*, *135*, 28–36.

Veras, A. B., Souza, T. G., Ricci, T. G., de Souza, C. P., Moryiama, M. C., Nardi, A. E., et al. (2015). Paranoid delusional disorder follows social anxiety disorder in a long-term case series: Evolutionary perspective. *The Journal of Nervous & Mental Disease*, *203*, 477–479.

Vercken, E., Wellenreuther, M., Svensson, E. I., & Mauroy, B. (2012). Don't fall off the adaptation cliff: When asymmetrical fitness selects for suboptimal traits. *PLoS ONE*, *7*, e34889.

Verona, E., Javdani, S., & Sprague, J. (2011). Comparing factor structures of adolescent psychopathology. *Psychological Assessment*, *23*, 545–551.

Verweij, K. J. H., Burri, A. V., & Zeitsch, B. P. (2014). Testing the prediction from sexual selection of a positive genetic correlation between human mate preferences and corresponding traits. *Evolution and Human Behavior*, *35*, 497–501.

Veselka, L., Schermer, J. A., & Vernon, P. A. (2012). The Dark Triad and an expanded framework of personality. *Personality and Individual Differences*, *53*, 417–425.

Vicario, C. M., Rafal, R. D., Martino, D., & Avenanti, A. (2017). Core, social and moral disgust are bounded: A review on behavioral and neural bases of repugnance in clinical disorders. *Neuroscience & Biobehavioral Reviews*, *80*, 185–200.

Vilares, I., & Kording, K. (2011). Bayesian models: The structure of the world, uncertainty, behavior, and the brain. *Annals of the New York Academy of Sciences*, *1224*, 22–39.

Vincke, E. (2016). The young male cigarette and alcohol syndrome: Smoking and drinking as a short-term mating strategy. *Evolutionary Psychology*, *14*, 1474704916631615.

Vinkhuyzen, A. A., van der Sluis, S., Maes, H. H., & Posthuma, D. (2012). Reconsidering the heritability of intelligence in adulthood: Taking assortative mating and cultural transmission into account. *Behavior Genetics*, *42*, 187–198.

Visintin, E., De Panfilis, C., Amore, M., Balestrieri, M., Wolf, R. C., & Sambataro, F. (2016). Mapping the brain correlates of borderline personality disorder: A functional neuroimaging meta-analysis of resting state studies. *Journal of Affective Disorders*, *204*, 262–269.

Visscher, P. M., Hill, W. G., & Wray, N. R. (2008). Heritability in the genomics era—concepts and misconceptions. *Nature Reviews Genetics*, *9*, 255–266.

Visser, J. C., Rommelse, N. N., Greven, C. U., & Buitelaar, J. K. (2016). Autism spectrum disorder and attention-deficit/hyperactivity disorder in early childhood: A review of unique and shared characteristics and developmental antecedents. *Neuroscience & Biobehavioral Reviews, 65*, 229–263.

Vitale, J. E., & Newman, J. P. (2013). Psychopathy as psychopathology: Key developments in assessment, etiology, and treatment. In W. E. Craighead, D. J. Miklowitz, & L. W. Craighead (Eds.), *Psychopathology: History, diagnosis, and empirical foundations* (2nd ed., pp. 583–615). New York: Wiley.

Vitt, L. J., & Pianka, E. R. (2005). Deep history impacts present-day ecology and biodiversity. *Proceedings of the National Academy of Sciences USA, 102*, 7877–7881.

Vitti, J. J., Grossman, S. R., & Sabeti, P. C. (2013). Detecting natural selection in genomic data. *Annual Review of Genetics, 47*, 97–120.

Vogelzangs, N., De Jonge, P., Smit, J. H., Bahn, S., & Penninx, B. W. (2016). Cytokine production capacity in depression and anxiety. *Translational Psychiatry, 6*, e825.

Voland, E., & Voland, R. (1989). Evolutionary biology and psychiatry: The case of anorexia nervosa. *Ethology and Sociobiology, 10*, 223–240.

Volk, A. A., & Atkinson, J. A. (2013). Infant and child death in the human environment of evolutionary adaptation. *Evolution and Human Behavior, 34*, 182–192.

Vorstman, J. A., Anney, R. J., Derks, E. M., Gallagher, L., Gill, M., de Jonge, M. V., et al. (2013). No evidence that common genetic risk variation is shared between schizophrenia and autism. *American Journal of Medical Genetics B, 162*, 55–60.

Vreeker, A., Boks, M. P. M., Abramovic, L., Verkooijen, S., Van Bergen, A. H., Hillegers, M. H. J., et al. (2016). High educational performance is a distinctive feature of bipolar disorder: A study on cognition in bipolar disorder, schizophrenia patients, relatives and controls. *Psychological Medicine, 46*, 807–818.

Vriends, N., Becker, E. S., Meyer, A., Williams, S. L., Lutz, R., & Margraf, J. (2007). Recovery from social phobia in the community and its predictors: Data from a longitudinal epidemiological study. *Journal of Anxiety Disorders, 21*, 320–337.

Wade, N. (2014). *A troublesome inheritance: Genes, race and human history.* New York: Penguin.

Wadsworth, M. E., Evans, G. W., Grant, K., Carter, J. S., & Duffy, S. (2016). Poverty and the development of psychopathology. In D. Cicchetti (Ed.), *Developmental psychopathology: Vol. 3. Maladaptation and psychopathology* (3rd ed., pp. 136–179). New York: Wiley.

Wai, J., Putallaz, M., & Makel, M. C. (2012). Studying intellectual outliers: Are there sex differences, and are the smart getting smarter? *Current Directions in Psychological Science, 21*, 382–390.

Wai, M., & Tiliopoulos, N. (2012). The affective and cognitive empathic nature of the dark triad of personality. *Personality and Individual Differences, 52*, 794–799.

Wakabayashi, A., Baron-Cohen, S., & Wheelwright, S. (2006). Are autistic traits an independent personality dimension? A study of the Autism-Spectrum Quotient (AQ) and the NEO-PI-R. *Personality and Individual Differences, 41*, 873–883.

Wakefield, J. C. (1992). The concept of mental disorder: On the boundary between biological facts and social values. *American Psychologist, 47*, 373–388.

Wakefield, J. C. (1999*a*). Evolutionary versus prototype analyses of the concept of disorder. *Journal of Abnormal Psychology, 108*, 374–399.

Wakefield, J. C. (1999*b*). Mental disorder as a black box essentialist concept. *Journal of Abnormal Psychology, 108*, 465–472.

Wakefield, J. C. (1999*c*). Philosophy of science and the progressiveness of the DSM's theory-neutral nosology: Response to Follette and Houts, part 1. *Behaviour Research and Therapy*, *37*, 963–999.

Wakefield, J. C. (2011). Darwin, functional explanation, and the philosophy of psychiatry. In P. R. Adriaens & A. De Block (Eds.), *Maladapting minds: Philosophy, psychiatry, and evolutionary theory* (pp. 141–172). Oxford: Oxford University Press.

Wakefield, J. C. (2015). Biological function and dysfunction: Conceptual foundations of evolutionary psychopathology. In D. M. Buss (Ed.), *The handbook of evolutionary psychology* (2nd ed., pp. 988–1006). Hoboken, NJ: Wiley.

Wakefield, J. C., & Schmitz, M. F. (2012). Recurrence of depression after bereavement-related depression: Evidence for the validity of DSM-IV bereavement exclusion from the Epidemiologic Catchment Area Study. *The Journal of Nervous and Mental Disease*, *200*, 480–485.

Wakefield, J. C., & Schmitz, M. F. (2013*a*). When does depression become a disorder? Using recurrence rates to evaluate the validity of proposed changes in major depression diagnostic thresholds. *World Psychiatry*, *12*, 44–52.

Wakefield, J. C., & Schmitz, M. F. (2013*b*). Normal vs. disordered bereavement-related depression: Are the differences real or tautological? *Acta Psychiatrica Scandinavica*, *127*, 159–168.

Wakefield, J. C., Schmitz, M. F., First, M. B., & Horwitz, A. V. (2007). Extending the bereavement exclusion for major depression to other losses: Evidence from the National Comorbidity Survey. *Archives of General Psychiatry*, *64*, 433–440.

Walderhaug, E., Varga, M., San Pedro, M., Hu, J., & Neumeister, A. (2011). The role of the aminergic systems in the pathophysiology of bipolar disorder. In H. K. Manji & C. A. Zarate, Jr. (Eds.), *Behavioral neurobiology of bipolar disorder and its treatment* (pp. 107–126). New York: Springer.

Waldman, I. D., & Lahey, B. B. (2013). Oppositional defiant disorder, conduct disorder, and juvenile delinquency. In T. P. Beauchaine & S. P. Hinshaw (Eds.), *Child and adolescent psychopathology* (2nd ed., pp. 411–452). Hoboken, NJ: Wiley.

Waldman, I. D., Poore, H. E., van Hulle, C., Rathouz, P. J., & Lahey, B. B. (2016). External validity of a hierarchical dimensional model of child and adolescent psychopathology: Tests using confirmatory factor analyses and multivariate behavior genetic analyses. *Journal of Abnormal Psychology*, *125*, 1053–1066.

Waldman, I. D., & Rhee, S. H. (2006). Genetic and environmental influences on psychopathy and antisocial behavior. In C. J. Patrick (Ed.), *Handbook of psychopathy* (pp. 205–228). New York: Guilford.

Walker, E., Mittal, V., & Tessner, K. (2008). Stress and the hypothalamic pituitary adrenal axis in the developmental course of schizophrenia. *Annual Review of Clinical Psychology*, *4*, 189–216.

Walker, E. F., Trotman, H. D., Pearce, B. D., Addington, J., Cadenhead, K. S., Cornblatt, B. A., et al. (2013). Cortisol levels and risk for psychosis: Initial findings from the North American prodrome longitudinal study. *Biological Psychiatry*, *74*, 410–417.

Walker, R. S., & Hill, K. R (2014). Causes, consequences, and kin bias of human group fissions. *Human Nature*, *25*, 465–475.

Walker, R. S., Hill, K. R., Flinn, M. V., & Ellsworth, R. M. (2011). Evolutionary history of hunter-gatherer marriage practices. *PLoS ONE*, *6*, e19066.

Waller, N. G., & Meehl, P. E. (1998). *Multivariate taxometric procedures: Distinguishing types from continua*. Thousand Oaks, CA: Sage.

Walsh, Z., Shea, M. T., Yen, S., Ansell, E. B., Grilo, C. M., McGlashan, T. H., et al. (2013). Socioeconomic-status and mental health in a personality disorder sample: The importance of neighbourhood factors. *Journal of Personality Disorders, 27*, 820–831.

Wang, C., Ji, F., Hong, Z., Poh, J. S., Krishnan, R., Lee, J., et al. (2016). Disrupted salience network functional connectivity and white-matter microstructure in persons at risk for psychosis: Findings from the LYRIKS study. *Psychological Medicine, 46*, 2771–2783.

Wang, L., Zhou, C., Zhu, D., Wang, X., Fang, L., Zhong, J., et al. (2016). Serotonin-1A receptor alterations in depression: A meta-analysis of molecular imaging studies. *BMC Psychiatry, 16*, 319.

Wang, X. J., & Krystal, J. H. (2014). Computational psychiatry. *Neuron, 84*, 638–654.

Wang, X. T., Kruger, D. J., & Wilke, A. (2009). Life history variables and risk-taking propensity. *Evolution and Human Behavior, 30*, 77–84.

Waters, R. P., Rivalan, M., Bangasser, D. A., Deussing, J. M., Ising, M., Wood, S. K., et al. (2015). Evidence for the role of corticotropin-releasing factor in major depressive disorder. *Neuroscience and Biobehavioral Reviews, 58*, 63–78.

Watson, D. (2005). Rethinking the mood and anxiety disorders: A quantitative hierarchical model for DSM-V. *Journal of Abnormal Psychology, 114*, 522–536.

Watson, D., & Naragon-Gainey, K. (2014). Personality, emotions, and the emotional disorders. *Clinical Psychological Science, 2*, 422–442.

Watson, D., & Stasik, S. M. (2014). Examining the comorbidity between depression and the anxiety disorders from the perspective of the quadripartite model. In C. S. Richards & M. W. O'Hara (Eds.), *The Oxford handbook of depression and comorbidity* (pp. 46–65). New York: Oxford University Press.

Watson, P. J., & Andrews, P. W. (2002). Toward a revised evolutionary adaptationist analysis of depression: The social navigation hypothesis. *Journal of Affective Disorders, 72*, 1–14.

Waynforth, D. (2012). Life-history theory, chronic childhood illness and the timing of first reproduction in a British birth cohort. *Proceedings of the Royal Society of London B, 279*, rspb20120220.

Weber, E. U., Blais, A. R., & Betz, N. E. (2002). A domain-specific risk-attitude scale: Measuring risk perceptions and risk behaviors. *Journal of Behavioral Decision Making, 15*, 263–290.

Wedig, M. M., & Nock, M. K. (2010). The functional assessment of maladaptive behaviors: A preliminary evaluation of binge eating and purging among women. *Psychiatry Research, 178*, 518–524.

Weeden, J., & Sabini, J. (2007). Subjective and objective measures of attractiveness and their relation to sexual behavior and sexual attitudes in university students. *Archives of Sexual Behavior, 36*, 79–88.

Weinberg, A., Klonsky, E. D., & Hajcak, G. (2009). Autonomic impairment in borderline personality disorder: A laboratory investigation. *Brain and Cognition, 71*, 279–286.

Weisberg, D. S., & Gopnik, A. (2013). Pretense, counterfactuals, and Bayesian causal models: Why what is not real really matters. *Cognitive Science, 37*, 1368–1381.

Weisman, O., Zagoory-Sharon, O., & Feldman, R. (2014). Oxytocin administration, salivary testosterone, and father–infant social behavior. *Progress in Neuro-Psychopharmacology and Biological Psychiatry, 49*, 47–52.

Weisman, O., Zagoory-Sharon, O., Schneiderman, I., Gordon, I., & Feldman, R. (2013). Plasma oxytocin distributions in a large cohort of women and men and their gender-specific associations with anxiety. *Psychoneuroendocrinology, 38*, 694–701.

Weiss, A., & Costa, P. T. (2005). Domain and facet personality predictors of all-cause mortality among Medicare patients aged 65 to 100. *Psychosomatic Medicine, 67,* 724–733.

Weller, J. A., & Tikir, A. (2011). Predicting domain-specific risk taking with the HEXACO personality structure. *Journal of Behavioral Decision Making, 24,* 180–201.

Wells, A. (2000). *Emotional disorders and metacognition: Innovative cognitive therapy.* Chichester, UK: Wiley.

Wells, A. (2005). The metacognitive model of GAD: Assessment of meta-worry and relationship with DSM-IV generalized anxiety disorder. *Cognitive Therapy and Research, 29,* 107–121.

Wells, J. C. K. (2007). Sexual dimorphism of body composition. *Best Practice & Research Clinical Endocrinology & Metabolism, 21,* 415–430.

Wells, J. C. K. (2012). Obesity as malnutrition: The role of capitalism in the obesity global epidemic. *American Journal of Human Biology, 24,* 261–276.

Wenzel, A. (2010). Relation to clinical syndromes in adulthood. In S. G. Hofmann & P. M. Dibartolo (Eds.), *Social anxiety: Clinical, developmental, and social perspectives* (2nd ed., pp. 177–206). London: Elsevier.

Wenzel, A., Haugen, E. N., Jackson, L. C., & Robinson, K. (2003). Prevalence of generalized anxiety at eight weeks postpartum. *Archives of Women's Mental Health, 6,* 43–49.

West, S. A., El Mouden, C., & Gardner, A. (2011). Sixteen common misconceptions about the evolution of cooperation in humans. *Evolution and Human Behavior, 32,* 231–262.

West, S. A., & Gardner, A. (2013). Adaptation and inclusive fitness. *Current Biology, 23,* r577–r584

West, S. A., Griffin, A. S., & Gardner, A. (2007). Evolutionary explanations for cooperation. *Current Biology, 17,* R661–R672.

West-Eberhard, M. J. (1983). Sexual selection, social competition, and speciation. *Quarterly Review of Biology, 58,* 155–183.

West-Eberhard, M. J. (2003). *Developmental plasticity and evolution.* New York: Oxford University Press.

Westen, D., & Harnden-Fischer, J. (2001). Personality profiles in eating disorders: Rethinking the distinction between axis I and axis II. *American Journal of Psychiatry, 158,* 547–562.

Westen, D., Shedler, J., Durrett, C., Glass, S., & Martens, A. (2003). Personality diagnoses in adolescence: DSM-IV Axis II diagnoses and an empirically derived alternative. *American Journal of Psychiatry, 160,* 952–966.

Westwood, H., Stahl, D., Mandy, W., & Tchanturia, K. (2016). The set-shifting profiles of anorexia nervosa and autism spectrum disorder using the Wisconsin Card Sorting Test: A systematic review and meta-analysis. *Psychological Medicine, 10,* S0033291716000581.

Wheelwright, S., Baron-Cohen, S., Goldenfeld, N., Delaney, J., Fine, D., Smith, R., et al. (2006). Predicting autism spectrum quotient (AQ) from the systemizing quotient-revised (SQ-R) and empathy quotient (EQ). *Brain Research, 1079,* 47–56.

Whelan, Y. M., Stringaris, A., Maughan, B., & Barker, E. D. (2013). Developmental continuity of oppositional defiant disorder subdimensions at ages 8, 10, and 13 years and their distinct psychiatric outcomes at age 16 years. *Journal of the American Academy of Child & Adolescent Psychiatry, 52,* 961–969.

White, J. L., Moffitt, T. E., Caspi, A., Bartusch, D. J., Needles, D. J., & Stouthamer-Loeber, M. (1994). Measuring impulsivity and examining its relationship to delinquency. *Journal of Abnormal Psychology*, *103*, 192–205.

White, T. P., Borgan, F., Ralley, O., & Shergill, S. S. (2016). You looking at me? Interpreting social cues in schizophrenia. *Psychological Medicine*, *46*, 149–160.

Whitehouse, A. J., Maybery, M. T., Hickey, M., & Sloboda, D. M. (2011). Brief report: Autistic-like traits in childhood predict later age at menarche in girls. *Journal of Autism and Developmental Disorders*, *41*, 1125–1130.

Whitfield-Gabrieli, S., & Ford, J. M. (2012). Default mode network activity and connectivity in psychopathology. *Annual Review of Clinical Psychology*, *8*, 49–76.

Widiger, T. A., & Gore, W. L. (2014). Mental disorders as discrete clinical conditions: Dimensional versus categorical classification. In D. C. Beidel, B. C. Frueh, & M. Hersen (Eds.), *Adult psychopathology and diagnosis* (7th ed., pp. 3–34). New York: Wiley.

Wiebe, R. P. (2004). Delinquent behavior and the five-factor model: Hiding in the adaptive landscape. *Individual Difference Research*, *2*, 38–62.

Wiecki, T. V., & Frank, M. J. (2013). A computational model of inhibitory control in frontal cortex and basal ganglia. *Psychological Review*, *120*, 329–355.

Wiecki, T. V., Poland, J., & Frank, M. J. (2015). Model-based cognitive neuroscience approaches to computational psychiatry: Clustering and classification. *Clinical Psychological Science*, *3*, 378–399.

Wiederman, M. W., Pryor, T., & Morgan, C. D. (1996). The sexual experience of women diagnosed with anorexia nervosa or bulimia nervosa. *International Journal of Eating Disorders*, *19*, 109–118.

Wig, G. S. (2017). Segregated systems of human brain networks. *Trends in Cognitive Sciences*, *21*, 981–996.

Wigman, J. T. W., van Os, J., Borsboom, D., Wardenaar, K. J., Epskamp, S., Klippel, A., et al. (2015). Exploring the underlying structure of mental disorders: Cross-diagnostic differences and similarities from a network perspective using both a top-down and a bottom-up approach. *Psychological Medicine*, *45*, 2375–2387.

Wilke, A., Sherman, A., Curdt, B., Mondal, S., Fitzgerald, C., & Kruger, D. J. (2014). An evolutionary domain-specific risk scale. *Evolutionary Behavioral Sciences*, *8*, 123–141.

Wilkins, J. F. (2011). Genomic imprinting and conflict-induced decanalization. *Evolution*, *65*, 537–553.

Wilkins, J. F., & Haig, D. (2003). What good is genomic imprinting: The function of parent-specific gene expression. *Nature Reviews Genetics*, *4*, 359–368.

Wilkins, J. F., Úbeda, F., & Van Cleve, J. (2016). The evolving landscape of imprinted genes in humans and mice: Conflict among alleles, genes, tissues, and kin. *Bioessays*, *38*, 482–489.

Willcutt, E. G., Doyle, A. E., Nigg, J. T., Faraone, S. V., & Pennington, B. F. (2005). Validity of the executive function theory of attention-deficit/hyperactivity disorder: A meta-analytic review. *Biological Psychiatry*, *57*, 1336–1346.

Willcutt, E. G., Nigg, J. T., Pennington, B. F., Solanto, M. V., Rohde, L. A., Tannock, R., et al. (2012). Validity of DSM-IV attention deficit/hyperactivity disorder symptom dimensions and subtypes. *Journal of Abnormal Psychology*, *121*, 991–1010.

Williams, D. R., & Bürkner, P. C. (2017). Effects of intranasal oxytocin on symptoms of schizophrenia: A multivariate Bayesian meta-analysis. *Psychoneuroendocrinology*, *75*, 141–151.

Williams, G. C. (1966). *Adaptation and natural selection*. Princeton, NJ: Princeton University Press.

Williams, J., & Taylor, E. (2006). The evolution of hyperactivity, impulsivity and cognitive diversity. *Journal of the Royal Society Interface, 3*, 399–413.

Williams, L. M., & Barry, J. (2003). Do sex differences in emotionality mediate sex differences in traits of psychosis-proneness? *Cognition & Emotion, 17*, 747–758.

Williamson, D. A., Gleaves, D. H., & Stewart, T. M. (2005). Categorical versus dimensional models of eating disorders: An examination of the evidence. *International Journal of Eating Disorders, 37*, 1–10.

Wilson, D. R. (1998). Evolutionary epidemiology and manic depression. *British Journal of Medical Psychology, 71*, 375–395.

Wilson, D. R., & Price, J. S. (2006). Evolutionary epidemiology of endophenotypes in the bipolar spectrum: Evolved neuropsychologic mechanisms of social rank. *Current Psychosis & Therapeutics Reports, 4*, 176–180.

Wilson, E. O. (2012). *The social conquest of Earth*. New York: Liveright.

Winegard, B., Winegard, B., & Boutwell, B. (2017). Human biological and psychological diversity. *Evolutionary Psychological Science, 3*, 159–180.

Winegard, B. M., Winegard, B., & Geary, D. C. (2014). Eastwood's brawn and Einstein's brain: An evolutionary account of dominance, prestige, and precarious manhood. *Review of General Psychology, 18*, 34–48.

Winterhalder, B., Lu, F., & Tucker, B. (1999). Risk-sensitive adaptive tactics: Models and evidence from subsistence studies in biology and anthropology. *Journal of Archaeological Research, 7*, 301–348.

Witherington, D. C., & Lickliter, R. (2017). Integrating development and evolution in psychological science: Evolutionary developmental psychology, developmental systems, and explanatory pluralism. *Human Development, 59*, 200–234.

Wlodarski, R. (2015). The relationship between cognitive and affective empathy and human mating strategies. *Evolutionary Psychological Science, 1*, 232–240.

Wolf, E. J., Miller, M. W., Harrington, K. M., & Reardon, A. (2012). Personality-based latent classes of posttraumatic psychopathology: Personality disorders and the internalizing/externalizing model. *Journal of Abnormal Psychology, 121*, 256–262.

Wolf, M., & McNamara, J. M. (2012). On the evolution of personalities via frequency-dependent selection. *The American Naturalist, 179*, 679–692.

Wolf, M., van Doorn, G. S., Leimar, O., & Weissing, F. J. (2007). Life-history trade-offs favour the evolution of animal personalities. *Nature, 447*, 581–585.

Wolf, M. B., & Ackerman, P. L. (2005). Extraversion and intelligence: A meta-analytic investigation. *Personality and Individual Differences, 39*, 531–542.

Wolpert, D. M., Doya, K., & Kawato, M. (2003). A unifying computational framework for motor control and social interaction. *Philosophical Transactions of the Royal Society B, 358*, 593–602.

Wonderlich, S. A., Crosby, R. D., Joiner, T., Peterson, C. B., Bardone-Cone, A., Klein, M., et al. (2005). Personality subtyping and bulimia nervosa: Psychopathological and genetic correlates. *Psychological Medicine, 35*, 649–657.

Wong, C. C. Y., Meaburn, E. L., Ronald, A., Price, T. S., Jeffries, A. R., Schalkwyk, L. C., et al. (2014). Methylomic analysis of monozygotic twins discordant for autism spectrum disorder and related behavioural traits. *Molecular Psychiatry, 19*, 495–503.

Wong, W. S., Solomon, B. D., Bodian, D. L., Kothiyal, P., Eley, G., Huddleston, K. C., et al. (2016). New observations on maternal age effect on germline de novo mutations. *Nature Communications, 7*, 10486.

Wood, D., Gardner, M. H., & Harms, P. D. (2015). How functionalist and process approaches to behavior can explain trait covariation. *Psychological Review, 122*, 84–111.

Woodberry, K. A., Giuliano, A. J., & Seidman, L. J. (2008). Premorbid IQ in schizophrenia: A meta-analytic review. *American Journal of Psychiatry, 165*, 579–587.

Woodley, M. A. (2011). The cognitive differentiation–integration effort hypothesis: A synthesis between the fitness indicator and life history models of human intelligence. *Review of General Psychology, 15*, 228–245.

Woodley of Menie, M. A., Cabeza de Baca, T., Fernandes, H. B. F., Madison, G., Figueredo, A. J., & Peñaherrera Aguirre, M. (2017). Slow and steady wins the race: K positively predicts fertility in the USA and Sweden. *Evolutionary Psychological Science, 3*, 109–117.

Woodley of Menie, M. A., & Madison, G. (2015). The association between g and K in a sample of 4246 Swedish twins: A behavior genetic analysis. *Personality and Individual Differences, 74*, 270–274.

Woodward, N. D., Cowan, R. L., Park, S., Ansari, M. S., Baldwin, R. M., Li, R., et al. (2011). Correlation of individual differences in schizotypal personality traits with amphetamine-induced dopamine release in striatal and extrastriatal brain regions. *American Journal of Psychiatry, 168*, 418–426.

Woody, E. Z., & Szechtman, H. (2011). Adaptation to potential threat: The evolution, neurobiology, and psychopathology of the security motivation system. *Neuroscience & Biobehavioral Reviews, 35*, 1019–1033.

Woody, S. R., Kellman-McFarlane, K., & Welsted, A. (2014). Review of cognitive performance in hoarding disorder. *Clinical Psychology Review, 34*, 324–336.

Workman, L., & Reader, W. (2014). *Evolutionary psychology*. New York: Cambridge University Press.

Wrangham, R. W. (1999). Evolution of coalitionary killing. *American Journal of Physical Anthropology, 110*, 1–30.

Wraw, C., Deary, I. J., Gale, C. R., & Der, G. (2015). Intelligence in youth and health at age 50. *Intelligence, 53*, 23–32.

Wu, K., Hanna, G. L., Rosenberg, D. R., & Arnold, P. D. (2012). The role of glutamate signaling in the pathogenesis and treatment of obsessive-compulsive disorder. *Pharmacology Biochemistry & Behavior, 100*, 726–735.

Wu, Y., Liu, X., Luo, H., Deng, W., Zhao, G., Wang, Q., et al. (2012). Advanced paternal age increases the risk of schizophrenia and obsessive-compulsive disorder in a Chinese Han population. *Psychiatry Research, 198*, 353–359.

Wu, Y. T., Maenner, M. J., Wiggins, L. D., Rice, C. E., Bradley, C. C., Lopez, M. L., et al. (2016). Retention of autism spectrum disorder diagnosis: The role of co-occurring conditions in males and females. *Research in Autism Spectrum Disorders, 25*, 76–86.

Wyman, M. J., & Rowe, L. (2014). Male bias in distributions of additive genetic, residual, and phenotypic variances of shared traits. *The American Naturalist, 184*, 326–337.

Wynn Owen, P. A., & Castle, D. J. (1999). Late-onset schizophrenia. *Drugs & Aging, 15*, 81–89.

Xu, G., Lu, W., Ouyang, H., Dang, Y., Guo, Y., Miao, G., et al. (2014). Association of affective temperaments measured by TEMPS-A with cognitive deficits in patients with bipolar disorder. *Journal of Affective Disorders*, *161*, 109–115.

Xu, Y., Norton, S., & Rahman, Q. (2017). Sexual orientation and neurocognitive ability: A meta-analysis in men and women. *Neuroscience & Biobehavioral Reviews*. doi:10.1016/j.neubiorev.2017.06.014

Xue, M., & Silk, J. B. (2012). The role of tracking and tolerance in relationship among friends. *Evolution and Human Behavior*, *33*, 17–25.

Yean, C., Benau, E. M., Dakanalis, A., Hormes, J. M., Perone, J., & Timko, C. A. (2013). The relationship of sex and sexual orientation to self-esteem, body shape satisfaction, and eating disorder symptomatology. *Frontiers in Psychology*, *4*, 887.

Yang, J., Benyamin, B., McEvoy, B. P., Gordon, S., Henders, A. K., Nyholt, D. R., et al. (2010). Common SNPs explain a large proportion of the heritability for human height. *Nature Genetics*, *42*, 565–569.

Yean, C., Benau, E., Dakanalis, A., Hormes, J. M., Perone, J., & Timko, A. (2013). The relationship of sex and sexual orientation to self-esteem, body shape satisfaction, and eating disorder symptomatology. *Frontiers in Psychology*, *4*, 887.

Yen, S., Shea, M. T., Battle, C. L., Johnson, D. M., Zlotnick, C., Dolan-Sewell, R., et al. (2002). Traumatic exposure and posttraumatic stress disorder in borderline, schizotypal, avoidant, and obsessive-compulsive personality disorders: Findings from the collaborative longitudinal personality disorders study. *Journal of Nervous and Mental Disease*, *190*, 510–518.

Yeo, R. A., Gangestad, S. W., Edgar, C., & Thoma, R. (1999). The evolutionary genetic underpinnings of schizophrenia: The developmental instability model. *Schizophrenia Research*, *39*, 197–206.

Yeo, R. A., Pommy, J., & Padilla, E. A. (2014). Strategic choices versus maladaptive development. *Psychological Inquiry*, *25*, 389–393.

Yeomans, M. R., & Gray, R. W. (2002). Opioid peptides and the control of human ingestive behaviour. *Neuroscience & Biobehavioral Reviews*, *26*, 713–728.

Yiend, J., Mathews, A., Burns, T., Dutton, K., Fernández-Martín, A., Georgiou, G. A., et al. (2015). Mechanisms of selective attention in generalized anxiety disorder. *Clinical Psychological Science*, *3*, 758–771.

Yildirim, B. O., & Derksen, J. J. L. (2012*a*). A review on the relationship between testosterone and life-course persistent antisocial behavior. *Psychiatry Research*, *200*, 984–1010.

Yildirim, B. O., & Derksen, J. J. L. (2012*b*). A review on the relationship between testosterone and the interpersonal/affective facet of psychopathy. *Psychiatry Research*, *197*, 181–198.

Yildirim, B. O., & Derksen, J. J. L. (2015*a*). Clarifying the heterogeneity in psychopathic samples: Towards a new continuum of primary and secondary psychopathy. *Aggression and Violent Behavior*, *24*, 9–41.

Yildirim, B. O., & Derksen, J. J. L. (2015*b*). Mesocorticolimbic dopamine functioning in primary psychopathy: A source of within-group heterogeneity. *Psychiatry Research*, *229*, 633–677.

Yorulmaz, O., Gençöz, T., & Woody, S. (2009). OCD cognitions and symptoms in different religious contexts. *Journal of Anxiety Disorders*, *23*, 401–406.

Yoshimasu, K., Barbaresi, W. J., Colligan, R. C., Voigt, R. G., Killian, J. M., Weaver, A. L., et al. (2012). Childhood ADHD is strongly associated with a broad range of psychiatric disorders during adolescence: A population-based birth cohort study. *Journal of Child Psychology and Psychiatry, 53*, 1036–1043.

Young, E., & Korszun, A. (2010). Sex, trauma, stress hormones and depression. *Molecular Psychiatry, 15*, 23–28.

Young, E. S., Simpson, J. A., Griskevicius, V., Huelsnitz, C. O., & Fleck, C. (2017). Childhood attachment and adult personality: A life history perspective. *Self & Identity*. doi:10.1080/15298868.2017.1353540

Yu, A. J., & Dayan, P. (2005). Uncertainty, neuromodulation, and attention. *Neuron, 46*, 681–692.

Zabelina, D. L., Condon, D., & Beeman, M. (2014). Do dimensional psychopathology measures relate to creative achievement or divergent thinking? *Frontiers in Psychology, 5*, 1029.

Zehr, J. L., Culbert, K. M., Sisk, C. L., & Klump, K. L. (2007). An association of early puberty with disordered eating and anxiety in a population of undergraduate women and men. *Hormones and Behavior, 52*, 427–435.

Zeigler-Hill, V., & Wallace, M. T. (2011). Racial differences in narcissistic tendencies. *Journal of Research in Personality, 45*, 456–467.

Zelazniewicz, A. M., & Pawlowski, B. (2011). Female breast size attractiveness for men as a function of sociosexual orientation (restricted vs. unrestricted). *Archives of Sexual Behavior, 40*, 1129–1135.

Zentner, M., & Mitura, K. (2012). Stepping out of the caveman's shadow: Nations' gender gap predicts degree of sex differentiation in mate preferences. *Psychological Science, 23*, 1176–1185.

Zerbo, O., Yoshida, C., Gunderson, E. P., Dorward, K., & Croen, L. A. (2015). Interpregnancy interval and risk of autism spectrum disorders. *Pediatrics, 136*, 651–657.

Zhai, J., Zhang, Q., Cheng, L., Chen, M., Wang, K., Liu, Y., et al. (2011). Risk variants in the S100B gene, associated with elevated S100B levels, are also associated with visuospatial disability of schizophrenia. *Behavioural Brain Research, 217*, 363–368.

Zhang, H. F., Dai, Y. C., Wu, J., Jia, M. X., Zhang, J. S., Shou, X. J., et al. (2016). Plasma oxytocin and arginine-vasopressin levels in children with autism spectrum disorder in China: Associations with symptoms. *Neuroscience Bulletin, 32*, 423–432.

Zheng, Z., Zhu, T., Qu, Y., & Mu, D. (2016). Blood glutamate levels in autism spectrum disorder: A systematic review and meta-analysis. *PloS ONE, 11*, e0158688.

Zhou, J., Yao, N., Fairchild, G., Cao, X., Zhang, Y., Xiang, Y. T., et al. (2016). Disrupted default mode network connectivity in male adolescents with conduct disorder. *Brain Imaging and Behavior, 10*, 995–1003.

Zietsch, B. P. (2016). Individual differences as the output of evolved calibration mechanisms: Does the theory make sense in view of empirical observations? *Current Opinion in Psychology, 7*, 71–75.

Zietsch, B. P., Morley, K. I., Shekar, S. N., Verweij, K. J., Keller, M. C., Macgregor, S., et al. (2008). Genetic factors predisposing to homosexuality may increase mating success in heterosexuals. *Evolution and Human Behavior, 29*, 424–433.

Zijlmans, M. A., Riksen-Walraven, J. M., & de Weerth, C. (2015). Associations between maternal prenatal cortisol concentrations and child outcomes: A systematic review. *Neuroscience and Biobehavioral Reviews, 53*, 1–24.

Zilioli, S., & Bird, B. M. (2017). Functional significance of men's testosterone reactivity to social stimuli. *Frontiers in Neuroendocrinology*. doi:10.1016/j.yfrne.2017.06.002

Zisner, A. R., & Beauchaine, T. P. (2015). Midbrain neural mechanisms of trait impulsivity. In T. P. Beauchaine & S. P. Hinshaw (Eds.), *The Oxford handbook of externalizing spectrum disorders* (pp. 184–200). New York: Oxford University Press.

Zuckerman, M. (2007). *Sensation seeking and risky behavior*. Washington, DC: APA Press.

Zuj, D. V., Palmer, M. A., Lommen, M. J., & Felmingham, K. L. (2016). The centrality of fear extinction in linking risk factors to PTSD: A narrative review. *Neuroscience & Biobehavioral Reviews*, *69*, 15–35.

INDEX

Page numbers followed by *f*, *t*, and *b* refer to figures, tables, and boxes respectively.